George Nelson Godwin

The Civil War in Hampshire, 1642-45

and the story of Basing House

George Nelson Godwin

The Civil War in Hampshire,1642-45
and the story of Basing House

ISBN/EAN: 9783337222178

Printed in Europe, USA, Canada, Australia, Japan

Cover: Foto ©ninafisch / pixelio.de

More available books at **www.hansebooks.com**

THE

CIVIL WAR IN HAMPSHIRE,

(1642-45)

AND

THE STORY OF BASING HOUSE.

BY THE

REV. G. N. GODWIN,

Chaplain to the Forces.

LONDON:
ELLIOT STOCK, 62, PATERNOSTER ROW, E.C.

1882.

TO

THE HONOURABLE W. T. ORDE POWLETT, J.P.,

DEPUTY LIEUTENANT FOR THE NORTH RIDING OF YORKSHIRE,

AND TO

THE REV. JAMES ELWIN MILLARD, D.D.,

VICAR OF BASINGSTOKE AND RURAL DEAN,

HONORARY CANON OF WINCHESTER CATHEDRAL,

THIS WORK IS, WITH MUCH GRATITUDE, DEDICATED.

PREFACE.

In the stern struggle between Charles I. and his Parliament, Hampshire played no unimportant part.

The capture, after a brief siege, of the strong fortress of Portsmouth, was no small gain to the Parliamentary cause, whilst, on the other hand, the gallant defence made by the Cavalier garrisons of Winchester Castle and Basing House, was eagerly watched, and warmly appreciated at loyal Oxford.

Lord Hopton's defeat at Cheriton "broke all the measures and altered the whole scheme of the King's counsels," nor did the fierce conflicts which took place at Arundel Castle and Salisbury, fail to influence the general result of the war.

To record in a complete, yet brief form, the part played by the County of Hampshire during that most eventful time, is the object of this work. The narrative has been most carefully compiled from original materials existing in our great national and private libraries, and other original sources. It is believed, indeed, that no known source of possible information has been left unexamined.

It was originally intended to quote many of the more interesting authorities *verbatim*, but the consideration of space, and the desire to render the work acceptable to the general reader as well as to the student, induced the method of judicious condensation, which has been now adopted.

In conclusion, the Author desires most heartily to thank the numerous friends who have assisted him in his researches, and to express a hope that his labours will prove to have supplied one more of those local histories which have become of increasing interest to English readers of late years, and which prove of good service to the historian of the great events of our country.

G. N GODWIN.

CURRAGH CAMP,
October 26th, 1882.

ERRATA AND CORRIGENDA.

Page 5, line 11, for "as" read "and."
,, 7, line 30, for "Aymey Loyante" read "**Aymez Loyante.**"
,, 8, line 37, for "Aymey Loyante" read "**Aymez Loyaute.**"
,, 9, line 15, for "Porta" read "Portu."
,, 9, line 49, for "Hachwood" read "**Hackwood.**"
,, 21, lines 24 and 25, for "he" read "they.'"
,, 24, line 51, for "Vikars" read "Vicars.'
,, 29, line 1, for "four" read "foul."
,, 29, line 3, for "a" read "all."
,, 29, line 25, for "Whykeham" read "**Wykeham.**"
,, 33, line 15, for "Aymey" read "Aymez."
,, 66, lines 1 and 21, for "Fairthorne" read "**Faithorne.**"
,, 76, line 17, for "some" read "come."
,, 90, line 25, for "light" read "eight."
,, 100, line 13, for "sabering" read "sabring."
,, 119, line 24, for "1812" read "1642."
,, 145, line 42, for "eight" read "light."
,, 165, line 35, for "line" read "lines."
,, 173, line 5, for "and wall as" read "as well **as.**"
,, 198, line 1, for "heopateld" read "field at the."
,, 200, line 48, for "Sadler" read "Sadleir."
,, 206, line 21, for "30,000" read "3,000."
,, 213, line 28, for "regiment" read "regiments."
,, 213, line 32, for "Welcher" read "Welden."
,, 217, line 22, for "600" read "600 horse."
,, 220, line 44, for "it" read "Winchester."

HAMPSHIRE FIGHTS OF LONG AGO.

CHAPTER I.—THE RUINED FORTRESS.

Stepping out of the ten o'clock up train at Basingstoke station, on a bright May morning, we find friends waiting for us than whom we cannot desire more genial companions or more reliable authorities, bound like ourselves for the famous, though now ruined, Cavalier stronghold of Basing House.

In company with another friend, who has many a time and oft given us most valuable assistance, are Mr. Cooksey and Mr. Sapp, who likewise take a warm and witthal discerning interest in all that concerns Basing famed in story.

The resistance of temptation is a virtue, and despite the many attractions of Basingstoke, we close firmly the eyes of our imagination, resolutely declining to describe the church or any other object of interest.

We pass the lower road leading to Basing, of which we shall hear much ere long. The Townhall, in the Market-place, contains several pictures, one of which is a portrait of the Merrie Monarch, by Sir Peter Lely. Others seem to have come from Basing House, and one of these is thought to be "the counterfeit presentment of the loyal Marquis" himself, with his baton of command.

As we turn to the left out of the Market-place, we note the "Falcon House." "That modern building," says Mr. Sapp, "stands on the site of a quaint old-fashioned hostelry, with the sign of the 'Fleur-de-lys,' which, according to constant local tradition, was for some days at least the head-quarters of Oliver, renowned in arms."

"Note also the 'Bell Inn' across the way, which was almost a century old when Basing House was taken," adds Mr. Cooksey. "Thither were brought as prisoners the Marquis and Sir Robert Peake, his Deputy-Governor, before being sent up to the Parliament in London."

On our right is the road leading to Hackwood, the stately home of the Dukes of Bolton, preferred by them to their old ancestral seat. Roundheads and Cavaliers alike have trudged, marched, as galloped along the road which we are now following. By this route "the puissant army" of Sir William Waller marched to face the house, and over these rolling hills, on which the grass then grew green and unbroken, advanced the Ironsides, who knew not the meaning of the word "defeat," who had conquered at Naseby and Marston Moor, and who failed not at Basing.

The valley below us is well watered, and in days when drainage was a thing little heeded the wide-stretching swamps must have aided the defence not a little. As we skirt the canal we reach a bridge, on the other side of which is a field still known as "Slaughter Close," where many a brave man on both sides died the death of a soldier. Close to the aforesaid bridge are two cottages, in one of which are some ancient beams, formerly belonging to a mill which was burnt during the siege, of which we shall hereafter have more to say.

Following the canal we see on the opposite bank a long ivy-covered wall, which two centuries ago did good service as a "curtain" for the defence of the fortress, being furnished with towers at either end, in one of which may still be seen the embrasures for five cannon. The cutting of the canal, some few years since, has considerably modified the outer defences, but still enough remains to interest the antiquary, the pleasure seeker, or him for whom the memory of bygone deeds of valour has a charm. Looking across the valley we cannot fail to remark the Basingstoke Workhouse, just in rear of which is the London and South-Western Railway.

The Workhouse and the railway mark the position of Cowdray's Down, whereon, as we shall see, Parliamentarian troopers kept watch and ward for many a weary month, and that clump of trees to the right beyond the railway is near a large chalk pit, known as Oliver's Delve, wherein regiment after regiment of the besiegers found shelter.

Closer at hand, but "severed by a wall and common roade, againe divided from the foot of Cowdrey's Downe by meades, rivulets, and a river running from Basingstoke, a mile distant, upon the west, is a farm house, which from a time long prior to the siege has borne the name of the 'Graunge,'" or "Grange." To Mr. Barton, the present tenant, we and all other visitors to the site of Basing House are much indebted for courteous permission to examine the traces of the deadly struggle here to be met with.

A noble barn, said by tradition to have been the former riding school, still retains a roof of which many a church might well be proud, and has evidently served as a target for Colonel Dalbier's hostile gunners. Just beyond the farm buildings by the roadside are two gateways, the brickwork of which justly attracts attention by its exquisite workmanship. A similar gateway, perhaps due to the same skilful workman, may be seen at Titchfield House.

Within these two ancient but now walled-up gateways is a level greensward, beneath which the crowbar meets everywhere with brickwork. This was probably the site of the Grange at the time of the siege, the present dwelling-house being of more modern erection. This idea gains confirmation from the fact that only a few yards distant from the level space just mentioned the wall is loopholed for musketry, apparently for the purpose of defending the Grange, which was, as we shall presently see, strongly fortified. Between the Grange and the railway flows the river Loddon, adjoining which may still be seen some of the ancient fish-ponds, now devoted to the cultivation of watercress. Tradition asserts that the dwellers in Basing House used to go to church by water, and old engravings show that a considerable lake formerly existed on this side of the house.

Great difficulty was experienced in building the railway viaduct in consequence of the swampy nature of the ground.

Looking across this low lying tract we note the neat houses of the pleasant village of Basing, called in the accounts of the siege "Basing Towne," the new rectory and the Church of St. Mary, which was more than once taken and re-taken. Nearly opposite to the aforesaid gateways is a wall, which has been battered by cannon shot, and just above, on the bank of "the barge-river, is a wall, which was formerly defended by a now ruinous tower, and which extends to the ancient garrison gate, the date of which, according to Prosser, is 1562, and on which may still be seen the ancient armorial bearings of the Paulets. Through that ivy-covered gateway have ridden chivalrous Colonel Gage, the deliverer of Basing in its time of need, stern Oliver, and Hugh Peters, "the ecclesiastical newsmonger," who brought word to waiting London of "The Sack of Basing House." Just within the garrison gate we cross the canal, and are joined by three friends, who give us much valuable local information. They are Hugh Raynbird, Esq., the Steward of the Hackwood Estate, Mr. Bartlett, who acts as the caretaker of this historic site, and Mr. Hall, the village blacksmith, to one and all of whom our best thanks are due.

To our right is a level greensward, surrounded by the canal and by deep moats. Along the bank of the canal are the foundations of towers of massive brickwork. Wherever the pick is used foundations are met with just below the surface, and we see to our left front evident remains of some stately building.

Considerable difficulty exists in determining the exact position of various sites at Basing House, but from the words of the "Loyal Marquis" himself, hereafter to be quoted, from the remains already met with and from the descriptions given of the position of the batteries, it seems almost, if not quite, certain that we are now standing on the site of what was called "the New House."

Climbing or creeping through a rail fence, we note a gap in the rampart where the brickwork has fallen inward, evidently shattered by some resistless force. We know that batteries were constructed to play upon this portion of the defences, and that practicable breaches were made hereabouts. Furthermore, Mr. Hall points out the spot, some six feet to the left, from which he himself saw a 32lb. cannon-ball taken. Let each decide for himself, but it seems, to say the least, very probable that this was "the imminent deadly breach" by which the besiegers, so long baffled, at last entered the stronghold. Beyond the moat to the south is an open space, still called the Park, as it was two centuries ago. Not long since two piers of fine brickwork stood at the former entrance, nearly opposite to which is a chalk-pit, in which several skeletons have been discovered. Those slain in the siege seem to have been buried where they fell. Some appear to have been interred with care and reverence, whilst the position of other remains seems to indicate haste and heedlessness. There was formerly a little wood between the House and the village of Basing. Leaving the very probable site of the New House, and retracing our steps, we note a bridge of brickwork, which was brought to light a few years since. Mark it well, for on that bridge brave men on both sides "fought it out at sword's point."

Huge earthworks, circular in form, faced with brickwork, over which grass and ivy grow green, invite exploration, but leaving the bridge behind us and walking over turf beneath which lie hidden yet more foundations, we soon reach a gate which opens into a spacious garden, in which the Boy-King Edward VI. sought health in our fresh Hampshire air; wherein Queen Mary and her Spanish bridegroom spent some hours of their all too brief honeymoon, and which saw Queen Elizabeth and the Ambassador of France in grave and earnest converse. Thomas Fuller, Wenceslaus Hollar, Oliver Cromwell, Sir Ralph Hopton, and Hugh Peters have each in turn visit d this pleasant garden. Along one side of it runs the long loopholed "curtain" wall, with its two conical towers, one of which, as we have already seen, did good service as a battery, as also probably did the other, which is now transformed into a dovecot. All around the sides are nest-holes, most literally and in truth "pigeon-holes." Around a stout oak post in the centre revolves a framework with a ladder attached to it, which gives easy access to the several pigeon nurseries. The ancestral doves must have had unpleasant experiences during the siege, but no doubt proved most useful

"With their heads down in the gravy,
And their legs up through the crust,"

when other provisions began to fail. A postern gate from this dovecot is now walled up. We cross an orchard on the opposite side of the garden to the dovecot, noting the ancient wall on our right, and enter a chamber of massive brickwork, locally styled "The Banking," or "Banquetting House." The latter designation seems by no means appropriate, but it may have been a kind of mediæval "strong room." Who can tell? Turning to the right, up a flight of steps we see, at the door of the pleasant "Cottage," a heap of mementoes of the famous siege, which have been brought to light by the excavations which have for some time past been carried on by Lord Bolton, and in which the Hon. W. T. Orde Powlett has taken a keen and lively interest. Nor can we proceed further without thanking the latter for his kind assistance to the writer in his endeavours to throw light upon the siege and sa k of Basing. Broken pottery mingles with fragments of carved stone work. Here and there are proud escutcheons having on them. "Honi soit qui mal y pense," and fragments of the glorious family motto, "Aymey Loyante." Blackened and discoloured here and there indeed are they, for flame-jets and smoke-eddies have done their worst, but "Love Loyalty" is still the text from which they preach, and spite of storm, sack, and spoil, Basing will be "the House of Loy lty" for evermore. Glass quarries have been found with "Aymey Loyante" painted on scrolls of a period evidently prior to the siege. This discovery destroys the pretty legend of Basing House being styled "Loyalty House," from the "Loyal Marquis" having written this motto on the window with a diamond ring, with a view to animate and inspirit the garrison. These quarries bear also the family badge (a key and garter). Several cannon-balls have been found. Mr. Hall says "Yes, I have seen a number recast in years gone by at the Basingstoke Foundry." Bullets, and a large number of fragments of shell have been met with ; and two swords were brought to light some years ago. Beautiful encaustic tiles, over which Queen Bess walked, even in her old age tripping lightly, quaint tobacco pipes, with bowls suggestive of the days when "the weed" was worth its weight in silver, and farmers chose their largest shillings to place in the tobacconists' scales, still tell of the past.

Dr. Hayes, of Basingstoke, has in his possession some ancient manacles from Basing, and do not those vitrified masses speak of intense and fervid heat? Hand grenades, and the jaws of horses that munched oats two hundred years ago, together with bones picked by hungry Cavaliers at the same distant period, are not wanting. The old ramparts are here gay with flowers, speaking not of war but of peace. Long may they continue so to do!

Retracing our steps towards the brick bridge, by which we paused awhile ago, we have between us and the Canal the supposed Bowling Green, oblong in shape, and formerly defended, says Prosser, by a rampart and covered way, whereon amused themselves—" "Stop," cried Mr. Sapp, "no historical disquisitions please, or we shall be here till to-morrow morning!"

Opening an iron gate, and as carefully closing it I chind us, we halt for a moment at the entrance to a huge circular embankment of earth face l with brickwork, and surrounded by a moat, the average perpendicular depth of which (except towards the Bowling Green) is 30 feet. Round the top of the earthworks runs a path commanding wide and extensive views over the neighbouring country. Prosser ("Antiquities of Hampshire, 1842") tells us that around the citadel or keep was a parapet wall, about four feet high from the gravel, now destroyed. Some such protection must have been necessary, since the besiegers' works were within pistol shot. Several towers also protected the circular rampart, which we will walk round presently.

We are standing on the supposed site of the lofty Gate House, and close beside us is a heap of fragments of carved stonework, which tell of past magnificence. Notice especially some fine brickwork or terra cotta, of the Tudor period, and very similar to that at Layer Marney, in Essex, which probably formed part of the stately mansion erected by the first Marquis, who was " a willow, and not an oak."

Mr. Cooksey now produces a recent reprint, entitled "A Description of the Siege of Basing Castle, kept by the Lord Marquisse of Winchester, for the service of His Majesty against the forces of the Rebells under command of Colonell Norton. Anno Dom. 1644. Oxford, printed by Leonard Lichfield, printer to the University, 1644." From this diary he reads the following extract:—

"Basing Castle, the seat and mansion of the Marquisse of Winchester, stands on a rising ground, having its forme circular, encompassed with a brick rampart, lined with earth, and a very deep trench, but dry. The loftie Gatehouse with foure turrets looking northwards, on the right whereof without the compasse of the ditch, is a goodly building, containing two, faire courts. Before them is the Graunge severed by a wall and common roade, againe divided from the foot of Cowdrey's Downe by meades, rivulets, and a river running from Basingstoke, a mile distant upon the west. The south side of the Castle hath a parke, and toward Basing towne a little wood, the place seated and built as if for Royaltie, having a proper motto, 'Aymey Loyalte.'"

"Having read this account of Basing in its glory by its lord and master, let us explore its ruins!"

Inclining to the right, as we enter the circular keep or citadel, we at once reach the excavations before referred to. Very curious and very puzzling are their results. The rooms at present explored seem to have been the kitchens of the mansion. Recesses in which some think the tinder-box formerly rested have been opened out, together with chimneys, fireplace, and ovens. Just within the rampart is what at present seems like a corridor, paved in some places with brick, and in others with flint. This paving has here and there disappeared, and there is reason to suppose that wood was used, as well as the more durable materials. Chalk also formed the floor in various places. A circular brick wall, three feet in height, a portion of which appears to have been hastily constructed, runs round the area parallel to the outer rampart. Drains have been met with, and a large culvert leads beneath the moat into the open country. In one portion of the wall are several recesses, the original use of which is shrouded in mystery. A large arch, which probably did duty as a silly-port, has been uncovered, and various chambers below the surface are being brought to light. The foundations of what was apparently a square tower are visible near the centre of the circular area, and close by is a large cellar, the arched roof of which was probably intended to be bomb proof. The stands for the beer barrel may still be seen, and light was admitted by shoots very similar to those in the crypt of Winchester Cathedral. The steps leading down to this cellar were of brick with stout oaken curbs. The all-consuming fire penetrated even here, as the charred timbers plainly testified. Indeed, this cellar was the probable scene of a tragedy as horrible as that of the Black Hole of Calcutta, of which Hugh Peters shall tell us more anon. The citadel was supplied with water from a well on the left of the entrance, and there is another well on the outer edge of the moat. Pursuing our walk round the circular rampart, we notice some masonry which seems to have formed part of the more ancient building which Adam De Porta called "home." Pleasant is the breezy walk along the path at the top of the rampart, where steadfast Cavaliers did "sentry go" for many a weary month. From the summit to the left of the entrance to the citadel we look down into the moat, more than 30 feet below, and the supposed site of the famous New House, beyond which is the canal, on the opposite bank of which some of the outworks of the fortress are still distinctly traceable. Further off is Basing Church, alternately occupied by both parties, and as we walk onwards we skirt the Park, in which the besiegers raised their strongest works. Close by, indeed within a stone's throw of where we stand, the foemen's trenches are still much in the same condition as they were after the final assault. Close quarters truly!

When we have completed half our circuit we see the well before mentioned on the outer edge of the moat, and we are evidently treading on foundations, probably of a tower, to defend a drawbridge, of the existence of which at this point there are some indications. A large mound to the right of the well perhaps marks the position of a hostile battery. Sir William Waller seems to have "faced the House" on this side. And now what a view we have! Away in the distance is Winklebury Circle, from whence, according to tradition, Oliver, on his all-conquering march, first surveyed from a distance the stately towers of Basing, doomed to fall. Rather nearer is Basingstoke, the head-quarters of the Parliamentarian Committee, and we fail not to remark pleasant Hachwood House, wherein most fittingly find place the portraits of the "Loyal" Marquis and Marchioness.

Close below us are Slaughter Close and the swamps which protected the fortress on the north. How clearly could the besieged discern the movements of the enemy's horse on Cowdrey Down, of the infantry quartered in the Delve, and of convoys moving along the lower road or "lane" from Basingstoke. Protected by the guns mounted upon and around the House, as well as by its own fortifications, was the Grange, which also was stoutly defended. Beyond the church, in a field called Priestcroft, which may be the land formerly belonging to the Chaplain of the free chapel of Basing, are the remains of fortifications, and across the River Loddon is Pyat's or Magpie Hill, from whence the besieged drew frequent and welcome supplies of corn.

One of our party produces a rare contemporary etching ascribed to Wenceslaus Hollar, the eminent engraver, who was himself one of the besieged, and Mr. Sapp has also a view of the House from a very ancient drawing, now in the Bodleim Library. The latter view shows a large expanse of water on one side, which is crossed by a causeway. In "The Soldier's Report of Sir William Waller's Fight," &c., we are told: "This place is very strongly fortified. The walls of the house are made thick and strongly to beare out cannon bullets, and the house built upright, so that no man can command the roofe; the windowes thereof are guarded by the outer walles, and there is no place open in the house save only for certain Drakes (or field-pieces) upon the roofe of the said house, wherewith they are able to play upon our Army, though we discern them not. The house is as large and spacious as the Tower of London, and strongly walled about with earth raised against the wall, of such a thicknesse that it is able to dead the greatest cannon bullet, besides they have great store both of ammunition and victualls to serve for supply a long time, and in the wall divers pieces of ordnance about the house." Cromwell speaks of taking "about ten pieces of ordnance." The Marquis says "Our courts being large and many;" and Hugh Peters states, "There were in both houses 16 courts, both great and small." Several towers aided the defence, but the lead was stripped from all the turrets during the siege, to be cast into bullets.

CHAPTER II.—BASING IN "YE OLDEN TYME."

Having now obtained a general idea of the ground on which once stood Basing House, we seat ourselves on the grassy slopes of the citadel, and one of our party (with an occasional comment from some one or other of his audience) speaks as follows:—"Before we speak of the Civil War, we must make brief mention of 'a fight fought long ago' on this very spot. A Danish host landed in the north, stormed York, and marched upon 'the Royal city called Reading.' Brave Earl Alfgar had tried to bar the Vikings' way, only to die as a soldier should, sword in hand beneath the oaks of Kesteven.

The lion-hearted Ethelred dwelt in the palace of the West Saxons at Winchester, and by his side was his young brother, Earl Alfred, 'the truth teller,' already known as a Dane fighter. Led by the two Royal soldiers, the men of Wessex, with their dragon standard, faced the Raven of the North on or near the site of Basing House. How thickly flew the arrows that day! how fiercely did Saxon and Northman hew and hack at one another! how cheerily rang out Alfred's battle cry! It was, we may be sure, not his fault that 'the Pagans remained masters of the place of death,' and that 'when the fight began hope passed from the one side to the other; the Royal army was deceived; the enemy had the victory but gained no spoils.' The grave of the slain is probably remembered in the name of the neighbouring farm of 'Lick Pit,' or 'Body Pit.'"

But we must hasten onwards. Camden says: "Beneath this (the Holy Ghost Chappell) Eastward lieth Basing, a towne very well knowne by reason of the Lords bearing the name of it, to wit, St. John, the Poinings, and the Powlets. For when Adam de Portu, Lord of Basing, a mightie man in this tract, and of great wealth, in the reigne of William the First, matched in marriage with the daughter and heire to the right noble house of St. John, William his sonne, to doe honour unto that familie, assumed to him the surname of St. John, and they who lineally descended from him have still retained the same. But when Edward St. John departed out of this world without issue in King Edward the Third his time, his sister Margaret bettered the state of her husband, John Saint Philibert, with the possessions of the Lord Saint John, and when she was dead without children, Isabell, the other sister, wife unto Sir John Poinings, bare unto him Thomas Lord of Basing, whose niece Constance by his sonne Hugh (unto whom this fell for her child-part of inheritance) was wedded into the familie of Powlet, and she was great grandmother to that Sir William Powlet who, being made Baron Saint John of Basing, by King Henrie the Eighth, and created by King Edward the Sixth first Earl of Wiltshire, and afterwards Marquess of Winchester, and withall was Lord Treasurer of England, having in a troublesome time runne through the highest honour, fulfilled the course of nature with the satietie of his life (and that is great prosperitie as a rare blessing among Courtiers), after he had built a most sumptuous house heere, for the spacious largenesse thereof admirable to the beholder, untill for the great and chargeable reparations his successors pulled down a good part of it. But of him I have spoken before." This keep or citadel, in which we now are, is probably an old camp, which has been utilised in turn by Celt, Roman, Saxon, Dane, Norman, and Cavalier. In a grant made to the Priory of Monks Sherborne, in the reign of Henry II., mention is made of "the old castle of Basing." This seems to have been rebuilt by William Paulet, or Powlett, the First Marquis of Winchester, of whom we are told that he was the son of Sir John Paulet, who was twice Sheriff of Hampshire. He was made Comptroller and Treasurer of the Household by Henry VIII., and became Lord Treasurer to Edward VI., by whom he was created Marquis of Winchester. "It has never been said that he possessed masterly abilities; he is only presented to us as a man of great policy and sagacity." He was the chief instrument in preserving the crown to Queen Mary, and died in 1571 at the age of 87, enormously wealthy, and leaving 103 descendants. He seems to have been remarkable for pithy sayings. Being asked how he had retained the favour of four Tudor sovereigns, he replied "I was born of the willow, not of the oak." He said also "that there was always the best justice when the Court was absent from London." He thus wrote:—

Late supping I forbear,
Wine and women I forswear;
My neck and feet I keep from cold,
No marvel then, though I be old;
I am a willow, not an oak.
I chide, but never hurt with stroke.

In 1560 he entertained at Basing his Royal mistress, who made the full fond confession, "By my troth, if my Lord Treasurer were but a young man, I could find in my heart to love him for a husband before any man in England." Entertaining Royal personages was expensive then as now. In January, 1569, the old Marquis received a letter from the Earl of Shrewsbury, who acted as jailor for the Queen of Scots, asking for a further allowance of wine in these terms:—"Truly two tuns have not sufficed ordinarily, besides that which is sacrificed at times for her bathings and such like use, which seeing I cannot by any means conveniently diminish, my earnest trust and desire is that you will now consider me with such larger proportions in this case as shall seem good unto your friendly wisdom, even as I shall think myself much beholden to you for the same, and so I commit you unto God. From Tutbury Castle, this 15 of January, 1569. Your assured friend to my power, G. SHREWSBURY." The second Marquis, who was one of the judges at the trial of the Duke of Norfolk in 1572, died in 1576, bequeathing his body to be buried in the church of Basing, and ordering that his funeral should cost 1000*l*. The third Marquis wrote poetry and gave large estates to four illegitimate sons. His son and successor impoverished himself by royally entertaining Queen Elizabeth in 1601, of which we have the following graphic account:

"Queen Elizabeth's entertainment at Basing House, in her progress in 1601.—Her Majestie was that night attended on to Basing, a house of the Lord Marquesse, where she took much quiet content, as well with the seate of the house, as honourable carriage of the worthy Lady Lucie, Marquesse of Winchester, that shee staid there thirteene dayes, to the greate charge of the sayde Lorde Marquesse. The fourth day after the Queen's comming to Basing the sheriffe was commanded to attend the Duke of Biron at his comming into that country, whereupon the next day, being the 10th of September, hee went towards Blackwater, being the uttermost confines of that shire, towards London, and then met the said Duke, accompanied with above 20 of the nobilitie of France, and attended with about 400 Frenchmen, who were met by George, Earle of Cumberland, and by him conducted from London to Hampshire. The said Duke was that night brought to the Vine, a faire and large house of Lord Sands, which house was furnished with hangings and plate from the Tower and Hampton Court, with 7-score beds and furniture, which the willing and obedient people of the countrie of Southampton, upon two dayes warning, had brought in thither, to lend the Queene. The Duke abode there four or five days, all at the Queene's charges, and spent her more at the Vine than her owne court for the time spent at Basen. During her abode there, Her Majestie went to him at the Vine, and he to her at Basen, and one day he attended her at Basen-parke on hunting, where the Duke staied her comming, and did there see her in such Royaltie, and so attended by the nobilitie, and costly furnished and mounted, as the like had seldome been seene; but when she came to the place where the Duke staied, the said sheriffe (as the manner is), being bareheaded, and riding next day before her, staied his horse, thinking the Queene would then have saluted the Duke, whereat the Queene, being much offended, commanded the Sheriffe to go on. The Duke followed her very humbly, bowing low towards his horse's maine with his cap off. About twenty yards Her Majestie on the sudden tooke off her maske, looked backe upon him, and most gratiously and courteously saluted him, as holding it not beseeming so mightie a Prince as she was, and who so well knew all kingly majestie to make her stay directly against a subject before he had shewed his obedience in following after her. She tarried at Basen thirteen dayes, as is aforesaid, being very well contented with all things there done, affirming she had done that in Hampshire that none of her ancestors ever did, neither any Prince of Cristendome could doe; that was she had in her progresse in her subjects' houses entertained a Royall Ambassador,and had Royally entertained him. At her departure from Basen, being the 14th of September, she made 10 Knights, having never in all her raigne made, at one time, so many before, whose names were : Sir Edward Citsell, second sonne to the Lord Burley ; Sir Edward Hungerford, next heyre to the Lord Hungerford ; Sir Edward Bainton, of Wiltshire, Sir W. Kingmil, Sir Care Rawleigh, Sir Francis Palmer, then sheriffe of the shire ; Sir Benjamin Tichbourne, Sir Hamden Paulet, Sir Richard Norton, of Hampshire ; Sir Francis Stoner, of Oxfordshire ; and Sir Edward Ludlow, of Wiltshire. Next day she went from Basen towards Farnham, a castle belonging to the see of Winchester, and in her way to Farnham she knighted Sir Richard White in his own house, having feasted her and her trayne very royally, neer unto which towne the sheriffe of Hampshire took his leave, and the sheriffe of Surrey met her, but the sheriffe of Hampshire and the gentlemen of that country went to Farnham by command, and there attended the next day, where they were feasted and kindly entertained by the learned prelate, Dr. Bilson, Bishoppe of Winchester, upon whose onely commendation two aunceient and worthy gentlemen of Hampshire, Sir Richard Mill and Sir William Udall, received there the dignity of knighthood. And thus much for that progresse to be noted." (Vide "Queen Elizabeth's Progresses," Vol. II.)

The Vyne or Vine just mentioned is near Sherborne St. John. Before the 16th century it was an old manor house, which Lord Sandys enlarged and beautified. It was afterwards greatly altered by Inigo Jones and his son-in-law Webb. Camden styles it " A neat house of the Lord Sandes, called from the vines introduced into Britain, more for shade than for the sake of the fruit, ever since the time of the Emperor Probus, who allowed the Britons and other nations to plant vines." Horace Walpole says " At the Vine is the most heavenly chapel in the world," which contains some stain'd glass brought from Boulogne after its capture by Henry VIII. by the first Lord Sandys. This glass has, therefore, like Hudibras's breeches and the hollow copper ball on Naseby Spire, " been at the siege of Bullen." The tomb room adjoining the chapel was built by John Chute, the friend of Horace Walpole. It contains an altar-tomb, with an effigy of Chaloner Chute, Speaker of the House of Commons, and one of the great lawyers of the time of the Commonwealth, who purchased the estate of the representatives of the Sandys family. For full particulars of the noble owners of Basing see Woodward's *History of Hampshire*, to which we are greatly indebted for much valuable information. The 5th Marquis at first managed his estates in peace, keeping up the old customs that " tenants were to make hedges for the wheat field by or within six days after St. Andrew's Day, and for the barley field on or within six days of Maie Daie. No wheat was to be sown until within a fortnight of Christmas, and no fallowing done until within a fortnight of Candlemas." But more stirring times were about to ruin, whilst immortalising, Basing, and to confer upon its noble owner the proud title of "the Loyal Marquis."

CHAPTER III.—THE CIVIL WAR BEGINS

It comes not within our province to discuss the causes of quarrel between Charles I. and his Parliament. Suffice it to say that the house of Pawlet declared for the King. On June 15th, 1642, Lord Pawlet was with the King at York, and was one of those who were styled by their opponents "the Popish and beggarly lords, and cavaliers for and about the King." On that day he, with 44 other noblemen, declared that "the King had no intention of making war upon the Parliament," and on June 20th he was one of 43 who undertook "to pay horses for three months (thirty days to the month), at two shillings and sixpence per diem, still advancing a month's pay, the first payment to begin so soone as the King shall call for it after the commissions shall be issued under the great scale. In this number are not to be reckoned the horses of the subscribers, or of those that shall attend them." Lord Pawlet promised to provide 40 horses, and the Lord Marquess of Hartford 60. Lord Pawlet and his son Sir John Pawlet were afterwards besieged in Sherborne Castle by the Earl of Bedford.

In Hampshire the Marquis of Winchester declared for the King, but his kinsmen, Sir Henry Wallop and Robert Wallop, who were members for the county and for Andover, were Parliamentarians. Of this ancient family Camden says, "After this, Test having taken into it a little river from Wallop, or more truly Wellhop, that is by interpretation out of our forefathers' ancient language 'a pretty well out of the side of a hill,' whereof that right worshipful familie of the Wallops of Knights' Degree dwelling harde by tooke name." Two other kinsmen, Richard and Sir Thomas Jervoise, represented the borough of Whitchurch in Parliament. Sir William Waller, the Parliamentarian general, was also a relative, and had just been returned a member for Andover.

Sir Henry Wallop and Richard Whitehead, Esq., who were both Parliamentarians, represented the county at Westminster. Sir Henry Rainsford and Henry Vernon, Esq., were the original members for Andover in the Long Parliament, but by a petition which bears the date of May 3rd, 1642, Mr. Vernon was unseated, and Sir William Waller declared duly elected, the return being amended on May 12th, 1642. Robert Wallop, Esq., a staunch friend to the Parliament, also represented Andover in the Long Parliament.

Henry Percy, Esq., was one of the members for Portsmouth, but on his electing to sit for Northumberland a new writ was issued on November 11th, 1642, and Nicholas Weston, Esq., was elected. The other member was the notorious Colonel Goring, who, deserting the Parliament, openly declared for the King early in August, 1642, and was, in consequence, expelled from the House of Commons on the 8th of that month.

The members for Southampton were George Gallop and Edward Exton, Esqs., who were likewise adherents of the Parliament. The representatives of Stockbridge were William Heveningham and William Jephson, Esqs., who supported the same cause, whilst at Whitchurch the Parliament had friends in Richard Jervoise, Esq., and Sir Thomas Jervoise, the sitting members. Clarendon speaks of "Norton, Onslow, Jarvis, Whitehead, and Morley, all Colonels of Regiments," and of "two Captains, Jarvise and Jephson, the two eldest sons of two of the greatest rebels of that country, both heirs to good fortunes." One of the members for Winchester was the celebrated John Lisle, Esq., the friend of Cromwell, and the husband of Dame Alicia Lisle, the victim of brutal Judge Jeffreys. His colleague, Sir William (afterwards Lord) Ogle, was a devoted Royalist, which caused him to be unseated on June 24th, 1643. Sir William Lewis, Bart., and Sir Wm. Uvedale supported the claims of the Parliament at Petersfield. Sir Benjamin Tichborne, who also represented Petersfield about this time, was obliged to "retire after the battle of Cheriton to the mansion at West Tisted. This is now a farm-house, and near it an old hollow oak is still shown in which the Knight contrived to secrete himself from the pursuit of the troopers who were sent to apprehend him. Sir Richard Tichborne was probably in the battle of Cheriton, as was also his brother, Sir Benjamin, and his son, Sir Henry. These members of the Tichborne family were unhappily arrayed against a kinsman in the Parliamentarian Army. This was Robert Tichborne, a zealous adherent of Cromwell, afterwards Lord Mayor of London, and called by the Protector to his Upper House in 1657. He sat as one of the Judges on the trial of the unfortunate Charles, and signed the warrant for his execution. He was arraigned, but never brought to trial. Sir Henry Tichborne, the son of Sir Richard, is the same baronet who is represented in Tilbourg's picture of the Dole. For his attachment to the Royal cause his estate was sequestered, but regained at the Restoration."

Colonel Norton, the friend of Cromwell, lived at the Manor House of Old Alresford, but Dr. Peter Heylin, the Rector, who wrote a History of the Reformation, was hateful to the Puritan party, having arranged his church according to the Injunctions issued by Archbishop Laud. The principal inhabitants of Alresford favoured the Parliament. Winchester Castle was a place of considerable strength. James I. had granted it to the Tichborne family in fee farm for ever. Sir William Waller laid claim to the office of Governor, but in 1643 Sir Richard Tichborne aided in bringing it under the aut'ority of the King. Bishop Curle and the Rev. W. Lewis, Master of St. Cross, were "stanch loyalists and Churchmen," whilst as to the inhabitants in general we know that when Charles I. was brought as a prisoner to the city under a guard of horse on December 21st, 1648, en route from Hurst Castle to Windsor, "At his entrance therein the Mayor and Aldermen of the city did, notwithstanding the times, receive the King with dutiful respect, and the clergy did the like. During his short stay of one night the gentry and others of inferior rank flocked thither in great numbers to welcome His Majesty." Most of the townsmen of Southampton appear to have been friendly to the Royal cause, whilst of the noble Lord of Titchfield House Clarendon says: "The Earl of Southampton was indeed a great man in all respects, and brought very much reputation to the King's cause." A large portion of the parish of Abbott's Worthy belonged to Arthur, Lord Capel, who desired that his heart,

after his execution in March, 1649, might be enclosed in a silver vase and presented to Charles II. at the Restoration, which was accordingly done. Of him the old rhyme ran:—

Our lion-like Capel undaunted stood,
Beset with crosses in a sea of blood.

Colonel Sandys, of Mottisfont House, Colonel Phillips, of Stoke Charity, Captain Peregrine Tasbury, and many others took up arms for the King. The Earl of Portland, who held sway in the Isle of Wight, was peculiarly obnoxious to the Puritans, who "objected to all the acts of good fellowship, all the waste of powder, and all the waste of wine in the drinking of healths, and other acts of jollity; whichever he had been at in his government from the first hour of his entering upon it."

The Marquis of Winchester seems to have been at first inclined to neutrality, for, after giving a description of Basing House, he says: "Hither, the rebellion having made houses of pleasure more unsafe, the Marquis first retired, hoping integrity and privacy might have here preserved his quiet, but the source of the time's villany, bearing downe all before it, neither allowing neutrality, or permitting peace to any that desired to be lesse sinful than themselves, enforceth him to stand upon his guard." The position of Basing House, commanding, as it did, the western road, could not escape notice, and on August 19th, 1641, "In the House of Commons one, Mr. Sewer, did this day give information that he did see on Monday was sevennight a great many arms in the Marquis of Winchester's house at Basingstoke, a recusant, and that the keepers of them told him there were arms for a thousand five-hundred men." On November 4th, of the same year, "It was ordered that the Lord Marquess of Winchester shall have liberty, by vertue of this Order, to sell off his arms to such tradesmen as will buy the same." Having thus, as they thought, rendered Basing House defenceless, some of its foes attacked it, which "enforceth him (the Marquis) to stand upon his guard, which, with his gentlemen armed with six musquets (the whole remainder of a well-furnished armory), he did so well that twice the enemies' attempts proved vaine."

"Portsmouth was at the time of the raising of the standard held for the King by one whose course, from first to last, devious, uncertain, and unprincipled, shed disgrace upon the nobleness of his name, and upon the honourable profession of a soldier. This man was Goring, than whom, on account of his private vices of drunkenness, cruelty, and rapacity, and of his political timidity and treachery, scarcely any one was more unworthy to be trusted with any important matters for counsel or execution. Clarendon says, " When the King returned to York, an accident fell out that made it absolutely necessary for the King to declare the war, and to enter upon it before he was in any degree ripe for action, which was that Portsmouth had declared for the King and refused to submit to the Parliament, which had thereupon sent an army, under the command of Sir William Waller, to reduce it."

" In the previous year Col. Goring had been a traitor to the King, and had betrayed the army plot. The Parliament now felt sure of him, but he was all the while in treaty with their enemies. Queen Henrietta Maria even thought of placing herself under his protection at Portsmouth. This plan he duly disclosed to the Parliament, and received large sums of money from both Puritans and Cavaliers to be expended upon the defences of the town. All which he performed with that admirable dissimulation and rare confidence that when the House of Commons was informed by a member, whose zeal and affection to them was as much valued as any man's, 'that all his correspondence in the county was with the most malignant persons (i.e., Royalists), that of those many frequently resorted to, and continued with him in the garrison; that he was fortifying and raising of batteries towards the land; and that in his discourse, especially in the seasons of his good fellowship, he used to utter threats against the Parliament and sharp censures of their proceedings, and upon such information (the author whereof was well known to them, and of great reputation, and lived so near Portsmouth that he could not be mistaken, in the matter of fact), (Was this informant Colonel Norton, or one of his family from Southwick Park?) the House sent for him, most thinking he would refuse to come. Colonel Goring came upon the summons, with that undauntedness, that all clouds of distrust immediately vanished, insomuch as no man presumed to whisper the least jealousy of him; which he observing, came to the House of Commons, of which he was a member, and having sate a day or two patiently, as if he expected some charge, in the end he stood up, with a countenance full of modesty and yet not without a mixture of anger (as he could help himself with all the insinuations of doubt or fear, or shame, or simplicity in his face that might gain belief, to a greater degree than I ever saw any man; and could seem the most confounded when he was best prepared, and the most out of countenance when he was best resolved, and to want words, and the habit of speaking, when they flowed from no man with greater power), and told them that he had been sent for by them, upon some information given against him, and that, though he believed, the charge being so ridiculous, they might have received, by their own particular inquiry, satisfaction, yet the discourse that had been used, and his being sent for in that manner, had begot some prejudice to him in his reputation; which if he could not preserve, he should be the less able to do them service; and therefore desired, that he might have leave (though very unskilful, and unfit to speak, in so wise and judicious an assembly) to present to them the state and condition of that place under his command. And then he doubted not, but to give them full satisfaction in those particulars, which, possibly, had made some impression in them to his disadvantage. That he was far from taking it ill from those who had given any information against him; for what he had done, and must do, might give some umbrage to well affected persons, who knew not the grounds and reasons that induced him so to do; but that if any such persons would at any time resort to him, he would clearly inform them of whatever motives he had; and would be glad of their advice and assistance for the better doing thereof. Then he took notice of every particular that had been publickly said against him, or privately whispered, and gave such plausible answers to the whole, intermingling sharp taunts and scorns to what had been said of him, with pretty application of himself and flattery to the men that spake it. Concluding ' That they well knew in what esteem he stood with others; so that if, by his ill carriage, he should forfeit the good opinion of that House, upon which he only depended, and to whose service he entirely devoted himself, he were madder than his friends took him to be, and must be as unpitied in any misery that could befal him as his enemies would be glad to see him.' With which, as innocently and unaffectedly uttered, as can be imagined, he got so general an applause from the whole House that, not without some apology for troubling him, they desired him again to repair to his government, and to finish those works which were necessary for the safety of the place, and gratified him with consenting to all the propositions he made in behalf of his garrison, and paid him a good sum of money for their arrears; with which, and being privately assured (which was indeed resolved on) that he should be Lieutenant-General of their Horse in their new army, when it should be formed, he departed again to Portsmouth; in the mean time assuring His Majesty, by those who were trusted between them, 'That he would be speedily in a posture to make any such declaration for his service as he should be required;' which he was forced to do sooner than he was provided for it, though not sooner than he had reason to expect."

"When the levies for the Parliament Army were in good forwardness, and that Lord had received his commission for Lieutenant-General of the Horse, he wrote the Lord Kimbolton, who was his most bosome friend, and a man very powerful, desiring 'That he might not be called to give his attendance upon the army till he was ready to march; because there were so many things to be done and perfected for the safety of that important place, that he was desirous to be present himself at the work as long as was possible. In the meantime he had given directions to his agent in London to prepare all things for his equipage; so that he would be ready to appear at any rendezvous, upon a day's warning.' Though the Earl of Essex did much desire his company and assistance in the Council of War, and preparing the articles, and forming the discipline for the Army, he having been more lately versed in the order and rule of marches and the provisions necessary or convenient thereunto than any man then in their service, and of greater command than any man but the General; yet the Lord Kimbolton prevailed that he might not be sent for till things were riper for action. And when that Lord did afterwards write to him 'That it was time he should come away, he sent such new and reasonable excuses, that they were not unsatisfied with his delay; till he had multiplied those excuses so long that they began to suspect, and they no sooner inclined to suspicion but they met with abundant arguments to cherish it. His behaviour and course of life was very notorious to all the neighbours, nor was he at all reserved in his mirth and publick discourses to conceal his opinion of the Parliament, and their proceedings, so that at last the Lord Kimbolton writ plainly to him 'That he could no longer excuse his absence from the Army, where he was much wanted; and that if he did not come to London by such a short day as he named, he found his integrity would be doubted, and that many things were laid to his charge, of which he doubted not his innocence, and therefore conjured him immediately to be at Westminster, it being no longer deferred or put off.' He writ a jolly letter to that Lord 'That the truth was, his Council advised him that the Parliament did many things which were illegal, and that he might incur much danger by obeying all their orders, that he had received the command of that garrison from the King, and that he durst not be absent from it without his leave:' and concluded with some good counsel to the Lord."

"This declaration of the Governor of a place, which had the reputation of being the only place of strength in England, and situated upon the sea, put them into many apprehensions; and they lost no time in endeavouring to reduce it; but upon the first understanding his resolution, Sir William Waller was sent with a good part of the army, so to block it up that neither men nor provisions might be able to get in, and some ships were sent from the Fleet, to prevent any relief by sea. And these advertisements came to the King as soon as he returned to York."

"Previous to the arrival of Sir William Waller, the troops of the Parliament were under the command of Sir John Merrick, who was at the time Serjeant Major-General of their army. He was afterwards superseded by General Philip Skippon, receiving the appointment of General of the Ordnance. Let us hear Clarendon once more. "It gave no small reputation to His Majesty's affairs, when there was so great a damp upon the spirits of men, from the misadventures at Beverly, that so notable a place as Portsmouth had declared for him in the very beginning of the war; and that so good an officer as Goring was returned to his duty, and in the possession of the town. And the King, who was not surprised with the matter, knowing well the resolution of the colonel, made no doubt but that he was very well supplied with all things, as he might well have been, to have given the rebels work, for three or four months, at the least."

This and other considerations induced the King to issue a proclamation calling on his loyal subjects to rally round his standard at Nottingham, and to send the Marquis of Hertford, with Lord Seymour, his brother, Lord Pawlet, Hopton, Stawel, Coventry, Berkeley, Windham, and some other gentlemen " of the prime quality and interest in the Western parts," into those districts to raise regiments for his service. But no sooner had the standard been displayed at Nottingham, on August 25, 1642, than "His Majesty received intelligence that Portsmouth was so streightly besieged by sea and land that it would be reduced in very few days. except it were relieved. For the truth is, Colonel Goring, though he had sufficient warning, and sufficient supplies of money to put that place into a posture, had relied too much upon probable and casual assistance, and neglected to do that himself which a vigilant officer would have done; and albeit his chief dependence was both for money and provisions from the Isle of Wight, yet he was careless to secure those small castles and blockhouses that guarded the passage; which revolting to the Parliament as soon as he declared for the King, cut off those dependences; so that he had neither men enough to do ordinary duty nor provisions enough for those few for any considerable time. And at the same time with this news of Portsmouth, arrived certain advertisements, that the Marquis of Hertford and all his forces in the West, from whom only the King hoped that Portsmouth should be relieved, was driven out of Somersetshire, where his power and interest was believed unquestionable, into Dorsetshire; and there besieged in Sherborne Castle."

SIEGE OF PORTSMOUTH IN THE YEAR 1642.

I have been favoured with the following extract from an exceedingly rare work, entitled "Jehoveh-Jireh, God in the Mount; or England's Parliamentarie Chronicle," in the possession of Mr. C. E. Smithers, of Queen-street, Portsea :—

" And much about this time came certain intelligence to the Parliament of the present estate, then of Portsmouth, how Colonell Goreing, the then Governour thereof (and that by the assent and good liking of the Parliament; Yet), had now deserted them; and declared himselfe solely for the King against the Parliament, and that he had strongly fortified himselfe both within and without against any forces that should come to oppose or supplant him; And that the Countrey much fearing he would now be but a bad neighbour, or unruly inmate to them, had already laid a strong siege about the Towne, but immediately desired the Parliament's assistance therein, which was accordingly performed, and the Parliament's forces built a strong Fort on the Bridge-foot before Portsmouth, and planted ordnance thereon, and forthwith the Parliament sent to desire the Earl of Warwick to place a Guard of Ships by sea, to prevent all passages and supplies to Portsmouth that way, which accordingly the said most Noble Earle faithfully performed, whereby the Collonell was now so hem'd in on all sides that it was not likely he could long keep house there in the Castle, the Townesmen also much disrellishing his doings therein. But because this was a piece of much concernment for the good of the whole kingdom, I shall here now take occasion for the Reader's more delight and fuller satisfaction, to give a particular narration of the siege and taking of this Town and Castle, wherein will be divers delightfull passages very obvious to the Reader's observation. Colonell Goreing, having about the beginning of August, 1642, declared himselfe openly (as was forementioned) to be for the King alone, and not for the King and Parliament, and having therefore resolved to keep it (as was pretended) for His Majesties coming thither, used all the care he could to fortifie himselfe therein, raised therefore in the first place a Mount at Portbridge, three miles from the Town, and the onley passage into the Island of Portsey, but upon the first comming of the Parliaments forces, which was about the tenth of August, he took away the Ordnance which he had planted in the said Mount, being foure pieces, and brought them back again into the Town, and kept the said Bridge onley with 10 or 12 Troopers with Pistolls and Carbines.

Now the Parliaments forces first showed themselves against Goreing about Pochdown in London way, halfe a mile from the Bridge. Hereupon the Colonells Troopes within the Town issued out in the night, and brought in all the sheepe and cattell that were in Portsey Island, and spoiled and pillaged the Inhabitans thereof, and of all their goods and substance, and of all their victualls, leaving them not so much bread as to live on for one day.

About the 12th of August our Parliament Troopers came in the night and beat the Govenours Troopers from the Bridge and the whole Island, tooke a Trooper prisoner, and another horse, the Rider hardly escaping, having leapt from his horse, and ran away over hedge and ditch. August the 13th, the Lord Wentworth, with about 60 Troopers, all they could make, issued out of the Towne half a mile into Portsey Island, to fetch in a piece of Ordnance, left behind them at first, and without resistance recovered it into the Towne."

Lord Wentworth was the Major-General of Goring's forces. The Cavalry under his charge received a severe check at Ashburton, in Devonshire, and on January 15th, 1646, he received the command of all the horse in the remnant of the King's Army in the West. He was constantly associated with Colonel Goring.

"But shortly after, our Troopers approached neere to a mill, fast by the Town Mount, whereon their Ordnance was planted, intending to fire the mill, to hinder their grinding of corne, which attempt on the mill, together with the Colonells Troopers endeavours to bring in the Cattell thereabout, caused many a hot skirmish, well performed on both sides, but little hurt done. Another time the Colonells Troopers sallied out of the Towne, and were chased by the Parliaments Troopers, and forced to retreat as fast as their horses could carry them, and at this there was a Scottishman, a brave soldier, followed the chase to the very Towne, within the gate, and being within the Gate, six of the enemies set on him altogether, and he most valiantly defending himselfe and fought most bravely, at last they gave him three gashes in his head, yet for all this he was retreating and had escap't them all, had not one very suddenly shut the gate upon him, and so he was taken prisoner, but they seeing him such a brave soldier, tooke care of him, and procured the best Chyrurgions they could to cure him, and suffered him to want nothing convenient for him, and for his valour the Colonell gave him three pieces at his departure, he being immediately exchanged for another prisoner which they tooke of the Colonells, at the Bridge as aforesaid.

Another time the Colonell himselfe and the Lord Wentworth with him sallyed out in the night, with all their Troopers in two Companies, to the Parliaments Workes, by the conduction of one Winter, one of the Aldermen of the Towne, who undertooke to guide them, and so brought them to the very Court of Guard, thinking thereby to doe them much mischiefe, but there they found opposition enough, and upon combating came off with the loss of three men, whereof one named Glover, the Colonells own man, was slain, and the aforesaid Winter, their Guide, was taken prisoner, one of the 3 was one Mr. Weston his man, brother to the Earl of Portland; they also lost a horse of the Lord Wentworth's, which Winter rode on, worth 30l. The Colonell also tooke six prisoners of our men, wereof five were musquetcers, such as had been Sentinells, the other was a Trooper, a stout fellow, who was also hurt by a thrust in the arme; the five musquetcers the Colonell gained to be labourers to carry baskets of earth at his workes, but the other stood it out stoutly and scorned to comply. Winter was kept prisoner in the Court of Guard, and his own son, a lad, was permitted to come out of the Towne, and to passe to and fro to bring his father cleane linen, and other necessaries; who once brought word from his father to the Governour, that the King was very neere the Towne, comming to their aid, which indeed was blazed abroad to be so in the Towne, of purpose to perswade the Garison souldiers that the King would now certainly and suddenly be with them, and liberally reward all their paines and good service. And t'was but need thus to take paines to perswade them, for the greatest part of the Garison-Souldiers were gone away from the Towne by night, sometimes four, sometimes six at a time; sometimes more and sometimes less, for a great many nights together, and the most of his best Gunners were gone from him to the Parliament side, and such as were left of the Garison, were even heartless and did but little, and that on compulsion: the expectation of the King's comming had so tryed and dul'd them, that they were even hopelesse thereof.

Now about August the 18th, the Governour plainely discerned from Gosport (a little Village, halfe a mile over the water from the Towne) that the Parliament Forces were framing some workes to make a Fort, whereat the Governour was much troubled, and presently shot at them from all his workes, that lay that way-ward, letting fly that night at least 60 bullets, but hurt but one man therewith and that by his owne folly, for he stood on his workes with a candle and lanthorn in his hand, whereby they had a right aime and so shot him; but for all this ours desisted not, but went on day and night till they had perfected two plat farmes, the one behind a Barne for ten pieces of Ordnance, the other behind a pile of Faggots for two pieces, though the Governor shot incessantly 14 dayes and 14 nights to have beaten them off, but could not. Shortly after this a parley was sounded but without any good successe, so then they fell to it again, the Governour letting flie his Ordnance apace, day and night, but not with any losse to us (blessed be the Lord for it), no not of a man or horse. All this time there being but two pieces of Ordnance planted on the small worke of Gosport, behind the Faggots, which played not at all on the Towne, though they could have done it, but some short time after, they shot thence and killed one of the Garison-Souldiers on their Mount, and cut off a French man's leg, near unto him above the knee, to the endangering of his life. The Governour himselfe, and the Lord Wentworth in their own persons (and all could be spared from other duties) wrought all one night to make a Trench on the top of the Mount that at the sight of the firing of our Ordnance, they might 1 ap down into it and save themselves from the like shot from Gosport.

On the Saturday following, ours played soundly from Gosport with our Ordnance and shot through the Tower of the Church and brake one of the Bells, and shot again against the same Tower, and that rebounded and fell into the Church, and shot down another top of a house that was near the Church, and the same Saturday morning they shot at the Water-mill, the Miller whereof commended it (by experience) for a good thing to rise early in the morning, for (as he said) if he had not risen early that morning, he had been kill'd in his bed, for a bullet tooke away a sheete and part of his bed. The reason why they shot so much at the Church-tower, was, for that at the top thereof was their Watch-tower, whereby they espied all approaches by sea and by land, and the tolling of a bell gave notice both what ships came by sea, and what number of horse came by land. That Saturday night ours shot but five bullets from Gosport, but every one of them did execution. It was well observed, that in a small time, as ours shot from Gosport; beginning at four of the clock on Friday afternoon, and ending at four on the Sabbath day in the morning, we did more execution with our two pieces of Ordnance than the Governour had with the Towne Ordnance in 14, or 16 daies, and so many nights, in which they shot, at least, 300 bullets, and kill'd but one man in all that time's, a most remarkable providence of the Lord, we having but two pieces of Ordnance at Gosport, whereas the Ordnance planted against Gosport, from their foure workes, could not be less than thirty pieces of Ordnance ; on Saturday, September the third, in the night, the Parliament forces took Sousey Castle, which lies a mile from the Towne upon the sea, and the way thither is on the sea-sands. The Captain of the Castle his name was Challmer, who on Saturday had been at Portsmouth, and in the evening went home to the Castle, and his Souldiers took horse-loads of Provision, Bisket, Meal, and other necessaries with them. They reported that he had more drinke in his head than was befitting such a time and service, and the Townsmen gave out that he had been bribed with money to yield up the Castle, but 'twas false, though the first may be true, yet was not that neither any furtherance to the taking of it, for, thus it was : there were about 80 musqueteers and others that came that night to the Walls of the Castle, and under their Ordnance, and had been with them a very good Engineer, and 35 scaling ladders, and the whole company in the Castle were but 12, Officers or Commanders, who all were not able to deal with ours in such a disadvantage. Wherefore ours having suddenly and silently scaled the Walls, called unto them, advised them what to doe, shewing the advantage we had over them, and therefore their danger if they resisted, who seeing the same immediately yielded the Castle to us ! whereupon the triumph at our taking it was plainly heard, about two of the clock in the morning, into the Towne, and so soon as they were masters of the Castle, they discharged two pieces of the Castle Ordnance against the Towne. Now hereupon the Governour perceiving that the Castle (which was the defence of the Towne both by sea and land) was lost and gone, and pelting already of the Towne with the Ordnance thereof, and having seen through a prospective glasse, so good and faire a Plat-forme for ten pieces of Ordnance at Gosport, in th t very morning, before break of day, he called a Councell of Warre to consult about their present condition, who soon agreed upon the sending out of a Drum to sound a Parley, which was done betimes, in so much that the Parley was begun about ten of the clock the same day, their hostages on each side being appointed. Out of the Towne, the Lord Wentworth, Mr.

Lewkner, and Mr. Weston, the Earl of Portland's brother. From the Parliament side, Sir William Waller, Sir William Lewis, and Sir Thomas Larvace." Of Sir William Waller we shall hear more. He and Sir William Lewis are thus described by Clarendon:—" Sir William Waller, Lewis, and other eminent persons, who had a trust and confidence in each other, and who were looked upon as the Heads and Governours of the moderate Presbyterian party, who most of them would have been contented, their own security being provided for, that the King should be restored to his full rights, and the Church to its possessions." "Lewis had been very popular and notorious from the beginning."

"The Parley was ended about five of the clock in the afternoon, but Articles of agreement not confirmed till seven, that a trumpet came, then, into the Towne from the Committee of the Parliament, and then the conclusion was fully made known, and Articles thoroughly agreed on, on both sides; namely, in brief, that the Towne and Castle was first to be delivered up to the Parliament, and the Colonell after some few daies, liberty to dispose of his estate there, to depart the Towne; which both he, the Lord Wentworth, Mr. Lewkner, and Mr. Weston, and all the Cavaliers with them, their servants, and adherents did accordingly; and Sir William Waller, and Sir Thomas Larvace, accompanied with Sir John Meldrum and Colonell Hurrey, together with a troop of Horse, and two companies of Foot took possession of the Towne." Is Sir Thomas Larvace a misprint for Sir Thomas Jervoise, one of the members for Whitchurch, and an active adherent of the Parliament? Sir John Meldrum belonged to a Scotch family. He was in command of the besiegers at the siege of Newark, and was signally defeated by Prince Rupert on March 22nd, 1643. Colonel Hurrey, or Urrey, deserted to the King in the following June, acted as guide to Prince Rupert at Chalgrove Field, again went over to the Parliament, revealing all that he knew of the King's affairs. He afterwards joined Montrose, was wounded and taken prisoner at Preston, and hanged straightway. "In the evening, at about nine of the clock, Colonell Goring took boat and rowed to a ship for Holland," leaving his garrison to effect a difficult and hazardous march to the King's quarters in the West." "This Colonell when he was first made Governour of this strong Towne of Portsmouth, expelled (as one of his first works of piety in this defection from the state) a good Minister out of the Towne, by name Mr. Tach, at the time of his first declaring himself, as aforesaid, which said godly Minister was brought in again by Sir William Waller, and Sir Thomas Larvace, and confirmed to be preacher to the Garrison. The greatest cause (as was conceived) that induced the Parliament side to agree to any Articles, was because the Colonell had vowed and threatened that if the Towne were taken by forceible assault, he would blow up the Magazine of the Towne, which lay in it, in two severall places; namely, in the square-Towre on the sea-side, where were, at least, 1200 barrels of Gunpowder, and very much Ammunition; and at the other end of the Towne, near the Gate, about 200 barrels more of Gunpowder and some Ammunition, and they having power over the Magazines, if they had fired them the whole Towne had been utterly spoiled, and not one person in the Towne could have been secured from destruction thereby. But they wisely considered that old militarie axiome, If thine enemie will flie, make him a golden bridge, better be mercifull to a few, though offenders, than to ruinate all, both nocents and innocents, which indeed was the divellish doctrine and hellish counsell in the Popish powder-plot, by that most wicked Jesuite Garnet, that Arch-Traitor.

Thus it pleased the Lord most graciously to finish the great worke of so high concernment to the Kingdome, as things now stand, and to doe it in a more than ordinarie way of mercie and goodnesse, both in respect of the speedie and also unbloodie effecting of it, so little hurt being done on both sides, especially ours, considering how desperately and diligently the Colonell discharged his Ordnance at our men in the siege, as you have heard, with so little successe. And who now can be so dull hearted, and so blind sighted, as not to conceive and see plainly from all those last forementioned premises, especially these of this Towne of Portsmouth, and therewith all ingeniously confesse and acknowledge, The Lord Jehovah to be on the mount of mercies to us, and for his believing peoples prosperity and welfare."

The surrender of Portsmouth produced a deep sensation in the Cavalier Court at Oxford.

Says Clarendon: "The King's enemies were, in a manner, possessed of the whole kingdom. Portsmouth, the strongest and best fortified town then in the kingdom, was surrendered to them. Colonel Goring, about the beginning of

September, though he had, seemed to be so long resolved and prepared to expect a siege, and had been supplied with moneys according to his own proposal, was brought so low that he gave it up, only for liberty to transport himself beyond seas, and for his officers to repair to the King. And it were to be wished that there might be no more occasion to mention him hereafter, after this repeated treachery; and that his incomparable dexterity and sagacity had not so far prevailed over those who had been so often deceived by him, as to make it absolutely necessary to speak at large of him before this discourse comes to an end."

Another account says: "The King's most able General, Colonel Goring, was an airy bacchanalian, who, in the most critical emergency, could not be enticed from the jollities of the table, slighting every alarmist till the carouse was concluded."

The Marquis of Hartford, with Lord Seymour, Sir Ralph Hopton, Lord Pawlet, and others, were at Sherborne, hoping to be able to relieve Portsmouth, but as soon as he heard of its surrender he withdrew into Glamorganshire with the Lords Seymour and Pawlet, leaving Sir Ralph Hopton to march into Cornwall with the cavalry under his command. Sir William Waller, with his forces, marched to join the Earl of Essex, after making himself master of Portsmouth.

Clarendon says of the surrender of Portsmouth: "This blow struck the King to the very heart." Ever since the days of the Eighth Harry the dwellers in the Isle of Wight had "furnished themselves with a parochial artillery; each parish provided one piece of light brass ordnance, which was commonly kept either in the church, or in a small house built for the purpose, close by the church. Towards the end of the last century some sixteen or eighteen of these guns were still preserved in the island; they were of low calibre, some being six-pounders, and all the rest one-pounders. The islanders, by frequent practice, are said to have made themselves excellent artillerymen. The gun carriages and ammunition were provided by the parishes, and particular farms were charged with the duty of finding horses to draw them." Of the Earl of Portland, who was the Governor of the Island at the outbreak of the war, Clarendon says that the Parliament "threatened the Earl of Portland, who, with extraordinary vivacity, crossed their consultations, that they would remove him from his charge and government of the Isle of Wight (which at last they did *de facto*, by committing him to prison, without so much as assigning a cause), and to that purpose objected all the acts of good fellowship, all the wast of powder, and all the wast of wine, in the drinking of healths, and other acts of jollity, whenever he had been at his Government, from the first hour of his entering upon it." "And when they were resolved no longer to trust the Isle of Wight in the hands of the Earl of Portland, who had long been the King's Governour there, and had an absolute power over the affections of that people, they preferred the poor Earl of Pembroke to it, by an Ordnance of Parliament; who kindly accepted it, as a testimony of their favour, and so got into actual rebellion, which he never intended to do. It is a pity to say more of him, and less could not be said to make him known." Colonel Brett them assumed command at Carisbrooke Castle.

A previously quoted writer, in the "Penny Magazine" for 1836, says, "Carisbrook Castle was in one instance made memorable by the heroism of a female, whose adventures in some respects resembled those of the celebrated Royalist the Countess of Derby, and Queen of the Isle of Man. At an early stage of the Civil War, Jerome, Earl of Portland, who had been Governor for Charles I. during many years, was removed by Parliament as a Catholic, or as one who, at least, was a favourer of Popery. Shortly after he was suddenly imprisoned in London on this ground, and further accused by the Commons of a thoughtless and profligate expenditure of public money in ammunition, entertainments, and the drinking of loyal toasts in Carisbrook. The principal inhabitants of the island drew up a petition in favour of their 'noble and much honoured and beloved Captain and Governor,' in which, dropping all allusion to his wasting of the ammunition, &c., they stuck to the more important question of his religious faith, declaring that not only was he a good Protestant, but that there was not one professed Papist or favourer of Papacy in the whole Isle of Wight. This petition being disregarded by Parliament, they drew up a spirited remonstrance, in which they spoke of defending themselves by arms, and admitting no new governor that was not appointed by the King. Twenty-four knights and squires signed this paper, but the people were very differently inclined. They were led by Moses Read, the Mayor of Newport, who declared in favour of Parliament, and transmitted a representation on the great danger accruing to the State from the Countess of Portland being allowed to continue in the Castle, and to retain Colonel Brett there as her warden. Read soon received order 'to adopt any measures he might think necessary for the safety of the island,' to siege the fortress, and to secure Colonel Brett, the Countess, her five children, and other relatives who had taken shelter within the walls. He marched upon Carisbrook with the Militia of Newport, and 400 sailors drawn from the vessels at anchor near the island. The garrison of the old Castle did not exceed 20 men, but the Countess resolved not to surrender except on honourable conditions. At the approach of the force from Newport she advanced to the platform with a lighted match, and declared she would herself fire the first cannon against the assailants. Moses Read, who had expected no resistance, soon came to terms with the bold Countess, and the Castle was surrendered on conditions. The Countess was soon afterwards removed from the island. No other attempt was made at resistance, and though somewhat agitated by Charles's residence in Carisbrook a few years later, the Wight remained invariably tranquil during the whole of the Civil War. This fortunate circumstance invited many families from the neighbouring counties, which were exposed to the horrors of warfare, to go and settle there; in consequence of which the rents of farms rose in proportion of from 20l. to 100l., and did not find their ordinary level until the Restoration."

"Carisbrook Castle was used as a State prison both by Cromwell and by Charles II. Towards the end of the Commonwealth period Sir William Davenant was confined here, and here completed his 'Gondibert.'"

The following account by Mr. Moody gives certain additional details :—" The Parliament obtained possession of the Isle of Wight at the beginning of these intestine wars by the removal and imprisonment of its Governor, the Earl of Portland, who was attached to the cause of the ill-fated and ill-advised King. The principal inhabitants of the Island petitioned in the Earl's favour, and afterwards signed a declaration to support the Royal cause ; but the popular voice sided with Parliament, to whom Moses Read, Mayor of Newport, stated that the safety of the Island was endangered while the Countess of Portland and Colonel Brett were suffered to retain possession of Carisbrook Castle. In consequence of this representation, the Parliament ordered the captains of ships in the river to assist Read in any measure he might think necessary for securing the island. Read accordingly marched the Newport Militia with 400 naval auxiliaries against the Castle, where Brett had not above 20 men, many well wishers to him being deterred from assisting them by the menaces of the populace, who threw off all respect for their superiors. Harvey, the Curate of Newport, a man under peculiar obligations to the Earl of Portland, distinguished himself by stirring up the feelings of the besiegers against the Countess and her children, saying that she was a Papist, and exhorting them in the canting phraseology of the times to be valiant, as they were about 'to fight the battle of the Lord.' The Castle had not at that time three days' provision for its small garrison, yet the Countess, with the magnanimity of a Roman matron, went to the platform with a match in her hand, vowing she would fire the first cannon herself, and defend the Castle to the utmost extremity, unless honourable terms were granted. After some negotiations, articles of capitulation were agreed on, and the Castle surrendered." "The other forts of the Isle of Wight were seized about the same time. This decisive step in favour of the prevailing powers prevented the occurrence here of those scenes of bloodshed which speedily desolated many other parts of the kingdom. Indeed, the security which was here enjoyed induced many families to become residents in the isle, and the rent of land increased about 25 per cent. in consequence, but fell again soon after the Restoration. After the fall of Carisbrook Castle, the small garrison at Portsmouth left the town, which was subsequently held by Parliamentarians. The Royalists made more determined efforts at Winchester, Basing House, and in some other parts of Hampshire."

CHAPTER IV.—THE CAPTURE OF FARNHAM CASTLE, MARLBOROUGH, AND WINCHESTER.

The dwellers in and about Farnham Castle were the next to suffer from the miseries of the Civil War. Clarendon says: "Farnham Castle, in Surrey, whither some gentlemen who were willing to appear for the King had repaired, and were taken with less resistance than was fit, by Sir William Waller, some few days before (the capture of Marlborough, on December 3rd, 1642) deserved not the name of a garrison." Says Warburton, " A few days previously Farnham Castle was taken by Sir William Waller, after an indifferent defence by Sir John Denham, Colonel Fane, a son of the Earl of Westmoreland, who was shot through the cheek, and died a few days after, being almost the only person slain. Denham was a poet and a wit, but to confess the truth, the poets do not appear to advantage in this war, even in a Tyrtæan point of view. Edmund Waller proved both a trimmer and a coward; Sir John Suckling, a poltroon ; Denham, no better ; William Davenant was dissolute and negligent, and the great Milton condescended to write the most rancorous and unworthy lampoons." To quote Lord Nugent, "Sir John Denham was more eminent as poet, gamester, and wit, than soldier. When George Wither was shortly after this brought prisoner to Oxford, and was in some jeopardy, having been taken in arms against the King, Sir John Denham begged the King not to hang him, for that 'while Wither lives, Denham will not be the worst poet in England.'" This good natured epigram contributed to save Wither's life, and was also afterwards the means of restoring to Denham some of his property in Surrey, which had been confiscated by Parliament, and given to Wither. But it would be unfair to refer a kind and gentle act to interested motives.

But it is time to take Carlyle's advice, and "Hear Vicars, a poor human soul zealously prophesying as if through the organs of an ass——in a not mendacious, yet loud-spoken, exaggerative, more or less assinine manner." In his Parliamentary Chronicle (before referred to) Vicars thus describes

THE TAKING OF FARNHAM CASTLE.

"Much about which time (the beginning of December, 1642), certaine information came to London that that noble and renowned knight and most expert and courageous commander Sir William Waller (who had also a prime hand in the recovery of Portsmouth from Colonell Goring), together with Colonell Fane and some other brave commanders, having suddenly assaulted Farnham-castle, within the space of three houres forced their approach to so neare the castle-gates that with a petard they blew open one of them, and most resolutely made forcible entrance thereinto; whereupon the Cavaliers within threw their armes over the wall, fell down upon their knees, crying for quarter (not so much as having once offered or desired to treat of any honourable conditions to depart like souldiers, before the castle was entered), which Sir William gave them. There were taken in this castle one Master Denham, the new High Sheriffe of Surrey, Captaine Hudson, Captaine Brecknox, a brewer in Southwarke, a most desperate malignant against the Parliament, and divers other prisoners of quality, with about an hundred vulgar persons, together with all the armes and ammunition in the castle, and about 40,000l. in money and plate, as was credibly informed, besides that the common souldiers had good pillage for themselves to a good value. The taking of this castle so terrified the Cavaleers in Sussex that those of them of the long robe (Master Luckener, the Corporation Proctour), Master Aderson, Master Heath (son to that dry and barren Heath the Judge, like father, like son), and others of the same stamp, began now to traverse the commands of their Cavaleers, and would then have gladly joined issue with the Parliament, on easie termes." This success of Sir William

Waller had a disastrous influence upon the fortunes of Basing House, as the Roundheads thus secured a most advantageous base of operations, of which they did not fail to make good use.

On November 21st, 1642, Lord Grandison's troope of horse and Colonell Greye's dragooners rode into Basingstoke, and 'one Master Goater' writes 'to a Merchant of good quality in Lombard-street' that they lay there 'eleven dayes; wee had emploiment enough to dress the meat and provide drinke for them. It hath been a great charge to our Towne, they demanded two thousand yards of woollen cloth and 500 yards of linnen at fourteene pence the yard; so the linnen Drapers brought theirs in, but the clothiers and wollen Drapers made no great haste, so they served themselves some at one shop and some at another.'" Part of the garrison of Basing House was added to Lord Grandison's force, which called forth a letter of remonstrance from the Marquis. All being prepared, "last Friday they went away, and as we heard, are gone to Marlborough, and many say they heard the guns goe off very fiercely." The cannons' roar told of the capture of Marlborough by Lord Wilmot, Lieutenant-General of Horse, on Saturday, December 3rd, 1642, after a sharp action. The towne was given up to pillage, and according to Vicars the Cavaliers committed great excesses. Sir John Ramsay, the Governor, was taken, "and other officers, who yielded upon quarter, above 1000 prisoners, great stores of Armes, four pieces of Cannon, and a good quantity of Ammunition, with all which the Lieut.-Gen. returned safe to Oxford." The weakening of the garrison of Basing House encouraged the friends of the Parliament to attack it, and they accordingly seem to have made one or both of those assaults which were repulsed, as we have seen, by the Marquis and "his Gentlemen armed with six musquets," probably aided, as they were on another occasion, by volleys of stones and tiles from the roof of the house. The loss of Marlborough was keenly felt by the Parliament, which had intended to make it a rendezvous for all their adherents in Wiltshire and the adjacent counties. Sir William Waller, Colonel Brown (of whom more anon), and others were sent to attack the victorious Cavaliers. Failing to meet with them at Marlborough, they pursued them to Winchester, with what result we shall presently see. "Mercurius Rusticus" thus describes the conduct of the Puritan force on the march. They seem to have, at any rate, possessed the virtue of impartiality, so far as plunder was concerned:—

"About December, 1642, the Collonels Waller, Brown, and others, marching from Ailesbury to Windsor, and thence by Newbury to Winchester, their soldiers in the march plundered every minister within six miles of the road without distinction, whether of their own party or of the other, whether they subscribed for Episcopacy, Presbytery, or Independency, whether they wore a surplise or refused it, only if they did not they afforded them the less booty. Those who were Confiders, whose Irregularity and Nonconformity armed them with confidence to appear, petitioned the House of Commons for relief and satisfaction, it being taken into consideration that this was not according to their new phrase, 'to weaken the wicked,' but the righteous and such as stood well affected to the Parliament, hereupon slandering the Cavaliers with the fact which their own soldiers had done; and to make the 'foolish citizens bleed free' there was an order drawn up and published, 'That in regard the petitioners were well affected men and plundered by the Cavaliers, there should be a general collection made for them the next Fast-day, and that the preachers should exhort the people and pray to God to enlarge the people's hearts, bountifully to relieve the petitioners.'" (Pp. 89-90). But mark the end of all this. Lord Grandison was despatched to the relief of the Marquis of Winchester. Let Clarendon speak:—:" This success (the capture of Marlborough) was a little shadowed by the unfortunate loss of a very good regiment of Horse within a few days after, for the Lord Grandison, by the miscarriage of orders was exposed at too great a distance from the Army, with his single regiment, consisting of 300, and a regiment of 200 Dragoons, to the unequal encounter of a party of the enemy of 5000 Horse and Dragoons, and so was himself, after a retreat made to Winchester, there taken with all his party, which was the first loss of the kind the King sustained; but without the least fault of the commander, and the misfortune was much lessened by his making an escape himself with two or three of his principal officers, who were very welcome to Oxford." John Vikars thus describes the failure of this attempt to succour Basing, and the subsequent occupation of Winchester, in his Parliamentary Chronicle, published in

1644. (P. 227 et seq.) "And about December the 7th, 1642, came a poste to the Parliament with letters from Winchester, setting forth a very great and famous victorie obtained by their forces against the Cavaliers in Winchester, which was in this manner effected: The Lord Digbie, Lord Grandison, Commissarie Wilmot, and some others of their confederacie, having possessed themselves of Marleborough, and most basely and barbarously pillaged and plundered the same, and like so many traiterous and lustfull bloodie thieves ravished and abused the women and maids of the towne (brave defenders of the Protestant religion, and showing themselves indeed to be the true sworne brethren of their bloody brothers in Ireland), these, I say, hearing that Sir William Waller, Colonell Browne (whose very names were, and that most justly, very dreadfull to them), Colonel Hurrey (who played both parties false), Colonel Middleton, and other forces of the Parliament were coming against them they thereupon thought it no boot to stay any longer there, but having, as I say, most cruelly got what they came for, viz., pillage and food, they speedily left poore Marleborough in most lamentable condition, and that audacious traitor Lord Digbie, with a part of their forces and a greatest part of their pillage, returned to Oxford, leaving the Lord Grandison with those other forces to see what further pillage he could meet with in those parts, but fearing to be caught nappiug by active Sir William Waller and his forces, and the better to protect himself and his Cavaliers from the pursuit of the Parliament's forces, he retreated to Winchester, a place more like to give him kind entertainment, being full of Malignant spirits, who indeed were not a little glad at his coming, thinking themselves now secure from danger, being under the wings of a bird of their own feather. But the Parliament forces with those commanders also comming to Marleborough and missing the Cavaliers there, resolved to follow in hot pursuit of them, and to revenge that cruelty exercised on that miserable town. Whereupon, after some coursing about the country, having notice by their scouts of the Lord Grandison's being now at Winchester, they bent their course with all speed thither, and by-the-way, strangely (if not wilfully in some of the commanders) failed of falling on the Lord Digbie's forces in their passage, and so they came before the citie of Winchester. Now the Cavaliers, having notice thereof, were not a little startled, and considering it altogether unsafe to keep themselves within the towne, and so give the Parliament's forces opportunity to besiege them, because they could not be able to hold out long for want of provisions fit for a siege, they resolved, therefore, to march out and to give them battell abroad, and so accordingly they issued out and prepared for a pitcht field, which the Parliament forces perceiving drew up all their forces also into a battalia, and came up most bravely and resolutely to them, and most stoutly gave them the first charge with their horse, and so there began to be a very hot skirmish between them for the time on both sides. But truly the Parliament's soldiers followed their business so closely and couragiously, and with such undaunted spirit, that after about halfe an houre's fight they inforced the Cavaliers from their ground and drove them violently into the towne againe, and, being very eager of their prey, resolved not to leave them, but most valiantly pursued them up to the towne walles, where the most part of their regiment fiercely assaulted the citie at one side of it, and notwithstanding the exceeding high and very steep passage up to the walls, even so steep that they had no other way to get up, but of necessity to creep up upon their knees and hands from the bottom to the top, which was as high as most houses, the enemie playing all the while on them with their muskets, and yet slew but three men in this their getting up, so at last (though with much danger and difficultie) our soldiers got up and plyed their businesse so hotly and closely that they had quickly made a great breach in the wall. And here Colonell Browne's Sergeant-Major (i.e., Major) deserved much honour in this service, he himself being also one of the first that forced upon the breach into the towne, though the enemies bullets flew thick about them, upon sight of whose ever invincible valour all the rest of his comrades followed close and drove the Cavaliers before them into the midst of the towne; who, having no place else of shelter, fled apace into the Castle, which yet was not so considerable a sanctuary or place of refuge to defend them long, especially it being destitute of ordnance, so our men beset the Castle round with musqueteers and horse, and lay per-dues under the wall, so that not a man of them could stir. Then about 10 or 11 of the clocke at night they sounded a parley, but our men would not accept it, and against the next morning we had prepared a great quantity of faggots and pitch barrels to fire the Castle-gate, in regard that we wanted ordnance and petards proper for such a worke. But as soon as it began to be light they, seeing no hope of helpe, sounded another parley, wherein the Lord Grandison himselfe, with five or six more, desired to be, which at last was accepted, and after some debate articles and conditions were agreed upon, viz., that they should all yeeld themselves up prisoners to the Parliament, presently resign the Castle into Sir William Waller's custody and possession, their armes, horses, money, and all to be seized on by the Parliament's officers in armes. But many of the townsmen, who had most of all infested our men, and shot most desperately at them, were now well repaid for that pains by our souldiers, who most notably plundered and pillaged their houses, taking whatsoever they liked best out of them, and so the souldiers dealt with all their common souldiers, or ordinary cavaleers, who only had quarter granted them for their lives. Here were taken prisoners the Lord Grandison himselfe, and his lieutenant-colonell, and betweene fourty and fifty other commanders of good worth and quality of Hampshire, about 600 horse, 200 dragooners, and 600 armes, together with great store of other pillage. In this fight from first to last there were about 30 or 40 slaine on their side, and but three or four on the Parliament's. Colonel Browne's regiment had the honour to take the city, and to make the first breach in the wall, and so to enter the towne. They assessed the townesmen and inhabitants for their base malignancy in so desperately opposing them at 1000l., or else to plunder the whole towne (which was hardly restrained in the common souldiers, especially in some houses), but chiefly some Papists' houses there, and the sweet Cathedralists, in whose houses and studies they found great store of Popish books, pictures, and crucifixes, which the souldiers carried up and downe the streets and market-place in triumph to make themselves merry; yea, and they for certaine piped before them with the organpipes (the faire organs in the minster being broken downe by the souldiers), and then afterwards cast them all into the fire and burnt them, and what (think'e you) was the case of those Romish Micky's, when their pretty petty Popish and apish-gods were thus taken from them, and burnt in the fire before them? And thus the Lord most graciously began in some measure to revenge the wrongs of his poore people of Marleborough, makeing these their enemies come short of long possessing their prey there gotten, which was thus by these most valiant Parliamentarians valiantly and violently regained out of their devouring teeth. And now to goe on" (p. 231). Truly "the good old times" must now and again have been somewhat unpleasant to live in! But let us hear the Royalist account of this matter. This we find in "Mercurius Rusticus, or the Countries' complaint of the barbarous outrages committed by the Sectaries of this late flourishing Kingdom."—

"Thy substance and thy treasure will I give to the spoil without price, and that for all thy sins, even in all thy borders."—Jer. xv., 13.

P. 144. " The rebels defying God in his own house; their sacrilege, in stealing Church plate and goods, their irreverence towards the King by abusing his statue, their heathenish barbarity in violating the bones and ashes of dead Monarchs, Bishops, Saints, and Confessors in the Cathedral Church of Winchester, &c. The next instance which I shall give of the rebels' sacrilege and profaneness is in the Cathedral Church of Winchester, which city, as it was the Royal seat of the King of the West Saxons in the time of the Heptarchy, so was it the seat of the Bishops of that people, after Kenwalchus, King of the West Saxons (not brooking the barbarous broken expressions of Agilbertus, his Bishop) divided this large diocese between Agilbertus and Wina, and leaving Agilbertus to reside at Dorchester, caused Wina to be consecrated Bishop of Winchester. Before we tell you by whom and in what manner this Church was robbed and spoyled of its ornaments and beauty, it will not be impertinent (while it may serve as an aggravation of their impiety) briefly to set down by whom this Church was built and so richly adorned, as lately we saw it. This magnificent structure, which now stands, was begun by Walkelinus, the 35th Bishop of that See, which work left innerfect, and but begun by him, was but coldly prosecuted by the succeeding Bishops until William of Wickham (the magnificent sole founder of two St. Mary Colledges, the one in Oxford commonly called New Colledge, the other a nurcery to this, near Winchester) came to possess this See. He, amongst many other works of Piety, built the whole nave or body of this Church from the quire to the west end, the Chappels on the east end, beyond the quire, had their several founders. The hallowed ornaments and utensils of this Church being many, rich, and costly, were the gifts of several benefactors, who, tho' their names are not recorded on earth, have found their reward in heaven. This Church was first differenced by the name of St. Amphibalus, who received a Crown of Martyrdom under the Persecution of Dioclesian. Next it exchanged this name for that of St. Peter, and again, this for that of St. Swithin, the 18th Bishop of this See. Last of all, it was dedicated to the Holy Trinity, whose blessed name is now called upon it; which holy name, though it could not but put the rebels in mind whose possession and house it was, did not at all afford it patronage and protection from their accursed rage and madness.

"The rebels, under the conduct of Sir William Waller, sate down before the City of Winchester on Tuesday, the 12th of December, 1642, about 12 of the clock, and entered the city that afternoon between two and three. Being masters of the city, they instantly fall upon the Close under a pretence to search for Cavaliers. They seize upon the Prebend's horses, and demand their persons with many threatning words. That night they break into some of the Prebend's houses, and such houses as they were directed into by their brethren, the seditious schismaticks of the city, and plundered their goods. But the castle, not yet surrendered into the rebels hands, something awed their insolency, which, being the next day delivered up to their power, did not only take away the restraint which was upon them, but incouraged them without check or control to rob and defie, both God and all good men, Wednesday, therefore, and Wednesday night being spent in plundering the city and Close. On Thursday morning, between nine and ten of the clock (hours set apart for better imployments, and therefore purposely in probability chosen by them, being resolved to profane all that was canonical) they violently break open the Cathedral Church, and being entred to let in the tyde, they presently open the great west door, where the barbarous soldiers stood ready, nay, greedy, to rob God and to pollute His temple. The doors being open as if they meant to invade God Himself, as well as His profession, they enter the church with colours flying, their drums beating, their matches fired, and that all might have their part in so horrid an attempt, some of their troops of horse also accompanied them in their march, and rode up through the body of the church and quire, until they came to the altar; there they begin their work, they rudely pluck down the table, and break the rail, and afterwards carrying it to an ale-house, they set it on fire, and in that fire burnt the books of Common Prayer, and all the singing books belonging to the quire; they throw down the organ, and break the stones of the Old and New Testament, curiously cut out in carved work, beautified with colours, and set round about the top of the stalls of the quire; from hence they turn to the monuments of the dead, some they utterly demolish, others they deface. They begin with Bishop Fox, his chappel which they utterly deface, they break all the glass windows of this chappel, not because they had any pictures in them, either of Patriarch, Prophet, Apostle, or Saint, but because they were of painted coloured glass; they demolish and overturn the monuments of Cardinal Beaufort, son to John of Gaunt, Duke of Lancaster, by Katharine Swinfort, founder of t e hospital of S. Cross, near Winchester, who sate Bishop of this See 43 years. They deface the monument of William of Wainflet, Bishop likewise of Winchester, Lord Chancellor of England, and the magnificent founder of Magdalen Colledge in Oxford, which monument in a grateful piety, being lately beautified by some that have or lately have had, relation to that foundation, made these rebels more eager upon it, to deface it, but while that colledge, the unparalleled example of his bounty, stands in despight of the malice of these inhuman rebels, William of Wainflet cannot want a more lasting monument to transmit his memory to posterity. From hence they go into Queen Marie's chappel, so called because in it she was married to King Philip of Spain; here they brake the Communion table in pieces, and the velvet chair whereon she sat when she was married. They attempted to deface the monument of the late Lord Treasurer, the Earl of Portland, but being in brass, their violence made small impression on it, therefore they leave that, and turn to his father's monument, which, being of stone, was more obnoxious to their fury; here, mistaking a Judge for a Bishop, led into the error by the resemblance or counterfeit of a square cap on the head of the statue, they strike off not only the cap, but also the head too of the statue, and so leave it. Amongst other acts of piety and bounty done by Richard Fox, the 57th Bishop of this See, he covered the quire, the presbytery, and the iles adjoining with a goodly vault, and new glassed all the windows in that part of t e church, and caused the bones of such kings, princes, and prelates as had been buried in this church and lay dispersed and scattered in several parts of the cathedral to be collected and put into several chests of lead, with inscriptions on each chest whose bones lodged in them. These chests, to save them from rude and prophane hands, he caused to be placed on the top of a wall of exquisite workmanship, built by him to inclose the presbytery. There never to be removed (as a man might think) but by the last trump, did rest the bones of many kings and queens, as of Alfredus, Edwardus senior, Cadredus, the brother of Athelstane, Edwinus Canutus, Hardecanutus, Emma, the mother, and Edward the Confessor, her son. Kiniglissus, the first founder of the Cathedral of Winchester, Egbert, who, abolishing the Heptarchy of the Saxons, was the first English monarch, William Rufus, and divers others. With these in the chests were deposited the bones of many Godly bishops and confessors, as of Birinus, Hedda, Swithinus, Frithestanus, S. Elphegus the Confessor, Stigandus, Wina, and others. Had not the barbarous inhuman impiety of these schismaticks and rebels showed the contrary, we could not have imagined that anything but the like piety which here inshrined them or a Resurrection should ever have disturbed the repose of these venerable, but not Popish reliques. But these monsters of men, to whom nothing is holy, nothing is sacred, did not stick to prophane and violate these cabinets of the dead, and to scatter their bones all over the pavement of the church: for on the north side of the quire there they threw down the chests wherein were deposited the bones of the Bishops; the like they did to the bones of William Rufus, of Queen Emma, of Hardecanutus, and of Edward the Confessor, and were going on to practise the like impiety on the bones of all the rest of the West Saxon Kings. But the outcry of the people, detesting so great inhumanity, caused some of their commanders (more compassionate to these ancient monuments of the dead than the rest) to come in amongst them and to restrain their madness. But that devilish malice which was not permitted to rage and overflow to the spurning and trampling on the bones of all, did satiate itself, even to a prodigious kind of wantonness, on those which were already in their power. And, therefore, as if they meant (if it had been possible) to make these bones contract a postnume guilt by being now made passive instruments of more than heathenish sacrilege and prophaneness, those windows which they could not reach with their swords, musquets, or rests, they brake to pieces by throwing at them the bones of Kings, Queens, Bishops, Confessors, or Saints, so that the spoil done on the windows will not be repaired for 1000l.; nor did the living find better measure from them than the dead, for whereas our Dread Sovereign that now is (the best of Kings) was gratiously pleased, as a pledge of his princely favour to the Church to honour it with the gift of his own statue, together with the statue of his dear father, King James of ever blessed memory, both of massy brass, both which statues were erected at the front of the entrance into the quire, these atheistical rebels, as if they would not have so much of the militia to remain with the King as the bare image and representation of a sword by his side, they breake off the swords from the sides of both of the statues; they break the cross from off the globe in the hand of our gratious Sovereign now living, and with their swords hacked and hewed the crown on the head of it, swearing they would bring him back to his Parliament.' A most flagitious crime, and that for the like S. Chrysostome (Hom. 2. ad populum Antioch), with many tears, complains he much feared 'the City of Antioch, the Metropolis, and head (as he calls it) of the East, would have been destroyed from the face of the Earth.' for when in a tumult, the seditious citizens of Antioch had done the like affront to Theodosius the Emperour in overturning his statues, how doth that holy Bishop bemoan? how doth he bewail that City? which, fearing the severe effects of the abused Emperor's just indignation 'of a populous City, a Mother boasting of a numerous issue, was on a sudden become a Widow, left desolate and forsaken of her Inhabitants, some' out of the sense and horror of the guilt abandoning the City and flying into the desolate wilderness, others lurking in holes and confining themselves to the dark corners of their own houses, thereby hoping to escape the vengeance due to so disloyal, so traiterous a fact, 'because of this four injury offered the Emperour's Statue. He (as that Father speakse was wronged, that was the supreme head of a) men, and had no equal on earth.' But what wonder is it that these miscreants should offer such shameful indignities to the Representation of his Royal Person and the Emblems of his Sacred power, when the heads of this damnable Rebellion (who set these their Agents on work) offer worse affronts to his Sacred person himself. and by their Rebellious Votes and Illegal Ordinances daily strike at the Substance of that power of which the Crown, the Sword, and Scepter are but emblems and shadows, which yet, notwithstanding, ought to have been venerable and aweful to these men, in respect of their Relation. After all this, as if what they had already done were all too little, they go on in their horrible wickedness, they seize upon all the Communion Plate, the Bibles and Service-Books, rich Hangings, large Cushions of Velvet, all the Pulpit Clothes, some whereof were of Cloth of Silver, some of Cloth of Gold. They break up the Muniment House and take away the Common Seal of the Church, supposing it to be silver, and a fair piece of gilt plate, given by Bishop Cotton ; they tear the evidences of their hands, and cancel their charter; in a word, whatever they found in the church of any value and portable they take it with them, what was neither they either deface or destroy it. And now, having ransacked the church, having defied God in His own house and the King in His own statue, having violated the urns of the dead, having abused the bones and scattered the ashes of deceased monarchs, bishops, saints, and confessors, they return in triumph, bearing their spoils with them. The troopers (because they were the most conspicuous) ride through the streets in surplesses with such hoods and tippets as they found, and that they might boast to the world how glorious a victory they had atchieved, they hold out their trophies to all spectators, for the troopers, thus clad in the priests' vestments, rode carrying Common Prayer Books in one hand and some broken organ pipes together with the mangled pieces of carved work, but now mentioned containing some histories of both Testaments, in the other. In all this giving too just occasion to all good Christians to complain with the Psalmist, 'O God, the heathen are come into Thine inheritance, Thy holy Temples have they defiled, The dead bodies of Thy servants have they abused, and scattered their bones as one heweth wood upon the earth. Help us, O God of our salvation, for the glory of Thy name.'—Psalm 79. It has been said that "of the brass torn from violated monuments might have been built a house as strong as the brazen towers in old romances." That acute and indefatigable antiquary Dr. Milner tells us that prebendaries were regularly installed in Winchester Cathedral until late in the summer of 1645. The Rev. Laurence Hinton, rector of Chilbolton, was installed on December 14th, 1644 ; the Rev. Thomas Gawen, rector of Exton, dates from June 17th, 1645 ; and the Rev. Nicholas Preston from July 23rd, 1645. As the result of an Act passed in 1643, all crosses, crucifixes, representations of saints and angels, copes, surplices, hangings, candlesticks, basins, organs, &c., were carried out of the Cathedral, and other churches' railings and altars were destroyed, raised chancels levelled, and according to local tradition cavalry were during these troublous times sometimes quartered, together with their horses, in the Cathedral. It is pleasant to find that a Whykehamist, who is said to have been Colonel Nathaniel Fiennes, the brother of Lord Say and Sele, who having been educated at Winchester, was also one of the Fellows of New College, and who possessed considerable influence amongst the Parliamentarians, was the means of saving from the spoiler Winchester College, together with the tomb and statue of him "whose rectitude, knowledge of humanity, talents for public work, and steady industry justify us in claiming for him a place in history close to, if not beside, such brightest stars of the time as Chaucer, Wycliffe, and Edward the Black Prince." Need we say that we speak of William of Whykeham, whom all dwellers beneath St. Giles's Hill love well ? The authority for all this havoc and destruction in Cathedrals and Parish Churches was "An order from the Parliament against divers Popish innovations, dated September 8th, 1641, being Wednesday : It is this day ordered by the Commons in Parliament assembled that the Church Wardens of every Parish and Chappell respectively do forthwith remove the Communion Table from the east end of the Church, Chappell, or Chancel into some other convenient place ; and that they take away the rails and level the chancells as heretofore they were, before the late innovations. That all crucifixes, scandalous pictures of any one or more persons of the Trinity, and all images of the Virgin Mary shall be taken away and abolished, and that all tapers, candlesticks, or basons be removed from the Communion Table. That all corporall bowing at the Name (of Jesus) or towards the east end of the Church, Chappell, or Chancell, or towards the Communion Table be henceforth forborn. That the Lord's Day be duly sanctified, all dancing and other sports, either before or after Divine Service, be forborn and restrained, and that the preaching of God's Word be permitted in the afternoone in the several Churches and Chappells of this Kingdome, &c."

"Die Mercurii, Sept. 8th, 1641 :—
"It is this day ordered by the House of Commons, now assembled in Parliament, that it shall be lawfull for the parishioners of any parish within the kingdome of England and Wales to set up a lecture, and to maintain an orthodox minister at their own charge to preach every Lord's Day where there is no preaching, and to preach one day in the week where there is no weekly lecture.

Hen. Elsyn. Eler. Dom. Com."

We have already quoted the words of Clarendon, that the misfortune of the defeat of Lord Grandison "was much lessened by his making an escape himself, with two or three of his principal officers, who were very, very welcome to Oxford."

But similar satisfaction was by no means felt in London. Vicars charges the fugitives with a breach of parole, saying, "About the middle of this December the Parliament had certaine information that those active and couragious champions, Sir William Waller and Colonell Brown, and the forces with them forementioned, having secured the prisoners they had taken at Winchester, in the strong towne of Portsmouth, whither they had sent them all, save only the Lord Grandison and Sergeant-Major Willis, who had perfidiously, contrary to their engagements to Colonel Goodwin, made an escape, were now bent for Chichester in Sussex."

Colonel Goodwin (here referred to) had been one of the members for Buckinghamshire two years previously. Here is a picture of him and his troopers from a Cavalier point of view. Listen to "Mercurius Rusticus":—"On Monday, the 29th of May, 1643, a boy of five or six years of age, attended by a youth, was comming to Oxford to his father, an officer in the King's army passing through Buckinghamshire, he fell into the hands of some troopers of Colonel Goodwin's Regiment, who not only pillaged him of the cloaths which he brought with him, but took his doublet off his back, and would have taken away his hat and boots, if the youth that attended on him had not earnestly interceded for them to save them. For one of the company more tender-hearted than the rest, moved with the child's cries and affrightment, and with the youth's earnest entreaty, prevailed with the rest not to rob the child these necessary fences against the injury of wind and weather. Yet tho' they spare him of these things, they rob him of his horse, and leave the poor child to a tedious long journey on foot. This barbarism to a poor child, far from his friends, almost distracted with fear, so prevailed with some, that they made Colonel Goodwin and Sir Robert Pye acquainted with it, hoping to find them sensible of so cruel practices on a poor child, but these great professors and champions of religion only laughed at the the relation, without giving any redress to the child's injuries. This want of justice in the commanders animated the soldiers to prosecute their villanies to a greater height, for that night they came to the place where the child lay, and the poor soul being in bed fast asleep, his innocent rest not disturbed with the injuries of the day, they dived into his and his attendant's pockets, robbed them of all their monies, and left them either to borrow more or beg for sustenance in their journey to Oxford."

"Mercurius Rusticus," says on the other hand that Colonel Brown in his letter to Isaac Pennington, the Lord Mayor of London, threw the blame of Lord Grandison's escape on Colonel Urrey, who, as we know, repeatedly changed sides during the war. The colonel, however, contrived to clear himself of this charge, and received compensation from the fund originally raised for the relief of the clergy who had been plundered by the soldiers of the Parliament. Let "Mercurius Rusticus" tell the story :—

"But Winchester being surprised and the Lord Grandison taken prisoner, Colonell Brown, in a letter to famous Isaac Pennington, magnifies the victory and enlarged the glory of it very much, but that circumstance of taking that noble Lord prisoner, but what did much eclipse the honour obtained that day, in the Letter he adds, that by the treachery of Colonell Urrey he was escaped. Little Isaac had hardly so much patience as to read out the Letter, but he summons his Mirmidons, and gives an Alarm to his Redcoats, the Messengers of his Fury, and sends them instantly to plunder Mistress Urries Lodging; it was no sooner said than done, they being as swift to act mischief as Isaac was ready to command it; what they had in charge they perform faithfully, and plunder her of no more but all. Mistress Urrey presently gives notice to her husband what measure she found in the City while he was in their service in the Country. The Colonell, upon the information, hastens to London to expostulate for this Injury, and for redress, complains to the House against the Ringleader Brown and Rout-Master 'little Isaac.' Upon hearing both parties, the House quits Colonell Urrey from any conspiracy with my Lord Grandison, or connivance at his escape, and for reparation of his losses they order him £100, to be paid out of the monies collected the last Fast Day for the plundered Ministers, who by this means were plundered twice, and so, one Order begetting another, they Order, 'That a new collection shall be made for the Petitioners the next Fast Day;' nor was this the first Debt by many that have been paid by the abused Charity of London, the 'great tax-bearing Mule,' as one justly calls it."

Leaving the imprisoned Cavaliers in safe custody at Portsmouth, let us follow Sir William Waller on his victorious march into Sussex.

CHAPTER IV. — THE GENERALS AND THEIR FORCES.

Before we speak of the stirring events which followed the capture of Winchester by Sir Wm. Waller at the close of the year 1642, it will be well for us to look at the generals on either side and at the forces under their command.

Sir William Waller belonged to an ancient family in this county, and laid claim to the ownership of Winchester Castle and to the office of hereditary chief butler of England. He had served with credit in the armies of the German Princes against the Emperor. When the Civil War commenced he was a member of the Committee of Safety, and raised a troop of horse for the service of the Parliament. Appointed to a subordinate command under the Earl of Essex, he, as we have already seen, made himself master of Portsmouth during the autumn of 1642, obliging Goring, the Governor, to take ship for Holland.

Winchester, Chichester, Malmesbury, and Hereford in quick succession opened their gates, and a swift and successful night march brought him to the Severn shore. Flat-bottomed boats speedily carried him and his troops across the stream, and he at once captured or dispersed a small Royalist force which had designs against Gloucester. The Parliament and the city idolised him, giving to him the proud title of "William the Conqueror." Effecting a junction with the Earl of Essex at Reading, that important town was taken by storm on April 27th, 1643. Essex loved him not, nor was Waller, truth to tell, the most loyal of subordinates. Essex wasted his army by inaction, whilst Waller lost his by desertion, "as the manner of him was."

The following letter from Sir William Waller to Sir Ralph Hopton, his constant and able opponent, is honourable alike to the writer and to the recipient :—

"My affections to you are so unchangeable that hostility itself cannot violate my friendship to your person, but I must be true to the cause wherein I serve. I should wait on you, according to your desire, but that I look on you as engaged in that party without the possibility of retreat, and, consequently, incapable of being wrought upon by any persuasion. That Great God, who is the searcher of all hearts, knows with what a sad fear I go upon this service, and with what perfect hate I look upon a war without an enemy. But I look upon it as *Opus Domini!* We are both on the stage, and must act those parts that are assigned to us in this tragedy ; but let us do it in the way of honour, and without personal animosity !"

Such was the man who was ere long to lay siege to Arundel, Chichester, and Basing. Waller's opponent at Portsmouth, "the King's most able general, Colonel Goring, was an airy Bacchanalian, who on the most critical emergency could not be enticed from the jollities of the table, slighting every alarmist till the carous was concluded." But Lord Hopton was a man cast in a more noble mould. Eliot Warburton says ("Memoirs of Prince Rupert," p. 113). "Sir Ralph, afterwards Lord Hopton, heir to one of the most powerful and ancient families in Somersetshire, was born in 1598. He was, early in life, distinguished by an aptness for study, and for the attainment of languages, to which he joined an ardent and enterprising spirit. He was at the battle of Prague, and aided in carrying off the poor Queen of Bohemia from her dangers. He was devoted to her as fervently and after as pure a fashion as the other heroes whom she fascinated. For her sake he passed five years of his youth in the wars of the Low Countries and the Palatinate. He was knighted at the Coronation of King Charles, and was elected to serve in Parliament for the City of Wells. Like most men of his disposition, he inclined at first towards the popular party, and was selected to read before the King the 'Remonstrance' of November, 1641. He, however, soon came to an opposite opinion, and henceforth applied himself vigorously to promote the interests of the Crown in his own county. He was almost constantly opposed to Sir W. Waller."

In January, 1646, when the King had only two small armies remaining in the field, the one in Cornwall, commanded by Lord Hopton, and the other on the borders of Wales under Lord Astley, things were looking serious. The Prince of Wales, abandoned by Goring and Grenville, still held sway in the west. He sent for Lord Hopton, and offered him the command of the seven or eight thousand men who still remained with the colours. "My lord," answered Hopton, "it is not a custom when men are not willing to submit to what they are enjoined to say that it is against their honour; that their honour will not suffer them to do this or that; for my part, I cannot at this time obey your Highness without resolving to lose my honour; but since your Highness has thought fit to command me, I am ready to obey, even with the loss of my honour."

Having shown himself a right skilful general, his own men at last obliged him to surrender. "Treat then," said he "but not for me," and neither he nor Lord Capel would be included in the capitulation. During the Commonwealth he found an asylum in Spain. He had been created a peer in 1643, and married the widow of Sir Justinian Lewer, but dying without children, the title became extinct. Sir William Waller was the assailant, and Lord Hopton the protector of the Cavalier strongholds in Hampshire and the neighbouring counties.

John, the 5th and "Loyal" Marquis of Winchester was thrice married. His first wife was Jane, daughter of Thomas, Lord Savage, by whom he became father to Charles, the 6th Marquis and first Duke of Bolton. He had the air of one born to command, and was a man of great determination, as we know from his answer to the arguments of Hugh Peters, "hat if the King had no more ground in England but Basing House, he would venture as he did, and maintain it to the uttermost." He also possessed considerable literary ability, and translated Quare's Devout Entertainments of a Christian Soul. In 1852 he translated The Gallery of Heroic Women, and Salon's Holy History in the following year. Having left the Church of England for that of Rome, his mansion naturally became a rallying point for the friends of the Queen in the south-western counties. "So early as September 23rd, 1642, the King wrote to the Earl of Newcastle, not only to permit, but to order him to enlist soldiers without considering their religion, or, in deed, anything except their fidelity to the Royal cause. We constantly find Basing described by its assailants as a Popish garrison. At first Roman Catholics and Protestants fought shoulder to shoulder, but during the last days of the heroic defence almost the whole garrison professed the same religion as the Marquis, who was at this time about 44 years of age. "Aymey Loyaulte, 'Love Loyalty,' not Royalty," says Mr. Mudie, "shows that the Marquis stood out thus gallantly for the King, not upon personal grounds, but from regarding him as the legitimate head of the government and administrator of the laws; that he was a loyalist in principle, not a party Royalist." Mr. Mudie adds: "Colonel Norton," who is so prominently mentioned in the diary of the siege, "was also a loyalist, though a loyalist having different views of the matter. He took the field, and took it bravely, for the privilege of the Parliament, which Charles had unquestionably invaded; but he had no hostility to the King according to law. It happened in that unfortunate contest in which England suffered more than in any other time since the Wars of the Roses that some of the most loyal men, the men most devoted to the whole constitution in all its three branches, were arranged upon each side, while mere courtiers mingled with the one party and enemies to both King and Parliament mingled with the other. Upon the side of Charles the loyal men stood only for the constitutional authority of the King, while the courtiers stood for him in disregard of the constitution. The loyalists on the side of Parliament stood only for its constitutional privileges, the rest of that party being enemies to all government. Between the first sections of the two parties it was merely a misunderstanding, but between the second it was implacable and deadly opposition. The former were anxious to save both constitution and country, the latter recked not for the ruin of both. This distinction is an important one, and necessary before we do justice to brave and good men upon either side—to such men as the Marquis of Winchester and Colonel Norton during this distracted and frequently misrepresented period of our history."

The Lady Marchioness of Winchester at this time was the second wife of the Marquis. She was named Honora, and was the daughter of Richard, Earl of St. Albans and Clanricarde, and was the mother of four sons and three daughters. Clarendon describes her as being "a lady of great honour and alliance, and sister to the Earl of Essex and to the Lady Marchioness of Hertford." She shared in all the dangers of the siege, and saw her maid killed by a grenade, she herself having a narrow escape. Together with the other ladies of the garrison, she aided in casting into bullets the lead stripped from the roof and turrets of the house, and it was in great measure owing to her representations and entreaties that Colonel Gage was despatched from Oxford to the relief of her beleaguered husband. Her brother was the celebrated General of the Parliament, "the slow-going, inarticulate, indignant, somewhat elephantine man," as Carlyle calls him.

Family strife once more! Colonel Richard Norton, already referred to, belonged to a family which had settled long before at Alresford, Southwick, near Portsmouth, and Rotherfield. His ancestor and namesake had been knighted at Basing House by Queen Elizabeth, and it was while Charles I. was the guest of Sir Daniel Norton at Southwick Park that he received the news of the assassination of the Duke of Buckingham by Felton at Portsmouth.

Colonel Richard Norton resided at the Manor House of Old Alresford, and is said to have distinguished himself in the battle of Cheriton by bringing up a body of Horse through bye ways, from his knowledge of the country, to charge the rear of the enemy. With this gentleman Oliver Cromwell was on familiar and intimate terms, distinguishing him in letters to his private friends by the appellation of "Idle Dick Norton." Clarendon says that the besiegers of Basing House were "united in this service under the command of Norton, a man of spirit and of the greatest fortune of all the rest," and speaks of "the known courage of Norton." He served under the Earl of Manchester, was a fellow colonel with Oliver in the Eastern Association, and became member for Hants in 1645. Cromwell addresses letters to him thus: "For my noble Friend Colonel Richard Norton. These," and commences "Dear Dick." Carlyle says of Norton, "Given to Presbyterian notions;

was purged out by Pride; came back, dwindled ultimately into Royalism." A relative of "the Loyal Marquis" married Elizabeth, the daughter of Sir Richard Norton, of Rotherfield.

A few particulars respecting the Cavaliers and their opponents may not be without interest.

In August, 1642, the Army of the Parliament was about 23,000 strong. There were 75 troops of horse, each 60 strong. The five regiments of dragoons had 100 in each troop, and 1200 was the strength of each of the 14 regiments of infantry, whilst 50 brass guns and a few mortars or "murtherers" formed the train of artillery. Iron guns had been manufactured at Buxted, in Sussex, by Ralph Hogge and his covenanted servant, John Jackson, as long before as 1543, but brass was now the favourite metal for guns. Sussex people used to say

Master Hogge and his man John
They did cast the first cannon.

Another version of this important transaction is as follows:—"Petrus Baude, Gallus Operis Artifex, worked with Ralph Hogge or Hugget, of Buxted, and first made cast iron guns.

Master Hugget and his man John,
They did cast the first can-non."

The Earl of Essex wore a buff-coloured scarf, which gave origin to the colours of the Parliamentarians. Royalist officers wore red scarves, whilst those serving the Parliament affected buff or deep yellow. Uniforms, so-called, existed but only in name. Buff coats were used by both parties, but red, orange, grey, purple, and blue regiments, with flags of the same colours, were to be seen, whilst John Hampden commanded a regiment of "Greencoats." The best discipline seems to have been maintained by the London Trained Bands, each regiment of which had the City Arms in the dexter canton of its flag. The Parliamentarian artillery had no distinctive uniform, and the cavalry, being Cuirassiers, required none. At Naseby the Cavaliers attacked one another, having no special distinguishing badges. In each troop of cavalry, or company of infantry, there was a subaltern officer, who, from the ensign which he carried, was styled a "cornet." £2, defrayed by the Council of State, was the price of a regimental colour. The officers of a Parliamentarian regiment were a lieutenant-colonel, captains, lieutenants, ensigns, a quarter-master, a carriage-master, a provost-marshal, a chirurgeon, and often a chaplain. There were ten companies in a regiment. The present major was then styled sergeant major, and non-commissioned officers were then, as now, known by the names of sergeants and corporals. One standard bore an arm painted, thrusting a bloody sword through a crown. They adopted Scriptural names. Cleveland alludes to this by a stroke of humour:—"With what face can they object to the King the bringing in of foreigners, when they themselves maintain such an army of Hebrews? One of them beat up his drums clean through the Old Testament; we may learn the genealogy of Our Saviour from the names in his regiment. The musterman uses no other list but the first chapter of Matthew."

The following names are given by John Squire as belonging to men "who joined us at the siege of Lynn, and came riding in full armed, and went into our second regiment; and who left us, many of them, after Marston Fight, on fancies of conscience, and turned Quackers (Quakers)":—"Hiram, Judah, Caleb, Danyel, Zachary, Saul, Aaron, Japhet, Jacques, Isaiah, Simon, Aminadab, Hezekiah, Christian, Zatthu, Ahimelech, Sheckaninh, Jobias, Jeheil, Selah, Manna, Eleazer, Ishmael, Vilellius, Zered, Israel, Amphilius, Gabriel, Premise, Gilead, Zack, Kesiah, Mathias, Pious, Malec, Je'sophat, Issachar, Shem, &c."

There are several publications intended for military service penned by ministers:—"The Soldier's Catechism, by Robert Ram, Minister, published by authority"; another, "A Spiritual Knapsack for the Parliament's Soldiers." The most extraordinary specimen of the temper of the times is one entitled "Military and Spiritual Motions for Foot Companies, with the Exercise of a single Company as they now ought to be taught, and not otherwise, by Capt. Lazarus Howard, 1645."

"It was a project of drilling and exercising a company of infantry at the same time by a double motion of soul and body. This full and whole exercise of a foot company spiritual and temporal may make us, like the Israelites, go up as one man, with one heart and in one form, a soldier of that Great Captain, Christ Jesus!"

"His scheme is to give the word of command to produce the military movement, and to every letter in that word he affixes some pithy and pious sentence to produce the accompanying spiritual one." He forms acrostics of

"To the Right About!"—"As You Were!" as thus:—

The Devil is let loose for a season, to try the patience of God's Church.
Our Enemies, O Lord, are near to hurt us, but Thou art near to help us.
The sword never prevailed, but Sin set an edge upon.
Hasten from the company of the wicked.
Every man shall sit under his own vine, nor hear any news or noises to affright us.
Religion made a stalking-horse for politics is odious.
It is a grievous judgment upon a nation when teachers sent for man's salvation shall become means of their confusion, &c., &c.

In the Royal army they had the field word given to know their friends in the heat of battle, "For God and the King," but the Parliamentarians had no word to recognise their fellows from the enemy, and several instances occurred of their firing on each other. This error was no doubt soon corrected. At the sanguinary battle of Marston Moor the field-word of the Parliamentarians, in contradistinction to the King's, was "God with us!" On that day the soldiers seem to have depended on the colour of their coats as a signal of recognition; these, however, were as various as their regiments, and it sometimes happened that both parties wore the same colour. The King had a red regiment, held to be "the Invincible Regiment," consisting of 1200 men. Among the Parliamentarians they had also a regiment of red-coats. (Vicar's *Parliamentary Chronicle*, Part 1, 200.) There were regiments of purple, of grey, and of blue. The Marquis of Newcastle had a regiment composed of Northumberland men, called from their dress, "White coats." These veterans behaved with the utmost gallantry, and though deserted at Marston Moor by all their friends they formed a ring to oppose Cromwell, and the White Coats fell in their ranks without the flight of one man. Whether from the colour of their coats, or their desperate courage, they also obtained the title of "Newcastle's Lambs!" There were 20 regiments of Foot, under as many colonels, including general officers, and 75 troops of horse under as many captains. These last were formed into regiments containing as many troops as occasion required. The complement of the regiment of Foot was probably 1000 men. Each troop of horse was to consist of 60 men, but the numbers were never full. There were five troops of Dragoons, each of 100, besides officers, and a troop of 100 Cuirassiers as a body guard for the Earl of Essex. The two chaplains were Dr. Burgess and Mr. Stephen Marshall. Hampden was colonel of the 20th Regiment of

Foot, with Richard Ingoldsby as his captain. Among the captains of Horse were, besides those who had also Foot regiments. Of the 67th Troop, Oliver Cromwell, with John Desborough as his Quarter-Master; of the 60th, John Fiennes, third son of Lord Saye, with Oliver's cousin, Edward Whally, as his cornet; of the 15th, Sir Wm. Waller; of the 8th, Lord St. John, with Oliver Cromwell, eldest surviving son of the member for Cambridge, as his cornet; of the 36th, Nathaniel Fiennes. The Parliamentarian colonels who had regiments appointed them were generally country gentlemen or students from the Inns of Court. The Parliament had recourse to military men, who had seen service in the Netherlands, to discipline their raw levies. Amongst these were many Germans, and in some accounts from the country we find noticed "the honest German" who drilled them. Cromwell writes, "Heed well your motions, and laugh not at Rose's Dutch tongue; he is a zealous servant, and we may go farther and get a worse man to our hand than he is." At York the King raised a body guard, in which the young Prince of Wales was a captain, and which was under the command of Lord Bernard Stuart, the brother of the Duke of Richmond. The King used to say that the revenues of those in that single troop would buy the estates of my Lord of Essex and of all the officers in his Army. Oliver Cromwell writes thus: "Buy those horses, but do not give more than 18 or 20 pieces each for them, that is enough for Dragooners. I will give you 60 pieces for that black one you won at Horncastle, if you hold to a mind to sell him for my son, who has a mind to him."

A pair of spurs cost 5s., "a feather for my basnet (i.e., helmet), 2 6d."; and "a new staffe for ye colours, 1s. 4d."

By an order made in 1629, the following prices were fixed for offensive and defensive arms and armour:—

	£	s.	d.
A breast of pistol proofe	0	11	0
A backe	0	7	0
A close caske (helmet) lined	0	17	0
A payre of pouldrons	0	12	0
A payre of vambraces	0	12	0
A payre of guissets	0	17	0
A culett or guarderine	0	7	0
A gorget lyned	0	3	6
A gauntlett gloved	0	3	6

See the whole price of the cuirassier's armour amounteth to 3 10 0

The prices of the parts, and of the whole corslet or footman's armour russetted, viz.:

	£	s.	d.
The breast	0	5	6
The backe	0	4	6
The tassets	0	5	0
The combed head piece, lyned	0	4	6
The gorgett, lyned	0	2	6

The total of the footman's armour 1 2 0
If the breast, back, and tassets be lyned with red leather the price will be 1l. 4s. 0d.

The prices of the parts and of the whole armour for a harquebuzier on horseback russetted, viz.:—

	£	s.	d.
A breast of pistoll proofe	0	9	0
A backe	0	7	0
A gorgett	0	3	0
A headpeece, with great cheeks and a barr before the face	0	11	0

The totall of the whole and all the parts of a harquebuzier or light horseman's armour is 1 12 0

A combed headpeece for a muskettier, russetted and lyned	0	5	0

Price of the pike:—

	£	s.	d.
The staffe	0	2	6
The head	0	1	8
Socket and colouring	0	0	4
Summe	0	4	6

For a new musket, with mould, worm, and scourer	0	15	6
For a new bandalier, with twelve charges, a prymer, a pryming wyre, a bullet bag, and a strap or belt of two inches in breadth	0	2	6
For a pair of horseman's pistols, furnished with snaphances, moulds, worms, scourer, flask, a charger, and cases	2	0	0

VI.—EVENTS IN PORTSMOUTH.—COLONEL GORING DECLARES FOR THE KING.—SKIRMISHES NEAR SOUTHAMPTON AND IN ISLE OF WIGHT.—CAPTURE OF SOUTHSEA CASTLE.—SURRENDER OF PORTSMOUTH.

Before proceeding further it will be well for us to note a few facts relating to this fratricidal strife not yet recorded in this o'er true tale. As early as June 21st the Deputy-Lieutenants, Colonels, and Captains of the County had made a Declaration in favour of the Parliament, which was assented to and with great cheerfulness approved of by the soldiers of the Trained Bands, about 5000 in number, who were speedily increased by the addition of numerous volunteers, who offered to serve in person.

On August 8th word was brought to the House of Commons that Colonel Goring had tendered an oath of allegiance to the King to the Mayor and Aldermen of Portsmouth, most of whom took it willingly. But Mr. Peck, a minister, Mr. Goodwin, Mr. Odell, Mr. Goodfellow, and several others refused it, and were in consequence obliged to leave the town. The Mayor took his wife and family to Salisbury, intending to leave them there, and to return himself to Portsmouth, after doing his utmost to raise men and money for the King. Twenty horsemen were posted at Portsbridge to keep watch and ward both by night and day. Four guns swept the approaches to the bridge, which was also protected by a strong frame of timber. The guns belonged to the *Maria*, pinnace. In order to encourage the townsmen, Colonel Goring showed them 3000*l*., and a rumour was current that 5000 French soldiers would speedily arrive as a reinforcement. The garrison was by no means unanimously in favour of the King. A certain Captain Wiles tried to win over his soldiers, but completely failed. After much discussion they fell upon him and slew him, the chronicler adding, " Alas, who knows whether, with his body, they slew his soul also !"

On August 2nd, 1642, the date of Goring's Declaration for the King, there were 300 men in garrison, 100 townsmen able to bear arms, and in the remainder of Portsea Island about 100 more. There were about 50 officers, with their servants. The Governor and officers possessed more than 50 horses, but there was only two days' provision in the town, which was unfortified and very weak in many places. Col. Goring ordered all men able to bear arms or to find substitutes to meet in the Bowling Green, on pain of imprisonment, knowing full well that only Cavaliers would put in an appearance. The friends of the Parliament were speedily disarmed, and 40 horsemen with pistols and carbines admitted into the garrison. At three o'clock on that August afternoon the Colonel addressed the meeting, urging them to stand fast for the King, promising money to the Cavaliers, and leave to depart to the adherents of the Parliament. The military chest was not empty, for Goring had received 3000*l*. from the Parliament for the payment of arrears to the garrison, and 9000*l*. from Mr. Weston, brother to the Earl of Portland, the Royalist governor of the Isle of Wight. At the conclusion of his harangue some of the soldiers shouted in token of assent, but others were discontented, and strife ran high in the town. Col. Goring at once sent out an officer to enlist recruits in the county, but only those who professed their willingness to fight for the King were admitted within the walls. All the soldiers and every townsman except three or four declared for the King, but within less than ten days more than half of them had found means to escape. The Parliament acted promptly. Orders were at once given to the Earl of Warwick to blockade the harbour with a squadron of five ships, and preparations for an attack on the land side were not forgotten. The Commission of Army was not put in force, but the Militia was duly embodied, with the result of making one or two companies of trained bands desert the cause of the King for that of the Parliament.

Many Hampshire gentlemen who had promised to bring in reinforcements of horse and foot were stopped en route, as was also Sir Kenelm Digby, one of Colonel Goring's principal allies and confederates. Only two days had elapsed before the County Militia began to blockade Portsbridge, rendering the provisioning of the garrison a matter of difficulty. On Saturday, August 6th, the supplies of provisions from the Isle of Wight were cut off, and on Monday, August 8th, the Earl of Warwick appeared off the mouth of the harbour with his blockading squadron. The Earl of Portland, Governor of the Isle of Wight, was committed to the custody of Sheriff Garret. His mother and most of his friends were Roman Catholics, and he was believed to be a member of the same communion. The Earl of Pembroke was duly appointed as his successor, and the House sent a messenger with orders to Colonel Goring to surrender Portsmouth to their authority.

The King despatched a gentleman to Portsmouth, with promises of help and reinforcements, but the gentlemen of Hampshire at once raised a besieging force, asking for the authority of Parliament, and offering to hazard their lives and fortunes in the maintenance of the true Protestant religion and the just privileges of Parliament. One hundred carbines, pistols, saddles, and much ammunition for the garrison were intercepted by the forces of the Parliament. The Bishop of Winchester sent five completely armed horsemen to Portsmouth, and Dr. Hinsham, one of the Prebendaries of Chichester, supplied the garrison with a load of wheat. Hackney coachmen were offered commissions, on condition of using their horses for the King's service. On August 11th the garrison was estimated to be 500 strong; "Papists and those ill affected to Parliament." The Grand Jury at the County Assizes in August presented a most loyal petition to the King, asking for aid against the Parliament.

On August 10th seven straggling Cavaliers robbed two Wiltshire gentlemen on the highway, about three miles from Winchester, of about 80l. in gold and 10l. in silver, shooting their horses dead and riding off. Pursued by two gentlemen of the county and their servants, they at length entered an inn in Romsey. Armed assistance having been obtained, they were promptly secured and imprisoned at Winchester to await their trial.

On Thursday, August 11th, there was a fight at Hosdown, a mile out of Southampton. The High Sheriff of Hampshire, escorted by some 80 men, endeavoured to raise the County Militia for the Parliament, but was attacked by 60 and odd Cavaliers and about 100 persons who disliked his proceedings. The fight lasted about an hour. Fifteen of the King's party were killed and nine mortally wounded, with a loss of five killed and none wounded on the other side. The country people came in great numbers to assist the Sheriff, as did also numerous well armed volunteers from the town of Southampton. At length many of the Cavaliers were captured, and put into safe keeping. The Mayor of Southampton addressed the assembled multitude, urging them to act only in a strictly legal manner, but most cautiously guarding himself from saying anything which might hereafter be construed to his hurt by either the King or the Parliament, "and so, taking his leave of the Sheriff, he returned home." Mr. Parker, a gentleman living at Upper Wallop, records all these proceedings with great satisfaction in a letter to a friend in London.

Meanwhile the Isle of Wight was preparing to rise in favour of the Parliament, though many of the leading men in it were favourable to the King. This was especially the case with the governors of the fortresses. Captain Burley, at Yarmouth, the Governor and Porter of Hurst Castle, and the Countess of Portland, at Carisbrooke, left no doubt as to which cause they favoured. Sir Robert Dillington tried to send over corn to Portsmouth, but it was intercepted on the way by one Master Buneckley. The adherents of the Parliament sent up a petition for horse and arms, saying that "they would serve the King in a Parliamentary way only." Whereupon 500 foot and two troops of horse were ordered to march to their aid, and to besiege Portsmouth. The arrival of the Earl of Pembroke was anxiously awaited, so that the malcontents might take active measures against Goring and his Cavaliers. On August 16th the Cavaliers made an attempt to secure the Isle of Wight under cover of darkness. The precise locality of the attack is not specified, but the people assembled, and Captain Johnson, "a man of most puissant courage," sallied from the town with 300 very well armed men. The assailants opened fire, wounding two men, but were at length obliged to retire. About 9.0 a.m. they began to show themselves in battle array, and "after some parley they fell to it like furious lions, and when they had felt the angry bullets on both sides they rested for the space of two or three hours, and then fell on again with as much fury as they did at first."

After a long skirmish the Cavaliers fled, having many killed and wounded. Only six or seven of Captain Johnson's men needed the aid of a surgeon. The defences of Newport were but weak, and Carisbrooke Castle was in sad want of ammunition and other necessaries. The Earl of Pembroke was ordered to proceed thither at once, and he accordingly started from Wiltshire on Monday, August 29th. On August 18th there were seven men-of-war, all of great force, blockading Portsmouth. In this squadron there were the *Paragon*, the *Cæsar*, the *Black James*, and four others. A letter from someone on board the *Paragon* says that the greatest harmony was the thundering of cannon both by day and night. On the arrival of the anxiously-expected land forces a general attack both by sea and land was to take place. Desertions from the garrison, which the worthy seaman estimated at 200, were of nightly occurrence. There were 100 guns mounted upon the works; only troops to man them were wanting. One ship of war was commanded by a Scotch nobleman, who, throughout the operations, did good service. On Tuesday, August 16th, he sent out his long boat and took prisoners Capt. Torney, the Governor of "Cowes Castle," and two other gentlemen, one of whom was brother to the Earl of Portland. They being safely secured, a body of seamen was landed, who took possession of the Castle, placing in it a garrison favourable to the Parliament. This same Scotch nobleman kept back provisions from Portsmouth, and captured a boat going to the Island laden with light horses, saddles, and equipments for the use of Cavaliers. The boatman saying that his fare was nine shillings, this active commander paid him, telling him at the same time that if he would bring the horses also alongside, he would give him another freight. This nobleman went on shore and threatened Captain Newland, "a great, fat tall man of a very heathenish behaviour," who had sent some corn to the garrison of Portsmouth, that if he offended again he should be sent up to the Parliament as a prisoner. "A captaine that is possessed of a castle near

the Cows" persuaded the countrymen to bring in their arms for safe keeping against the Cavaliers. Having got possession of them, he declined to surrender them until the ubiquitous Scotch nobleman threatened to batter the castle about his ears. This threat had the desired effect. Ships' guns were landed for the purpose of battering Portsmouth, and a naval brigade, 400 strong, took part in the operations which compelled the surrender of Carisbrooke Castle. The Countess of Portland, who held command there during the enforced absence of her husband, and who, as we have already seen, displayed considerable courage, was permitted to occupy a few rooms in the castle, and was at length indebted to the kindness of some seamen for the means of leaving the island. Colonel Brett, the Governor of the castle, Master Nicholas Weston, brother to the Earl of Portland, and the garrison received free passes to repair to any part of the island which they might think fit. Captain Browne Bushell was put in charge of the castle by Captain Swanley till further order of Parliament, and on August 27th, 1642, a letter from Newport thus ends:—

"So now our whole Island is at peace! Colonel Norton at once raised a force of musketeers, who took post at his house at Southwick Park. Some of the trained bands and a force of cavalry from the county speedily assembled, and more were expected. Sir William Waller and Colonel Urrey were each in command of a troop of horse, and there are some 20 firelocks that look like desperate soldiers." Colonel Goring made a proclamation that all women and children who were afraid should leave the town by noon on the following Sunday, and good cause had women to quit Portsmouth when troopers like his held sway in it. Terrible indeed are the accounts given by ancient journalistic scribes, too bad, indeed, to be quoted here!

Of the 200 men said to compose the garrison on August 15th, it was believed that fully one half would at once desert if opportunity offered. One man who went to sell his butter at Portsmouth was forcibly impressed, and there were many similar cases. Lord Wentworth was at Portsmouth, and some say Lord Goring; however his soul is there we may be assured."

Colonel Goring sent an officer to Salisbury with a party of 30 or 40 horse, in search of plunder and reinforcements, but on their arrival they were all captured and imprisoned.

Cruel, indeed, was the pillaging of Portsea Isle, which had then 2000 acres of standing corn upon it. One thousand cattle and more than a thousand sheep were carried off by the all-devouring garrison. Bread, cheese, bacon, and everything shared the same fate, the plunderers not even leaving half loaves behind them for the starving population. The owners were obliged to drive their own cattle within the walls, and were then themselves retained for military service.

On Wednesday, Thursday, and Friday, August 10-12, this plundering was at its worst. To aid the miserable rustics, the Earl of Warwick landed men from the blockading squadron at the east end of Portsea Isle, with two guns. Goring's horse were thus held in salutary check, whilst the seamen ferried numerous women and children over to Hayling Island. About 200 sheep and 100 cattle were also taken over to the same place of refuge, ropes being thrown over the horns of the cattle to make them swim after the boats. One hundred and thirty-five quarters of wheat were bound from Fareham to Portsmouth, but one Master Allen, of Gosport, succeeded in stopping the carts upon the road and altering their destination, by the aid of a few watchmen. Great was the rage of Goring. He threatened to bombard and utterly destroy Gosport with the guns of Portsmouth, and it was only after the humble prayer of the Mayor and others, upon their knees, that he consented to desist from his purpose for the sake of the women and children dwelling there. As it was, he terrified the Gosport people exceedingly. His gunner, Meader by name, had already fled from the town, but he summoned "a cannoneer," and ordered him to fire at Gosport. Upon his refusal the Colonel threatened to run him through, whereupon he shot, "but it was over the houses, and did no harm."

But deliverance was at hand for the unhappy, plundered dwellers in Portsmouth and Portsea Island. About 6.0 p.m. on Friday, August 15th, 1642, twenty soldiers made an attack upon Portbridge, not knowing what resistance they would meet with. They found but eight men on guard, one or two of whom were taken prisoners, the rest making their escape. One who saw the attack said that it would make a faint-hearted man a soldier to see their spirit and resolution. Colonel Hurry and Sir William Waller behaved themselves bravely on this occasion. The attack would have taken place before if the weather had not been very wet, confining the besieging forces to their quarters at Southwick and Havant. This success not a little encouraged the friends of the Parliament, and further measures were at once taken.

Captain Browne Bushell, a very active commander, held a consultation with Captains Martin and Swanley as to the possibility of cutting out the *Henrietta Maria* pinnace from under the guns of Portsmouth. They agreed with him that the enterprise was feasible, though the service was desperate and beset with difficulties. Nothing daunted, and encouraged by the taking of Portbridge, Captain Browne Bushell the same night manned some long boats, and under cover of the darkness pulled for the *Henrietta Maria*. She had a crew of 14 men, two of whom were officers, according to Goring's account, and Goodwin, the master, was suspected in the garrison of Parliamentarian leanings. On the other hand, the newspaper account says that she mounted eight brave pieces of ordnance, and had forty soldiers on board, being fitted for service. Goring says that the pinnace surrendered without receiving a blow, but his opponents say that the crew were overpowered and driven below. At any rate the capture was complete. Sail was at once made, and the *Henrietta Maria* began to stand out of the arbour. When out of range of the batteries two ships were descried, laden with corn for the garrison, which were summoned to surrender, and at once struck their colours. Four days previously the blockading squadron had intercepted a ship, on board of which were several hundred barrels of powder and 41 "most stately horse." The steeds were forthwith sent to London.

On Saturday, August 16th, Colonel Norton's forces marched from Portbridge almost to the gates of Portsmouth, whereupon Colonel Goring sent out two guns loaded with musket bullets, and two gunners to guard one of his guns, which he had been obliged to leave behind a mile distant from Portbridge, when he withdrew his guns on the preceding Wednesday. Watching his opportunity, a Parliamentary trooper rode between the guns and the town, his carbine being charged with two bullets, and shot one of the gunners, he himself escaping uninjured. Many now began to desert to the besiegers, offering to prove their sincerity by serving in forlorn hopes against the town. A contingent from Chichester had reached Portsmouth, who treated the townsmen with considerable severity. On August 17th there were said to be only 80 or 90 horses and no great strength of men in the town, whilst the Parliament had under its command 240 troopers and 500 infantry. The town was well provisioned, and ammunition was plentiful. Numerous were the devices employed to convey intelligence from the beleaguered town. A woman was caught at Portbridge carrying a bundle which looked like a baby, in the head of which was a black box full of letters. About 5.0 p.m., on Saturday, August 16th, a suit of clothes was intercepted at Havant, going to Mr. Bellingham, in Portsmouth, with ten letters sewn up in the linings. The man carrying it was detained, together with his horse. Letters from Lord Wentworth and others in Portsmouth likewise fell into Norton's hands.

The Royalists at Chichester were in the meantime not idle in seeking to aid their friends at Portsmouth. On August the 19th Sir Thomas Boyer, Sir William Morley, Mr. Lewknor, the Recorder, and others demanded the city magazine for the service of the King. Captain Chitty, a staunch adherent of the Parliament, refused to surrender it, and placed a strong guard over it. Mr. Lewknor and the clergy of the Cathedral made overtures to Colonel Goring, who asked them to aid him to the utmost of their power. One Mr. Bellingham, a young gentleman, rode fully armed from Chichester to Portsmouth. He afterwards tried to make his escape from the garrison, keeping a boat in readiness, for which he paid 5s. per diem. The Rev. Mr. Bringsted, parson of Havant, "a most pestilent man," had sent a light horse to Portsmouth. For this Colonel Norton made him pay dearly. Ten light horse were quartered on him, "and lately one of the Scotsmen, being aggrieved with him, fell upon him, basted him well-favouredly, and fain he would be gone ; but they will not let him. So he is forced to stay, waits upon them daily, gives them good words, and tells them that he will gladly lie out of his own bed to make them room !"

On August 10th a letter brought in with difficulty from the King, promising relief, had greatly cheered the garrison, but communication with the outer world became day by day more difficult. "Three gallant gentlewomen" tried to get a boat for Stokes Bay. They failed to reach their destination, and were brought back in a friendly manner to Sir Thomas Boyer's house in his coach. Having no man with them, they were strongly suspected to be men in women's apparel. These were evidently not times for ladies to travel alone. At Havant a traveller was caught with letters from Portsmouth concealed in his boots. The letters were taken from him and given to Colonel Norton, who sent out "a few lusty men with muskets" to arrest the messenger. Another envoy coming from Chichester to Portsmouth through bye lanes was met by apparently a most boorish rustic, who proved to be an officer in disguise, and who carried him and his despatches to Colonel Norton, at Southwick.

On August 25th Chichester declared for the Parliament, but the Cavaliers there continued to intrigue, the Cathedral clergy being especially active. The power of the pulpit was energetically used on behalf of the King. Parliament at once ordered that all Popish recusants, all who should put in force the King's Commission of Array, or any who should furnish horses, arms, money, &c., to the King should be disarmed. Dr. Hinsham, a Prebendary of Chichester, sent a load of wheat to the Portsmouth garrison, and there was daily drilling in the Close of light cavalry raised by the Cathedral clergy. The Mayor, Mr. William Cawley, firmly refused to listen to any Royalist overtures what ever made to him by the Bishop and clergy.

On Friday, August 26th, information was given to both Houses of Parliament of a ship coming from St. Domingo with a cargo, valued at 600,000*l.* Her name was the *Sancta Clara*, and she was laden with silver, cochineal, &c. Prevented from entering Portsmouth harbour by the Earl of Warwick's squadron she was, according to Cavalier opinion, treacherously carried into Southampton by Captain Bennett Strafford. The cargo was seized by order of the Parliament and sent up to London, the silver alone requiring three waggons and a cart to convey it to the Guildhall, in charge of Major Burrell and a troop of horse. Don Alonco de Cardenes, the Spanish Ambassador, remonstrated, and on January 2nd, 1643, the King issued a proclamation, warning all his subjects against illegal handling of the silver, &c. in question. The ultimate fate of this prize money does not appear.

On August 27th the siege works at Portsmouth were almost ready to open fire. Strong forts had been constructed, which commanded

CAPTURE OF SOUTHSEA CASTLE.

the town, and from which it would be easy to batter the walls. On this day a soldier "much drunk" found means to pass the line of the besiegers' sentries, thinking to take the town single-handed. With a lantern and candle in his hand he advanced, the garrison firing more than 40 cannon shot in the direction of the light, all of which missed him, "but he approaching nearer the walls was laid asleep with a musket shot!" Letters were intercepted showing that the Chichester Cavaliers were strongly bent upon the relief of Portsmouth.

On August 29th a messenger from Portsmouth brought up to the House of Commons a Romish priest, two other ministers, and the Town Clerk of Portsmouth, who were committed to various prisons until further order.

On Saturday, August 27th, Colonel Goring's trumpets from within the town sounded twice for a parley, which took place on the following day. Colonel Goring "entertained the Commissioners very nobly, and carried himself like a gentleman." He asked leave to send a messenger to the King, asking for relief by a certain day. Failing such relief, he expressed his willingness to resign his allegiance to the King, and to hold the town for the Parliament, as he had previously done. He refused to surrender at once without orders from the King, and the parley closed without result. Goring threatening to hold out to the last. That night the cavalry of the garrison attacked the besiegers, but were repulsed. Their leader was slain, two men were wounded, two taken, together with three of the best horses, and the whole party was chased back to the gates. One estimate considered the number of soldiers in the town at this date to be 300. The want of salt and corn now began to make itself felt in the garrison, and the Parliament despatched 1000 soldiers into Hampshire, who as they marched found profitable amusement in pillaging the houses of any whom they chose to consider Papists, and making them fly. Sir John Meldrum gained considerable credit as an engineer for his construction of batteries against Portsmouth at this time. The soldiers of the garrison, disappointed of relief, were on the point of mutiny, and their discontent was still further increased when batteries from Gosport, one of which may still be seen upon the beach, opened fire on September 2nd, and continued their bombardment until the morning of Sunday, September 5th.

On Saturday, September 4th, after long conference and discussion, Colonel Norton decided to attempt Southsea Castle, then considered to be the strongest fort in England for its size. It was surrounded by a wall three or four yards in thickness and about 30 feet in height. The moat was three or four yards deep and five yards broad. The Castle mounted 14 guns, all of which, with the exception of two, were 12-pounders, besides other smaller pieces of artillery. "It hath dainty chambers fit to entertain a Prince." Another account says that there were nine or ten guns actually in position, and as many more ready for mounting. The Governor of the Castle was Challender, a suspected Roman Catholic. On this Saturday night he remained in Portsmouth carousing with Colonel Goring until 11.0 p.m.

The storming party consisted of two troops of horse and 400 infantry, who were provided with 20 scaling ladders. Marching from their quarters about 1.0 a.m. on Sunday morning, singing psalms as they went, the garrison of Portsmouth opened a random fire upon them, which did no harm. At 2.0 a.m. they arrived within a couple of bow shots from the Castle, and halted for an hour. Meanwhile a feigned attack upon Portsmouth from Gosport was in progress. Two men were killed in the town, and in addition "we heard a very pitiful lamentation." At 3.0 a.m. the storming party advanced, and got between the Castle and the sea, as all the guns were pointed landward. They then jumped into the moat, some men falling and hurting themselves. Capt. Bushell and a trumpeter then went to the Castle, and standing upon the bridge the Captain ordered the trumpeter to sound a parley. The parley commenced, the assailants offering fair quarter to the garrison. Governor Challender, "being something in drink, and withal newly awakened out of his deep sleep" suggested that if they would kindly defer their visit until the morning he would take the matter into consideration. The infantry then scaled the walls, Challender begging quarter for himself, lieutenant, ensign, and small garrison. This was granted, and the garrison was disarmed, without the loss of a man on either side. Challender, nothing loth, at once began to drink the health of the King and Parliament with his new friends, whom he requested to fire three guns as a signal to Goring that the Castle was taken.

Goring replied with at least 30 shot, one of which narrowly missed the leader of the storming party. Ten men retreated behind a piece of timber upon the drawbridge, which was immediately afterwards struck by shot. No one was, however, injured. Some 80 men were left to keep the Castle for the Parliament, and a mutiny at once broke out in Portsmouth. The Mayor, a lieutenant, an ensign, and many soldiers fled from the town, and nearly all the rest of the garrison threw down their arms. Only some 60 were still willing to fight, most of whom were gentlemen and their servants, who were unskilled in the use of muskets and in the working of heavy guns. Colonel Goring therefore sent a drummer to solicit a parley, and surrendered Portsmouth on the following conditions:—Two companies of Parliament troops were to be posted in the town about 6.0 a.m., on September 7th, for the prevention of disorder and the safety of the magazine. The garrison to have free passes to any place except to an army in arms against the Parliament, with horses, swords, and pistols, but with no other arms. Twenty days to be allowed for the journey. All stores to be delivered up uninjured. Free passes, without arms, to be granted to those wishing to proceed beyond sea. Those belonging to the old garrison of Portsmouth to remain or depart at their pleasure. An amnesty to be granted to all except deserters from the Parliament. The magazine to be left uninjured. Carriages to be provided on payment, if required, for those leaving the town. The prisoners on both sides to be released, except those that are to be sent up to the Parliament. The Governor, if he wishes, to send a gentleman elected by him to the King. After the capitulation Colonel Goring, as we already know, took ship for Holland.

CHAPTER VII.—OUTRAGES IN WILTSHIRE.—SURRENDER OF FARNHAM AND WINCHESTER.—SOUTHAMPTON DECLARES FOR THE PARLIAMENT.

Whilst Colonel Goring was fighting at Portsmouth, some of his friends had been trying to aid him by making various plundering forays in the neighbouring county of Wiltshire. After the surrender of Portsmouth, the Earl of Pembroke proceeded to deal summarily with these disturbers of the public peace. We have already noted his departure for the Isle of Wight. Having reduced that portion of his government to tranquillity he returned towards Wiltshire at the close of September. Cavalier marauding in those districts was at its height on October 1st, 1642, but was speedily destined to receive a severe check. The Earl of Pembroke brought with him from Hampshire three hundred horse and foot, and was joined on his march by some of the trained bands. On October 4th, at some place unspecified by the annalist, he found himself confronted by Lord Coventry and 1000 Cavaliers. The contest was short, but decisive, forty Cavaliers being slain and 10 captured, Lord Coventry himself escaping in disguise. Ten men were lost by the Parliament, and the Earl, having "settled that county in a very good posture and peaceable condition," returned home to Wilton House on October 13th, with much honour. A week later the three counties of Berks, Hants, and Surrey were raising troops of Dragoons, some of which had already reached Windsor Castle, whilst others were on their march thither, intending to fortify it on behalf of the Parliament. Throughout the war the excesses committed by those who, rightly or wrongly, styled themselves Royalist partisans did much to strengthen the cause of the Parliament in these counties.

Hampshire men of those days were by no means devoid of either military spirit or experience. Only three years before the county had sent forth, at the King's command, against the Scottish foe 1000 foot and 100 horse, and in 1640 no fewer than 1200 Hampshire soldiers marched beneath the banner of the Earl of Northumberland, stout old Sir Jacob Astley commanding another hundred meanwhile. These military companies seem to have been considerably wanting in discipline, for on October 11th, 1642, a letter written to Lord Grey by Lord Stourton was read in the House of Lords, complaining of "the great unruliness of the soldiers in Hampshire," especially finding fault with the infantry, who were then on the march between London and Portsmouth. The unfortunate nobleman complained that he had been plundered of his property, and that the robbers had threatened him with repeated visits. He therefore asked for protection to his house, stating that in Wiltshire also the soldiers had paid him four most unwelcome visits. On two occasions he bribed them to depart. Once they came to the number of 300, hacking and hewing at his gates, and vowing that they would, if refused admittance, cut the throats of men, women, and children indiscriminately. The county trained bands were usually about 600 in number, but on October 19th, 1642, those of London obtained permission to double their effective strength. The Committee for the Defence of the Kingdom were ordered e Upper House to afford hapless Lord Stourton all necessary protection. Soldiers who had been wounded or maimed in the service of the Parliament used to attend daily at the Savoy Hospital to receive the aid of a physician and certain surgeons. These sufferers were allowed 8d. per diem till cured.

On November 6th the Earl of Essex was ordered to draw out his army at once to check the plundering of Rupert and his troopers. On the 24th of the month Prince Rupert was in bed suffering from an attack of measles, but squadrons and parties of horse were sent every day into Hampshire, returning to Reading and Oxford with hostages and prisoners. Sheep, oxen, horses, carts laden with corn, and plunder of every kind were to be met with in many a country lane. Chichester was at this time very weak in defences, but early in November, 1642, the inhabitants presented a petition to Parliament expressive of their willingness to fortify the city. Permission was at once granted, and the citizens were allowed to retain seven guns with which they had been furnished by Sir William Lewis, the Governor of Portsmouth. Ten barrels of powder were also ordered to be issued from the magazine at Portsmouth for the defence of Chichester. £1000 had been collected for the payment of the Portsmouth garrison whilst Goring held command in the town. This sum was now handed over to Sir W. Lewis to be paid to his soldiers. A year's pay for the garrison amounted at this time to 5030*l*.

On November 18th the Commission of Array, as attempted to be carried out in Sussex by Sir Edward Ford, the Royalist High Sheriff, was declared to be illegal, and he himself was to be arrested as speedily as possible. The Commission of Array was declared to be illegal throughout Sussex, and Captain Ambrose Trayton was ordered by Parliament to raise and command 200 men, volunteers or otherwise, for the defence of Lewes. One-fifth of the proposition-money, plate, &c., collected in Lewes was to be applied to the protection of the town, and the security of the public faith was offered to all Sussex men willing to lend money or plate to the Parliament.

On Wednesday, November 30th, Farnham Castle was taken by Colonel Brown and his Dragoons, in the manner already described in these pages. Eighty, or, according to another account, 120 prisoners taken on this occasion were sent to Windsor Castle, and from thence to London, in carts which were hired for their conveyance. Forty of them arrived in London on December 1st without having suffered the loss of any of their clothes. Distributed amongst various prisons, they were released next day, and every man of them had money given him. Very different treatment to that received by prisoners on both sides at later periods of the war! Winchester House, in St. Mary Overies, Southwark, was taken as a prison for Cavaliers on November 11th; Lord Petre's house in Aldersgate-street, and the Bishop of London's house, near St. Paul's being similarly appropriated on January 5th, 1643.

On December 17th, 1642, Winchester surrendered, as we have already seen. Contemporary accounts give certain additional details. On the preceding 18th of November the Corporation had voted money for "swords, bullets, and providing the Citie armes." Two Regiments of Foot which belonged to the King's Life Guard made a sortie from the city, and were nearly all captured, and Sir William Waller reports "we cut off two regiments, one of horse, another of dragooneers, 600 of which were gallant horse. We began our fight five miles wide of Winchester, toward Salisbury way, in pursuit whereof we took fifty commanders, besides Viscount Grandison, and killed divers, but the number we know not. The city joined against us, yet pursuing them into it, we took them all prisoners, and when they were taken they gave us all the gold and silver they had, and the city compounded with us for 1000*l*." Cornet Sterly, who was present, writes that Winchester offered 200*l*. to be saved from pillage. One account says that Lord Grandison, 65 other officers and commanders, 1000 foot, 600 horse, 200 dragoons, and 600 arms fell into the hands of Sir William Waller. Lord Grandison had the rank of Lieut.-General in the King's army. He was afterwards mortally wounded at Bristol on July 26th, 1643. Dying at Oxford on September 29th, 1643, he was there buried beneath a stately monument in Christ Church Cathedral. One who took part in the assault says:—" The most part of our regiment assaulted the city at one side of it, where the wall was broken down. The greatest part of the opposition was from the townsmen, who have since sufficiently paid for it (for they have been the greatest opposers of us), having been plundered by our unruly soldiers. We stood in arms all that night."

The writer goes on to admit, with evidest disgust, that the prisoners were despoiled, contrary to the articles of capitulation, even of their clothes, "four or five pulling at one cloak like hounds at the leg of a dead horse." Gold was given to the soldiers by the hapless Cavaliers by the handful, and Cornet Sterly says that only the officers were retained, all the rest being stripped and sent away. The writer of the above quoted letter speaks of "many other disorderly passages," and says that only his zeal for the right cause prevented his quitting the army. Cornet Sterly gives the best list of prisoners, whose names were, according to him, as follows: Colonel Lord Grandison, Sir Richard Willis, Sir John Smith, Major Hayborne, Captains Garret, Honeywood, Barty, Booth, Brangling, Wren, Beckonhear; Lieutenants Williamson, Rogers, Elverton, Rodham, Booth, Cornets Bennet, Savage, Ruddry, Gwynn, and Bradlines. The county gentlemen taken with the Cavaliers were: Sir John Mills, Sir Thomas Phillips and his brother, Sir Francis Powre; Masters Ranford, Saunders, Griffin, Foyle, and his son, Powlet, and his son. Some of the prisoners taken at Winchester were confined at Portsmouth, whilst others were committed to the charge of Dr. Layton, the keeper of the Lambeth House Prison. On February 24th, 1645, it was ordered that all standards which had been or should hereafter be taken by the forces of the Parliament should be committed to the care of W. Riley, Esq., Lancaster Herald at Arms at the Herald's College.

Winchester Castle, which played no unimportant part in many a Hampshire contest, is said by Milner and others to have been about 850 feet in length north and south, and 250 feet in breadth, east and west, becoming much narrower at its northern extremity, where a wall that followed the slope of the ditch united it to the West-gate. The keep was about 100 feet square, and connected by a wall with the southern defences of the city. It was flanked by four towers, one at each corner, and another tower above the entrance faced the north. The main gate of the castle faced the west, and stood near the centre of the west front of the more modern King's house. Directly opposite, on the other side of the ditch, was a strong barbican or turret, in which a guard was posted, and in front of which was the place of execution. Square towers at intervals looked down into the moat, which was of varying depth, but which near the keep must have been at least 100 feet deep and as many wide. There was a good deal of anxiety felt at Southampton at this time. Master Goter sent a letter to a merchant of good quality in Lombard-street, on Dec. 9th, 1642, from which we learn that Captain Richard Swanley, an active partisan of the Parliament, had summoned the Mayor and Corporation to decide as to their future course, telling them that on December 3rd, 1642, he was in possession of Calshot Castle, and had disabled Nutley (Netley) and St. Andrew's Castles, having also stopped the boats going with provisions to Southampton from the Isle of Wight and Hythe. Calshot Castle had a chief captain in receipt of 1s. 8d. per diem, an under captain, four soldiers at 8d., one porter at 8d., and eight gunners at 6d. each per diem. The whole annual expenditure was 107*l*. 7s. 6d., whilst St. Andrew's Point fortress was maintained for 85*l*. 3s. 4d. per annum. Southampton had been for the levying of shipmoney assessed at 195*l*., Winchester paying 190*l*., Portsmouth 60*l*., Basingstoke 60*l*., and Romsey 30*l*. The whole county was required to provide one ship of 600 tons burden, with a crew of 260 men, at a cost of 6000*l*. The Parliament had many friends in the town, and when Prynne and Burton landed at Southampton, on November 28th, 1640, after their release from their prison in the Channel Islands, they were escorted in triumph through the town towards London. The Mayor and some of the richer burgesses were, however, inclined to favour the Royal cause, and when Captain Swanley's letter was read an animated discussion took place. The result, however, was that a deputation was sent to Portsmouth to declare that the town would henceforth submit to the authority of the Parliament. "Yet every man underwrit it not; it was thought that Swanley would have come up the river with his ships, and beat the town about our ears!"

CHAPTER VIII.—RIVAL PARTIES IN SUSSEX—THE CAPTURE OF ARUNDEL AND CHICHESTER.—DESECRATION OF CHURCHES.—HAMPSHIRE DEFENCES.

We must now march with victorious Sir William Waller for awhile over the pleasant Sussex Downs, taking with us as most trusty and withal right pleasant guides W. H. Blaauw, Esq., M.A., F.S.A., and G. Hillier, Esq., who have most successfully investigated the whole subject. Nor shall the Rev. H. D. Gordon be left out, who has also laboured in the same field. Through the exceeding kindness of J. Dudmey, Esq., Secretary of the Sussex Archæological Society, and Mr. St. Leger Blaauw, who have aided me greatly, we need not dread losing our way in any historic by-road. Sussex had shown its loyalty in 1640, when the clergy of the diocese contributed 985*l*. 16s., and the county sent 640 foot and 80 horse to swell the ranks of the army which marched against the invading Scots. But on February 17th, 1643, there was an ominous sounding petition sent up to the House of Commons praying for "a thorough reformation of religion" in the county. Arundel and Chichester took opposite sides. The former, together with Portsmouth and Winchester, was in safe Cavalier keeping, but Chichester was devoted to the Parliament, being considerably under the influence of a great brewer, William Cawley by name, whose memory is still preserved by "Cawley's Lane," at Rumboldswyke, where he possessed certain broad lands. The son of an Alderman of Chichester, he sat in Parliament, first for Midhurst, and afterwards for his native city, steadily opposing the King whenever opportunity offered, and resisting all Royalist overtures. He signed the King's death warrant, but represented Chichester in the Convention Parliament of 1660. Being exempted from pardon at the Restoration, he died in exile in Switzerland, his estates being granted to the Duke of York. Lewes was represented in Parliament by Colonel Herbert Morley, who was a firm Puritan partisan, and possessed immense influence in the county. On November 7th, 1642, the King published a general amnesty for Sussex, from which Colonel Morley and Henry Chittey were specially excepted.

On August 28th, 1642, it will be remembered that a parley took place between the besiegers of Portsmouth and the beleaguered garrison, in which Mr. Christopher Lewknor took part. He was the Recorder of Chichester, and is styled "the man appointed by his Majesty to take in money and plate on his behalfe." After the surrender of Portsmouth, Goring was allowed six days. Lewknor and the other officers two, to leave Portsmouth. Goring finished his restless life as a Dominican monk in Spain in the year 1662. In August, 1642, Chichester was reported to be "in a good state of defence, and resolved to maintain the Protestant religion, but some ill affected persons had plotted to betray the town, and some ministers had made seditious sermons, saying that the irreverent clergie had preached down the bishops, and the reverend tradesmen had preached down the clergie." When the King's scouts, ten in number, appeared in Hyde Park on November 16th, and his army was at Brentford, there was a general expectation on both sides that it would have turned towards Chichester, and the party in possession prepared for defence. An ordinance had been passed for associating the forces in the four counties of Hampshire, Surrey, Sussex, and Kent made Sir W. Waller as Major General, and the Parliamentary journalist states that a popular dread of the cruelty of the King's army prevailed in Chichester. "Such was the terror of the townsmen; yea, and of the cathedral men too (having heard of their plundering at Brainford), that they put themselves in armes, and out of their subscribed monies maintained a considerable strength." Captain Ambrose Trayton was, on November 18th, authorised to call in 200 men, or more if necessary, for the defence of Lewes, and to command them. By an ordinance hastily passed on November 21st, Mr. Morley and others were sent down to put Sussex "into the like posture of defence as is Kent, and to disarm all such as shall refuse to join with them in securing the county." In West Sussex the Royalists mustered strongly, whilst Colonel Morley was supreme in the Eastern Division. Several of Colonel Morley's relatives, Sir Edward Ford, of Up Park, and many other gentlemen, were on the side of the King. It was remarked of Sussex, as of other counties in the south and east of England, that though many of the chief gentry were for the King, yet the freeholders and yeomen being generally on the other side, as often as they attempted to show themselves they were crushed and their efforts defeated. Sir Edward Ford had been just made High Sheriff of Sussex, not three days old in his place, according to Vicars, and had offered the King a thousand men, and to undertake the conquest of Sussex, though 60 miles in length.

The Mayor of Chichester (Robert Eaton) had been too loyal to please the prevailing party in the city of Chichester, of which the Bishop and Christopher Lewknor (the Recorder), with many of the clergy, were Royalists, and after publishing the Royal Commission of Array had fled to join the King, though he afterwards, in September, made his peace by paying a fine of 150*l*. His successor, William Bartholomew, had b. en active on November 2nd in procuring seven pieces of ordnance from Portsmouth, with license to introduce 200 men from the County Militia for the defence of the city against the Cavaliers, but nevertheless by a concerted movement the Royalists assembled in such numbers on November 22nd as to seize the cannon and the magazine, take the city keys away from the Mayor, and imprison some of the trained bands of the enemy. The news of this surprisal was sent up to Colonel Morley in Parliament next day. The two M.P.'s for Chichester (Sir W. Morley and Christopher Lewknor) were expelled the House. "An impeachment was ordered November 23rd against Sir William Morley, while Sir John Morley and Sir E. Ford were voted delinquents and ordered into custody."

The report to Parliament was of course from a hostile pen. Parliament was then also informed that " the county of Sussex is in a great combustion, and that there is some thousands of the Papists and malignants in the county gathered together in Chichester, it being also reported that a great number of the Cavaliers are come in thither to assist the Array men in opposing the ordinances of Parliament." Instructions were at once given to seize High Sheriff Ford, to exact money from Papists, and to take other precautions.

After the surrender of Winchester in December, 1642, Sir William Waller, in spite of rumours that Prince Rupert had led 20 troops of horse towards Chichester marched against Arundel Castle. A few days previously the forces of the Parliament had gained a considerable success. On December 8th news reached London that the High Sheriff, Sir Edward Ford, when marching from Chichester to Lewes in company with the Earl of Thanet, had ordered all men capable of bearing arms to join him on pain of death, and of having their houses burnt to the ground. Some recruits were obtained by this summary order, but they were by no means zealous for the Royal cause. At Hayward's Heath, some two miles from Cuckfield, the Cavaliers were faced by a somewhat less numerous force. Neither party had any artillery. The fight began by a fierce attack by the Parliamentarians, and lasted at least one hour. "The fight was performed with their muskets at first, and after some volleys our horse broke into their van, our footmen just at that instant charging courageously into their quarters." The Parliamentarian reserves now came up, and completed the rout, the Cavaliers losing, it is said, not less than 200 men. The countrymen who had been forced into Sheriff Ford's ranks threw down their arms and ran away as fast as their legs could carry them to Hurst, Ditchling, and the neighbouring ...lages. Sir Edward Ford and the Earl of Thanet's horse "flying with all speed up to the not distant downs, and so to Wissum (Wiston ?) to the Earl's house," and from thence to Chichester. The victors marched to secure Lewes. The troops which had taken part in the capture of Winchester marched from thence to Havant, many deserting on the road, their pay being in arrears, and returning to London, intending there to re-enlist in other regiments. At Havant Sir William Waller and Colonel Ramsay joined them at the head of 2000 men. The prisoners taken at Winchester having been safely disposed of at Portsmouth, and at Lambeth House, London, the whole force was ready to march towards Chichester and Arundel on the morning of Monday, Dec. 17th, when a sudden order was received from the Earl of Essex, recalling Colonels Hurrey, Goodwin, and Browne, with four regiments. These troops however, seem to have remained a few days longer under Sir W. Waller's command. The march into Sussex was by no means unopposed. There are somewhat vague accounts of a fight "with a great party of the King's army in a great field for seven hours very courageously." At length Sergeant-Major Skippon came up with eleven troops of horse, and the Cavaliers fled, many of them being captured, and some 200 slain. The loss of the victorious army is said to have been about 40. Sir William Waller and Colonel Browne, his energetic second in command, then marched with the main body of their troops to Chichester, sending at the same time a detachment of 100 men to make themselves masters of Arundel Castle, which had "a garrison, though not numerous or well provided, as being without apprehension of an enemy," and which had been during the previous year abandoned in despair by its owner, Thomas Earl of Arundel, the friend and patron of the artist Hollar. Whilst the remainder kept the Royalist townsmen in check, 36 daring spirits assaulted the castle, which, if well garrisoned, would have been impregnable. Their arrival was unexpected, but the gates of the castle were, nevertheless, closed. Thereupon "they set a petard to the gate, and blew it open, and so most resolutely entered the castle, surprising all there, amongst whom they took one Sir Richard Lechford and his son, a great Papist, and one Captain Goulding, raising men and armes in Sussex to assist the malignants in Chichester, which said prisoners," being sent up to London, were speedily placed in durance vile. Another account styles these prisoners Sir Richard Rochford and Mr. Rochford. The capture of 100 horse, together with arms and stores, rewarded the victors, who claimed to have captured this important stronghold without the loss of a man. Weapons having been sent from London, the Trained Bands of Sussex, who had been disarmed by Sir Edward Ford, the Royalist High Sheriff, informed the Parliament that they were resolved "to regain and fetch their arms from Chichester, or else to lose their lives in the attempt thereof:" They were as good as their word.

After the fall of Arundel Castle, the fate of Chichester was sealed. The newswriter of the day says of the Royalists:—"These silly persons, being deluded with expectation of the Cavaliers to assist them, would gladly submit, if it might be accepted, with satisfaction out of their estates." Mr. Blaauw says, "Although Clarendon speaks of the city as being uncompassed with a very good old wall easy to be fortified (B. vi.), yet soon after Waller and Sir W. Lewis had blockaded it, they informed the Parliament that they find it of no great strength to hold out long." Clarendon thinks it would not have yielded "if the common people of the country, out of which soldiers were to rise, had been so well affected as was believed;" but he confesses that the cause was unpopular, and that in fact "their number of common men was so small that the constant duty was performed by the officers and gentlemen of quality, who were absolutely tired out." Colonel Browne (who is called by Sir Philip Warwick "a woodmonger," and "a man of a clear courage and good understanding, and very crafty," and who was afterwards knighted by Charles II. on account of his civil usage of his father when a prisoner, was during the siege withdrawn to resist a pressing danger at Windsor, leaving Waller only 1000 horse, 300 dragoons, and six guns: but Sir Arthur Haslerig was present, and was both now, and again in 1647 when invited by W. Cawley, "the especial scourge of the city."

Vicars has, fortunately for posterity, preserved in his *Parliamentary Chronicle* (pp. 234-240) Sir W. Waller's own account of the siege as given in a letter written to the Earl of Essex. From this letter it appears that Sir William was joined, on the evening before his arrival at Chichester, by three troops of horse and two companies of "Dragoneers" under the command of Colonel Morley and Sir Michael Levesey, making his troops amount to some 6000. On his arrival before the town on December 21st, 1642, the garrison made a sortie, but were repulsed, one of their number being slain, and another taken prisoner. The besiegers suffered no loss, and secured their position "upon a Downe called the Broils, the onely commanding ground about the towne." The guns of the town were not silent,

CAPTURE OF CHICHESTER.

and the rest of the day was spent in the construction of siege batteries. With the approval of Sir Arthur Haslerig and other officers, Sir William Waller summoned the garrison to surrender. A parley took place. Says Sir William, "The persons I sent were Major Horatio Carey and Captain Catre: the hostages from them were Colonel Lindsay and Lieutenant-Colonel Potter." Sir William Waller demanded an absolute surrender of the city, with the giving up of Sir Edward Ford, of all Papists and of all persons considered by Parliament as delinquents. The soldiers were to depart without arms; but officers were to retain their swords and horses, giving a pledge never again to take up arms against the Parliament.

After long debate, the garrison declined to accede to these terms, but offered to give up any Roman Catholics within the walls. "Whereupon the next day our battery played, but our cannoneers overshot the towne extremely." Cannonading continued, and towards evening the besiegers received a letter from the Earl of Essex, announcing the approach of Prince Rupert. Scouts were immediately sent out, and on the following day Waller brought his guns nearer the town. The suburbs of the West Gate were occupied after a fierce struggle, but the burning with wild-fire of certain houses by the garrison obliged the besiegers to beat a retreat. The garrison also fired some houses at the East Gate, " but we got possession of the Almes Houses, within halfe musket shot of the North Port, and then planted our ordnance very advantagiously, which played through the gate up into the Market Place of the City." Two companies of foot and two troops of horse which Lieut.-Col. Roberts had brought from Arundel took post after vigorous opposition at the South Gate. The suburbs of the East Gate were also occupied by the besiegers, who kept up a brisk fire upon any of the defenders who showed themselves upon the walls. A whole culverin was now placed in position within pistol shot of the East Gate. The West Gate was also to be set on fire, and Sir William intended "to petard a back gate that issued out of the Deanery through the town wall into the fields, and was walled up by a single brick thick." But whilst arrangements were being made for the attack a trumpet was sent out of the city at ten o'clock at night asking for a parley at nine o'clock the next morning. This request was granted, and at the appointed hour Sir William Balnidine and Captain Wolfe were sent from the garrison to treat for a surrender. A cessation of arms was agreed upon during the progress of the negotiations, but Sir William Waller declined to grant any more favourable terms than " Quarter, and with it honourable usage." This being refused, " not without hot indignation," the besieged prepared to sell their lives dearly, and Sir William "to proceed roundly and speedily with them." But at the last moment, before the assault, a trumpet was sent out of the city desiring a respite until seven o'clock on the following morning, at which hour a surrender was agreed upon. In spite of the futile opposition of some of Lord Crawford's Scotch troopers, the city was delivered in the afternoon to Sir William Waller, " the gates being set open for us and then set fast againe. Then the first thing we did was to release and fully set at libertie all the honest men of the towne whom they had imprisoned, who being thus enlarged, we imployed in places of trust in the city." In the evening a train of powder was discovered near Sir William Waller's quarters, but the gunner, on being apprehended, and all the Royalist leaders disclaimed all knowledge of the matter. During the eight days that the siege lasted no rain fell, which greatly facilitated the operations of the besiegers, but within half-an-hour after the victors had entered the gates there were "continual incessant showers." Vicars also records with exultation that the surrender took place at the very time of the observance of a solemn fast. Sir William Waller at once sent up to London Sir Edward Ford, who was soon afterwards released, through the influence of his sister Sarah, who had married the Parliamentarian General Ireton. Sir John Morley. Colonel Shelley. Christopher Lewknor. Colonel Lindsay. Lieutenant-Colonel Porter, Sergeant-Major (i.e., Major) Dawson, and Major Gordon were amongst the prisoners, with some 60 other officers and commanders, who were for the most part Scotchmen, "with all their brave horses, which were dainty ones indeed." About 400 "excellent dragooneers" and three or four hundred infantry laid down their arms. Most of the humbler captives were sent up by sea and speedily imprisoned in London.

Dr. King also ("a proud Prelate, as all the

rest are, and a most pragmaticall malignant against the Parliament, as all his cater-capt companions are") did not escape. Seventeen captains, thirteen lieutenants, and eight ensigns were found in the garrison. Mr. Blaauw says, "The Parliament accompanied their thanks with a special charge to the commanders at Chichester 'to be careful of the prisoners;' and they were hurried off to London, where they were confined in the deanery of St. Paul's, and in Lord Petre's house, in Aldersgate-street, until January 11th, 1643, when some were sent to Windsor Castle. Ensigns Richard and Thomas Shelley were in March removed from Lord Petre's to Plymouth for security. Lewknor was kept as a close prisoner, and none allowed to speak to him in private. The prisons often at this period overflowed, and Colonel Morley was one of a committee 'to dispose of the prisoners, either by sending them to the Indies or otherwise.' Some were kept in vessels at Gravesend, and Colonel Goring was kept in custody at the 'Red Lion' Inn, Holborn, even though Parliament considered it not safe, and wished him to be removed to the Tower, but it was courteously resolved that 'Lady Goring shall have liberty to see her son, Colonel Goring, a prisoner to the Parliament, in presence and hearing of his keeper.' He was released March 12th, 1644, by exchange with Lord Lothian."

Dr. Bruno Reeves, the Dean of Chichester, was fined 120*l.*, and received no benefit from his deanery for many a long year. He has left an account of the damage done to the Cathedral, which was printed in "Mercurius Rusticus." We may add that at the invitation of Mr. William Cawley a party was sent in the year 1647, under the command of Sir Arthur Haslerig, to finish the work of destruction, which is alleged had been left incomplete, and they did finish it. Dr. Reeves says that on the day after the surrender of the city the Marshal and some other officers entered the vestry, and took possession of the vestments and church plate, leaving "not so much as a cushion for the pulpit, nor a chalice for the Blessed Sacrament. . . . As they broke down the organs and dashed the pipes with their pole-axes they scoffingly said, 'Hark, how the organs goe!'" They broke the rail and the Communion Table to pieces, together with the Ten Commandments, and the pictures of Moses and Aaron. Prayer-books and musicbooks, torn to pieces, were everywhere to be seen, whilst gowns and surplices were appropriated, with a view to their speedy conversion into shirts. The portraits of bishops and kings were destroyed, and "one of those miscreants picked out the eyes of King Edward the Sixth's picture, saying 'That all this mischief came from him when he established the Book of Common Prayer.'"

On the following Tuesday there was a solemn thanksgiving in the Cathedral for Sir William Waller's victory, and after the sermon "they ran up and down the church with their swords drawn, defacing the monuments of the dead, hacking and hewing the seats and stalls, scratching and scraping the painted walls." Sir William Waller stood by with his sword drawn, as if in fear of his own men, whereat Dean Reeves makes merry. The Sub-Deanery Church in the north transept was then treated in a similar manner, the Bible being "marked in divers places with a black cole," prayer-books torn up, the surplices appropriated, and the chalice broken in pieces as fair and lawful plunder. Five or six days afterwards Sir Arthur Haslerig, who had been informed "by a treacherous officer of the church of the hiding place of the remaining church plate, entered the Chapter House at the head of a party duly provided with crow-bars and ordered them to break down the wainscot. Sir Arthur's tongue was not enough to express his joy, it was operative at his very heels, for, dancing and skipping (pray mark what musick that is to which it is lawful for a Puritan to dance), he cryed out 'There, boys, there, boys; hark! it rattles, it rattles, it rattles!' and being much importuned by some members of that church to leave the church but a cup for the administration of the Blessed Sacrament, answer was returned by a Scotchman standing by 'that they should take a wooden dish.'"

Mr. Blaauw says: "Before quitting Chichester it is fitting that antiquaries should especially lament some of the accompaniments of this capture, such as the loss of the ancient city records, and the destruction of the north-west tower of the Cathedral. After a few years' trial as a garrison town, part of the time under the famous Algernon Sydney, as governor, the Parliament fortunately resolved to disgarrison Chichester, March 2nd, 1646, and its ordnance was transferred to Arundel." The bastion of the North Wall of Chichester between the two

West Lanes was built at this time with the stones of the two churches of St. Pancras and St. Bartholomew, which stood without the walls Sir William Waller after the surrender requested permission to visit London, he himself being in bad health and his troops being worn out with fatigue.

A curious extract from an old register throws some light on the route taken by Sir William Waller's troopers on their way to Chichester from Winchester. Some few years since in a shop at Bishop's Waltham an old book was rescued from destruction, which upon examination proved to be one of the registers of the neighbouring parish of Upham. It contains the following entry, for which, together with very much valuable information, I am indebted to F. Baigent, Esq., of Winchester: "Item, for cleansing ye church against Christmas (1642), after ye troopers had abused it for a stable for their horses, 2s." This entry proves that local traditions of some of our Hampshire churches having been used as stables are not without foundation. The old register above-mentioned contains frequent entries of relief given to sick and wounded soldiers, and in the year 1647 certain soldiers were relieved "on their march home." A year or two afterwards the writer of the entry referring to the troopers, altered the words "had used it for a stable" into "had abused it for a stable." A slight alteration, but clearly indicative of the political creed of this rural keeper of the records.

Churches in Winchester fared no better, for in 1660 we read "the little church of St. Clement having been much dilapidated while the soldiers occupied it as a guard-house, was used as a place to lay faggots in, yea, to keep hogs in, and wherein to receive oxen, horses, &c., at times of fairs." On January 1st, 1643, it was ordered by the Parliament that the Cavaliers taken at Chichester should be sent to Windsor Castle, and other prisoners outside the City of London. Lambeth House was already so full of Royalist captives that Lord Petre's house in Aldersgate-street was utilised as a prison on January 5th, 1643.

On Wednesday, January 4th, 1643, it was ordered "bellsand expressions of joy this night to be done as is usual," and on Sunday, January 8th, a solemn thanksgiving for the taking of Chichester was appointed in all churches within the City of London. On January 16th Colonel Herbert Morley received the thanks of the Speaker in his place in Parliament "for the great service he did in the taking of Chichester." Other members of the Paulet family, beside the Marquis of Winchester, had meanwhile been doing the King good service. On December 10th, 1642, the Earl of Pembroke was, by a declaration of both Houses of Parliament, appointed Lieutenant of Wilts and Hants, "as the Lord Paulet, Sir Ralph Hopton, and others, their accomplices, have gotten together great forces in the western parts of this kingdom." We already know that Lord Paulet was with Sir Ralph Hopton and the Marquis of Hertford at the outbreak of the war, and after the surrender of Portsmouth by Goring retired with them into Glamorganshire. In Ireland also Sir John Paulet gained a great victory over the Irish rebels near Bandon Bridge, in the county of Cork, on November 23rd, 1642. After Alderman Gallop and another burgess had, as we have seen, signified at Portsmouth the fidelity of the town of Southampton to the Parliament, Calshot Castle, which was considered a place of considerable strength, was duly supplied with shot. Windmill fortress, near Portsmouth, had a captain who received 9d. per diem, two soldiers at 6d., and eight mariners at 8d. per diem. The annual cost was 100*l*. 10s. Portsmouth had a captain with 13 gunners, the latter receiving 6d. per diem. Annual cost, 188*l*. "Sportsmaking," a bulwark, had three guns, whose daily pay was 6d. each. Calshot Point had a chief-captain at 1s. 8d. per diem, an under captain at 8d., four soldiers at 8d., one porter at 8d., and eight gunners at 6d. each per diem. The annual cost was 107*l*. 7s. 6d. Hurst Castle had a captain at 1s. 8d. per diem, an under captain at 10d., ten soldiers at 6d., a chief gunner at 8d., one porter at 8d., and six gunners at 6d. per diem. Total yearly cost, 264*l*. 13s. 4d. St. Andrew's Point fortress cost 85*l*. 3s. 4d. per annum. At Portsmouth town and isle there was a new fortress, with a captain whose pay was 10d. per diem. The daily pay of the 20 soldiers under his command amounted to 13s. 4d. Sandown Castle in the Isle of Wight had a captain at 4s. per diem, an under captain at 2s., thirteen soldiers at 6d. per diem, one porter at 8d., a master gunner at 8d., and seven gunners at 6d. each. Annual cost, 363*l*. 6s. 8d. The Captain and Steward of the Isle of Wight received 47*l*. 7*s*. 6d. per annum. The town of Lymington, which contained friends to both of the contending parties, sent its records about this time to Hurst Castle for safe custody.

On December 27th the Earl of Portland, the imprisoned Royalist Governor of the Isle of Wight, was released from custody, and two days before the close of the year 1642 a terrible explosion announced the partial blowing up of some of the defences of Farnham Castle. We say partial, because in July, 1648, it was referred to the Committee at Derby House " to take such effectual course with Farnham Castle as to put it in that condition of indefensibleness as it may be no occasion for disturbing the peace of the country." A rate was accordingly levied to defray the expense of this service. Bishop Morley expended 7000*l*. after the Restoration in repairing the damage done at this period.

CHAPTER IX.—FIGHTING AT ALTON.—SIR WILLIAM WALLER PLUNDERS WINCHESTER AND DEFACES ROMSEY ABBEY—ROAD WAGGONS SEIZED NEAR BASINGSTOKE.

On Tuesday, February 24th, 1643, it was announced that the counties of Kent, Surrey, Sussex, and Hampshire had entered into a mutual agreement to raise and maintain 3000 foot and 300 horse for the service of the Parliament. On hearing of this project the King, at Oxford, issued a proclamation, declaring all such levies illegal, and calling upon all soldiers already embodied to retire to their homes, under pain of being considered guilty of high treason.

On Feb. 11th, 1643, it was ordered by the Parliament that two troops of horse and a regiment of dragoons should be raised for their service in and about Hampshire, the cost being defrayed out of the sequestered estates of Papists and delinquents. A committee was appointed to manage this business, of which Sir Thomas Jervoise, Knight, was the President, and John Leslie, Esq., the Receiver. Sir William Waller was also permitted to raise money for the maintenance of his army from the four associated counties of Hants, Surrey, Sussex, and Kent.

On Sunday, Feb. 5th, "Mercurius Aulicus," the Court Gazette of the Cavaliers, hears at Oxford that there was much discontent amongst the soldiers of the Parliament at Portsmouth, whose pay was considerably overdue, and that numerous desertions had taken place in consequence. At the end of the month 1500*l.* was paid to Sir William Lewis, the Governor, for the supply of the garrison. Frequent entries occur during this troublous period of large sums expended for the same purpose.

On Monday, Feb. 27th, a petition from the Isle of Wight was presented to Parliament. It stated that the defences of the island were very weak, and that there was good cause for fearing a foreign invasion, and asked that all monies raised in the island for purposes of defence might be expended within its limits. A supply of heavy guns, muskets, match, powder, bullets, corslets, &c., was requested for immediate issue to the various forts and castles, together with a guard of ships. The petitioners were also anxious that the troops on the mainland of Hampshire might be warned to hasten to their assistance as soon as an alarm was given. The subscribers to the fund for the defence of the island seem to have been numerous. and on Monday, April 4th, 1643, a Committee was appointed by Parliament to carry their wishes into effect, consisting of Sir Henry Worsley, Bart., Colonel Thomas Carne, John Lisle and John Bulkley, Esqs., all Deputy-Lieutenants of the Isle of Wight. Hearing that Sir William Waller was anxious to march towards the West Prince Rupert, on Feb. 22nd, rode out of Oxford at the head of a considerable force, and tried to intercept four guns and seven cartloads of ammunition, which were on their way to join the Parliamentary Army. Rupert and his troopers reached Basingstoke, and exchanged greetings with the stout old Marquis of Winchester, but failed to secure their prize, Waller having received intelligence of their arrival, and sent orders to the convoy to halt upon its march, whilst he himself retreated to Guildford. Detachments of his forces had already reached Winchester and Alton, and orders were at once despatched to recall them. The party from Winchester retired without molestation, but the Alton detachment was not so fortunate. It was 200 strong, and was reconnoitring the roads into Gloucestershire and Wiltshire, and reached Alton on February 22nd. Scarcely had the wearied troopers unsaddled, before 1500 of Rupert's wild riders beset the town. Thinking

FIGHTING AT ALTON.

that resistance would be useless, they cried for quarter, which was scornfully refused, whereupon they prepared to sell their lives dearly. Having a field-piece with them, they loaded it with musket bullets, and calmly awaited attack. The Cavaliers came boldly within range, the gun was fired, and when the smoke cleared away 80 of the assailants were seen to be either killed or wounded, and the rest retreating in confusion. Night was falling fast, but on came the attacking party once more. Again did that murderous field-piece scatter its deadly hail, and again did 40 soldiers of the King fall *hors de combat*. Darkness put an end to the strife, and the Cavaliers deferred their intended capture until the following morning, only to find at dawn that the gallant defenders of Alton had skilfully escaped, and fallen back in good order on the main body during the night. During the last week of February, 1643, Sir William Waller was still at Chichester with three or four hundred horse, some of his ten troops being but 10 or 15 strong. He was asking for and expecting reinforcements, as the Cavaliers were said to be meditating the re-capture of Winchester and Chichester, and had nearly the whole of Wiltshire at their mercy.

On February 28th he had reached Farnham, but was said to have only 400 dragoons, all my Lord General Essex could spare, and ten troops of horse, " which being put together, will make three good ones," to oppose the Princes Maurice and Rupert, who were said to be at the head of 5000 horse, and at least 2000 Welshmen. Poor Hampshire paid weekly 750*l.* for the service of the Parliament, and on Friday, March 3rd we have reports of much indiscriminate plundering of friends and foes by Prince Rupert's soldiers. The county had formerly refused to join the Association for Defence entered into by Kent, Surrey, and Sussex, fearing to incur the vengeance of the King, whose army had taken post in and around Reading. The miseries inseparable from civil war at length turned the scale, and Hampshire became one of the Associated Counties. Prince Rupert was to a considerable extent successful in preventing Waller from obtaining horses upon which to mount his infantry, and would probably have given him a severe defeat had not his scouts, who were always active and well informed, given him timely warning of a threatened attack upon either Reading or Oxford. Reluctantly, therefore, he fell back from Basingstoke and Cirencester, and re-entered Oxford on March 28th. According to a letter from Henley-on-Thames, he had on April 7th taken up a position at Reading. Prince Rupert having retired, Sir William Waller was now at liberty to make, in company with Sir Arthur Haslerig, what Clarendon calls a quick march through Wilts. The same authority states that he had under his command a light party of horse and dragoons some 2000 in number, belonging to the army of the Earl of Essex. "Mercurius Aulicus" says that he had 500 foot, a regiment of horse, another of dragoons, six field-pieces, and four cart-loads of muskets to be distributed amongst the recruits who might join his standard. His banner was a somewhat singular one. At the Battle of Agincourt one of his ancestors had been fortunate enough to capture the Duke of Orleans, who, after a residence in England of some 25 years, paid 100,000 crowns of ransom money. In memory of this event the Waller family were granted as armorial bearings a leafy tree, from which was suspended a shield bearing the lilies of France. The motto was "Fructus Virtutis" (the fruit of valour). His second in command, Colonel Brown, had upon his banner a skull and a wreath of laurel, with the motto "One of These!" and his constant associate, Sir A. Haslerig, had adopted the device of an anchor suspended from the clouds, and the motto "Only in Heaven!"

On March 3rd, 1643, Sir William Waller marched into Winchester, "and being an inhabitant and a freeman of the city, he promised that no man should suffer any loss or damage by him, and he performed it for as much as it concerned himself, but when he went away on Saturday (March 4th) he left behind Sergeant Major Carie, with a troop of horse, to levy 500*l.* upon the same. A most unreasonable sum to be imposed upon a town so lately and so miserably plundered. But say what they could in their own behalf, no less than 500*l.* would be accepted, and that accordingly was raised, viz., 350*l.* out of the inhabitants of the city, 150*l.* on one Sir Henry Clerke, a neighbouring gentleman." Master Say, a son of a prebendary of the Cathedral, who probably fared none the better on that account, had entrusted his horses for purposes of concealment to his servant. Having been betrayed by some of his neighbours, he was brought before Sir William

Waller, who questioned him as to the whereabouts of the steeds. Master Say pleaded ignorance, and was forthwith handed over to the Provost Marshal, who received orders to make him confess. This official conducted him to the "George" Inn, which dates back to the days of the Fourth Edward, and led him into what is now known as "the 18-stall stable." Placing a halter round his neck, the Marshal renewed his cross-examination. Obtaining no information, he hoisted him up to the rack, allowing him to hang until he was almost strangled, and then gave him a little breathing space. This process was repeated several times, until the spectators of this barbarous scene quitted the stable in disgust. Finding torture ineffectual, the Marshal with many kicks and blows dismissed Master Say, who a few days afterwards was reported to be dangerously ill, a circumstance scarcely to be wondered at.

On Saturday, March 4th, Sir William Waller and his army marched to Romsey, where they at once began to deface the Abbey Church, pulling up the seats and destroying the organ. "Which was no sooner done, but a zealous brother of the ministry, dwelling not far off, got into the pulpit, and for the space of two hours, in a furious zeal, applauded that religious act, encouraging them to go on as they had begun!" The chronicler laments that this stately church, having escaped destruction at the time of the dissolution of the monasteries, had been reduced to ruin in these dissolute times.

From Romsey Sir William Waller marched to Salisbury, being constantly joined by numerous recruits. He seized many horses in various places, and by an ingenious stratagem did considerable damage to the Royal cause. He sent out orders as if from Prince Rupert to all the neighbouring Cavaliers for a general muster at Salisbury. Some 3000 responded to the call, and were astonished, on March 10th, 1643, to find themselves unhorsed and disarmed by their wily opponent. They not unnaturally remonstrated, but without effect, Sir William politely requesting the loan of the steeds until the conclusion of the war. During the year 1643 horses were valued at 4l. each, but they had previously been procurable for 30s. and 50s. Hay cost 6d. for a day and night, and the price of oats was 2s. per bushel.

On leaving Salisbury Waller's army had increased to the number of 3000 men, and it was said that he had with him, strange to say, two troops of French and Dutch Papists under the command of Sergeant-Major (i.e., Major) Carie (or Carew) and Captain Carr. Some of these men afterwards came over to the King's army and said that when they were brought over to England they fully understood that they were to fight for the King, and not against him. After taking possession of Malmesbury and making the small Royalist garrison prisoners, Sir William Waller marched into Dorsetshire, putting to flight Sir John Strangeways and the Cavaliers of Dorset and Somerset.

During the month of March, 1643, some of the Cavaliers from the garrison of Reading marched to Basing House, and in the neighbourhood of Basingstoke (another account says near Wokingham) succeeded in intercepting several waggons laden with cloth, belonging to certain clothiers of the western counties. The spoil was worth from 10,000l. to 12,000l., and the merchants went to Oxford and petitioned the King for redress. Their prayer was heard, and on March 22nd the cloth-laden waggons reached London in safety. Certain bales, however, belonging to Mr. Ash and his brother, who were both members of the House of Commons, were confiscated. The merchants, who recovered their property, were obliged to take the new protestation of allegiance, and to pay their fees, as if they had been prisoners to Smith, the Provost Marshal of Oxford. This officer seems to have been terribly severe, and in fact most brutal in his treatment of the prisoners entrusted to his care. Frequent complaints were made to Parliament of his barbarities, and the House of Commons addressed a remonstrance to the King on the subject. My Lord General the Earl of Essex was by a resolution of the House of Commons passed on March 16, 1643, officially informed of these proceedings, and also that certain passers by Basing House had been fired upon from the windows. The day of trial for "Loyalty House" was now near at hand.

CHAPTER X.—PRINCE MAURICE AT SALISBURY.—FAST DAY AT SOUTHAMPTON AND PORTSMOUTH.—COLONEL NORTON REPULSED.—BASING HOUSE BECOMES A GARRISON.

On Wednesday, April 19th, 1643, we catch a passing glimpse of the home-life of a famous divine. "Ordered that Mr. Dr. Fuller shall have a pass to carry his wife to Salisbury, and to return back again."

On Saturday, April 15th, 1643, the Earl of Essex sat down before Reading, which surrendered twelve days afterwards. The terms of capitulation were not faithfully observed, which served as a pretext for excesses on both sides on various subsequent occasions. On April 21st "Dalbier, a German Engineer," was said in London to have been slain before Reading. Rumour spoke falsely, and Colonel Dalbier lived to do much harm to Basing House, which the emboldened friends of the Parliament hoped would speedily share the fate of Reading.

On Thursday, May 4th, the Hampshire Cavaliers were again raising their heads, but were once more doomed to disappointment. Two ships bound from Dunkirk to Ireland, and laden with ammunition for the King's forces, were driven into Portsmouth, and were at once seized by Sir William Lewis, the Governor. An ordinance of both Houses of Parliament passed on May 4th provided that the whole of the King's revenues from the county of Hampshire should be applied to the repair, maintenance, pay, &c., of the garrisons and fortifications of Portsmouth, Hurst, Calshot, and Southsea Castle.

On Wednesday, May 13th, a petition was read in Parliament which bore the signatures of most of the inhabitants of Portsmouth, asking for the appointment of Sir William Waller as Governor of the town, and declaring their "readiness to serve them in the defence of that place with their last drop of blood." The Earl of Essex was thereupon recommended to appoint aller, but from "Mercurius Aulicus" of June 28th we learn that Sir William Lewis having been superseded "Master Wallop" was temporarily appointed. Sir William Waller having marched to the westward from Salisbury, Prince Maurice, the Earl of Carnarvon, and the Marquis of Hertford reached that pleasant cathedral city about nine o'clock on the morning of Whit Sunday, May 20th, with, it was said, 2000 men. Before the arrival of the Prince, Lord Seymour and some Cavaliers "took divers well affected persons prisoners, amongst which Mr. Dutton, the Mayor, was one." Sir William Waller, Sir Edward Hungerford, Sir John Horner, and other friends of the Parliament were preparing to offer opposition, "so that now this town, which, under the pretence of standing as neuters, it is thought hath afforded no small supply unto Oxford, is now like to speed no better than Marlborough and other places which have been utterly ruined by the Cavaliers." Before Prince Maurice and his army entered the city proclamation was made by the High Sheriff of the county "that none should be plundered without order, which it is confessed was indifferently kept, but we were forced to give them free quarter." On the following day the Prince, Marquis, and Earl of Carnarvon dined at Wilton, and there took two special horses, "and shot a gallant stallion of the Earl of Pembroke's, which they could not take, but the horse is like to recover." On their return to Salisbury an order was issued that all the citizens should give up their arms, on pain of having their houses searched. Many useful weapons having been thus obtained a collection was made in the city, to defray the cost of the Prince's table during the stay of the army. On Wednesday, May 23rd, two guns and two barrels of powder were discovered by the Cavaliers not far from the Council House, and a party of horse brought in four waggons laden with wool and oil from London, together with several pack horses. Another detachment found a gun and two or three drakes or field-pieces concealed at Wilton, which were likewise secured. Next day two loads of pikes and corslets arrived, which had been collected in the neighbourhood by dint of armed search. The following day was Friday, May 25th, and Prince Maurice and the Marquis of Hertford marched out over Harnham Hill to Dogdean, where a general muster of the county had been ordered to take place. All partisans of the King were at once enrolled as soldiers, whilst the friends of the Parliament were either disarmed, or, if unprovided with weapons, obliged to contribute various sums of money. Two loads of arms were brought back to Salisbury in the evening.

On Saturday, May 26th, the Prince's army, now increased to not less than 4000 horse and 1000 foot, was drawn up in battle array at Dogdean, from which place one detachment marched towards Warminster, whilst another was sent to plunder the Earl of Salisbury's house at Cranborne. About six o'clock on the morning of Sunday, May 27th, the whole army marched away from Salisbury towards Dorchester, to the great joy even of their own friends in the city. The Mayor, who had all this time been kept in durance vile, was released when they departed, but Master Hunt, a Parliament man, and some others were taken away in safe custody.

On June 6th the Prince, Marquis, and Lord Carnarvon were once more at Salisbury, intending to join Sir Ralph Hopton on his march towards Oxford. A journalist of that day says: "They would willingly now give him 2000*l.* to be gone, who before gave him 1000*l.* to welcome him. The Canons and Prebends had before their first coming taken down their organs themselves, and hid two hundred of their pipes, for fear of the Parliament's forces, hoping hereafter to have them up, and play their old tunes, but now they may take them, and help their countrymen to play the new tune of 'Fortune my Foe.'" Sir William Waller, who with Sir Edward Hungerford, Sir John Horner, and others was striving to keep both the Prince Maurice and Sir Ralph Hopton in check, was deficient in cavalry, but was early in June joined by Sir Arthur Haslerig and a welcome reinforcement of 500 horse. Notwithstanding this accession of strength, Prince Maurice and the Marquis of Hertford were able to defeat Waller's army on Monday, June 12th, to which "Mercurius Aulicus" thus refers: "Friday, June 9th. The rebels had solemn fast at Southampton, Portsmouth, and Hursley, for the speeding of Sir William Waller's great design against His Majesty's forces in the west, where Master Strickland, that learned, devout Levite, was pleased to say in his prayer these very words, 'O Lord, Thy honour is now at stake, for now, O Lord, Antichrist has drawn his sword against Thy Christ, and if our enemies prevail, Thou wilt lose thine honour!' But how God Almighty was pleased with this blasphemy and treason the issue of Waller's design hath manifested to the world!" On Saturday, June 24th, it was ordered that two foot companies, 300 strong, should be raised for the protection of the Isle of Wight from amongst its own inhabitants.

On July 7th we hear that Sir William Waller had sent a letter to Dorchester, asking that two troops of horse and one hundred dragoons should be sent to Colonel Norton, of Southwick Park, who was already in command of an equal number of men, and who was speedily joined by this welcome reinforcement.

On July 15th, after the complete defeat of Waller by Sir Ralph Hopton and the Cavaliers of the west upon Roundway Down, near Devizes, the House of Commons strongly urged the City of London and all friends of the Parliament in the counties of Hants, Surrey, Sussex, and Kent to send money, men, horses, and ammunition to the aid of either Fairfax or Waller, upon the security of the public faith for repayment. Towards the end of July it was deemed necessary to raise 7000 men for the service of the Parliament. London and Middlesex were to provide a contingent of 1500, and the four associated counties just mentioned were also to do their part, the Earl of Pembroke being appointed to the command of the cavalry raised in Hants, Surrey, Sussex, and Berks. Sir William Waller was to march to meet these new levies, who were to muster in London, and at Windsor, Cambridge, and Bedford.

On Wednesday, July 19th, 1643, "Mercurius Aulicus" tells us that the Parliament had ordered all possible aid to be sent to Sir William Waller from Portsmouth and other places of Hampshire. "Colonel Norton of Southwick, the great incendiary of that country, being made a Colonel amongst the rebels,

St. Barbe and others having the command of some troops of horse," marched to Winchester, and plundered it for the third time of all arms and horses. From thence he proceeded to Salisbury, where he arrived on Thursday, July 13th, where he also seized all the horses and arms to be found, and plundered the houses of the Cathedral clergy, even taking away their servants' clothes, and confiscating about 80*l.*, which belonged to an hospital of poor people, of which one of the prebends was governor. On his march from Salisbury to Devizes to join Sir William Waller, hearing of the defeat of the latter upon Roundway Down, he retreated to Wardour Castle, and from thence to Wilton. Preparing to attack Salisbury once more, he found the citizens, who had heard of the defeat of Waller, in arms to oppose him, and thinking discretion the better part of valour returned to Hampshire by a safer way, because, to him, the furthest way about was the next way home. Towards the end of July the Marquis of Winchester, who since the surrender of Reading had seen his enemies increasing in numbers, and forming strong garrisons in his neighbourhood, found that Colonel Norton was threatening a visit to Basing House, "as being a place in which he hoped to find much spoil and little opposition, for to say truth, he is a very valiant gentleman where he meets with no resistance." Clarendon, on the other hand, speaks of Norton as being a man of undoubted bravery. The Marquis made a journey to Court, and obtained permission to have one hundred musketeers of Colonel Rawdon's regiment sent under the command of Lieut.-Colonel Peake with speed and secrecy to Basing. He then returned home, nor did he reach Loyalty House a moment too soon. Scarcely had he arrived before "Colonel Norton, with Capt. St. Barbe, with his troop of horse, and Capt. Cole, with a ragged rabble of Dragoons, begirt the house and pressed the siege exceeding hotly." Within the walls there were, besides servants, only "six gentlemen, armed with six muskets, the whole remainder of a well furnished armoury." They had already proved their prowess, for with them the Marquis had done so well that twice the enemies' attempts proved vain.

But now surely, on this 31st of July, 1643, the odds are overwhelming, for see, two regiments of dragoons, under Colonels Harvey and Norton, have made their way through the park palings, and are bent upon an attack in force. Another half-hour, and the hopeless struggle will be at an end. But hark to yonder musket shots, and listen intently. Surely that is "Rupert's call" from cavalry trumpets, and see how the rebels are flying in all directions. Yes, aid is at hand. Lieutenant-Colonel Peake has come from Oxford by forced marches, and is now beating the foe from Basing village, clearing house after house. But the King, hearing of Norton's threatened attack, has, although he is about to march towards Bristol, and surely needs the help of every available man, sent Colonel Bard with some troops of horse to the relief of beleaguered Basing. The cavalry arrive just as the musketeers have cleared a way to "The Castle," as Basing House was often styled by the Cavaliers. Lieut.-Colonel Peake deserves full credit for his victory, for Harvey and Norton's two regiments of dragoons "ran quite away" from his musketeers. Basing being thus at liberty, Colonel Norton and his allies retreated that night to Farnham, and from thence to Portsmouth, "plaguing and plundering all the country as they passed along, for fear it should be thought that he had made so long a journey, and lain out so long, to undo nobody." A letter was at once written by the Parliamentarian Committee at Portsmouth to the Lord General Essex, and read in the House of Lords on September 7th, asking for more troops for the protection of the town, as the Cavaliers had succeeded in surprising both Dorchester and Weymouth. Colonel Norton's repulse at Basing was doubtless another cause for alarm to the adherents of the Parliament in Portsmouth. Colonel Harvey, who aided Colonel Norton in this attack upon Basing, had formerly been a captain in one of the regiments of the London Trained Bands. He had been unfortunate in business, and is described as a "decayed silkman." When the war broke out he was appointed to the command of a troop of horse and of a regiment of dragoons. The women of London presented a petition for peace to the House of Commons, and, refusing to disperse, Colonel Harvey, with his troop of horse, was ordered to charge the unarmed crowd. The order was rigorously obeyed, and not a few women were killed or wounded. Col. Harvey's standard bore the device of a Bible with the motto "Lex Suprema" (the supreme law!) and below a city, with the motto "Salus Patriæ" (the safety of our fatherland). During the Commonwealth, Colonel Harvey was the temporary owner of Fulham Palace and of various revenues belonging of right to the See of London. One who knew him says "He came off bluely in the end."

The standard of the Marquis of Winchester was like those of other contemporary commanders, square in form, bearing a scroll with pendent ends, on which was the motto "Aimez Loyaute." The musketeers, who proved so timely a reinforcement to the defenders of Basing House, belonged to the Regiment of Foot commanded by Sir Marmaduke Rawdon, of whom, and of the other officers of the garrison we will speak more at length hereafter. Warburton says ("Memoirs of Prince Rupert," p. 116): "During the early part of the Civil War the pikemen held the post of honour. The pikemen, as well as the musqueteers, wore a leathern doublet, steel cap, cloth hose, and square-toed shoes, with a large rosette. The pikeman, when he could get it, wore a back and breastpiece of steel, with an iron hook on the former, whereon to hang his steel cap while marching. The musqueteer wore a 'bandolier' or broad belt with charges of powder hung by little cords. The bullets were carried in a little bag or in the mouth for immediate use, over the left shoulder; a sword belt over the right; his match-lock rest was sometimes attached to his left wrist, while not in use, and sometimes he had a boy allowed him to carry this cumbrous piece of artillery for him. There were locks to the pistols and petronels (the latter so called 'because it hangeth on the breast') of the Cavalry, but none, I think, to the Infantry musket. The former were wound up like a watch by an instrument called a spanner, and when let off by the trigger the flint was brought against a rough surface that gave the spark by friction. These were called 'snaphaunces.' The charges of powder suspended from the bandolier being often 12 in number, were often styled 'the twelve Apostles.' The pay was 8d. a day for the Infantry and 16d. for the Cavalry." Such were the men who manned the walls and towers of Basing House.

After the repulse of Harvey and Norton. Basing House "is then begunne, according to the quantity of men now added, to be fortified." Cavaliers evidently knew how to use pickaxe and spade, as well as musket and pike. The whole area of the fortifications was 14½ acres, and many a now grass covered rampart is still in existence. Whilst batteries were in course of construction at Basing, certain ships asked and obtained convoy from the Earl of Warwick, who was in command for the Parliament at Portsmouth. He thereupon ordered Captain William Thomas, who commanded the *Eighth Whelp*, to escort these vessels from Southampton, Torbay, and Lynn to the coast of France. the *Charity*, frigate, being also in company. Off Brest the men-of-war were attacked by one of the ships which had gone over to the King's party. The result of the fight was the spending of prize money at Portsmouth by Parliament men-of-war's men. The story is a stirring one, but comes not within our province.

CHAPTER XI.—ALARM AT SOUTHAMPTON—CAVALIERS FINED AND IMPRISONED—COLONEL POWLET SLAIN NEAR WINCHESTER—SOUTHAMPTON AND THE ISLE OF WIGHT FORTIFIED.—WINCHESTER RE-OCCUPIED BY THE CAVALIERS.

Captain Swanley having persuaded Southampton, not without dread of possible bombardment, to declare for the Parliament, the opponents of the Royal cause took care to make their power felt, not however without some opposition from their fellow townsmen, and occasional fears for their own safety.

On Saturday, August 5th, 1643, "Mercurius Aulicus," at Oxford, had received letters from Winchester to the effect that "Legay, Wolfrey, Mercer, and the rest of the pack of the town of Southampton have sent their goods into the Island, and upon the least noise of the Royal army's approach will fly themselves likewise." Murford, the Parliamentarian Governor, had serious thoughts of sailing for New England, and had lately exchanged 500l. worth of silver for gold, he "being not worth 5l. when he came thither." Colonel Nathaniel Fiennes, the brother of Lord Say and Sele, who had been educated at Winchester College, and had been admitted to a fellowship at New College, Oxford, in quality of founder's kin, had surrendered Bristol to Prince Rupert on July 26th, and on the last day of the same month reached Southampton, at the head of 80 horse, each of whom had a woman riding behind him. This arrangement may have been, and probably was, productive of mutual satisfaction, but would sorely wound the sensitive feelings of an adjutant in this prosaic nineteenth century. Governor Murford at once took measures to secure the election of Colonel Fiennes as a burgess of Southampton, "and his (Murford's) chaplain, in his sermon the day before, like a desperate wretch, charged the King with dissembling protestations. Murford, like a brave villain," threatened to imprison a townsman for affirming that "the Queen's Majesty was joyfully entertained at Oxford, for (said Murford) it will discourage the well affected to hear that the Queen is beloved in any place." The poor townsman would most assuredly have been placed in durance vile had not the wife of the Governor, who is described as "the hired Governess" been induced, by a seasonable gift, to mollify the wrath of her lord and master. A youth, who relieved a half-starved Cavalier prisoner, had a narrow escape from imprisonment, for, in the opinion of Governor Murford, "if such were not relieved, there would be fewer malignants alive!"

Before supper one evening he assembled some 30 young apprentices, whom he ordered to take the Solemn League and Covenant. On their refusal he threatened them with imprisonment, saying that "their refusal disparaged his Government," and the same night three women were arrested, merely for saying that "they thought the King was too wise to be led by ill counsel."

On the following day Colonel Whitehead and Mr. Fielder, two of the authorities of Portsmouth, came to Southampton, and at once sent orders to various Cavaliers to pay them large sums of money. Sir John Mills was ordered to contribute 500l., whilst Master Thomas Mill was assessed at 200l. Mistress Clerk was to pay 200l., Alderman Raymond 100l., and others in proportion. Those who demurred were imprisoned, plundered, or carried away to Portsmouth, Colonel Whitehead playfully remarking that "he had been at a great charge to build a cage at Portsmouth, where many Hampton birds should sing very suddenly!"

About August 12th Colonel Powlet, who seems to have been a relative of the Marquis of Winchester, attacked Winchester with a party of horse, who probably belonged to the garrison of Basing House. He was at first successful, and levied contributions from most of the friends of the Parliament within the city. He at length retreated, carrying with him some 40 prisoners, but at a distance of some two or three miles from Winchester was attacked by a party of dragoons from Southampton. In the skirmish that followed Colonel Powlet and two of his men were killed, 60 others were made prisoners, and the captive citizens of Winchester released. "Mercurius Aulicus" loved not the Governor of Southampton, and learns on Saturday, August 12th, that "Mudford, alias Murford, that infamous Brownisticall Governor of Southampton," had that week shipped off "Mr. Jones, a learned ingenuous gentleman," with certain others, to New England, "making him pass his own door, without allowing him speech of his wife, or necessaries from his friends." Another version of this story is that Mr. Jones, being suspected of having written a pamphlet in answer to certain observations on His Majesty's Declaration, was kept for a long time in custody at Portsmouth, on an allowance of a penny farthing per diem for bread and water, but at length, in company with the Town Marshal, escaped to Oxford. Colonel Whitehead is reported to have said that "Cruelty to Cavaliers was acceptable work to God," and that he need not fear even if the King should prevail, for that he had secured his lands, had sufficient to maintain him, and had taken care to have a friend at Court, who had undertaken to save his life.

The good people of Southampton were strongly urged by Governor Murford's chaplain to take the Solemn League and Covenant. Here is a quotation from his prayer : "Bless the King, O Lord ; mollify his hard heart, while delighteth in blood ; open his eyes, that he may see that the blood of Thy servants is dear in Thy sight. He is fallen from faith in Thee, and become an enemy to Thy Church. Is it not he that hath sinned and done evil indeed ? But as for these sheep, what have they done ? Let Thine hand, we pray Thee, O Lord, be on him and on his father's house, but not on Thy people that they should be plagued." Colonel St. Barbe, after taking the Covenant, said aloud, before many witnesses, that "he had rather see the kingdom in a flame than that the King should prevail against the cause they have undertaken." Governor Murford sent Thornborough, Riggs, and certain other apprentices to a most noisome dungeon at Portsmouth, and "the Mayor, a very ancient man," was imprisoned for eleven weeks. Colonel Whitehead had ordered him to give up the keys of the town to him for the service of the Parliament, the good old Mayor answering him, being a Jerseyman, "Me no hang for you Master Whitehead, you hang for yourself." When he was at length released Murford, to please Colonel Whitehead, gave orders to the soldiers on guard to prevent the Mayor by force from going out through any of the gates of the town.

"Mercurius Aulicus" remarks : "Aug. 29th a seditious Levite at Portsmouth, one Tooker, Master Whitehead's own Chaplain, in a fast sermon prayed God 'to open the eyes of five Lords who lately deserted Him and His cause, and were gone to the King.' And 'tis somewhat strange those Lords should have their eyes shut, and yet should find the way from London to Oxford. Whitehead last week starved two prisoners to death at Portsmouth, refusing their bodies the service or attendance of friends at their funeral."

On Tuesday, Sept. 5th "Mercurius Aulicus," whose statements can, however, be digested only with the aid of a whole peck, if, indeed, a bushel be not preferable, of salt, is informed from Winchester that all ministers in the neighbourhood of Southampton have been replaced by Murford with men of his own party. Robinson, his own chaplain, prayed thus the last fast day : "O God, many are the hands lifted up against us, but there is one God ; it is Thou, Thyself, O Father, which doest us more mischief than they all." Mistress Murford, "the other day a poor seamstress," is said to be "most devout." Two of Captain St. Barbe's troopers attempted to rob a poor labourer near Milbrook, who, however, although he had no other arms than "a prong and a good heart," unhorsed them both, fully armed as they were, beat them well, and brought them and their horses into Southampton.

On Wednesday, Sept. 20th, both Houses of Parliament were informed that Hampshire, Portsmouth, Southampton, the Isle of Wight, and the western parts are in great danger, and may be possessed by the enemy speedily if some course be not taken. Sir William Waller was ordered to march thither at once, leaving some of his troops to follow, and on Monday,

October 2nd, Sergeant-Major Struce or some other Engineer was to proceed at once to the Isle of Wight, and to fortify in the manner that the Deputy Lieutenants of the Island shall think best. Eleven culverins or 18 pounders, and 20 Sakers or five pounders, had already been provided for these new defences, and the necessary timber was ordered to be cut in the New Forest, and transported to the Isle of Wight. At the end of September Governor Murford was actively engaged in fortifying Southampton. He threatened to hang the tythingman of Stoneham for negligence in execution of the warrants sent out for the raising of men and levying of money in the neighbourhood, and his sub-committee voted that the King's proclamation forbidding the payment of rents to those in arms against him should be burnt by the common hangman. "The good old Mayor," however, possessed sufficient influence to prevent this plan being carried out. The Earl of Southampton's house was also seized, and made to do duty as a gaol. On Saturday, November 4th, the Association of Hants, Sussex, Kent, Surrey, and the town and county of Southampton was officially announced, and Thomas Mason, Mayor of Southampton, was one of the Parliamentarian Committee for Hampshire.

On November 22nd the Parliament was of opinion that Southampton stood in need of further protection, and that it would be well to raise an additional local force for that purpose. The cost of so doing was to be defrayed from certain new excise duties, and by the sequestration of the estates of Papists, Cavaliers, and delinquents. The following Committee was therefore appointed:—Richard Norton, Esq., Thomas Mason, Mayor of Southampton, Richard Major, Esq., and Aldermen Edward Hooper, George Gallop, Edward Exton, Robert Wroth, and Henry Bracebridge, Esqs. All things considered, the year 1643 must have witnessed some stirring scenes in Southampton. The Fleming family, who were relatives of Oliver Cromwell, and had settled at Stoneham in the days of Good Queen Bess, were staunch adherents of the Parliament.

Dr. Milner is of opinion that there was no garrison in either the city or castle of Winchester during the early part of the year 1643. But in a history of Winchester, published in 1773, we are told that Sir William Waller left Lord Grandison and some of his troops under a small guard confined to the Castle. Soon after Waller's departure, Lord Grandison, with a few of his friends, found means to escape, and joining the Royal army at Oxford, prevailed with Lord (then Sir William) Ogle, at the head of his troops to attempt the retaking of the Castle, and setting the prisoners at liberty. This enterprise was so effectually performed by his Lordship that in three days he found himself not only in actual possession of the castle, but also of all the arms, ammunition, and effects of the enemy. Dr. Milner says that the King's secure hold upon the western counties at the close of the year 1643 was a great incentive to Hampshire and Sussex Cavaliers to exert themselves, and that Sir Richard Tichborne, its owner, was mainly instrumental in gaining possession of Winchester Castle. But whatever was the date of the Cavalier re-occupation of Winchester, it is certain that Basing House maintained throughout the year an attitude of firm and uncompromising resistance. Let us return thither.

CHAPTER XII.—THE GOVERNOR OF BASING HOUSE AND OTHER OFFICERS OF THE GARRISON.

Andover was in safe Royalist keeping, as was also Donnington Castle, near Newbury. These garrisons rendered communication easy between Kent, Surrey, and Sussex on the one side, and on the other Abingdon, Wallingford, Oxford, and the west.

"This House hath not onely been a great annoyance to all the country round about, but hath been a meanes to stop the trading out of the west to London by robbing and pillaging the carriers and clothiers that come from them, it standing near unto the direct road." So speak my Lord Denbigh and Sir Thomas Middleton. The Marquis was also able to enforce the payment of the 180*l*. demanded weekly by the King from each neighbouring hundred of Hants, Berks, and Wilts. A number of women and children had found refuge at Basing House, "wee not having lesse then scavenscore uselesse mouthes," and many Royalists had stored their valuables within its walls. Sir William Waller had hitherto been far too busy to be able to think much of either the Marquis or his doings. But having at length returned from his campaign in the western counties, where he had most assuredly lost all claim to be styled "William the Conqueror" for the future, he was at liberty to turn his attention to "Loyalty House." The "pure and spotless" Lord Grandison, who had formerly done his best to protect the Hampshire fortress, had lately died of wounds received at the taking of Bristol, which surrendered to Prince Rupert on July 26th, 1643.

The garrison of Basing were not taken unawares. "Upon report of a puissant army under command of Sir William Waller, to be appointed for the taking of it in, Colonell Rawdon (or Roydon) with the rest of his Regiment (being about one hundred and fifty more) is commanded thither. The Lord Marquisse taking forth commissions, as Colonell and Governor, for the raising of more forces for the defence of the same." Lieutenant-Colonel Peake was also appointed Lieutenant-Governor.

The town of Basingstoke favoured the cause of the Parliament, and on Friday, May 19th, 1643, it was ordered that whenever a fast was appointed for Wednesday, Basingstoke market should be held on Tuesday. In one of the volumes published by the Camden Society we find many interesting particulars concerning Colonel Rawdon, the Governor of Basing House. He was descended from the ancient family of that name near Leeds, in Yorkshire, and at the age of 16 was taken to London by his elder brother Lawrence, who placed him in business there, and laid the foundation of his fortunes. Mindful of his kindness, when in after years his younger brother died at Leeds he requested that his nephew and namesake Marmaduke Rawdon, then a boy of sixteen, might be committed to his parental care.

"When the younger Marmaduke became a member of his uncle's household the London merchant was in the prime of life, and at the height of prosperity. He had married a wealthy heiress, and was the father of a numerous family. He enjoyed the reputation of being one of the most enterprising and successful of the English mercantile adventurers of his day. His transactions extended to almost every part of the known world. He traded largely in the wines both of France and the Peninsula through agencies or factories established at Bordeaux and Oporto. From the merchants of Holland and the Netherlands he purchased the produce of the vintages which flourished on the banks of the Rhine and its tributaries. To encourage the introduction into this country of the wine recently produced in the Canary Islands, he joined in forming an important factory at Teneriffe. He was among the earliest of the adventurers who invested capital in the cultivation of the sugar plantations of Barbadoes. This island was first settled under the authority of letters patent granted by James I. A subsequent grant was made by Charles I." (See "Verney Papers," ed. Camden Soc, p. 193, note.) We learn from the "Calendar of State Papers," 1628-29, that Mr. M. Rawdon was either sole or part owner of the following ships in the years 1626 and 1627 :—"1626, Sept. 15.—Owners, M. Roydon, Rowland Wilson and others.—*Transport*, of London, tonn, 200. Capt. H. West. 1627, Jan. 30.—Owner, M. Roydon.—*Patience*, of London, tonn, 300, *George*, tonn, 80, Capt. Christopher Mitchell. 1627, Feb. 21st.— Owners, M. Roydon and others.—*Vintage*, of London, tonn, 140, Capt. R. West."

"It is said that he was one of the first who rigged out a ship for the discovery of the N.W. Passage. He was a member of the Company of Turkey Merchants, and he possessed the confidence of the French merchants who traded with England, and acted as their friendly advocate when negociations with our Government to them were before the council-table. We are not surprised to be told that he was much esteemed by the Royal favourite Buckingham, and that he received marked attention from both the great Duke's masters, King James I. and King Charles I. That Mr. Rawdon was upon terms of friendly and familiar intercourse with the latter monarch is apparent from a letter addressed by him to the Secretary of State, Sir John Coke, which happens to be preserved among the State papers of the year 1627:— 'Right Honorabl',—After his majestie had read that p't of the Spanish letter that is hear translated, his majestie saide it was of great importance, and commanded me and Cap. Marsh to deliver both the oregenall with the p't translaited, and this letter from the fathers at Rome, unto your honneur, till his further pleasure was known. Thes letters I had wth. a number of others in a shipp which we tooke at sea with sugars newly comed from Brasill, and finding it of consequence I thought it my dewty to present it to his majestie; thus humbly kissing your honeurs hands I wish all health and good fortunes may attend you,— Your honeurs servantto to dispose, MARMADUKE RAWDON. Tottnam, this 7th Septembers, 1627.'—Addressed—'To the Right Honorable Sir John Coke, Knight, one of his majesties secretaries att Tottnam, thes.'—We gather from this letter that Mr. Rawdon and the Captain of one of his merchant ships had called at the palace and been admitted to an interview with the King. A Spanish vessel freighted with sugars from Brazil had been captured by the Englishman, and her papers seized. Among them were letters which the merchant thought of sufficient importance to be presented to the notice of his Sovereign. The King was of the same opinion, and in the usual manner commanded them to be laid before his Secretary of State. In the year 1628 Mr. Rawdon sat in the House of Commons as one of the representatives of the commercial and shipbuilding town of Aldborough, in the county of Suffolk, but it does not appear that he was returned to any subsequent Parliament. At an early period of his career he was made a member of the Municipal Corporation of the City of London, but upon being afterwards elected an Alderman he refused to accept the office." He was, under Major-General Skippon, Lieut.-Colonel of the 1st Regiment of the London Trained Bands, the regimental ancestors of "The Buffs." The standard of this regiment is thus described : "Gules. The Distinction Argent being Piles Wavey." As soon, however, as Lieut.-Colonel Rawdon perceived that "the citizens were inclined to the Parliament" he resigned his commission, and in 1643 joined the King at Oxford. He soon raised a regiment at his own cost, of which he took command. Having been ordered to Basing House, he there played a gallant part, winning for himself the well-earned honour of knighthood. His banner, square in form, bore the device of a spotted animal with a long bushy tail and an elongated snout, and the motto "Mallem mori quam tardari" (I'll rather die than stop my course).

Lord Capel, a relative of the Marquis of Winchester, who had large estates in Hampshire, had the device of a crown and sceptre, with the motto "Perfectissima gubernatio" (Monarchy the best of Governments).

A hostile writer says, "Colon l Royden, a decayed merchant of London, who lived at Clerkenwell, and went to Basing to recruit being the Governor of that Garrison." Small wonder was it if he were "decayed," for the Parliament loved him not. On Friday, May 9th, 1643, we hear of " a ship of rich trafique belonging to Captain Royden" being taken by the Earl of Warwick, and on Thursday, September 14th, we know that his goods and those of others taken in certain ships from the East Indies were " to be sold by the candle," and that the first 400*l.* of the proceeds were to be devoted to the maintenance of Waller's army, which was then meditating an attack upon Basing House. Lieutenant-Colonel Peake, the Lieut. Governor of " Loyalty House" was "sometime picture seller at Holborn Bridge," according to Symonds, and "a seller of picture babies" said his opponents. His name is affixed to numerous prints and engravings, which are now rare. He was a man of venerable appearance in his later years, with a long white beard, like a ball of cotton, as his portrait, in the possession of Mr. Sapp, of Basingstoke, gives proof.

Under his orders was another artist, William Fairthorne, his former pupil, who had worked with him for some three or four years previous to the breaking out of the Civil War. In the garrison was also the celebrated " Wenceslaus Hollar," who belonged to an ancient Bohemian family, and was born at Prague in 1607. His parents destined him for the profession of the law, but his family being ruined and driven into exile by the capture of Prague, he was compelled to support himself by a taste and ability which he had very early exhibited, by the use of the pen and pencil. In 1636 Thomas, Earl of Arundel, an accomplished connoisseur, when passing through Frankfort, on his way to Vienna, as Ambassador to the Emperor Frederick II., met Hollar, and was so pleased with the unassuming manner and talent of the young engraver that he attached him to the suite of the embassy. On his return to England the Earl introduced Hollar to Charles I., and procured him the appointment of drawing master to the young Prince, subsequently Charles II. For a short period all went well with Hollar, for he now enjoyed the one fitful gleam of sunshine which illumined his toil-worn life. He resided in apartments at Arundel House, and was constantly employed by his noble patron in engraving those treasures of ancient art still known as the Arundelian marbles. But soon the great Civil War broke forth; Lord Arundel was compelled to seek a refuge on the Continent, whilst Hollar, with two other artists, Peake and Fairthorne, accepted commissions in the King's service.

Of Lieut.-Colonel Johnson Dr. Chalmers gives the following account (abridged) :—" Thomas Johnson, an English botanist of the 17th century, was born at Selby in Yorkshire, and bred an apothecary in London. He afterwards kept a shop on Snow Hill, where, says Wood, by his unwearied pains and good natural parts he attained to be the best herbalist in England. He was first known to the public by some botanical works, published in 1620 and 1622, which were the first local catalogues of plants published in England. He soon after acquired great credit by his new edition and emendation of 'Gerard's Herbal.' He wrote an account of the flora of the southern counties, and was one of the first to botanise in Wales and on the slopes of Snowdon. The University of Oxford, in consideration of his merit, learning, and loyalty, conferred upon him the degree of M.D. on May 9th, 1643. In the army he had the rank of lieutenant-colonel to Sir Marmaduke Rawdon, Governor of Basing House."

Major Cuffand, Cufand, Cuffel, Cuffles, &c. (his name is variously spelt) belonged to an ancient family, who dwelt in the old Manor House of Cuffand or Cuffell, which formerly stood at no great distance from the Vine, and of which the site is marked by an orchard, which is encircled by a brick-lined moat. On the tomb of Simon Cuffand, who was interred at Basingstoke in 1619, he is described as " Simon Cufand, of Cufand, in Hampshire, 500 years the possession and habitation of gentlemen of that name, his predecessors." On his mother's side " Simon Cufand was extracted from the Royall blood of the Plantagenets. He was a man of examplar virtue and patience in grievous crosses, who always lived religiously." Major Cuffand had both Tudor and Plantagenet Royal blood in his veins, and was in religion a Roman Catholic. Lieut. Cuffand also did good service. Major Langley had been "sometime a mercer in Paternoster-row." The senior captain in Colonel Rawdon's regiment had been a cordwainer or shoemaker!

Major Rosewell had been an apothecary in the Old Bailey. " Captain Rowlet (Rowland), a scrivener, next door to the sign of the ' George' at Holborn Conduit, and Lieutenant Rowlet, his brother. Lieutenant Ivory (Emery) sometime a citizen of London (a vintner). Ensign (Ancient) Coram was son of one Coram, a Papist in Winchester. William Robinson, a Papist, was surgeon to the Lord Marquis of Winchester." Captain Peregrine Tasburgh was a Hampshire gentleman, and of the deeds of Cornet Bryan we must speak hereafter.

CHAPTER XIII.—SIR WILLIAM WALLER'S PREPARATIONS—LORD CRAWFORD DEFEATED AT POOLE—NECESSITIES OF PORTSMOUTH—THE ASSOCIATED COUNTIES—LONDON TRAINED BANDS ORDERED TO BASING—OPERATIONS NEAR FARNHAM—DESPERATE ASSAULT ON BASING HOUSE—REPULSE OF SIR WILLIAM WALLER AT BASING HOUSE—CAPTURE OF LORD SALTOUN—ADVANCE OF SIR RALPH HOPTON—SIR WILLIAM BEATEN AT BASING HOUSE—RETREAT TO FARNHAM.

The testing time for Basing House was now fast approaching. On Wednesday, September 13th, 1643, an ordinance of Parliament was passed permitting Sir William Waller to impress as soldiers any persons with the exception of the servants of peers, assistants, and attendants of Parliament, and on the following Wednesday he received orders to march at once with all available forces, leaving the remainder of his army to follow as speedily as possible, information having reached Westminster that Hampshire, Portsmouth, Southampton, the Isle of Wight, and the western parts were in great danger, and might be speedily possessed by the enemy if measures of defence were any longer delayed. Sir William had previously declared to the Committee of Safety that if the sum of 4000*l.* was paid to him for the support of his army he would march forthwith. On September 13th it was decided that he should be appointed Governor of Portsmouth, that important office being vacant, and winter coming on, it being moreover necessary to guard against the attacks of Cavaliers and foreign enemies. "Certain information" had been told on September 13th that Lord Crawford, who, in the Army List of 1642-3, is said to have been in command of three troops of horse, had been attacked near Lymington by a force from Sussex. Lord Crawford was at the head of three hundred Royalist horse, but his opponents slew seven of his men and took 24 prisoners. Had they followed up the pursuit as far as Christchurch, it seems probable that Lord Crawford must have surrendered at discretion. On Monday, September 18th, there was a force of some 2000 men said to be under the command of Prince Maurice, Lord Crawford and others reported to be approaching Southampton with a design of laying siege either to that town or to Plymouth, and of afterwards marching into Sussex.

Towards the close of the month Lord Crawford offered a bribe of 200*l.* for the surrender of Poole. A letter was intercepted, to the effect that the attack would take place upon Sunday, September 24th. Preparations to repel it were at once made, and the assailants fell into a carefully planned ambuscade. Lord Crawford had 200 men killed and 50 wounded, according to one journalist, but "Mercurius Aulicus" says that only ten men were slain and four taken prisoners. Lord Crawford had a horse killed under him, and he and his party owed their escape to the fact that the gunners of the town did not sufficiently depress their guns. Three hundred arms were taken, and 140*l.* which had been paid as a bribe found its way into the pocket of Captain Sydenham, who did good service for the Parliament during the siege of Corfe Castle. Colonel Dalbier, "of name and reputation, and good experience in war," was wounded at Newbury Fight about this time, but lived to do much harm to Basing and its stout-hearted garrison. The goods of Sir Marmaduke Rawdon and other merchants having been duly "sold by the candle," as the order of September 14th directed, the first 4000*l.* of the proceeds was paid to Sir William Waller according to his request, and his army of 5000 foot, and between 30 and 40 troops of horse, was ordered to meet him at Windsor on Friday, September 22nd, 1643. A regiment of Dragoons left London for the appointed rendezvous on Tuesday, September 26. One who saw them depart writes thus: "The common saying is Dragooners are a rude multitude, but though they marched not very soberly, yet we will hope better of them." The same writer adds that

Sir William Waller had 2000 horse and 3000 foot already with him at Windsor, and was in daily expectation of reinforcements. Governor Mudford was fortifying Southampton during the closing days of September, and Waller was mustering his army upon Hounslow Heath on October 12th.

In the regiments of the Parliament the Colonel's company was 200 strong, the Lieut.-Colonel's 160, and the Sergeant-Major's (or Major's) 140, whilst seven captains had command of 700 men. Each regiment could muster 1200 men besides officers, whilst those in the service of the King were 1000 strong. Each of the Parliament's troops of horse had in it two trumpeters, three corporals, a saddler, a farrier, and sixty troopers. Sir William Waller in 1642-3 was captain of the 15th Troop of Horse, and had associated with him Lieut. Richard Newdigate, Cornet Foulke Grevill, and Quartermaster Francis Grey.

On Monday, October 16th, Dr. Harris, the Warden of Winchester College, represented to Parliament that being bound by oath to reside at Winchester, he could no longer attend the Assembly of Divines at Westminster, whereupon Mr. Cawdrey, of Great Billinghurst, in the county of Northampton, was appointed in his stead. Sir William Kingsmill, the Sheriff of Hampshire, had summoned the Knights, Baronets, Esquires, and Gentlemen of the county to meet at Winchester on Monday, October 30th, to devise measures for securing the peace of the county, and for checking depredations. Sir William Waller, who had lately been appointed Lieutenant of Farnham Castle, took action at once, obliging the Sheriff to resign his office a week before the appointed time, and issuing an order on October 29th, warning all men not to appear, saying that the whole business was a plot of the Cavaliers.

On October 28th Parliament was informed that Portsmouth was in want of a Governor, and also of men, money, powder, and match. Either Sir Robert Harley or Sir William Erle "stopped the relation of such things in the open house ' for this is no place to mention the state of Portsmouth in, for 'tis likely His Majesty may come to the knowledge of it.'" After long debate a Committee was appointed to go to Lord Wharton, " who hath a commission from the General (Essex) to be Governor of that place," and to ask him to resign. Sir Arthur Haslerigg, the constant friend and comrade of Waller, reminded the House that Sir William Waller had formerly been appointed Governor of Portsmouth. Nothing was, however, settled, for fear of offending my Lord General Essex, between whom and Sir William Waller there was most assuredly no love lost.

On Saturday, November 4th, a Decree of Association united in the cause of the Parliament the counties of Sussex, Kent, Surrey, Hampshire, the Isle of Wight, and the town and county of Southampton. Sir William Waller was appointed Major-General of the Association, and a Committee was duly formed to further the interests of the Parliament, of which Richard Love, of Basing, and Thomas Mason, Mayor of Southampton, were members.

On Friday, November 10th, we hear of the Earl of Essex complaining that the formation of this Association would be very prejudicial to the forces under his command, and saying that his troops were to the full as much in need of provisions and money as were those of Waller.

As we have already seen, Farnham was the Parliamentarian base of operations, and from thence Sir William Waller determined to advance against Basing. The four associated counties of Hants, Sussex, Surrey, and Kent paid 2638*l*. per week for the support of his army, which was usually 5000 strong. It was resolved to occupy Odiham and Alton, and from thence to proceed by gradual approaches towards Basing, taking possession of or destroying anything that might prove of service to the enemy. Some of the military authorities thought that 1200 horse and 800 dragoneers (who did duty both as infantry and cavalry) would be sufficient to "give a good account" of the House. Others advised that 800 horse, as many dragoneers, and half as many musketeers should be detailed for this service.

The Red Trained Bands of Westminster, the Green Auxiliaries of London (Colonel Conyngham was in command when this regiment afterwards surrendered in Cornwall), and the Yellow Auxiliaries of the Tower Hamlets, under Col. Willoughby, were also ordered to Basing, which had at this time, according to a letter written by Lord Winchester, a garrison of 400 men.

Through the kindness of the Rev. T. Millard, D.D., Vicar of Basingstoke, who has given me very much valuable assistance, we shall be able to follow the proceedings of the attacking force without difficulty. Dr. Millard has kindly sent me the account given by Lieutenant Elias Archer, who himself held a command in the force, in his "True Relation of the Marchings of the Red Trained Bands of Westminster, the Green Auxiliaries of London, and the Yellow Auxiliaries of the Tower Hamlets (London, 1643)." On Tuesday, Oct. 17th, 1643, the Yellow Auxiliaries marched from Wellclose, and on Wednesday, the 25th, effected a junction at Windsor with their comrades (Green) of London, and (Red) of Westminster. On Monday, October 30th, the whole force was in motion, and on their march through Windsor Forest met by appointment some of Waller's horse, his regiment of foot, and a company of blue coats. Sir William Waller had just before lost 800 men by desertion, and on October 24th, being Tuesday, 14 others, "belonging to the regiment of one Duett, a foreigner," followed the example of their comrades. But let Lieutenant Archer speak for himself. The "Snaphan musket" mentioned by him is thus described by Mr. Boutell ("Armsand Armour," p. 294.): "The snaphance, snaphaunce, or flint lock, succeeded towards the close of the 16th century, probably about the year 1580. Evidently suggested by the wheel-lock, it substituted a piece of flint for the pyrites, and instead of the wheel it had a rough plate of steel. The pull of the trigger caused the flint to strike the steel plate, and by that same act the pan was uncovered, so that the priming powder might be exposed to receive the shower of sparks that would fall upon it. It seems to have been a Dutch invention, and to have by no means a dignified origin, for this lock is said to have been brought into use by certain marauders who by the Dutch were called 'snap-haans,' hen-snappers, or poultry-stealers. These worthies could not afford wheel-locks, and the lighted matches were likely to lead to their detection, so they devised their own 'snaphance,' little suspecting, doubtless, that their ingenious invention would be universally adopted, and would maintain its supremacy during the greater part of three centuries."

Lieut. Archer says : "Oct. 30th, we marched to a Greene about a mile from Windsor, where we made Alt and Rallied our men, each Regiment drawing into a Regimental forme, where likewise our Traine of Artillery and Waggons of warre came to us, and so we marched towards Farnam through Windsor Forest, where in the Afternoone we met some of Sir William Waller's Troopes of horse, his owne regiment of foot, and one company of Blew-coats with Snap-han muskets, which guard the traine of Artillery onely; all these marched with us." The whole force halted at nightfall within a mile of Bagshot. After an hour's rest they again advanced, reaching Farnham between one and two o'clock on Tuesday morning.

On the following day, Wednesday, November 1st, all the infantry, with the exception of the Green Regiment, which was quartered at a distance of two miles from the town, was drawn up in Farnham Park. Including a reinforcement of four companies belonging to the garrison of Farnham Castle, there were present 29 companies of infantry, besides horse and dragoons. On the same day a clerk of a company of Sir William Waller's own Regiment of Foot was sentenced to death by a council of war on a charge of having endeavoured to cause a mutiny in the army. On the next day he was hanged on a tree in the park in the presence of the whole force. The Londoners were not unmindful of their kinsmen in the field, sending much provision to them, which was very thankfully received. On November 2nd Waller was said to have at Farnham and Guildford between five and six thousand men, and had surprised at Alton 100 Cavaliers under the command of Colonel Bennet. The King's forces were concentrating near Reading, intending to attack Waller's army, and on Tuesday, October 30th, the county of Hants was ordered to pay the sum of 260*l*. towards the fund for the relief of the maimed soldiers of the Parliament and of widows and orphans who favoured the same cause.

On Friday, November 3rd, the regiments marched from Farnham towards Alton, and were reviewed by their General on Bentley Green. The "field state" showed that there were present 16 troops of horse, eight companies of Dragoons, 36 companies of Foot, and a train of Artillery, consisting of ten heavy guns, and "six cases of small drakes." After an hour's halt the march towards Alton was resumed, and that night Elias Archer's regiment was quartered at the little villages of East and West Worldham, two miles distant from Alton. Sir Ralph Hopton's forces retired from Winchester towards Andover and Salisbury at the approach of Waller's army. The pieces of ordnance mentioned above may have been either demi-culverins throwing a 9lb. shot, with a 9lb. charge of powder; culverins, throwing an 18lb. shot, with an 18lb. charge of powder; or demi-cannons, throwing a 30lb. shot, with a 28lb. charge of powder, but were most probably demi-culverins. We know, however, that Sir W. Waller had with him at least one demi-cannon. The small "drakes" were light field-pieces, sometimes called "saker drakes," which threw a 5lb. shot, with a 5lb. charge of powder. Two "drakes" were often attached to a regiment.

On November 4th Sir William Waller was said to have with him 46 troops of horse, numbering in all 2000, whilst 13 troops from Kent were on the march to join him. He had four regiments of foot raised in Kent, Surrey, and Sussex, and further reinforcements from the latter county were expected, as was also Colonel Wems with some leather guns (of which more hereafter) and a train of artillery. Lord Crawford with a large body of horse was trying to assist the garrison of Basing House. Several skirmishes had taken place, with but slight loss on either side. In one of these skirmishes Waller surprised and made prisoners two troops of Cavaliers bound for Oxford. He also took 512 head of cattle coming south for sale, "the property of a great man in Oxford," and sent a party of horse towards Andover to keep in check Lord Crawford, who was advancing from Salisbury. Saturday, the 4th of November, was a day of rain and snow, which compelled Waller's troops, who had mustered in force about two miles from Alton on the road to Winchester, to return to their quarters.

The 5th of November witnessed a great muster in the neighbourhood of Alton, and the army took the road to Winchester, but towards evening, when about nine miles distant from that city, turned to the right, halting for the night at the village of Chilton Candover, between Alresford and Basingstoke. The night was bitterly cold, and the Londoners, unused to campaigning, failed to appreciate their camping-ground, although at Windsor and elsewhere they had been usually quartered in barns and outhouses.

The Earl of Crawford's army from Salisbury was in the neighbourhood of Andover, and advancing to the relief of Basing, so that the Yellow Auxiliaries, being on the extreme left of Waller's army, were kept constantly on the alert. On Monday (November 6th) the reveille sounded long before the dawn, and about an hour before daybreak the whole force was in motion. The fog was dense, the roads were heavy, and marching difficult, so that it was past noon before the Marquis saw "Waller with the expected army (consisting of 7000 horse and foot) before the house." "Mercurius Civicus" describes the garrison as consisting of "the Woodheads, who are for the most part certaine malignants of the City of London, and parts adjacent." "The Scottish Dove" says "There are in it divers Ladies and gentlemen, and many citizens, and it's conceived much wealth." "The True Informer" states "They say that the souldiers and other persons within it, being about 500, are very resolute and desperate, by reason that many of them, being Papists of great estates in those parts, have secured the greater part of their treasures and riches in that house."

"The souldier's report concerning Sir William Waller's fight against Basing House on Sunday last, November 12th," says that the garrison consisted of some 500 men, "all in a manner Papists," and that considerable treasure had been brought thither for safety, Basing being the only Cavalier stronghold in the neighbourhood.

The writer adds that the defences of the house were sufficiently strong to resist cannon shot, and that the house was as large and spacious as the Tower of London. The house was "built upright, so that no man can command the roof," upon which certain field-pieces were mounted. These guns were able to harass the besiegers, without danger to the gunners who served them. The windows were protected by the out-works, and earthworks had been thrown up, upon which the besiegers' guns failed to make any impression. The garrison was well supplied with provisions and ammunition, and had mounted several guns upon and near the house.

"Mercurius Aulicus" of Wednesday, November 15th, says:—"But that which was the chief news of the day was an express relation of the siege of Basing Castle, given by those who were eye-witnesses, and behaved themselves too gallantly in the service to be guilty of a lie, which was impartially thus. Sir William Waller, having hovered some eight or ten days

THE FIRST ASSAULT.

about Farnham and Alton, came before Basing House on Monday, November 6th, and though his drums, trumpets, and guns proclaimed his approach, yet the Lord Marquesse and the rest could not get sight of him through the greatness of the mist, till about one of the clock, when the sun, breaking and dispersing the mist, discovered Waller's whole body to the garrison." A survey was made from "the stately gate house of the Castle," and the Marquis estimated the number of his foes at about seven thousand horse and foot. Warm work was but too evidently near at hand.

One chronicler says that Sir William Waller sent out a party into the park under the pretence of hunting deer, who placed some of their number in ambush, and took prisoners about forty of the garrison, who sallied out upon them. "Mercurius Aulicus," however, says that a few rebel horse rode out in front, and that a slight skirmish took place between them, and some cavalry from the house, with no loss on either side. A forlorn hope of about 500 musketeers was then selected from Sir William Waller's army, Captain William Archer being in command of the detachment of the Tower Hamlet Yellows, and was sent to storm the house. "Mercurius Aulicus" says that the strength of this forlorn hope was only 100 men. They boldly advanced "into a lane between two hedges towards the lower walls, giving fire amain," and for a while gained ground. They fought until they had expended all their ammunition, and were then relieved by a regiment of Dragoons, who continued the attack until "the edge of the evening."

Meanwhile "the army and train" (i.e., the artillery) marched towards Basingstoke, and, crossing the river there, returned "and came upon a hill over against the house, upon the side of which hill our ordnance were planted." "Mercurius" says that the enemy took post "on the N.W. side of the house," and, says Woodward, "near where now stands the turnpike-gate." About four o'clock in the afternoon some ten or twelve shots were fired against the house, whereupon a parley was demanded. Lieut. Archer says that the garrison asked for a conference, but "Mercurius Aulicus" says that Waller sent a trumpeter to demand a parley and to tell the Marquis "that Sir William Waller, being there in person, had sent him to demand the castle for the use of the King and Parliament, and that he offered fair quarter to all within the castle."

Whilst negotiations were in progress two drakes or field pieces were suddenly fired from the besiegers' batteries. Suspicions of treachery were excited, and the trumpeter was at once arrested until a satisfactory explanation was given. It appears that some "scattering powder" became ignited by accident and fired the guns. Mr. Boutell says ("Arms and Armour," p. 222) "In order to fire the cannon the touch-hole was filled with fine powder that would ignite and burn with great rapidity, and to this was joined a train of slowly-burning powder, which was laid along the length of the cannon; this train was fired at the end most distant from the touch-hole, and while the fire was passing leisurely along, the gunners had time to retire to a safe distance. The larger the cannon the longer would be the train, and the gunners would have a proportionately longer time for their movement out of danger."

Pending explanation, Lord Winchester sent out a drummer with this answer. "That he understood very well the words 'King and Parliament,' that as they were now taken, 'the King' was one thing and 'the King and Parliament' another. That Basing was his own house, which the law told him he might keep against any man. That it was now more particularly commanded by His Majesty, who had put a garrison into it, beyond which command he knew no obligation."

Two hours afterwards the drummer returned with an apology from Sir William, "excusing the rudeness of his disorderly guns during the parley," and chivalrously offering free passage to the Marchioness, with her children, and also to all women and children within the house. His guns still fired, and the Marchioness returned answer "that she thanked God that she was not in that condition to accept of fair quarter at Sir William Waller's hands, being resolved to run the same fortune as her Lord, knowing that there was a just and all-seeing Judge above, who she hoped would have an especial hand in this business, from whom Sir William Waller could pretend no commission. Whatever befel, she was not unprepared to bear it, and so thanked Sir William for his offer of fair quarter."

After the receipt of this answer, the besiegers' guns ceased their fire for an hour, and their trumpeter was sent out of the house "by a strange way which he knew not," probably in the direction of the river. "They said that there was onely one small leap over part of a little brooke," instead of which the hapless "music," as trumpeters were then styled, found himself stuck fast in a deep morass. He was obliged to leave his horse," a very stout one, and of about 20*l*. valew," and with difficulty returned to head-quarters, considerably bemired.

Orders were given for an attack in force the next morning, and 36 cannon shot were discharged against the house about ten o'clock that night, or, as some say, between midnight and four o'clock in the morning. Then came a lull until day-break, the guns being protected by a hastily constructed breastwork. Says Lieut. Elias Archer, "Some wounded, not four slain outright."

At daybreak on Tuesday, Nov. 7th, a very hot fire was poured into the devoted garrison from Sir William Waller's batteries, which were on the north-west side of Basing House, and which directed their efforts against the front of the Gate House. There were in position five small guns and a demi-cannon. This latter threw a 30lb. shot, with a charge of 28lbs. of powder. The garrison could bring only one gun to bear upon those of the assailants, but it did good service, and slew a large number of the enemy. No one was as yet hurt in the house, and the damage done to the stately structure itself was not considerable. As soon as it was light the Cavaliers had fired all the houses which could possibly provide cover for the assailants, and about nine a.m. Waller again despatched "a forlorne hope" against the house, having previously sent a strong party of horse towards Andover to keep the Earl of Crawford's cavalry from Salisbury from raising the siege. Here is an account from one of the "forlorne hope":—"I sent you a letter last Tuesday morning, which no sooner I had done but our forces were drawn into a body and 500 men commanded (for) the forlorne hopes. It fell to my captaine's lot, Capt. Warrene, to be commander. We fought from ten till six, but two of our company wounded. Never in the world was there such desperate service on the very mouths of the cannon with so little loss."

On the other hand, "Mercurius Aulicus" states, on the authority of some of the garrison, that the forlorn hope was sent down the hill to take the Grange and the New House. "the Castle being to defend both." The attacking force came on boldly through a narrow lane, but a heavy fire was opened upon them from a half-moon, and from "divers holes made in the walls, so that they were obliged to retreat with heavy loss. Fresh attacks continued to be made in the same quarter, and three guns were brought to bear on the north side of the New House, whilst other troops were sent to storm the Grange, the attack and defence of which have many points of resemblance to the fierce struggle in and around the chateau of Hougomont at Waterloo.

Captain Clinson, Sir William Waller's Captain-Lieutenant, a man of great courage and resolution, "took the Grange with very little loss," whence having steady aim at the holes, and sighting from easy places, they much annoyed the garrison." All along the north side of the fortifications and outworks, some of which were captured, the fight raged fiercely.

The attacking force was exposed within pistol shot to the fire of the enemy, and could find scarcely any cover except the church, most of the surrounding buildings having been burnt by the garrison at daybreak. The stormers were at length obliged to take shelter in such buildings or ruins as remained standing, from which they continued to pour in a well-sustained fire of musketry. Sir William Waller's guns "battering the Castle and the New House" meanwhile. So says "Mercurius." On the other hand, "The Soldier's Report" speaks as follows: "Our Army had no shelter, not so much as any village hovill, nay, not very many trees, save only by Basing Park side some few young groves, which could not shelter them to any advantage; they were constrained to fight in a champien place, which was a great disadvantage to Sir William's army, yet did nothing at all discourage their resolutions." In spite of all disadvantages, however, the forlorn hope gained a partial success, and, as we have seen, "gained all their outhouses, wherein was much provision of bread, beere, bacon, pork, milk, creame, pe ise, wheat, oats, hay, and such like, besides pigs and poultery, and diverse sorts of household goods, as brasse, pewter, feather beds, and the like."

Thus did the Grange, "severed by a wall and common road," fall into the foeman's hands. A good encouragement, truly! Some of the assail ants sat down to eat and drink, whilst others continued fighting, "and came unto the very gates of the house, beat down the turret and divers chimnies." Was this turret part of "the loftie gate-house, with foure turrets, looking northwards?" Dire indeed was the destruction of chimney pots by the besiegers. This was due to their anxiety to dismount "certaine drakes which are upon the roofe of the said house, wherewith they are able to play upon our army, though we discern them not." Fighting and feasting went on simultaneously, revellers and warriors alike being constantly relieved by fresh parties, each of which had some men killed or wounded. Sir William Waller failed to secure his prize "by reason of the absence of his Granadoes, petards, and other engines to blow in the gates;" but the garrison were so hard pressed that they again sounded a parley, and offered to surrender if they might depart, bag and baggage. These terms were refused, and to it they went again.

It would never do to allow the Roundheads to feast on Cavalier stores at the very gates, and accordingly, hard as was the necessity, the Marquis decided to destroy the provisions which had been intended to feed the garrison during many a long month. Lieutenant-Colonels Peake and Johnson determined upon a desperate sortie. Meanwhile the strife continued with unabated fury all along the line of the defences on the north side. At least one sergeant (whose name has not been left on record, but who was nevertheless a brave man) and a few men were selected for this dangerous duty. The gallant old Governor, Colonel Marmaduke Rawdon, aged as he was, had still a heart of fire, and sallied forth likewise with the little band of heroes. Deadly, indeed, was the fire poured upon them, and desperate were the hand-to-hand combats that took place. But right gallantly was the service performed. They "fired the onthouses and barns adjoining to them, which were full of wheat and other grain," old Colonel Rawdon cheering on his musketeers and saying that "he knew that Waller would not stay it out." Lieut.-Colonel Johnson, at the head of twenty-five men, penetrated as far as "the very Grange yard." Here he was singled out as an antagonist by Captain Clinson, and a hand-to-hand struggle followed. Colonel Johnson's life was only saved "by two or three stout fellows of the garrison." Overpowered by numbers, Capt. Clinson was slain, his commission being afterwards found in his pocket. Lieutenant Archer says that the manner of his death was as follows:—"Sir William Waller's Captain-Lieutenant, a man of great courage and resolution," lost his way, and was killed, with many men, in a lane by two drakes, or field-pieces, loaded with case shot. The lower road to Basingstoke, in all accounts of the siege, is called "the lane," and, as may easily be seen, it is commanded by a tower pierced for guns of small calibre, such as were then styled drakes, minions, &c. It is possible, therefore, that the present cross-road was the scene of this slaughter. Lieutenant Archer states that none of the assailants were killed during the fight at the Grange, although some were wounded. "Mercurius" says, however, that they lost many killed and wounded, some of them being burnt to death in the barn. The party in the house found that retreat was to the full as hazardous as their sallying forth had been. "The sergeant which led them was killed, and most of his men, in the yard between the house and the barn." How is it possible to reconcile such a statement as this with the declaration of the Marquis that only one of the defenders was killed and another wounded, or with the statement of "Mercurius" that the loss of the garrison was only two slain, one of whom was "their youngest gunner and three wounded," or, the assertion of the same journal that only one of the garrison was wounded, and not one slain? At any rate the approach of night and the combined influence of "fire, sword, and water" compelled Sir William Waller's men to relinquish their hold upon the fiercely contested, and now completely destroyed Grange, leaving behind them some arms, and many killed and wounded. The assailants once more bivouacked in the fields, "wherein our lodging and our service did not well agree, the one being so hot, and the other so cold." Their loss was estimated at Oxford to have been at least 150 killed and as many wounded.

On the following day, Wednesday, November 8th, Sir William Waller, who is said to have meanwhile kept a detachment at Winchester, drew off his forces, and retired to the town of Basingstoke, which was full of wounded men, one doctor alone having no less than eighty under treatment. The Marquis of Winchester sent into Basingstoke a cartload of Waller's wounded, and Cavaliers at Oxford asserted that

Sir William detained both the carter and his team. But this statement was but too probably a partisan slander, as such a meanness would have been totally at variance with the character of Waller, who, by the way, had his best gun broken during the attack. There was urgent need for wariness on the part of Sir William, who, repulsed at Basing, had now to prevent, if possible, the advance of Sir Ralph Hopton.

On Saturday, November 11th, news had reached London that Hopton had concentrated his forces from Salisbury, Andover, Malmesbury, and elsewhere at Winchester, and that Sir William Waller, in no wise loth to give him battle, had drawn off from Basing House, and had quartered his men at Basingstoke, the Vine, and intermediate places. The remainder of the week was devoted to rest and refreshment, but the Roundhead horse were by no means idle, scouring the country far and wide, and making raids into the adjacent counties. The reasons assigned for Sir Ralph Hopton's delay in succouring Basing were that Sir William Waller was both able and anxious to fight; that the noblemen and gentry under the command of Hopton were unwilling to risk another battle similar to that fought at Newbury only a few weeks before (Sept. 20th, 1643); that they wished to await the arrival of some Scottish reinforcements, and that the army was in want of arms and gunpowder.

On Thursday, Nov. 9th, there assembled at the house of Master Legay, an active adherent of the Parliament at Southampton, some two hundred of the townsmen, who had taken the Solemn League and Covenant, to keep a solemn fast, and to pray for the success of Sir William Waller. On the same day there was a motion made in the House of Commons that " all records and writings of antiquity in Basing and other places might not be as common plunder!"

On the day of the retreat from Basing, the Roundhead troopers secured a rich prize. Lord Saltoun, or as one writer styles him, Lord Sultan, in company with a certain Friar King, his confessor, and several companions, whose number is variously given as three, twelve, and thirty, had landed on the coast of Sussex, after having been successfully employed in France as a collector of monies in aid of the Royal cause. He had with him a sum of money variously estimated at 300*l.*, 500*l.*, 2000*l.*, 3500*l.*, 4000*l.*, 5000*l.*, and 6000*l.*, with which he intended to raise two troops of horse in the western counties. He was also the bearer of important despatches from the French Court. Sir William Waller had a week's notice of his intended arrival, and sent out Captain Gardiner, who was commonly styled the Mayor of Evesham, with his own troop and some other horse, who intercepted him and his party at Newbury, on their way to Oxford. Captain Gardiner brought his prisoners to Basingstoke, in which town the present "Bell Inn" was the usual place of confinement. From Basingstoke they were afterwards transferred to Farnham Castle, and were at length sent up to London to be dealt with according to the good pleasure of the Parliament. After Waller had retired, the Marquis wrote an account of the fight to Secretary Nicholas, who writes thus to Prince Rupert:—

"Monday last Waller sat down before Basing House, and Wednesday last he drew off all his ordnance and forces to Basingstoke, a mile distant, where he now lies with all his forces, and threatens to return thither to assault the place again, and hath sent for scaling ladders to Windsor for that purpose. The Marquis of Winchester writes cheerfully, saith he hath 400 men and three weeks victualling, and that he hath killed divers of the rebels, and lost only one man and one hurt. Sir F. Berkeley was, on Wednesday last, at Huntington, twenty miles on this side of Exeter, with four regiments of foot, and will, we hope, be at Winchester on Monday next." The Earl of Newport was at this time Master-General of the Ordnance. He was appointed on September 2nd, 1634, and held office until the Restoration, when he was suspended. He at once despatched the scaling ladders asked for by Waller, but fortunately for Basing House they came to hand too late for the great assault, which took place on Sunday, November 12th, 1643. Concentrating his forces from the various positions which they occupied between Basingstoke and the Vine, and being now furnished "with new supply and fireworks from London," Sir William Waller, at the head of from 6000 to 8000 infantry, together with five regiments of dragoons and ten guns, marched towards Basing on that November Sunday morning. He had an ample supply of petards, grenades, as shells were then styled, and ammunition, nor had ladders, which Lieut. Archer says were not scaling ladders, been forgotten. The cavalry reached Basing about an hour before noon, and halting within musket shot of the house, began to taunt the garrison, saying, "Where's your Hopton? Prince Rupert hath but three men," &c. This martial raillery continued until a gun, which had in the meantime been placed in position, opened fire, not without reply from one of the field-pieces mounted upon the roof of the house. The artillery duel was kept up with spirit until the neighbouring clocks struck twelve, when the assailants, who had previously formed up in three divisions well supplied with petards and ladders, rushed forward for a simultaneous attack. Lieut.-Colonel Johnson had foreseen this manœuvre, and, before the storming party on the south-west side of the house could enter the defences opposed to them, he led out thirty musketeers into a lane under the half moon. This little force suddenly appeared, fired a volley, and retreated. The enemy pursued into a winding lane, until they came within range of the half moon, the fire from which proved fatal to not a few. Thrice was Lieut.-Colonel Johnson successful in thus luring the enemy to their own destruction.

Sir William Waller sent a party of 500 men from the middle of the park, to storm "the Castle," but a small gun upon the ramparts loaded with case shot killed about a dozen of them, and wounded many others, whereupon the survivors refused to advance again. The stormers came sufficiently close to permit the women to take part in the fight by hurling bricks, tiles, and stones from the roofs of the various buildings. The artillery had by this time made several breaches in the defences, which seemed practicable, at any rate, so says the chronicler, but practicable breaches are not usually made in so short a time with guns of small calibre. On the north and north-east the enemy having the protection of a small wood, felt sure of gaining the New House with ease, and concentrated here most of their guns and about 2000 men. The Westminster Trained Bands and the St. Katherine's Regiment, better known as the Auxiliaries of the Tower Hamlets, were posted at this point. For two full hours did Waller's guns awake the echoes with their deep toned voices, which must have sounded but grimly on that Sunday afternoon, until about two o'clock, when the stormers were seen issuing from the wood, bringing with them drakes or field-pieces, "and two load of ladders." They advanced until they came within a few yards of the Castle, the circular site of which is still hugely conspicuous, crowded into the ditch, forced the garrison to beat a hasty retreat from a half-moon, and planted an ensign in the ditch. Under the eye of Sir William Waller himself, and guided by two deserters from the garrison, who had undertaken to point out the weakest points of the defences, they fixed a petard on the jamb of the gate, which, however, fortunately for the garrison, was so strongly barricaded that the explosion did little or no harm. And now the courage of some began to fail. We are told "that the St. Katherine's Regiment was also faulty at Basing, especially the officers of those regiments whom Sir William could not get to some up so far as the front of his horse, where he stood in person." They absolutely refused to relieve their comrades, who gallantly maintained the fight until ammunition failed them, and fixed a petard in the wrong place. " upon a gate so strongly rampired within that it could not be stirred. Some of the officers and soldiers were very valiant." Those belonging to Sir William Waller's own regiment received especial commendations for valour, advancing as they did close to the very gates, and taking aim at the soldiers of the garrison. All those within the house are said to have done their duty manfully. Colonel Rawdon and his officers armed with muskets fought side by side with their men, and the Marchioness of Winchester, and all the ladies who had found shelter within the walls, cast bullets with the lead hastily stripped from roofs and turrets. At some period or other of the operations at Basing during the Civil War, the Chapel of the Holy Ghost at Basingstoke was also despoiled of its lead, which was found useful to kill Cavaliers. The lead from Basing Church also disappeared, each party in this case laying the blame on the other. In no wise disheartened by the failure of their petard, the stormers in the ditch shouted loudly. " All is our own." But they reckoned without their host. " An ingenious and vigilant German in the Castle" was on the alert. Was his name " Humphrey Vanderblin, engineer?" We know that " the foreign engineer" did much to strengthen the defences of Loyalty House, and in the list of prisoners taken by Cromwell at Basing we find the name of " Humphrey Vanderblin, engineer." Whatever his name may have been, " the ingenious and vigilant

German" saved Basing House that day. Whilst the petard was being fixed to the gate by the storming party, the wily Teuton was busily knocking a hole in the north end of the buildings, with a view of opening fire upon the right flank of the assailants. His intention was perceived, and he was greeted with a few volleys of musketry. In no wise daunted, he, with two or three comrades, completed the opening, and returned the leaden compliments with interest killing three or four of the opponents. Encouraged by this success, and by the failure of the enemy's petard, the garrison, by a determined attack, retook the half-moon, "whereupon the rebels lose heart, and many men as well." Their ammunition was beginning to fail, and they looked in vain for support from their faint-hearted comrades. Whilst the dragoons and many of the other soldiers fought with great courage, the Westminster Regiment is said to have been less eager for the fray than were certain others. Some thought that "Captain White, the keeper of my Lord Petre's house" in Aldersgate-street, then used as a Cavalier prison, "would not go on for fear of displeasing his prisoners," his office being worth 1500l. per annum to him, whilst others were of opinion that the soldiers of Westminster were unwilling to proceed to extremities, hoping as they did for the speedy return of the King to his Palace at Whitehall.

The *Complete Intelligencer*, of November 21st, 1643, says that "the house was extremely well fortified, and inaccessible for storming. The Trained Bands offered their lives to Sir William Waller in any service against men, but were loth to venture further against walls. We must excuse them, they being young and raw soldiers, and not yet frosted abroad."

Small wonder was it, therefore, that unsupported, without ammunition, with an active and inspirited foe pressing them hard both in front and on their flank, and perceiving the repulse of the other columns, that Sir William Waller's men at length fell back in considerable disorder, and retreated through the little wood in all haste. They left behind them their two field pieces, their ladders, and the colour which they had planted in the ditch. This latter trophy of victory "the soldiers wished to take, but were held back for fear of ambuscade." During this day's fighting seventy or eighty of the Westminster men were accidentally shot by their comrades. The front rank fired too soon, and whilst in the act of retiring had to face a volley from their friends in the rear, and the garrison, firing one or two field pieces at the same moment, increased the slaughter. Lieutenant Archer speaks of the Westminster Trained Bands as "being designed to set upon the south-west part of the house through the park, being upon a plain level ground before the wall without any defence or shelter."

Sir William Waller himself shunned no danger, and proved himself on that day, as indeed he had ofttimes before, a valiant soldier. Fighting continued until it was too dark to distinguish the loopholes and embrasures. About three o'clock in the afternoon of that short November day the wind began to rise, and heavy rain fell.

Darkness and stress of weather combined obliged Sir William to sound a retreat, and drawing off his forces to the distance of half-a-mile he himself lay all night in the midst of his men upon some straw in the open meadow, intending to renew the attack upon the morrow. About ten o'clock at night "the London youths of the Auxiliary Regiment" were sent towards the house to bring off the field pieces, &c., which had been perforce abandoned that afternoon. They succeeded in removing the guns and some petards without loss to themselves, according to their own account, but "Mercurius Aulicus" says this bold enterprise cost about twenty of them their lives. For this achievement the Regiment was publicly commended and rewarded by Sir William Waller. The "Green Regiment," of which Colonel Rawdon had formerly been the lieutenant-colonel, suffered most of all the regiments engaged, and a lieutenant in Waller's army writes thus:—" Basing House is absolutely the strongest place in England, and requires a summer's siege. By report of some prisoners, we have taken a great number of their men, and divers gentlewomen and ladies of great quality. The Green Regiment did bravely at Basing. Captain Web, therefore, to be Sergeant-Major (i.e., Major); his Lieutenant Master Everet to be made a Captain upon the next opportunity."

It rained all that sad Sunday night, the hours of which, though comparatively free from war's alarms, were mournfully employed in the burial of the dead, with the exception of about thirty, whose bodies were lying close to the defences of the house. The garrison made prize of "more than 120 muskets with rests, two great brass petards, divers hand granadoes, three barrels of powder, much match, several heaps of bullet which lay upon the ground, halberts, half pikes, and scaling ladders."

One of the deserters who gave information to Waller had formerly served under that General. He had been taken prisoner at the battle of Roundway Down, and had taken service in the army of the King, only to desert at the first opportunity, but now found a grave at Basing. One wounded man who lay very close to the fortifications, with his leg shattered by a cannon shot, was asked "What the King had done to him that he should take up arms against him?" His only reply was to take his knife and to cut his own throat. During the first day's fighting "the youngest gunner" of the garrison was killed, and Sir William Waller having reasons to suspect the fidelity of one of his own gunners, placed him under arrest, and afterwards hanged him.

On the morning of November 13th "much rain" was but too evidently the order of the day, and it was decided by a Council of War to retire to Basingstoke and Farnham in order "to refresh the army to receive the western Woodheads." This complimentary title referred to Sir Ralph Hopton and his relieving force, which, according to the reports of spies sent out in search of information through by-ways and our pleasant Hampshire woodlands, was said to be at least 5000 strong. When Waller's men reached Basingstoke they found scaling ladders, grenades, and ammunition from London awaiting them. Sir William's loss was variously estimated, but Lieutenant Archer considered that it amounted to some 250 to 300 in the three days' fighting, whilst "Mercurius Aulicus" says that he lost 1000 in killed and wounded. One account says that how many of the Cavaliers "are hurt we cannot tell, nor what detriment they received, save only one of their cows, which being frighted with the noise of the guns, leaped over the wall, by which it seems to be of great thickness." It was suggested that mining would prove more successful than a direct attack, and such was the expectation of success in London that wagers were laid upon the Exchange that Sir William Waller was actually in possession of Basing House. Lieut.-Colonel Peake was falsely reported to have been killed, as indeed he was on several other occasions, together with certain other officers and "malignant citizens."

The Marquis of Winchester says that the result of the nine days' blockade and three days' fighting was the retreat of Waller, "having dishonoured and bruised his army, whereof abundance were lost, without the death of more than two in the garrison, and some little injury to the house by battery."

Monday, November 13th, being a very tempestuous day, the besiegers, as we have seen, retired to Basingstoke, and spent the day in refreshing themselves and drying their clothes. The next day there was an alarm that Sir Ralph Hopton was advancing to the relief of Lord Winchester, and a detachment of Cavaliers drove in the Roundhead picquets at Basingstoke, whereupon Waller's army quartered in the fields two miles from Basing. On Wednesday, the 15th, the whole besieging force retreated to Farnham, which was reached at two p.m., the Marquis being by no means sorry to see them depart, though without any ceremonious leave-taking. "Mercurius" says that Sir William Waller had 1000 men killed and wounded at Basing, and that he speedily lost 1200 others by desertion. So ended the first attack in force upon Basing House. Upon his arrival at Farnham, Waller established his head quarters there, and at once asked for reinforcements, which were readily granted by the Parliament. He also "began to fortifie the towne with breast workes and the like."

CHAPTER XIV.—DEFENCE OF THE ISLE OF WIGHT—THE MARQUIS OF WINCHESTER ACCUSED OF HIGH TREASON—AFFAIRS AT PORTSMOUTH—SIR WILLIAM WALLER AT FARNHAM—ADVANCE OF LORD HOPTON—OCCUPATION OF WINCHESTER—SKIRMISH AND TROUBLES AT ODIHAM—EXPEDITION TO MIDHURST—FIGHTING AT FARNHAM—HOW SIR WILLIAM WALLER WAS REINFORCED.

Leaving Sir William Waller for awhile at Farnham, we must briefly chronicle the course of events in other parts of the county. The Generals of the Parliament had not been on the most friendly terms.

In August, 1643, the Earl of Manchester having been appointed Sergeant-Major-General or Commander-in-Chief in the Eastern Counties, the Earl of Essex, not without some grumbling, conceded to Sir William Waller the chief command of a force to be raised in London. At length, on September 28th, Essex assured the Parliament "that he will begin upon a new score, and give Waller the best encouragement he can."

On October 7th thirty pieces of ordnance with their due proportion of shot were ordered by the House of Commons to be sent to the Isle of Wight, and on Monday, October 16th, in consequence of a petition numerously signed by the inhabitants, an order was given that the Earl of Warwick should send some ships of strength speedily for the defence of the island. Mr. Lisle, one of the Members for Winchester, was directed to bring in an ordinance for the raising of soldiers to be stationed in the Isle of Wight and at Hurst Castle. Colonel Carne, the Lieutenant-Governor of the island, was called in, and gave an account of several things which he considered needful to be done, whereupon he received the thanks of the House for his care and fidelity, and was ordered to repair to his command without delay.

On Wednesday, October 18th, an intercepted warrant for the raising of money which had been issued by the Marquis of Winchester was read in the House, whereupon it was ordered "That the Marquis of Winchester's estate be forthwith sequestred. That the Marquis of Winchester be accused of high treason, and Mr. Browne is to bring in a charge against him."

On the following day Mr. Lisle was deputed to request the Earl of Essex to grant Sir Gregory Norton a commission to raise 100 men for the defence of the Isle of Wight, and on Tuesday, Oct. 24th, Sir William Waller was to be officially informed of the arrival of some of the King's troops at Horsham in Sussex.

On Thursday, Nov. 2nd, Mr. Walter Erle, Mr. Lisle, and Mr. Long received directions to go forthwith to the Earl of Essex, and to ask him on behalf of the House of Commons to consider in what dangerous condition Sir William Waller is in at this present, to acquaint His Excellency that the enemy has drawn his main force towards Sir William, and to request all the assistance which Essex may be able to give. Two days later my Lord General Essex reports that most of the enemy having withdrawn in the direction of Northamptonshire, Waller is in no immediate danger, and that as to Portsmouth "he would have the House settle a constant pay for that garrison, and he would keep it in his own hands and put in a sufficient deputy." He wishes that the present Committee may continue to be responsible for the defence of Portsmouth. This was agreed to, with the addition of three members, viz., Sir Thomas Jervoise, Mr. Button, and Mr. Lisle. On Friday, Nov. 3rd, the Earl of Warwick, the Admiral of the Parliament, was ordered not to allow any strangers or aliens, with the exception of merchants, to land in England, and three days afterwards 1000*l*. was directed to be paid for the supply of the garrison of Portsmouth.

On Tuesday an order was passed "for sequestring the rectory of the parish church of Alverstoke, in the county of Southampton, whereof Mr. Roolfe is now rector, into the hands of Mr. Anthony Prouse, Master of Arts, a godly, learned, and orthodox divine, who is appointed to officiate said cure, and to preach diligently to the parishioners, and to receive the rents and profits belonging unto it, paying all duties due unto His Majesty." The various high-constables received orders not to send in any more money or provisions to the quarters occupied by Sir W. Waller's army for the present, and it was settled that 42 ships, viz., 18 of the King's ships and pinnaces and 24 merchants' ships and pinnaces, "be forthwith sent for as a winter guard for the safety and security of the English, Irish, and Scottish coasts."

On Friday, November 10th, Lord Inchiquin was ordered to be charged with high treason for having sent troops from Ireland to fight against the Parliament, and on Wednesday, November 22nd, men-of-war from Bristol and Wexford were reported as being at Dublin in readiness to bring over a larger force. We shall meet this "Irish Brigade" again on Cheriton Down.

On Saturday, November 11th, Sir J. Lee and Mr. Lisle are to be repaid from the funds destined for the defence of the Isle of Wight all expenses incurred by them in sending soldiers thither. On Monday, November 13th, the Committee of Safety was exhorted to send speedily the 1400 foot and the horse commanded by Sir A. Haselrig to Sir William Waller, "and to consider of a settled way of payment" for his men. On Wednesday, November 15th, Sir A. Haselrig and Mr. Trenchard were bidden to write a letter to Sir W. Waller to explain why the House of Commons has sent 500 of his men to the siege of Plymouth, and to ask if he can possibly spare 500 others, who are still to be under his command, for the same destination.

After his repulse at Basing House Sir William Waller reached Farnham at two o'clock in the afternoon of Wednesday, November 15th, and at once made proclamation by drum-beat that all soldiers under his command should forthwith muster in the park. The names of all deserters and of men absent without leave were then duly recorded, and several of the culprits, being soon afterwards arrested in Westminster and Clerkenwell, were ordered to be sent down to Farnham, there to be tried by a council of war, or, as we should now say, by a court-martial. Lieutenant Archer says, "In the time that we lay there (Farnham) we had divers alarms and other accidents."

Sir William Morley, M.P., who had fought for the King at Chichester during the previous year, about this time paid a fine of 1000l. to the garrison of Portsmouth, and the sequestration of his estate ceased on September 9th, 1643. Lord Hopton had meanwhile been doing his utmost to assist the Hampshire Cavaliers. Towards the end of the year 1643 the King was in possession of Bristol and the whole West of England. The Parliament had no stronghold in Wiltshire, and possessed only one or two towns in Hampshire, the people of the county being strongly opposed to them. We learn from Clarendon (Book VIII.) that both armies having retired into winter quarters, great efforts were made in London to despatch Sir William to the west, with a powerful force. Prince Maurice was besieging Plymouth, which was expected to surrender ere long. The King therefore determined to oppose Waller's march, so that he might be unable to raise the siege of Plymouth. Sir William, afterwards Lord, Ogle, with the assistance of Sir Richard Tichborne and eight other Hampshire Cavaliers, secured Winchester Castle for the King, and materially strengthened its defences, with the idea of making it a rendezvous for an army then collecting in the west. Sir William Waller, who was Major-General of the four associated counties of Kent, Surrey, Hants, and Sussex, was not without well-wishers in Winchester, to the Castle of which indeed he laid claim, and they did not fail to exert themselves on his behalf. In his "Vindication of the Character and Conduct of Sir William Waller, Knight," he says (p. 202), with reference to his leaving England for Holland in 1647, "As for that suggestion that I should make over or transport with me great sums of money, it is as untrue as that fiction of the butter barrels was ridiculous. I acknowledge the sending of some goods of mine into the Low Countries to Rotterdam about two or three months, if I remember not, before I was inforced to take that course with myself: all was nothing but household stuff; the best part whereof I had, by the care of a good friend, saved out of Winchester Castle but a few hours before the King's party seized upon it, and the rest I bought at London; but there was neither penny of money nor ounce of plate that travailed with it. But whatever there was, it was viewed and allowed at the Custom House before the ship went off with it, which I hope may serve to give satisfaction to all reasonable people that I meant plainly and honestly, and may shew that there was nothing acted to put any cheat upon the state." So that the fittings of Winchester Castle must be sought for in the homes of the portly burghers of Rotterdam and the Hague. Sir William Waller speedily frustrated Lord Ogle's plans by his vigilance and activity. But for a while things seemed as favourable as the most ardent Royalists could desire. There is evidence that the Cavaliers occupied Winchester during the month of October, 1643, for, in the Corporation records, which I have been permitted to examine through the kindness of the Mayor, E. D. Godwin, Esq., and of W. Bailey, Esq., the Town Clerk, the following significant entry occurs:— "27th October, 1643. Fifty pounds lent to Sir William Ogle and Collonell Gerrard." In vain, however, do we search for any record of repayment of these monies. A history of Winchester published in 1773, which has been already referred to, says of Sir William Ogle, "His first care was to strengthen his newly acquired garrison, and render it as inaccessible as art could invent, wisely considering that its situation rendering it the principal key of the whole western country, it might be made a convenient and serviceable rendezvous for his Royal master. He, therefore, lost no time in putting this business into execution, and happily meeting with the concurrence and mutual assistance of the Mayor and citizens, he not only re-fortified the Castle, but put the city itself into a much better posture of defence than it had been in for many years before; immediately after which the western army marched into it, consisting of 3000 foot and 1500 horse under the command of Lord Hopton." Francis Baigent, Esq., to whom also my best thanks are due, says:—"The defences to the west of the Castle were some entrenchments thrown up at the spot known as Oram's Arbour, which was formerly the training ground for the City Trained Band and the place where the people assembled for the county elections. There were traces of these entrenchments visible some 30 or 40 years ago, if not later."

The city was also fortified in a more modern style towards the east, on St. Giles' Hill, &c. As Christmas drew near Lord Hopton arrived, in company with Baron Stratton, at the head of a force which his influence had collected in the west, together with a portion of the garrison of Bristol. "He had in a short time got a pretty body of foot and horse." Sir Charles Vavasour and that veteran soldier Sir John Pawlet joined him with two very good though numerically weak regiments, which, together with a good troop of horse under the command of Captain Bridges, had been brought over from Munster to Bristol at the cessation of hostilities. Lord Hopton now found himself sufficiently strong to advance first to Salisbury, and shortly afterwards to Winchester. Here he was joined by Sir John Berkeley with two other infantry regiments which he had raised in Dorsetshire, making his whole force amount to some 3000 foot and 1500 horse. Winchester was an admirable base of operations, and ere long became such a centre of Royalist activity that Waller was obliged to halt at Farnham on his westward march, and to request additional reinforcements from London, with which, as we have seen, he was duly furnished.

Two days after Sir William Waller had been repulsed at Basing Lord Hopton made an advance from Winchester, with either the whole or a portion of his force, and the garrison of Loyalty House had "the liberty of farther fortifying, which thus, as time and number would permit, made up, is rather strong than regular."

Lord Hopton was a brave man and excellent officer, who sought not for preferment at Court, checked pillage, and protected rustics, "fulfilling what he esteemed the duty of a faithful subject with all the humanity of a good citizen."

On Thursday, November 16th, there was despatched an account to the Parliament of the operations at Basing, and on the same day a strong force of cavalry and infantry was sent by Sir William Waller to beat up Lord Hopton's head-quarters at Odiham. The hedges were found to be lined with musketeers, who kept up a galling fire. The country people, on being questioned, gave information that the main body of the Cavaliers had fallen back towards Alton and Alresford, so that "only some of their straggling, pillaging forces were taken." The quiet little town of Odiham, of which all men know the broad street and huge chalk pit, had its full share in the troubles inseparable from the Civil War. The present Vicar has done much to throw light upon Church matters during this stormy period. He has ascertained that the Rev. Bezaleel Manwaring, Vicar of Odiham, was buried on January 10th,

1641. According to local tradition, his successor was ejected in the depth of winter, and turned into the street when the snow lay deep upon the ground. His wife's sufferings were so great that some kindly-hearted neighbours were scarcely able to give her shelter before an infant made a premature appearance in what was indeed to its parents a world of sorrow.

The Rev. Mordecai Kaddons, a Presbyterian minister, occupied the vicarage during the Commonwealth, but for what length of time is uncertain. In the record of his burial, on Oct. 10th, 1703, he is described as "minister." It is some six times noted in the register that at this time banns were published in the market-place. "1654, Nov.—The intent of marriage between Edward Demole, husbandman, and Barbara Cope, spinster, both of Newnham, was published in the market, 11th, 18th, 25th Nov." It was in those days, even as now, "well to be off with the old love before you are on with the new," for we are told: "Mar. 3rd, 1654.—Received by the hands of Thomas Washam, in the behalf of Alice Washam, his sister, an interdiction of publishing the intent of marriage between William Knight, of Upton Grey, gentleman, and Anne Millingate, upon occasion of a pre-contract." If, however, the course of true love ran smoothly on, despite all proverbs to the contrary, the Magistrates' aid and blessing was invoked: "1653, Nov. 2nd.—The marriage between Edward Mills and Mary Draper was solemnised by Francis Tylney, Esq., Justice of the Peace, according to an Act of Parliament of the 24th of August, touching marriages."

Parish registers and other records could be only imperfectly kept at this time. The conscientious Parish Clerk of Odiham made the following entry:—"There will come a time that men will come to search in this book (the baptismal register) for the names of their children, and in regard that they cannot find their names here written, let them not blame me for it, but look upon their own selves, for since the wars began in this land there have been many that have been baptised that I never knew of, neither have I had timely notice of them; nevertheless I know that the blame will be laid upon me. Thomas Hooker, Parish Clerk, 1652." The parish register of Basing previous to and during the Civil War has perished, and John Chase, Notary Public and Chapter Clerk and Registrar of Winchester Cathedral, signs his name to the following entry, dated 10th of April, 1643:—"In Domo Munimentorum Ecclię, Cathis Sctrę Trinitatis, Winton. This should have been placed in the beginning of this book, being the first time that I began to order the muniment house after the same was the first time defaced and spoiled, and divers writings taken away (14th December, 1642). The muniment house (after I had ordered the writings, charters, deeds, and muniments found there, and bound them up according to the table mentioned in this book, in their several boxes and places, thereby to find them by the direction of this book), was the second time by the army and soldiery broken up, and all my ledgers and register books taken away: the records, charters, deeds, writings, and muniments lost; divers of them burnt; divers of them thrown into the river; divers large parchments, they made kites, withal, to fly in the air, and many of the old books lost, to the utter spoiling and destruction of the same muniment and charter house; many of which deeds and writings may be supposed to have been kept and to have been there for many hundred, of years, as by the dates taken by me, and mentioned in this book, doth appear." Strangely enough, quiet, peaceful Odiham felt also the remote effects of the great Napoleonic wars. A number of French officers resided there on parole in the cottages round the Chalk Pit. A fine oak on the Winchfield-road, still known as the Frenchmen's oak, about a mile from the town, marks the limit of their permitted walk. Two of them died here, to one of whom there is a monument in the churchyard. But to resume our narrative of events.

On Friday, November 17th, Sir William Waller was at Farnham, and Lord Hopton at Basing. Cavalier scouts were everywhere on the alert, and news had reached London from Portsmouth that some of Hopton's men having organised a foray, the country people fired the beacons, which had been placed in readiness, rose as one man, and forced the plunderers to return to their quarters. On Friday, November 17th, Waller on his part likewise sent out Captain Oakley with 45 men, who made a march of twelve miles into the enemies' quarters to a market town, called Methouse (Midhurst), a few miles from Petworth. Two other troops of horse had been also detailed for this expedition, but coming late to the rendezvous, Capt. Oakley marched without them. When he and his small detachment were within six miles of Midhurst, some rustics informed him that 150 Cavalier horse had visited the town that morning, but had just left for Petworth, intending to return to Midhurst that same night. "It was thought that if we came not (to Midhurst) with a very strong party, the town, being very malignant (i.e. loyal), and store of Papists in it, would have risen against us; yet was this valiant Captain nothing at all discouraged, but resolved to march thither." On his arrival Capt. Oakley posted his sentries at all the entrances into the town, of which he kept possession for two hours. Three Cavaliers who had been left in the town by their comrades were made prisoners, several horses were seized, "and some store of cloth which was taken from Papists and malignants there to clothe the foot." The little band then returned unmolested to the headquarters of the army.

On Saturday, Nov. 18th, Lieutenant Archer makes a note: "There came to us much provision of victuals and strong waters to our regiment, which was very thankfully received, although, thanks be to God, we had no great scarcity before." On the same day the Committee for Westminster, sitting at Worcester House, was directed to furnish a list of all deserters from the Westminster Regiment, with a view to their apprehension. A sum of 5000*l*. was to be paid to Sir William Waller, to whom Mr. Reynolds was to write a letter of encouragement, assuring him that as many soldiers as possible should be sent without delay. The four associated counties of Kent, Surrey, Sussex, and Hants were to be warned "to send all the assistance that may be." Sundry deserters ere long found themselves in durance vile at Westminster and Clerkenwell, awaiting the decision of a Court-Martial. In the armies of the King it was the rule to execute deserters immediately after their capture. Sir William Waller himself was by no means happy, but was, on the contrary, full of anxiety. He complained that his men were in want of pay, "and also that they were not so at command as was to be desired." He therefore begged for reinforcements from the Committee of Militia for London, saying that he had only from 1200 to 1400 foot and 15 troops of horse, 12 of which were from Kent. Colonel Morley's

Sussex Regiment refused to march to join him until they had received their arrears of pay, and Colonel Norton's Hampshire Regiment had not yet effected a junction with him. His spies, whom he had sent out to lie in the woods, reported that Hopton had at least 5000 men with him, and some prisoners stated the Cavaliers were only two or three miles distant, with a force of 2000 foot and 10 troops of horse. Sir William, almost despairing of success, adds "that he put himself into God's protection!" The Westminster Trained Bands were anxious to recover their reputation for valour, which had been somewhat discounted at Basing; but it seems probable that if Hopton had but attacked in force upon that memorable Saturday, the result of the campaign in the Southern counties would have been very different. But the golden opportunity thus lost never again presented itself. Instead of pressing their attack home, the Cavaliers contented themselves with giving an alarm to Waller's Kentish Horse, who were quartered at Guildford, by means of small reconnoitring parties who penetrated as far as Pirbright and other places in the neighbourhood. Lord Hopton meanwhile made a leisurely advance towards Farnham. Waller, who was anxiously awaiting the arrival of the Kentish Horse from Guildford, drew out the few troops which he had with him, and boldly faced his foe on a heath, at a distance of three or four miles from Farnham. Both forces sent out forlorn hopes, which faced each other for about an hour. Waller's men then received orders to charge, whereupon their opponents fell back upon their main body. Waller, seeing their retreat, advanced in force, on which Hopton drew off his troops in good order without fighting. It was generally supposed that the Welshmen, who were numerous in the Royalist ranks, were much indisposed to fight at so great a distance from their mountain homes.

Before the dawn of Sunday, November 19th, the Kentish Horse, 400 in number, had joined Sir William Waller, who now felt somewhat more at ease. He, however, sent an express to London, urging the immediate despatch of the 1500 men which he had been promised as a reinforcement, saying that Hopton was within a mile of him with an army collected from Reading, Oxford, and elsewhere, which was at least twice as numerous as his own.

During the morning hours the Cavaliers

FIGHTING AT FARNHAM.

appeared "upon Beacon Hill, a mile from Farnham," or, according to another account, "upon a hill two miles from Farnham," causing Waller's men to muster in the Park. An artillery duel was carried on at long range, and the two armies watched one another for some hours, Lord Hopton fearing to make an attack in force, as his enemy had received an accession of strength. At length Sir William Waller sent out some cavalry to fire upon the hostile ranks, and "our horse faced theirs until three o'clock in the afternoon, and sent forth scouts, who fired upon the enemy (the Cavaliers) and killed some of them, but we had not one man hurt."

November days are but of short duration, and as yet Waller's scouts had only "slain two straggling Cavaliers and taken three horses besides those who were hurt." Their Roundhead comrades were becoming impatient, and towards evening a strong party of horse and foot, including the red-coated Trained Bands of Westminster, made a vigorous charge, and made the Cavaliers retire down the hill towards Crondall, which was only a mile distant from the scene of action. As they retreated they lined the hedges of the narrow lanes with musketeers, and Waller, fearing an ambuscade, drew off towards Farnham. During the night a party of Lord Hopton's horse tried to beat up Sir William Waller's quarters, but the latter, having received timely warning, sent out three bodies of cavalry with a total strength of 300 sabres, who took prisoners, 30 or 40, or 60 troopers, as chroniclers variously relate, a sergeant-major (or major), two captains, with others, and slew some 25 more. But following up the pursuit too hotly, the victors, when they at length drew rein, were saluted with volleys of musketry from the hedges, which " did much hurt, killing some and wounding others ; so that the purchase proved not much worth, costing some men's lives, a few of whom being worth many horse." During this week there was also a skirmish in Wiltshire, in which Lord Crawford was wounded, losing 12 horses and having several men placed hors de combat, whereupon he fell back upon a position nearer to Lord Hopton's main body.

On Thursday, November 16th, all the horsemen under the command of Sir Arthur Haslerig, " being all compleat and experienced soldiers," were summoned by beat of drum, upon pain of death, to appear on Friday, November 17th, in the New Artillery Ground, in order to march to Sir William Waller. Clarendon thus graphically describes this regiment :—" A fresh regiment of Horse, under the command of Sir Arthur Haslerig, which were so compleatly armed that they were called by the other side the regiment of lobsters, because of their bright iron shells with which they were covered being perfect cuirassiers, and were the first so armed on either side, and the first that made any impression upon the King's Horse, who, being unarmed, were not able to bear a shock with them. Besides that they were secure from hurts of the sword, which were almost the only weapons the others were furnished with."

Invincible, however, as they had hitherto proved, these bold cuirassiers had been charged by Lord Byron at the head of his gallant "Blacks" on Roundway Down on July 13th of this same year, and had, after a fierce struggle, in which Sir Arthur received many wounds, at length been broken.

The early hours of Monday, November 20th, saw them on the march from London in the direction of Farnham, where Sir William Waller was anxiously awaiting their arrival, as well he might, for by nine in the morning a strong body of Cavalier horse and foot appeared upon the hill between Crondall and Farnham, which caused a muster of the Parliamentarians in the Park. Their guns, which were originally planted at a distance of a mile and a-half from Lord Hopton's cavalry, were, in consequence of the advance of the latter, able to open fire about an hour before noon, a party of Roundhead troopers having ridden up the hill and formed up to support them in rear. The gunners speedily got the range, and, according to the reports of prisoners, did great execution. Seven men were killed by the first discharge, and few shots missed their mark. After a protracted artillery duel, the Roundhead cavalry made a charge, and diverted the attention of the enemy from a body of infantry, who, advancing without molestation, charged in their turn. Sir William Waller's men had the field word of "The Lord of Hosts," their opponents having selected "The Prince of Wales." Thus charged by cavalry and infantry simultaneously, the Cavalier horse "wheeled about and fled down the hill, and their foot, being always behind the horse on the side of the hill, were not drawn up at all, and retreated while their horse stood for their reserve." In other words, Lord Hopton's cavalry covered a retreat in good order. Eight Cavaliers were captured, one of whom was a trumpeter, or "music." Lord Hopton carried off his killed and wounded, estimated by their opponents to be more than 40 in number, " but the next day we found four of their horse killed, and much blood." So says the Parliamentarian scribe, who only admits the loss of one man on his own side. On this eventful Mond y the Kentish regiment reached Farnham from Guildford, and five companies of Sir A. Haslerig's regiment of foot were also a welcome reinforcement to Sir William Waller.

Before sunset on Tuesday, November 21st. Colonel Richard Norton, the "Idle Dick Norton" of the hero of Naseby Fight, had reached Waller's head-quarters from Southampton at the head of his famous corps of "Hambledon Boys," and Colonel Morley had arrived from Kent, his regiment having at length consented to march, on the understanding that they were to receive their full arrears of pay on reaching Farnham. The county of Kent had already sent 500 horse and foot, and was raising 1500 more men for Waller, whose strength was now estimated at 4000. On this day some of his soldiers went to a park called " The Holt," about a mile and a-half from Farnham, to kill deer, and, taking advantage of a thick mist, the Cavaliers' scouts surprised and captured nine of Captain Levett's men.

On Wednesday, November 22nd, as various merchants had been sending frequent requisitions for convoy, Parliament ordered that 19 men-of-war and 23 merchant ships should be detailed as a winter guard for the shores of Great Britain and Ireland. This was the more necessary, as the Cavaliers were known to have sixteen ships at Bristol and Barnstaple, and to be fitting out others. The House of Commons passed an ordinance on Wednesday, November 22nd, directing the Governor of Poole to send up to London the horses captured when Lord Crawford unsuccessfully attacked the town. The steeds were to be sold, and the proceeds divided amongst the garrison of Poole. Some rings and tobacco which had been seized *en route* for Oxford were likewise ordered to be sold " by the appointment and directions of Mr. Jennour." The money realised by the sale was to be spent in sending to Sir William Waller

" those forces that lie on the County of Middlesex," after the informer had received his promised reward. " Mr. Trenchard, Chairman to the Committee of Accounts," was to send these men, together with certain arms, to Sir William Waller. The arms in question were in the custody of Captain Ellingworth, of whom we read on December 9th, 1643. " Captain Ellingworth shall be tried by a Council of War for cheating the State by false musters, and selling and pawning, and embezzling his soldiers' arms allowed by the State."

Says Lieutenant Archer, on Nov. 23rd : " There came to us at Farnham a very fair regiment of horse, and a company of dragoons, consisting of 120 out of Kent, under the command of Sir Miles Lowsy (Livesay) " Sergeant-Major, or, as we should style him, Major Webb, who had, as we have seen, earned promotion before the walls of stubbornly defended Basing, with some of the green-coated London Trained Bands was this day sent, together with other forces, from Farnham, to aid in the relief of Plymouth, to which Prince Maurice and Sir Richard had laid siege. Sir William Waller also wrote a letter to the Parliament, which was read in the House of Commons two days afterwards, when it was agreed that 5000*l.* should be raised for the supply of his army, " upon the credit of the Excise," 2000*l.* of which was to be paid to him without delay. This latter sum was promptly furnished by Alderman Towse, in consideration of interest at the rate of eight per cent. Sir William thus writes in his " Vindication," " And for the payment of arrears I may say I was for it to the uttermost farthing. I may not say who were against it, but those who seemed to be pillars, or somewhat, whatsoever they were it maketh no matter to me, contributed nothing, nay, gave their flat negative to it. And, truely, herein I did but discharge my conscience, for I was ever of opinion that a soldier's pay is the justest debt in the world. For if it be a crying sin to keep back the wages of an hireling, that doth but sweat for us, it must needs be a roaring altisonant sin to detain pay of the soldier that bleeds for us. There is a cry of blood in it, and God will make inquisition for it!" Well and nobly said, Sir William! He also stated in his letter that a battle was imminent, and that he was in great need of " some able officers." The Earl of Essex received orders to send him some, and

Mr. Trenchard was to "take speedy order to send unto Sir William Waller Capt in Carr's troop."

There was a report on Friday, November 24th that the King had marched to Basing House at the head of 2000 horse, intending to co-operate with Lord Hopton in an attack upon Farnham Castle. Accordingly, about ten o'clock in the morning the colours were hoisted on the castle, and the army was drawn up in the park, where it to no purpose awaited an attack. A party of horse was on the same day sent from Farnham into Sussex after Sir Edward Ford, "to make an end of his Sheriff year." After the morning's "alarm" the Cavaliers retired to Odiham, and their enemies were able to refresh themselves. A report reached Oxford that Hopton had beaten Waller back to London, and the Queen, overjoyed at the intelligence, "gave the messenger 4l. 10s., all she had in her purse!" But the tidings were false, for on Saturday, November 25th, the Earl of Essex was preparing to send reinforcements to Farnham, and the county of Kent was raising a force of 2000 infantry, and was likewise fortifying Tunbridge and Sevenoaks to check the advance of Hopton. It seems somewhat doubtful whether there was a skirmish on Sunday, November 26th, in which Lord Hopton gave Sir William Waller a few shot, losing, however, about 100 of his own men, or whether the somewhat vague account does not refer to the day of the retreat to Crondall. The Surrey troops having been withdrawn from their homes towards Farnham, it seemed not improbable that Lord Hopton would march upon Guildford. To keep him in check until his own main body could arrive from Farnham Sir William Waller summoned all the men of Surrey between the ages of sixteen and sixty to muster at Guildford in defence of the county. Entrenchments were being constructed at Farnham, and several challenges to fight a pitched battle were sent to Hopton by his old friend and ever courteous antagonist Waller, who also on several occasions hung out flags of defiance at Farnham Castle. Sir William's own words are, "The war I abhorred, though I acted in it as upon the defensive, which I thought justifiable, but it was ever with a wish that the sword, as it was fabled of Hercules his, might be dipped in oil rather than in blood; that the difference might end rather in a peace than a conquest; that, as it fell out in the decision between Zenocles and Euripides, the one party might not have the worse, nor the other the better, but such an accommodation might take effect as might be with saving of honour to King and Parliament, whereby both might have the best."

Certain stragglers from Lord Hopton's force plundered an old woman's cottage near Farnham, and stole her bedding, of which the Parliamentarian newspapers did not fail to make much stern and satirical mention. Captain Bithy, a deserter from the army of the Parliament, was taken and condemned to death by a council of war, and we learn from Lieutenant Archer that during these operations Bartholomew Ellicot, who had formerly been a butcher near Temple Bar, and who had also been a captain in the army of the Parliament, was taken prisoner, whilst fighting for the King. He had not only deserted from the army of the Earl of Essex, but had also appropriated money intended for the payment of the soldiers. He could expect no mercy, and on Wednesday, December 6th, he was hanged in the market-place at Farnham. He had, in addition to his other offences against the Parliament, done his best to betray the town of Aylesbury to the Cavaliers. One who saw the execution has left on record that "he died in a miserable condition, justifying himself in the Acts, and condemning the Council of Warre which found him worthy of death."

Lord Hopton's forces were scattered throughout Hampshire, and on the morning of Monday, Nov. 27th, he sent a party towards Farnham from the direction of Crondall, which was greeted by a hot fire from the artillery of the castle, and from some guns placed in position in the park. Three shots killed 17 horses and 15 men. There was a report that the King was to dine at Basing House that day, having brought with him "2000 or 3000 horse and some strength of foot," with the intention of carrying off the garrison and treasure, and of "slighting" or dismantling the fortress, and that a party had in consequence been sent out to Crondall in order to prevent any unwelcome intrusion on the part of the Farnham garrison. This rumour probably arose from the fact that "divers of His Majestie's servants and attendants" had lately come "from Oxford with the Prince's (Rupert's) owne regiment to the aid of the Lord Hopton." Clarendon says that "Sir Jacob Astley was likewise sent to him (Hopton) from Reading with 1000 commanded men, of that garrison, Wallingford, and Oxford; which supply no sooner arrived at Winchester, but the Lord Hopton resolved to visit Waller's quarters, if it were possible to eng ge; however that he might judge by the posture he was in whether he were like to pursue his purpose for the West. Waller was then quartered at Farnham and t e villages adjacent, from whence he drew out his men, and faced the enemy as if he intended to fight, but after some light skirmishes for a day or two, in which he always received loss, he retired into the Castle of Farnham, a place of some strength, and drew his army into the town." Galled by this artillery fire, the Cavaliers were obliged to retreat towards Crondall, hotly pursued by the cavalry of Sir William Waller. Beaten out of the village, they were soon galloping at headlong speed toward Odiham and Basingstoke, some of them having only lately reached Farnham from Basing House, to the garrison of which they belonged. When the muster roll was called that evening, a Major, a Lieutenant, and 60 horses were reported as having fallen into the hands of the enemy, whilst thirty men were either killed, wounded, or missing. The pursuers, who returned laden with various kinds of booty to Farnham, only admitted a loss of six men.

Tuesday, November 28th, witnessed the despatch of a party of horse and dragoons from Farnham towards Odiham, under the command of Colonel Van Rosse, to beat up the enemy's quarters. They slew some Cavaliers and took a few prisoners. But a whole troop declined to follow Colonel Van Rosse, who was dangerously wounded in the shoulder. The cowards were next day deservedly cashiered and disarmed!

Meanwhile Lord Hopton was making a formidable demonstration in force near Farnham. Sir William Waller is said to have had with him only six troops of horse, the rest of his cavalry having been despatched to Odiham and other places, but his scouts were active and intelligent. It seems probable that Lord Hopton only intended to prevent the retreat of his infantry from being discovered, he having sent off part of his foot towards Alresford either on this or the previous d y. He had also, in a proclamation, in which he styles himself "Field-Marshal-General of His Majesty's Western Forces," summoned all Hampshire men between the ages of sixteen and sixty to appear in arms for the King at Winchester. Upon the near approach of the assailants two guns were fired, which made complete lines through the Cavaliers, who were said, probably with exaggeration, to number eight thousand. A preliminary skirmish took place between 300 horse of each party, and the main fight was in the park. After a few shots had been fired the Cavaliers made a retrograde movement. A pursuit was ordered, and proved very successful, although the retreating troops "rallied upon a hill near adjoining." The Roundhead newswriter says that Hopton's men, after a few hours, became disordered, that they lost many officers and horses, and that about two o'clock in the afternoon they fled, going for the most part towards Basing House; that many hundreds were slain, and that prisoners reported that Lord Hopton was being carried off the field, as if dangerously wounded; that only one of Waller's men was missing, and that his wounded were not numerous.

But according to "Mercurius Aulicus" Sir William's great victory was nothing after all He says that Hopton faced Farnham, and that Waller, not daring to come forth, fired two guns from the castle "over every house's head," until towards the close of "that dark misty day" the Cavaliers fell back, followed by the Roundhead cavalry, who killed only one dragoon, but lost five men themselves. The pursuers did not give up the chase until they reached Hook, on the other side of Odiham, and Waller despatched a messenger to the Parliament, who reached London on the afternoon of Wednesday, November 29th, and found the members of both Houses listening to the Fast Sermon at St. Margaret's, Westminster. Master Bridges was the preacher, and his subject was "Though God do suffer the enemies of His Church to be great and exceeding many, yet God will raise up a power to withstand and overpower them." "After the sermon was done the House of Commons went to the Parliament House, and there sat very late." But in those "good old times" Parliament met at nine o'clock in the morning, and every unpunctual member was to be fined twelve pence!

On Wednesday, November 29th, the Roundheadhorse penetrated to Odiham and Basingstoke, giving divers alarms that day and the following night, and bringing back five of Lord Crawford's troopers, together with their horses.

On Thursday, November 3'th, Hopton withdrew his outposts from Odiham, Basingstoke, and Long Sutton, and retired towards Winchester. Lord Crawford with his cavalry took post at Alton, Lord Hopton himself quartering his men at Andover, Winchester, Alresford, Petersfield, and the intervening villages. Basing House was left to take care of itself, but Sir William Waller was at present in no mood to try conclusions with the Marquis and his brave little garrison.

On November 30th the counties of Sussex and Surrey were ordered by the House of Commons to raise, " either by press or volunteers, the 800 Foot set upon them," and Sir William was to send officers "to receive them as they are levied." Within three or four days Waller went himself to London more effectually to solicit recruits than his letters had been able to do.

Listen to his own account of the treatment he received ("Waller's Vindication," pp. 13-18): " I confess after that defeat which I received at the Devizes (July 13th, 1643), upon my return to London, I found, contrary to my expectation, a multitude of friends, *populum amicorum*, in the Independent party that appeared for me. In that heat, as the sun is ever hottest after a cloud, I had an offer from them of a very considerable army, to be raised and put under my command, with a constant maintenance for it, if I would engage myself to maintain none but godly officers, such as should be recommended to me. Unto which I replied that I desired nothing more than to have such officers about me as might be remarkable for that spot, as Moses calleth it ; but I wished them to consider that there went more to the making up of an officer than single honesty. *Alia ratio boni civis et boni viri*, as Aristotle said in another case. A good man might make a good soldier, but there must go the good man and the good soldier to the composition of a good officer. I besought them likewise to weigh my condition, how I stood answerable with my life and honour, for any miscarriage that should fall out in the service, and that it would be a poor plea for me to say that it was the officers' fault, when it might be justly retorted upon me as my fault that I took such officers. This I assured them, that where I could find persons qualified with piety and ability, such faithful centurions as knew how to command, and when to say go, come, do this, I would prefer them before all others. But in the want of those I looked to be excused if for the advantage of the service I made bold to employ such as should appear to be able soldiers, although they were not otherwise so refined men as I might wish. And to the end that there might be a fair choice, and to obviate all exceptions, the Parliament having voted a considerable body to be raised for me, I appointed a council of war, whereof Sir Arthur Hesilrigg was President, to examine the merits of every man that should stand to bear any office in that army, with power to cross all such out of the list as should be judged unfit or unworthy to be employed. But this did not satisfy, and I then found that they had it in their design to model and form an army that should be all of their own party, and devoted to their own ends. Upon this we differed. I trusted not them, nor they me, and so we agreed. From that time forward I may date the expiration of their friendship. It is true that long after, and so long indeed as I held my command, I was kept up by them, but I could plainly perceive it was but in the nature of a stale, in opposition to that noble Lord the Earl of Essex, whom they feared, and therefore hated implacably, and they were willing enough to foment those differences between his lordship and me, to the prejudice of the public service, that they might make their ends upon us both, and gain the better pretence to bring on their new model. In what condition I was maintained may be demonstrated by the Treasurer, Mr. John Trenchard, his accounts, where it will appear that from the time of my setting forth unto my disbanding I never received full 104,000l., an inconsiderable sum compared with what others had, and yet out of that stock I was fain to play the good husband, and to be at the charge to pay for part of my arms and ammunition Besides this they would be sure I should never have an entire body of my own, but so compounded of city and country regiments that when they pleased they might take me in pieces like a clock, and this was the true reason why I could never improve any successes, because these adventitious borrowed forces, having no dependence upon me, but upon those that sent them, would not follow me further than pleased themselves, but would be ready to march home when they should have pursued their point, as if they had done enough when they had done anything. Yet such were the charities which I met with in the world, that it was made my fault that, like Joash, I gave over shooting sooner than I should have done, when, in truth, I had no more arrows left to shoot. From time to time I was put upon all disadvantages that might lessen me in my reputation, and expose me to ruin. . . . So that, in effect, I was in no better condition than those gladiators of old among the Romans, preserved awhile, to perish in the end, and kept only to be lost. This was the friendship I parted with!" Thus speaks Sir William Waller.

It has been a difficult task to describe these somewhat confused operations at and near Farnham, owing to certain discrepancies in the accounts given by the various actors in the drama, but every statement which I have made rests, not on conjecture, but on the authority of contemporaneous records.

CHAPTER XV.—DEFENCE OF THE ISLE OF WIGHT—NAVAL ESTIMATES—CAPTAIN SWANLEY'S PRISONERS—THE SUSSEX CAVALIERS—LORD HOPTON IS REINFORCED.—LETTER TO PRINCE RUPERT—FORAYS INTO SUSSEX—FIGHT AT SOUTH HARTING.

The early days of December, 1643, saw due provision made for naval matters, and for the defence of the Isle of Wight. On Thursday December 7th, the Deputy Lieutenants and Treasurers of the Isle of Wight were instructed to pay Captain Scofield the sum of 80l. "towards his raising and conveying thither 100 soldiers," and four days later we hear of 500 men being embodied for the same destination, in addition to 200 formerly enrolled, and duly ferried across the Solent. We learn also that "whereas several fortifications are making in the said Island by Ordinance of Parliament," William and Thomas Bowreman and Thomas Carne, Esquires, were to be a standing Committee for the purposes of defence.

On Saturday. December 9th, the Naval Estimates for the year were discussed in Parliament, and 5000 men were voted "for next year's fleet," which was to consist of 46 ships. Of these two were to be second rates, whilst the third rates were to be nine in number. There were to be 20 fourth rates, 10 fifth rates, and five sixth rates, 26 of the whole fleet being men-of-war, and 20 hired merchant ships; light ships were to cruise to the westward, 10 watching the estuary of the Severn and the coast of Ireland meanwhile. The Downs, the coasts of Scotland, and the northern shore of the Emerald Isle were protected by three squadrons, each consisting of eight ships. Three thousand men were to be employed in 30 men-of-war, and the merchant ships for the next winter guard, which was to last for five months, at a cost of 60,000l. The expenditure for 5000 men during the eight months summer guard of the year 1644 was estimated to amount to 130,000l. The ordinary expense of the whole Navy in harbour during the year 1644 was to be 18,000l. The sum of 20,000l. was voted for "extraordinary and ordinary service in the office of the Ordnance." The cost of victualling 4000 men for six months in forty ships " supposed to be sent to sea as reprisals, according to a late ordinance," was to be 24,000l. The " payment of ordinary for this year, the winter guard now at sea, the freights of sundry merchant ships already discharged, arrears, sundries, &c.," amounted to 140,000l., and the whole vote for naval expenditure for the year 1644 was 392,000l.

Lord Clarendon was horrified to hear that the Parliament had laid a weekly assessment of 10,000l. upon the City of London, and that their weekly revenue from the whole kingdom was no less than 33,518l., or 1,742,936l. per annum. He says that 20,000l. was the largest sum ever raised by taxation in any previous year. What would the worthy Chancellor think of the Budget for the year of grace 1882 ?

An amusing description of the willingness of the citizens of London to aid the Parliament by their contributions is as follows :—

" And now, my Lord, since you have London left,
Where merchants' wives dine cheap, and as cheap sup,
Where fools themselves have of their plate bereft,
And sigh and drink in the coarse pewter cup;
Where's not a silver spoon left, not that given them
When the first Cockney was made Christian:
No, not a bodkin, pin-case; all they send,
Or carry all, whatever they can hap on,
E'en to the pretty picktooth whose each end
Oft purged the relics of continual capon.
Nothing must stay behind, nothing must tarry.
No, not the ring by which dear John took Harry."
—*Penny Magazine* for 1844.

Nor were the ladies more backward in behalf of the cause, for in a satirical ballad, entitled " The Sale of Rebellion's Household Stuff," the following lots are, amongst others, offered for sale :—

"Here's the purse of the public faith,
Here's the mo.er of the sequestration,
Where the good wives upon their good troth,
Lent thimbles to revive the nation.

Our old acquaintance Captain Swanley, who was formerly expected to bombard Southampton, was in command of one of the ships sent to the coast of Ireland.

A truce had been made at Sigginstown, in the County Kildare, on September 16th, 1643, which allowed two regiments of infantry of excellent quality, though numerically weak, under the command of Sir Charles Vavasour and Sir John Pawlet, and a good troop of horse under the command of Captain Bridges, to be brought over from Munster to Bristol, to the aid of Lord Hopton, who, thus reinforced, advanced to Salisbury, Winchester, Basing, and Farnham, as has been already described.

Speaking of this truce, the Rev. C. P Meehan says: "Every creek and harbour suddenly became infested with the Parliamentary cruisers, so much so that it was difficult to send men or money out of Ireland. The orders issued by the Parliament to their partisans on the land were only equalled by the Algerine ferocity of their cruisers on the seas. Out of 150 men, who about this time sailed for Bristol, and who were taken by one Swanly, at sea, 70, besides two women, were thrown overboard, because they were supposed to be Irish. Nor did the Irish retaliate, for soon afterwards, falling in with a ship which had on board 50 Kirk ministers deputed to preach up and administer the Covenant in Ulster, they contented themselves with making them prisoners. This fatal truce was the source of all these miseries, and the coast, which hitherto had been so watchfully guarded, was now swarming with rebel ships, whose commanders showed no mercy to such as had the misfortune to fall into their hands."
In addition to the troops from Ireland mentioned above, Lord Hopton had also two regiments of infantry under the command of Sir John Berkeley, who had raised them in Devonshire, so that his whole force amounted to at least 3000 foot, and about 1500 horse, with the advantage of a most advantageous base of operations at Winchester.

For some time the Cavaliers of Sussex and of the adjacent districts of Hampshire had, according to Clarendon, unfortunately, like their friends of the same party in other counties, formed "so good an opinion of their own reputation and interest that they were able, upon the assistance of few troops, to suppress their neighbours who were of the other party, and who, upon advantage of the power they were possessed of, exercised their authority over them with great rigour and insolence."

Accordingly no sooner had Lord Hopton established himself at Winchester, the castle of which had been re-fortified by Sir William, afterwards Lord, Ogle, than he received confidential messages from these friends to the King with offers "That if he would advance into their country they would undertake, in a short time, to make great levies of men for the recruit of his army; and likewise to possess themselves of such places as they should be well able to defend, and thereby keep that part of the country in the King's obedience."

Clarendon says that the county of Sussex was one in which "the King had hitherto had no footing." The Rev. H. D. Gordon says, "This evidently means no army or garrison, for the majority of the Sussex gentry, with one or two marked exceptions, at that time were staunch Roy lists. The most notable exception was at Petworth, whose owner, Algernon Percy, tenth Earl of Northumberland, was one of the great Parliamentarian leaders, second only to the Earl of Essex, the General. One Henry Percy, however, seems to have commanded the ordnance at Gloucester for the King ('Match—The ordinary rate is 30s. per cent.; for locks and breets, 1s. a-peece; for iron shot, 1 li. (£) a tonne. Asher Comper, before Gloucester, the 21st Aug., H. Percy, General of the Artillery.'—State Papers, Domestic,' 1643, No. 336), and afterwards Oliver Whitby, the Royalist Rector of Petworth, lay hid in a hollow tree for shelter, as Charles II. did in Boscobel Oak. With the exception of Petworth House and the famous Mr. Yalden, of Blackdown Hill, who entertained Cromwell, the remaining powers of West Sussex and the neighbourhood of Hampshire were Royalists. On the immediate frontier of Hampshire, the seat of war, Sir William Ford, of Up Park, and Sir Edward Ford, his son (knighted at Oxford and made Sheriff of Sussex, and afterwards the commander of Arundel), and Sir John Caryll, his son at Harting Place, Parson Caryll, of Harting, and the Coopers, of Ditcham, near Petersfield, were the most active and daring Cavaliers. If, therefore, the King had 'no footing in Sussex,' it was not for want of friends. Of course, on the seaboard the Parliament cause was supreme."

Sir Edward Ford was in command under Lord Hopton of a regiment of horse, in which many Sussex gentlemen had enrolled themselves. These all urged Lord Hopton to send some troops into Sussex, as Waller was not likely to advance from Farnham, so that they might the better be able to raise men for the King's service. They undertook also to secure Arundel Castle, which, "standing near the sea, would yield great advantage to the King's service, and keep that rich corner of the country at His Majesty's devotion." Lord Hopton finding that he could not make any further impression upon the garrison of Farnham, and having certain information that Sir William Waller had gone to London to be "feasted and lectured," thought it a fitting opportunity to comply with the importunities of the Sussex Cavaliers, whose estates had, since the preceding April, been entirely at the mercy of certain Parliamentarian sequestrators, one of whom was Colonel Herbert Morley, who in the following year played no unimportant part during the siege of Basing House.

Lord Hopton paid a hurried visit to Oxford during the month of December, 1643, probably with a view of urging in person an advance into Sussex, which he had already recommended by frequent letters. He was extremely anxious to compel Sir William Waller to give battle, and informed the King that the design was perfectly feasible "if he had the addition of a regiment or two of foot, the quarter of Sussex he proposed to visit being a fast and enclosed country, and Arundel Castle having a garrison in it, though not numerous or well provided, as being without apprehension of an enemy."

The King had only intended during the winter to stop Waller in the west, and to recruit his own forces so as to take the field early in the following spring, knowing that his enemies meant to be stirring betimes. But Lord Hopton's strong position at Winchester and the oft-repeated solicitations of the Sussex Cavaliers made many persons think that the opportunity ought not to be lost.

The Cavaliers of Kent were anxious to strike a blow for the Royal cause, and it was thought that the union of Kent and Sussex might form the basis of a powerful association of the southern counties on the King's behalf. Lord Hopton accordingly received permission to prosecute his design, if at the same time he felt sure of being able to check Waller's march towards the west. Stout old Major-General Sir Jacob Astley was sent towards Winchester from Reading with 1000 disciplined troops, drawn from the garrisons of Reading, Wallingford, and Oxford, Colonel Boles, of whom we shall hear more hereafter, being in command of the detachment from Wallingford.

Lord Hopton being thus reinforced, and finding that Sir William Waller had concentrated his army at Farnham under the protection of the Castle, had betaken himself to London to solicit reinforcements, determined to march at once into Sussex. Just then he received a most unwelcome letter from Prince Rupert ordering Colonel Gerrard's regiment to rejoin the Prince's own force, from which it had recently been detached. Mr. Warburton gives the reply of Lord Hopton, which throws considerable light upon the state of affairs at this critical juncture. It is as follows:—

"May it please your Highness,—Your Highness's commands concerning Colonel Gerrard's regiment, as all other your commands, I shall ever be most ready to obey. I shall only offer to your Highness my present difficulty, which is, that we being here, near the enemy, and our horse decreasing much, I am doubtful lest, in sparing a good old regiment, I may give the enemy too great an advantage upon me in this champaign country; unless your Highness will please to do me the favour to send me some other regiment that hath had rest, till this be recreated. The truth is, the duty of the service here is insupportable, were it not in this cause, where there is so great a necessity either of prevailing through all difficulties, or suffering them to prevail, which cannot be thought of in good English, therefore, if your Highness resume the horse regiment, I should be glad to give these some ease as I could.—I rest in all humility and faithfulness, your Highness's most humbly devoted servant, RALPH HOPTON.—Alresford, Dec., 1643.

For a full account of Colonel Gerrard and his gallant kinsmen, the reader is referred to p. 79 of the admirable and exhaustive work on "The Two Battles of Newbury," by W. Money, Esq., F.S.A.

The time seemed propitious for an advance into Sussex, into which county a party of Cavaliers had already made a raid some few

FIGHT AT SOUTH HARTING.

weeks previously. The *Scottish Dove*, of October 27th, 1643, says:—" The Cavaliers have lately been at Petworth (in Sussex), the Earle of Northumberland's house, from whence they tooke twenty brave horse, and carried them to Oxford."

From the *Perfect Diurnall*, of Friday, November 23rd, 1643, we learn that a portion of the garrison of Basing House had also rein orced Lord Hopton, "and the common vote of the people speak him to be 8000 horse and foot, but very much unarmed. That they press hard towards Kent, and some of them are got as far as Petworth, in Sussex."

The detachment which thus visited Petworth for the second time was under the command of Lord Crawford, who was, however, speedily obliged to retire, and to take post at Alton.

On the night of Thursday, November 23rd, 1643, there was a fight at South Harting, in Sussex. The register of that parish contains the following entry, "There were 3 souldiers buried. Novr. 24th, 1643." The Rev. H. D. Gordon says, " Following this hint, and assuming from the loyalty of the parish that the 'three souldiers' were King's men, I found, on inquiry, that there was a vague local tradition that there had been some fight under the Downs in a field on the east side of Harting, named the 'Culvers,' adjoining Harting Vicarage, and that Oliver had been in the town. Subsequent search verified this entry of the register to an hour, and the exact spot indicated by the old men's traditi n. These three soldiers were part of the Royalist cavalry on their way to Arundel, detached from Alton or Basing by Ludovic Lindsay, 15th Earl of Crawford, who was Lord Hopton's chief cavalry officer."

"The register dates the burial on Friday, November 24th. On the previous night, Thursday, November 23rd, there had been, as the 'Mercurius Aulicus' or 'Court Mercury' of Sunday, December 10th, p. 7 7, describes, a fight at South Harting. It appears that the Royalist cavalry entered the village first, very weary from a long march, and took up their quarters. Some 400 of the much despised Parliamentarian dragoons, under Colonel Norton, accidentally, it seems, caught the King's men asleep in South Harting. But the six officers of the King's force who were quartered at Sir John Caryll's house near the church (Harting Place) were equal to the occasion, and passing along a lane at the back of the church, named Typper-lane, they cleverly placed themselves in the Culverrs fields between the hills and their enemy. Then, relying on the fact that none are so much exposed to panic as those who are trying to fix ten others, they charged the enemy, giving the signal ' Follow, follow,' which in the darkness would give the impression to the Parliamentari ns that some of the King's forces on the way to Arundel had been signalled back, and were coming down the hill like an avalanche."

The following is the text of the "M rcurius Aulicus" of Sunday, Dec. 10th, 1643 (spelling modernised):—"This day I was certainly informed by an eye-witness of credit of one of the noblest pieces of cowardice that ever attended a bad cause and conscience. It happened on Thursday, the 23rd of November last, about in the dead of night about six score of the tail of Crawford's regiment came into a village in Sussex, called South Harting, a place sufficiently known by reason it is the constant seat of the noble Knight and brave housekeeper Sir John Caryll. They entered the village very far spent with travel, want of sleep, and food, and extremely weather beaten with a rainy, stormy night. These their sufferings and indispositions caused them presently to quarter themselves in the several houses of the town, only six of the chief officers and a boy lay in the Knight's house. Within less than an hour after, when all of them were now taking their rest, the famous Colonel Norton, of Hampshire, enters the village, not knowing till he was in the town that any of the King's soldiers were there, but having notice thereof and of the assurance, by taking them utterly unprovided for defence, that he might safely shew a bravo proof of his valour, he caused his men to rank themselves ten and ten, and so to make good every door and house of the town that none might escape, which being done, the rebels cry ' Horse, horse,' in the street, which the King's soldiers mistaking to be the call of their own commanders, offered in divers places to come forth, but were presently shot or killed, so that seeing no possibility of bringing forth themselves or their horses into the street, almost all of them fled by backways on foot to save themselves, leaving the rebels outrageously domineering in the town, shooting into all houses and at all persons, and barbarously using such of the King's men as their valour enabled to make any opposition.

"In this hurly-burly word was given to the six officers in the Knight's house how the town and their soldiers were surprised by the rebels. These six men, with one boy, took horse, rushing out by a back lane upon the 400 rebels, for so have some of their own company since protested to have been their number, and crying out Follow, follow, follow,' as if they had already chased them, charged in upon them with so much fury and undaunted courage that they routed them, and presently drove them, killing and wounding them, quite through t e town, forcing them over hedges and ditches, killing as many as the rebels had done of theirs, that is, some half-a-dozen, taking two prisoners, one of which being the trumpeter, wounding very many, having but five or six of theirs, and but one of these much wounded, the Earl of Crawford's own cornet, but not dangerously, and brought off all their own arms and divers of the rebels' horse, with all Captain Betsworth's suit of arms (probably Betsworth of Milland).

" The rebels having since been faithfully acquainted with the truth of their beating, and how that their 400 horse and dragooners were so lamentably beaten and chased away by only six men and a boy (but when they were in their chase and flight here and there two or three soldiers stept out of their places where they hid, and lent some blows to their fellows), one of the rebels swore solemnly in these true and remarkable words, ' By ——, we deserve all to be chronicled for the veryest cowards that ever lived ! ' " Such was the fight at South Harting.

On Friday, December 1st, we hear of Lord Hopton's troops being at Andover and Winchester, and that Sir William Waller was receiving reinforcements from Kent. Prince Maurice was half inclined to raise the siege of Plymouth, and to march to join Lord Hopton at or near Basing House. On the afternoon of Saturday, December 2nd, Sir William Waller reached London from Farnham, and had a conference with the Earl of Essex at his house in the Strand. He asked for and obtained reinforcements, and set out again for Farnham on the following Monday morning. On Tuesday, December 5th, Mr. Trenchard, the Chairman to the Committee of Accounts, was directed to give three days' pay " to Colonel Pottley's men that lie here in Middlesex, to carry them to Sir William Waller." These troops were to be sent at once under an officer appointed by Mr. Trenchard. Colonel Pottley himself meanwhile writes from Farnham that Hopton's forces had beaten up one of their opponents' quarters, but had done but little harm. On Saturday, Dec. 9th, Mr. Trenchard was ordered to write to Sir William Waller, requesting him to send officers to take command of Colonel Pottley's men, each of whom was to receive a fortnight's pay upon arrival at Farnham. Soldiers refusing to march were " to be proceeded against according to the Law Martial," and Colonel Pottley was to be ordered to cashier those captains of his regiment that Mr. Trenchard had certified to be unworthy of their command.

There was a report that the King had slept at Basing House on the night of Sunday, Dec. 3rd, having brought with him 2000 horse, besides foot, and that he had since returned to Reading, taking with him much plate and treasure from Basing House, intending to cut his way through Waller's army, and to march into Kent. Another statement was to the effect that the King had sent for " plate and other ornaments for ceremonies of State from Basing House to Reading, where His Majesty intends to keep his Christmas," but the sole foundation for these reports seems to have been that some of the Royal cooks came to Basing House about this time with the Prince's regiment. On Saturday, December 9th, a lieutenant of the Green Regiment of Trained Bands, quartered at Farnham, says that for some time past there had been alarms both by night and day, and that on Monday, Dec. 4th, he had been sent out in command of a forlorn hope of 80 musketeers to face the Cavaliers, who, "after some small firing and some great gun shot, ran away." On Tuesday, December 5th, a strong regiment joined Sir William Waller at Farnham from Kent. This reinforcement was the more welcome, as the London Trained Bands were now eagerly desirous to turn their faces homewards. On Monday, December 4th, a letter from the Earl of Essex was read in the House of Lords to the effect that Sir William Waller reports the King to be advancing towards Basing with all his forces, whilst his own army is but weak, and is in great want of recruits. The sum of 1000*l*. was at once voted for the relief of Sir William Waller, who asserted that Lord Hopton's army was three times as numerous as his own. There were said to be 8000 men in arms for the Parliament in Kent, Sussex, and Surrey, who were "not willing to have Sir John Culpepper made Viceroy, nor Sir Edward Deering Bishop of Canterbury." The only road for Cavaliers towards Kent lay through Sussex, " which they will at this season not be able to do."

Lord Hopton, however, meant to try what could be done, and taking advantage of an exceptionally hard frost, made his way with great ease over roads which were usually at that season of the year almost impassable, " and he came to Arundel before there was any imagination that he had that place in his prospect."

The Rev. H. D. Gordon says " The cavalry force of Hopton in this brilliant feat passed over the downs to Arundel, viâ Petersfield, Harting, and Marden, and in order to secure the line of communication, Petersfield and Harting Place were for the time garrisoned for the King. Colonel Sir Edward Ford's own regiment was quartered at Up Park throughout December to guard the passes in the hills, which were their chain of communication with Winchester and Oxford, and the possession of which secured their retreat."

"The pleas of Sir William Ford, of Up Park, and John Caryll, of Harting," at the close of the war, are to be found amongst the Royalist Compositions, and show clearly the positions stated above. Caryll pleads " That your petitioner being at his father's house, called Harting in Sussex, which is in the midway direct from Winchester to Arundel, and the King's forces having made a garrison in the said house about December, 1643, Sir Ralph Hopton coming thither with part of his army, commanded your petitioner to attend him to Arundel, where he detained your petitioner until the Castle was taken by Sir William Waller." Sir William Ford, of Harting, Knight, complained that " 2000 coards of wood had been cut down in Harting Park (Up Park) for satisfaction of wrongs done to certaine countrey people thereabout by some parties of horse of Col. Ford, his sonne's, regiment."

Whilst himself on the march to Arundel Lord Hopton despatched a detachment of cavalry to attack Lord Lumley's house at Stanstead, in the parish of Stoughton, in Sussex, " which was then a castellated building, with a turreted gateway and a courtyard. As one of the possessions of the FitzAlans it had passed in 1580 on the death of the last Earl of Arundel of that name to Lord Lumley, the husband of Jane, one of his co-heiresses. It had, however, since his death been sold to Richard Lewknor." The Royalists were repulsed with loss by Col. Morley, or, as some say, by Colonel Stapley, or by Colonel Norton, of Southwick Park, and Endymion Porter's son, or brother (accounts vary) was "sore wounded and taken prisoner." Lloyd's Memoirs says "Loyal blood like Harvies' went round the Porters' from the highest to the meanest, 26 of the name having eminently suffered for His Majesty." Colonel Stapley is said to have faced the assailants with his regiment of horse, and to have fired guns at them, killing 250 men and capturing 500 horses This account, however, lacks confirmation.

Colonel Norton, who was in command, during the absence of the Earl of Pembroke, of the cavalry raised in the four associated counties of Hants, Surrey, Kent, and Sussex, seems to have been posted at Cowdray House, the noble mansion of Lord Montague, which was taken by Lord Hopton, who placed a garrison in it, and also in Lord Lumley's mansion at Stanstead, which soon afterwards fell into his hands. Colonels Norton and Stapley commanded at Stanstead and Cowdray, but it is difficult to state which of these two commands either of them held.

Colonel Anthony Stapley, of Patcham, as we are told by Mr. Blaauw, had in the preceding September prepared the garrison of Chichester, of which city he was the Governor, to march to the assistance of Sir William Waller, who was then in Dorsetshire. He was in 1640 and 1656 returned both for Lewes and the county, and in both instances, sat for the county. Although he had married the sister of the Royalist Lord Goring he was a zealous adherent of the Parliament, taking the Covenant on Feb. 5th, 1644. He was one of the King's Judges, and signed his death warrant. Clarendon ranks him "in the number of the blackest offenders." He died in 1658.

Various preparations were made to check Lord Hopton's advance, but to no purpose, and a Parliamentarian officer, who is thought to have been Colonel Edward Apsley, of Worminghurst, has left an interesting account of his adventures and capture at this period. It is too long for insertion here, but is given *in extenso* both by Mr. Blaauw and Mr. Hillier. Lord Hopton reached Arundel on Wednesday, December 6th. Clarendon tells us that the position was naturally a strong one, and that the somewhat antiquated fortifications were in good repair, the moat being both broad and deep. The garrison of fifty-five men, although not sufficiently numerous to hold out for any considerable period, was nevertheless strong enough to repel any sudden assault. But neither provisions nor ammunition, though often demanded, were abundant within the walls, and Captain Capcot had not expected so unwelcome an arrival. Accordingly, on Saturday, December 9th, 1643, being the third day after Lord Hopton's entry into Arundel, a threat of severity in case of assault was sufficient to effect the surrender of the castle. The besieging force was estimated at fully 2000 men. On December 7th the Committee at Lewes informed Parliament that the town of Arundel had been taken, and the castle besieged and in great danger, " whereupon, on December 9th, John Baker, of Mayfield, was appointed High Sheriff of Sussex, and the four associated counties of Kent, Sussex, Surrey, and Hampshire were ordered to try to relieve Arundel Castle, "to clear the County of Sussex," and to secure that county, consulting to that end with the Earl of Northumberland, Lieut. of Sussex. Some of the Parliamentarian garrison joined Lord Hopton, others were made prisoners, and the townsmen of Arundel, who favoured the Parliament, were severely dealt with. Sir Edward Ford was appointed Governor, with a garrison of above 200 men, provisions were collected, and the Rhodes ditch made, as well as an earthwork connecting the Swanbourne Lake with the works surrounding the Little Park. Lord Hopton, who had also left a garrison at Cowdray, and had been checked by Colonel Herbert Morley, at the Bramber Bridge, near Lewes, was only able to remain six days at Arundel Castle. The Committee of Safety wrote at once to the Earl of Essex, urging him to assist Sir W. Waller against the increasing Royalist forces in Hampshire and Sussex, and a contemporary journalist observes "no doubt the rot was in Hantshire as well as Sussex, for it came thence!" Waller's journey to London had a successful issue. He exaggerated the strength of Lord Hopton's army, and easily obtained all necessary supplies and reinforcements. The *True Informer* of December 9th, 1643, has the following :—" That renowned and unmatcheable engineere, Collonel Wems, Lieutenant-Generall of the Ordinance and Traine unto Sir William Waller, according to the desire and appointment of the House of Commons in Parliament, went down from London on Tuesday night last, December 5th, with waggons laden with leather pieces of ordinance, and much other ammunition, and is by this time at Farnham with Sir William Waller. These leather pieces are of very great use, and very easie and light of carriage. One horse may draw a piece, which will carry a bullet of a pounde and halfe weight, and doe execution very farre. This is the said Colonel's particular invention, and will be of very great service unto Sir William's army, especially for this winter season." These leather guns were afterwards captured at Cropredy Bridge, loaded with case shot. " 8000 from Kent, Sussex, and Surrey are in armes against the Cavaliers." We shall meet some of these Surrey and Sussex men before rising ere long. The City of London was now requested to allow " the longer stay of their forces," 500 men of the Windsor garrison were ordered to join Sir William Waller, the Kentish Committee wrote from Westerham to offer assistance, and Sussex was required immediately to pay 1080*l*. 5s. 5d., and to raise 125 horse.

Numerous Cavaliers of rank had taken refuge at Winchester, amongst whom we may mention Bishop Curle and Dr. Peter Heylin. The latter was Rector of Alresford, and had written a "History of the Reformation." The Presbyterians hated him for having arranged his church according to the late injunctions. Chillingworth, the clever author of " The Religion of Protestants." accompanied Lord Hopton to Arundel Castle, and was there left with the office of what we should call Commanding Royal Engineer.

The Parliamentarian regiments were recruited by means of impressment, voluntary enlistment, and also by allowing apprentices to count their time of military service as if it had been spent with their masters. But in this emergency the White and Yellow, two of the strongest regiments of the London Auxiliaries, were on December 13th, 1643, by consent of the City of London, which could re-call them at pleasure, ordered to march with all speed to Farnham ; officers and men not marching out were to be fined and imprisoned. Sir William Balfour, with 1000 horse, was detached from the army of the Earl of Essex and placed under the command of Sir William Waller, who at once repaired to Farnham, and speedily ascertaining that Lord Hopton's forces were quartered at too great distance from each other prepared to strike a decisive blow.

CHAPTER XVI.—COLONEL NORTON'S VICTORY AT ROMSEY—LORD CRAWFORD ASKS FOR SACK—SIR WILLIAM WALLER ATTACKS ALTON—THE CHURCH STORMED—DISPOSAL OF PRISONERS—WALLER'S MARCH TO ARUNDEL—SIEGE OF ARUNDEL CASTLE—SKIRMISH AT HAVANT—WARBLINGTON CASTLE—ARUNDEL CASTLE SURRENDERS—LORD CRAWFORD—TRACES OF THE CONFLICT.

Sir William Waller now determined to attack Lord Hopton's scattered forces in two places at once, " as beating up of quarters was his master piece." Colonel Norton, the " Idle Dick" of Cromwell, and now Governor of Southampton, received orders which he was not slow to execute. His old friend and comrade, Captain Francis St. Barbe, of Broadlands, had been slain in the first battle of Newbury, on the 20th of the preceding September, but he had as his subordinates Sergeant-Major (or Major) Murford, of whom frequent mention has already been made, and Captain Bowen. Major Murford's company was 130 strong, whilst that of Captain Bowen mustered 96. Another account says Norton had less than 220 men. An attack was planned upon the town of Romsey, which was then garrisoned by Col. Bennet's regiment of horse, variously estimated to be both 130 and 200 strong, and a regiment of foot commanded by Colonel Courtney, said to number 300, with a view of keeping in check the Parliamentarian garrison, which was ordered on Tuesday, November 29th, 1642, to be established at Southampton. Sir Humphrey Bennet was, says Mr. Money, one of the Bennets of Pythouse, Wilts. Colonel Thomas Bennet was Prince Rupert's Secretary, and the family were staunch adherents to the Royal cause. Sir Humphrey Bennet himself was High Sheriff of Southampton, and commanded a brigade of horse at the second battle of Newbury, which was fought on Saturday, 26th October, 1644. On this occasion his regiment consisted of nine troops, almost full, but having only two colours. We learn from a letter written at Southampton, on December 13th, that Colonel Norton's force left that town at three o'clock on the morning of December 12th. The forlorn hope was led by Lieutenant Terry, the first division by Sergeant-Major Murford, the main body by Colonel Norton, whilst Captain Bowen, with his men divided into two parties, brought up the rear. In this order they marched in silence to Romsey, which was reached about an hour after daybreak, whereupon the forlorn hope was sent to force its way over a bridge into the town. Major Murford, with some of his men, "fell upon their strong traverse, which was presently quitted by their sentinels." He at once followed up his success, fought his way into the town, capturing the main guard, whereupon the Cavaliers threw down their arms and fled. Murford then entered several houses, and secured various prisoners, one of whom was "Captain Lieutenant Norton, brother to Colonel Norton, and a far honester man than himself." Seven Cavaliers were killed in the market-place, two of whom were captains. "Murford hath one of their commissions." Colonel Norton then entered the town with the main body of his forces, and the Cavaliers fled, most of them probably taking the direction of Winchester. The prisoners, either 25 or 40 in number, included three captains, two lieutenants, one corporal, and several gentlemen. Nearly two hundred horses, numerous arms, and the magazines were captured. Many muskets were broken by the victors, who also threw several barrels of powder into the river, and the triumphant Roundheads returned unmolested to Southampton. On the same night a party of thirty men sent from Southampton to Romsey brought back some plunder without opposition, and on the following day there was a solemn thanksgiving for Colonel Norton's success at Southampton.

The news of this disaster was but a sad welcome to Lord Hopton, who returned to Winchester from Arundel on the evening of December 26th, but more doleful tidings still were to follow. It will doubtless be remembered that Lord Crawford had taken post at Alton. Our old friend Lieutenant Archer says on Friday, December 1st, 1643, "towards the evening intelligence came that the Lord Crawford was come to Alton with a regiment of horse and another of foot, and began to fortify that town with all the speed he could, and that Sir Ralph Hopton had quartered many of his men at Alresford and Petersfield, which was done in policy to keep our forces from Winchester, while their main body got into Sussex and Kent, at which time they took Arundel Castle, or within a day after." The infantry regiment here referred to was largely composed of Welshmen and Irishmen, and had been recently sent from the garrison of Wallingford to reinforce Lord Hopton. Clarendon says that it was about 500 strong, but the epitaph of its Colonel states that it was not less than 1300. It was under the command of Colonel John Bolle, second son of Sir John Bolle, who died in 1606. He was an ancestor of the present Warden of Winchester College, to whom I am indebted for much information concerning him. This gallant soldier was a brother of Sir Charles Bolle, of Louth Hall, in Lincolnshire, who on one occasion concealed himself beneath the arch of a bridge near the gaol at Louth, whilst the enemy's troopers galloped unsuspectingly above his head. He raised a regiment amongst his tenants for the King, and gave the command of it to his brother John.

Colonel John Bolle did great deeds at Edgehill and other places at the head of his regiment, whose ranks, sadly thinned by the ravages of war and disease, seem to have been afterwards filled with Welsh and Irish recruits.

On the evening of Saturday, Dec. 9th, most of Waller's men were drawn up in Farnham Park, and a party was that night sent towards Alton, which beat up Lord Crawford's quarters, and afterwards fell back upon Farnham. But more stirring work was at hand.

An attack in force upon Alton having been decided upon, Lieut. Archer says, "Tuesday, Dec. 12th, most of our men went presently into the town (Farnham) to refresh and prepare themselves for the service, where, although they before gave their general consent, many of them stayed behind, and went not with their colours. Nevertheless we advanced without them."

During the morning hours of this memorable 12th of December Lord Crawford had sent a messenger to Farnham, asking Sir William Waller to send him to Alton a runlet of sack, promising to send a fat ox in exchange." Our worthy Sir William sent in a loving compliment to the Lord Crawford half a hogshead of sack, who, mistrusting the matter and the messenger, caused the messenger and divers others to taste thereof, and then caused it to be carefully laid by for his own drinking." Sir William Waller demanded the promised ox, whereupon Lord Crawford replied that he would bring it himself. Waller "fails not at nightfall to go in search of his ox, and, instead of a beast, brought away 565 prisoners." His men, 5000 in number, mustered without beat of drum in the park at Farnham, and commenced their march about seven o'clock in the evening, going in the direction of Basing House. But after advancing about two miles the cavalry halted for an hour upon a heath between Crondall and Farnham, and awaited the arrival of the infantry, and thus reinforced continued their march, which was favoured by the hard frost, which at this time lasted for six weeks without intermission. Lieut. Elias Archer says: "But having marched that way about two miles we returned to the left." Another eye-witness says that the whole force marched as if towards Basing until one o'clock in the morning, and then "faced south towards Alton between the hills." Lieut. Archer says that they "in a remote way between the wood and hills marched beyond Alton, and about nine o'clock on Wednesday morning, December 13th, came upon the west side of the town, where we had both the wind and hill to friend." Sir William Waller's scouts were vigilant, so that his main force arrived without attracting observation. "Mercurius Aulicus" admits that the Cavalier scouts had concentrated their attention on the main road leading from Farnham to Alton, not expecting an attack from any other quarter. Some of Sir William's scouts were captured, but others brought information that Lord Crawford was quartered in the town with between 300 and 500 horse, in addition to the infantry regiment of Colonel John Bolle. Scarcely had they made their report before Lord Crawford and his troopers were both seen and heard galloping at speed out of the town towards Winchester, having promised their comrades of the infantry that they would speedily return with reinforcements. They quitted Alton on the eastern side, but being unexpectedly headed back by the Parliamentarian horse, they galloped back through the town, and rode to the southward direct for Winchester, whilst in their rear, now sabering one, now capturing another, rode the pursuing mail-clad squadrons of Sir Arthur Haslerig, known as "Lobsters," from their iron shells, and, says the stern Puritan chronicler, "our Foot made the woods ring with a shout." Three or four Cavaliers were slain in the pursuit, which was followed for about half a mile through narrow lanes, and about 30 horses and some prisoners were taken by Sir Arthur's men, who then returned and blocked up all the entrances to the town, leaving Lord Crawford and his men to make the best of their way to Winchester.

Nor were the infantry idle meanwhile. Lieut. Archer says, "Then Sir William's own regiment of foot, Sir Arthur Haslerig's five companies, and five companies of Kentishmen went on upon the north and north-west side, and gave the first onset by lining of hedges and the like, but could not as yet come to any perfect execution, in respect that our London Regiments were not come in sight of the enemy, and therefore they bent all their force against those three regiments, and lined divers houses with musqueteers, especially one great brick house near the church was full, out of which windows they fired very fast, and might have done great prejudice to those men, but that when our train of artillery came towards the foot of the hill they made certain shot, which took place upon that house, and so forced them to forsake it. In the meantime our London regiments and four companies that belong to Farnham Castle came down the hill; then the Red Regiment and the Green coats and the four companies of Farnham Castle, set upon a half moon and a breast work, which the enemy had managed, and from which they fired very hot and desperately till the Green Auxiliaries marched on the other side of a little river into the town with their colours flying, and being in the wind of the enemy, fired a little thatched house, and so blinded them that this regiment marched forwards, and coming in part behind the works, fired upon them, so that they were forced to forsake the said half-moon and breast work, which they had no sooner left but presently the Green-coats and part of the musqueteers of the Red, and our Yellow regiment entered, while the rest of our regiment marched into the town with their colours flying." Another eye-witness, already referred to, says that the infantry advanced as far as the Market Place.

Lieutenant Archer continues: "Now was the enemy constrained to betake himself and all his forces to the church, churchyard, and one great work on the north side of the church, all which they kept near upon two hours very stontly, and, having made scaffolds in the church to fire out of the windows, fired very thick from every place."

The other account says that the Cavaliers, being all musketeers, retired to the works near the church, "where they had double trenches and a half-moon." The church and a barn close by were their "chiefest refuge;" and there was "a very hot fight near two hours by reason of a malignant, who willingly fired his own barn and other houses." The smoke caused much annoyance to the assailants, who lost about three men "by reason of which smoke." The battle word of the Cavaliers was "Charles," that of their opponents being "Truth and Victory."

The fight continued, says Lieutenant Archer, "till divers soldiers of our regiment and the Red Regiment fired very thick upon the southeast of the churchyard, and so forced them to forsake that part of the wall, leaving their muskets standing upright, the muzzles whereof appeared above the wall as if some of the men had still lyn there in ambush, and our men seeing nobody appear to use those muskets, concluded that the men were gone and consulted among themselves to enter two or three files of musqueteers, promising Richard Guy, one of my captain sergeants, who was the first that entered the churchyard, to follow him if he would lead them. Whereupon he advanced, and coming within the churchyard door, and seeing most of the Cavaliers firing at our men from the south and west part of the churchyard, looked behind him for the men which promised to follow him, and there was only one musqueteer with him."

"Nevertheless, he, flourishing his sword, told them if they would come the churchyard was their own; then Symon Hutchinson, one of Lieutenant-Colonel Willoughbie's sergeants, forced the musqueteers, and brought them up himself. Immediately upon this one of the sergeants of the Red Regiment, whose name I know not, and, therefore, cannot nominate him as his worth deserves, brought in another division of musqueteers, who, together with those which were there before, caused the enemies' forces to betake themselves towards the church for safeguard, but our men followed them so close with their halberts, swords, and musket stocks that they drove them beyond the church door, and slew about ten or twelve of them, and forced the rest to a very distracted retreat. Which, when the others saw who were in the great work on the north side of the churchyard, they left the work, and came, thinking to help their fellows, and, coming in a disorderly manner to the south-west corner of the church, with their pikes in the rear (who furiously charged on in as disorderly a manner as the rest led them), their front was forced back upon their own pikes, which hurt and wounded many of the men, and brake the pikes in pieces. By this time the churchyard was full of our men, laying about them stoutly with halberts, swords, and musket-stocks, while some threw hand granadoes in at the church windows, others attempting to enter the church, being led on by Sergeant-Major Shambrooke, a man whose worth and valour envy cannot stain, who in the entrance received a shot in the thigh, whereof he is very ill." Major Shambrooke is elsewhere said to have been wounded in the thigh in the church, by the pistol of a prisoner, to whom he had given quarter. "Great hopes there is of his speedy recovery." An entry having been forced into the church, the exterior and interior of which still bear many a bullet mark, Colonel Bolle declared with an oath that he would "run his sword through the heart of him which first called for quarter." Clarendon says that he hoped to defend the church " for so many hours that relief might be sent to him, but he had not time to barricade the doors; so that the enemy entered almost as soon, and after a short resistance, in which many were killed, the soldiers, overpowered, threw down their arms, and asked quarter, which was likewise offered to the Colonel, who refused it, and valiantly defended himself, till, with the death of two or three of the assailants, he was killed in the place, his enemies giving him a testimony of great courage and resolution." According to a family tradition the Colonel was shot in the pulpit, but, according to "Mercurius Aulicus," he was knocked on the head with the butt end of a musket. The *Weekly Account* of Dec. 2 th, 1643, says, "I am certainly informed there were not above fifteen pieces found in the pocket of Colonel Bolles, who, until he fell himself, did bravely encourage and lead on his soldiers."

This gallant soldier's epitaph is inscribed on two brasses, one of which is affixed to a pillar near Bishop Morley's monument in Winchester Cathedral, and the other is in Alton Church. It states that the strength of his regiment was 1300, and that he took refuge in Alton Church with about 80 of his men; that the fight lasted six or seven hours, and that Colonel Bolles killed six or seven of his assailants before he was slain, together with sixty of his men. The author of this epitaph, who claimed kinship to the gallant Colonel, erroneously stated the date of Alton Fight as 1641, instead of 1643, and it has been justly remarked " As no hero was ever perhaps more deserving of an honourable commendation to posterity so never perhaps was there an epitaph more devoid of grammar and orthography than that which is here erected to his memory." It thus concludes:

"His Gratious Soueraigne, hearing of his death, gave him his high Commendation in ys pationate expression:—

Bring me a Mourning Scarffe, I have Lost one of the best
Commanders in this Kingdome.
Alton will tell you of that famous Fight
Which ys man made, and bade this World good night.
His Vertious Life fear'd not Mortality,
His Body must, his Vertues cannot die,
Because his Blood was there so nobly spent,
This is his Tombe; that Church his Monument.
Ricardus Boles, Wiltoniensis in Art. Mag.
Composuit Posuit que Dolens.
An. Dm. 1689."

According to Lieutenant Archer, "He being slain, they generally yielded and desired quarter, except some desperate villains which refused quarter, who were slain in the church, and some others of them wounded, who afterwards were granted quarter upon their request." The Lieutenant says that Waller's loss was "not above eight or nine at the most, besides what were wounded, and I conceive their loss of men to be about fifty or sixty, most of which were slain in the church and churchyard after we had entered." Other accounts say that the Cavaliers had 40 or 100 killed, and that Waller lost only five killed, five or fifteen wounded, "and about six scorched with powder by reason of their own negligence." "Mercurius Aulicus" says that "27 of the King's men fell at Alton, and that only 3 0 were made prisoners, whilst Waller had 200 men killed in the church and churchyard!"

Master Elias Archer says that when all resistance was at an end the prisoners who had been taken in and about the church were placed in a large barn "which joyned to the churchyard, and after the church was cleared of our men, they were all put into the church, and the rest which were taken in several houses in the town were put to them, and there they were coupled together and brought to Farnham, the number of them being 875, amongst whom were about fifty commanders besides horsemen, which were taken in pursuit of the Lord Crawford, who ran away from the town as soon as we gave the first assault upon their works." Archer thinks that Waller's cavalry " made our number of prisoners near 1100, many of those prisoners being men of considerable respect in the King's army." Another account says that there were 700 prisoners taken in the church, nearly 100 in the barn, near the churchyard, and more than 100 in the field with, "divers Irish men and women," and significantly adds that "there was great wrath against the Irish." Another writer gives the number of prisoners as 760. From 100 to 200 horses were captured, and 1000 arms, most of which were given to certain auxiliaries from Kent, who soon afterwards joined Sir William Waller, armed only with clubs. Amongst the prisoners were one Colonel, one Lieut.-Colonel, one Major, and 13 Captains. Three cornets were taken, one having upon it the letters "C. P." and the Prince of Wales's arms, another with the arms of the Earl of Strafford, together "with divers other colours hid in the church." Waller at once employed the inhabitants of Alton to "slight," or demolish the fortifications which had been constructed in and about the town by the Cavaliers. The prisoners were fastened together in couples with match, "and are now in Farnham Church and Castle, where they may hear better doctrine than they have heard at Oxford or amongst the Irish rebels."

Some of Waller's west country recruits are said to have fought up to their knees in dirt. The *Weekly Account* says, with reference to the Cavaliers, "I cannot learn of any store of money they had," but another writer asserts that the victors took much spoil "insomuch that divers of our soldiers strutted along with their hands full of gold and silver, saying " Look here, boys, when was it thus with me before!" They also made prize of good arms and clothes.

Lord Crawford left his hat and cloak behind him at Alton, and owed his escape to the speed of his horse. It will be remembered that he had on the previous day received with due tasting precautions a present of some wine from Sir William Waller. This he also left behind him in his flight, and it was ever afterwards remembered against him that he "left his sack at Alton. By reason of this unexpected company he was struck with a panic fear, and left the wine without a compliment for Sir William Waller's own drinking, who was the right owner thereof, whose soldiers wanted no tasters of the same !"

The following characteristic letters from Hopton and Crawford were read in the House of Commons on Monday, December 18th, together with a letter from Sir William Waller, whose first messenger, announcing his victory, had reached London on December 13th :—

" To Sir W. Waller.—Sir,—I hope your gaining of Alton cost you dear. It was your lot to drinke of your own sack, which I never intended to have left for you. I pray you favour me so much as to send me my owne chirurgion, and upon my honour I will send you a person suitable to his exchange. Sir, your servant.
CRAFORD."

" To Sir W. Waller.—Sir,—This is the first evident ill successe I have had. I must acknowledge that I have lost many brave and gallant men. I desire you, if Colonell Bolles be alive, to propound a fit exchange ; if dead, that you will send me his corps. I pray you sende me a list of such prisoners as you have, that such choice men as they are may not continue long unredeemed. God give a sudden stop to this issue of English blood, which is the desire, Sir, of your faithfull friend to serve you,

Winton, 16th Dec. RALPH HOPTON."

Clarendon adds—"The Lord Hopton sustained the loss of that regiment with extraordinary trouble of mind, and as a wound that would bleed inward; and therefore was the more inflamed with desire of a battle with Waller to make even all accounts." A little more patience, my Lord Hopton, and your wish shall be fully gratified.

It was noticed that Alton was taken at the very time when the Cavaliers at Oxford were making "bon-fyers with much triumph" for the death of Pym.

On Friday, December 15th, Sir Arthur Haslerig and Sir Gilbert Gerard were ordered by the House of Commons "to prepare a letter to be written to Sir William Waller to acknowledge the great service he has done, and how it has pleased God to bless it with good success." The House thanked the officers and commanders, including those belonging to the city, for their valour and good service, and wished "to encourage them in the perseverance."

One thousand horse-shoes and eight thousand nails were ordered to be issued from store on payment to Sir William Waller. Cavalry shoeing smiths now use only six nails per shoe, whilst civilian smiths still use eight. Three hundred muskets, bastard muskets, and calivers (the caliver was a lighter kind of musket), three hundred swords, one thousand clubs, fifty barrels of powder, and four tons of match, the two last items being drawn from the Navy stores, were to be sent to Waller's army, and 20*l* was to be spent on arms and saddles for Capt Savile's troop. About 40 prisoners were taken by Waller during the week following the Alton fight, and were secured with their comrades in Farnham Church and Castle. On the third day they were offered freedom on condition of taking the Covenant and engaging to serve the Parliament. A number of them, variously stated as being 300, 500, and 600, accepted these terms, took the Covenant in the chancel of Farnham Church, and during the following week proved the groundlessness of the doubts which were freely expressed as to their fidelity by a fierce assault upon their former comrades at Arundel. About 500 others, many of whom were Irishmen, refused these offered terms, and were detained in custody.

On Monday, December 18th, the Committee of Safety was directed to dispose of the prisoners taken at Alton, "and it any be Irish rebels, to consider what is fit to be done with them." The Committee for Prisoners was to decide about those who were not exchanged or who refused to take the Covenant. The London trained bands now marched homewards, and the prisoners, tied together with match, were brought up to town, some being consigned to the custody of each regiment.

On Tuesday, December 19th, the trained bands, with their captives, halted at Hammersmith, and on the following day 57 officers, 330 soldiers, and four servants to the principal officers were marched under a strong guard to the Royal Exchange. Ten principal officers and forty others were committed to Lord Petre's house, in Aldersgate-street, 20 were sent to the Gatehouse, 50 to the Marshalsea, 30 to Winchester House, 50 to Lambeth House, 5 to the Fleet, 40 to Bridewell, 40 to Maiden Lane, 30 to London House, 20 to Ely House. Thirty-two others were lying sick and wounded at Farnham and Alton, and were said to be well cared for. On the same day the House of Commons voted that a sum of 26*l*., realised by the sale of some raw hides which had been seized on their way to the Mayor of Reading, should be paid "to a lieutenant in Sir Arthur Haselrigge's regiment that hath lost a leg in the service at Alton."

Lady Butler, a well-known courtesan, who often appeared in public clad in male attire, on hearing that her paramour, Sir Giles Porter, had been wounded at Alton, shot herself with a pistol. The chronicler adds, "Qualis vita, finis ita. As was her life, so was her end!"

Thus did Lord Crawford "leave his sack at Alton!"

There must have been sad hearts at Basing when news arrived of the disaster at Alton, in the immediate neighbourhood. But misfortunes never come singly, and a more grievous blow was ere long to be given to the Royal cause.

On Friday, December 15th, the newspapers in London stated that the King had marched from Oxford to Reading, and that the Prince's own regiment, which had lost a cornet at Alton, had brought from Basing much money "in trunks iron chests, boxes, and the like," much plate having been there deposited in safe keeping together with "crucifixes, candlesticks, jewels, and Popish trinkets," a large proportion of which was promptly sent to the Mint established in loyal Oxford during these troublous years.

The Committee of Safety had meanwhile been urging the Earl of Essex to come nearer to Sir William Waller, or at any rate to send him some infantry, "or otherwise he will not be able to prosecute this advantage which he has now gotten, for the King's forces increase in Hampshire and Sussex, and divers new regiments are raising there, which would be very prejudicial to the public, unless presently prevented," and a newswriter observes "No doubt the rot was in Hantshire as well as in Sussex, for it came thence." The Earl of Essex grumbled on December 14th, and four days later the Committee of Safety informed him that Prince Rupert was marching to join Lord Hopton, with a view to forcing Waller to an engagement with 6000 horse and foot, desiring him to advance to Windsor, or to go to the assistance of Sir William Waller. Another account says that Rupert was marching southwards from Northamptonshire, and had with him ten guns, in addition to his cavalry and infantry.

This order of the Committee was confirmed by the Parliament on December 20th, Sir William Waller having gone towards Arundel, leaving a garrison at Farnham, "and that Sir Ralph Hopton, as the Houses are informed, hath drawn all the forces he can make towards Basing."

On Monday, December 18th, also, measures were taken to reinforce Waller, as the King was drawing all his forces towards him. 500l. was ordered to be spent "for the better enabling and encouraging 500 men to march to Waller from Windsor," 500 men of the city regiments being sent to supply their place.

On December 20th the answer of the Earl of Essex was read in Parliament. It was to the effect that he considered Sir William Waller to be in no great danger, since he had such a strong base of operations as Farnham, which had lately been regularly fortified, and "that the enemy, especially at this season of the year, will not be able to do him any harm;" that he was, nevertheless, sending to Sir William Waller Colonel Behre with nearly 600 horse, "and so well commanded" that they will easily be able to face 1000 Cavaliers. This letter was written at St. Albans on December 18th, 1643. Sir William Waller was, however, perfectly capable of securing his own safety, and of this he speedily gave proof.

On December 27th the sum of 300l. was ordered to be spent in purchasing arms and warlike stores for the Parliamentarian garrison at Southampton, and Ludlow records in his Memoirs that just before the commencement of the siege of Wardour Castle, of which he was the Governor, he went to Southampton to buy all the ammunition which Colonel Norton could spare. On Saturday, December 23rd, 1643, the Governor of Poole received permission to compound with the prisoners whom he had taken at Dorchester, "and also with Mr. Wyatt, that endeavoured to betray Poole." The money thus realised was to be expended upon the defences of Poole.

"Mercurius Aulicus" of December 25th has preserved the following warrant sent to the tenants of the Marquis of Winchester by Col. Jones, the Governor of Farnham Castle :—

"These are to give you notice, in regard you have made such a return to my warrant, issued out to the High Constable of your Hundred, that except you send into Farnham Castle, by Monday next, without further delay, the several proportions of wheat, malt, barley, and other things assessed and charged upon you, according to the said warrant, you are to expect the same penalty with which the Marquesse of Winchester threatens you, there being more reason that you should serve a Protestant before a Papist. Given under my hand at Farnham Castle, the 8 day of Novemb., 1643.

SAMUEL JONES, Collon.

To the Tythingman of Sherfield."

On which the journalist satirically remarks, "Yes, Master Jones, wee'l call you Master Colonel when you know how to spell the word; it is most reasonable such a personage as yourself should be served before the Lord Marquesse of Winchester, especially of such as are his Lordship's tenants." The women of England found that the long duration of the war had a very depressing effect upon the matrimonial market, and in the *Harleian Miscellany* are three witty but coarsely worded petitions purporting to emanate from the maidens, wives, and widows of the kingdom, urging on the Parliament the desirability of a permanent and lasting peace. The maidens one and all express their eagerness to marry at once, if only the men would return from the wars; the wives deplore the absence of their husbands; and the widows unanimously express their determination to marry at the least once more, as soon as the war is over. As it is now, so was it then. But one soldier's wife, Susan Rodway by name, lonely at home, with a sick chil 1 to care for, wrote a letter to her husband, which is here transcribed, with the original spelling, as some readers may like to see how soldiers' wives wrote two centuri s ago:—

"Most deare and loving husbane, my king love —I remember unto you, hoping that you are in good helth, as I ame at the writting heareof. My little Willie have bene sicke this forknight. I pray you to come whome ife yone cane cum saffly. I doo murfull that I cannot heere from you ass well other nayberes do. I do desiere to heere from you as soone as youe cane. I pray youe to send me word when youe doo thenke youe shalt returne. You doe not consider I ame a lone woemane; I thought you woald never have leave me thuse long togeder, so I rest evere praying for your saveso returne,

Your loving wife,
SUSAN RODWAY,
Ever praying for you tell deth I depart.

To my very loving husbane, Robert Rodway, a traine soudare in the Red Reggiment, under the command of Captaine Warrin. Deliver this with spide, I pray youe."

Alas! poor Susan! Your letter, duly entrusted to "Robert Lewington, the Hampshire carrier," was intercepted by a lieutenant of Lord Hopton's army, and never reached your husband's hands. Forwarded to Oxford, it, after some weeks' delay, was published for the information of the whole kingdom in the columns of "Mercurius Aulicus." And it is much to be feared that there was an ominous reason for your husband's long silence, for Captain Warren led on his men as a forlorn hope during one of the fiercest assaults at Basing House, in Nov., 1643, and your dearly loved Robert may even then have been sleeping in a soldier's grave beneath the stately ramparts of "Loyalty House." We may wonder too what was the fate of "Little Willie," who "have heene sicke this forknight," about whom his mother is so anxious! But a truce to moralising.

Sir Edward Ford had been left by Lord Hopton in command at Arundel Castle, and had under him more than 200 men and "many good officers, who desired or were very willing to stay there, as a place very favourable for the levies of men which they all intended, and it may be that the more remained there out of the weariness and fatigue of their late marches, and that they might spend the rest of the winter with better accommodation." So says Clarendon, and continues: "The Governor was a man of honesty and courage. but unacquainted with that affair, having no other experience in war than what he had learned since these troubles. The officers were many without command; many whereof were of natures not easy to be governed, nor like to conform themselves to such strict rules as the condition of the place required, or to use that industry as the exigence they were like to be in made necessary." Amongst them was "Colonel Bamford, an Irishman, though he called himself Bamfield; who, being a man of wit and parts, applied all his faculties to improve the faction, to which they were all naturally inclined, with a hope to make himself Governor." Lord Hopton also left in the castle the Rev. Dr. William Chillingworth, a native of Oxford, and a Fellow of Trinity College in that University. He was a very distinguished controversialist, and was the author of the well-known "Safe Way to Salvation, or the Religion of Protestants." Dr. Calamy, quoted in "Dallaway's Arundel," says: "In the beginning of the war he was with the Earl of Essex, and when with him in Cornwall, he showed himself a person of great strength and undaunted courage. His commands were as readily obeyed by any colonel in that army as the General's own. He invented at the siege of Gloucester engines after the manner of the Roman 'testudines cum pluteis,' which ran upon cart wheels, with a blind or planks musket proof, and holes for four musketeers to play out of, placed upon the axletree, and carrying a bridge before it. The wheels were to fall into the ditch, and the bridge to rest upon the town's breastwork, so making several complete bridges to enter the city." At Arundel Castle he had under his charge two small guns, called "murderers," the only ones mounted on the works. "Some say that he was actively engaged during the siege in constructing machines after the Roman method, and that the vexation arising from their failure greatly hastened his death. He was a good logician, and used his logic to some purpose in theology; but he left out an important consideration in his military elenchus when he forgot that the Romans did not employ "villainous saltpetre" in their sieges." Lord Hopton laid in a good store of provisions, and left these orders with th· garrison, "In the first place, setting all other things aside, to draw in store of provisions of all kinds, both for the numbers they were already and for such as would probably in a short time be added to them; all which from the great plenty that country then abounded with was very easy to have been done." But Sir William Waller "found that garrison as unprovided as he could wish. For instead of increasing the magazine of victual by supplies from the country, they had spent much of that store which the Lord Hopton had provided." Sir William Waller having determined to attempt the recovery of Arundel Castle, the City of London was requested "to allow the longer stay of their forces;" five hundred men of the Windsor garrison were, as we have seen, ordered to join him; the Kentish Committee wrote from Westerham to offer assistance, and Sussex was required to pay immediately 1080*l.* 5s. 5d., and to raise 125 horse.

And now, as Mr. Gordon tells us, Sir William Waller marched in pursuit of the hitherto victorious Cavaliers, with a larger army than had entered Sussex since the battles of Senlac and Lewes. From his own letter we learn that he marched from Farnham on Sunday, December 17th, 1643, and a letter from one of his officers, preserved by Mr. Gordon, which originally appeared in the "Mercurius Civicus" of Dec. 21st, of that year, states that the hour of departure was "about two of the clock in the afternoon, marching towards Hazleworth (Waller himself says Haslemere), our noble general seeming to go another way, to amaze the Papists and malignants, and the better to prevent intelligence, and about midnight came with his whole army to the said town, where the rendezvous was that night. Monday sunrising, his honour wheeled about towards Medhurst, where my Lord Mountacute's (Montague) house is (Cowdray), which said lord is a known and profest Papist." Sir William Waller, writing from Arundel, on Friday, Dec. 22nd, said that the garrison of Cowdray consisted of four troops of Cavalier horse and 100 infantry. "I determined to give them the good night." Accordingly, two regiments of cavalry were sent to block up the various roads in the neighbourhood, "but they were too nimble for me, and escaped hither, where I overtook them on Tuesday night." The officer continues, "The house is now possest by the Parliament forces, where we staid that night, and furnished the said castle, for indeed it may well be called so in regard of the strength thereof, with all necessaries for defence to awe the Papists and malignants, wherewith the said town is much infested and infected. Tuesday morning we marched from Medhurst, sending out a party of horse to Petworth, having thought to surprise the enemy there, but they fled before our success. Hopton and the great ones to Winchester, and the rest to Arundel with bag and baggage; all that night we lay on a heath, within a mile of Arundel." The Parliament ordered the goods plundered at Cowdray to be brought to London and "sold to the best value." Other contemporary accounts say that Lord Hopton evacuated Petersfield and Alresford in great haste, leaving many arms behind him at the former place. Having concentrated his forces at Winchester, he was "entrenching apace," 1000 men being daily employed as a fatigue party. Forced labour was also exacted from the country people, and Lord Hopton was summoning all men between the ages of sixteen and sixty to join his standard. Five or six who refused to take service under him were hanged at Salisbury, as were also certain others in various places.

Mr. Gordon says, "The march of the main body of Sir William Waller's army over Blackdown Hill must have been an imposing sight, as it passed the friendly mansion of the Yaldens, and it is strange that no local records or traditions remain concerning it. Probably some detachments went south, and leapt upon the Sussex Weald by the bowery slopes of Hollycombe and Milland. Medhurst (*i.e.*, Midhurst, still so called by our peasants, who never say Mi*d*hurst) found itself the centre of a flood of men on that Monday night, and Cowdray Park must have been full. Would that some of the old trees now standing could tell us of the camp fires that they saw that December night."

Meanwhile it was reported in London that Colonel Norton had surprised and taken 200 Cavalier horse, who were quartered at Twyford, about three miles from Winchester. Sir William

Courtney, of Brambridge, a Cavalier, afterwards paid a fine of 25*l*. 3s. 4d. as a composition for his estate. Colonel Norton was the son-in-law of Sir Walter Erle, a staunch adherent of the Parliament, and, according to Mercurius Aulicus, of Wednesday, August 16th, 1643, his mother was as devoted as himself to the Puritan cause. "Mercurius" is, as usual, uncomplimentary, but journalistic satire is by no means of modern origin:—

"It was also signified from thence (Portsmouth) that the Lady Norton, mother to that most noble Colonel who hath done such wonders of late days, and governess for the present of the town of Portsmouth, for the Committee dare do nothing without her advice, was very busily employed in making some new works about Portsey Bridge; and was not only every day in person amongst the workmen, whom she encouraged much by her presence, but brought with her also with her every day 30 or 40 maids and women in a cart (they may live to be so coached hereafter) to dig and labour in the trenches. To the great honour of her sex, of her person more, who in a short time will grow as able to command-in-chief as the good Lady Waller to possess the pulpit. It was further signified from thence that the Committee by her direction had caused a dungeon to be made there as dark as hell, that if the liberty of the subject should be laid up there nobody should have hope to find it, intended for such malefactors, as it now appears, who either do refuse to take the new oath or to pay their taxes, or otherwise shall show any good affections to his sacred Majesty."

On Wednesday, December 20th, 1643, the 17 days' siege of Arundel Castle commenced. Mr. Blaauw, Mr. Hillier, Mr. Dallaway, Mr. Gordon, and others have treated this subject with much care, and it is only necessary here to rapidly sketch the course of events, with due gratitude to those who have thus facilitated our task.

From a letter written by Daniel Border, from Arundel, on January 9th, 1644, "to a gentleman dwelling in Mugwell-street," it appears that Sir William Waller's chief engineer was captured by the garrison. From the account given by "Mercurius Aulicus," it seems that Waller must have despatched a reconnoitring party to Arundel, on Tuesday, December 19th, in advance of his army. "Just as Sir William Waller approached Arundel Castle the Governor had taken in more ammunition and match from Weymouth, who, going up to the castle, caused a house to be fired. Instantly there came staring four or five rebel commanders, and were seized by the garrison soldiers, who being asked why they came hither, answered that Sir William Waller bade them fall on where they saw fire. Soon after this a barn was fired, and eight more were taken in the same manner; one of them they call 'the devil with one leg,' a famous engineer, but he was too busy with the fire."

At early dawn on the morning of Wednesday, December 20th, Sir William Waller surveyed the enemy's position, and says that he speedily found a place " to flank their line with our ordnance. We fell on upon the north side of the works, which we did so scour a woody hill in the park on the west side of the pond with our pieces, that we made it too hot for them." Another account says that an attack on the north-west and south-west of Arundel commenced at eight o'clock in the morning. The encouraged assailants at once stormed a very strong new retrenchment, probably constructed by Lord Hopton " from the town gate down to the aforesaid pond by the mill." Another division simultaneously " forced a very strong double work in a narrow passage by the mill." The outworks, together with some 80 prisoners, were taken after about half an hour's fighting, and about ten o'clock the Cavalier horse made " a brave sally," but were repulsed. The storming party " beat them into the castle, and entered the first gate with them; the second they made good and barricaded, and there they are welcome." A forlorn hope was then ordered to scour the streets, and captured a captain, a lieutenant, and several other prisoners. Certain townsmen having taken refuge in the Church of St. Nicholas, preparations were made to smoke them out, whereupon they speedily surrendered at discretion. The struggle had been severe though brief, and the beleaguered garrison, which Waller knew to be in great want of supplies, kept up a brisk fire of musketry from the castle, but were not able to command any considerable portion of the town. Only three or four men are said to have been killed whilst entering the town, but one man was wounded in the thigh upon the bridge, and Captain Butler received a shot in the holster as he rode over The number of wounded was not large, but included Lieut.-Colonel Burcher, wounded in the

THE SIEGE CONTINUES.

stomach. He, however, speedily recovered. Lieut.-Colonel Ramsay, who was one of the first to enter the town, "whilst casting his eye towards the castle, was unfortunately slain with a musket bullet from thence; he was interred on the following Saturday, six trumpeters going before the corpse with a mournful sound, his sergeant-major, to whom his place fell, following, and then all the officers of his regiment." The besieged hoisted a red flag of defiance, for, says Whitelock, "The Earl of Essex's colours were a deep yellow; others setting up another colour were held malignants, and ill-affected to the Parliament's cause. So small a thing is taken notice of in the jealousies of war!"

The prisoners taken at Alton, and who had joined Sir William Waller here, proved their fidelity by a vigorous attack upon their former comrades, and great praise was bestowed upon the blue-coats, who ran up the enemy's works, and beat them off with the butt-ends of their muskets. One of Waller's men, actuated either by anger or treachery, tried to shoot him, but his musket missed fire, and the would-be assassin was hanged without delay. Sir William Waller says, "I am very weak in foot, and my horse so hacknied out that they are ready to lie down under us. I expect Colonel Bayne here this day, and Colonel Morley." The first-named officer was, it will be remembered, bringing up the cavalry reinforcement, 600 strong, sent to Waller by the Earl of Essex. That night most of Waller's infantry were quartered in the town of Arundel, whilst a regiment of cavalry was on the alert to check any attempt to relieve the castle.

On Thursday, December 21st, Colonel Morley arrived with his regiment, and some of the adherents of the Parliament in the neighbourhood, hearing of scarcity in Waller's army, sent in as a present six loads of provisions, an example which was speedily followed by others. The besieged refused either to give or to take quarter, and the long frost, which had aided the operations alike of Hopton and of Waller, at last ended in a thaw. Jacob Travers, writing from the army, says that the weather was cold and the nights long, and that the soldiers were exposed to "high winds and extraordinary showers of rain." In order to check the fire of musketry from the castle, Major Bodley, "perceiving divers in the castle look forth in a balcony," posted himself and twelve musketeers "in a private place of advantage," and by a well directed volley "slow and wounded divers of the enemy."

That night two "saker drakes," or light field pieces, together with certain musketeers, were placed in the tower of the church, from which, on the following day, a heavy fire was directed upon the upper portion of the castle. Many of the garrison were captured whilst endeavouring to escape. Sir Miles Livesay arrived with a regiment of horse from Kent, and Sir William Springate brought up his regiment of Kentish infantry. Preparations were made to draw off the water of the Swanbourne Lake, which supplied the wells of the castle. There were 100 prisoners in Arundel Church, who had been captured when Waller entered the town. A certain Richard Smith, a deserter from the army of the Parliament, "for twenty shillings, whereof he had twelve pence in hand, by them hired to go to Hopton for aid," was arrested at a court of guard four miles distant. When questioned by the captain of the guard, he said that he had lost the letter addressed to Lord Hopton. Having been proved to be "an arch spy in our army," he was hanged on the bridge, within sight of the castle. He said that "the enemy's strength in the castle was 1000 foot and 100 horse, but no provender for them. That they had store of oxen, but no beer or wine, save water only, which in the castle well; that the common soldiers with him had that day half a pound of bread weighed out to them."

On Saturday the draining of the lake was completed, and many fugitives let themselves down from the castle walls by ropes, but were for the most part captured. The besiegers strengthened their guards, and Sir Henry Heyman came with his regiment from Kent.

On Sunday desertions from the garrison were frequent and a heavy fire was directed against the castle from the guns in the church tower. Colonels Head and Dixie arrived with two Kentish regiments, which, together with "divers regiments from Sussex," made Waller's force amount to not less than 10,000 men. A number of starving horses were turned out of the castle, and one of Waller's men, in his anxiety to secure one or more, ventured too near the castle and was slain. About noon on Monday, December 25th, about thirty Cavaliers attempted to make a sortie, but upon Waller's drums beating and his trumpets sounding to arms they hastily retreated. Sir William Waller refused to exchange prisoners, and to promise quarter to the garrison if they surrendered the castle. On Tuesday, December 20th, some guns were planted in "a new place," which made the besieged garrison afraid to show themselves, and other measures to check the advance of any relieving force were also taken.

Lord Hopton was meanwhile most anxious to relieve the beleaguered Cavaliers. But there were, unfortunately, sad dissensions in his army. The English—Irish who had come over to reinforce the Cavaliers—constantly styled the Cornish men, who were numerous in the army, Cornish Choughs, Puritans, and Roundhead rogues; whilst the men of Cornwall in return retaliated with the epithets of Irish Kernes and Popish dogs. From words they came to blows. Several Cornishmen were killed, and many of their comrades, variously estimated at 50 and 1500 in number, deserted their colours and returned to their homes.

Whitelock in his "Memorials" says that 800 native Irish landed at Weymouth in January 1644, under the command of Lord Inchiquin, to aid the cause of the King. They were attacked by the garrison of Poole, and suffered considerable loss in killed and wounded. Two of their guns were also captured, and their magazine of gunpowder was blown up. Whitelock remarks, on March, 1644, "Divers of the Irish, about 1500, were cast away at sea coming to serve His Majesty. It was observed that these bloody Irish coming over hither never did any service considerable, but were cut off, some in one place, some in another. In all places the vengeance of God follows bloodthirsty men."

Determined, however, to make an effort to relieve Arundel Castle, Lord Hopton ordered the county to send one hundred carriages to Winchester for the use of his army, and on Tuesday, December 26th, news had been received in London of his having sent an armed force to break down the bridge over the Test at Redbridge, thus cutting off the town of Southampton from supplies from the New Forest, in the hope that Sir William Waller would send troops from Arundel, if he did not altogether raise the siege. This proceeding had, however, only the effect of stimulating Sir William Waller to greater exertions. The two Houses of Parliament ordered necessaries for the supply of Southampton to be furnished by the Isle of Wight, and Lord Hopton's men retired to Winchester without gaining any advantage, except killing three or four of Colonel Norton's men.

Lord Hopton himself now marched across the county to Petersfield, which he reached on Wednesday, 27th, with 2000 cavalry and 1500 infantry. Waller's scouts at once reported the approach of this relieving force, and stating that they had actually seen it upon the march. "On the news of this the besieged began to hope again in Winchester and Oxford, and came forth to the balcony again," only to be shot down by certain musketeers who had been posted in the ruins of an old chapel. An oxhide boat was discovered in the river "which runneth near the east side of the castle," which had been used to ferry over a messenger sent to Lord Hopton with a request for immediate relief.

No sooner had the royalist general marched out of Winchester towards Arundel than the ever active Colonel Norton, with the garrison of Southampton, boldly advanced to within two miles of Winchester, and made prize of more than fifty fat oxen.

On Thursday, December 28th, there were further desertions from Arundel Castle. A flag of truce was hoisted, and an application was made by the garrison to Sir William Waller for a supply of sack, tobacco, dice, and cards, in return for which they offered beef and mutton. They complained of a want of both bread and water, and sent numerous oxen out of the castle that night. On this day "a party of His Excellency's horse encountered with a party of Sir Ralph Hopton's near Petersfield, and took prisoners two quartermasters, one sergeant, and two common soldiers."

At seven o'clock on the morning of Friday, December the 29th, Sir William Waller recovered possession of Chichester, which, partly through the influence of Sir William Ford, of Up Park, Sir Edward's father, had been secured for the King on the 22nd of the preceding month. The constables and tythingmen of Singleton and West Dean were ordered to impede Lord Hopton's march by every possible means, and the besiegers removed some ammunition from Midhurst to Arundel for safer custody. As the Cavaliers were now close at hand Sir William Waller left 1500 men to continue the siege, and marched to meet them. The two armies faced each other on North Marden Down and at West

Dean. A few shots were exchanged, and three or four men killed on each side, whereupon Lord Hopton retreated nine miles to Heaveen (Havant?). Another account says that the scene of this skirmish was only three miles from Arundel.

On Saturday, Dec 30th, notwithstanding Sir W. Waller's proclamation that no quarter would be given to deserters, fugitives continued to quit the castle. One of them was a sergeant, who complained of a scarcity of food, with the exception of "powdered beef" and "a few live beeves." Beef was plentiful to the last, but no bread was served out to the garrison after Christmas Day.

Among the State Papers (Domestic), 1643, is one dated 28th December, written by a Royalist of the name, real or assumed, of Harrison, to a "Mr. Jean Bradley, English gentleman, of the College of Tournay, Paris."

It is quoted by Mr. Gordon, and is as follows: "28, 10br, 1643, ... Sir William Waller was bravely repulsed and soundly beaten from Basing about five or six weeks ago, with the loss of the best part of 1000 of his men and the diminution of his credit with the citizens. But since it hath been his fortune, he being four or five thousand strong, and the other but weak for number, to surprise at unawares, and, after firm fight, with the slaughter of more of his side, to take two or three hundred of my Lord Crawford's men, who were brought to this town (Farnham or Guildford?) in triumph about a week ago from South Harting, as I think the place is called in Sussex."

This account evidently refers to a skirmish between Sir William Waller's forces and those of Lord Hopton about the time of the march of the former general to Arundel, where he commenced the siege of the castle on December 20th, 1643. Mr. Gordon is of opinion that it has reference to the retreat of Lord Hopton after the failure of his attempt to relieve Arundel Castle, and that Colonel Norton was the victor in this encounter. It may well be that "Idle Dick Norton" was Lord Crawford's antagonist, but as Lord Hopton did not retreat from Arundel until December 29th, this engagement must have taken place some eight days previously.

On Saturday, December 30th, relief was urgently requested by the Parliamentarian garrison of Wardour Castle, of which Colonel Ludlow, whom we shall hereafter meet at Basing House, was the Governor. In the journals of the House of Commons of this date we find mention of "the British Army" in Ulster, so that this much used phrase can boast of an existence of nearly two centuries and a half. The Earl of Essex was also ordered to march either to Windsor or to some place from which he would be able to assist Sir William Waller, as Lord Hopton was known to be in motion.

On January 2nd, 1644, Colonel Norton wrote a letter giving an account of a successful brush with the Cavaliers on their retreat from Arundel. From this letter it appears that on Saturday, December 30th, he marched to join Sir William Waller, but could obtain no intelligence of the whereabouts of Lord Hopton's army. Stress of weather obliged him to quarter his troopers less than a mile distant from the enemy, who were "upon a hill undiscovered." Scouts, however, speedily brought word of the proximity of a hostile force, and Colonel Norton prepared to repel an attack. After facing the Cavaliers for some time, he saw that their numbers were hourly increasing, and accordingly began to retire in the direction of Chichester, covering the retreat in person with fifty men of his own troop. The pursuers attacked in force, striving to cut off the rear guard, whereupon Colonel Norton "was fain to make a stand," and to retire so as to form up on an adjacent heath. After some manœuvring, his men continued their retreat in good order, but on reaching Havant met "the two regiments of Dragoons, so they say, of Lord Crawford and Colonel Ennis, coming out of a cross lane. Some of them faced us, while the rest marched by," wearing red uniform. At once Colonel Norton charged them, heedless of superior numbers, and as soon as he came within half pistol shot the Cavaliers broke and fled. Not many of them were killed, except a captain and a captain lieutenant, "but I think few escaped without broken pates." Several prisoners were secured, with a loss of two or three of Colonel Norton's men, who were killed. Their victorious comrades safely escorted the prisoners to Chichester, and Colonel Norton proceeded to Portsmouth, from which place, on January 2nd, 1644, he despatched the letter from which we have learned the foregoing particulars.

Between Saturday, December 30th, 1643, and Thursday, January 4th, 1644, there were continual desertions from the garrison of Arundel

Castle, and those who still held out were anxious to treat for a surrender, but Sir William Waller requiring them to surrender "at mercy," the negotiations proved fruitless. On January 1st, 1644, Mr. Nicoll was directed by the Parliament to request the Earl of Essex to grant Sir William Waller a commission as major-general to command the forces of the four associated counties of Hants, Surrey, Sussex, and Kent, "according to the ordinance for that association," and the storekeepers were directed to furnish Sir William Waller with any necessaries which were not in store in the Tower of London. The commission was at once granted by the Earl of Essex, but not without an energetic protest, and was delivered to Sir William on January 3rd. On the same day it was ordered that the regiment of horse which had been ordered to be raised for service under Sir Richard Grenville should be completed by the Committee of the four associated counties, and that Mr. Trenchard should pay on account 40*l*. to Lieut.-Colonel Cooke, 40*l*. to Colonel Van Hust, and 20*l*. to Captain Smith, "to fit and despatch them away to the service of Sir William Waller."

On January 5th we read of a skirmish near Petersfield between 200 Cavaliers and 80 of the cavalry lent by the Earl of Essex to Sir William Waller. The latter were victorious, and, with a loss to themselves of six men, captured five Royalist officers. A day or two before a body of 500 or 800 (accounts vary) well-armed soldiers, whilst on the march from the western counties to join Lord Hopton, suddenly mutinied, and, marching to Poole and Lyme Regis, enrolled themselves as soldiers of the Parliament.

Lord Hopton himself tried to aid the garrison at Arundel by laying siege to Warblington House, between Chichester and Portsmouth, which Colonel Norton in the early days of January occupied with a garrison variously said to number 40, 50, 60, and 80 men. Of this castle, the ruins of which are well worthy of a visit, Mr. Moody says that it "appears to have been built with brick, faced on the outside with hewn stone, and was originally a square pile of about 200 feet, surrounded by a quadrangular court, but the only part now standing is a gateway and tower, fast mouldering away. The whole was surrounded by a fosse ten feet deep, and included about an acre of ground. Before the northern angle appears to have been an entrenched camp of five acres, now overgrown with wood, surrounded by a bank nearly eight feet high, and a ditch of a similar depth to that around the castle." ("Antiquarian Sketches of Hampshire," p. 340.)

The Rev. W. Norris, M.A., to whose kindness I am much indebted, says: "Henry VIII. conferred Warblington on Sir Richard Cotton, the Controller of his Household. To him I am disposed to attribute the erection of the present castle, of which the tower remains, the style of the architecture of which is that of a Tudor rather than of an earlier age. It remained in the hands of the Cottons till the Civil War. Sir Richard Cotton received King Edward VI. in it in the year 1552, and, according to a terrier of the manor, it was in perfect repair in the year 1633. After that we know only of a ruined tower, a broken arch, and a few nondescript mounds, and remains of a moat; but the story is soon told. The Cottons were Royalists, the Civil War broke out in the year 1642, and those who adhered to the Royal cause suffered for their loyalty." "The church as well as the castle must have been battered in the Civil War. A fragment of a tomb now in the vestry was once built into the south-west wall of the chancel, showing only one flat side, on which was engraved a cross in a circle. Some thought it was a Saxon altar, some that it was the dedicatory stone of the church. When restoring the church in 1860, and trying whether there were any remains of a window in that place, I had it taken out, and it turned out to be part of a broken monument of about the age of Queen Elizabeth. So it appears that the Republicans were not behind the Reformers in destructive zeal. The church, like most other churches at the Restoration, was imperfectly repaired. Much was done in the year 1800 to remedy the evils it had suffered, which considerably facilitated the still further restorations which were made in 1859, 1862, and 1864."

A contemporary writer says that Lord Hopton "after long siege and loss of more men than were there in garrison," took Warblington Castle, and another remarks, "Sir Ralph Hopton has spent his time frivolously against Warbleton House, betwixt Winchester and Portsmouth, where we leave him till divine justice finds him."

On Saturday, Jan. 6th, 1644, the Parliament ordered 100*l*. to be given to Major Scott, and Captain Cochram, the Mayor of Rye, "in testimony of their good services to the State."

The Commissioners of Excise were also directed to advance 4000l. "in regard of the great extremities that Sir William Waller's army was in."

Sir William had now a force of 10,000 men under his command, and had received either four or six heavy guns from Portsmouth, which on Thursday, Jan. 4th, opened fire upon the castle. Discord reigned within the walls, and Clarendon says, "By some of the soldiers running out to him, he found means to send in again to them; by which he so increased their faction and animosity against one another that after he had kept them waking, with continual alarms, three or four days, near half the men being sick and unable to do duty, rather than they would trust each other longer they gave the place and themselves up as prisoners of war upon quarter, the place being able to have defended itself against all that power for a much longer time."

On Friday, January 5th, the defenders of the castle, reduced to extremities, were extremely anxious to come to terms with Sir William Waller. A message was sent out by a drummer, who, being hungry and seeing abundance of food in the besiegers' lines, surrendered himself as a prisoner, whereupon a second drummer was sent out of the castle. Three commissioners were appointed on either side to draw up articles of surrender. The Cavaliers named Colonel Bamfield, Major Bodville or Bovill, and a captain, Sir William Waller nominating Col. Wems, Major Anderson, and a Kentish captain. He invited the Cavalier officers to dine with him, as he did also Lady Bishop, the daughter of the Earl of Thanet, with her two daughters, one of whom, Diana, only fifteen years of age, was the young wife of Henry Goring, the only son of Lady Goring, who, with her daughters, met her here. No definite agreement was come to, as the Cavalier demands to depart unmolested were refused by Sir William Waller. That evening the Commissioners returned to the castle, but the ladies with their maids were provided with quarters by Sir William Waller. "The soldiers and Governor himself were in a miserable distress and perplexity all the night."

The youthful Mrs. Henry Goring returned to her husband, and soon afterwards a drum was sent out with Colonel Rawlence and Major Mullins, who promised the speedy surrender of Sir Edward Bishop and Sir Edward Ford. The drum was sent back to the castle, but returned after midnight "with a letter of simple demands." The guards around the castle were at once trebled to prevent anyone from escaping, and the drum was sent back, with an order that the two hostages were to come forth at once if they desired a further cessation of hostilities. They gave themselves up about two hours after midnight, and the fortress was formally surrendered about nine o'clock in the morning of Saturday, January 6th, 1644, upon the following conditions :—

"*Propositions made by Sir William Waller to the besieged in Arundel Castle.*

First.—I require the Castle of Arundel to be delivered into my hands by to-morrow morning, ten o'clock.

Second.—That all Colonels of horse and foot, and all horse, arms, ammunition, and military provision whatever be then delivered to me entire and unspoiled.

Third.—That all Commanders, officers, and gentlemen have fair quarter and civil usage.

Fourth.—That all soldiers shall have quarter for their lives.

Fifth.—That for security of performance, Sir Edward Bishop and Sir Edward Ford be immediately delivered into my hands.

Explanation.

One.—By fair quarter, I mean giving life to those that yield, with imprisonment of their persons; but civil usage, which is sufficient security that they shall not be plundered.

Two.—Concerning the place they shall be sent to, it shall not be determined, but will be left to mine own freedom, without further capitulation.

Three.—The ministers are included in the articles, and are prisoners, as well as the soldiers.

Four.—When I send away the officers, I shall take care that they shall not want horses to carry them, but will not be bound to let them have their own horses."

The condition as to ministers was added with a view to securing the person of Dr. Chillingworth, who was in the castle. Seventeen colours of foot and two of horse were taken, and more than 1000 prisoners, besides 100 taken at the capture of the town, and those who were caught whilst escaping from the castle. An eye witness says : "I never saw so many weak and feeble creatures together in my life, for almost all the common soldiers were half starved, and many of them hardly able to set one foot before another." There were amongst them about 100 officers, 50 country gentlemen, and about 800 soldiers, five hundred of whom joined Sir William Waller. The rest were sent up to London guarded by four troops of horse, some in carts, some on foot. Three days were required for the journey, and on arrival the Committee of Militia assigned the captives to various prisons. A Committee consisting of Mr. Downes, Mr. Ravenscroft, and Colonel Alexander Popham was ordered to decide the fate of those who refused to take the Solemn League and Covenant. Sir William Waller was empowered to determine the amount of ransom to be paid by the "gentlemen, not soldiers," who had been captured, and was to send up to the Parliament a list of the ransoms paid.

A complete list of the officers and gentlemen who thus became prisoners of war will be found in Mr. Dallaway's " History of Arundel." Sir Edward Ford and Sir Edward Bishop were declared by Parliament incapable of any employment. Sir John Morley was allowed to compound for a fine on Oct. 23rd, 1644. On Sir William Waller's letter describing the taking of Arundel Castle being read in the House, on January 8th, it was ordered that Mr. Cleere, surgeon, should be recommended to the Masters and Governors of St. Thomas Hospital as the successor of Major Mullins, who had been taken in arms at Arundel. On Saturday, January 27th, the governing body of the Hospital claimed their right of free election. Their petition was referred to the Committee for Hospitals, who, on January 30th, ordered the election of Mr. Cleere. It was also ordered on January 6th that Dr. Chillingworth, Master of the Hospital at Leicester, having been taken in arms at Arundel, should be deprived of his office, which was to be conferred upon "Mr. Gray, Minister, brother to the Earl of Kent." Vexation, inclement weather, privations, and the harsh treatment of the Puritan ministers did their work, and before the end of the month Dr. Chillingworth breathed his last at Chichester. The circumstances of his death are graphically described by Mr. Dallaway.

About 200 horses, 2000 arms, many oxen both alive and dead, 20 barrels of powder, and 4000*l*. in money rewarded the victors. Great was the subsequent destruction. The north-west side of the castle was dismantled, and the great hall with the adjacent buildings were destroyed. The College of the Holy Trinity was also greatly injured, and its windows, which contained a series of portraits of the Earls and Countesses of Arundel, were irretrievably ruined. Sir William Waller now sent "2000 horse and foot and two drakes to besiege my Lord Lumley's house in Sussex." This was at Stanstead, and, as we have already seen, had been garrisoned by Lord Hopton when he made himself master of Arundel Castle. It surrendered at once, and the ironworks in St. Leonard's Forest, where the Royal ammunition had been made, and which belonged either to the Crown or to Royalists, were destroyed at the same time. Amberley Castle is also said to have been dismantled at this period of the war. Sir William Waller now resolved " that if Sir Ralph Hopton will not find out him, he will find out Hopton," and asked the Parliament to at once send him the City Regiments, under Major-General Browne, as he was anxious to give battle to the Cavaliers, who were still at Havant, leaving these regiments to garrison Arundel, under the command of Colonel Morley and Colonel Springett.

On January 8th, 1644, Sir H. Vane, jun., and Sir Arthur Heselrig were directed by the House of Commons to prepare a letter for Sir William Waller, which was to be signed by Mr. Speaker Lenthal, " to congratulate him on his great and good success, and to encourage him according to his intentions to prosecute the advantages it has pleased God to bless him with." The Committee of Safety was to consider how to improve the advantages which Waller had gained, and Mr. Downes, Mr. Ravenscroft, and Colonel Alexander Popham were ordered by the Parliament to proceed to Arundel to thank both the victorious General and his officers and men, and to inform them that the Parliament would do its utmost to enable them to advance against the enemy.

On January 6th Colonel Potley, who held a command under Waller, was maliciously wounded by one of his own men, who was of course hanged forthwith.

On January 8th Sir William Waller, having been reinforced by the London Brigade, wrote from Broadwater to the Parliament reporting that a large vessel named the *St. James*, of Dunkirk, having been chased by a Dutch man-of-war, and being unaware of the surrender of the castle, had entered the river Arun for safety, and had taken the ground "at Heene, near Arundel Castle." She mounted 24 brass guns, and had on board about 100 barrels of powder, "with good store of arms for the English-Irish that make havoc in Cheshire," said to be 2000 in number, besides other valuables. Several Cavalier officers were also on board. She was ordered to be detained, and the cargo was stored in Arundel Castle till the question of prize money should be decided by the Court of Admiralty. If she should prove lawful prize, the soldiers were to profit by the capture.

On January 15th another letter was witten by Sir William Waller from Arundel, asking that the ship might be sold, so that his men might receive their arrears of pay. This letter was referred to the Committee of Safety. A large picture of St. Ursula found in this ship, which had been painted for the Church of St. Anna at. Seville, was exposed to view at Westminster, and pamphlets were written to prove that it represented Queen Henrietta Maria urging King Charles to surrender his sceptre to the Pope!

Mr. Green and Sir A. Heselrig were directed to write to thank Sir William Waller for his care in this matter. The Spanish Ambassador interfered, and various merchants claimed the cargo, and at length the *St. James*, of Dunkirk, was released on August 24th, 1644. Colonel Morley, as Governor of Arundel Castle, was ordered to pay 4000*l*. salvage to Waller's army as compensation, and to account to the claimants for what had been already sold or used. Colonel Stapley, the Governor of Chichester, objected to quarter some of Sir W. Waller's troops in that city, but on January 19th the Earl of Essex ordered him to obey Waller in all things, as being his commanding officer.

On Tuesday, January 16th, Mr. Trenchard received instructions to provide 1000*l*. worth of shoes, stockings, and boots for Waller's army, the value of which was to be deducted from their pay. Three hundred muskets and three cartloads of ammunition for the same army passed through Lewes on January 8th. Sir William Waller in his "Vindication" says, "All that I got in the war by way of purchase or booty was one month's pay, as a Colonel of Horse, upon the surrender of Chichester. . . I had likewise 700*l*. for my part of the salvage of a ship that was driven on ground near Arundel when I lay before the castle, of which I gave the House a clear information when I delivered in my account. Besides this, of gift at several times I received 100*l*. from Mr. Dunch, of Pewsey, as I take it, who with a great deal of kindness sent it to me, though a stranger and utterly unknown to him, when I lay at Newbridge, and 50*l*. I had presented to me from the town of Lewes, in acknowledgment of my poor service at Arundel, which I likewise reported to the House; and in plate at Gloucester, Hereford, and Poole, to the value of 100*l*. or 150*l*. at most. And this is the utmost reckoning I can make, if it were my last reckoning, except I should put to account every horse gotten from the King's party upon the service, and bring in a little painted cabinet and some toys, worth 12*l*. or 14*l*., presented to my wife by the merchants of that forementioned ship, as a token of their thankfulness for the care I had shewed to preserve their goods."

Mr. Hillier, in his admirable "Sieges of Arundel Castle," gives some congratulatory verses presented to Lady Waller after her husband's signal success in Sussex.

Much mention has been made throughout these operations of Lord Crawford. A few particulars concerning him will, therefore, not be out of place.

Ludovic Lindsay, 15th Earl of Crawford, joined Charles I. at the raising of the standard at Nottingham. He "was made welcome and created commander of the volunteers." He was with his regiment at Edgehill, on October 23rd, 1642, and at Chichester, on December 29th, in the same year, Colonel, Major, and Captain Lindsay, of his regiment, together with about sixty other officers, chiefly Scotsmen, were taken and sent up to London. Vicars says that their horses " were very dainty ones!" Lord Crawford speedily made good this loss, and took part in the battle of Lansdown, on July 5th, 1643. Soon afterwards, having been sent to bring up some powder, he was intercepted by Sir William Waller, and lost one or two troops, besides the ammunition. He, however, played a distinguished part at the great battle on Roundway Down, fought at the first battle of Newbury, on September 20th, 1643, and had, as we have seen, a very narrow escape at Poole, only five days afterwards. At Alton, on December 13th, he had "got out with his troops," but being overpowered, was obliged " to get away with a few," leaving his "sack," hat, and cloak behind him, and owing his safety to the speed of his horse. He went north with Montrose, but soon returned to England, and held command as a major-general at Marston Moor, on July 2nd, 1644, " incurring the greatest hazard of any." Captured when the town of Newcastle was stormed, on October 9th, 1644, he was sent to Scotland, and condemned to death. Reprieved for a short time, the victory of Montrose, at Kilsyth, where his regiment suffered terribly, set him free once more. After Montrose's defeat at Philiphaugh, on September 13th, 1645, Lord Crawford took refuge in France and Spain. He was at Badajoz in June, 1649, and took part in Paris in the tumults of the Fronde, guarding Cardinal de Retz, in his citadel of Notre Dame, in company with fifty Scottish officers, who had seen service under Montrose. He is said to have died in France a childless man, in the year 1653. Such was the stirring life of " a steadfast Scottish Cavalier, all of the olden time!"

Gladly, did space permit, would we insert the Rev. H. D. Gordon's description of the entrenchments still plainly visible at South Harting, but we can only note that Harting Place, the residence of the Caryll family, was plundered several times, and the church converted into a stable or hospital. On the summit of the downs are several mounds immediately facing the park palings, near Two Beech Gate, from which several skeletons have been disinterred and carefully laid to rest in the churchyard. Mr. Gordon tells us that a lane in the neighbourhood is still euphoniously styled " Kildevil Lane," and says " There is a large green mound south of Up Park House, in which tradition says a number of horses were buried, and there is a similar tumulus further to the south at the fern-beds between Compton and East Marden, called " Solomon's, *alias* Baverse's Thumb." Some years ago a man grubbing a fence near Compton Down pulled up an ash stump that disclosed a nest of silver pieces of the time of Queen Elizabeth, no doubt hidden there before some local fight. In fact, that the fighting spread far and wide over this portion of the Downs is shown from the circumstance that the Rev. A. Locke, Vicar of Chalton, recently picked up some cannon balls of the period of the Civil War in digging the ground for his school. An axe-pike of the period, and other relics, point to the same conclusion ; these were found, together with a skeleton, at Stonewood, near Petersfield, by the Rev. G. Taswell, in making a garden. The axe-pike is 22 inches long. It is handled like a modern spade, so that the wooden shaft was enclasped by the iron, the older pikes were driven into their wooden handles like modern hay-forks. Some skeletons were also discovered at Bepton, in the neighbourhood of Midhurst, by Mr. Eames, who found that the skull of a very large specimen had been fractured as if by a sword-cut or shot.

In South Harting Church there is the following inscription :—" Major John Cowper lost his life in Winchester Castle in the service of King Charles the First ; he was plundered and sequestered of all he had by the rebels."

CHAPTER XIX.—RIVAL PARTIES AT WINCHESTER—H.M.S. "MAYFLOWER"—CAPTAIN BALL AND TOBIAS BAISLEY—COLONEL LUDLOW TAKEN—CALENTURE—THE ISLE OF WIGHT AND LYMINGTON—GOVERNOR MURFORD AT SOUTHAMPTON—ROYALIST PLOT—SKIRMISHES NEAR SOUTHAMPTON—OUTRAGES AT WINCHESTER—PREPARATIONS FOR BATTLE—FIGHTING AT BASING HOUSE AND ROMSEY—SIR JOHN OGLANDER.

The "Perfect Diurnall," of January 8th, 1644, announced that Lord Hopton was hemmed in between Chichester and Winchester, and that it would be difficult for him to escape from Sir William Waller's army. Despite all predictions to the contrary, the Royalist Commander "made a nimble retreat to Winchester," whither Waller prepared to follow him, leaving Colonel Norton to hold Cowdray House, so that we read in February, 1644, of "the garrison of Colonel Norton in Cowdray House, which lies indeed as a forlorn hope between them and their enemies."

The city of Winchester certainly contained some friends to the Parliament, for in a Royal Message addressed to its citizens in December, 1642, the King declared with reference to the capture of the city by Sir William Waller, that "you have openly declared yourselves enemies, and evil entreated those whom you had cause to entertain with all love and respect, flatly opposing our authority, and betraying those to ruin that were the instruments of our preservation," concluding with a threat of forgetting that they were his subjects in the severity of his chastising them. The citizens justified their conduct, which they declared was sanctioned by all laws, human and divine, saying that "we cannot be justly blamed for endeavouring to secure our lives, and to keep our wives and daughters from rapine and inevitable destruction," and concluding by asserting at one and the same time both their loyalty and their resolution to continue the same course of action.

But on December 30th, 1643, we find the following entry in the Corporation records:—
"Taken out of the coffer, plate delivered to Mr. Jasper Cornelius, appointed to receive the same for His Majesty's use, by virtue of an ordinance sent by His Majesty to the Mayor and Aldermen of the City for the loan of money or plate for the maintenance of the Army, by the consent of the Mayor and all the Aldermen of the City, one silver ewer, weighing 32oz. 4-1oz.; three silver bowls, 31oz. 4-1oz.; two silver wine bowls, 15oz. 4-3oz.; one gilt bowl with the cover, 31oz. 4-2oz.; one great silver salt, weighing 28oz.; one silver tankard, 19oz. 1-2oz.; one silver basin, 74oz.; total, 225oz. 4-1oz., at 5s. an ounce, amounting to 58l. 16s. 3d." A loan never destined to be repaid! Mr. Jasper Cornelius was an attorney by profession, and was a firm supporter of the Royal cause.

At the end of the year 1643 and during the spring of 1644 there were four Parliamentary armies in England, besides garrisons and local forces—Essex's own main army; Waller's, raised, or to be raised, also for action, chiefly in the south and west; Manchester's, of the seven Associated Eastern Counties; and the Army of the Fairfaxes in the north.

One of the King's ships, named the *Mayflower*, which had been flagship at Falmouth, was taken by the Parliament's ship, *the Eighth Whelp*, and brought as a prize to Portsmouth. On January 8th, 1644, the storekeeper at that port was ordered to deliver to "Henry Dolling, part owner of the ship *Ark of Poole*, appointed by the House to lie before that town for defence and safeguard thereof, six pieces of ordnance, with carriages, ladles, emptions, shots, and other gunner's stores," forming part of the armament of the *Mayflower*, allowing Captain Dolling to select his own guns. Alderman Towse and other Commissioners of Excise had advanced 500l. from their own purses "for supply of the pressing necessities of the town of Southampton," paying the money to George Gallop and Edward Exton, Esqs., M.P.s for the town, at the time when Lord Hopton had broken down the bridge at Redbridge. They were now reimbursed from the Excise duties.

But we must return for a moment to Basing House, which had steadily held its own, doing as it had done after the first Battle of Newbury, when we read "the Marquesse of Winchester with his forces at Basing hath also gathered up many stragglers, whereof some are officers." But now some within the walls began to lose heart, and on Jan. 11th we are told of various Cavaliers with their horses coming from Basing House to Major-General Browne, who was in command of some London Trained Bands at Croydon, saying that they had been forced to take up arms, offering to serve the Parliament, and being enlisted accordingly. The Marquis had not only to contend with open enemies and faint hearts, but he also had some trouble in controlling the lawless spirits of certain of his own partisans, who thought that loyalty and plunder were synonymous terms. A certain Capt. Ball complained that he had been deprived of his horses by Major-General Astley, after he had at his own expense raised a whole regiment for the King. Warburton, in his Memoirs of Prince Rupert and the Cavaliers (p. 212), gives the old General's letter to Prince Rupert, with the original spelling, which does not make Captain Ball appear to much advantage. Mrs. Ball seems to have been a help-meet for her husband : "May it pleas your Highnes,—As conserninge one yt cales himselfe Capne. Ball, yt hath complayned vnto yr Highnes yt I have tacken awaie his horsses from him, this is the trewth. He hath livede neare this towne ever since I came heather, and had gotten not above twelve men togeather and himselfe. He had so plundered and oppressed the pepell, paying contributions as the Marques of Winchester, and the Lord Hopton complayned extreamly of him ; and he went under my name, wtch ho vsed falsecly, as givinge it out he did it by my warrant. Off this he gott faierly offe, and so promised to give no mor caues of complaynt. Now, ewer since, he hath continewed his old coures in so extreame a waie as he and his wife and sone, and 10 or 12 horsses he hath togeather, spoyles peepell, plunders them, and tackes violently thear gooddes from them. As vpon comphyntes of the contrie and the Committie hier, I could do no lese then comitt him, and took awaie som nine or ten horsses from him and his, for he newer had mor, and those not armed ; which horsses ar in the custodie of Sir Charles Blunt. Divers (persons) claime satisffaction from him for thear goodes he hath taken from them ; as one man 30 powndes worth of hoppes he took from them vpon the high waie. And this day to Comittie heir hath given warninge that both he and his complaynt shall be heard ; all wtch shall be amplie informed hereafter to yr Highnes yt yr Highnes may so no wronge shall be don him. Yr Highnes most humbell and obedient seervant, Jacob Astley. Reading, this 11th Jan., 1644."

After Captain Ball had thus be n rendered harmless, the Marquis, feeling sure that he would not be long left in peace, was anxious to obtain accurate information as to the state of affairs in London. He selected as the fittest man to act as a spy a certain Tobias Baisley, who, a porter by occupation, had formerly servd the Parliament, but had deserted their cause, and taken service under Prince Rupert, who left him at Basing. He was employed "at 4s. a week with meate and drinke in Basing House to make bullets," and was now and again sent forth to gain intelligence. In this he was so far succesful that he had "betrayed divers c rriers with their waggons too and carriages to the Cavaliers." Poor Tobias paid dearly for his visit to town He was arrested in London as a spy, and "Mercurius Civicus," from whence the true and veracious story of Tobias is taken, tells us the result. "A Covncil of War" assembled on Thursday, Feoruary 6th, 1644, and Tobias was condemned to die. On Tuesday, February 18th, he was taken to Smithfield, "guarded by Mr. Quarterman, the Marshall, and divers others of the City Officers, and a company of the trained bands." Arrived at the place of execution the Marshall appeared in a second capacity, viz. that of Chaplain, and catechised the prisoner at length as to his religious belief. This done. " and thereupon the people being satisfied, the excentioner, Brandon (who is said to have afterwards beheaded the King), was commanded to doe his office, whiche he did, though the porter shewed much unwillingnesse to go off the ladder."

All things considered, the reluctance of poor Tobias is not greatly to be wondered at.

Wardour Castle, of which Colonel Ludlow was Governor, had long been besieged by the Cavaliers, and about the middle of January Sir William Waller assured the garrison that if they would hold out for another fortnight he would either relieve them or lay his bones under the castle walls. Poole and Southampton were strongly garrisoned for the Parliament, and between these two towns Colonel Ludlow's troop had taken post, with the double object of harassing the enemy, and if possible raising the siege. The troopers fell into an ambuscade, and Cornet, afterwards Major, William Ludlow's horse was wounded in two places. A bullet passed completely through the Cornet's body, notwithstanding which he recovered, to the astonishment of every one.

Colonel Ludlow having discovered a considerable amount of treasure concealed in the Castle, offered the garrisons of Poole and Southampton 700*l.* or 800*l.* if they could succeed in raising the siege. All efforts and offers, however, were in vain, and Lord Hopton having reinforced the besiegers with a strong detachment of Mendip miners, commanded by Sir Francis Doddington and an engineer, Ludlow was obliged to surrender on February 18th, 1644.

He was conducted by his captors that night to the house of Mr. Awbery, at Chalke, and from thence was sent to Oxford by way of Salisbury and Winchester. At the latter city Lord Hopton strongly urged him to desert the service of the Parliament for that of the King, as did also " a relation of mine, Colonel Richard Manning, who, though a Papist, commanded a regiment of horse in the King's service." But all solicitations were fruitless. His captivity was not of long duration, and on the 17th of April the House of Commons was informed of his release by exchange. He was soon afterwards appointed Sheriff of Wiltshire, and accepted a commission as Major under Sir Arthur Haselrig. During the month of May, 1644, he did good service under Waller, who blockaded Oxford on one side, whilst Essex took post on the other.

Before Friday, January 12th, Lord Hopton had been reinforced by 28 colours, or 500 men, and five days later he was reported to be planning with the advice of his cavalry to place guns and a fixed camp in a commanding position upon "Warhill," or Weyhill. One fortified post was to be established at Winchester, another at Weyhill, and a third at Reading, at a distance of 15 or 20 miles from each other, so as to maintain an easy communication with Oxford. On January 19th Hopton's forces were in motion towards Salisbury and Andover, but operations were greatly impeded by a hard frost and a deep fall of snow. Sir William Waller was in London on January 24th, and five days afterwards Colonel Turner's regiment of horse, which had lately been under the command of the Earl of Essex, was ordered to join his army, in which, since the capture of Arundel Castle, much sickness, especially calenture, had prevailed. Mr. Blaauw says, "Calenture needs a dose of archæology now-a-days, though formerly an item in the London Bills of Mortality. This fatal fever especially attacked those who lay exposed to unwholesome night air. In the delirium peculiar to it, surrounding objects assumed the aspect of verdant meadows to the eyes of the sufferer, who when at sea would madly throw himself into it, as if seeking the refreshment of a cool walk upon land. Dryden and Swift have made fine poetical use of this delusion. Probably Falstaff died of it, for Mrs. Quickly, describing his last symptoms, after lamenting that he was 'so shaked of a burning quotidian tertian,' says, 'after I saw him fumble with the sheets and play with flowers, I knew there was but one way, for 'a babbled of green fields'. Hen. v., Act 2nd."

Amongst the victims was Colonel Springet, who was joint Governor of Arundel Castle with Colonel Morley, and on February 3rd, 1644, he was buried at Ringmer, his native place.

On January 17th the Parliament ordered the sum of 3,000*l.* to be paid to Colonel Norton, the Governor of Southampton, for the purchase of arms, and about a week afterwards several letters from Thomas Carne, Esq., the Deputy-Governor, and from several Deputy-Lieutenants of the Isle of Wight, were read, asking the Parliament to allow the *Charles*, man-of-war, to remain at her present station for the protection of Hurst Castle and Lymington Fort. They also asked that Parliament would provide for the defence of the island, and place a strong garrison in Hurst Castle, as 800 native Irish rebels, under Lord Inchiquin's command, had landed at Weymouth and were plundering Dorsetshire. Five hundred others were expected. During the following month a party of them plundered Lady Drake's house in Dorsetshire, burning it to the ground. She herself escaped to Lyme, wearing, indeed, a pair of shoes, but otherwise almost naked. On January 24th the Lords at a conference desired the Commons to provide for the safety of the Isle of Wight. The *Charles* was ordered "to reside where she is now," for the period for which she was victualled. The Earl of Warwick was ordered to send ships to lie off the Isle of Wight and all the western coasts for their protection. The Committee for the safety was to provide for Hurst Castle and Lymington Fort, for the strengthening of which 500l. was voted on February 17th. The necessary funds were advanced by the Commissioners of Excise, of whom Alderman Towse was one, together with 200l. for Newport garrison.

Some extracts from the "Lymington Records," which are given by Mr. Wise in his book on the "New Forest," throw light upon the condition of the country at this period. They are as follows :—" 1643. Quartering 20 soldiers one daie and night, going westward for the Parliament Service, 10s. 2d." " 1646. For bringing the towne chest from Hurst Castell, 2s." " Watche when the allarme was out of Wareham, 4s." "For the sending a messenger to the Lord Hopton when he lay at Winton with his army, with the towne's consent, 14s." Notice here that there were evidently two parties in the town, " with the towne's consent." " 1646. For keeping a horse for the Lord General's man, 3s. 10d." " 1650. Paid to Sir Thomas Fairfax, his souldiers going for the Isle of Wight, with their General's passe, 12s." " 1643. Billeting of seamen, 4l. " " 1645. For cheese and beer for the souldiers, 10s. 10d." " 1646. Warning the Watch when the alarme was for Watch and Wards, and Beer, 7s. 5s., 5s. 6d., in all 17s. 6d. For 2lb powder, 2s. 8d." " 1650. For quartering of souldiers at the Mayor's house, 4s. 6d., and grasse for their horses, 4s. 8d." We learn also from Woodward that there were also influential Cavaliers in the town. The Dore family made great sacrifices both for Charles I. and for the Duke of Monmouth, and when in 1644 Prince Charles (afterwards Charles II.) appeared off Yarmouth (Isle of Wight) with 2000 men and 19 ships, in the hope of rescuing his father, he was aided by Barnard Knapton, the Mayor, and certain burgesses of Lymington.

"Mercurius Aulicus" tells an amusing story on October 2nd, 1643 :—" One John Stanley, who was Purser to a ship, was pleased to send his powerful warrant for venison in these very words, · These are to will and require you upon sight hereof to kill, or cause to be killed, one fat buck of this season, and send him to the " George," in Limmington, to be sent aboard our ship, and this shall be your warrant. Per me John Stanley. To Mr. George Rodney, Master Keeper, or to any of his Under Keepers.' "

Did the Purser get his venison after all ?

On February 5th, 1644, a very interesting letter was written to Captain Thomas Harrison, who was afterwards one of the regicides, by Mr. Peter Murford, who had been Governor of Southampton, but had been superseded by Colonel Norton, under whom he was now acting as Sergeant Major, or, as we should now say, Major. As his name frequently occurs about this time in connection with Southampton affairs, a few notices of him may be of interest, albeit they are drawn from the hostile "Mercurius Aulicus." Mr. Murford was a tailor by trade, as plainly appears from this extract, bearing the date of Wednesday, Sept. 30, 1842:— "And the members may well think to tax all the world when Murford, the pretended Governor of Southampton (nine of whose profession make one man), hath power to fine that town as seemeth best to his greatness. For as by letters from Winchester we were this day certified, Colonel Morley, the Sussex rebel, having at Ringwood surprised two or three straggling soldiers of His Majesty's forces and brought them into Southampton, was as a grateful welcome entertained with a banquet at the Councell House of the town by that imperial seamstris Mistris Murford, and after dinner was created burgess of Southampton by Murford himself. But the poor townsmen paid for all ; it so pleasing this mighty Governor that he assessed the town at 650l., which they were forced to pay suddenly to avoid plundering, which he threatened, especially the old Mayor, who was constrained to ransom his goods with 40l. And in the same letters it was further signified that this infamous Governor pulled down the picture of Queen Elizabeth from over the north gate of that town (called the Bar Gate), saying that the Queen was the occasion of all these troubles, for if she had made a thorough reformation all this fighting would have been spared. But if nothing but religion had stirred this good man's spirit, he might still have governed the shears and thimble and let corporations alone."

On October 2nd, 1643, we hear of stirring scenes at Southampton. "The good Governor this last week, as this day we were certified, had a full commission to exercise marshall law, and therefore made the Earl of Southampton's house a common gaol, on such delinquents as His Mightiness shall think convenient. By virtue whereof he sent abroad his strict warrant commanding all villages near unto Southampton to assist him with men and money in fortifying the town, among whom the Tythingman, of Stoneham, was convented before him for negligence in executing of his Worship's new warrants, whereupon Murford said unto him, 'Sirrah, if the King send to you, then you can presently go, run, and ride; but when I send, you will not step a foot, but, Sirrah, when I speak the word hereafter, I'll make you fly, or you shall hang for it." In imitation of whom, his own Sub-Committee, Richard Major, Paul Mercer, Peter Legaye, and others, moved very eagerly at the meeting in Southampton, that the King's proclamation for non-payment of rents to rebels might be burned by the hand of the common hangman at the market-place, but were prevented by the good old Mayor of that town, who hath sufficiently smarted for his loyalty."

Once more, on Tuesday, October 14th, 1643, we are told "Nor is the city of Coventry only happy in a good servant, the town of Southampton being able to match Purefoys with her famous Governor, Master Murford, one who, though I know not the man, is resolved still to trouble me with his weekly actions. For having, as we told you heretofore, decreed to make the Earl of Southampton's house a prison, this week he sent in fifty prisoners to take possession, and to show his mightiness, he assembled his Committee, viz., Mercer, Legay, Major, and the rest, at their meeting place in Southampton, where, after a serious debate, it was concluded that all the coal in Netley House, a house belonging to the Lord Marques of Hertford, now Chancellor of the University of Oxford, should be removed to Southampton by some of the rebels of Master Murford's garrison, which, in obedience to the just authority of this rebellion, was quickly performed; whether they will fetch coals so easily from Newcastle we shall see ere long, but if they do not they tell us that they will cut down all the woods within three-score miles of London." Governor Murford's chaplain was the Rev. Nathaniel Robinson, a friend of Oliver Cromwell, who, in 1649, was settled in the Rectory of All Saints' Church, Southampton, and who negotiated between Oliver and Richard Major, of Hursley, concerning the marriage of Richard Cromwell and Dorothy Major. Murford and his friends, Legay, Mercer, and others, towards the end of the year 1643 announced the discovery of a real or pretended plot to betray the town to the Cavaliers, "but the offenders were only the inhabitants of the town, and such only as had somewhat to lose, as appeared by a good round assessment levied on them within few hours after breaking open of the plot."

From Murford's letter of February 5th, 1644, we learn that after destroying the bridge over the Test at Redbridge, Lord Hopton's troops retired to Winchester. On the following day a letter reached Mr. Robert Mason, a merchant of Southampton, from Mr. Jasper Cornelius, a Royalist attorney at Winchester, asking him to persuade Murford to betray the town to Lord Hopton. Murford talked the matter over with Colonel Norton, who ordered him to send a favourable reply. Mr. Jasper Cornelius offered him 1000*l.* in money, a better office than that which he then held, a pardon under the Great Seal, and an assurance of the King's favour. By Colonel Norton's secret directions, Murford asked for either the 1000*l.* at once, or else 500*l.* and the Royal pardon. Colonel Norton meanwhile informed the Earl of Essex and Sir William Waller of the offers made by Cornelius. The pretended treaty was protracted, in order to gain time, in the hope that Lord Hopton would blockade Southampton, and be defeated by Sir William Waller on his return from Arundel. The promised pardon was at length sent, but no money. The reward was only to be paid when the work was done. A month went by, and eight letters passed between the negotiators, Mr. Robert Mason being bound to secrecy by oath. At length Murford told him that Colonel Norton knew everything. Mason made an earnest appeal for mercy, for the sake of his wife and large family, but in vain. He was, however, allowed to return to his own house, three doors distant from Murford's, and profiting by the opportunity, before he could be arrested he made his escape to Winchester, where he was welcomed and employed in a confidential position. Lord Hopton now despatched troops to blockade Southampton, and several skirmishes took place, in all of which the soldiers of the Parliament had the advantage. On January 31st, 1644, a cornet, five soldiers, and their horses were taken prisoners. Two days afterwards two men of the town were captured with their horses and arms, three or four being wounded. One of the latter, a captain, was on February 5th dying of his wounds, at Romsey. On a previous occasion we find the Mayor and some of the richer burgesses favoured "the Malignants," or Cavaliers. On February 5th the Lord Admiral, the Earl of Warwick, sent the *Maria* pinnace to Southampton Water, to guard the town, which was then threatened by the Royalists, Lord Hopton's men having committed certain depredations on the land side, so that there was in the whole county "hardly anything left for man or beast." Lord Hopton was expecting to be reinforced either from Oxford or the West. Major-General Browne with the City Brigade was fortifying Petworth, in order to prevent a Cavalier inroad into Sussex. Lord Hopton's army was about 7000 strong at Winchester, and was recruited with Irishmen, horse raised in the western counties, and pressed men. The persons and estates of those refusing to serve the King were alike liable to be seized. The Cavaliers at Winchester were now "fortifying apace," but many of them, who were Protestants, declared that they would not serve with the Irish troops, who had either arrived or were daily expected. In one of the skirmishes near Southampton, a Parliamentarian officer was taken prisoner. His men followed the retreating Cavaliers, and brought them to action again at the village of Twyford. The prisoner was placed in the front rank, but the Parliamentarians fired hotly, killed eight of their opponents, put the rest to flight, and rescued their officer. On February 9th the counties of Kent, Surrey, Sussex, and Hants were raising 5000 men to check the movements of Lord Hopton, who had formed the plan of aiding Col. Massey in Gloucestershire and Wiltshire.

Sir Benjamin Tichborne, M.P for Petersfield, a staunch Cavalier, dwelt in the old moated, oak-panelled family mansion at West Tisted, which is full of interest to the archæologist. His home was, however, seized upon by Sir William Waller, who established there a cavalry outpost. This circumstance would have been forgotten if a casualty had not occurred, which was duly recorded in the parish register. For the following entry, which speaks for itself, I have to thank the Rev. Mr. Stewart :—

"A soldier, one Leiftenant Vernon, under a gentleman, one Captayne Gibbon, of ye Kentish regiment of Horse for the Parliament against the King, in the tyme of ye Civil Warr betweene King Charles and his Parliament, being quartered at Sir Benjamin Tichborne's house, was buried in the Charnell of West Tisted, on the north side, directly under the little window. He was unfortunately killed by his Captayne's Groome of his horse in the kitchen standing by the fire on the Monday before, being February the 10th, being about 9 of the clock at night. Shott into his left shoulder through the bare (breast?) bone, with a pistoll charged with two bulletts. The Captayne's man that did it was tried by a Councell of Warre as a thing of infortune, and not on set purpose maliciously. The Colonell of the Kentish regiment was one Colonel Lacy, Feb. 12, 1644. A memoral accident!"

"Mercurius Aulicus" tells us that the good people of Odiham were sadly disturbed whilst at church on February 11th. Some of the garrison of Farnham Castle rode into the church during the service, and "presented their pistols at Master Holmes, the minister, saying with a loud impudence, 'Sir, you must come down, for we do not allow of such kind of preaching.'" One trooper fired his pistol in the church ; a number of women fainted, "and one Bushell's wife fell down dead."

On Thursday, February 15th, it was known in London that two troops of Hopton's men had reconnoitred Southampton. Colonel Norton sallied out upon them, and "many were wounded in their wheeling." No less than 80 of them were killed and taken, the fire on both sides being well sustained. One hundred good horses, 120 arms, and other plunder rewarded the victors, whose loss is not stated, and the rest of the Cavaliers fled in disorder. Hampshire men were ordered either to supply Lord Hopton's cavalry with horses, or to pay 10*l*. per man in lieu of each horse. A weekly payment of 2*s*. per week was levied "upon such as are but meanly landed." Imprisonment and plunder awaited those who refused payment. Almost all the sheep, not omitting pregnant ewes, are said to have been devoured by the Cavaliers, who were charged with having eaten up 3000 sheep within twelve days at Odiham without payment.

On the 19th of the following month a petition was presented by "the Master and Almesfolk of the Poore Hospitall of St. Mary Magdalen, neare Winchester, to the Right Honourable Ralph, Lord Hopton, Baron of Stratton, and Field Marshall General of His Majesty's Western Forces." The petitioners stated that they could not live without charitable additions to their endowment, and that 16 acres of barren arable land and dry common for 120 sheep was all the land they possessed, which they diligently cultivated. That about Christmas, 1643, Lord Hopton's men had killed 36 of their sheep, necessitating the removal of the rest to a distance of sixteen miles. Of this they had made no complaint. "But your petitioners do farther shew that within four nights last past the soldiers keeping their rendezvous there have not only devoured nine quarters of their seed barley for this season, being the full provision for the same, and have broken down and burnt up the great gates, all doors, table boards, cupboards, gyses, timber partitions, barnes, and stables there, but have also used violence to the house of God, burning up all the seats and pews in the church, also the Communion table, and all other wainscot and timber there that they could lay hands on, and have converted the said house of God into a stable for horses and other profane uses, to the great dishonour of God and grief of soul of your poor petitioners, being very aged and impotent persons, and thereby made destitute of the means of having either temporal or spiritual food." Lord Hopton endorsed this petition with an order that Henry Foyle, Esq., and Commissary Fry should protect these distressed almsfolk.

About the middle of February, 1500 of Lord Hopton's cavalry were at Salisbury marching to the westward. Having been suddenly recalled to Hampshire, some 500 of them deserted their colours. The rest were "badly armed, not worth much, as were many Cavaliers elsewhere." Lord Hopton had ordered some dozens of maps of Kent, Sussex, and Surrey to be sent to him from London, for the use of his officers. His supply of ammunition was now fast failing him.

On Saturday, Feb. 17th, Sir William Waller was quartering his army near Chichester and Arundel. The London Brigade was at Petworth. Its officers maintained strict discipline, and on Feb. 20th, " a corporal was to be tried by a Council of War for revealing the watchword in the night time." Some of Colonel Norton's men were in garrison at Cowdray House, near Midhurst, five miles from Petworth. Detachments of Cavaliers from Winchester were hovering about Alton, and giving constant alarms to the garrisons at Cowdray and Petworth, but inclement weather prevented any important military operations.

On February 20th, the Parliament passed an Ordinance for giving an allowance of 12,000*l.* per month to the Scottish Army, to commence on the 1st of March, and two days afterwards news reached London that Lord Hopton and Sir William Ogle were discussing the advisability of demolishing the fortifications of Winchester, and evacuating the city, for the double reason that it was difficult to provide for the wants of 400 cavalry as well as infantry, and that Sir William Waller was threatening a personal advance in force. "Mercurius Aulicus," on February 23rd reports a mutiny of some of Waller's troops, and that Captain Guthred and some others had come over to the Cavaliers. Waller was expecting to be reinforced by 3000 foot, 120 horse, and 500 dragoons, which had been lately raised in the four associated counties of Kent, Surrey, Sussex, and Hampshire.

On February 27th Hopton was impressing men, many of whom deserted at the first opportunity. Of 600 men thus forced into his ranks 100 deserted at once, and 200 more were missing when the detachment reached Winchester, despite the exertions of a guard of horse. Many country gentlemen were said to be preparing to abandon Hopton, and to welcome Waller whenever he should advance into Hampshire. The 29th of February brought news that Sir William Waller's rendezvous was to be at Chesterfield, and that he would march towards Winchester after another ten days. The Kentish men were to be there, also 1200 foot, 400 horse, and 200 dragoons, Sussex and Surrey sending their due proportion under "that valiant soldier Sir Richard Grenville."

And now the greatest disaster of all for the King's troops was at hand. After the capture of Arundel Castle and his victory at Alton,

Sir William Waller was eager to proceed on his march into the western counties, more especially as the 10.0 horse which, under the command of Sir William Balfour, the Earl of Essex had been obliged, sorely against his will, to lend his subordinate but rival Waller, might be withdrawn at any time. Besides, the Auxiliary Regiments of London were anxious to return home, their period of service having nearly expired. Accordingly, as an old writer observes, "Sir William Waller, after his reducement of Arundel Castle, marched to find out my Lord Hopton, to cry quits with him for his defeat at Roundway Down" (near Devizes).

Lord Hopton, on his part, was nothing loth, especially after the disaster at Alton, which "inflamed him with desire of a battle with Waller to make even all accounts." The King, having heard of the strong reinforcements granted to Sir William Waller, sent a large force of volunteers from Oxford to reinforce the army under Hopton. They were under the command of the Earl of Brentford, a man whom Clarendon says had been a very good officer and had seen much service. His courage and boldness no man doubted, but long-continued and heavy drinking bouts had weakened his mental powers, which never had been very great, "he having been always illiterate to the greatest degree that can be imagined!" Being an intimate friend of Lord Hopton, and wishing to pass the winter in active service rather than in repose, he asked permission to march to Winchester, which was very readily granted by the King. On his arrival, Hopton gave him a most cordial welcome, and offered him the supreme command of the whole force. This offer, however, he refused, but promised to aid in all expeditions to the best of his ability. If the fortune of Cheriton fight had been different, the two generals would have marched together to the aid of the Cavaliers of Sussex and Kent, and would have made the King supreme in those two counties.

Sir William Waller was massing troops near Farnham, meaning to seek the Cavaliers, and "they cheerfully embraced the occasion and went to meet him." A contemporary account says: "Both armies were near one another a good space, for my Lord hovered about Winchester and those parts."

On the 1st of March, 1644, Hopton was said to have barely 6000 men at Winchester, and desertions from that garrison were frequent.

Sickness was decimating both armies, but the Cavaliers were the greatest sufferers. The town and garrison of Portsmouth were distressed for provisions, as Hopton's outposts were in occupation of Southwick, Bishop's Waltham, Fareham, and other places in the neighbourhood. One hundred barrels of powder were ordered to be stored in Arundel Castle for the supply of Waller's army, and on March 7th orders were given that forty other barrels from the powder mills, near Guildford, should be sent for the same purpose to Farnham Castle, the garrisoning of which at this time caused some anxiety to the Parliamentary Committee of both kingdoms. All the officers of cavalry and infantry regiments raised in Kent, and the Governors of all the garrisons in the four associated counties of Kent, Surrey, Sussex, and Hants, were to obey the orders of Sir William Waller as Major-General of the Association. Sir William himself, when present in the House of Commons about this time, obtained authority to make a summary levy of horses in three days in West Sussex, so as to complete the proportion of cavalry to be provided by the county for the regiment then being raised for Sir Richard Granville. The Committee of Militia wrote "to encourage the City Regiment, now in Sussex, to continue for yet longer upon the service, the necessity for it at this time being so important." Sir John Trevor was raising money in Sussex for Sir William Waller, and on Thursday, March 7th, the Committee of Militia and Mr. Molins, Comptroller of the Ordnance, delivered to that General's army, "One demi culverin, called Killcow, three drakes at Leaden Hall, one demi culverin drake, and one sacre drake, upon shod wheels, with their carriages, and for carriages, with provisions for sixty shot round." Hampshire and Sussex Puritan recruits were coming in apace, and Kentish Volunteers nearly 5000 strong destined for the same service were being maintained at the expense of their county. On Sunday, March 10th, eighteen loads of ammunition left London for Waller's army. Sir John Evelyn and other Hampshire gentlemen had promised allegiance to the Parliament, and had taken the Covenant, but on March 2nd it was debated whether or not they were again eligible for seats in the House.

Colonel Harvey, who was beaten at Basing House, in company with Colonel Norton, on August 2nd, 1643, was now sent with his regiment of horse to join Sir William Waller at Farnham, and our old acquaintance, Captain Swanley, the terror of Southampton, about this time made prize of a ship of Bristol, laden with arms and ammunition for the King. On or about March 9th some of Lord Hopton's cavalry from Winchester faced Southampton. Colonel Norton sent out a party to skirmish with them until some other troops who had made a long and circuitous march could attack them from an ambuscade in their rear. The result was most disastrous to the Cavaliers. One of the sons of Sir John Stawell was killed. This family was constantly active on the side of the King. The Cavaliers are said to have carried off five cartloads of their dead, and the slain and prisoners are variously estimated at 80 and 140. Between 60 and 80 horses were brought back to Southampton, together with two cornets and other officers. Colonel Norton lost only three men, according to one writer; but all concur in stating that his losses were but slight. Sir William Balfour, Major-General of Horse under Sir William Waller, was now in Hampshire with 4000 horse and dragoons, and on his march from Reading to Devizes took a few straggling Cavalier horsemen, who were billeted at Andover, and immediately afterwards occupied Newbury, which now had a garrison of 5000 horse and foot, and from whence Captains Dolbery, Turner, and Thompson were sent with about 200 horse to face Basing House. "The foxes and wolves there came out," and followed the retreating Roundheads as far as Odiham, plundering meanwhile and capturing a waggonload of provisions. Thereupon they halted and retired towards Basing House, their strength being almost the same as that of their opponents. Now, in their turn. did Balfour's men advance to the attack, killing twenty Cavaliers, routing the others, recapturing the waggon, and taking many prisoners, or, according to two chroniclers, capturing "many troops of horse and provision carriages," or "six waggons of beef, malt, and bacon going to Basing House."

Sir William Balfour's troopers then advanced, somewhat to the alarm of the garrison at Winchester, but "that good knight, Sir John Smith, beat up the rebel quarters at Bramdean, Petersfield, and Alton." recapturing the provisions, and making the unwelcome Parliamentarian intruders retire. On Tuesday, March 12th, Lord John Stuart, one of the Duke of Richmond's brothers, who was in command of Lord Hopton's cavalry, led by Captain Thomas Evan, had a party of Sir Edward Stawell's horse and foot "to a place near Alresford." The same day a party of Cavaliers marched out of Romsey, and when approaching the New Forest met a party of their comrades, who did not recognise them, and shots were exchanged. This mistake having been rectified, the w' ole force returned to Romsey, which some of Colonel Norton's men from Southampton, led by Captain Thomas Evan, had that evening occupied. "where they had but a short night's rest." Early in the morning of March 13th the Cavaliers entered the town, surprised their opponents, who were about 120 in number, and very well armed. From 80 to 100 prisoners were taken, the rest by different ways escaping. Captain Evans had in his pocket a commission as Governor of Romsey. Six of the prisoners were found to be deserters from Lord Hopton's army, and were summarily hanged, at the especial request of their own regiment.

Meanwhile things were by no means going on smoothly in the Isle of Wight. On Tuesday, March 12th, the petition of Captain Scofield, John Baskett, and Richard Bury, gentlemen, and others against Col. Carne, "the present Deputy Governor of the Isle of Wight." was read in the House of Commons, and referred to the Committee for the safety of the Isle of Wight. Another petition was in course of signature in the Island, which the Committee received orders to suppress. Colonel Carne, who was accused first of discountenancing the friends of the Parliament, and secondly of countenancing those of the King. was to be summoned to appear in London to answer these charges. The Earl of Pembroke, the Governor of the Isle of Wight, wrote to the standing Committee there " to take care of the safety of the Island, especially of Carisbrooke Castle and Sandown Fort. And that James Millis and Captain Hunt may be secured, or sent out of the Island by the Committee, that they may do no prejudice to the safety of the Isle." On Friday, March 22nd, a petition of the knights. gentlemen, and inhabitants of the Isle of Wight was read, and the Earl of Pembroke received further orders to take care of the Island until the matter should be decided by authority. Colonel Carne was afterwards acquitted of the two charges brought against him by a majority of 21 and 20 votes respectively.

Notice was also taken on March 22nd of "the demeanour and carriage of one Oglander in the Isle of Wight." On this point "Mercurius Aulicus" enlightens us on Monday, August 14th, 1643:—

"This day also we received intelligence that Sir John Oglander being in the Isle of Wight, one, who is a sufficient brother, said to him that the King's ships were goodly ships. 'Yes,' said Sir John, 'but they would be better if they were restored to their true owner,' meaning His Majesty. The Roundhead replied, 'Why, what would you gain if the King had them all?' 'No matter for gain,' said Sir John. 'I would I had given 500*l.* of my own purse so as the ships were in the right owner's possession.' 'And verily,' said the other, 'it shall cost you 500*l.*,' and so presently informed against him, and caused him to be fetched to prison, where now the good knight is kept close only for discovering a good wish to His Majesty."

On Tuesday, March 19th, 1644, two letters from the Earl of Warwick, dated, one, three days previously, and the second the day before, were read in Parliament, enclosing "extracts of Captain Jorden's letter and Captain Thomas, his letter from Portsmouth and Stokes Bay," to the effect that they had chased the Earl of Marlborough, "and had taken four prizes of good value, the one of thirteen guns, belonging to Lyme."

On March 25th it was decided that the Summer Guard should consist of eighteen merchant ships. The two second rates and one third rate men-of-war previously ordered to be sent to sea were countermanded. A strong escort was to be provided for certain ammunition carts which were to be sent to Sir William Waller. But all these matters of detail were in the following week to be dwarfed by the great struggle which has been variously styled the Battle of Cheriton, Alresford, Brandon Heath, Brandon, Bramdean, and Winchester, as well as Cheriton Down Fight and Cheriton Fight. Truly manifold are the appellations of this dread and stern reality!

CHAPTER XX.—A BATTLE IMMINENT—SIR WILLIAM WALLER'S ADVANCE—LORD HOPTON'S ENTRENCHMENTS—WEST MEON OCCUPIED—CAVALIERS AT ALRESFORD—SKIRMISH AT TISTED—CHERITON FIGHT—STRUGGLE IN THE WOOD—THE TIDE TURNS—HOPTON RETREATS—A CAVALRY CHARGE—KEEN PURSUIT—TROPHIES OF VICTORY—LOSSES ON BOTH SIDES—THE EARL OF FORTH—WINCHESTER SURRENDERS—LADY HOPTON TAKEN PRISONER—REJOICINGS IN LONDON.

Encouraged by the presence of the Earl of Forth, his firm friend and superior officer, and sorely grieved by the late disasters at Alton and at Arundel, Lord Hopton, having been also reinforced from Oxford, was anxious to try conclusions with Sir William Waller. He and Lord Forth intended, if successful, to advance into Sussex and Kent, in which counties Rushworth says "they were like to find many to join them." The same author says that the Cavaliers were 13,000 or 14,000 strong, and that Sir William Waller, Sir William Balfour, who commanded the cavalry, Sir Michael Livesay, who had brought up a force from Kent, and Major-General Browne, who led the London Brigade, had upwards of 10,000 men. But most authorities give the numbers on each side as being from 8000 to 10,000. The Parliamentarian Generals, especially Sir William Waller, "who wished to cry quits with Lord Hopton for his defeat at Roundway Down" on July 13th, 1643, were by no means reluctant to stake the issue of the contest upon the result of a battle. Waller was elated by his previous victories gained at Alton and Arundel, and knew that his London Brigade was exceedingly anxious to march in the direction of the metropolis. Moreover he feared the speedy recall of the cavalry which had lately been lent to him by the Earl of Essex.

According to a letter from Petworth we learn that the White and Red Regiments and the Southwark Regiments, which composed the London Brigade, were to advance on March 16th from Petworth to Midhurst, at which latter town they halted for five days. Lord Hopton, who on March 19th was said to have under his command 10,000 men, the majority of whom had been impressed, was now concentrating all his forces from the western counties, preparatory to a general rendezvous on Tichborne Down. Many of his pressed men were expected to desert, if opportunity offered, and there was a report that 10,000 arms had been landed at Weymouth from Dunkirk for the Cavaliers. Sir William Balfour, who was in command of 4000 horse and dragoons, was on March 18th, says "Mercurius Britannicus," "betwixt Winchester and Romsey, and the rebels in Oxford are betwixt fear and despair." Sir William Waller was on his march from Sussex with six or seven thousand horse and foot, the county of Kent having sent him 500 cavalry and 1200 infantry. The armies were nearly equal in number, and Lord Hopton was busily fortifying Winchester, and "building a great fort about one mile thence, to keep off all approaches thereunto, but the hills so command that city that his labour will be lost, and his great sconce" or redoubt "prove useless." Is not this great fort or sconce the well-known earthwork, with its clump of fir trees visible from afar, known to all men as Oliver's Battery, so called probably from having been occupied by that stern soldier, Cromwell, in October, 1645?

On March 18th, Sir William Waller reached Chichester with his train of artillery, and on the following day a solemn fast was observed by his army, just one week before the appointed time, as the following week was likely to prove somewhat eventful. All the farmers' teams were impressed by Waller for the transport of his baggage and guns. Sir William Balfour had also taken up a position nearer to Portsmouth, and on March 20th the whole army was to advance towards Winchester. On the 21st Sir William Waller himself was still in Chichester, but some of his forces had marched to Catherington, and others were quartered at Havant. The London White and Yellow Regiments, under Major General Browne, were at Midhurst, and the horse and foot from East Kent, under Sir Michael Livesay, had effected a junction with the rest of the army. Sir William Balfour's 4000 horse and dragoons were " at Portchester, Portsmouth, Petersfield, Lippooke, &c." The Surrey forces of the Parliament were on the march towards Godalming, and a traveller reported that for nineteen miles together all the towns and villages were filled with the soldiers of the two opposing armies, each of which was said to be 10,000 strong. On March 21st, a solemn Day of Humiliation was observed at the Church of St. Martin's in the Fields, for the success of Sir William Waller, who was even then expected to act upon the defensive, as he was advised to do by the Parliament. He had appointed Tichborne Down as a rendezvous for the London Brigade, and also for the cavalry force under Sir William Balfour. When it was known in London that Waller was actually on the march towards Winchester through Petersfield, "two gallant pieces of ordnance, fit for battery, with divers carriages and ammunition," were at once sent to him.

Lord Hopton and the Earl of Forth had previously challenged Waller to fix the day and place for a battle, and by the night of Saturday, March 23rd, some of the troops on either side were within six miles of one another. Some of the Cavaliers were posted on the downs a mile distant from Winchester, whilst others were constructing entrenchments upon Tichborne Down. Mr. Duthy says ("Sketches of Hampshire," p. 194) :—" There is a tradition that when Alresford was occupied by the Royal Army under Hopton, before the battle of Cheriton, some of the outposts were on the ridge of Ovington Down, where the present turnpike road now skirts Sir Thomas Dyer's park, and a field, which is still known by the name of Butcher's Close, is pointed out as the spot where the Commissary collected and slaughtered cattle for the use of the King's Army. Marks of entrenchments are visible, or were lately so, which were probably thrown up at the same period." Other entrenchments are also to be traced upon Gander's Down,

apparently intended to protect the old road from the Four Lanes, Beauworth, to Winchester. But Lord Hopton's soldiers were mostly "young boys, forcibly taken from their parents and masters, who also want arms and military exercise!"

For information as to the manœuvres on both sides we are much indebted to Mr. Duthy's "Sketches of Hampshire," Woodward's "History of Hampshire," and other sources. Major-General Browne was in command of the London Brigade, and in an account of the battle, "presented to the Right Honourable the Lord Mayor" by one "imployed in the service of the City and State to attend the London Brigade," we are told that "upon Thursday, the 21 of this instant, March (our Brigade being quartered at Midhurst), our major general received orders from Sir William Waller to advance towards Winchester, to a town called Traford, which accordingly he did with incredible speed, almost at an hour's warning, and that night arrived there, which we found to be a small village, not above seven or eight houses to quarter all our men. There we met with much hardship." No long halt was made in the village, for from "an account published three days after the battle, as sent in a letter from an intelligent officer in the armie to his friend in London," we learn that "on Monday last, March 25, we (the writer was one of the London Brigade) were drawn forth from a town called Traford into a heath appointed by Sir William Waller for the meeting of all his forces." Traford is evidently Treyford.

At this rendezvous three disorderly soldiers of the London Brigade were executed. One was tied to a tree and shot for killing his comrade. Another, who belonged to Sir William Waller's own regiment, was hanged as a deserter, as was also the third for mutiny, and for levelling a musket at his captain in order to rescue an offender. Towards evening on Monday, March 25, the London Brigade approached West Meon, which village they were informed was five miles distant from Alresford, six miles from Bishop's Waltham, and nine from Winchester. This brigade, forming the advance guard of Waller's army, also ascertained that the Cavaliers were assembled in force only some five miles off. Lord Hopton's outposts had already occupied the village, and "as the quarter masters came riding in, with a piece of a troop for their guard," a brisk skirmish took place, which resulted in the retreat of the Cavaliers, leaving behind them in captivity their commanding officer, "with a good horse under him, and good store of money." Soon afterwards a rumour was circulated that 600 Cavaliers were entering the village, which caused the Londoners to evacuate it. Some few shots seem to have been exchanged, but Captain Robert Thompson bravely led on a forlorn hope of musketeers, and secured the possession of West Meon to Sir William Waller. Lord Hopton, being duly informed of this brush with the enemy, quitted Winchester on Tuesday, March 26th, on which day Sir William Waller and his staff had reached Petersfield, from whence he advanced as far as East Meon. During the day six troops of his cavalry encountered sixteen troops of Royalist horsemen near West Meon. Three of Lord Hopton's men were made prisoners, and the rest retired, having probably accomplished their object of ascertaining the strength of the enemy.

On Wednesday, March 27th, Sir William Balfour, who had under his command Sir Arthur Haslerig's cuirassiers, known to fame as "The Lobsters," from their iron shells, was sent by Waller with a large force of cavalry to occupy the town of Alresford. But Lord Hopton was too quick for him. Putting himself at the head of 800 horse and dragoons, and ordering the infantry to follow with all speed, he hastened to secure the town. His force and that of Sir William Balfour marched in full view of one another nearly all the way, but the Cavaliers were the first to arrive, and Balfour and his troopers reluctantly fell back to quarter themselves in the neighbouring villages.

On Wednesday, March 27th, the Cavaliers received a considerable accession of strength, and made an attack in force, hoping to surprise the enemy, whom they expected to find at church, the day having been set apart for a solemn fast. But in this they were disappointed, for the Londoners had taken advantage of their halt at Midhurst to keep the fast during the previous week. "Thus the Royalists found them prepared for their reception, full of confidence instead of humiliation, under arms instead of at prayers." The assailants, however, succeeded in capturing some stragglers, and "appeared in a great body upon the hill on the left hand of the town," or, as we should rather call it, the village of West Meon. On the same day Major-General Browne, in obedience to orders received, marched out of West Meon towards Cheriton, the enemy meanwhile threatening an attack in force. Some tumuli called "The Devil's Jumps," West Tisted Common, which are said by local tradition to be the graves of soldiers, perhaps cover the remains of those who fell on this day. "We drew our men into a body near the town (West Meon) and marched as forlorn," in hourly expectation of an attack, until at length they were obliged to halt "a mile or more from the village in extreme danger." So writes one who styles himself "an Eye-Witness." This gentleman had been sent by the Lord Mayor and the Committee of the City Militia to follow Sir William Waller's army, and to report the proceedings of the London Brigade, and seems to have been the first specimen of a war correspondent on record. Unfortunately, his excessive modesty has buried his name beneath the obscurity of two centuries, and to us moderns he can only be a nameless "Eye-Witness."

At length Sir William Waller brought up his brigade from East Meon, and the united force advanced until they "came near to Cheriton, to a place called by some Lamborough Field," a name which it still retains. There and on the adjacent common they quartered for the night, "the enemy lying upon Sutton Common, and some part of them nearer to us, so near that the sentinels could hear one another talk." On Wednesday and Thursday nights Waller's troops "lay in the open field about three miles from Alsford, where the enemy kept a garrison."

On the morning of Thursday, "a commanded party sent to view the enemy" met with a Cavalier forlorn hope of considerable strength. The cavalry fought desperately, and two heroes, whose names are unfortunately not recorded, gained for themselves great renown.

Then spur and sword was the battle word, and we
   made their helmets ring;
Shouting like madmen all the while "For God and
   for the King;"
And though they snuffled psalms, to give the rebel
   dogs their due,
When the roaring shot poured thick and hot, they
   were steadfast men and true.
                    (THE OLD CAVALIER).

At length a gun, which did great execution, was brought to bear upon the Royalists, who thereupon retreated somewhat hastily. "Mercurius Aulicus" gives an account of this day's proceedings, which Mr. Duthy thus admirably summarises :—

"It would appear from the accounts published by the Cavaliers, in what may be termed their *Court Gazette,* that Lord Hopton made a partial attack upon Waller during his march from West Meon, and having driven him from an eminence on which he was stationing his troops, sent Colonel George Lisle with a body of men to retain possession of it, which that officer gallantly executed, bivouacking there all night. If this be correct, it must have been Waller's original aim to have occupied ground nearer Alresford, on the ridge extending from Tichborne to Bramdean Common, and the less elevated swells to the south of it between the wood called Sutton Scrubbs and East Down Farm, and that he was driven from his position and compelled to take up his quarters farther off, in the vicinity of Cheriton. On these eminences Colonel Lisle was probably posted, for on the morning of Thursday, the 28th, it was discovered that his post was commanded by still higher ground, to which the enemy had retired. Skirmishes now ensued, and each party seems to have claimed the advantage. The Cavaliers assert that, notwithstanding the strength of Waller's position, which was such as he usually chose, a spot intersected with hedges and trees, behind which his men were strongly posted, and from which they poured such tremendous vollies as few soldiers had ever experienced before, yet the gallant Colonel Appleyard, being ordered to drive them from it, 'so led up his men, and they so followed their leader, that the confident rebel, with all his odds, was forced from his seat, and made give place to his betters.' If this was the case, he certainly recovered it again, for here he was posted on the ensuing morning. In their account of the transactions of the 28th, the Roundheads state that parties of theirs, in making reconnaissances, were attacked by the enemy, who were received with great gallantry by their horse, and on a considerable body of the Royalists coming to the relief of their comrades who were engaged, a gun was brought to bear on them, which did considerable execution, and caused them to retreat in disorder." Appleyard was wounded, either on this or the following day. He was taken prisoner at Naseby, in 1645, together with the following officers of his regiment, some, if not all, of whom fought at Cheriton :—Captains Triwhit, Masters, Sanderson, and Hubbart, Lieutenants Middleton, Thompson, Lewen, and Baker." They wore yellow uniform."

It is evident that the skirmishes on this day were by no means of a decisive character. Whitlocke's memorials say that the armies for "two or three days faced each other, and had some light skirmishes with the horse, and Sir William Waller's men took about thirty of the enemy, and slew one captain and an Irish rebel." Councils of War were held this day in both camps, and on either side it was decided to fight on the morrow, the setting of whose sun many a brave soldier both of King and Parliament was fated never to behold.

Early on the morning of Friday, March 29th, Sir William Waller's men were seen to be strongly posted on the high ground which extends from the neighbourhood of the village of Cheriton to the farther end of Cheriton Wood, which lay in the front of their extreme right, at which part of the line the London Brigade was posted. Lord Hopton's regiment took advantage of the numerous lines leading from Alresford and the neighbourhood of Bishop's Sutton to crown the eminence that extends from Tichborne to Bramdean Common. Before the battle began, the Cavaliers employed "a subtle device, such that none could fathom," which was the announcement of a victory over the Scotch army by the Earl of Newcastle, at the very time that the Scottish warriors had defeated the Earl, and also of an exaggerated account of Prince Rupert's success at Newark.

The contest is variously said to have commenced at eight, nine, and ten o'clock in the morning. The "Field Word" was the same in both armies, "God with us," which Sir William Waller discovering, substituted for his own men "Jesus bless us," which towards the close of the struggle was exchanged for "Glory to God alone !"

The gaining of Cheriton Wood "was conceived to be of extraordinary advantage," and four files per company of the London Brigade were formed up 1000 strong as a forlorn hope, and were sent to occupy it under the command of an officer who is variously styled Captain, Sergeant Major (*i.e.*, Major), and Colonel Thompson, or Tompson, and who, it will be remembered, had commanded a forlorn hope at

West Meon on the previous Monday evening. The attack proved successful, in spite of the efforts of the forlorn hope of the Cavaliers, who fought hand to hand, and from tree to tree. Lord Hopton had foreseen this attack, and had planted some drakes or field pieces upon the high ground at the north-eastern side of the wood which commands the rest, "which they so furiously discharged that we were forced to retreat," and although reinforced by musketeers, the Londoners did not hold the wood for more than an hour, during which time their casualties were numerous, and they lost Captain-Lieut. Milton wounded and taken. Was he a relative of the poet? A map of this neighbourhood still gives the name of Gunner's Castle to some houses at a cross road close to the position said by the contemporary historians to have been selected by the Royal artillery. Colonel Thompson's leg was so badly shattered by a cannon shot as to render amputation necessary. After the retreat of the Londoners Lord Hopton's cavalry began to charge, "and our men bravely received their first shock, and answered them blow for blow, and bullet for bullet." Nevertheless, although they had the support of a large force of musketeers, who, posted in coppices and enclosures kept up a heavy fire, the Parliamentarians were forced to give ground. But the country was unfavourable for cavalry manœuvres, being of a heathy nature, and a Parliamentarian writer remarks that "the ground where the enemy's horse stood was so uneven that they could not march in any order." This circumstance, together with the warm greeting which they had met with, no doubt damped their ardour in this "sharp battle."

Clarendon says, "The King's horse never behaved themselves so ill as on that day, for the main body of them, after they had sustained one fierce charge, wheeled about to an unreasonable distance, and left their principal officers to shift for themselves," and he speaks in another place of "the few horse that stayed and did their duty."

On the other hand Sir William Waller's horse "did little for the space of an hour after their retreat."

The "foot regiments on both sides fought stoutly on both sides, and came up to push of pike; the London forces and Kentish men with Waller, and Sir Arthur Haslerig and Balfour did brave service." Mr. Duthy says, "The position originally occupied by each army was strong. The ground rapidly descending in front of the Parliamentarians formed a regular escarpement, and before the Royalists it was equally but more irregularly steep, while the wood and detached hedges and coppices lay between them both. It was necessary, however, in order to come into contact, that one party at least should descend from their vantage ground, and it seems as if the Cavaliers, encouraged by the success of their first onset, at which time the Roundheads acknowledged 'that the day was doubtful, if not desperate,' pushed forward with more valour than prudence across the broad valley which separated the armies, up to the rising ground, where Waller's men lay entrenched behind hedges and thickets. This took place chiefly on the left of the Parliamentarians soon after the discomfiture of their horse, and the vantage ground which they occupied enabled them to throw their enemies into confusion and to become assailants themselves. They drove the Royalists from hedge to hedge till they forced them to the top of the hill, probably to the edge of Tichborne Down." The fighting on the right and in the centre seems to have been less severe than it had been on the left.

But now Major-General Browne collected 100 musketeers from the hedges, and led them in person to attack the wavering, but not as yet routed Royalist cavalry. It was now about one hour past noon, when "the London regiments drove the enemy from the hedges, which they had lined with musketeers, and gained a passage to a wood, which stood the Parliament's forces in great stead." They "falling unexpectedly upon the enemy's horse, gave fire so bravely on them that they were forced to wheel about, and thereupon our body of horse came on again, and gave them so hot a charge that they were forced to a disorderly retreat." These London musketeers fought "most gladly and courageously. They charged quite through the enemy's body, and put them to a rout, so that they were forced to retreat to the top of the hill where they first appeared." This hill was probably Tichborne Down. Seeing that the fortune of the day was going against him, Lord Hopton, who, by the admission of his enemies, "managed his forces soldier-like" on this and many other occasions, sent off his baggage and artillery and a portion of his infantry towards Alresford, so that "only the horse and a few of the foot were left to fight us," and to cover the retreat of the main body of the army. 300 Roundhead musketeers now left the shelter of the hedges, and advanced at speed, so that the Royalist foot, "who all the day till then had stood to it, perceiving their horse begin to fly, do seek for shelter by flight themselves, and throw down their arms." To make matters worse, Sir William Balfour, with his 4000 well-armed cavalry, including Sir Arthur Haslerig's iron-clad "Lobsters," who had been repulsed in the earlier part of the day, once more charged the disheartened infantry, completing their discomfiture. Sir William Waller, as this living torrent of cuirassiers swept past him, making the very earth tremble beneath with the trampling of their chargers, "bravely encouraged them to second the example and courage of their leader, and they did notably serve to increase the victory. The Kentish regiment of horse, assisted with Col. Norton's regiment, stood manfully to it, and never lost ground." Colonel Norton, who had lived much at Alresford, was well acquainted with every lane in the neighbourhood, and is said to have brought up his renowned troop of Hambledon Boys, and charged the Cavaliers in the rear, thus not a little contributing to the victory. The Kentish regiment gave no quarter to the Irish, "who first ran for it, and threw down their arms. They were mostly red coats of Lord Inchiquin's regiment, led by his brother." Another account says, "The first of the King's men that are said to run away were two regiments of Irish." The officers did their best to rally the fugitives, "beating and cutting them with their swords," but to no purpose. "There was a hollow betwixt both bodies, which each endeavouring to gain, many men found it for their graves on both sides." This is probably the lane leading from Sutton Scrubbs towards Cheriton, which, on that fatal day, according to village tradition, ran with blood. The victory was complete. Those who followed the pursuit found nearly 2000 arms under the hedges, and many of Lord Hopton's newly-raised Hampshire levies made the best of their way to their homes without opposition from the victors. Lord Hopton in person did his best to cover the retreat with a body of cavalry composed of the regiments of Colonels Butler, Nevill, and Howard. Colonel Butler received a wound in the leg, but reached Oxford in safety.

Sir W. Balfour and Sir A. Haslerig were energetic in the pursuit, and, in spite of the efforts of the Royalist cavalry, succeeded, after a chase of between two and three miles, in overtaking the retreating infantry, who, according to rustic report, shouted to their mounted comrades "Face them, face them once more; face them!" Thus urged, the cavalry made a final charge, only to be broken and chased until the infantry were a second time overtaken and attacked, losing many men. It was five o'clock in the afternoon before the battle was at an end, and neither army was sorry to perceive the coming on of night. As the Cavaliers retreated through the town of Alresford they set fire to it at both ends, probably in revenge for the Parliamentary politics of some of its principal inhabitants. The soldiers of the victorious army, however, speedily arrived, and aided the inhabitants to extinguish the conflagration, which only destroyed four or five houses. Sir William Balfour, who commanded the cavalry, in his account, written on the following day, said that the pursuit was kept up till Winchester was not four miles distant, and informed the Parliament that he was drowsy for want of sleep, which he considered a sufficient reason for curtailing his official report. Misled by unfriendly rustics, and seeing that most of the infantry were retreating in the direction of Winchester, Sir William Waller urged on the chase towards that city, and so failed to secure all the fruits of his victory. "Mercurius Aulicus" asserts that Lord Hopton took three colours from him, carrying them off in triumph. The same newspaper says that Hopton lost neither guns, colours, nor carriages. Another account says that Waller captured seven guns, but Rushworth says that only two guns fell into his hands. It is expressly stated by one writer that two hours before the defeat became general, Lord Hopton sent away nine guns towards Winchester, with an escort of 300 men, leaving only two on the field, which were afterwards captured. Six of the nine guns were buried in a place of security, and the other three were conveyed in safety to Basing House. One hundred loads of corn, meal, and provisions, two waggons conveying field pieces and muskets, and 30 other conveyances are said to have rewarded the victors.

Favoured by the darkness Lord Hopton, "with his horses and carriages, it being in the night, wheeled about through a narrow lane, and so went unperceived to their garrison at Basing House," which he himself reached in company with the Earl of Forth and fourteen other officers. The line of retreat seems to ave been through Avington, and thence towards Basing House, which a considerable body of troops succeeded in reaching in good order. All through the night did the disheartened Cavaliers march in haste, exclaiming as they hurried towards Alton, Basing, and Winchester. " The kingdom's lost ! the kingdom's lost !" and killing more than 200 horses in order to block up the narrow lanes with their bodies so as to impede pursuit.

The slaughter was considerable, most of the Irish neither giving nor receiving quarter. The number of the killed and wounded is variously stated, but the most reliable estimate gives 900 as the loss on the side of the Parliament, and 140J as that in Lord Hopton's army. Few men of note fell in Waller's army. Major Bosville, or Bovill, who had been one of the Commissioners to arrange the terms of surrender at Arundel, received a mortal wound in the stomach, and Colonel John Meldrum, who in 1642 had been Lieutenant of the 2nd Troop of Horse, was shot in the arm and wounded in the head. In his will he is described as being " very much wounded." After the Restoration his remains, in common with others, were exhumed, and thrown into a common pit in St. Margaret's church-yard. Colonel Dolbeir, or Dalbier, hereafter to prove a foe to Basing House, was wounded, and Colonel Thompson lost his leg, as we have already seen, during the attack upon Cheriton Wood. Captain Fleming was also wounded, but recovered. On April 17th, two members of the House of Commons were sent to visit him, and to present him with thirty pieces of gold, promising him at the same time further supplies of money.

The losses on the King's side in killed, wounded, and prisoners were indeed grievous. The death of Lord John Stuart, second brother to the Duke of Richmond, who commanded Lord Hopton's cavalry, was especially lamented. He was "a young man of extraordinary hope, and whose courage was so signal in this action that too much could not have been expected from it, if he had outlived it, and he was so generally beloved that he could not but be very generally lamented." He was little more than twenty-one years of age, and was far more at home in the camp than he was at Court. Lloyd tells us that he 'not only led a vanguard of light horse, charging the enemy most gallantly, but also discreetly composed a difference arising in the command and service with these words, 'Let us dispute the main with the enemy, and we shall have time enough to dispute punctilios between ourselves.'" He was wounded in six places during the action, and had two horses killed under him, and is thought to have received his death wound in the hollow way before referred to. from Colonel John Meldrum, who was, like himself, a gallant soldier.

Sir John Smith, brother to Lord Carrington, and Commissary-General of the Horse, was also mortally wounded. He belonged to an ancient Roman Catholic family, had seen much service in Flanders, and had long been celebrated as an experienced cavalry officer. He had done many deeds of valour during the war, made a daring escape from his prison in Windsor Castle, and recovered the Royal Standard at the Battle of Edge-hill. This exploit is thus described by Mr. Warburton: " Then Captain Smith, an officer in Lord Bernard Stuart's 'Show troop,' resolved to rescue it or die ; there were none to second him but Robert Walsh, an Irishman, and one or two more, and the stoutest brigade of cavalry could scarcely penetrate that serried line of pikes, through which the musketeers still kept up a continuous fire. Smith and his comrades snatched some orange scarves, the hated badge of Essex, from the dead, and easily mingled in the confusion among the enemy; so they approached the Lord General, whose secretary, Mr. Chambers, was waving the standard in triumph above his head. Smith rode up, and unceremoniously told him that a penman had no business to carry such a standard in a field like that. So saying, he snatched it from him and moved quietly away until he had a clear course before him to the hill ; then galloping off with his precious prize, he restored it in triumph to the King. That evening he was knighted under its shadow, the first knight banneret made in England for one hundred years. He afterwards received a gold medal, with the King's portrait on one side and the banner on the reverse. 'He wore it by a green watered ribbon across his shoulders until his dying day.'" Both he and Lord John Stuart were carried off the field to Reading, and from thence, on the following day, to Abingdon, " by the few horse that stayed with them and did their duty, but they lived only to the second dressing of their wounds, which were very many upon both of them. The death of these two eminent officers made the names of many who perished that day the less inquired into and mentioned." They both found soldiers' graves at Oxford. The number of Royalist gentlemen slain on this fatal day is said to have been four hundred and eighty-five, of whom two-fifths were Roman Catholics. It is noteworthy that Sir Richard Tichborne, the second baronet, probably took part in this battle, as did also his brother, Sir Benjamin, and his son, Sir Henry. On the other side fought Robert Tichborne, a zealous adherent of Cromwell, who was afterwards Lord Mayor of London, and who was afterwards one of the regicides. He was at the Restoration arraigned, but was never brought to trial. Sir Benjamin Tichborne was M.P. for Petersfield, and after Cheriton Fight retired to the family mansion at West Tisted. Some troopers were sent to arrest him, but he escaped by concealing himself in a hollow oak, which still stands in an adjacent field, and to this day is known as "Sir Benjamin's Oak." Sir Henry Tichborne, the son of Sir Richard, who is represented in Tilbourg's celebrated picture of the Tichborne Dole, was a staunch Cavalier. He recovered his sequestered estates at the Restoration in 1660.

In "England's Black Tribunal" we read:— "Colonels Sandys, Scot, and Manning, persons of great worth and eminency, whose valorous minds scorned danger, and hated no man so much as a coward, these gallant sons of Mars were all slain in the battle between my Lord Hopton and Waller, on Cheriton Down, March 29th, 1644. Colonel Phillips, slain near Winchester (Gentlemen Volunteers.) Mr. Sands, slain at Alresford." Lord Powlet, of Somersetshire, and Sir George Wilmot were erroneously said to have fallen. Sir John Powlet reached Basing with Lord Hopton. Colonel Sandys was father-in-law to Sir John Mill, those of Newton Bury, and representative of Sandys of Estwaite Furness and Sands of the Vine. The son of Colonel H. Sandys of the Vine, himself a Cavalier, was obliged to sell the estates in 1653. Sir William Balfour says that Colonels Gray and Butler were also killed, but Colonel Butler at any rate escaped to Oxford, although he received a wound in the leg. Colonel Manning, a Roman Catholic, also fell. Of him the "Brief Chronicle" says that he was "father to the person who betrayed the King to Cromwell while he resided at Colen, in the design of Colonel Penruddock, for which he was shot to death in the Duke of Newburgh's country." Colonel Phillips was probably one of the family that resided at Stoke Charity.

The Earl of Forth, who, it will be remembered, had come to the assistance of Lord Hopton, was confined to his quarters at Alresford by an attack of gout, probably brought on by his notorious intemperance. When word was brought to him that the London Brigade had been driven from Cheriton Wood with great slaughter, and with the loss of a thousand prisoners, he called for a pack of cards. At length a messenger came in haste to tell him that the Royal horse was routed, and that his presence was imperatively necessary, upon which he went at once to the scene of action. He was wounded, but in company with Lord Hopton and fourteen other officers reached Basing House in safety. Mr. Money says that "he had seen service in Sweden under Gustavus Adolphus, in Denmark, Russia, Livonia, Lithuania, Poland, and Prussia. In England alone the number of his wounds had equalled that of the battles in which he had exposed himself. At Edgehill, says Lloyd, he modelled the fight. He was at Brentford and Gloucester, was shot in both the fights at Newbury, at Cheriton, and at Banbury. He had been shot in the head, in both arms, the mouth, leg, and shoulder, and, as if all this had not been enough for his scars and his story, the catalogue was finished by a fall from his horse that broke his shoulder. He survived to wait upon Charles II. in exile, and, returning to his native country, was buried in 1651 at Dundee."

There were on the King's side "divers other persons of quality wounded, among whom was Sir Edward Stawell, eldest son to Sir John, and Sir Henry, now Lord Beard." They were both taken prisoners. The former was "a Major-General of a brigade, a man of a great estate," and is said by Sir William Balfour to have been dangerously wounded. Colonel Sir Henry Beard was "Colonel of a regiment of horse, and of a regiment of foot," and had been in the service of the Parliament in Ireland, which country he had only recently left. Four days after the fight he was brought up to London as a prisoner by Sir Arthur Haslerig, and was confined in Lord Petre's house in Aldersgate-street. He was soon afterwards exchanged for Captain Hacker and Mr. Stanley, who had been captured by the Royal army.

"Colonel Cary, a Renegado" from the service of the Parliament, was a prisoner with a severe wound, and Colonel Seymour shared his captivity. The prisoners taken during the fight and in the course of the next few days were said to be 120 officers and 560 soldiers. Much ammunition was also taken during the pursuit. The retreating Cavaliers were reported to have carried off several cartloads of dead, in addition to others interred at various places. There is a large mound in Lamborough Field, near Cheriton, which is the last resting-place of many of the slain. When it was opened a few years since, a layer of black earth alone remained of what had once been valiant soldiers. In Cheriton Wood also there are some mounds on the rising ground, wherein rustic tradition says that three generals were buried, and which probably cover the remains of the London Trained Bands and their opponents who fell during the struggle for the possession of the wood. These mounds are overgrown with brambles, but are easily recognisable, the more so as the neighbouring underwood was cut away last year (1880).

Lord Hopton's army released fifty of their prisoners, one of whom, who was left behind in a wounded condition, reported that not more than 20 of his comrades were detained after the battle was at an end. Lieutenant-Colonel Kingston, Captains Price, Chidleigh, Jackson, Audley, and Seymour, Lieutenant Kite, Ensigns Cowper, Mellis, Marsh, and Midley, Cornets Constable and Ducket, Physician John Morsey, and a nameless priest, all fell into the hands of Sir William Waller, and "a captain left behind at Alresford sorely wounded, doth swear the devil is in the Roundheads, they are such firemen." Lord Hopton's cornet for his troop of guard was a standard gules, bearing for device a cannon or; above, this motto, *Et sacris compescuit ignibus ignes.*"

Only one day did Lord Hopton remain at the friendly garrison of Basing House, for on Sunday, March 31st, leaving his wounded behind him, he continued his march to Reading, proceeding from thence to Oxford. The late Mr. W. Cooper, of Cheriton, had in his possession a cannon ball weighing about nine pounds, and I now have another of smaller calibre. Such relics of the great fight are of late less frequently upturned by the plough than they formerly were, but not many years since some of the dwellers at now peaceful Cheriton utilised them for the game of bowls, and the late T. Lipscomb, Esq., of Alresford, exhibited at Winchester in 1845 a basket-hilted sword, which was found on the battle-field. Captain Wickham, of Tichborne Park, also has a 12-pounder shot, cast like a bullet.

A week before Cheriton Fight, the King had issued a proclamation at Oxford that all holders of office under the Crown should repair to that city by April 20th at the latest, on pain of forfeiture of office, intending to commence the campaign early in the season. But these hopes were now blighted. Clarendon says, "This battle was fought on the 29th day of March, which was a very doleful entering into the beginning of the year 1644, and broke all the measures and altered the whole scheme of the King's counsels. For whereas before, he hoped to have entered the field early, and to have acted an offensive part, he now discerned he was wholly to be upon the defensive, and that was like to be a very hard part too!"

The London Brigade halted at Alresford, but some of Waller's men marched fourteen miles beyond that town in pursuit of the fugitives. Some of the prisoners gave information that detachments of the Queen's and Prince Maurice's regiments had taken part in the fight, and that a Council of War had decided upon the destruction by fire of the town and castle of Farnham, if Lord Hopton had gained the day. Sir William Waller himself marched towards Winchester, which he reached on the day after the battle. A messenger whom he despatched to Major-General Browne, at Alresford, was "interviewed" by the "Eye-Witness," and informed him that there were not 200 of the Cavaliers left together, and that Sir William Waller would attack the city, from which he was only a mile and a-half distant. Lord Hopton having retreated to Reading and Oxford, there was no longer any hope of defending the entrenchments constructed at Winchester with so much skill and labour, and Sir William Ogle was satisfied with keeping possession of the castle itself for the King. Accordingly, leaving about one hundred soldiers, most of whom were Irishmen, to hold that important fortress, most of the Cavaliers who had taken refuge in the city marched from thence to Andover. Sir William Waller, who claimed Winchester Castle as his own by right of inheritance, expected that his success at Cheriton would give him immediate possession of it, but on reaching the city he found the gates closed against him. Bishop Milner says that the inheritance of Winchester Castle certainly belonged to Sir Richard Tichborne, who had married Waller's sister. Waller's second wife was the daughter of the Marquis of Winchester. As soon, however, as he had summoned the garrison, the Mayor and Corporation came out and presented him with the keys of the city, declaring their adherence to the cause of the King and Parliament, " and desiring to be preserved from violence, which they were accordingly." They doubtless shared the opinion that "the battle near Winchester is the greatest wonder that hath happened in our days." Colonel Norton was meanwhile scouring the country at the head of his troopers, and captured without resistance 160 horsemen, who had taken refuge in a wood the night after the battle. Sir William Balfour chased the retreating Royalists as far as Andover, for which town Waller himself was one of the members, and took post there. The officer in charge of the prison at Winchester was so terrified by the news of the disaster at Cheriton that he opened the prison doors and released the eighty prisoners who had been taken at Romsey a few days previously.

Sir William Waller, not thinking it worth while to spend time in the reduction of Winchester Castle, merely halted to refresh his men, and then hastened towards Salisbury in pursuit of the Royalist cavalry. On his arrival there he found that he had again failed to meet with Lord Hopton, but he "made all the Cathedral men run for it." Sir William Balfour, who was at Wilton on April 4th, and Waller then sent out detachments on all sides, and thus captured numerous prisoners " in woods and by-houses every day," sometimes securing a whole troop at a time. Sir William Balfour whilst at Andover was informed that Lady Hopton had reached Newbury on her way to join her husband, who having received reinforcements from Oxford, was now engaged in rallying his forces, and was at Marlborough on April 6th. Sir William Balfour promptly despatched a party of horse to Newbury, who succeeded in surprising Lady Hopton, together with her escort of 200 men, two coaches, and twelve coach horses. "Order was given to treat the lady with the respect due to her quality, and she was quickly dismissed, and conveyed to Oxford, being permitted to take with her what plate and jewels properly belonged to her or her attendants, but the rest was made prize of."

Sir William Balfour's letter to the Earl of Essex, describing Cheriton Fight, was read in the House of Commons on Monday, April 1st, 1644, and James Pitsome, or Pattison, and Ralph Norton, the two scouts, who brought the intelligence to London, received 10/. each. On the following day Sir Arthur Haslerig gave a full account of the matter to the House of Commons. The Lord Mayor of London, John Wollaston, had already directed that Sunday, March 31st, was to be observed as a day of solemn thanksgiving by "every minister within the City of London, liberties, lines of communication, and bills of mortality," and the House of Commons now ordered that Tuesday, April 9th, should be a day of public thanksgiving for the victory in all churches and chapels in London and Westminster, and within the lines of communication. April 14th was to be the Day of Thanksgiving in all provincial churches and chapels on the south side of the Trent, whilst on account of the difficulty of communication, April 28th was to be the Thanksgiving Day in all parishes north of the Trent. "The printer to bring a convenient number of notices to the members of the House to be sent into the several counties." It was also ordered that on Tuesday, April 9th, being the Day of Thanksgiving in the metropolis, every minister should publish the resolution of the Parliament "to draw all their forces together to pursue this victory, and to put it to a day, and to fight with the enemy," so as to put an end to the war. They were also "to exhort the people to contribute to their utmost for the sending forth what possible strength can be had." A collection was to be made on behalf of "poor maimed soldiers."

The Rev. Obadiah Sedgwick, D.D., Pastor of Coggeshall, in Essex, preached the thanksgiving sermon before the House of Commons at St. Margaret's Church, Westminster, in the morning, choosing as the motto for his discourse I. Sam., vii., 12: "Hitherto hath the Lord helped us;" and selecting as his text Psalm iii., 8: "Salvation belongeth unto the Lord. Thy blessing is upon thy people. Selah!"

"Master Thomas Case, Preacher at Milkstreet, London, and one of the Assembly of Divines," occupied the same pulpit in the afternoon. The motto chosen by him was Psalm ix., 10: "And they that know thy name will put their trust in thee; for thou, Lord, hast not forsaken them that seek thee!" and his text was Daniel xi., 32: "And such as do wickedly against the covenant shall be corrupt by flatteries; but the people that do know their God shall be strong, and do exploits."

On the same day the preachers received the thanks of the House of Commons at the hands of Sir W. Brereton and Sir W. Massam, for their sermons, which were ordered to be printed. We learn from Rushworth that on the evening of this eventful April 9th there was a great meeting in the city, "to whom repaired a Committee of Lords and Commons." Speeches were made by the Earl of Warwick, Sir H. Vane, the Earl of Essex, the Earl of Pembroke, Colonel Hollis, and Mr. Recorder, who all concurred in urging the speedy raising of men and money for the service of the Parliament, in order that the advantages gained at Cheriton might be improved to the utmost. But Colonel Ludlow subsequently wrote as follows:—"We were not yet so happy as to improve our advantages, by which negligence we got little more than the field and the reputation of the victory."

CHAPTER XXI.—DR. FULLER AND ARMY CHAPLAINS—TRAITORS AT BASING HOUSE—THE ASSOCIATED COUNTIES—WALLER'S SUCCESS AT CHRISTCHURCH—THE ISLE OF WIGHT IN DANGER—WALTHAM HOUSE TAKEN—RECRUITING IN LONDON—OPPOSITION AT WINCHESTER—AFFAIRS AT SOUTHAMPTON, ODIHAM, BASING, AND SALISBURY—OPENING OF THE CAMPAIGN OF 1644.

The Battle of Cheriton would, of itself, have committed Sir William Waller irretrievably to the cause of the Parliament, but long before, in a proclamation of "grace, favour, and pardon to the inhabitants of his county of Southampton," published at Reading on November 28th, 1642, the King had spoken thus : " Except Sir Thomas Jarvise, Sir William Waller, Knights, and Richard Norton, Esquire, against all which we shall proceed according to the Rules of the Law."

In this hour of their disaster and defeat, Basing House was of great service to the Cavaliers as a rallying point. The "Weekly Accompt," published on Wednesday, April 10th, 1644, thus speaks of the retreat from Cheriton :

" We shall find that Sir William Waller, with as much courage as successe, hath pursued his advantages, and forced the Lord Hopton from Winchester to Basing, who cannot but lament his unhappinesse ; our men still pressing on him and gaining ground as he fled back, until they had routed the army of his men, and sent out many of his men from the world."

Sir John Pawlet retired with Lord Hopton to Oxford. Many of the wounded were probably left at Basing House to receive surgical aid. This is the more likely, as Lord Hopton left in the garrison his own Chaplain, who was no other than Dr. Thomas Fuller, the author of " The Worthies of England." He joined Lord Hopton in the capacity of Chaplain to the Forces in 1643, preached every Sunday to the troops, and wherever the army went made careful personal inquiries, to the no small benefit of literature. He was present at Cheriton Fight, and was, as we have said, left at Basing House when the Royalist forces retreated to Reading and Oxford. He animated the garrison to repulse the assaults of a portion of Waller's army, and seems to have remained some months under the hospitable roof of Lord Winchester, writing of " the troutful streams" and " natural commodities" of Hampshire, and confessing to some slight interruptions from the noise of the cannon. He' thus speaks of Basing House and Bramshill :—

" As for civil structures, Basing, built by the first Marquess of Winchester, was the greatest of any subject's house in England, yea, larger than most (eagles have not the biggest nests of all birds) of the King's Palaces. The motto, 'Love Loyaltie' was often written in every window thereof, and was well practised in it when, for resistance on that account, it was lately levelled to the ground.

"Next Basing, Bramsell, built by the last Lord Zouch in a bleak and barren place, was a stately structure, especially before part thereof was defaced with a casual fire."

In Russell's memorials of Dr. Fuller we are told : " Lord Hopton came to Oxford in Dec., 1643, having already distinguished himself, both in and out of the field, as one who could command not only others, but himself. Amongst his chaplains were Fuller and Richard Watson, of Caius College, also an author of several curious collections." Fuller's anonymous biographer observes of the Lord Hopton : "This noble Lord, though as courageous and expert a captain, and successful withal as any the King had, was never averse to an amicable closure of the war upon fair and honourable terms, and did therefore well approve of the

Doctor, and his desires and pursuit after peace. The good Doctor was likewise infinitely contented in his attendance on such an excellent personage, whose conspicuous and noted loyalty could not but derive the same reputation to his retainers, especially one so near his conscience as his chaplain, and so wipe off the stain which, the mistakes of those men (the zealots, who, with Heylyn, were not satisfied with Fuller's measure of loyalty) had cast upon him."

Dr. Fuller afterwards rejoined Lord Hopton and when that general was driven into Cornwall obtained permission to take refuge at Exeter, where he resumed his studies, and preached constantly to the citizens.

The army chaplain played no unimportant part in the Civil War.

John Vicars informs us ("Jehovah Jireh," p. 200) that at Edge-hill "the reverend and renowned Master Marshall, Master Ask, Master Mourton, Masters Obadiah and John Sedgwick, and Master Wilkins, and divers others eminently pious and learned pastors rode up and down the army through the thickest dangers, and in much personal hazard, most faithfully and courageously exhorting and encouraging the soldiers to fight valiantly and not to fly, but now, if ever, to stand to it and fight for their religion and laws!" In 1639 chaplains attached to the Lord General's train, or as we should now say, to the Staff, received 6s. 8d. per diem, but the pay of the preacher to the train of Artillery was only 3s. per diem. Amongst the officers general of the horse we read of a preacher with a daily stipend of 4s. On Monday, May 6th, 1644, the House of Commons increased the pay of all chaplains serving with the armies of the Parliament to 8s. per diem, but on February 27th, 1659, we learn that "the preacher was one of the field and staff officers of a regiment of Foot," and was paid 6s. 8d. per diem.

The defeat at Cheriton sorely discouraged the little garrison at Basing, some of whom grew weary of further resistance. A plot was formed within the walls to surrender the fortress to Sir William Waller, with whom a correspondence was carried on by "the Lord Edward Pawlet, brother to the Marquis of Winchester, and then with him as unsuspected as a brother ought to be." Everything was arranged, and Sir Richard Granville, who had been after Cheriton Fight appointed by Waller to command his cavalry, "was sent before with a body of the horse, that all things might be well disposed and prepared against the time Waller himself should come to him. He appointed a rendezvous for the horse at Bagshot, and the same day marched out of London only with his equipage, which was very noble, a coach and six horses, a waggon and six horses, many led horses, and many servants. With these, when he came to Staines, he left the Bagshot-road, and marched directly to Reading, where the King's garrison then was; and thence, without delay, to Oxford, where he was very graciously received by the King, and the more because he was not expected. He communicated then to the King the whole design of the surprise of Basing; upon which the King sent an express immediately to the Marquis with all the particular informations; who thereupon seized upon his brother and the other conspirators, who confessed all, with all the circumstances of the correspondence and combination. The Marquis prevailed with the King that he might only turn his brother out of the garrison, after justice was done upon his complices. This very happy and seasonable discovery preserved that important place, which without it had infallibly been lost within few days." So speaks Clarendon. Lord Edward paid dearly for his share in the plot, and the name of Edward has never since been borne by any of his family. The Marquis seems to have been stern enough in his punishment of his brother, having apparently compelled him to act as the executioner of his accomplices and of all criminals belonging to the garrison, for in the most complete list of the prisoners taken at Basing House which has been preserved, we find this terrible entry, "Edward Pawlet, the hangman." The subject is a painful one, and nothing but stern duty as an impartial chronicler induces me to refer to it.

On Saturday, March 30th, 1644, the day after Cheriton Fight, the House of Commons ordered that 3000 foot, 1200 horse, and 500 dragoons should be raised and maintained for Sir William Waller in the four associated counties of Kent, Surrey, Hants, and Sussex. Hampshire, in which the Isle of Wight was on this occasion not included, was ordered to pay a weekly assessment of 680*l*. 16s. This payment was to begin from the 10th of February, 1644, and to continue for four months at least. The ordinance states that a considerable portion of these troops had been already raised, "and whereas the said counties have bought many arms and ammunition, and must buy many more, and must be at great charge in raising, maintaining, and recruiting the said forces, making and erecting of fortifications, magazines, courts of guard, &c.," it was ordered that all monies levied in Hants and Sussex on the estates of Papists and delinquents, and two-thirds of all monies paid to the County Treasurer, were to be devoted to the discharge of these liabilities. The whole weekly amount to be raised in the four counties for the raising and maintenance of the Association forces was to be 2638*l*. 1s. 6d. Kent was to pay a weekly sum of 930*l*. 16s.; Surrey, with the exception of Southwark, and the lines of communication, as the defences of London were styled, paid 345*l*. 13s. 6d. per week, whilst the contribution of Sussex for the period was 680*l*. 16s. The Committee charged with the sequestration of the estates of delinquents was urged to be active and diligent in the good work of raising funds at the expense of the friends of the King. Sir William Waller was styled Sergeant-Major-General under the Earl of Essex. This weekly assessment was, in point of fact, continued for a much longer period than the four months during which it was originally imposed, and was renewed on Saturday, June 15th, 1644. All officers and men belonging to the associated forces of the four counties were to subscribe the Solemn League and Covenant on enlistment. Officers were to make good any horses or arms which might be embezzled or lost in any way except in actual warfare. No free quarter was to be permitted, and the Association regiments were not to march beyond the limits of the four counties without the consent of Sir William Waller and of a Committee. A liberal scale of pay was laid down, but with the understanding that all officers whose pay amounted to 10s. per diem were only to receive half that amount until the close of the war, whilst those whose pay was 5s. per diem were likewise obliged to look upon 1s. 8d. of that amount as deferred pay.

Leaving Winchester Castle with its small Cavalier garrison unassailed for the present, Sir William Waller, accompanied by Sir William Balfour and his victorious 40 0 horse and dragoons, made a rapid southward march from Cheriton and Alresford. He was reinforced from Poole and by the garrison of Southampton, under the command of Colonel Norton, and on his arrival at Salisbury "made all the Cathedral men run for it." Steadily following up the pursuit, Waller and Balfour fell upon a regiment of Cavalier horse and 100 foot, who had attempted to rally near Whitchurch, in the neighbourhood of Dorchester, routed them, and chased them as far as Weymouth, with the loss of many killed, some of whom were men of note. Three hundred prisoners were taken. 70 of whom were officers and gentlemen, together with 500 arms. Kent was sending to Waller 200 horse and 300 foot. Other troops were to follow these, not only from Kent but also from the other associated counties. Continuing his westward march, Sir William Waller despatched a body of 1000 horse and dragoons, with orders to relieve the towns of Poole and Lyme Regis, which were in danger of capture by the Cavaliers, to clear the county of any hostile force, and afterwards to march and occupy Weymouth. These orders were successfully executed by this force of cavalry, which, according to another account, was 2000 strong. It also gained an important success at Christchurch.

Sir John Mills, the Governor, had summoned several Royalist Commissioners of Array to meet in consultation as to the best means of recruiting Lord Hopton's army. Waller's cavalry arrived unexpectedly, and, as he himself stated, in his letter to the Parliament written from Ringwood on April 5th, 1644, captured the whole of the assembled Cavaliers " without striking a stroke." One hundred horses, 400 infantry, and more than that number of arms rewarded the victors. The prisoners were sent under escort to the town of Poole. One hundred of them are said to have been gentlemen of position, and "a valiant Lady Captain," who is elsewhere styled "the cornet or captain of the oyster women petitioners to Parliament," was detained in custody.

One writer says that "twenty-two Commissioners of Array for Hopton, and Royalist gentlemen of Hants and Wilts, as well as 280 brave horses," were captured. Amongst the officers were Colonel Sir John Mills, Sir John Stowell, Mr. Coventry, Lieut.-Colonels Goddard and Paulet, Sergeant-Major (*i.e.*, Major) Turney, Captains Gogill, Mill, and Barrow; Captain-Lieutenant Sheiling; Lieutenants Willis, Hitchcocke, Jenkins, Philpott, Harvey, two Lewins, Cockeram, and Scullard; Cornets

Lane, Johnson, Baily, and Thorneburgh; Quartermasters Complin, Crofts, Egerley, and Legate; Marshall Richard Michael; Dr. Thornbury; Mr. Todd, Captaine; Gentlemen in ranks, Messrs. Worsleys (two), Thornburnes (two), Lovell, Jenkins, Fitch, Hencocke, and Cockes; also, "Mr. Imber, minister, who was plundered and imprisoned." Mr. Todd is, in another account, said to have been not a captain, but a chaplain. Two centuries ago the respective duties of captains and chaplains were often easily amalgamated.

Christchurch Castle, near the church on the N.E., close to the Avon, was probably built by Richard de Redvers. Some ruins of the keep, and also of a stone building about a hundred yards to the eastward still remain. The latter, the walls of which are of considerable thickness, was probably the hall of the Constable or Governor, whose yearly fee in 1559 was 8£. 0s. 9d. The keep stood upon an artificial mound about twenty feet in height. Portions of its eastern and western walls remain. The walls of the castle are in some places twelve feet in thickness, but the whole structure was probably dismantled about the year 1656, when Sir Henry Wallop, second of the name, had been High Constable. The havoc wrought in the Priory, of which, as elsewhere, Cromwell bears the blame, may perchance have been wrought by Waller and Balfour's troopers after this victory at Christchurch in 1644.

The Isle of Wight now gave proofs of its devotion to the cause of the Parliament, sending abundance of corn, butter, cheese, and other provisions to Southampton for the supply of Waller's army, and refusing to receive any payment for them. A welcome reinforcement of 300 men was likewise sent to swell the Puritan ranks. Mr. Lisle, the well-known member for Winchester, was, on April 8th, directed by the House of Commons " to bring in a letter of thanks to be written to the inhabitants of the Isle of Wight for their forwardness in sending provisions to Sir William Waller's army." On the same day the Lieutenant of the Ordnance was directed to forward to Waller " one hundred barrels of powder, match, and bullet proportionable."

But on April 17th the Earl of Pembroke addressed a very strong remonstrance to Parliament, stating that the Isle of Wight was in great danger, the town of Wareham, in Dorsetshire, having been taken by the King's forces. He complained also that Colonel Carne, the Deputy-Governor, was detained in London, awaiting examination as to whether he had not discountenanced those who were well affected to the Parliament, and countenanced the Malignants or Royalists, and asked that the Colonel might be either acquitted or sentenced, and that in any case precautions might be taken for the defence of the Island.

This remonstrance was supported by a numerously-signed petition from the inhabitants of the Island, dated at Newport, on April 20th, which declared that Colonel Carne was wanted at his post at once. The House of Commons thereupon took the matter into consideration on April 24th, with the result that Colonel Carne was acquitted of the two charges brought against him by majorities of 21 and 20 votes respectively. The Isle of Wight petitioners further requested that monies might not be collected in the Island by strangers, " but by some of our own honest country gentlemen," that the Island Militia should be reduced to three companies at most, and that " the present officers, who are much beloved," might retain their commands. They asked that the new excise duties levied in the Island might be expended upon the local forces and garrisons, as they were in dread of an invasion on behalf of the King from Spain and elsewhere. They begged for an issue of at least 200 barrels of powder, warlike stores, and more especially swords, there being none of these weapons in store. They were also urgent that the Earl of Pembroke, who was the Lord Lieutenant, should pay them a visit. " though it was but for one week, for the better establishing of peace and quietness."

The Island can scarcely have been in the spring of 1644 a desirable sea side residence!

On Friday, April 5th, Colonel Jonas Van Druschke, " colonel over a regiment of horse, under Sir William Waller," of whom we have heard before, presented a petition informing the House " of his long sickness by reason of his great wounds." He had, however, recovered, and was " desirous to go again to his charge if he had part of his arrears." His request was granted, and on April 17th it was also ordered that a sum of 30*l.*, belonging to a person named Brasier, which had been seized by the Committee for Examinations, as being intended to be conveyed together with other property to Oxford, should be paid by Sir Arthur Haslerig and Sir Philip Stapleton to Captain Fleming, who probably belonged to the family at North Stoneham, and who had been wounded at Cheriton Fight. From this grant being paid through Sir Arthur Haslerig and Sir Philip Stapleton, who were both distinguished cavalry officers, it is probable that the recipient was Christopher Fleming, Esq., afterwards captain and adjutant general of horse, who fell during the siege of Oxford in 1644. Another Colonel Fleming was appointed Governor of Pembroke Castle in 1647, and Sir Oliver Fleming was on November 2nd, 1643, appointed by the Parliament as their Master of the Ceremonies. Mr. Brasier, however, stoutly denied the justice of the confiscation of his 30l., and he was ordered to be compensated if he succeeded in proving his case. Sir William Waller about this time bought in London 30l. worth of confiscated Royalist property, which he afterwards conveyed to Holland, and on which, as he in his " Vindication" takes great pains to prove, he paid all lawful tolls and excise duty.

Even before the great day of Cheriton Fight the London Brigade under the command of Major-General Browne had been anxious to return home, and after the defeat of Lord Hopton, the Londoners refused to serve any longer for the present. Clarendon says, in his account of Cheriton Fight, "There could not then be any other estimate made of the loss Waller sustained, than by the not pursuing the visible advantage he had, and by the utter refusal of the Auxiliary Regiments of London and Kent to march farther, who, within three or four days left him, and returned to their habitations, with great lamentations of their friends who were missing." These Kentish Auxiliaries were probably under the command of Colonels Head, Dixie, and Sir Miles Livesay.

The Londoners, before they returned home, did good service for the Parliament. They marched under the command of Major-General Browne, from Southampton, intending to proceed to Wareham, in Dorsetshire. But they seem to have first proceeded to the eastward, through Botley, to the little village of Wickham. Intelligence reached them there that Colonel Whitehead, M.P. for Southampton, with a force of 200 men, was besieging an equal number of Cavaliers, commanded by Colonel Bennet, at Bishop's Waltham, in the stately palace belonging to the Bishop of Winchester, then known as Waltham-house, and of which the stately ivy-grown ruins now arrest the attention of even the most heedless passer-by. Bishop Robert Poynet, the successor of Bishop Gardiner in the see of Winchester, surrendered the palace and manor to John, first Marquis of Winchester, who in his turn was obliged in the reign of Queen Mary to restore the property to its former episcopal owner. Hearing of the proximity of the London Brigade, Colonel Whitehead asked for and readily obtained assistance from its commander. Major General Browne marched from the village, wherein William of Wykeham was born, to destroy the stately palace in which, in a good old age, that never-to-be-forgotten prelate gently breathed his last. On his arrival he placed his guns in position, and local tradition asserts that they fired many rounds before the besieged consented to treat for a surrender, which they at length did when they perceived that every preparation had been made for an assault.

The duration of Colonel Whitehead's operations against the garrison is unknown, but the London Brigade reached Bishop's Waltham on April 6th, and the capitulation was signed on April 9th. The conditions agreed to were " That the commanders and officers then in the house might pass away with their horses, and their swords by their sides, and the common soldiers only with a rod or staff in their hands." The garrison left all their arms and ammunition to the victors, who permitted their soldiers to treat the whole contents of the palace as common plunder. One writer says that one hundred of the garrison were detained in captivity. " Mercurius Aulicus" says that the rebels obtained only 42 muskets, no pikes, powder-barrels, guns, or baggage, and not much besides soldiers' clothes, to secure which they stripped the garrison to their shirts in a field near the palace.

On the other hand, we have it on record that the articles of surrender were so strictly observed that a soldier who had taken a poleaxe from Colonel Bennet, who commanded the garrison, received orders from Major-General Browne to immediately restore it. Local tradition says that Bishop Curle was in the palace during the siege, and succeeded in escaping in a cart, a layer of manure being placed over him.

Prosser says that a folio black-letter Bible, printed in 1613, with the arms of King James I. on the cover, and having a manuscript inscription that it had "come out of the Place-house," was formerly preserved at Bishop's Waltham. Much bacon was found by the victors, who asserted that the place " had been a plundering garrison." After the division of the spoil, the London Brigade marched away, leaving "Colonel Whitehead to pull down the house if he chose."

On Thursday, April 11th, we read "Waltham House in ashes. Poor England, the glory of the nations, now growing into a wilderness!"

The Manor of Bishop's Waltham was sequestered, and in the year 1646 was sold by the Parliament to Robert Reynolds, Esq., for the sum of 7999*l*. 14s. 10½d. Mr. Moody, in his antiquarian sketches of Hampshire (p. 307) says Grose, the antiquarian, who visited Waltham soon after the Restoration, thus describes the palace :—" Its area was in its figure a right angled parallelogram, the four sides nearly fronting the four cardinal points, its east and west sides measuring 300ft., and its north and south sides 180ft. It consisted of two courts, one of which, the outer or northern court, was considerably the largest. The entrance was near the northern end of the west side. Through this lodge were the servants' offices and lodging rooms, with the gate leading to the second or inner court. On the west side was a great hall, lighted by five noble Gothic windows: its length was 60ft. by 27ft., and its height was 25ft. At the south end of this room were niches for seats or statues. Near this spot was a double row of pilasters, now almost covered with rubbish, which seem to have supported some arches. Opposite, on the east side of the court, was a chapel of the same dimensions as the hall. The north aisle had probably a cloister, and over it lodging-rooms, or a long gallery. The south aisle was seemingly the body of the house, the rooms of which are said to have been from 20 to 22 feet high. On the angles, made by the concurrence of this side with those of the east and west, were two square towers, part only of one on the south-west angle is remaining; the other is entirely down; each of its sides measures 17 feet. All the outer walls were six, and the inner walls four feet thick. Most of them have been pulled down and carried away for the sake of the materials. On the west side ran a ditch 25 feet wide, between which and the wall was a walk. About 40 feet of the ditch formed a large pond, which is said formerly to have been nearly half a mile long and a furlong broad; and to the east of the house are two large gardens, walled around with brick, and the remains of two lodges."

Mr. Moody continues: " For two centuries these interesting remains have suffered equally from the ravages of time and the cupidity of man, but they still arrest the eye of the stranger and afford contemplation and study to the antiquarian. A portion of them, supposed to have been the offices, is now used as a barn. The great hall, in the second or inner court, the front wall of which remains almost entire, was 65 feet in length, 27 in width, and 25 feet high, and was lighted by five large windows of magnificent proportions, now mantled with ivy. Besides the hall, there are the remains of a tower, 17 feet square, in the southern end of which may be discerned traces of the minstrel gallery, and at the south-west corner a curious corbel remains, which supported its part of the framed timber roof. In the front of the building there is a large sheet of water, artificially formed for the necessary supply of fish at the palace in Catholic times; and into it several small streams pour their water, and from it issues the river, which, passing through Durley and Botley, discharges itself into the Southampton estuary near Bursledon."

Great exertions were made in London to fill up the gaps made in Waller's army by disease, battle, and the departure of the London and Kentish auxiliaries. On Saturday, April the 6th, the Committee of Both Kingdoms received orders " to send away such forces as now are, or speedily may be ready, to Sir William Waller, as the King is drawing all his forces against Sir William Waller, and is going in person with them." Two days afterwards it was decided that the Committee of Militia of the City of London might send out to any destination or recall the Trained Band Regiments at pleasure, imposing " reasonable fines" upon officers or soldiers who refused to march, the Parliament undertaking to give the men when on service the pay of regular troops. On Saturday, April 13th, Mr. Ellis reported that the Committee of Militia had sent the two City Regiments to reinforce Waller, that the Westminster Regiment was to follow, that three other regiments would reach the rendezvous at the appointed time, and that even then there would remain "three more regiments to be drawn forth as a reserve." These London Regiments were each about 1000 strong, and had already displayed great courage and endurance at the first Battle of Newbury, which was fought on September 20th, 1643.

The county of Kent had sent 400 additional horse and a regiment of foot to reinforce Waller, and Colonel Harvey, the former assailant of Basing House, was, with his regiment, to receive a month's pay and to march in the same direction. The train of artillery was likewise to receive a month's pay and to march, as were also Lord Gray's Regiment of Horse, and the Hertfordshire regiment, which was 700 strong. The Earl of Manchester's horse had already set out for the rendezvous, so that Essex, Manchester, and Waller were all expected speedily to be in a position to act with vigour. A sum of 1700*l.* was voted for powder for the army of the Earl of Essex. This force was to consist of 7500 infantry, besides officers, forming in all seven regiments. The General's own regiment was to be 1500 strong, and the other six 1000 each. Every regiment was to be composed of eight companies and no more. Essex's cavalry was to muster 3000 men besides officers, arranged in six regiments of 500 each. Six troops made up a regiment. The Colonel's troop was to be 100 strong, and the remaining five were to be 80 in number. There was to be also "a suitable train of artillery." The cost of maintaining this army was to be 35,504*l.* per month, and was to be provided by means of Excise duties. Essex, whose headquarters were alternately at Windsor and St. Albans, was now recruiting diligently.

Sir William Waller was about this time displaying considerable personal activity. On March 29th he gained a great victory at Cheriton, on April 5th he was at Ringwood, and a day or two afterwards at Romsey. On April 8th he was meting out chastisement to the city of Winchester, and on the following day we hear of him at Andover. On the 11th he was at Bishop's Waltham urgently demanding stores from the Committee of the West, and on the 17th we find him at Farnham.

It will be remembered that after Cheriton Fight the safe keeping of Winchester Castle had been entrusted by Lord Hopton to a slender garrison, who were for the most part Irishmen. Lord Hopton was reported to have reached Oxford, suffering from a bullet wound in the back, received either at Cheriton or during the subsequent retreat. But early in the month of April, 1644, information reached the loyal Mayor of Winchester that the King in person was marching towards the city at the head of a large force, and that Lord Hopton's army had been largely recruited. The loyal citizens flew to arms, attacked, disarmed, and imprisoned the 100 men whom Waller had left to observe the movements of the Cavaliers, who occupied the Castle. News of these proceedings speedily reached Romsey, where Sir William Waller then was, together with the intelligence that the Cavalier garrison of the Castle "were received into the town and billeted there." The Parliamentarian General, who, in the opinion of his own party, had hitherto treated Winchester too leniently, at once marched thither from Romsey with a portion of his army on Monday, April 8th, 1644. On his arrival he found the gates closed against him. After marching round the city, and being denied admission at all points of ingress, he blew open one of the gates, the position of which is unfortunately not stated, with a petard, and "entered by force, which occasioned great damage to the inhabitants, by the unruly soldiers, who could not be restrained from plundering." They also released their comrades who had been imprisoned by the citizens, took 1000 arms, as well as 100 Cavalier prisoners, both officers and men, and refreshed themselves at the expense of the city. On the following day Sir William Waller had reached Andover, from which place he marched by way of Bishop's Waltham (April 11th) to Farnham.

On Tuesday, April 16th, an ordinance was read in the House of Commons, for the association of Wilts, Hants, Berks, and some of the western counties. "Mercurius Aulicus" two days previously stated that at Southampton two of the Parliamentary Committee in that town, named Mercer (a native of Dunkirk) and Legay (a Walloon), having seen some boys playing at being Hoptonians and Roundheads, had taken measures to have the urchins well whipped, and afterwards sent to the workhouse. It is somewhat remarkable that Messrs. Mercer and Legay, who were both active assistants of Governor Murford at Southampton, are mentioned as being foreigners by birth, and that "the good old mayor, a very ancient man," was a native of

Jersey. Sir Arthur Haslerig was now Governor of Southampton, and Colonel Norton was acting as Major-General of Horse under Sir William Waller. On April 26th, 1644, he was at the head of 800 cavalry, whom he had himself raised, but on the 15th of the following month he presented a humble petition to Parliament, "desiring pay for his soldiers, who have received very little since their first entertainment." A sum of 2000l. was granted out of the revenues of the Court of Wards towards the payment of these arrears. On Thursday, April 25th, money was sent by the Parliament to Major Beare, who was at the head of 400 horse in the neighbourhood of Southampton. This officer, who is elsewhere styled Colonel, and not Major, had been lent with the force under his command by the Earl of Essex to Sir William Waller, who, before April 17th, had reached Farnham, where he was joined by Lady Waller, who seems to have sometimes preached to the soldiers, if the satirical remarks of the Cavalier journals are in any degree founded on fact. Some of Waller's troops were posted at Odiham, and others at Alton, with a view to check the forays of the garrison of Basing House.

On April 16th a party of his cavalry attacked a Cavalier outpost at Sonning, in the neighbourhood of Reading, taking prisoners two lieutenant-colonels, three captains, divers other officers, twenty-one soldiers, together with their arms, and forty horses. In his letter, describing this affair, which was dated from Farnham, on April 16th, 1644, Waller begs for a supply of money and stores. He renews this application on April 27th and 29th, and also on May 2nd, until at length on May 5th a Committee of Parliament assembled to devise means for the regular payment of his army, and to order Cols. Stroud, Pyne, and Popham to join him at once. On April 17th Waller said that the City Regiments were quartered in and about Farnham, and that he expected four troops of Kentish horse to effect a junction with him on the morrow. On April 20th a muster of his whole force near Farnham showed that he was at the head of 10,000 men.

On April 20th ten troopers were towards evening sent to Odiham, whereupon a party of Cavaliers, stated by a hostile writer to have been 100 strong, fell back upon their main body, which had taken post nearer to Basing House. The Roundheads pursued them, capturing "one, who was the worst horsed."

Some of Prince Maurice's troops were said to be in the neighbourhood of Salisbury.

On Monday, April 22nd, Mr. Boate, one of the Master Shipwrights of Portsmouth, was, with certain others, placed on the list of "the Commissioners and Master Shipwrights for the felling of the timber of Delinquents for the use of the Navy," and three days afterwards the House of Commons granted "100l. worth of books out of the particular and private study of the Archbishop of Canterbury" (Laud) to Chaplain Hugh Peters, whom we shall meet hereafter at Winchester and Basing House.

On Wednesday, April 24th, Sir William Waller having received intelligence of a large convoy of provisions and much cattle destined for Basing House, sent out a party of horse, who intercepted it, and captured a master gunner, three sergeants, three corporals, forty soldiers, "one thousand sheep and other fat cattle," and some contribution money intended for the pay of the garrison.

Waller was by no means inclined to leave Basing House in peace. The Diary of the Siege says:—

"The ensuing spring (1644) the rebels, as well consulting the importance of the place as the injuries suffered by it both in their trade and force. resolve, having before assayed it by surprise and storm, to try by starving it, to which their armies' six weeks quartering at Farnham, Odiham, Grewell, and Basingstoke was a preparative, harrowing the country round about until their march to Oxford." This plan of operations was similar to that pursued in the following year.

About the middle of April the King, believing that Waller intended to march into the western counties, mustered an army in person at Marlborough, consisting of 6000 foot, and more than 4000 horse, which remained inactive for some weeks, vigilantly observing Waller's every movement.

Finding, however, that recruiting in London was going on vigorously, and that neither Essex nor Waller would be able to march until they were strongly reinforced, the Royal army advanced to Newbury, where it remained for nearly a month, observing the enemy's motions.

and ready to succour either Reading or Wallingford, in case of need.

On Friday, May 3rd, Sir W. Waller received a welcome supply of 3000*l*., and four days afterwards he cut off some stragglers from Basing House, recovering some contribution money which the Cavaliers had collected from the neighbourhood, and making prisoners of about twelve horses and their riders, most of whom were officers, one being "Captain Rosewell, sometime apothecary in the Old Bailey."

Captain Rosewell was speedily conveyed to Farnham Castle, where he fared but badly. "Mercurius Aulicus" says on July 6th, 1644, "'Tis true the rebells are most revengeful against Basing, as appears by their usage of Captain Rosewell, who (because he belonged to the garrison of Basing) was clapt up in prison at Farnham Castle, and there lodged in so noysome a hole (the rebels made it so) as 'tis not conceivable how a man should breathe in it above two houres."

On May 9th the Speaker wrote to the Sussex Committee, requesting that the county regiment of the Association might march to reinforce Waller. Military arrangements were not always perfect even in " the good old times." All London had long been preparing for the expeditions of Essex and Waller, but it was at the last moment discovered that " provision was wanted for roundshot, for demi-culverin, sacre and minion, hand granadoes and granadoes for mortar-pieces." The General of the Ordnance was not unreasonably called upon to state his reasons in writing " why in all this time notice was not given to the Office of the Ordnance to make this provision."

On Friday, May 10th, Waller's men had another skirmish with foragers from Basing House, with unrecorded result, and on the same day Salisbury was the scene of strife.

Either two troops or four hundred horse (so greatly do accounts vary) of Prince Maurice's army were known to be at Salisbury, and 120 horsemen from Southampton, many of whom were natives of Salisbury, and, therefore, well acquainted with the posts of the various sentries, reached the city between two and three o'clock in the morning of Friday, May 10th. There were only thirty or forty Cavaliers left in Salisbury, the rest having gone on an expedition to levy contribution money from the neighbourhood. A sentry gave the alarm, and killed one of the assailants, but the attack was nevertheless a complete success. A captain was roused from his slumbers to find himself a prisoner, together with fifteen of his comrades, some of whom were men of considerable position and influence. The rest of the Cavaliers beat a hasty retreat from the city. The victors, who secured a good deal of valuable booty, losing only the one man who was killed by the sentry, retired unmolested with their prisoners to Southampton. On Tuesday, May 14th, Col. Jephson, M.P. for Stockbridge, was appointed Lieutenant-Governor of Portsmouth under the Earl of Essex, and five days previously an ordinance of the House of Commons had directed the Tower Hamlets, Westminster, and Southwark regiments, amounting in all to 4200 men, to march with arms, guns, ammunition, and carriages to join Sir William Waller. Three other regiments, "raised in London and the liberties," also numbering 4200 men, were to be placed under the orders of the Earl of Essex. Whilst on service they were to be paid by the Parliament. On Wednesday, May 15th, the Parliament ordered these regiments to be ready to march at two hours' warning, and, in fact, Sir William Waller in the course of the day marched with them to Farnham, where his army, which until a few days had been posted in detachments extending from Farnham to Chichester, was now concentrated. Deserters from the City Regiments were ordered to be arrested and to be forwarded to their respective corps for punishment. Careful watch and ward was to be maintained in London after the departure of the troops. On Monday, May 13th, a supply of " knapsacks, shirts, shoes, and coats" was ordered by the Parliament to be sent to the garrison of Gloucester. So that the knapsack can claim a respectable antiquity of two centuries at least. It is also about this time called a "snapsack," which, perchance, throws eight on the etymology of this useful, but, on a long march, ponderous article.

The Royal army had now been quartered at and about Newbury for more than three weeks, without having received any accession of strength since the King had reviewed it at Marlborough, about the middle of April, when it could muster 6000 foot and more than 4000 horse. Finding that the Earl of Essex had marched out of London with his army to Windsor, and that Waller had proceeded to the parts between Hartford Bridge and Basing, without any purpose of going further west, the King's army marched to Reading, and, in three days, His Majesty being present, they slighted and demolished all the works of that garrison, and then, which was about the middle of May, with the addition of those soldiers, which increased the army 2500 old soldiers more, very well officered, the army retired to the quarters about Oxford, with an opinion that it would be in their power to fight with one of the enemy's armies, which they longed exceedingly to do. Thus speaks Clarendon. The friendly garrison of Reading being thus dismantled, and Waller, his old adversary, close at hand, there was indeed need for the Marquis of Winchester at Basing House to stand upon his guard. How well and gallantly he did so must, however, be told in another chapter.

The fortifications of Reading were demolished by the evening of Tuesday, May 14th, and on the following day the Royal army retired to Caversham, the King proceeding to Oxford. On the following day, May 16th, Lord Hopton had under his command at Newbury 5000 horse and foot, and other detachments of the King's troops were stationed at Witney. Either on this or the previous day Sir William Waller had reviewed his troops at Farnham. His army had been largely reinforced from London, Kent, and Sussex, and consisted of about 10,000 men. He had eight regiments of horse, and eight of foot, sixty baggage and ammunition waggons, and twenty four guns of various calibres. He had also a considerable number of guns made of leather, which had the advantage of lightness, and were, strange to say, effective, throwing case-shot to a considerable distance.

The Earl of Essex, whose reputation as a general was inferior to that of Waller, his second in command, now marched to Windsor with 10,000 men. These were his former army, which had wintered near St. Albans and in Bedfordshire, and which had been lately reinforced by four regiments of the Trained Band and London auxiliaries, which were 4200 strong. The day after the Royal army evacuated Reading Essex sent troops from Windsor to occupy the town, and without difficulty persuaded the City of London to place a garrison there. Essex and Waller henceforth conducted their operations with a view to their mutual defence and support, though they never actually united their armies.

The King, at Oxford, was anxiously, but with indifferent success, striving to ascertain their probable plan of operations. His cavalry were posted at and about Wantage and Farringdon, whilst his infantry occupied Abingdon, as to the defence or evacuation of which town specific instructions were given to Lord Wilmot, who was in command of the garrison. Sir William Waller marched from Farnham in the direction of Wallingford, on Saturday, May 18th, and had an interview with the Earl of Essex on the following day at Henley on Thames, from whence he returned at the head of a body of cavalry to Basing House. He spent several days at Basingstoke, having at the same time posted a detachment at Andover with a view of checking the advance of any relieving army from the west, but the relation of his proceedings must be deferred for a while.

On May 21st Essex was still at Henley, but four days afterwards he had gained possession of Abingdon, which Lord Wilmot had disgracefully abandoned in a fit of ill-humour. Essex had marched from Henley by way of Reading, where he arrived on May 23rd, on which day Colonel Popham, with his regiment of horse, received orders from London to report himself to Waller for duty. Sir William, with his army, then occupied Wantage, so that the whole of Berkshire was now in the possession of the Parliament, and the King was almost besieged in Oxford.

Lord Hopton was despatched to Bristol, where Waller had many friends, and on Monday, the 3rd of June, the King, with all his effective cavalry and 2500 infantry, succeeded in escaping from Oxford.

Sir William Waller, "who had the lighter ordnance and the less carriages," was ordered to follow the Royal army, which he did in a most irate mood; whilst the Earl of Essex, "who had the greater ordnance and the heavier carriages," marched westwards to Blandford, made himself master of Weymouth, and proceeded to Exeter.

Clarendon says (Bk. VIII.), "The Earl of Essex, by slow and easy marches, and without any opposition or trouble, entered into Dorsetshire, and by his great civility and affability towards all men, and the very good discipline in his army, wrought very much upon the people. Insomuch that his forces rather increased than decreased. . . . . It can hardly be imagin'd how great a difference there was in the humour, disposition, and manner of the army under Essex and the other under Waller in their behaviour and humanity towards the people; and, consequently, in the reception they found among them. The demeanour of those under Waller being much more ungentlemanly and barbarous than that of the other; besides that the people, in all places, were not without some affection, and even reverence, towards the Earl, who, as well upon his own account as the memory of his father, had been always universally popular."

Another writer says:—"Essex's popularity was equally great with the common soldiers, who familiarly called him 'Old Robin,' and never saw him off duty without throwing up their caps and crying out, 'Hey for Robin!'"

These details, although not strictly relating to the Civil War in Hampshire, are nevertheless necessary in order that we may be enabled to understand the subsequent events of the year 1644.

Henceforward the strife assumes a new and changed character. The great armies which have so long been traversing the country have now, for a time at least, passed off the scene, and we shall henceforth be able to concentrate our undivided attention upon the gallant defence of Basing House, by the heroic Marquis of Winchester, and our narrative will really and actually be the story of Basing House.

CHAPTER XXII.—WALLER AT BASING—CAVALIERS REPULSED AT ODIHAM—A SIEGE IMMINENT—HOSTILE PREPARATIONS—BASING VILLAGE OCCUPIED—DESULTORY SKIRMISHES—WATCH AND WARD—SIR MARMADUKE RAWDON—NIGHT ATTACKS—THE SIEGE CONTINUES—CROPREDY BRIDGE—RELIEF A NECESSITY—BUFF COATS AND MORTARS—RIVAL PREACHERS.

We learn from "Mercurius Civicus" that on Sunday, May 19th, 1644, Sir William Waller was at Henley-on-Thames in consultation with the Earl of Essex, and that he returned from thence with some troops to Basing House. "Whether he hath any intention to set upon the house we cannot say. The place is considerable, and worthy some pains in the taking, but the field service is now principally to be looked after." "The Parliament Scout" of the same date says, "It is affirmed with much confidence that Sir William Waller is before Basing House; we wish him good success, but we fear the contrary." The proceedings of the detachment sent towards Basing are described as follows, in "A True Relation of the Progress of the London Auxiliaries since their joining with Sir William Waller until their return homewards":—

"On Tuesday, the 21 (of May), we marched (from Bramley) to Basing House, where we came about 3 or 4 of the clock in the afternoon. They welcomed us with 2 or 3 pieces of Ordnance, and hung out 3 or 4 several Colours; the Ordnance did no hurt, only scared our under marshal; the blast blowing off his hat, our horse went round, faced the house; the enemy charged upon them, slew 2 horse and 1 man of ours, we saw 2 of their men fall on the breast work, but no more to our view. There we lay until evening, and it not being thought convenient to lay siege to the house, we marched round the park to Basingstoke. The enemy thinking we had an intention to beleaguer the house, burns all the houses, and 2 mills near adjacent, because we should have no shelter there. We lay at Basingstoke three nights, and had indifferent good quarter for our money, but the inhabitants were fearful they should be ill dealt withall after our departure for entertaining us; they pay 40l. per week towards the maintenance of the house, and that morning before we came in they had payed that week's money. On Thursday, the 24th, we marched towards Abington, and making a halt two miles onward in our way, there were brought unto us 20 prisoners or thereabouts, horse and foot. That night we lay at Aldermaston."

The 20 prisoners were probably a party belonging to the garrison, sent out to observe the movements of the retiring Parliamentarians. Waller wrote to the Parliament from Basingstoke on May 23rd. There were faint hearts still among the Cavaliers, for Waller, as he marched away to join the Lord General (Essex), as above described, asked for "some power given him to receive such into mercy as would come in. It will add much to the service of the Parliament, and to the diminution of the King's forces, and that he had good grounds to make that motion." At the end of May Sir William Waller was in the neighbourhood of Abingdon. On Saturday, the 1st of June, as we learn from a pamphlet entitled "A Victory obtained by Colonel Norton and Colonel Jones," "Colonel Norton's Watch of Horse faced Basing House." The Diary of the Siege, says, "At what time Colonel Norton drawing some forces from the adjacent garrisons, by order of their pretended Parliament is to block up the house."

"Whereupon," continues the pamphlet and other accounts, "as it was certified by prisoners since taken, Colonel Royden, a decayed merchant of London, who lived at Clerkenwell and went to Basing to recruit, being the Governour of that garrison with the Lord Marquis of Winchester, a known Papist, called a Council of War in Basing House, by which Council of War it was thus agreed :—

I. That forces should be drawn out and sent forth to fall upon Colonel Norton and Colonel Jones, their quarters at Odyam.

II. That they should give no quarter, but put all to the sword.

III. That two men should go along with them, one with a dark lanthorn, and the other with torches to fire the town of Odyam.

IV. That they should have all the plunder of the town for the same.

V. That they should have each man five shillings before the march.

By these and other proceedings of the enemy we may easily see the danger of their cruel and bloody counsels."

But there was a traitor within the walls of Basing. Scarcely had the Council broken up before the result of its deliberations was confided to the enemy. The Diary says :—" (By the treachery of a soldier giving intelligence two days before)—Thus forewarned, Colonel Jones, the Governor of Farnham Castle, drew forth 200 men from that garrison on Thursday last (May 31st) to Odiam, within four miles of Basing House, where, it is said, Colonel Morley, the Governor of Arundel Castle, was to meet him, and so to have straightened that place, which exceedingly annoys the country thereabouts, but by reason of other emmergent occasions, Colonel Morley came not thither, whereupon the enemy thought to have taken Colonel Jones in a trap." Unaware that their opponents were upon the alert, "they drew out all their horse and most part of their foot which was able to march (80 horse and 200 foot), about eleven of the clock at night, none being left in the house, only those which were upon the guard or not able to march by reason of sickness. Prisoners say that for their better encouragement herein the Marquis of Winchester came part of the way with them, and at his return back gave the common soldiers five shillings a piece." They thought "before morning not to have left a man to have brought tidings, for the town was unfortified, and many ways into the same, and the street very broad."

"About two of the clock on Sunday morning, a gentleman of Colonel Norton's troop, being sentry, hailed them at Walnborough (Warnborough) Mill, being about half a mile from Odiam, who giving an alarm to the town, the Watch of Horse drew out, who faced them, and fought with them in the lane above the mill. It pleased God to put such courage and resolution into the hearts of Colonel Jones and his men, that when the alarm was given they resolved to bandy with the enemy and to try whether they would fight without Basing walls." "They (the Watch of Horse) being forced to retreat, with the loss of one man only, who died valiantly ; afterwards the enemy set upon the foot in their guards, who were all ready to give them an answer, and accordingly defended themselves very valiantly. Colonel Norton, in all this losing no time, had by this got most part of his horse and drew them into the field, leaving the rest for the town, and marching close to the enemy very furiously, fell upon them with great valour, which caused the enemy presently to retreat, so that when Colonel Jones fell on the front with his foot, the horse came in on the rear, at which the enemy's horse fled, and all the foot with their arms were taken, and the horse pursued almost to Basing House."

"Upon their retreat were taken as followeth :—
Major Langley, sometime a Mercer in Paternoster-row, was taken prisoner, wounded, but being in poor habit, more like a tinker than a gentleman, was let go again.

Captain Rowlet (Rowland), a Scrivener, next door to the sign of the "George" at Holborn Conduit, also is taken, and Lieutenant Rowlet, his brother, two superstitious cringing malignants. Lieut. Ivory, sometime a citizen of London, Ensign (ancient) Coram, son of one Coram, a Papist in Winchester (Roger Coram was a gentleman residing at Abbot Barton, and was a parishioner of the Church of St. Thomas, in Winchester. He held Cranbury, and, dying in 1683, was buried in St. James' Cemetery, at Winchester). William Robinson, a Papist, surgeon to the Lord Marquis of Winchester, also three Gentlemen of the Arms, three sergeants, five drums, and three drummers, seventy-five (72) common soldiers, whereof some of them are such as have formerly run from the Parliament service, and are likely to receive their just reward. One quartermaster, five corporals, and one sutler to the Army."

"There were also taken 100 (150) foot arms

beside horse and arms, every man keeping what horse he took himself.

Four found dead upon the place, many wounded, some very dangerously.

We lost on our side only one man (2 men) and about 7 or 8 shot, which was all the loss we had, one being a Lieutenant of those that were hurt of our men.

The enemy's word was 'Honour' ours, 'God with us.'

They that are taken prisoners report that they were encouraged to come forth of Basing House against Colonel Norton's forces, to take from them their buff coats and new shillings which Colonel Norton had newly paid the men, but they were disappointed of their hopes; we showed them half-crowns as well as shillings after they were taken prisoners."

"About 4 of the clock in the afternoon, Colonel Norton's horse marched again up to Basing, and four of his trumpeters sounded first a challenge, and afterwards 2 or 3 levets flourishing before the enemy, but the enemy appeared not." (A levitt or levite was a sound of mirth. H. Teonge says, in 1676, "Our trumpets sounding merry levitts all the way.")

The Diary speaks briefly thus of Colonel Norton: "By the treachery of a soldier giving intelligence two days before, defeating a party of the Garrison drawn out to Odiam, and taking divers prisoners, upon the fourth of June faced the House with a Regiment of Horse and Dragoones, and after some hours stand quartered in Basingstoake." Three troops of Colonel Norton's horse were present on this occasion.

Captivity at Basing House must have been somewhat unpleasant, for we read, "The same night 10 of our men, which they had formerly taken prisoners, and used them barbarously, and stripped naked to their very shirts from their backs, having an hop bag in their prison, with the same made means by cutting into slips to lengthen it, to let them down, and made an escape, and came to our forces to Odyam, one of them being a Kentish Corporal, and most of the rest taken when Sir William Waller was before Basing, who tell us that there is but 7 of our men prisoners in Basing left." Colonel Jones sent a report of Odiham Fight to the House of Commons. This skirmish was fought near a spot whereon a gallant deed had been done four centuries before. Camden says, "Whose castle (Odiam) in the reign of John was gallantly defended for a fortnight by thirteen English soldiers against Louis, King of France, who had closely beleaguered it with his whole army, and surrendered at last (in the year) 1216."

Colonel Norton sent the prisoners taken at Odiham, who were estimated by their captors to be half of the whole garrison of Basing House, to Southampton, from whence they were a few days afterwards sent up to the Parliament in London. The closing days of May saw great preparations for an attack in force upon the Marquis of Winchester and his stronghold. Colonel Sir Richard Onslow, Colonel Jones, the Governor of Farnham Castle, and Colonel Norton, with their regiments, were all destined for this important service, and were to be further reinforced by some horse from Kent. On June 8th a letter from Guildford says that "the country came in very freely and courageously. There met many gallant trooper men, stout soldiers; they were never known to go out before so heartily and freely, and they carried themselves so civilly in the town as ever any gentlemen did, and on Sunday morning, at five of the clock, Captain Cufly, an honest godly minister of Gilford, who goes out with them upon this design, preached unto them, and after sermon they marched towards Farnham, and so for Basing." The four associated counties of Hnts, Surrey, Sussex, and Kent had raised 3000 men, most of whom were now on the march towards Basing. The same number were to be held in readiness as a reserve in the event of the Earl of Essex's ordering the besieging force to effect a junction with his own army, with which he was about to march to the relief of Lyme, in Dorsetshire, which Prince Maurice was unsuccessfully besieging.

Colonel Richard Onslow was to be in chief command of the Surrey forces at Basing House, and his officers were Lieutenant-Colonel Jordan, High Sheriff of Surrey, and his son, Captain Jordan, Sergeant-Major (*i.e.* Major) Hill, of Guildford, Captain Cufly, Captain Wesbrook, of Godleman (Godalming), Captain Perham. Captain Warren, who had already commanded a forlorn hope during Sir William Waller's attack upon Basing, and others. Lieutenant-Colonel Dunscombe remained at Guildford to raise the 3000 men of the reserve, and Colonel Richard Norton commanded the men of Hants, who formed two regiments, one of foot and the other of horse. The Marquis of Winchester was levying contributions in the neighbourhood, and in consequence we read of "Those plunderers who have cossed the country at 80*l.* or 100*l.* presently to be brought in unto them." The "Kingdom's Weekly Intelligencer" exultingly says:—"Hampshire hath shewed a good example. They have agreed among themselves to maintain forces to keep in those thieves and robbers at Basing, ... This service will be of great advantage, for there is nothing to hinder the trade of the clothiers in Wiltshire to London except that garrison," which did oftentimes, as we shall see, lay violent hands upon goodly bales of broadcloth destined for the metropolis. Other Hampshire men were at the same time doing their best to harass loyal Oxford, under the command of Major-General Browne, who laid siege to Greenland House, near Henley-on-Thames, the capture of which was considered to be of more importance than even that of Basing. It was surrendered after an heroic defence, together with all the arms and ammunition, on June 18th, 1644, the garrison marching out with all the honours of war.

The Marquis of Winchester thus describes the week ending June 11th: "Colonel Norton (his foot not yet come up), keeping his guards of horse upon our avenues to stop the fetching in provisions."

On June 15th Colonel Jones, the Governor of Farnham Castle, came up to London, accompanied by a gentleman who was the bearer of a letter, which duly appeared in the "Weekly Account" on June 25th, and from which we glean much information concerning the commencement of the siege. After the disaster at Odiham, the garrison, which was thought to be either about 140 or 200 in number, pressed yeomen's sons and others as soldiers, and sent out parties of horse to levy contributions in the neighbourhood. The Parliamentarians at Basingstoke, hearing that a party of the garrison had marched towards Reading, sent out about 50 horse and 20 musketeers to cut off their retreat. Chased to a broken down bridge which probably spanned the Loddon, the Cavaliers dashed through the stream, but left in the hands of the enemy nine horses which had stuck fast in the mud. Colonel Norton himself was on June 15th daily expected to return to Basing, having gone with his regiment of horse a week previously to Andover, which was said to be occupied by the King's forces.

But his subordinates were nevertheless active, for we read : " Colonel Norton hath possessed himself of the town of Basing, and seized on many cattle and much corne, which the Marquis of Winchester, a grand Papist, but nevertheless one whom His Majesty employs for the good of the Protestant religion, had provided to be sent to him at the garrison of Basing House, but it will now be better employed." The town, or as we now call it, the village of Basing, is said to be "within half musket shot" of the House, the garrison of which was much harassed when in search of provisions or forage. Two companies of Roundheads had occupied "a great house on the east side" of Basing House. Colonel Jones was at Odiham with three companies, and Colonel Onslow held Basingstoke with four companies of his Surrey regiment.

On June 11th, Colonel Norton received his expected reinforcements of infantry. Colonel Morley, who possessed great influence and many friends in Sussex, appeared at the head of "sixe Colours (or Companies) of Blew" from that county. Sir Richard Onslowe's Regiment of Surrey Red-coats was five companies strong, and Colonel Jones contributed two White companies from Farnham. Colonel Norton's regiment was also strengthened by the addition of three fresh troops of horse.

The whole force was "drawne up before the House upon the south of Basingstoake." At the approach of night the companies of white coats, with one troop of horse, marched to Sherfield, Sir Richard Onslowe, with his troop of horse, to Andwell House, "near the ruins of the Priory," whilst "Morleye's Foot and Norton's Horse quartered in Basingstoake."

This state of things lasted for the three following days. The Parliamentarian troopers faced the house daily, challenging the Cavaliers to sally forth, and try the issue of battle. Nothing loth, as soon as the enemy showed signs of retiring to his quarters, the Royalist troopers dashed through the garrison gate, and harassed the rear guard to some purpose, with but little loss to themselves.

As a party of Roundhead troopers were patrolling the neighbourhood they received information from some countrymen that about 30 horse from Basing House had gone towards the Vine. Pursuit was ordered, and the two parties met upon a heath. The Cavaliers halted, and formed up, but eventually, perceiving their opponents' preparations to charge, wheeled and galloped off, with the Roundheads close in their rear. One horseman suddenly rode back to the pursuers, saying that he was one of their own army, who had been captured that morning. His statement was at first doubted, "thinking that knowing himself to be badly horsed, and so in danger to be taken he used that policy to escape," and he was placed under arrest, until recognised as being an officer of the Parliament "who was carelessly out of his quarters." On June 14th it was reported in London that the besieged garrison was in great want of a mill to grind corn, the two mills having been burnt on the occasion of Sir William Waller's visit about three weeks before. Salt and other necessaries were also in great request within the walls.

On June 15th there was a sharp skirmish. "To see the countenance of the enemy, fifty foot are sent towards Basingstoke under covert of a mill and hedge," [Was this Eastrop mill, or the mill nearer to Basing?] "whilst our horse forced theirs into the Town." The Roundheads are reinforced, and the Cavaliers retreat in good order, drawing on their pursuers until the infantry can pour a volley into their ranks from the mill and hedge. The Parliamentarian foot soon come up, and several vollies are exchanged, until the Royalist infantry "are commanded in."

Two days after this skirmish, as two teams were fetching provisions for the house from Sherfield, the enemy's horse made a sudden dash and carried them off, making prizes likewise of three horses grazing in the Park, at no great distance from the house. That night the two white companies from Farnham venture to quarter in the village of Basing, attacking the garrison, doing good execution, and fortifying the Church. They only admitted the loss of one man killed, and another wounded, and placed marksmen in the adjacent houses, from whence they on the following day picked off two of the garrison.

"Idle Dick Norton," who had returned to Basing by June 17th, was evidently very much in earnest. A friendly journalist says : "Valiant Colonel Norton sits close upon Basing House, and hath possessed himself of the town, they of Hampshire have agreed to maintain a regiment of horse and foot for the service of the State under that Colonel ; it is pity such spirits should want instruments to work with, it is pity such good workmen should not have good tools."

Meanwhile the Earl of Essex, on his march to relieve Lyme Regis, sent out scouts, who, "having discovered the Queen's regiment, near their quarters, a party of horse was sent out towards them, which caused them to fly further westward, and so Hants is rid of those plunderers." This account is amplified by the following statement, which bears date June 17th: "His Excellency is advanced in his march beyond Amesbury, leaving Salisbury on the left hand, and hearing that there were 300 of the King's horse in Salisbury, sent two regiments of horse thither, under the command of Sir William Balfour, but they were gone an hour before they arrived. They pursued them seven miles, but could not overtake them."

The Royal army having retreated towards the west, Basing was now indeed in danger, and, says the Diary of the Siege, "We divide our men into two parts, leaving two thirds on duty, whilst the other rest, appointing to each Captain and his company a particular guard, dividing the quarters of the garrison to the Field Officers. The works adjoining to the park "were entrusted to the charge of Major Cuffand. Major Langley, whom we have seen captured at Odiham looking like a tinker, was responsible for 'the works in the gardens. The dispose (or arrangement) of the guns' was superintended by Lieutenant-Colonel Peake, the printseller, before referred to, some of whose musketeers were to act as a reserve for supply of all places as any need required. The troopers were supplied with muskets, and no one was exempt from duty. 'The Lieutenant Colonels and Majors being Captains of the Watch, Colonel Rawdon only in this excused, by reason of his years."

Colonel Rawdon, the Governor of Basing House, had not long before received a visit from his son Marmaduke, whom he had at the commencement of the troubles in England sent with a cargo of valuable merchandise to the Canary Islands, and with a letter recommending him to the care of his own nephew, Marmaduke Rawdon, who was a thriving and prosperous merchant there, and who cared not to take part in the fierce fratricidal strife then raging in his native land. He, however, welcomed his young kinsman most warmly, and entertained him in a most hospitable manner until the end of the year 1643, when he sent him back to England, says an interesting volume published by the Camden Society, with a cargo of wine, "for both their accounts, desiring him when he was in England to go and see his father, who was then Governor of Basing Castle, and to present him, as a token of his love and duty, with a curious gold hatband of goldsmith's work and a gold chain, and that of 500*l.* he carried with him, he should show it to his father to take it all or part, as he should best please. He arrived safely at Mount's Bay, in Devonshire, I would say, Cornwall, and, according to his cousin's request, went straight to his father at Basing, having a convoy from my Lord Hopton. When he came to his father his father asked him how he left his nephew. He told him very well, in good health, and that he had sent him a small present of a gold hatband and a gold chain, with order likewise that of 500*l.* he had there of Barbary gold he might take part of it or all, if he had occasion for it. He said, 'Let me see your gold,' so his son poured it out of a great silk network purse upon the table, which looking upon, he bid his son pick him out half-a-score of the best ducats of the finest gold, and told him, 'This I take to make the King's picture to wear with the chain of gold your cousin hath sent me; for the rest, put them up and carry them with you; it may be my nephew and you may have more occasion for them than I shall.' Here (at Basing) he stayed some few days with his father, and then went to Oxford, where he coined part of his gold (King Charles I. had his mint at Oxford for several years during the Civil War), and from thence went to London to meet the ship, where he disposed of his wines and gold in commodities proper for the main of Spain."

But troubles were in store. He was arrested, and on June 18th had reached London in custody. A contemporary journal says that "he makes himself a stranger in England, and pretends that he was a merchant or factor in foreign parts, yet when he came over he could find the next way to Basing House before he came to London, and, as he saith, was going now for Spain. So he was committed to custody, till further examination." He seems, however, to have been speedily released, and to have sailed for Seville, where he sold his merchandise, and, lading his vessel with oil and other things suitable for the Canary Islands, returned home about the middle of the year 1644, a considerable gainer by his expedition, and took no further part in the Civil War.

Thomas Rawdon, the eldest son of Sir Marmaduke, was a colonel in the Royal army, "fought in both the Fights of Newbury, and accepted many dangerous commissions for the service of the King. Having thus become a marked man, he fled from the persecution of the ruling powers, and took refuge with his kinsman and younger brother in the Canaries. By them he was cordially received and entertained for a considerable time with princely hospitality. In the 'Catalogue of lords, knights, and gentlemen who have compounded for their estates,' printed in London in 1655, are these names—' Rawdon, Thomas, of London, merchant, 400*l.*; Royden, Marmaduke, D.C.L., per Edmund Hardman and William Green, 559*l.* 3s. 2d.'"

On June 18th, a day hereafter to be memorable for a fight at Waterloo as well as at Basing, the blue-coated regiment from Basingstoke relieved the white companies who had occupied the church, which they converted into a stable, breaking open the vaults, and casting the coffins of Lord Winchester's ancestors into bullets, as was clearly proved a few years since by actual observation.

Just as the new comers had "taken over" their quarters, and the church clock had struck the midnight hour, there was heard the clash of steel and a hurried rush, and then a jet of flame made the old tower stand out in bold relief. The Cavaliers had fired one of the neighbouring houses, from the windows of which their comrades had been shot. Next evening there was a terrible hurly-burly. The garrison set fire to all the buildings between Basing House and the church, and the blue-coats themselves fired some of those beyond. Half Basing was in a blaze, and the Roundheads abandoned their works in a panic to shelter in the hedges, others continuing their flight to a considerable distance. But now, above the din, rang out the church bells, and help came from all sides. The Cavaliers retreated, and their opponents spent the night and the whole of the next day under cover of the hedge and palings of the park. Firing continued, one sentry was killed and his comrade wounded. On June 20th the besiegers took heart, and leaving the protection of the park palings, returned to their works.

But Colonel Norton was ill at ease. On Thursday, June 19th, he wrote to the House of Commons, asking for money, and was granted 2000l. from the Revenue of the Court of Wards. He likewise asked for and obtained from the Committee of the four Associated Counties of Hants, Sussex, Surrey, and Kent, to whom his letter was referred, a much needed supply of saddles, pistols, swords, and muskets. He said that he expected reinforcements from Southampton, and at his request an ordinance was passed " to remove malignant priests and clergymen that do much infest the country thereabout." Colonel Norton also complained that "the gentry of that county did not second his expectations, and that to the great discouragement of his soldiers they received but little favour or assistance from them." Mr. Lisle, M.P. for Winchester, was directed to reply to this letter, and to give the thanks of the House to Sir Richard Onslow, Colonels Norton and Morley, and Lieut.-Colonel Jordan, the High Sheriff of Surrey, " for their good service at Basing."

On June 20th a strong guard of Colonel Norton's men was posted at the church, but Lord Winchester's cavalry was not idle. Some of Norton's officers were descried riding along the lower road from Basingstoke, which they thought perfectly secure. A dozen musqueteers were posted behind the hedge at the corner of this road, which was then known as "the Lane," and greeted them with a well-directed volley. Some of them were wounded, and the whole party turned their horses' heads and galloped at their best speed towards Basingstoke, the Cavaliers in fierce pursuit meanwhile. Well was it for the fugitives that Colonel Norton had posted "a guard of horse on Cowdreye's Downe, who perceiving it, troop to the rescue," or none of the fugitives would have escaped that day. The Cavaliers drew rein, and wheeling to the right, galloped up to the besiegers' works near the Grange, took them by a sudden dash, set them on fire, and carried off a prisoner to the House.

Colonel Carne, the Deputy-Governor of the Isle of Wight, Colonel Whitehead, M.P. for Southampton, Colonel Button, Captain Jervoise (the son of Mr. Jervoise, of Herriard), and "one Master Graves, a kinsman of Colonel Graves, now rode through the lane to the entrenchments, our men being then at the burial of one of our soldiers." The Royalist musketeers behind the hedge were still at their post, and felt sure of their prize. But one of them fired too soon, "and shot Master Grave's horse, which gave warning to the rest." Master Graves was captured, but the rest of the party escaped, and rode off towards the west. Two hours afterwards Colonel Norton sent in a trumpeter with a flag of truce " to demand his liberty, being a traveller," but the Marquis sent back the messenger with a proposal for an exchange of prisoners.

On the following day (June 21st) there was a skirmish in the Park. Two of Sir Richard Onslow's Surrey redcoats were captured, and another was killed. Colonel Norton himself towards the end of June marched to join Sir William Waller. Let "Mercurius Aulicus" speak once more : " Norton himself is gone to Sir William, and left the work to others, thinking it ill manners to attempt that for which his general was so handsomely basted, who found it as difficult to enter Basing as to get into his Worship's own Castle at Winchester !" *Basting House* was a title often given by rejoicing Cavaliers to the brave little garrison. The two fortresses of Basing House and Donnington Castle completely commanded the great road from London to the western counties, and on June 20th there were no less than 2000 horse and foot employed in besieging Basing House and keeping the roads open for traffic. A convoy of 80 waggon loads of cloth and other merchandise reached London in safety on Monday, June 17th, but on the following Sunday the garrison of Donnington Castle, of which stout-hearted Sir John Boys was Governor, sallied forth, and made prize of two waggon loads of merchandise and six heavily laden packhorses, which were going from London to Marlborough, and carried them into the Castle. In spite of protestations that these goods were the property of Cavaliers residing in the neighbourhood, they were declared to be lawful prize, and were turned to good account by the garrison.

But during the evening of the day on which the waggons in question were seized, Colonel Norton, on his way from Basing to join Sir

William Waller, at the head of two troops of horse and thirty dragoons, made a sudden attack upon Donnington Castle, killing a sentry and securing eight horses in an adjacent stable. Unable to effect anything further, owing to his having no infantry with him, he and his party continued their march without the loss of a man, and reached in safety the army of Sir William Waller, with whom Sir Arthur Haslerig, at the head of his bluecoats, and Major-General Browne, with the London Brigade, were also expected to effect a junction.

The King and Sir William Waller had been manœuvring throughout the month of June. His Majesty had been enabled to return to Oxford, and from thence to pass into Buckinghamshire and Northamptonshire, and at length succeeded in forcing Waller to fight at Cropredy Bridge, which spans the Cherwell. Colonel Norton took part in this battle, in which Waller lost his leather guns, of which mention has been already made. The strength of his army was, on June 28th, ordered to be 70.0 foot, 3000 horse, with field and other officers, and "a train of artillery proportionable." Carlyle says (Letters of Oliver Cromwell, vol. 1, p. 172), " Waller's last action was an undecisive, rather unsuccessful fight, or day of skirmishing, with the King, at Cropredy Bridge, on the border of Oxford and Northamptonshires (29th June, 1644), three days before Marston Moor, after which both parties separated, the King to follow Essex, since there was now no hope in the north ; Waller to wander London wards, and gradually lose his army by desertion, as the habit of him was." Henceforth the star of his glory grew dim, and he was no longer known by the proud title of " William the Conqueror." Colonel Norton, after the fight at Cropredy Bridge, returned to Basing.

On or before June 24th two companies from Portsmouth had joined the white-coats from Farnham, and now the siege began in grim earnest. Colonel Morley's pikes and muskets were quartered in the park, while on his right was Colonel Onslow, who took charge of "the Lane and the Close towards Basingstoake, where, having forced their quarters, they presently breake ground, shutting us up on three sides with their foot, and on the other side their guards of horse keeping on Cowdroye's Down at night, busying themselves with spade and pickaxe to secure their quarters." Colonel Norton repaired the dismantled works which had been thrown up by Sir William Waller, erected fresh batteries, and dug and delved until his men might well in their love for Scripture parallels, compare themselves to the workmen of Nehemiah, who laboured with a tool in one hand and a sword in the other. There were still faint hearts in Basing House, and "three of ours runne to them."

On the 26th Royalist musketeers find full occupation. They wore iron pot helmets and swords with curiously curve-shaped hilts, many of which were forged in Holland, and were of the value of 7s. 6d. each. Every man's musket cost 18s. 6d., whilst the rest for the somewhat unwieldly piece was valued at 10d. Bandoliers for powder could be purchased for 3s., gunpowder was sold at 18d. per lb., match at 1l. 10s. per cwt., and bullets (called musket shot) at 18s. per cwt.

Thus equipped, the musketeers were sent forth " by the point of Basingstoake (a bulwarke) to view their lodging in the Lane, and to cut downe some Trees, climbing a ruined mill, from which they played on us, both which are done, and divers of them killed, with losse of two of ours." "The lane" is the lower road to Basingstoke, and the mill here spoken of stood nearly opposite to the conical tower in the garden, which is now a dove-cot. In the " True Relation of the Progresse of the London Auxiliaries" the garrison are said to have burnt "two mills neere adjacent." But darkness favoured the besiegers. "At night they run a Line (i.e., a trench) towards the mill, where we had galled them the day before," and the defenders of " Basingstoake bulwarke" have to keep themselves under cover for the future. But with true English tenacity of purpose Colonel Norton still holds his own, trusting to the help of a powerful ally within the walls, to whom men give the dread name of—famine ! No foraging parties are able to scour the country ; the hay in the meadows is stacked not for the benefit of Royalist, but of Roundhead chargers ; the stores in the cellars and vaults are sadly diminished, and the sentinels of the garrison fear that none of the corn which harvestmen will soon be busily reaping just beyond Colonel Norton's lines will find its way to the Basing House barns and granaries. A message must be sent to Oxford at all hazards, and on the night of June 27th "a Party of horse, Firing upon their Sentinells upon Cowdreye's

Downe, much amuse their guards, whilst others of them are sent by to Oxford," to ask that a relieving force may be despatched to Basing.

Clarendon thus graphically describes "a party of horse" (Book VI.) : "Among the horse the officers had their full desire if they were able to procure old backs and breasts and pots (iron skull caps), with pistols and carabines for their two or three first ranks, and swords for the rest; themselves (and some soldiers by their example) having gotten, besides their pistols and swords, a short pole-axe."

Lacy the player says, "The honest country gentleman raises the troop at his own charge; then he gets a Low-Country Lieutenant (one who had served in the Low Countries) to fight his troop safely; then he sends for his son from school to be his cornet; and then he puts off his child's coat to put on a buff coat: and this is the constitution of our army." (Note to Scott's "Rokeby," Canto iv.)

"In the reign of King James I," says Grose in his "Military Antiquities," "the buff coat or jerkin, which was originally worn under the cuirass, now became frequently a substitute for it, it having been found that a good buff leather coat would of itself resist the stroke of a sword; this, however, only occasionally took place among the light-armed cavalry and infantry, complete suits of armour being still used among the heavy horse."

These buff coats were usually lined with silk or linen, secured before with buttons or by a lace, and were often richly decorated with gold or silver embroidery. The owner of one of these coats, just after the Restoration, says, "I would not have taken 10*l*. for it." Cavalry corslets, consisting of back, breast, gorget, and head-piece, were valued at 22s. each. Some of Colonel Norton's men were probably armed only with Danish clubs, 1000 of these primitive weapons having been issued from store to Sir W. Waller's army in December, 1643.

"Mercurius Aulicus" and other Cavalier journals were beginning to make merry at the expense of Colonel Norton's fruitless siege of Basing House, and the Parliament was determined to take the Hampshire fortress at all costs.

The "Weekly Account" has the following paragraph :—"Two mortar pieces went this day (June 20th) also to Basing, and divers granadoes, which we hope will prove good instruments in gaining Basing House, for we are certified that the besiegers have intrenched themselves, and hope to render a good account of that service."

The brass mortar pieces ranged in calibre from 18½ to 4¼ inches, those of iron being from 12½ to 4¼ inches in calibre. In 1620 it is ordered that "The twentie pieces of great ordinance before mentioned, two mortar pieces for fireworks must be all mounted upon field carriages with foure wheels, and lymmers (limbers) ready compleate, and to be furnished and attended with spare carriages and wheeles, blocke carriages, copper ladles, furnished with spunges and rammers, and with all other habiliments and utensells of warre, and with many other small provisions which are soe necessary for the trayne of artillery, that without them they cannot march nor be used." ("Scott's British Army," Vol. I., p. 391.)

In the year 1639 an establishment of a train of 30 pieces of artillery consisted of one Master of the Ordnance, one Lieutenant of the Ordnance, one Comptroller, four Gentlemen of the Ordnance, one Master Gunner, 30 Gunners, and 40 Matrosses. These last (then first mentioned) seem to have been of lower rank than the Gunners. In 1618 we read of "One General of Artillery, 25 Conductors of Artillery, one Petardier, one Captain of Miners, 25 Miners, one Captain of Pioneers, one Surgeon, and one Surgeon's Mate;" and in 1620 mention is made of "Three Master Gunner's Mates and three Constables, or Quarter Gunners." ("Duncan's Hist. of R. Artillery," Vol. I.)

These "mortar pieces" thus forwarded to Basing were intended to fire shell "gernadoes." Some of these were 80lbs. in weight, as we learn from the Diary of the Siege, the accuracy of which is attested by numerous fragments recently discovered. They were also styled Granada shells.

"The first shells were cast in 1543 (in which year iron guns were made by three foreigners at Buckstead in Sussex), for mortars of 11 inch calibre, described as 'certain hollow shot of cast iron, to be stuffed with fireworks, whereof the bigger sort had screws of iron to receive a match, and carry fire to break in small pieces the same hollow shot, whereof the smallest piece hitting a man would kill or spoil him.'" (Duncan's Hist. of Royal Artillery, vol. I.)

Hand grenades have also been found during

the progress of the excavations. These are small iron shells, about three inches in diameter, filled with powder, fitted with a time fuze, and either thrown by hand, or projected from a hand-gun or "musketoon" fired from a rest. These missiles are said to have been first used in the year 1594. The grenadier was originally armed with these deadly missiles, hence his name.

On June 29th, hereafter to be famous for the Restoration of "The Merrie Monarch," whilst the ponderous mortars were slowly making their way towards Basing, Colonel Morley, who was now in command of the besiegers, had brought a sconce or detached fort in the park "to some perfection," and by noon the watchers on the walls can see that "cannon baskets" (i.e., gabions, or hollow cylinders of basket-work, varying in size from a diameter of 20 inches to six feet, with a height of from two feet nine inches to six feet) have been ranged in order, indicating that a culverin has been placed in position. The culverin weighed nearly 36cwt., had a bore of 5¼ inches in diameter, threw an 18lb. shot, and required a charge of 18lbs. of powder. They are not mistaken, and during the afternoon six 18lb. shot came crashing into the House and works. "Next day being Sunday (their Cause allowes not now for Sabbath), doubling their diligence throughout the Leaguer (or siege works), the besiegers are busy all day in completing the Redoubt at Morley's Quarters in the Park, and on the Towne (Basing) side towards a Mill, drawing a Line from the Church." This latter operation seems to have been designed to prevent the garrison from communicating with Pyat's Hill and Sherfield. Nor was Colonel Onslowe idle in the lower road from Basingstoke, his red-coats "raising a platforme in the Lane with so much speed that the next morning a Demy Culverin playes from it." The Demi Culverin weighed about 27cwt., with a bore of 4½ inches in diameter, and threw a 9lb. shot with a charge of 9lbs. of powder.

There was not much sleep on the following night. A messenger from loyal Oxford makes his way through the besiegers' lines under cover of the darkness. He is the bearer of glad tidings "informing us of His Majestie's success against Waller at Cropready" (only two days before). "We Eechoe it to our neighbours with Volleys both of small and great, they answering with their Guns, battering our Kitchen and Gatehouse, till a shot from our platforme spoyling the Carriage silenced their Demi Culverin" (in the lane.)

It will be remembered that some of the guns were mounted on the House *en barbette*. The Gatehouse stood at the entrance of the circular citadel, and this nocturnal artillery duel seems to have been principally fought on the northern side of the garrison.

In Sir Sibbald Scott's British Army (vol. I. p. 464) there is an amusing description of artillery practice in 1642. "A man upon his tower, with a flag in his hand, cryed them aime whilst they discharged their cannon, saying 'Wide, my lord, on the right hand; now wide two yards on the left; two yards over, my lord, &c." Some few events of importance took place during this month of June, 1644, in other parts of the country, which claim brief notice at our hands.

On the last day of May the Speaker issued his warrant "for pressing a bark at Portsmouth to go upon special service" to Lyme Regis, then besieged by Prince Maurice. This naval reinforcement probably contributed to the subsequent raising of the siege.

On Tuesday, June 5th, ever zealous Captain Swanley received the thanks of the House, and a gold chain, of the value of 200*l*., "for good service at the Isle of Wight, Pembroke, and Caermarthenshire," Captain Smith, "his Vice-Admiral," being at the same time presented with a gold chain worth 100*l*. Both these officers also received medals, a fact which is specially noted, these honourable badges of distinction being then far less common than they are at present.

The Earl of Warwick, Lord Admiral of the Parliamentarian fleet, having captured 2000 stand of arms at sea, 200 of them were sent forthwith to the Isle of Wight, as 10,000 had been ordered to be distributed "about Hants and those parts."

On June 3rd it was ordered by the House of Commons, that Sir Thomas Jervoise, Knight, Robert Wallop, Richard Whitehead, Esq., should be directed to take steps within one month, for the sequestration of the estates of Papists and delinquents of a less value than 12,000*l*., within the cities of London and Westminster, and to apply the proceeds to the liquidation of the 8000*l*. due as arrears to the garrisons of Portsmouth, and of Hurst, Southsea, and Calshot Castles. On Saturday, June 22nd, an ordinance was brought forward for the appointment of John Lisle, Esq., M.P. for Winchester, as Master of the Hospital of St. Cross, in the place of William Lewis, who had shown himself a staunch adherent of the King. Two days previously Captain Baxter, Mr. Matthews, of Newport, Mr. William Maynard, and Sir Gregory Norton, were added to the Parliamentarian Committee for the Isle of Wight, five members of which were to form a quorum. The weekly assessment of the Island was not to exceed 50l., and Mr. Lisle was directed to write to the Committee requesting them "to give countenance and encouragement to the godly ministers sent into that island." On Saturday, June 22nd, it was known in London that the Rev. Aaron Crosfield had been brought before the Committee of the Isle of Wight, for saying that "he that would not join with Prince Rupert against the Parliament was a traitor and a rebel." Parson Crosfield had been shut out of his own church by some of his parishioners "who desired to hear an honest godly man sent to them by the Parliament, but this Crosfield was cross indeed," and, sending for his surplice, he preached to a small congregation in the church porch, whilst the "honest godly man" addressed a numerous audience in the school house. Lady Norton, the wife of Sir Gregory Norton, "had repetition of sermons in her house," which so greatly enraged the adherents of the Rev. Aaron Crosfield, that they were ready to demolish the knight's mansion. Sir Gregory Norton, Mr. Edwards, and Mr. Lisle were firm friends to the cause of the Parliament in the island, "countenancing good ministers there, such as Bellars, &c.," and also sending 300 bushels of corn to supply the wants of some scantily supplied troops.

On Thursday, June 27th, Hugh Peters, whom we shall meet again, as a chaplain at the sack of Basing House, and who had already received a grant of books to the value of 100l. from Archbishop Laud's "particular private study," was presented by Parliament with the volumes still remaining there, which were valued at 40l. more. It would be interesting to know the nature of the 140l. worth of books which filled the shelves of Laud's "particular private study!"

On Sunday, June 30th, a party of Cavaliers in the neighbourhood of Andover took possession of sixteen waggons laden with cloth on their way from Wiltshire to London. The same detachment on another occasion seized 40 pack-horses which were going to the west from London, and only released them on payment of 40l. Thus ended the month of June. 1644.

CHAPTER XXIII.—FORAYS IN HANTS—WINCHESTER CASTLE—THE "THE GOLDEN SUN"—AFFAIRS AT BASING—THE SIEGE CONTINUES—SUMMONS TO SURRENDER—BOMBARDMENT—MESSAGES TO OXFORD—ATTACK AND DEFENCE—SALISBURY CATHEDRAL.—A NIGHT ATTACK—DEFENCE OF ISLE OF WIGHT—STUBBORN BASING—EXPECTED SURRENDER — SUCCESSFUL SORTIES—HOPES OF RELIEF — CORNET BRYAN CAPTURED—HOSTILITIES CONTINUE—ESSEX SURRENDERS.

On Monday, July 1st, 1644, the House of Commons ordered "500 musquets to be lent with their equipage to the Basing House forces, and 200 musquets with their equipage, borrowed of the gentlemen of the Isle of Wight, to be returned to them." A man-of-war equipped by certain London merchants had lately brought into Cowes a ship having on board 3000 stand of arms and much ammunition, all of which were supposed to be "going to Exeter." The aforesaid 700 muskets were now ordered "to be taken out of the prize ship at Cowes," and if the ship should not prove to be lawful prize, the merchants who claimed to be the owners of her cargo were to receive compensation "out of the Segovia wools brought from Weymouth."

The Cavalier garrison of Winchester Castle still held out, and "Mercurius Aulicus" says on July 2nd, "Since Alresford Fight (March 29th), the rebels have often faced Winchester Castle, but have still been repulsed, and never went off without their errand." But on the following day a journal of opposite politics asserts that the Cavaliers were plundering the neighbourhood of Winchester, had cut the throat of a miller, had outraged women, and were carrying about a petticoat upon the point of a sword, exclaiming, " This is the Parliament's colours!" On Wednesday, July 10th, Lord Hopton was said to be raiding in Hampshire at the head of 1000 horse, Colonels Popham and Ludlow, the latter of whom is described as "that faithful patriot, Colonel Ludlow, High Sheriff of Wiltshire," being unable to keep him in check as Colonel Norton had done, more especially as the mass of the people were but ill-affected towards the Parliament. On the same day the Committee for Hampshire, three of whom constituted a quorum, were ordered by Parliament to be diligent in raising both men and money, so that a force of 600 infantry, 100 horse, and 100 dragoons might be ready to march on July 20th, for service near Oxford, and at the discretion of Parliament. This contingent formed part of the 10,000 foot, 1700 horse, and 1350 dragoons then being raised in several counties for the service of the Parliament.

During this month the House of Commons ordered the sum of 250l. to be paid of Lord Capel's woods "to the widow of Colonel Meldrum," slain in their service (at Cheriton), and 50l. to another like widow." Great must have been the havoc wrought by the order in the pleasant woodlands at Abbot's Worthy. Although Colonel Norton was actively besieging Basing House, Sir Richard Norton, of Rotherfield, who had been created a baronet on May 23rd, 1622, was a staunch Cavalier, and one of the Commissioners of Array for Hampshire. He was now ordered to appear before a Committee of Parliament, and on July 15th, 1644, a letter, written by the Committee at Basingstoke four days previously, was read in the House. It stated that Sir Richard had been sent up to London under arrest, whereupon he was "committed to Lord Petre's house during the pleasure of the House." This loyal and persecuted baronet paid a fine of 1000l. for his estate on March 6th, 1645, and died in 1652.

On Thursday, July 18th, a hostile newspaper tells us that Sir William Ogle, the Governor of

Winchester Castle, "a great plunderer," had some fourteen days previously sent out a force consisting of 50 horse, 60 musketeers, and 40 pikemen. The cavalry entered the town of Andover, the infantry having meanwhile halted at a distance of some three miles. A convoy was intercepted, and sixteen waggons, laden with cloth, cheese, oil, &c., 60 (or 94) oxen, and 36 horses, coming from the western counties, were captured. With this plunder, which was valued at more than 6000*l.*, the Cavaliers retired unmolested to Winchester. Sir William Ogle had taken from "the Master of Winchester College fifteen oxen and three hogsheads of beer, upon suspicion that he was a Roundhead." The College authorities sent a complaint to Oxford, whereupon Sir William Ogle compensated them with fifteen oxen which he had taken in a foray, thus "robbing Peter to pay Paul."

On July 22nd "Mercurius Aulicus" says "Winchester Castle is made fit by Sir William Ogle for entertaining Sir William the Conqueror (Waller), and the enemy often face Winchester Castle, and are still repulsed." Mercurius Britannicus also admits "by the same token they about Winchester Castle have not yet recovered it." The ever active Colonel Norton was on July 20th reported to be attacking Donnington Castle, near Newbury, and five days afterwards to be watching with his cavalry to hinder the garrison of Winchester Castle from plundering. On Wednesday, July 24th, we hear that the garrison of Portsmouth had been largely reinforced, and was in future to be maintained at a cost of 500*l.* per month from the excise duties levied throughout Hampshire, with the exception of the town of Southampton, and the Isle of Wight.

A ship belonging to the King of Denmark, named the *Golden Sun*, and under the command of Captain Nicolas Ruter, had been detained at Portsmouth on suspicion of having been chartered by the Cavaliers. On Saturday, Oct. 5th, 1644, it was ordered that "Lieut.-Colonel Roe do deliver from store to the Committee of the West 500 Danish Forks, Clubs, or Roundheads taken on board the Danish ship." On December 4th, the ship was reported to be leaking, and the House of Commons authorised the caretakers to break open the hatches and to remove the cargo to a place of safety, to be appointed by the Committee of the Navy. The ship and cargo were, after long delay, eventually released by order of Parliament. After the battle of Cropredy Bridge, which was fought on June 29th, Sir William Waller lost half his army by desertion, and "had been roaming about Oxford with his rapidly decreasing forces in a very unoffensive manner." Writing from Farnham he asks for supplies, and "expresseth his forwardness to assist the Lord General (Essex), and calls the God of heaven to witness it is not his fault, and wisheth the blood and infamy may rest on the heads of them that lay obstructions in the way, averring that if money cannot be had he will march without it. That he desires nothing more under God than to be able to march, and that no fault shall be found in him."

But let us return to Basing House. On Wednesday, July 3rd, the garrison was said to be well supplied, especially with corn and bacon, although malt and beer were somewhat less plentiful. The besiegers had captured ten foragers from the House, and from the "Weekly Account" of the same date we learn that the siege works were already within pistol-shot, or, according to the "Diary of the Siege," "within half musket-shot." The enemy kept up a continuous fire, and two or three of the garrison were killed or wounded daily whilst on duty within the House. "They shoot the Marquisse himself through his cloathes. The carriage of their piece being now repaired, they now renew their battery on the House, unto the detriment and topping of our towers and chimnies."

On Thursday, July 4th, there was "stinking beef thrown over Basing Walls," owing to a deficiency of salt. The "Weekly Account" contains a letter written about this time in the besiegers' lines :—" Sir,—I doubt not but you would gladly heere how things stand with us, for this House hath not onely been a great annoyance to all the country round about it, but hath been a meanes to stop up the trading out of the West to London by robbing and pillaging the carriers and clotheers that came from them. It standing near unto the direct road, and therefore, both for the subduing of those that are in it in arms against the Parliament (which are Papists and Arch-Malignants), and for the prevention of the foresaid mischiefs hereafter, we have closely besieged the same, and are intrenched within Pistol shot of the House, so that none can enter in or out. Since our throwing up a trench against them the Enemy are very still, which before were lavish in their Powder, though to little purpose. Captain Warn came lately from Plimmouth unto us, and we hope they cannot long hold out.

From before Basing, July 5th, 1644."

Force having hitherto failed, the besiegers try the effect of stratagem, and on the morning of the 8th of July "they assay to draw us forth by making an alarme to themselves (leaving their piece neglected without a guard), but," says the Diary, "faile." In the evening a Cavalier prisoner makes a bold dash for freedom, and escapes to the house under fire of a hundred muskets. This "so chafed them that they continue firing untill midnight, and shot two of our men." Next morning Colonel Onslowe's Surrey redcoats are reinforced by four companies of their comrades. The new comers advance somewhat heedlessly. At once there is a flash and a sharp report, followed by two others in quick succession as they "have three shot placed amongst them from our minion, making them change their march to troop at further distance." A minion was a gun weighing nearly 10cwt., with a 3¼in. bore, throwing a 4½lb. shot with a 4½lb. charge of powder.

On July 11th a company from Southampton, seven score strong, marched up from Southampton to join Colonel Morley, by way of Hackwood, "unto Hollowaye's Mill" (the site of which is not easily to be fixed with certainty). Having been thus strongly reinforced, Colonel Morley thought fit to summon the Marquis to surrender the stoutly defended fortress. Colonel Norton being absent, he would, if successful, obtain much credit by gaining possession of the house.

The besieged were keeping a fast on July 12th, when he "sends by a drum this harsh demand, written with his left hand, for which he was afterwards marked in the shoulder, which spoiled his Clearkship ever since : "—

"My Lord,—To avoid the effusion of Christian blood, I have thought fit to send your Lordship this summons to demand Basing House to be delivered to me for the use of (the) King and Parliament ; if this be refused the ensuing inconvenience will rest upon you (yourselfe). I desire your speedy answer, and Rest, My Lord,

Your humble servant,

HERBERT MORLEY."

The messenger had not long to wait. " The Marquisse upon small deliberation returned Mr. Morley this answere." (" And had this sodain answer "). To this my Lord Marquis sent a speedy answer, which not long after he sealed with a bullet, which seemed to relate to these his Lordship's words sent to Master Morley :—

"Sir,—It is a crooked Demand, and shall receive its answer suitable. I keep this House in the Right of my Soveraigne, and will do it in despight of your Forces. Your Letter I will preserve (reserve) in testimony of your Rebellion.

WINCHESTER."

"This is returned by a drum, with directions. 'Hast, hast, hast, post hast' upon the letter. Morley speaks his choller from his gunns, which now and some daies following played on our Waterhouse."

Things were getting serious in Basing House. The "True Informer" states on July 13th that the besiegers numbered some 3000 horse and foot, who " have planted two pieces of battery against it, which hath beat down divers of the chimneys and made some breaches in the house. They are in some distress for want of salt and wood, without which they cannot long subsist, so that they are in great expectations that the house will be surrendered, or otherwise they are resolved to batter and storm it."

The "Scottish Dove" of July 12th is jubilant : "Greenland House is taken, and it will not be long before Basing House be in the same case to beg for a Parliamentary passe."

Greenland House was surrendered after a brave resistance of six months. Clarendon says (Bk. VIII.) : " Greenland House could not possibly be longer defended, the whole structure being beaten down by the cannon." With playful sarcasm it is recorded on July 12th :— "Colonell Onslowe's men courteously permitting eight of our foot to fetch six beasts grazing before their workes. At night Coronet (Cornet) Bryan and some troopers passing a messenger by Cowdreye's Downe (to Oxford) bring in two prisoners." This capture was of great service to the besieged, for it was announced in London on July 15th that an assault would have been made upon Basing House had not "two men through negligence taken prisoners," given information to the garrison. A letter written at Basing on July 15th alluding to the construction of mines, says that Colonel Norton was then quartered in Basingstoke, and that

Colonel Jones, the Governor of Farnham Castle, occupied Basing Church, whilst Colonels Onslow, Morley, and Whitehead were entrenched round the House. The besiegers were 3000 in number. Some of the chimneys of the house had been battered down, and a few small breaches had been made. The garrison was very quiet, and a prisoner reported a scarcity of meat, and that there was " only puddly and bad water to drink."

On July 18th a flaring bonfire in the park and two volleys along the whole line proclaimed a welcome to the Parliamentary Committee sent to Basingstoke to urge forward matters at stubborn Basing.

Clarendon says that the weather at the end of June was very warm, and heat now began to increase the distress of the defenders. The "Court Mercurie" of July 20th has the following :—" The Seidge at Basing House still continues, as wee are credibly informed (however the Malignants may pretend the contrary), the besiegers have planted some pieces of battery against it, and made divers breaches through the house, and are resolved in case they refuse to surrender it speedily to storme it, the besiedged say that they have plenty of ment, but so tainted by reason of the weather and for want of salt and seasoning, that it is very infectious, and many of them have dyed lately through the extremity of the disease it has bred amoung them." The water supply seems at all times to have been abundant, though not always of good quality.

Foreign engineers had done their best to strengthen Basing, for in " A Looking Glass for the Popish Garrisons " we read :—" Could those tall walls, bulwarkes, and forts that were cast up by the subtill art of the forraign engineers be scaled without a fall ?" Having, however, been thrown up in haste they were "in many places slender, and nowhere finished."

On July 20th a party of musketeers sally out, and do some execution in the lane before they are ordered to retire, and at the same time a captain of Colonel Morley's regiment is killed by a shot from the works. Two hours afterwards a drum is sent into the garrison with letters for the exchange of prisoners, but really to inform the Cavaliers that Colonel Norton had returned in safety from the defeat of Sir William Waller at Cropredy Bridge, and to gain time to draw one if not two mortar pieces secretly to the trenches, from which as soon as the drum had returned, a shell of 80lb. is fired during the evening into the house, "concluding their devotion and the day with thundering from their culverins, two (shot) passed through the quarters where our sick men lay, but without hurt."

At Donnington Castle, the friend and ally of Basing House, there were fired " a 500 and odd bullets, most of them 36lb., some six, some 12."

Mr. Boutell says (Arms and Armour p. 251) : " Until about the middle of the 17th century mortars were invariably discharged by double firing. The process of loading, while this system of firing prevailed, was very slow and tedious. After the powder had been placed in the chamber of the mortar it was closed in by a wooden board or shutter made to fit the bore of the piece ; then this board was covered with turf, and, over the turf, again, earth was placed ; and, finally, on the earth the shell with its live or lighted fusee was made to rest in such a manner that it was only partially enclosed within the mortar. All this required time. The gunner lighted the fusee of the shell with one hand, while with the other hand he fired the mortar from which it would be discharged."

The morning of the 22nd, says the " Diary of the Siege," saw the enemy's lines much advanced, and a sconce or redoubt finished, which was intended to prevent their battery in the Park from being attacked on the flank. The Marquis himself is wounded by a bullet, and two men are killed by chance shot. Another account says, " The hurt within is not much, the Marquis hurt, two men killed by chain shot." A small gun called a cabonet had its carriage broken by a shot from one of the besiegers' culverins. The cabonet fired projectiles of not more than 2lbs. in weight. The following night being dark and stormy, tried and trusty Edward Jeffrey, whose name is still continued in Basingstoke, is despatched to Oxford. But the same night that favoured the muffled-up trooper with his load of despatches close to his heart, favoured also the stealthy flight of 8 Roundhead prisoners, who got back to their leaguer with reports that made " our allowance of great shot to be next day doubled, and at night more granadoes."

Honest Edward Jeffrey was, no doubt, in disguise, for we are told that the Royalists were constantly passing through the country for Parliament men, with orange tawny scarfs and ribands. He carried news of successful resistances, which was, of course, speedily exaggerated, for to the Royal army near Crediton in Devonshire came "Newes this day (Satterday, 27th July, 1644) that Bising House had slayne many of the besiegers, and had raised the siege which had layne before to it long."

Wednesday, July 24th, must have been a very wet day, and on the following day the low grounds were flooded, and "the trenches on the towne (Basing) side in the Meads flote with the quantity of rain that fell, thereby forcing them to lye more open to our towers, from whence our Markes men spoyled divers."

Nor did the enemy fare better elsewhere. On the other side towards the Basingstoke Bulwark, the garrison had constructed "a Blind," or a structure of timber, covered with earth and loopholed, from which sped forth a deadly leaden hail.

Under cover of the darkness a strong Puritan working party is sent into the trenches near the lane, but "two pieces charged with case (shot) so luckily are placed upon them that they were heard complain their suffering."

Early next morning, the musketeers are again at their loop-holes in "the Blind," and pick off an officer and several men. A cow is seen grazing, and the grunt of poor piggy is heard near the blind and the Basingstoke Bulwark. A trooper gallops forth in search of milk and bacon, and piggy and the cow are led away captive, under cover of volleys from both sides, Colonel Norton's men getting the worst of it. All the evening long is heard the cannon's roar, and six shells in addition hurtle through the air. One falls in the granary and spoils some corn, and two others fail to explode. Shell practice and half rations combined are too much for weak nerves, and "at night two souldiers run to them."

The morning of July 27th shows a traverse or mound of earth, about the height of a man, across the meadow from the burnt mill (nearly opposite the present dove-cot) commanding the way to the blind, which had proved so disastrous to the enemy on the previous day. Nor had Colonel Morley been idle. He had made his quarter more secure by enclosing the nearer side of an old orchard.

Stone shot can do good service sometimes. During the night six stones of the same size as the 36lb. shells are hurled from one of the mortars. "Each day continuing like allowance, these and the granades for awhile seemed troublesome, but afterwards become by custom so familiar to the souldier, that they were called as they counted them, Bables (i.e. Baubles), their mischiefes only lighting on the house, and that the losse, our courts being large and many."

"Mercurius Aulicus" tells us that Sunday July 28th, was an eventful day. Lieutenant Cuffand, of the Marquis' regiment, and Cornet Bryan, of Lieutenant-Colonel Peake's troop, sallied forth at the head of forty horse, charged the rebels in their works, killing between twenty and thirty of them, and capturing ten prisoners. They also "took an Orange Colour of Horse, and one Trumpet, and pursued the rebels to Basingstoke's towne's end, slashing and doing execution all the way." On the 30th of July a jet of flame from Basing Church tells that a culverin has been planted there, for the purpose of breaching a tower from which Cavalier marksmen had caused much annoyance to the enemy in that direction. Firing continued from the other guns already in position. So "ends the yeare of the place's being garrisoned, and the second month of the Leaguer" (i.e. siege.) The Cathedral clergy at Salisbury now shared in the troubles of the Civil War. On August 3rd, Lieut.-General Middleton wrote to the House of Commons, saying that certain plate, hangings, copes, cushions, and a pulpit cloth had been "seized on by the common soldiers in Salisbury Church," and five days afterwards the articles in question were "all brought in to the view of the House." It was thereupon ordered that the plate and pulpit cloth should be restored to the Cathedral, the superstitious representations upon them having been first defaced. The copes, hangings, and cushions, having first been similarly defaced, were to be sent back to Sir William Waller to be sold, and the proceeds were then to be shared "among the soldiers that took them, and brought them up!"

Amongst the earliest Laws and Ordinances of War established for the army under the Earl of Essex in 1643, it was ordered "all such who shall violate places of public worship to undergo severe censure." But if the proceeds of such violation were thus shared amongst the plunderers, few would hesitate to incur the censure.

On August 4th it was reported from Southampton that 100 infantry from that town, together with four troops of horse under Capt.

Braxtone, brother to the Mayor of Winchester, and Captains Fielder, Santbrook, and Thomas Bettworth, jun. (Bettesworth, whose home was in the Cathedral Close), were facing Winchester, as the gates both of the city and castle had been, at the instigation of the clergy, shut against the forces of the Parliament.

Captain Thomas Beesworth (Bettesworth) with some fourteen horse had ridden forth from the headquarters, which had been established within two miles of Winchester, in order to transact business with some other officers. Returning "about midnight he found his watch of horse not set," which made him suspect the presence of a hostile force. None such, however, appeared, and Captain Bettesworth and his men advanced up to the city wall without attracting observation, and by the help of a heap of rubbish effected an entrance through an unguarded breach. Two men were left in charge of the horses of the party, and the rest hurried through the silent streets hoping to secure the sleeping Mayor, together with some of the Royalist clergy. They were, however, discovered, and at once there rang out the cry of "Arm! Arm!" forcing them to beat a hasty retreat. They, however, succeeded in carrying off four Cavalier prisoners, who were forthwith sent under escort to Southampton.

A letter written in the Isle of Wight on August 8th, states that "persecuted godly ministers" were taking refuge there, and gaining over numerous adherents for the Parliament. Sir Gregory Norton was a staunch partisan of the same cause. Many of the inhabitants objected to the raising of a large force for the defence of the island, which was already protected by 100 men and 30 guns. The Parliament allowed 3000*l.* per annum for purpose of defence, and had also given the local Committee authority to raise a larger amount if necessary. The Earl of Pembroke had been settling various matters in the island, and was said to be "much affected with honest godly preachers; he hears their sermons frequently, and is in converse with them ordinarily, and hath much improved his own and the public's good." On Wednesday, August 21st, the "Committee for placing well affected ministers in Hants," was ordered to assemble at three o'clock in the afternoon at the Exchequer, and also at whatever other times they might think fit, six members forming a quorum. The Earl of Pembroke found that "all the companies they had there except Bonelman's were disbanded, and three of them gone out of the island, whereof Sir Gregory Norton's was one," but he nevertheless persuaded the Commissioners and gentlemen of the island "to send 500 able and expert soldiers" to the army of the Earl of Essex, who was then in Cornwall. On Monday the Lieutenant of the ordnance was ordered to send "a ton of bullet, with proportion of match, to the Isle of Wight." The Committee of the West were also to send thither five hundred swords and three hundred bandoliers, which were to be paid for from the fine of one-twentieth part of his estate assessed upon Mr. Palmer, then a prisoner in the Fleet.

On August 1st, a Kentish regiment under the command of Sir Michael Livesay, was quartered at Chobham, in Surrey, in readiness to aid the besiegers of Basing House. Sir William Waller was himself in London, but his army, consisting of 3500 horse, and 1500 foot, was at Abingdon, Newbridge, and other places near Oxford, with the garrison of which city there were continued skirmishes. The siege of Basing House was meanwhile in active progress, and on July 31st it is evident that the enemy mean to come to close quarters. One of the defences of the house is known as "Basing Bulwarke," and within half musket shot of this by the woodside, "towards Basing towne a little wood" another platform is commenced. "Towards evening praying, the shot (it having been their fast) they spared all day." At night they ran a trench from the church to their work at the woodside. Four of the garrison deserted, and exaggerated the damage done by stones and grenades, whereupon they "send us store, one whereof firing our hay, falling into the barne, had done much hurt, had not our diligence soon quenched it."

Hitherto the soldiers had been on guard for 48 hours at a time, but this being found too harassing, the garrison was divided into two parts, who relieved each other every 24 hours. Gentlemen and troopers also did their part, and the Marquis highly commends them for having throughout the siege performed the duties of both cavalry and infantry (with the exception of standing sentry). They took part in all sallies, sometimes on horseback and at other times on foot, armed with muskets or brown bills. For seven weeks did they maintain their horses with grass and sedge, which they cut at night, at the risk of their lives, close to the enemy's works.

A letter sent from Basingstoke to London on Thursday, August 1st, stated that the besieged had suffered considerable loss from the shells which had been hurled into the garrison. Nine prisoners had escaped from the house, which they said was still well provisioned, but was held only by "250 men very weary of the fort. They are very still in the house, and answer neither by drum, trumpet, nor cannon."

There was good reason for this ominous quietness, for on Saturday, August 3rd, the terrible malady of small-pox was reported to be raging in the garrison, so that many officers were endeavouring to escape, either through fear of infection or on account of private quarrels. Some writers have concluded from an expression in the "Diary of the Siege" that the garrison were suffering from the effects of their own licentiousness, but a hostile writer distinctly states that small-pox was the malady which was working havoc within the walls. It was said that the King had counselled a surrender, but that Lord Winchester had made reply "that, under His Majesty's favour, the place was his, and that he was resolved to keep it as long as he could." The besiegers about this time received thirty more shells and some additional mortarpieces.

On August 4th, an unsuccessful attack was made upon the house, but one shell damaged the building, as did also another "beating down part of the mill wall." There was now a rumour in the besiegers' line, that provisions were diminishing, and that a surrender might be expected ere long. Colonel Norton preferred starving out the garrison, to taking the place by storm. The cavaliers had hitherto been careful of their men, expecting that the besiegers would be strongly reinforced, but seeing that their number did not increase, bolder counsels were adopted. "Our" men were few in number, much spent with labour, discouraged by divers wants, and the prevalence of disease. The rebels could be annoyed, and their works retarded, whilst prisoners could be compelled to give useful information. An able writer in "All the Year Round" (April 4th, 1874), says:—"Almost at that moment an opportunity set fire to the powder. A party of Puritan foot can be seen from the tower lying loosely like stray sheep in Waller's Work, on the green slope of Cowdry Down. There the knaves are, the lazy loons, sprinkled about like so much black pepper on a green cloth. Out dash twenty cavalier horse (commanded by Lieutenant Cuffand, a relative doubtless of Major Cuffand) while Cornet Bryan, with 20 more wild fellows, slips in between the other rogues and the hedge. Their guard of horse stand in somewhat too loose order. Hark, forward! Hey there! spur all together; away run the louts flying like mad dogs to Basingstoke; every moment one is sabred or shot down, or torn off his horse, with a shake and a curse and a slash and a stab; and here comes Cornet Bryan, with eyes only for one fair face blushing at him from the battlements, with a trumpet in one hand and their colours red and wet over his dusty shoulder. Seven horses and three sour trooper prisoners follow at his heels. Eleven of their foot were left stretched out dead, and four bound and dragged in prisoners—a pretty good haul for one throw of the net, our men returning under command of their cannon without the loss of a man." At the commencement of this skirmish the besiegers thought that the long-expected relief had arrived, and began to fly in confusion from their works in the Park, but speedily discovering their mistake, they returned, and kept up a hot fire of shot and shell. Meanwhile the prisoners who had been captured by Cornet Bryan stated that the deserter from the garrison had given information to the enemy that Basing Bulwark was especially weak (as was indeed the case), and that the next attack would be made in that quarter. All hands to work! and Basing Bulwark and other weak points are strengthened with hastily-constructed defences. The assailants said that this sortie was made "to the Grange Field about evening sermon time," and admitted the capture of an ensign and a trumpeter. On August 5th, which "Mercurius Aulicus" notes as being the anniversary of the celebrated Gowrie Conspiracy, Lords Saye and Maitland reached the Hampshire Committee at Basingstoke with instructions from the Parliament. Colonel Norton was not to be caught napping a second time, and it was now easy to see that the guard at Waller's Work on Cowdrey Down had been doubled, and pikes, evidently intended to repel a cavalry charge, could be seen glinting in the sun-light. The besiegers' cavalry were also much more on the alert. In the Park the siege works were now very close to the defenders' batteries, especially near the wood on the side of the village. Cannonading went on incessantly, great shot, stones, and three kinds of shell b. ing literally rained upon the House. The assailants were now close enough to throw in hand-grenades as well.

Such is the daily programme until August 10th, when Colonel Whitehead brings up his regiment, five companies strong, through Basingstoke to Cowdrey Down, and occupies the Delve, a still existing chalk pit, which is now known as Oliver Cromwell's Delve. This regiment had scarcely been a month raised before it thus marched to Basing, but it fought bravely nevertheless. Special mention is made of Cornet Doven, who "being a mighty proper man flew out so desperately" that he took two helmets. He is also said to have distinguished himself in some unrecorded manner at Romsey Abbey Church.

To give welcome and amusement to the new comers, and to show what their guns can do to "proud, stubborn, and malignant Basing," a heavy fire is concentrated on "a round tower in the old castle," which at length falls with a heavy crash. In the etching ascribed to Hollar we see "The Tower that is Halfe Battered Downe." As the siege guns were placed in the Park, this statement throws some light on the disputed question of the position of the old and new houses. (See Chap. I.)

But the Marquis paid them back next morning in their own coin. Major Cuffand, in command of six files of musketeers and 20 troopers, armed with brown bills, sallied forth into the Park and attacked their outward lines, killing some of them, burning their "blinds" and baskets, and bringing off a mortar with store of arms and tools, with a loss of only two men wounded. During "the amazement" caused by this bold sortie, Lieutenant Snow (who, from his name, seems to have been Hampshire born) with 20 musketeers and 12 men armed with bills, attacked the works in the lane (or lower road) and did considerable execution, breaking their demi-culverin, setting fire to their guard-house and baskets, and capturing, besides arms and tools, a welcome supply of ammunition, which proved most serviceable. The enemy were so chafed by their misfortunes that Captain Oram (who commanded the guard that day) was tried by a court-martial for neglect and cowardice, and cashiered, narrowly escaping with life. The "Diary of the Siege" is poor Captain Oram's best witness, "For neglect and cowardice (running as others then and after did), holding correspondence with the place (where no man knew him), and sending in ammunition (which was never received) with the hazard of life is cashiered their service. A sentence much like that against the Earle of Strafford made with caution not to be brought to president (precedent) for after times, least it too nearly might concern themselves."

Captain Oram's family lived in the lower part of the city of Winchester, and a token issued in 1664 by William Oram, who dwelt near the Eastgate, and was the founder of the Winchester Free School, is still in existence.

On Saturday, August 10th, Colonel Francis Thompson, who had lost his leg at Cheriton Fight, presented a petition, which was referred from the Upper to the Lower House, to the effect that he was "very infirm through the many wounds he has received, and was in great want for supply of monies which are due unto him for his pay." Nine days afterwards Sir William Waller was ordered to march westward forthwith from Farnham with his horse and dragoons. He was empowered to seize horses for his expedition in the five western Associated Counties, upon the security of the public faith, and his infantry were when mounted to "have the pay, officers and soldiers, as dragooneers." Waller writes from Farnham on August 28th, and also on September 1st, saying that he is willing to march, on receipt of 500l., and of horses for his mounted infantry.

Forage was scarce in Basing House, and, during the night of August 11th, the encouraged Cavaliers constructed an earthwork near the Grange, near the foot of Cowdrey's Down, in order to secure the meadows for the troopers, who were obliged whenever the nights were dark to sally forth to cut grass and sedge for their horses.

During the next few days the besiegers continued to fire their culverins, but were chiefly busied in the preparation of gabions, brushwood, and turf, with a view to future operations, and in filling gabions with grass, so that they might the less readily be set on fire.

During this partial lull, let us see what measures were being taken for the relief of "Loyalty House." Clarendon says (Bk. viii.), of Basing:—"It was so closely begirt before the

King's march into the West, and was looked upon as a place of such importance, that when the King sent notice to Oxford of his resolution to march into the West (he set out on Monday, July 1st), the Council humbly desired His Majesty that he would make Basing his way, and thereby relieve it, which His Majesty found would have retarded his march too much, and might have invited Waller to follow him, and therefore declined it. From that time, the Marquis, by frequent expresses, importuned the Lords of the Council to provide in some manner for his relief, and not to suffer his Person, and a place from whence the Rebels received so much prejudice, to fall into their hands. The Lady Marchioness, his wife, was then in Oxford (in Murray's handbook for Hampshire, she is credited with the authorship of the Diary of the Siege), and solicited very diligently the timely preservation of her husband; which made every body desire to gratify her, being a Lady of great honour and alliance, as sister to the Earl of Essex, and to the Lady Marchioness of Hertford; who was likewise in the town, and engaged her husband to take this business to heart, and all the Roman Catholics, who were numerous in the town, looked upon themselves as concerned to contribute all they could to the good work, and so offered to list themselves and their servants in the Service."

"The Council, both on publick and private motives, was very heartily disposed to effect it; and had several conferences together, and with the officers; in all of which the Governour too reasonably opposed the design as full of more difficulties, and liable to greater damages than any soldier who understood command would expose himself and the King's Service to; and protested that he would not suffer any of the small garrison that was under his charge to be hazarded in the attempt." (The Governor of Oxford was Sir Arthur Aston, who was afterwards killed at the storming of Drogheda.) "It was very true, Basing was near 40 miles from Oxford, and in the way between them, the enemy had a strong garrison of Horse and Foot at Abingdon, and as strong at Reading, whose horse every day visited all the highways near, besides a body of Horse and Dragoons quartered at Newbury; so that it appeared to most men hardly possible to send a party to Basing, and impossible for that party to return to Oxford, if they should be able to get to Basing."

Stout "Loyalty House" was therefore left for the present to shift for itself, which it was very well able to do. Messengers still contrived to make their way to the King, for about this time "a party of horse broke out by night and rode away for Wallingford or Oxford." At the dead of night on August 12th, Colonel Norton's drums beat to arms and the Cavaliers expect an assault, but do not cease their labour at their new works on the side towards the village. Between three and four o'clock in the morning a trumpet sounds clear and shrill from out the Delve or chalk pit on Cowdrey's Down, and at once 50 musketeers made a fierce attack upon Lord Winchester's working parties, but are speedily repulsed. Simultaneously 60 other musketeers, under cover of the little wood which proved such an annoyance to the besieged, succeed in reaching the moat close to the royalist batteries, but are received with well-directed volleys by the guard stationed at the park bulwark which flanked the ditch, whereupon they retire in haste, some of them flinging away their arms in their flight. Three guns loaded with case shot open fire upon the fugitives, whose retreat is covered by a heavy cannonade from their own works. Thinking it necessary to connect the large fort in the park with the works in and about the lower road or line, Colonel Norton's engineers commence a trench for that purpose. The cannon are silent all the next day, but after dark there is another false alarm.

Towards the evening of Wednesday, August 14th, Lieut. Cuffand and that wild horseman Cornet Bryan pull on their big buff boots, toss off a sufficient dose of sack, and ride forth each at the head of twenty horse and forty musketeers to Cowdrey's Down, where they drive the foot from Waller's Work, rout the guard of horse, and chase them as far as Basingstoke. Reinforced, the Roundheads roll back the tide of victory. Brave Cornet Bryan and a trooper are knocked down and hemmed in, three others being wounded meanwhile, and Ensign Amory, a London vintner, killed. The sortie is, nevertheless, successful. The loss of the enemy is heavy, and there are captured, Lieut. Cooper, a corporal of horse, and seven others, who say that four days previously, Colonel Morley had been wounded by a bullet in the shoulder, whilst inspecting the works in the park. The accounts published in London of this affair stated that about fifty horsemen rode out of the house on the Basingstoke side, intending to break through Colonel Morley's quarters in the park, but they marched up to Colonel Onslowe's quarters in the lower road and close towards Basingstoke, because " upon the borders of these two Colonels' quarters they intended to break through." The enemy were, however, on the alert, and gave them a warm reception, killing seven of them, capturing five, and cutting off the retreat to the house of either ten or seventeen others, who fled, "among which one is supposed to be a very eminent commander," either Lord Winchester, Sir Marmaduke Rawdon, or some person of distinction, but who was, in reality, brave Cornet Bryan. The rest of the party were beaten into the house with loss, and some of them were wounded. The captive Cavaliers on being questioned said that "the garrison holds out, because the king's party will show them no favour if they surrender, and were they out, they know not how to live or where, most of them being broken citizens and notorious Papists."

The capture of Cornet Bryan was duly reported to the House of Commons on August 21st, by Colonel Jones, who reached London on that day. He also stated that Farnham Castle was in a good state of defence, being threatened by no enemy, and that as the besiegers of Basing House had three infantry regiments before it, he had withdrawn his two White Companies from Basing to Farnham. The besiegers had made a large breach on the east side of the house near the park. Two days, August 15th and 16th, were spent in negotiations for an exchange of prisoners. One wounded Cavalier was exchanged for three of the enemy in like condition. The garrison "offering Lieutenant Cooper and the Corporal (both stout men, wounded, and taken fighting) for our Coronet (Cornet Bryan), but would not be accepted, so much they valued him!" You would have been a V.C. now-a-days, Cornet Bryan!

The parley being at an end, hostilities recommenced, three shells being thrown in during the night, one of which did not explode.

From Sir Edward Walker, Secretary of His Majesty's Council of War, we learn that preparations were now actively making for the relief of the gallant little garrison. In "His Majesty's Happy Progress and Success from the 30th of March to the 23rd of November, 1644," we read : —" August 14th. Now in this time of expectation we had leisure to enquire after the actions of those rebels we had left behind us, and in what conditions His Majesty's Garrisons stood, whereof Basing we left besieged, and Banbury and Donnington Castles were since surrounded by the Rebels."

On the night of August 16th, a deserter from the garrison gives information of an intended sortie in the direction of Waller's Work and the Delve on Cowdrey Downe, to protect which latter point a battery has been for some days in process of construction. Thus forewarned, they strengthen Waller's Work with gabions. The sortie is, however, at first most successful. The 300 men of Colonel Whitehead's regiment, who were quartered in the Delve, fly from it for their lives, carrying their colours with them. The Royalist troopers are over keen in pursuit, and the enemy are speedily reinforced. It is now indeed time to draw rein, for, see, the musketeers from Holloway's Mill are lining the hedges of the meadows in force. Only the coming up of the infantry from the house saves those bold riders from destruction. During the evening a culverin is placed in the newly-raised battery at the Delve, which, together with the culverin near the church, keeps up a fire upon the house. During the night three more of the garrison desert.

The 19th of August is a full noisy day. A demi-cannon, throwing a 30lb. shot, with a charge of 28lbs. of powder, is got up to the battery near the wood, and the enemy fire 48 shot. On the two following days they expended eight score more rounds, the least shot discharged weighing 18lbs., besides shells. Two men are killed and two others "mischieved." Lord Winchester's best iron gun is "broken," and a breach made in one of the square towers, besides damage to the battery in front of it. This last injury officers and soldiers alike take spade in hand to repair, with the result of making it able to resist 60lb. shot, whereas before field pieces had left evident traces upon it.

A hostile letter from Basing, which was published in the "Weekly Account" on Friday, Aug. 23rd, speaks of the capture of Cornet Bryan, of the great breach which had been made in the house, and of considerable damage done to Lord Winchester's private apartments by cannon shot. The writer continues, "and that a bullet came through in his own bedchamber, himself being at that very instant time in bed, which had like to have put him into the very same deportment as his father the old Marquis was in . . . . for he was so struck with fear that he leaped out of his bed, and ran into another room without his breeches, crying out that he wondered how the Roundheads could find him out, for he thought he had been safe in his bed!" During the week ending August 27th, ten Roundhead prisoners "in the New prison at Basing" had made a rope ladder, and endeavoured to escape, but were caught in the act, and only one got clear off. This seems to show that the garrison prison was situated in the New House.

The fire slackens on Thursday, August 22nd, and they "permit the night enjoy its proper silence, disturbed only by such whose bascnesse prompted them with hope to gaine by craft what by their force they could not, shooting Notes fixed to arrowes with proffers of preferment to the souldier perswading mutinies, and labouring divisions 'twixt the regiments, leaving no stone unturned, but all in vaine, except the gaining some faint-hearted knaves."

We may judge of the character of these missives from what occurred at the siege of Gloucestary, as related in John Vicar's Parliamentary Chronicle (p. 405), "Sunday, Sept. 3rd, 1643:—

In which said dayes afternoone a paper was shot upon an arrow into the towne, wherein were these words:—

"These are to let you understand that your God Waller hath forsaken you, and hath retired himself to the Tower of London. Essex is beaten like a dog. Yield to the King's mercie in time, otherwise if we enter perforce no quarter for such obstinate traiterly rogues. From a WELL-WISHER."

To which presently upon another arrow was returned this answer:—

"Waller's no god of ours, base rogues yee lye;
Our God survives from all eternity.
Though Essex beaten be, as you do say,
Rome's yoke we purpose never to ol ey,
But for our cabages which ye have eaten,
Be sure, ere long, ye shall be soundly beaten.
Quarter wee'l aske ye none; if we fall downe
King Charles will lose true subjects with the townc.
So sayes your best friend, if you make timely use of him Nicholas cudgell you well."

"Roundheads," "carrott beards," and "Essex calves" were some of the pleasant names applied by the Cavalier to his opponents in this fratricidal war.

The 23rd and 24th of August are signalised in Basing House by the unwelcome arrival of cross bar shot, logs of wood bound with iron hoops, and shells, "whereof two miss firing. Two more run to them."

The heavy battery near the wood with its 30-pounder having greatly torn the tower, the besiegers on the 25th August commence a battery within pistol shot on the side of Basing village, in order to complete its demolition. Two men of the garrison are killed, and a third maimed by artillery fire in other quarters. "In the park they shew a Sow made for their musquetiers, thrusting before them for to play behind." The Sow was "made with boards lined with wool to dead the shot." There is a sketch of this very curious machine in Groso's Military Antiquities. At Corfe Castle, in the preceding year, boards, hair, and wool for making a sow against the Castle cost 2l. 3s. 4d. The machine had three truckle wheels, and its failure at Corfe Castle is thus described:—

"The first that moved forward was the sow, but not being musket proof she cast nine out of eleven of her farrow; for the musketeers from the castle were so good marksmen at their legs, the only part of all their bodies left without defence, that nine ran away as well as their broken and battered legs would give them leave, and of the two which knew neither how to run away nor well to stay for fear, one was slain."

Two desertions from Basing House on this, and four more on the following night! This will never do. One would-be deserter has been caught in the act, and is at once hanged, whereupon "for a long time not one man that stirred, though our necessities grew fast upon us, now drinking water, and for some weeks making our bread with pease and oats, our stock of wheat being spent." Hard times, truly!

The besiegers now extend their lines almost completely round the house, forming the line of circumvallation which, according to Hugh Peters, was more than a mile in circumference. A hostile redoubt is also constructed opposite to the Basingstoke Bulwark. Its site is perhaps marked by a still existing mound. The garrison are reluctantly compelled to abandon the work on Cowdroy Down, which secured to them the command of the meadows, as it is too much exposed, and they have not sufficient men to hold it. The enemy's culverin in the battery at the Delve having been broken, another is substituted, which opens fire on August 28th. The next night five horses grazing in the meadows are carried off to Norton's lines, and twenty-four hours afterwards two troopers cutting grass are also captured.

The over-active foe now divert the course of the river Loddon, hoping thus to be able to get possession of the Grange, but the construction of a dam, which increases the depth of water, frustrates their hopes.

So ends the month of August, 1644, the events of which are thus summarised by another author :—

"For a fortnight the besiegers fell a-battering. Having torn the Tower, they fall upon the House side next the Town, making a work within pistol-shot, and, because of short commons within, some of cowardice got out to the enemy. Whilst necessities increased, no beverage but water, no bread but of pease and oats, other corn all spent."

Two of the besiegers' cannon had been rendered useless during the recent bombardment, either through being overloaded or from too rapid firing, but other heavy guns had recently been sent from Portsmouth, and others were expected to arrive from thence ere long.

The Earl of Essex agreed, at the instigation of Lord Roberts (or Robartes), a man of impetuous disposition and full of contradictions, to invade loyal Cornwall, whither he was quickly followed by the King in person, and speedily reduced to extremities. The Parliament were extremely anxious that Waller, who on August 29th was at Farnham with no large force, should at once march to the relief of Essex. This he professed his readiness to do, on being joined by some Kentish regiments numbering 1500 horse and foot, by Colonel Stapley, who was on the march from Chichester with 500 old soldiers, and by 500 additional troops from the Isle of Wight. Various reinforcements had, on September 10th, raised the strength of his army to 4000 men. But on August 31st, "the slow-going, inarticulate, indignant, somewhat elephantine man," as Carlyle styles the Earl of Essex, was forced by the King to surrender at Fowey, in Cornwall.

After the surrender it was agreed that Essex's infantry (his cavalry had escaped without the loss of a man) should be secured from plunder, by the protection of a convoy to either Poole or Southampton.

Clarendon (Bk. VIII.) continues:—" Of the 6000, for so many marched out of Foy,- there did not a third part come as far as Southampton, where the King's convoy left them ; to which Skippon gave a large testimony under his hand 'that they had carried themselves with great civility towards them, and fully complied with their obligation.'"

We shall meet with Essex and his army again ere long.

CHAPTER XXIV.—RECRUITING—BASING AGAIN SUMMONED—RENEWED BOMBARDMENT—PROPOSED RELIEF—SORTIES IN FORCE—LADY WALLER—A PURITAN ARMY—RELIEF AT LAST—COLONEL GAGE—THE RELIEVING FORCE—THE MARCH TO BASING—LOYALTY HOUSE SAVED—RETREAT TO OXFORD.

On Sunday, September 1st, Sir William Waller had received a reinforcement of 1200 or more infantry at Farnham, and on the same day the House of Commons voted a weekly assessment, to continue for twelve months, by which 125*l.* per week was to be raised in Hampshire, in which county Winchester, Southampton, and the Isle of Wight were by name included. On September 1st, likewise it was ordered that 6000 foot arms, 6000 coats, breeches, shirts, stockings, shoes, and caps should be sent to Portsmouth for distribution to the infantry of Essex's army, "and 500 pairs of pistols for recruiting the Lord General's horse." Many of these arms and stores, together with much powder and ammunition, were sent to Portsmouth on Sunday and Monday, September 8th and 9th, Essex having appointed that fortress as a place of rendezvous for his army. He himself was at Portsmouth on September 14th. The following Chronogram was circulated amongst Cavaliers after the defeat of Essex in Cornwall:—

"VIVat Rex CoMes EsseXIV's DIssIpatVr."

For the large Roman capital letters substitute the equivalent Arabic numerals, add them up, and the result gives the correct date, 1644.

The Earl of Pembroke received the thanks of the House of Commons on September 2nd, for raising soldiers in the Isle of Wight. The Parliamentarian Committee for the Island were ordered to send these men by sea to Lymington, Christchurch, or Weymouth, so as to meet at any convenient rendezvous Sir William Waller, who on September 6th wrote from Farnham, saying that he was starting westward with all diligence.

On September 7th Waller was supplied with 118 barrels of powder, at a cost of 490*l.* 7s. 6d., and he on the same day granted a commission to Colonel Popham, Major Ludlow, and others to raise a regiment of horse from the western counties, in which Ludlow was to command a troop. Essex had shamefully left his army in Cornwall to its fate, but on September 7th, within a week of his disgraceful flight, he was informed by the Speakers of the two Houses, "that his fidelity and merit in the public service is not lessened; and they are resolved not to be wanting in their best endeavours for the repairing of this loss."

Prince Rupert was expected to march into the southern counties, and orders were accordingly issued on September 7th to Sir William Waller and the Earl of Manchester to advance with all speed towards Dorchester, so as to check the advance of the King's army. The Earl of Manchester reached Huntingdon with his army on Sept. 8th, and was directed to march westward towards Abingdon with all possible expedition, and to send advertisement of his progress as he advanced. The town of Wareham, in Dorsetshire, had been held for the King by some 500 Irishmen, who about this time surrendered their trust to the Parliament, and on September 7th Colonel Jephson was ordered to billet these 500 soldiers at Hayling Island. They were to receive the sum of 1200*l.* and 300 old muskets, which were then in the public magazine, under the charge of Lieut.-Colonel Roe. Ships were also to be employed or chartered at a cost of 200*l.* to convey these men back to Ireland. Sir William Waller was at Blandford on September 20th, and on the previous day Essex writes from

Portsmouth concerning the defence of the town against the advancing army of the King. A portion of Essex's army was on September 21st at Southampton, daily receiving much needed supplies, and four days afterwards he wrote to the Parliament saying that he had received 30 cartloads of clothing for his infantry. On Sept. 24th it was decided that the old establishment of Hurst Castle, which was costing 50*l.* per month, should be defrayed by the Committee of the Revenue, but that all extra expenses were to be charged upon the Hundred of Christchurch.

Two days afterwards Colonel Butler, who had been put under arrest together with Colonel Weare, they having experienced some reverses in the retreat from Lostwithiel, and being suspected of a design to betray the army of Essex to the King, was sent up in custody from Portsmouth to London, and committed to the Tower, where he was "to have none come near him, or attend upon him, but such as he will be answerable for."

Authority was given to Sir William Waller, on September 27th, to impress 500 horses for his cavalry, and 600 for his train of artillery. £9000 was also voted for artillery for the Earl of Essex. Of this sum 3000*l.* was to be paid at once, 3000*l.* at the end of three months, and the remainder at the expiration of six months. Essex was also empowered to impress horses in Berks, Hants, Wilts, Dorset, Oxford, Somerset, and Devon. Not more than two were to be taken from any one team, and they were to be paid for by the Committee of the County. The Markmaster was to mark them, and he and his assistants were to be both cashiered and punished if they spared the horses of any one except Members or Assistants to Parliament.

On September 28th many of the Earl of Manchester's horse, under the command of Colonel Oliver Cromwell, were between Andover and Salisbury, in readiness to effect a junction with Sir William Waller, if the King should march in that direction, as were also 500 horse which Essex had sent to Marlborough.

The last day of September saw 500 saddles and furniture voted for the army of the Earl of Essex, and also a sum of 240*l.* for the supply of the chests of sixteen surgeons, who were to be attached to this force. 15*l.* was allowed for each surgeon's chest, the money was paid to the Master and Wardens of the Barber Surgeon's Company, and the Master and Wardens of the Apothecaries' Company were directed to examine the chests and drugs.

Mrs. Jane Fane, the daughter of Colonel Anthony Fane, who fell during Waller's attack on Farnham Castle in 1642, presented a petition saying that she had been granted, but had never received, a sum of 1500*l.* out of the profits of the Court of Wards. This money was now ordered to be paid. William Kingsmill, Esq., late Sheriff of Hants, was with others directed to collect the arrears of the weekly assessment of 125*l.* Sir William Waller was at Shaftesbury, and the Earl of Essex at Portsmouth.

Colonel Norton, at Basing, was hopeful that famine and bombardment had at length broken the spirit of the little garrison, and accordingly, on Monday, 2nd Sept., after keeping up a hot fire all the morning, he sent, together with proposals for an exchange of prisoners, the following summons:—

"MY LORD,—These are in the name and by the authority of the Parliament of England, the highest Court of Justice in this kingdome, to demand the House and Garrison of Basing to be delivered to me, to be disposed of according to Order of Parliament. And hereof I expect your answer by this Drum, within one hower after the receipt hereof. In the mean time I rest,
Your's to serve you,
RICH. NORTON.

From the quarters before Basing,
the 2 of Sept., in the afternoone,"—
("forenoone" says "Mer. Aulicus.")

It does not take long to write an answer, and "the noble Marquis sufficiently understood the language of these three last yeares, and therefore instantly returning the Rebel this answer":—

"SIR,—Whereas (your demands pretend authority of Parliament) you demand the House and Garrison of Basing by a pretended authority of Parliament, I (make this) answer, that without the King there can be no Parliament, but by His Majesties Commission I keep this (the) place, and without his absolute command shall not deliver it to any pretenders whatsoever.
I am, your's to serve you,
Basing, 2 Sept." WINCHESTER.

No sooner has Colonel Norton read this reply than his new battery on the Basing side of the house fires within six hours 120 shot of 18 and 60 lbs. weight, small shot likewise coming thick and fast, with the result of foundering one of the great brick towers, probably that of which the foundations are still distinctly visible on the slope above the canal, and which seems to have been situated at one of the corners of the house, and wall as killing three men, and wounding a woman. The *débris* of the tower completely blocked up one end of an adjacent curtain (a line of wall connecting two bastions), necessitating the construction of a traverse or mound of earth, from seven to ten feet in height, to prevent the other end of the curtain from being enfiladed by shot, which would speedily have dismounted the guns and proved altogether ruinous. A traverse being a defensible parapet, is a formidable obstacle to a storming party. Its thickness varies according to the fire to which it is exposed. All hands are busy in strengthening the neighbouring bulwark, which had been damaged by the heavy cannonade. Next day only 20 great shot are fired, and the enemy's guns having been damaged by too rapid firing, are drawn off to Farnham, and new ones substituted, which had been sent from Portsmouth. During the night the line of circumvallation is brought nearer to the Grange from the side of Basingstoke, thus almost completely encircling the garrison. No more sorties can now be made to Cowdry's Down, and the earthwork there which the Cavaliers have not occupied for some days, on account of its exposed position and their own paucity of numbers, is "slighted" or destroyed.

The Marquis has all this time been sending messengers to Oxford with new importunities and a positive declaration " that he could not defend it above ten days, and must then submit to the worst conditions the rebels were like to grant to his person and to his religion ;" and new instances from his Lady prevailed with the Lords to enter upon a new consultation, in which the Governour (Sir Arthur Aston) persisted in his old resolution "that he would not suffer any of the small garrison that was under his charge to be hazarded in the attempt 'as seeing no cause to change it !' "

" In this debate Colonel Gage (of whom more hereafter) declared 'that though he thought the service full of hazard, especially for the return, yet if the Lords would, by listing their own servants, perswade the gentlemen in the town to do the like, and engage their own persons, whereby a good troop or two of horse might be raised (upon which the principal dependence must be). he would willingly, if there were nobody else thought fitter for it, undertake the conduct of them himself, and hoped he should give a good account of it; which being offer'd with great cheerfulness by a person of whose prudence, as well as courage, they had a full confidence, they all resolved to do the utmost that was in their power to make it effectual." (Clarendon, Bk. VIII.)

The garrison at Basing is told to expect relief on Wednesday, the 4th of September. The anxiously expected day finds every man on the alert, but noon strikes, and no signs of relief appear. To raise the spirits of the disappointed soldiers, Lieuts. Snow and Byfield, and Ensign Outram are ordered to command a sortie in force. Lieut. Byfield seems to have been related to the Rev. Adoniram Byfield, rector of Collingbourne Ducis, and one of the few persons who have been by name stigmatised by Butler in Hudibras. Adoniram Byfield was a Parliamentarian, chaplain to Colonel Cholmondeley's regiment, and the father of Dr. Byfield the celebrated " Sal Volatile Doctor," who in his epitaph is said to be " Din volatilis,tandem fixus" —" Long volatile, fixed at last !"

The three officers above named are each in command of twelve troopers armed with brown bills, and eighteen musketeers, and without delay are sent to attack Colonel Onslowe's quarters in the park, in three several places. They succeed beyond expectation, capturing the enemy's redoubts, and a demi culverin or 9 pounder. This gun they draw nearer to the house, but are obliged to retreat, with a loss of three men killed and one wounded, some guns having opened fire upon th m with case shot. They bring in three prisoners, in order to obtain useful information, but make no effort to secure more, " our gaole being full." There is plenty of cannonading on both sides, and a successful sortie is made to the Delve on Cowdry's Down. Sir William Waller at the head of two troops of horse, has reached Basingstoke two hours before the commencement of the skirmish, and " came forth to see the sport, and with his horse facing the House, too near on Cowdrey's Down, they had their Captaine killed with round shot from our works." The enemy acknowlege a loss this day of 60 privates, two gunners, and two lieutenants killed, and twelve dangerously wounded. One of the lieutenants belonging to Sir William, and brought by curiosity to see the Leaguer, is there slain. Three others of the garrison are slightly wounded by earth and stones thrown up by an 18lb. shot. At night an attempt is made to bring in the culverin captured in the park, but it proves too heavy a task. The enemy's guards are doubled, and twelve royalist musketeers keep a strict watch over the gun.

" Mercurius Aulicus," on Wednesday, September 4th, says that Sir William Waller arrived " with his pretty portable army and his wonderful lady." Lady Waller had considerable reputation as a preacher, and the journalist adds that the sortie was successful, through the soldiers running " out of the trench to see, or rather to hear her," their comrades keeping but careless watch meanwhile. The captured gun is said to have be. n one of the largest of those in position against the House, and was brought within pistol shot of the defences, when it was unfortunately overturned. The Cavaliers at Oxford hoped that during the following week Basing would be relieved, and that they would hear that " Colonels Onslow, Norton, Whitehead, Jones, and horrible Herbert Morley, are all grinning mad !" Burton's War's in England says (p. 93.)—" And now comes Sir William Waller again, and with some troops faces the House, on whom the besieged played from their works."

On September 5th, however, it was reported in London that a Puritan prisoner who had escaped from the House had brought word to the besiegers that various officers of the garrison had sewn up money and plate in their clothes, hoping to be able to escape, which they often attempted to do, but to no purpose, all sorties being repulsed with loss, so that a speedy surrender was expected " upon reasonable composition."

The Parliamentarians, in their account of the night attempt to carry off the overturned gun to the House, said that their watch was asleep, admitted a loss of eight men killed and twelve others taken prisoners, and added that the besieged made a second sortie, in the hope of securing a dray laden with beer, but were repulsed with the loss of some prisoners.

During this and the following day (September 5th) the assailants fire fifty shot from their new battery near the wood, in the direction of the village, battering down a stack of chimneys, and making a wide breach in the New House. Towards evening Sir William Waller's army comes in sight, marching westward. Two companies of infantry go by way of Hackwood, and are followed next evening by two other companies, two waggons, and twelve troops of horse. On the next day (September 7th) the fire from the enemy's batteries ceases at noon, and the garrison have leisure to watch two strong regiments of twenty companies marching in the same direction as the cavalry. Two companies of white-coats turn in to Basingstoke, together with ten guns of various sizes, which are guarded by a yellow company. For the last four nights all the men have been kept at their posts, as they are also to-night, as an attack is by no means improbable. But the only disturbance is that of tongues, some of Colonel Norton's men asserting that Sir William Waller will storm the place next morning, and disputing with the new comers as to the distribution of the expected plunder. But Waller is anxious to move westward, and has learnt already by bitter experience the strength of Basing, so that he is by no means eager to try conclusions with it again. So he marches away and " We againe with our old guests are left to try it out, grown now so mute upon this parting as in 48 houres we heare but of two Culverin (18lb.) shot, next day recovering heart, they tell us 22, and resting some daies past now find their worke again." But the long looked for relief was now near at hand. Although the King had been fighting the Earl of Essex in the west, he was by no means unmindful of the necessities of Lord Winchester, for on Wednesday, September 11th, Sir Edw. Walker, Secretary of His Majesty's Council of War, thus writes : " Having many difficulties to pass before he (the King) made his winter quarters, likewise remembering that Basing and Banbury were then closely besieged, &c."

Preparations had for some time, as we have already seen, been making at Oxford to despatch a party to the relief of the Hampshire fortress, and the garrison had been led to expect aid on September 4th, but a week's delay was unavoidable, and eventually proved the safety of the expedition. For had Sir Wm. Waller been still hovering with his forces about Farnham, as he had been the week before, it would have been " in probability a hazard, whether they had releived us, or preserved themselves."

But all things being now prepared, action was at once taken. Several somewhat varying accounts of this gallant enterprise are found in

"Clarendon" (Bk. VIII.), Colonel Gage's "Official Report," the "Life of Sir Henry Gage," published at Oxford in 1645, the "Diary of the Siege," "Woodward's History of Hampshire," "Mercurius Aulicus," "Whitelocke's Memorials," &c.

In the last chapter we have seen Colonel Gage offering himself as the leader of the relieving expedition. Let us now learn what manner of man he was. He had been in command of the English regiment in Flanders, and at the commencement of the war had unsuccessfully tried to procure for the King from the Spanish Government of Flanders 6000 infantry and 400 cavalry. He afterwards obtained leave to make offer of his services to the King, and had not long reached Oxford, where he was appointed to the command of one portion of the town, and to assist the very unpopular governor, Sir Arthur Ashton. Colonel Gage "was in truth a very extraordinary Man, of a large and very graceful Person, of an Honourable extraction, his Grandfather (Sir John Gage) having been Knight of the Garter; besides his great experience and abilities as a Soldier, which were very eminent, he had very great parts of breeding, being a very good scholar in the polite parts of Learning, a great Master in the Spanish and Italian Tongues, besides the French and Dutch, which he spoke in great perfection; having scarce been in England in 20 years before. He was likewise very conversant in Courts; having for many years been much esteemed in that of the Arch-Duke and Duchess, Albert and Isabella, at Brussels; which was a very great and regular Court at that time; so that he deserved to be looked upon as a very wise and accomplished Person. Of this Gentleman, the Lords of the Council had a singular esteem, and consulted frequently with him, whilst they looked to be besieged; and thought Oxford to be the more secure for his being in it, which rendered him so ungrateful (unpopular) to the Governor, Sir Arthur, that he crossed him in anything he proposed, and hated him perfectly, as they were of Natures and Manners as different as men can be."

Colonel Gage and Sir Arthur Aston were both Roman Catholics. Such a gallant deliverer had Loyalty House.

Clarendon says, moreover (Bk. VIII), "There was about this time, by the surrender of Greenland House (which could not possibly be longer defended, the whole structure having been beaten down by the cannon) the regiment of Colonel Hawkins marched into Oxford, amounting to near 300, to which as many joined as made it up 400 men." Colonel Gage says "with somewhat more than 400 musquetiers of Her Majesty's and Colonel Hawkin's regiment, and 250 horse of my Lord Treasurer's Regiment, commanded by Colonel Webb of Sir Arthur Aston's regiment (or "the Governour's Troops") commanded by Lieutenant-Colonel Buncle." According to "Mercurius Aulius" Major Windebank, who in the following year was shot for surrendering Bletchington House to Cromwell (April 13th, 1645), commanded the foot. The cavalry, or "Horse Gentlemen Volunteers," are thus described by Clarendon: "The Lords mounted their servants upon their own horses, and they with the Volunteers, who frankly listed themselves, amounted to a body of 250 very good horse, all put under the command of Colonel William Webb, an excellent officer, bred up in Flanders in some emulation with Colonel Gage, and who, upon the Catholic interest, was at this time contented to serve under him." Colonel Gage was therefore in supreme command, Colonel Webb acting as Brigadier, whilst Lieut.-Colonel Buncle commanded the 250 horse of my Lord Treasurer's regiment. There was also another body of horse under the command of Lieut.-Colonel Sir William Campion, who was Governor of Boarstall House, a stronghold on the western verge of Buckinghamshire, two miles from Brill, and half way between Oxford and Aylesbury, which Colonel Gage had not long before retaken and garrisoned for the King. Sir William Campion in this time of need ventured to bring his cavalry force to the relief of Basing. Twelve barrels of powder and 1200lb. weight of match were taken for the supply of the besieged garrison. Sir S. D. Scott says (British Army, vol. II. p. 311), "Match was made of cotton or hemp, spun slack, and boiled in a strong solution of saltpetre, or in the lees of wine. It was generally hung in reserve at the girdle, or tied to the bandoleers; it was sometimes coiled round the arm or hat." By the 15th of Charles II., cap. 4, every musketeer was bound to attend every muster with "half a pound of powder, half a pound of bullets, and three yards of match."

With this "regiment of bold blades," a small

party for so great an action. Colonel Gage marched out of Oxford about ten o'clock on the night of Monday, the 9th of September, with orders to relieve Basing House (long besieged by the Rebels), and to put in such provision of victuals as the country there affords." As the object of the expedition was the relief of Basing House, it was important that the enemy should not receive notice of the approach of the Cavaliers. They therefore "passed through the country for Parliament men, with orange tawney scarfs, and ribbands on our hats." Col. Hawkins' regiment wore white uniforms.

The march lasted all night, and early on Tuesday morning the force reached Cholsey Wood, near Wallingford, where it was joined by Captain Walters with about 50 horse of his troop, and as many foot of that garrison, which was the last in Berkshire to hold out for the King, only surrendering to Fairfax in 1646.

The wearied soldiers here rested for three hours, and says Colonel Gage : " I despatched an express to Sir William Ogle, Governor of Winchester Castle, who had promised Mr. Secretary Nicholas 100 horse and 300 foot of that garrison to help to raise the siege of Basing whensoever the Lords should have any such design. I sent by this express a letter of credit of Mr. Secretary's to Sir William Ogle, desiring him with his men to fall into Basing park, in the rear of the Rebels' quarters there, betwixt 4 and 5 of the clock in the morning, being Wednesday, the 11th of September" (a presumption upon this aid was the principal motive for the undertaking, says Clarendon), whilst I, with the troops of Oxford, fell on upon the other side (by the Grange), and my Lord Marquess from within the House plyed them with sallies."

In the "Life of Colonel Gage" the reinforcement from Wallingford is said to have numbered 80 horse and the same number of foot.

"Having despatched this express, and refreshed my men, I marched forward with as much speed as the foot soldiers could manage (through by lanes) to Aldermaston (a village out of any great road, seven miles distant from Reading,) where I intended to repose and refresh again. Thither I sent Captain Walters before with his Troop, and the Quartermasters of each Regiment to have provisions in a readiness against the soldiers arrived, intending only to refresh and rest two or three hours. But Captain Walters finding some Parliament scouts in that town, forgot his orange tawny colours, and fell foul with the enemy, taking six or seven of them prisoners, by which he unmasked and discovered us to be Royalists."

"Mercurius" says that the Roundheads had come from Reading, and admitted that their object in visiting Aldermaston was to burn the prayer book and surplice. One of them was killed, and six were captured, together with their horses and pistols. The Royalist infantry were already so much fatigued that Colonel Gage set the example, which was followed by the officers and troopers, of dismounting and marching on foot for three miles, placing the foot soldiers in the saddle meanwhile.

Notice was quickly sent to Basing of the approaching danger, which accident made their stay shorter at that village than was intended, and than the weariness of the soldiers required. Whilst Colonel Gage was on his march from Wallingford to Aldermaston, the besiegers of Basing House were, strange to say, quiet all day, but fired ten shots from their cannon during the evening. After dark they received warning of the rapid advance of Colonel Gage, and prepared to give him a warm reception. But trusty and tried Edward Jeffery, who had carried so many messages to Oxford, was also on the alert, and made his way into the garrison with news of the doings at Aldermaston. Quickly were beacon fires made ready upon the roof of the lofty gatehouse looking northward, in sign of welcome and of readiness to aid. There was, unfortunately, a thick fog rising from the meadows, and scarcely could those welcoming lights be seen, even on Cowdry Down. Leaving willing hands to tend the midnight fires, let us return to Colonel Gage, whose main body reached Aldermaston about eight o'clock on Tuesday night, and halted for three hours. "Aulicus" says that the halt was between nine p.m. and one a.m. The almost exhausted soldiers "then set forwards again, and marched all night, arriving within a mile of Basing, betwixt four and five of the clock on Wednesday morning." The diary of the siege says, "By seven next morne, the noble Colonell Gage with horse and foot past through so many hazards, had obtained Chinham Downe (Chinham lies between Basing and Sherborn St. John), where Colonell Norton with his strength, having intelligence, did stand in readiness." To quote Colonel Gage once more, " Our foot being extreamly surbated and weary, though I had endeavoured to ease them what I could in the whole journey, either by setting them up behind the horsemen, or making the horsemen alight and the foot ride, or by encouraging them with hopes of great pillage, or with promises of money when they returned to Oxford." "Aulicus" says that the infantry were not only rested, but also much gratified by Colonel Gage's consideration in mounting them behind the troopers, and were now again ready to fight vigorously, whereas when they first came within two miles of the enemy they were falling out and lying down on the road through sheer exhaustion. Burton says ("Wars in England," p. 93), that Col. Norton being in readiness on Chinham Down, "Gage makes his approach, appearing first on an hill near the highway which leads to Andover." To quote Colonel Gage once more, " I was no sooner arrived there (at Chinham Down), but Lieutenant Swainely met me, sent by Sir William Ogle from Winchester, to tell me that he durst not send his troops to assist me, in regard some of the enemy's horse lay betwixt Winchester and Basing, so that I was forced to enter into new councils, and call the officers together to take new resolutions." It was indeed time to take counsel, for both horse and foot were already almost worn out with fatigue, whilst Norton's men were fresh and unwearied, with the advantages of a strong and previously selected position, and of "a fog so thick as made the day still night, helping the shrouding of his (Norton's) ambuscades, and clouding passes unto such who neither knew nor could discern a way, more than their valour and the sword did cut," whilst Gage had now no hope of aid from Winchester. The force which kept Lord Ogle and his garrison in check at Winchester was probably the cavalry, commanded by Major Ludlow, which was principally raised in the western counties. Ludlow had a few days previously been attacked upon Warminster Heath, from whence he made a skilful retreat to Salisbury. With 30 horse he entered the city, "where divers persons, ill affected to the Parliament, made a great shout at our coming into the town, rejoicing at our defeat." Ludlow continued his retreat over Mutton Bridge, where he succeeded in checking pursuit by showing a bold front upon a causeway only three feet in broadth, and through White Parish to Southampton. Only two days after his arrival at the latter place, he, at the request of Colonel Norton, marched with his wearied horsemen to face Winchester Castle. Sir William Ogle, the Governor, anxious if possible to assist Colonel Gage's expedition for the relief of Basing House, sent out some men, amongst whom Ludlow recognised his old acquaintance and schoolfellow, Mr. William Neale. " I called to him," says Ludlow, "telling him that I was sorry to see him there," and offering to exchange shots with him. Neale retreated, at the same time shouting " Come on," and another Cavalier greeted Ludlow with a brace of bullets, one of which wounded his horse in the belly so severely that it died that night, whilst the other struck the rider within half an inch of the bottom of his breastplate. Not long afterwards Ludlow retired with his command into Wiltshire, having effectually hindered Sir William Ogle from co-operating in the relief of Basing House. Colonel Gage continues, " And because we were disappointed of so considerable a party as that of Winchester, and foreseeing the enemy might draw to a head, having notice of our coming, we resolved not to dismember our forces and fall on in several places, as we would have done if either the Winchester forces had arrived, or we would have surprised and taken the enemy at unawares, but to fall on jointly at one place. In order to which I commanded the men to be ranged into battalions, and riding up to every squadron, gave them what good words and encouragement I was able, though I confess it needed not (most of them being so well resolved of themselves) and delivered them the word ('St. George'), commanding every man to tie a white tape, ribband, or handkerchief upon their right arm above the elbow, which was the sign and word I had formerly sent to my Lord Marquis (lest by his sallying and our falling on we might for want of a distinctive sign fall foul upon each other). We marched on, Colonel Webb leading the right wing, Lieut.-Colonel Bunele the left wing of the Horse, and myself the Foot. (The "Life of Colonel Gage" says that he dismounted, and led the infantry on foot with his sword drawn) till at the upper end of a large champion field (Chinham Down), upon a little rising or ascent of a hill, near certain hedges lined by the enemy's musqueteers, we discovered a body of

five cornets (or troops) of horse (very full) standing in very good order to receive us. But before we could come up to them we were saluted from the hedges with a smart volley of musquet shot, more terrible than damageable, for Col. Webb, notwithstanding, with the right wing of my Lord Treasurer's Horse, charged the enemy (Col. Gage's biographer says that their strength was six troops, not five) so gallantly that in a movement they all turned head and ran away. Lieut.-Col. Bunele with our left wing falling in likewise after them, and following the chase with the right till the Rebels' horse were gotten into a place of safety. In this pursuit what men or horse of the enemies' were lost, I cannot learn certainly; but certain I am we took a colour or cornet of theirs, which I understand was Col. Morley's, the motto of which was *Non ab Aequo sed in Aequo* ('Victory is not by Right, but in Right'), a motto not so proper to theirs, as our cause, the equity of which gave us the victory with the true and genuine signification of the motto." The diary of the siege says that Norton was forced to retreat, " the fogge befriending him, serving as covert for his safer flight through Basingstoke." Clarendon speaks thus : " After a shorter resistance than was expected, from the known courage of Norton, though many of his men fell, the enemies horse gave ground, and at last plainly run to a safe place, beyond which they could not be pursued."
" Aulicus " says that the wind was also unfavourable to the operations of Colonel Gage, who as soon as he approached the enemy ordered his drums and trumpets to sound, thinking to take the besiegers by surprise. They were, however, on the alert, within musket shot, and their drums and trumpets at once made reply. The cavalry fight lasted not long, but was fiercely contested. The rebel horse fled ere long, and two troops of the Lord Treasurer's regiment then chased five troops of Norton's horse without even firing a pistol. The rebel foot fought better, more especially Colonel Morley's regiment, but the musketeers of the Queen's Life Guard, and of Colonel Hawkins' regiment beat them from hedge to hedge, until, abandoned by their mounted comrades, they retreated, aided by the fog " and a lane of which they had possessed themselves."
Burton, on the other hand, says that when Colonel Gage's force was first descried, " Norton charges with courage, and breaks through the other's horse, who, having a rescue of musketeers, with more than ordinary valour forced Norton to retreat as far as the church and through Basingstoke, the same time the besieged, sallying out at several places, brought in many prisoners." Whitelocke says that Colonel Gage had "about 1500 of the King's foot out of several garrisons mounted for dragoons." He adds that when the fight began Norton charged and broke them, " but they with great courage wheeled about, and charged Norton's whole body, who retired unto Colonel Morley's quarters," in the park.

At all events the Cavaliers remained masters of the field, and Colonel Gage now advanced with his infantry, sounding his trumpets, to give notice to the garrison of his approach. The fog began to clear away, and the besieged soon found that friends were close at hand. Says Clarendon, " The foot disputed the business much better, and, being beaten from hedge to hedge, retired into their quarters and works. which they did not abandon in less than two hours." The garrison also sent forth some musketeers, commanded by Lieut.-Colonel Johnson (the botanist) by way of The Grange. who beat the enemy from their works, pursuing them to Cowdry Down, and from thence " unto The Delve, clearing that quarter, with so small defence as is incredible. The passe (by The Grange) thus cleared, meeting our welcome friends, our joyes are echoed, whilst the sad prisoners are led in to see the House they lay so long about, their number 64 common soldiers. two sergeants, one lieutenant, whereof the wounded were next day sent forth unto the care of their own chirurgeons, and," grimly adds the Diary, " two that ran from us had execution !"

Army physicians and surgeons received 6s. 8d., apothecaries 3s. 4d., barber surgeons 2s., and under barber surgeons 6d. per diem. " Such surgeons must weare their baldricke, whereby they may be knowen in the tyme of slaughter ; it is their charter in the field." For gunshot wounds it was recommended " to cauterise them with the oil of elders, mixed with a little treacle."

" Aulicus " says that in the first encounter and sortio fully 120 rebels were killed, and more than 100 captured, 17 of whom were dangerously wounded. The latter " were dressed in the house, and sent out to the leaguer" (*i.e.*, siege works). A writer on the other side says: "Norton had a slight hurt in the hand, and lost but one man, but the House was relieved." A loss of nine Cavaliers slain, two of whom were officers, is admitted by "Aulicus." Captain Sturges was killed, whom Colonel Gage calls "a gallant young man of the Queen's Life Guard," and whom "Aulicus" describes as "a gallant daring young man, who, with Colonel Gage, both at the taking of Boarstall House, at Abingdon, and here also shewed exemplary courage."

"Young Mr. Stonor (of Stonor Park), Cornet of the Troop of Wallingford, who gallantly kept his colours, though he lost his life," also died like a gallant soldier. The seven others who fell were common soldiers. Four Cavaliers were taken prisoners, "whereof one was Master Stanhope, Gentleman of the Horse to the Lord Marquis of Hartford, who, engaging himself to gain a standard of the rebels, for want of seconds was hemmed in, after he had run a Captain Lieutenant of their's through the body."

Colonel Gage at once placed in Basing House, the twelve barrels of powder, which Burton says formed many a horse-load, and the 12cwt. of match brought from Oxford," paid my Lord Marquess the respects due to a person of his merit and quality," and Colonel Hawkins told off 100 of his white coated musketeers to strengthen the little garrison. "That lovers met that day, and blushed, and kissed, and old grey-bearded friends embraced each other, and aye marry pledged each other too; that good Catholic comrades exchanged prayers at Basing altar, that brave fathers kissed the wives and children they had left shut up in brave old 'Loyalty,' needs no telling. But not alone in kissing and quaffing did Gage and his troops spend those two merry days."

A speedy return was made to Cowdry Down, and the cavalry from Oxford retreated to Chinham, under fire of Norton's guns. From thence, leaving a force to observe the enemy's works, marching to Basingstoke, they took possession of it with small resistance (for the Parliament Committees who lodged in that town, having notice of our coming, quitted the town the night before, and drew most of their forces into one head, which we broke.) "From thence all that day I continued sending to Basing House as much wheat, malt, salt, oats, bacon, cheese, and butter as I could get horses and carts to transport. There I found a little magazine of 14 (whole) barrels of powder, with some (100) musquets, which I likewise sent into Basing House, and thence I sent also 40 or 50 head of cattle, with 100 sheep." "Aulicus" says that it was the market day at Basingstoke, and that Col. Gage "brought in 100 cattle, whereof divers were excellent fat oxen, as many or more sheep, and 40 and odd hogs."

"Whilst these things were doing at Basing stoke my Lord was not wanting in himself in Basing House, but from thence with the 100 white coats I left him commanded by Captain Hull, and 100 musqueteers under command of Major Cuffand, he sallied out into Basing Town, from whence he chased and utterly beat the enemy." The siege works were captured, and the church, which had been fortified, was carried by assault.

In Basing Church were captured and sent into the houses young Captain Jarvise (Jarvas) and Captain John Jephson, whom Gage calls "sons of Aulicus" is very hard upon Captain Jarvise, styling him "Captain Jarvas, son to Sir Thomas (who is so famous in Hampshire that when any man speaks an untruth big enough to be noted, they call it Jarvasing.")

Captain Jarvise had previously distinguished himself at the siege of Corfe Castle. Captain Jephson afterwards changed sides, and was governor for the King at Bandon-bridge in Ireland. One lieutenant, two sergeants, and about 30 (33) soldiers were captured in Basing Church, the rest by several ways escaping, but 40 rebels were killed either in the church or in the village of Basing.

During the 18 weeks' siege the Puritans claimed to have expended 1500 barrels of powder against Basing House. They stripped the lead from the roof of Basing Church, "and gave it out that the Cavaliers in Basing House had attempted it before." So says "Aulicus," adding, "Some conceive the chief receivers took two parts in powder and one-third in money, which is the usual method of their reckoning. For the rebels' soldiers are cozened by their officers; the members cheat them both; the devil cozens all three; and the Scots tug hard to deal with all four!"

During the struggle in the morning, the guns mounted upon Sir Richard Onslowe's batteries on the Basingstoke side of the House had been removed to the works in the park, and, taking advantage of this circumstance, Lieutenant-Colonel Peake led out some musketeers, who captured the works, destroyed the redoubts, and fired the tents and huts near Holloway's Mill, "the enemy so hastening from these works as scarcely 3 could be made stay the killing. Thus might we see at once three of their quarters (in Basing, at Holloway's Mill, and on the side of Basingstoke) blaze." The rest of the enemy were obliged to retire into the strong fort which they had constructed in the park. Lieut.-Colonel Peake and his musketeers also brought in "a goodly demi-cannon (30 pr.) from Sir Richard Onslowe's works."

By the time all this was done, says Colonel Gage, "the day began well near to be spent, and the enemy having received some fresh supplies of horse, appeared much more numerous and gay than in the morning, and made a show of a desire to fight with us again, advancing for that purpose over a large champion almost within musquet shot of our horse, which stood ranged in a field without Basingstoke, betwixt large hedges lined by me with musquetoeers. There we stood facing each other, till at last I perceived our squadrons of horse to grow thin, many men stealing privately out of their ranks, and both our horse and men extremely tired and fasting, I gave orders to the horse to retire by degrees and pass through the town (Basing) towards Basing House, whilst I, with the foot, made good the avenues or passages on this side the town, where the enemy appeared. And when I understood the horse were all passed through the town, and put again into their squadrons on the other side towards Basing House, I myself, with most of the foot, retired likewise through the town to our horse, leaving Captain Poore with 60 or 70 musqueteers to make good that avenue, and being come to our horse, I sent orders to Capt. Poore (of an old Wiltshire family), to retreat likewise with most of his men, leaving only a sergeant at the avenue with 20 musqueteers, to dispute till we were all entered into Basing House. From thence I sent afterwards for the sergeant and his men, who all came off safe, the enemy not once attempting to enter into the town, but retiring to their quarters not long after they had perceived our horse retire."

Continues the Colonel, "I durst not lodge that night in the town, as well because I saw the enemy grow strong, and our men and horse extreme weary and fasting, as because there were many avenues which must have been maintained; and I feared our men would quit their guards and betake themselves to the houses, drinking and committing disorders in the night. But the next day early I sent Lieutenant-Col. Buncle thither (to Basing and Basingstoke) again with all the horse and foot, as well to refresh the soldiers as to be sending continually all that day provisions into the House."

The garrison also made a sally into the park, and brought off a culverin, "a faire brass gun," which the enemy in their flight had abandoned near the wood between the House and the village, the enemy making no resistance. Emboldened by this, the Cavaliers attacked the fort in the park, but were recalled, as most of the infantry were busied elsewhere. A sergeant and five men were mortally wounded in this affair, and the surgeons of the garrison had their hands full, many of the troops from Oxford having been wounded on the previous day. Towards evening intelligence was received of the enemy's mustering in force near Silchester, and advancing towards Kingsclere.

"Meanwhile," says Colonel Gage, "I spent the day in contriving our retreat to Oxford, and, sending out several spies to observe the motions of another enemy drawing to a head from Abingdon, Newbury, and Reading to hinder our retreat homeward.

"And I fouud by the unanimous relation of all my several spies that they of Abingdon (500 horse and dragoons under Major-General Browne) were lodged at Aldermaston, they of Nowbury (300 strong) at Thatcham, they of Reading (and all the horses which the country could rake together) at Padsworth, places upon the river Kennet, over which I was to pass in my retreat; and that Norton with his horse and foot was to follow me in the rear whensoever I began to march, which he conceived I could not do but he should have notice of it. I resolved, therefore, in my own breast, without acquainting any man, to make my retreat that very night, having during the short time I had been at Basing House, partly out of Basingstoke, partly out of Basing Town, put at least a month's provisions into the House (the country people are said to have driven away their cattle, and to have hidden provisions on hearing of Gage's approach), and drawn in two pieces of artillery of the enemy's (the one a demi-cannon, which lay engaged betwixt the House and the enemy's trenches, neither of them daring adventure to draw them off)." An iron cannon was at least 9½ft. long, weighing about three tons. The culverin and demi-culverin were each ten feet long. One averaged 43cwt., the other 35cwt.

"But the more to amuse the enemy and give him cause to think that I thought of nothing less than of so sudden a retreat, I sent out certain warrants that afternoon, which I knew would fall into the enemy's hands, to the towns of Sherborne and Sherfield, to bring speedily a certain quantity of corn into Basing House, upon pain (if they refused) of sending them 1000 horse and dragoons to set their towns on fire before next day at noon."

"Having thus disposed of all things, and being unable to serve my Lord Marquess much more than I had done by any longer stay there (though by staying any longer I might have endangered the loss of the Oxford troops), somewhat before night I sent orders to Lieut.-Colonel Buncle to retire with the men from Basingstoke and march to Basing House, as the night before, but not to permit his men to enter into the House until further orders. Whither, when the men were arrived, I told my Lord Marquess of my resolution to depart that night, and of the necessity of it, and begging of him two or three good guides, which he readily gave, (was Edward Jeffrey one of them?), I took leave of his Lordship and began to march away without sound of drum or trumpet, about 11 o'clock on Thursday night, and gave order to all my scouts, in case they met with any Parliament scouts in the night, they should likewise give themselves out to be Parliament troops marching from before Basing House to the River Kennet, to lie in wait for the Oxford forces that were to come that way. And thus we passed the Kennet undiscovered, by a ford near Burghfield Bridge (the bridge itself having been broken by the enemy), our horse taking up the musketeers en croup; and afterwards the Thames, by another ford at Pangbourne, within six miles of Reading, about eight or nine o'clock on Friday morning, (the bridges at Henley and Reading had been also broken down), and from thence marched into the town of Wallingford, where we rested and refreshed our wearied men and horse that night, and the next day (Saturday, Sep. 14th) arrived safe at Oxford, having in this expedition lost Captain Sturges, a gallant young man of the Queen's Life Guards, young Mr. Stonor (of Stonor Park), cornet of the troop of Wallingford, a servant of Sir W. Hide's, with some others, to the number of eleven in all, and 40 or 50 hurt, but not dangerously." On Thursday, September 12th, a Colonel, a Lieutenant-Colonel, and two Lieutenants of Foot of Gage's force seem to have been captured, but again rescued by their comrades. Another account says that Gage lost a Colonel, a Major, 100 killed, and many prisoners. Some of his scouts were captured during his masterly retreat. Colonel Gage continues: "What loss the enemy had we cannot yet learn, (his biographer estimates the Puritan loss at six score slain, and from 100 to 150 taken prisoners), but we took about 100 prisoners of them. And thus, my Lord, to comply with the order I received, I have troubled your Lordship with a tedious relation, for which I humbly beg your pardon, and the honour to be esteemed.

My Lord, your Lordship's
    Most humble Servant,
        HENRY GAGE.
Oxford, this 16th of September, 1644."

All Oxford turned out to greet the returning deliverers of Loyalty House, and many were the eyes that looked eagerly for noble Colonel Gage. But they looked in vain. Wishing not for the applause of the multitude, and satisfied with having done his duty, he turned his horse's head into a back street, and rode quietly away unnoticed to his quarters. Wherever we meet with Colonel Gage we always find cause to admire him, and in concluding this account of the relief of Basing House we fully endorse these words, penned full two centuries since:—
"I say you must needs grant the whole action to have been, for wise conduct, gallant and skilful manage, the most souldier-like piece these Warres have ever yet afforded!"

CHAPTER XXV.—FIGHT IN BASING VILLAGE—LIEUTENANT-COLONEL JOHNSON—RENEWED BLOCKADE—ATTACK ON THE CHURCH—GATHERING ARMIES—THE KING'S ADVANCE—ANDOVER FIGHT—RENDEZVOUS AT BASING—WELCOME SUPPLIES—GAGE'S SECOND RELIEF THE SIEGE RAISED.

In order to still further conceal his retreat Colonel Gage had given orders that the next morning a letter should be sent to Colonel Norton, offering to exchange Captain Jephson for Captain Love, which was accordingly done. The exchange was effected by noon, and the enemy then discovered too late that the relieving force was beyond their reach. Captain Love's family resided at Basing (Woodward's "History of Hampshire"). As we here see, he was a Royalist, but his relative Nicholas Love was a member of the Committee of Parliament for Hampshire. Verily, houses were divided in those days!

Numerous Hampshire recruits were now joining the forces of the Parliament, but Col. Ludlow, having first duly notified his intention to Colonel Norton, withdrew his command from Winchester to Salisbury. On reaching the latter city he called for a list of the principal adherents of the King residing there, whom he ordered to pay the sum of 500*l*. The citizens made many excuses, but Ludlow secured 200*l*. and quarters for his men, after which he himself went to London to recruit and procure arms.

On Friday, September 14th, Colonel Norton did not venture to re-occupy the village of Basing, but kept his men shut up in their strong fort in the park. All the carts belonging to the garrison were busily employed in carrying corn and provisions from the village to Basing House, under the protection of 100 musketeers, commanded by Captain Fletcher. Towards evening, when, as "Aulicus" confesses, the Cavaliers "were drinking in the town, and in no good order," Colonel Norton in person headed an unexpected attack. Making a circuit, he fell upon Captain Fletcher's party in the church-yard " before the horse centinells could give timely notice to the officers to draw all the soldiers into a body," and drove the Cavaliers from the church. Reinforcements speedily arrived from the house under the command of the field officers, and "one hour's very sharp fight followed," at the end of which time the besiegers were driven from the church and retreated " to their onely work in Basing Park," with a loss of either 16 or 32 men killed on the spot and in the pursuit, very many wounded, and eleven prisoners.

Captain John Jephson, who had been exchanged on the previous day for Captain Love, "led on the rebels' van, where Captain Love made haste to meet him, but Jephson, though wounded, retreated too fast towards Colonel Norton, who valiantly brought up their rear, and came, good gentleman, almost to the churchyard, where, being minded of his grave, he was the first man that ran away." ("Mer. Aul.." Sept 14th). Clarendon, however, speaks of " the known courage of Norton." Some arms were picked up by the victors, who lost one ensign and two (4) common soldiers killed, six (7) wounded, four mortally, and eight prisoners. "Lieutenant-Colonel Johnson, Doctor of Physique (the best herbalist in England), was here shot in the shoulder, whereby contracting a fever he died a fortnight after, his worth challenging funerall tears, being no less eminent in the garrison for his valour and conduct as a soldier than famous through the kingdom for his excellency as an herbarist and physician." He was, there is reason to believe, in the meridian of life. Woodward says, "Thomas Johnson, of Hull, a London apothecary, May 9, 1643, made an honorary M.D. of Oxford. His itinerary through Bristol, Southampton, the Isle of

Wight, and Guildford, was published under the title of 'Mercurius Botanicus.' At Basing he served as Lieutenant-Colonel to Sir Marmaduke Rawdon, the Governor."

In the 1662 edition of the "Worthies of England," p. 204, we are told :—" Thomas Johnson was born in this county of Yorkshire, not far from Hull, bred an apothecary in London, where he attained to be the best herbalist of his age in England, making additions to the edition of Gerard. A man of such modesty that knowing so much he would own the knowledge of nothing. The University of Oxford bestowed on him the honorary degree of doctor in physic, and his loyalty engaged him on the King's side in our late civil warre. When in Basing House a dangerous piece of service was to be done, this doctor, who publickly pretended not to valour, undertook and performed it. Yet afterwards he lost his life in the siege of the same House, and was, to my knowledge, generally lamented of those who were of an opposite judgment. But let us bestow this epitaph upon him :—

'Hic Johnsono jacet, sed si mors cederet herbis,
Arte fugata tua cederet illa suis.'

'Here Johnson lies, could physicke fence death's dart,
Sure death had been declined by his art."

(Fuller.)

" Jacet" would seem to be an error for "jaces."

During the whole of the following week the garrison maintained their hold upon Basing, fetched in provisions, and destroyed hostile batteries and fortifications, without the least resistance.

On Friday, September 19th, it was ordered "that the horse which are now under the command of Colonel Norton shall advance into some other places of the kingdom for the service of the State, as it shall please the Committee of Both Kingdoms to give directions."

The gallant defence of "Loyalty" or "Basting" House was widely known, and Sir Edward Walker writes as follows from Exeter on Sept. 20th :—" And now it will be fit to observe the gallant behaviour of His Majesty's garrisons of Banbury, Basing, &c."

Things now went on much as before, except that no bombardment took place, and the siege assumed rather the character of a blockade.

By September 23rd some weeks' provisions had been brought in. The enemy on this day attacked the guard at Basing, which, being few in number, was obliged to retire. The enemy having re-occupied the church, once more confined the garrison within the house, and exchanged two gentlemen belonging to Colonel Gage's force who had been captured near Reading for three of their own comrades.

Next day (September 24th) a score of fat hogs are seen on Cowdry Down, and are fetched in by the infantry, a party of cavalry which had been sent out by way of the Grange protecting the foot meanwhile. The enemy's picquets were driven in, and fell back on the guard posted near Basingstoke. Five troops of cavalry quickly issued from the town, and the Cavaliers retired in good order until a body of Royalist musketeers, who had previously lined a hedge, checked the pursuit by a well-directed volley. Much ado about a few pigs.

On the following day there was a similar skirmish, and the garrison succeeded in destroying the hostile battery at the Delve on Cowdry Down, and took possession of the planks and timber. The same day a Committee of the House of Commons was appointed to settle a controversy which had arisen, Sir John Maynard and Colonel Jones, Governor of Farnham Castle, being vehemently accused by the Parliamentarian Committee for Surrey. Colonel Jones seems to have been generally successful in quarrelling with some one. Sir Richard Onslowe was thanked for raising men for the defence of Surrey and to besiege Basing House, and the county of Surrey was ordered to continue to maintain his forces. Two hostile accounts state that on Thursday, September 26th, the besiegers "took an outwork with a captain and twenty-eight (30) soldiers who defended it," but no mention is made of this disaster in the "Diary of the Siege," from which we learn that on Friday, September 27th, the Royalist horse were once more on Cowdry Down engaging the attention of the enemy, whilst others carried off six of the Puritan infantry close to the works in "the park lane towards Basingstoke," together with a water leveller employed to draw off the waters of the Loddon. Colonel Morley himself narrowly escaped capture. The Roundhead foot tried to cut off the retreat of the Cavalier horse, but were driven back by some musketeers previously placed in ambush. An hour afterwards Colonel Norton sent in a message by a drum, asking that a day might be fixed for the exchange of prisoners, which was accordingly done. The diary continues: "The stage of Cowdrey furnished again with actors, a coronet (cornet), and three more of their's are killed, and one of ours. At night, the morrow being a fair at Basingstoke, six foot with pistol and brown bill are sent to try the market, and four miles off at a Committee-house finding to serve their turn, from thence bring in 23 head of cattle by the Delve, which pass our daily skirmishing kept free."

On the last day of September the garrison received information that the enemy's working parties, who were engaged in fortifying the church, sometimes kept but a careless guard, whereupon Major Cuffand, with a hundred musketeers, was sent to take possession of the church. The storming party captured a battery close by, but had no means wherewith to force an entrance. The enemy rallied in force, and Major Cuffand was beaten back, with the loss of a sergeant and six men wounded, most of them mortally. The defenders had an ensign and some others slain.

The first days of October saw the Earl of Manchester still lingering at Reading, whilst Sir William Waller's army was at Salisbury, Dorchester, Shaftesbury, and Weymouth, with a view of checking the march towards Oxford of the King, who, on October 2nd, had reached Sherborne on his return from Cornwall. The infantry, under the Earl of Essex, were quartered in Portsea Isle, at Southampton, and in the Isle of Wight. Six thousand arms and thirty waggon loads of cloth had reached Portsmouth, and the Earl was asking for further supplies of necessaries, to be sent him with all speed. He himself was constantly journeying to and fro between Southampton and Portsmouth, as necessity required, and was exceedingly anxious to force the King's army to fight. Colonel Butler was committed to the Tower on October 1st, and on the same day it was reported that the breaches already made in Basing House were becoming larger, that the besieged had plenty of ammunition, but that provisions were by no means abundant.

The 2nd of October saw Captain Rosewell, who had been released from his loathsome prison at Farnham, and Captain Rigby sent to treat for an exchange of prisoners, hostages having been given for their safe return. The same night M. Greaves, the brother of Colonel Greaves, whose capture we have already described, and Captain Jarvis were released, and the next day two lieutenants and divers more in exchange for Captain Rowlett (the scrivener who lived next door to the sign of the George at Holborn Conduit, a near neighbour of Lieut.-Colonel Peake, a superstitious, cringing malignant), a lieutenant, and two of the three sergeants lost at Odiham. The lieutenant was Lieutenant Ivory, "sometime a citizen of London." Some days afterwards Cornet Bryan received glad welcome back again, together with three gentlemen of Colonel Gage's force who had been captured, and with Cornet Bryan had been released to Oxford.

Pass two days more, and the cavalry on both sides exchanged pistol shots on Cowdry Down, the enemy having the advantage of numbers, and the garrison that of a hedge lined with musketeers. The odds were on the side of the Cavaliers, "and three or four of theirs were daily carried off, we all the while (this and the eight days following) losing one horse and two foot soldiers. At night (Oct. 4) send forth our chapmen well furnished, and good market folks; in five hours' time return again with 25 beasts, under the noses of their sentinels, some musketeers of ours lying abroad for their protection."

On October 4th the foes of Basing reported the garrison to be losing heart on account of the delay in the King's advance out of the West to their relief, and "Mercurius Aulicus" tells us that on the next day the Derby House Committee had sent orders to the Committee at Basing to give continual alarms, as the garrison was in great want of match. Mr. Moncy says, "The Derby House Committee consisted for the English Parliament of seven selected Peers and fourteen selected Commoners. Essex, Manchester, Waller, and Cromwell were of the English part of this Committee. Derby House, Cannon-row, Westminster, being the meeting place of the Committee, it received the name of the 'Derby House Committee.'"

The Earl of Manchester wrote from Reading on October 3rd, saying that he had sent four troops of horse to Basing at the earnest request of the Committee for Hampshire, and from the 4th until the 9th of the month he was without success, endeavouring to compel the surrender of stoutly defended Donnington Castle, near Newbury. Failing in this object, he returned to Reading.

On October 4th Lieut.-General Cromwell obtained for his regiment 300 pairs of pistols with holsters, 140 heads, 140 backs, and 140 breasts, at a cost of 580*l*. 10s.; and on the same day the Earl of Essex was ordered to receive "from the Tower Wharf two brass demi-culverins, four brass sacres, and two 6lb. bullet drakes." In contrast to this, it was ordered on October 5th that "Lieut.-Colonel Roe do deliver to the Committee of the West 500 Danish forks, clubs, or roundheads taken on board the Danish ship," of whose detention at Portsmouth previous mention has been made. On the same day a month's advance of pay was made to the Waggon-Master-General for 200 horses and 64 drivers for the train of artillery. Each horse was to cost 1s. 3d. per diem, each man 1s. 6d., and the total cost was to be 17*l*. 6s. per diem.

On October 4th Mr. Lisle, M P. for Winchester, was ordered to bring in an ordinance for the felling of 2000*l*. worth of wood belonging to various Royalist delinquents in Hants and Sussex. No timber trees were to be felled, except at a reasonable time. The Governor of Portsmouth was directed to raise the strength of his garrison by recruiting to 1000 infantry, arranged in seven companies. The Earl of Essex, having received 6000 stand of arms, was ordered to deliver to the Garrison of Portsmouth 300 snaphance muskets, 200 muskets, 100 pikes, 500 bandoliers, 600 swords, 12 drums, 12 halberts, and some partizans, the Parliament undertaking to make good these weapons to him, if necessary. The Committees for Sussex and Hants were ordered to raise and pay a troop of 100 well armed horse, who were to garrison Portsmouth and to defend these two counties.

The Earl of Manchester's army was meanwhile waiting for orders at Reading. Major-General Laurence Crawford, who held a command under the Earl of Manchester, and who charged Cromwell with cowardice, had made a survey of Basing House, and was expressing his hope of speedily reducing it, if he were but reinforced by a thousand men. There was no good feeling between Cromwell and Crawford, for "the regiments of Colonels Pickering and Montague are mentioned in chief among those that on Cromwell's instigation absolutely refused orders from Major-General Crawford."

On October 8th, the King was only five miles distant from Shaftesbury, marching eastward with 12,000 horse and foot, according to his opponents, or with 5500 foot and 4000 horse, according to Clarendon, causing Waller to fall back from Shaftesbury to Salisbury. Colonel Dalbier, the future besieger of Basing House, was at Blandford with his command. The Earl of Manchester was daily expected to march from Reading to effect a junction with Sir William Waller. Lieut.-General Cromwell was near Marlborough with Manchester's cavalry. These troopers were on the left of the Parliamentarian army at Marston Moor. "They were raised out of the associated counties of Bedford, Cambridge, Suffolk, Buckingham, &c., commonly called the Eastern Associates, and both for arms, men, and horses the completest regiments in England. They were more completely at the command of Colonel Cromwell, then Lieutenant-General, an indefatigable commander, and of great courage and conduct."

In a "Statement by an Opponent of Cromwell" we read:—

"Colonel Fleetwood's regiment, with his Major Harrison, what a cluster of preaching officers and troopers there is. Other regiments, 'most of them Independents, whom they call godly, precious men, indeed, to say the truth, almost all our horse be made of that faction.' Colonels Montague, Russell, Pickering, and Rainsborough's regiments, all of them professed Independents, entire."

The 4000 infantry commanded by Essex, at Portsmouth, were already mostly re-clothed and armed, but in the army of the King, who was at Blandford on October 11th, and who was said by Waller to contemplate marching through Winchester or Newbury, to Oxford, there was much sickness, and desertions were numerous, especially amongst the Cornishmen, who did not care to fight at so great a distance from their homes.

On October 9th the Committee at Basing wrote to the House of Commons asking that reinforcements of infantry might be sent thither, either by Manchester or Essex. The letter was referred to the Committee of Both Kingdoms, and Waller, Essex, and Manchester were, on October 15th, ordered to unite their forces, a plan previously suggested by Essex, and Basing was named as the rendezvous of the armies.

Clarendon says that the King "was now most intent to return into his winter quarters at

Oxford, which was all he could propose to himself; in which he expected to meet with all the obstructions and difficulties his enraged enemies could lay in his way. He knew well that Waller was even then ready to come out of London, and that Middleton (an old foe to Basing) was retired from Tiverton to join him; that they had sent to the Earl of Manchester to march towards the West with his victorious army. So that if he long deferred his march he must look to fight another battle before he could reach Oxford. His Majesty had a great desire in his march to Oxford to relieve Donnington Castle and Basing, which was again besieged by almost the whole army of the enemy."

Such was the posture of affairs, according to Clarendon (Bk. viii.), at the end of September, 1644.

It was time to help Basing once more, as we see from the following letter from the King to Prince Rupert:—

"Nephew,—I am advertised by a despatch from Secretary Nicholas that the Governors of Banbury, Basing, and Donnington Castle must accommodate, in case they be not relieved within a few days. The importance of which places, and consequently (illegible) hath made me resolve to begin my march on Tuesday towards Salisbury, where Prince Rupert may rely upon it the King of England shall be, God willing, on Wednesday next, where I will desire Prince Rupert to come with what strength of horse and foot you can, and the two demi-cannon (30 pounders), many of my men being unarmed. I have sent to Bristol for muskets, which I desire Rupert to speed to me. I desire to hear daily from you, and particularly when you will be with me, and which way you will march, and how strong you can come to

"Your loving uncle and most faithful friend,

"Blandford, 11thOct., 1644. CHARLES R."

Prince Rupert had, on October 5th, left the King for Bristol, and the latter had promised not to engage until the Prince returned to him with reinforcements of Gerrard's and Langdale's troops. Desertions, sickness, want of pay, food, shoes, and stockings thinned the ranks of the Royal army, which was obliged to make frequent halts in order to secure the payment of forced contributions, so that the King did not reach Salisbury until October 15th. He here received information that Waller lay at Andover with his troops, that Manchester was advanced as far as Reading with 5000 horse and foot and 24 pieces of ordnance, that the London Trained Bands, consisting of the red and blue regiments of the City of London, the red regiment of Westminster, the yellow regiments of Southwark and the Tower Hamlets, making in all about 5000 men, commanded by Sir James Harrington, were beginning their march to him, and that 3000 of the horse and foot of the Earl of Essex's army were near Portsmouth, expecting orders to join with the rest. Prince Rupert was unable to meet the King at Salisbury, and, after a halt of three days, the Royal army was again on the march. Instead of proceeding directly to Oxford and relieving Basing House and Donnington Castle on his way thither, the King, over-persuaded by Lord Goring, determined to attack Waller, who, with three thousand horse and dragoons, had occupied Andover, at a considerable distance in advance of the supporting army of the Earl of Manchester. He had marched thither from Salisbury, through Winterbourne Stoke, from which village he wrote a letter on October 14th, stating that the King was advancing towards him. Essex, Waller, and Manchester held a Council of War on October 12th, at Basingstoke, and on the evening of the following day, which was Sunday, four regiments of the London Brigade reached the town, the fifth being left to garrison Reading. Waller returned to his troops at Winterbourne Stoke, near Amesbury, at which place he still was on October 15th, and from whence he fell back upon Andover. He, together with Lieutenant General Middleton, hoped by thus retreating to gain time, so that Essex's recruited, re-clothed, and re-armed troops might be able to effect a junction with the army of Manchester. Sir Arthur Haslerig was still serving under his old commander (Waller), and Lord Hopton was near Bristol. A critic unfriendly to the King observes, "when haste is in the saddle, repentance is in the crupper." Daily skirmishes took place between the King's forces and Waller's rear guard, but on October 14th Lieutenant-General Cromwell reached Reading from the siege of Banbury with a detachment of horse, and two days afterwards Manchester at length marched in bad weather with his infantry and 32 guns towards Newbury and Basingstoke, which he reached on the following day, his intention being "to have our foot to be betwixt Newbury and Basingstoke, and there to meet with our Lord General (Essex)." He sent on most of his horse, under Cromwell, to reinforce Waller, but it was afterwards made a matter of accusation against him that he had not joined Waller with his whole force instead of marching to Basing. At Basing he met "Sir Archibald Johnston, of Warriston, and Mr. John Crowe, sent by the Committee of Derby House to attend the movements of the Generals and to stimulate them."

The Parliamentarian Committee at Basingstoke made on October 14th an earnest appeal for reinforcements, and two days afterwards Mr. Boyce, the Lord General's messenger, carried orders to the Earl of Manchester to send forces to Basing "for the reducing of that garrison, which is a service of very great concernment." Manchester answered this letter on October 19th, reporting his arrival with his army at Basingstoke. He was now so anxious to fight that the Commissioners, in company with Sir W. Balfour, Major-General Skippon, and other officers, selected the positions to be taken up by the several regiments in the event of a battle.

The Earl of Essex at Portsmouth was now again ready to take the field. Some of his men were "sea and weatherbound" in the Isle of Wight, where Sir Gregory Norton and other good people were doing them much kindness, and boats were sent to fetch them on Tuesday, October 15th. The Earl of Pembroke had two days previously been thanked by Parliament for his care of the Isle of Wight, and had been empowered to seize any boats "upon the continent" of Hants for its security. He was also ordered, in consequence of a letter written on October 14th, by the Mayor and inhabitants of Newport, to direct Colonel Carne, the Deputy-Governor, to repair to the island forthwith.

On landing on the shores of Hampshire, Essex's men marched at once to Titchfield, which had been appointed as a rendezvous for the various detachments of their comrades quartered in Portsea Isle, Southampton, and elsewhere. Essex finding that the King was advancing with some 10,000 horse and foot, sent on his cavalry under Sir William Balfour to Basingstoke, whilst he himself followed with between three and four thousand infantry. Both armies were eager to fight, weather permitting. The King's rendezvous was "about Andover, and in a heath near Whitchurch between Andover and Basing." Some of the Royal horse had on Sunday, October 13th, appeared on a hill not far from Basing, but on their scouts giving timely warning of the advance of some Roundhead troopers, they fell back in good order. The garrison or force to which this adventurous party of bold riders belonged is not stated.

The Earl of Manchester was in charge of the train of artillery destined for Essex's army. The guns had previously been sent by water from London to Reading. Essex marched on October 17th from Portsmouth to Petersfield, and on the following night quartered his men at Alton. The Parliament had now therefore troops posted from Abingdon to Basingstoke, as well as at Alton, Midhurst, and Petworth, and could easily hinder the King from invading Sussex, in which county Colonel Temple was also raising forces on behalf of the Parliament.

On Friday, October 18th, Sir William Waller was granted 300 backs, breasts, and pots, 300 pair of pistols, and 300 saddles for the cavalry under his command, and was also to be reinforced by Colonel Ludlow and Major Dewett, with their horse. But disaster now befel "Sir William the Conqueror," which made him less eager " to go a king-catching" than he had previously been.

The King "had left all the cannon that he had taken from the Earl of Essex at Exeter; and now he sent all his great cannon to a garrison he had within two miles of Salisbury, at Langford, a house of the Lord Gorges, where was a garrison of one hundred men, commanded by a good officer. The rest of the cannon and carriages were left at Wilton, the house of the Earl of Pembroke, with a regiment of foot to guard them, and the King appointed a rendezvous for the army to be the next morning (October 18th), by seven of the clock, near Clarendon Park, and good guards were set at all the avenues of the city, to keep all people from going out, that Waller might not have any notice of his purpose, and if the hour of the rendezvous had been observed, as it rarely was (though His Majesty was himself the most punctual, and never absent at the precise time), that design had succeeded to wish. For though the foot under Prince Maurice came not up till eleven of the clock, so that the army did not begin it's march till twelve, yet they came within four miles of Andover before Waller had any notice of their motions, when he drew out his whole body towards them as if he meant to fight, but upon view of their strength, and the good order they were in, he changed his mind, and drew back into the town, leaving a strong party of horse and dragoons to make good his retreat. But the King's van charged and routed them with good execution, and pursued them through the town, and slew many of them in the rear, until the darkness of the night secured them, and hindered the others from following farther. But they were all scattered, and came not quickly together again, and the King quartered that night at Andover. The scattering of this great body under Waller in this manner, and the little resistance they made, so raised the spirits of the King's army, that they desired nothing more than to have a battle with the whole army of the enemy, which the King meant not to seek out, nor to decline fighting with them if they put themselves in his way. And so he resolv'd to raise the siege of Donnington Castle, which was little out of his way to Oxford. To that purpose, he sent orders for the cannon which had been left at Langford and Wilton to make all haste to a place appointed between Andover and Newbury, where he staid with his army, till they came up to him, and then marched together to Newbury, within a mile of Donnington." (Clarendon, Bk. viii.)

We learn from Symonds' Diary that this battle was fought on October 18th, 1644, and that the King slept that night at the "White Hart" Inn, at Andover. This writer says, "Friday, 18th October, 1644, His Majesty, &c., left Sarum and marched towards Andever. Gen. Goring raised a forlorn of horse, consisting of about 200 gentlemen, who were spare commanders of horse, beat them out of Andever, took Carr, a Scot colonel, and another captain, a Scot, that died, who a little before his death rose from under the table, saying he would not die like a dog under a table, but sat down on a chair and immediately died of his wounds. Took about 80 prisoners, followed the chase of them two miles, who all ran in great confusion. Had not night come so soon it might have been made an end of Waller's army, for our intention was to engage them, but they disappointed our hopes by their heels."

Waller's men are said to have been routed in a lane leading into Andover, and to have been afterwards chased through the town. This affair was styled "a fierce alarum." The fighting continued for two hours. Some accounts say that Waller lost about thirty men, others that the King and Waller each lost 20 or 30 men, whilst another chronicler states 10 men as the loss on either side, describing the affair as being only a skirmish with Waller's rear guard.

It was, however, considered much more serious, for Waller at once retreated towards Basingstoke, sending at the same time to the Earl of Manchester to ask for assistance. The latter general thus writes from Basingstoke on October 19th, "Yesternight late I received a very hot alarm from Sir William Waller's quarters, that the King with all his army was come to Andover, and that he was upon his retreat towards me, whereupon I drew out my foot and those horse that were with me in order to help Sir W. Waller, who reached Basingstoke with little or no loss." Manchester was evidently frightened, and prepared to retreat from Basing. He was afterwards charged with having "retreated to Odiham, out of the way, though he had 7000 horse and 7000 foot, enough to face the King's whole army." Cromwell stated that Manchester at this time would have retreated to Odiham, leaving the besiegers at Basing House exposed to the whole army of the King, if Sir W. Waller and Sir A. Haslerig had not arrived just in time to hinder him from so doing. Cromwell indignantly adds: "We being at Basing with near 11,000 foot, and about 8000 horse and dragoons, and the King with not above 10,000 horse and foot!"

The Earl of Essex at Alresford was promptly informed of Waller's disastrous retreat, and, says Manchester, on October 19th, "notwithstanding some difficulties, is marched this night to Alton." The "difficulties" referred to seem to have been some Cavalier horse, who were said to be under the leadership of the gallant Hopton. A party of Sir Arthur Haslerig's regiment of horse, 120 strong, commanded by the celebrated Major (afterwards Colonel) Okey, met the King's cavalry near Alresford. The Cavaliers charged boldly, but ere long fell back upon their reserve, leaving a lieutenant, a quartermaster, and four troopers in the hands of the enemy. Essex then proceeded without molestation to Basing, arriving there on October 21st. He had two days previously asked that Colonel Dalbier might be sent to him.

On October 17th, being Thursday, a little after mid-day, the watchers on the towers of Loyalty House descried the vanguard of Manchester's army marching to Basingstoke and Sherfield. Next day some of his cavalry rode up to the siege works, two of them being picked off by the marksmen of the garrison. The following day (October 19th) eight regiments of infantry and some of cavalry, with all the baggage and artillery (24 guns), halted and faced the house for some hours, drawn up on the south of Basingstoke. Towards night the infantry retired and quartered in Basingstoke, most of the cavalry, which all day long had been drawn up near Rook's Down, two miles distant, riding at speed to their quarters near Farnham.

On October 19th Manchester wrote to London that the King had halted, "only I hear that some of his horse were drawn up about White Church."

On Saturday, October 19th, the King advanced from Andover to Whitchurch, where he was to remain until his General, Lord Brentford, who was behind, and the Earl of Portland, who had been detained with the siege of Portland, should come up with the remainder of his forces. Some of the Royal cavalry were only five miles distant from the enemy, and the Earl of Northampton, with his brigade of 1500 horse, was sent to unite with Colonel Gage, who led a regiment of foot and some horse from Oxford for the relief of Banbury, which had been besieged for thirteen weeks by Colonel John Fiennes with all the forces of Northampton, Warwick, and Coventry. Sir William Compton had bravely defended the town and castle, and the garrison, "though they had but two horses left uneaten, had never suffered a summons to be sent to them." Reduced, however, to great distress, these gallant soldiers gladly hailed the arrival of the relieving force, which completely routed the besiegers. Colonel Webb, who had accompanied Colonel Gage on this expedition, as he had formerly done to Basing, was here seriously, but not mortally wounded.

Mr. Money says: "On Sunday (October 20th), a party of horse was dispatched to relieve Donnington Castle, and returned the next morning. On Monday night, October 21st, 1644, a spy in the service of the Parliament returned to camp with the following intelligence: His Majesty's army was in Whitchurch all Sunday night, and that town was full of soldiers, both horse and foot, but their train of artillery was not there, only a few waggons belonging to officers. That their train stood on Andover Downes, within two miles of Whitchurch, or thereabouts. The King was last night (Sunday) at Whitchurch, but by some reported to be at Winchester, and by others at Andover. The last night, about eight of the clock, went out about 400 horse out of Whitchurch to give an alarm, and returned this morning about break of day. (This was the party which was sent to relieve Donnington Castle.) Yesterday it was ordered that the train should be drawn up to Whitchurch Downes, but was hindered by the wet weather, and so staid two miles short. And that this day (Monday) the rendezvous was to be kept upon Sevenborough (Seven Barrows), the drums beat up at Whitchurch at break of day. This day, about eight o'clock, there stood at Whitclear (? Whitway or Highclere), a great body of horse, as he conceiveth to be 2000, on this side Sevenborough. That about twelve o'clock there were going to Kingsclere some empty carts, accompanied with some troops of horse, which carts he supposeth were to carry provisions that were summoned to be brought to Donnington Castle. (These apparently were the empty carts returning from the Castle). That it is generally reported the King quarters at Donnington the next night. Carriages were warned at Bawgus (Banghurst), and the parishes adjacent, to appear this morning at Whitchurch. From Newbury that great provisions of victuals are made, and all towns adjoining, for the army which is expected there this night. That a great party from Oxford and Wallingford is to be there to meet the King's forces this night." ("Parliamentary Scout," 24th to 31st October, 1644.)

On Saturday, October 20th, the sum of 200*l.* was voted for the defences of Hurst Castle, and on the next day 800 suits of clothes and 200 carbines were ordered for Waller's dragoons. Forty loads of cheese, a due proportion of biscuit, six tons of match, and six tons of musquet ball were to be sent to Farnham Castle as a magazine for the armies.

Sir Archibald Johnston, of Warriston, and Mr. John Crewe, Commissioners in the Parliament's army, reported from Basingstoke on October 21st the arrival of the Lord General Essex with his army.

The combined forces of Essex, Waller, and Manchester, together with the London Brigade, at least 5000 strong, under Sir James Harrington, amounted to 11,000 foot and 8000 horse and dragoons, whilst the King had not more than 10,000 horse and foot. Nine days previously the House of Commons had voted 20,000*l.* for the maintenance of the London Brigade.

Essex on reaching Basing approved Manchester's determination to fight, and at once sent orders to Reading for the destruction of all the bridges over the Thames and Kennet, in order to cut off the King's retreat to Oxford.

On October 21st the Parliament Commissioners stated the King was at Overton. Waller, who was now at Basingstoke, had captured two captains and divers common soldiers. One estimate reckoned the strength of the Royal army to be from 16,000 to 20,000, composing three brigades. One of these was said to be with Hopton at Winchester, the second with the King at Andover, and the third marching towards Marlborough, intending either to reach Oxford or to relieve Banbury. Captain Symonds, in his "Marches of the Royal Army," says: "Munday, Oct. 21st. His Majesty lay at King Cleer (at Mr. Tower's), seven miles from Basing. the troop (*i.e.* of Life Guards) at Newtown (between Kingsclere and Newbury), the head quarters of the horse at Newbury. This day the enemy visit Essex, Manchester, Waller were with all their forces, and made assault upon Basing."

On the other hand we are told "near that house they gathered into one body, but attempted not the place. Here joined the Earls of Essex, Manchester, Sir William Waller, with some Trained Regiments of London," and according to "Aulicus," of Oct. 28th, "They durst not adventure the bruising of their army upon Basing Garrison, but left it on Tuesday last, after their outguards within half a mile of Basing had been beaten up by Captain Markham, with a party of horse of the Queen's regiment. His Majesty's army being then at Kingsclear."

A battle being now imminent, several surgeons were sent down on Oct. 21st to Basingstoke, by the Parliament, and the following day was set apart in London as a day of humiliation and prayer. Cromwell and some other commanders wished to fight at once, but the Earl of Manchester decided to march back to Reading, with the object of making the attack from the north or left bank of the Kennet. The King had marched to Kingsclere, which lies midway between Basing and Newbury, with the intention of attempting the relief of Basing. But finding this position indefensible against an enemy so greatly superior in cavalry, he, after one night's halt, continued his march towards Newbury with his infantry and a party of horse. Sir William Waller, eager to avenge his defeat at Andover, skirmished with the Cavaliers, "but His Majesty facing the Parliamentarians with a party of horse, drew off his infantry from King's Cleer, and marched to Newbury." Waller was, however, not to be denied, and Captain Fincher was ordered to push home a charge upon the retiring Cavaliers, which resulted in the capture of several officers and 60 men.

Mr. Money says: "In the year 1839, in digging a grave in the nave of Ewhurst Church, on the Basingstoke-road, near Kingsclere, the remains of two soldiers, with portions of military ornaments, were found at a shallow depth. These interments had the appearance of having been hastily conducted, and were supposed to have been the bodies of officers slain in a skirmish in the neighbourhood during the operations before Basing." May they not have fallen during Capt. Fincher's cavalry charge?

The King having thus departed, Essex and Manchester marched on Oct. 22nd from Basingstoke through Swallowfield to Reading. On Oct. 27th was fought the second Battle of Newbury, which has been so graphically described by Mr. Money, to whose admirable work the writer is greatly indebted for many important facts.

On Oct. 29th the House of Commons sanctioned the following scale of daily pay for the garrison of Windsor Castle:—A colonel, 2*l.* 5s.; one captain, 15s.; two lieutenants, 4s.: two ensigns, 3s.; five sergeants, 1s. 6d.; five corporals, 1s.; five drummers, 1s.; 12 gunners, 2s.; 12 matrosses, 1s.; one minister, 8s.; his man, 8d.; one marshal, 5s.; one gun-smith, 1s. 6d.: one armourer, 1s. 6d.; one surgeon, 4s.; his man, 8d. The knapsack was then called a "snapsack." "Aulicus" speaks on Monday, Oct. 28th, 1644, of "three days' provisions prepared in their snapsack."

But to return to Basing House. The "Diary of the Siege" says:—"On Oct. 20th, three foot soldiers coming too near to see the House receive the curtesy of fetching in, and next day by our foot in ambush in the lane a cornet of Sir William's (Waller) regiment, and two dragoons were taken ; our horse from off the hill fetch in two straggling foot, at noon some regiments of horse and foot belonging to the Earl of Essex join to the Leaguer ; their army toward evening drawn in Battalia that night keep the field, the van near Rocke's Downe, the battle (i.e., main body) at Basingstoake, and rear by Hackwood ; next day marching the army towards Reading, the foot by Sherborne, and the horse keeping along their left (to repel any attack from the King's cavalry)." The following day (Oct. 23rd) three more troopers were brought in, Lord Winchester's cavalry venturing forth to harass the enemy on their march. At night a storm brought down a tower, which had been almost destroyed by the artillery, upon the heads of five of the garrison, killing one, and somewhat bruising the rest.

Skirmishes marked the closing days of October. Lieut. (Captain) Cuffand, with some 40 horse, checked the besiegers on Cowdry Down, wounding five horses and as many men, and capturing a prisoner, losing only one man himself. Next day he faced their horse again, whilst Cornet Bryan, ever in the saddle, with some few horse, carried off a load of corn driving near to their guard, "and riding through the garrison from off the other side, bring in a cart and team passing to Basingstoke." These carts were sent out on each of the three following nights, with a strong guard, and brought in five quarters of threshed corn from Piat's (i.e., Magpie's) Hill, on the other side of the river Loddon, together with 12 loads in the sheaf. Fourteen beasts were also brought in from the same place. To stop these proceedings, the enemy posted a guard of horse and foot at the barns on Piat's Hill, the said guard being relieved daily at nine p.m.

After the second Battle of Newbury, which was fought on Oct. 27th, 1644, it was reported that Prince Rupert would do his best to raise the siege of Basing House. A Council of War ordered the three armies of horse to prevent any such attempt. The King, having left Marlborough, was expected to head a relieving force in person. Manchester accordingly marched to Aldermaston, where he encamped in the fields, in order to intercept him. At a Council of War, "no man speaking so much against fighting as Cromwell," it was unanimously decided to concentrate the Parliamentarian infantry at Reading and Henley, and the horse at Farnham, Okingham, Windsor, Maidenhead, and Staines, in preference to adopting more vigorous measures. On November 6th the Committee of Both Kingdoms sent Messenger Bulmer to the Earl of Manchester with orders to send the City Regiment from Reading to Basing siege, relieving it either by one of Manchester's own, or by some other suitable regiment. Colonel Ludlow's regiment, which had been cut up at Newbury, "being that day on the guard," was ordered to be sent at once into Wiltshire.

The month of November opened with gloomy prospects at Basing House. All the beer barrels were empty, and the stock of bread and corn but slender. Lieut.-Colonel Peake was therefore despatched with a party of horse and foot to Piat's Hill, which was reached about 8 p.m. The enemy's fires were still burning, but the guard was nowhere to be seen. Two prisoners only were made, and the loading and sending of carts to the House went on without interruption until midnight. Then some cavalry from Sherfield came down the hill, and together with some infantry from Basing attacked the Royalists, who lined the hedges, according to their usual practice, with musketeers. A fierce and protracted cavalry skirmish ensued, but volleys of musketry from the hedges turned the scale in favour of the Cavaliers. Norton's foot, who knew every inch of the ground, fought desperately to dislodge the musketeers, but being charged by the royalist horse, and a diversion being made by an attack upon Basing Church by a party from the House, they were put to the rout, and driven through the river Loddon in confusion. Lieut.-Colonel Peake and his foragers then fell to work again, "and before morning carry in 16 cart loads in sheaf ; our drovers at same time passed through our guards eight beasts, and at noon next day some soldiers skipping out seize on twelve sides of mutton and some pork loaded upon a horse as contribution food going unto the church." Short allowance at church that day.

Listen again to Chronicler Symonds : "His Majesty, when he came to Oxford (Satterday, 2 Novembris, 1644) knighted Colonel Gage for his good service of relieving Banbury and Basing." An honour well and worthily won ! Four days afterwards Colonel Sir Henry Gage commanded the Queen's Regiment of Foot, 150 strong, out of Oxford at the rendezvous on Shotover Green.

For ten days before the 5th of November the officers at Basing House had been reduced to one meal per diem., the soldiers being allowed two. Beer now failed completely, and everyone was obliged to drink water. The soldiers were persuaded by their officers to follow their example, and content themselves with one meal a day. This was more than one hungry man could bear, and at night he deserted to the enemy, who were almost inclined to raise the siege in despair, and disclosed the necessities of the garrison. The deserter's information caused the besiegers to persevere a little longer, more especially as they had been reinforced from Newbury by Colonels Strode and Ludlow, with a good strength of horse and some dragoons. Colonel Strode was "one of the Deputy Lieutenants of the Militia for Somerset, a man much relied on in those parts, and of a good fortune. No man wished the King's army worse success." Clarendon speaks, Bk. vii., of his dread of the King's soldiers.

Colonel Ludlow, whom Carlyle describes as "solid Ludlow," was afterwards one of the King's Judges, and succeeded to the command of the Army in Ireland, after the death of Ireton, on November 26th, 1651. He came to Basing with his regiment at the special request of Colonel Norton. By way of welcome to Colonel Strode's regiment, Cornet Bryan rode forth on November 6th, under cover of a fog, with a party of horse, down the valley nearly to Basingstoke, and carried off three sentries. Posting his own men in their stead, he soon afterwards took prisoners, without even firing a pistol, a corporal and two troopers, who came to relieve the three luckless sentries. The same night Major Cuffand made a sortie with some horse and foot, killed a sentry, beat off the enemy's horse, and cleared the road to Pint's Hill, sending out foragers, who, however, returned empty handed, on account of the vigilance and numbers of the opposing cavalry. Two desertions from the garrison, one of the runaways taking his horse with him. A messenger was sent to Oxford, but was unfortunately captured by the watchful foe. The weather was "fair for that season."

Major Rosewell led out the same party on the night of November 9th, and having lined the hedges with musketeers, was able to keep the enemy's horse at a distance. He stormed the works at the Delve on Cowdry Down, and again despatched a foraging party to Pint's Hill, who within four hours afterwards brought in 18 beasts and six loads of corn in sheaf, besides sending two messengers safely on their way to Oxford. The long nights were now favourable to any attempt to raise the siege. A letter from the King, in which he declared his intention to relieve the garrison "in spite of heaven and earth," was about this time intercepted by the besiegers, and certain Cavaliers, who sallied forth to obtain some hop-poles for firewood " were so pelted by some of our City forces that they left 18 behind, besides that went halting in." Five regiments from Newbury were ordered to check any effort on the part of Prince Rupert to succour Basing, "which, if not prevented, would exceedingly encourage the enemy, and be very prejudicial to the public affairs."

Warburton says "Rupert appeared before the stout old walls on the 11th November, and exchanged compliments with the garrison." It may be to this period that the following paragraph in "Mercurius Aulicus" (p. 101-2), which gives a not over pleasant picture of the condition of Royalist prisoners, refers :—

"There was a poor man living near Moor Park, whom, when Prince Rupert was in those parts, he commanded to show him where the pipes lay which conveyed water to the Castle. For this crime they apprehend him, and commit him prisoner to the Castle, where they fed him with so slender diet that they even starved him, and when upon his wife's tears and lamentable cries that she and her children were like to starve at home while her husband starved at Windsor, they having no subsistence but what he got by the sweat of his brows, he was released. He was not able to stand on his legs, and whether dead since we have no information."

Prince Rupert's stay in the neighbourhood, both on this and other occasions, was not of long duration, for on the 21st he attempted to surprise Abingdon, and on the 23rd entered Oxford with the King.

Upon Cowdry Down Colonel Ludlow's trumpeter, or "music," was captured on November 13th, and on the following day a regiment of foot was seen at Chinham, marching to Basingstoke.

The 15th brought a trumpet from Sir William Waller to arrange terms for the exchange of his cornet, who had been taken prisoner in the lower road to Basingstoke on October 20th. Another trumpet brought in two officers of the garrison that had long been prisoners at Farnham. Were these officers "Ensigns (Ancient) Coram, son of one Coram, a Papist, in Winchester, and William Robinson, a Papist, surgeon to the Lord Marquesse of Winchester," the only two officers captured at Odiham on the 2nd of June, of whose release by exchange we have not already heard? For these two officers the trumpet took out "seven of theirs, we taking care to fill their roomes again within two hours after, fetch in one, and kill two more abroad." Dates are now somewhat obscure. The "Diary of the Siege" seems to imply that the besiegers finally struck tents and departed about November 15th, whilst from Symonds we gather that the siege was raised on the 20th. Clarendon says "the enemy was in the meantime marched from thence to Basing, which, they thought, would, upon the sight of their whole army, presently have yielded, but, finding the Marquis still obstinate to defend it, they were weary of the winter war, and so retired all their force from thence, and quitted the siege the very day before Gage came thither, so that he easily delivered his provisions, and retired to the King without any inconvenience." Symonds tells us, "Monday, 18th November.—The enemy left Newbery and marched near Basing. This day, Tuesday, 19th November, Colonel Gage was sent towards Basing to relieve it with 1000 horse." The Diary says that the siege lasted 24 weeks. It commenced on June 4th, and according to this computation ended about November 18th. Symonds states that Colonel Gage was sent to the relief of Basing on November 19th, and Clarendon says that his force was to "march so as to be at Basing House the next morning after they parted from the army." "Aulicus" gives the date as November 13th, the anniversary of Waller's repulse in 1643. The question is a difficult one. The sight of the whole army of his foes did not in the least dismay the "Loyal" Marquis. The Diary says "their army now again hovering about, afford us sport, each day killing or taking some of their curious ones, and seize two carts, one with a load of hay, passing too near our works."

But help was at hand. In Clarendon (Bk. viii.) we read, "The King had not yet done all he meant to do before he took up his winter quarters, and since he heard the enemy lay still at Newbury, he marched to Marlborough, where he found all things to his wish. His heart was set upon the relief of Basing, which was now again distress'd; the enemy, as is said before, begirt it closely from the time that Gage relieved it. He had a great mind to do it with his whole army, that thereby he might draw the enemy to a battle; but upon full debate, it was concluded that the safest way would be to do it by a strong party, that 1000 horse should be drawn out, every one of which should carry before him a bag of corn, or other provisions, and march so as to be at Basing House the next morning after they parted from the army, and then every trooper was to cast down his bag to make their retreat as well as they might, and Colonel Gage, who had so good success before, was appointed to command this party, which he cheerfully undertook to do. The better to effect it, Hungerford was thought the fitter place to quarter with the army, and from thence to despatch that party. So His Majesty marched back to Hungerford, which was half way to Newbury."

Colonel Sir Henry Gage led his 1000 horse to Basing, but found that there was no need of sudden withdrawal from thence. Let the Diary speak. "The enemy wearied with lying 24 weeks, diseases, with the winter seizing them, his army wasted from 2000 to 700, fearing the forces of His Majesty now moving about Hungerford, raiseth his leaguer, and at eight this morn drew off his waggons and two gunns, three days before brought in. The foot at noon march towards Odgiham, the huts being fired, and some troops of horse left to secure their rear. On whom a party of our horse with Coronet Bryan waiting their opportunityes disorder their retreat."

"Next night honoured Sir Henry Gage (the enemies' remove not knowne), sent by his Majesty with 1000 horse, brings in supplies of ammunition and provision, each trooper in a bag bearing his part, having a skein of match swadled about his waist, besides what was brought in carts, and staying here three days most amply victualled the garrison, drawn down by length of seige almost unto the worst of all necessityes, provision low, the soldiers spent and naked, and the numbers few, having besides our hurt and maimed, and such as ran from us lost near 100 men by sickness, and the siege, whereof a Lieutenant-Colonel (Johnson), two ensigns (one of whom was Amory), three sergeants, and seven corporals." It was said in London on November 26th, that "Basing garrison had neither stockings nor shoes, drank water, and looked all as if they had been rather the prisoners of the grave than the keepers of a castle."

Some of the warrants issued by Col. Gage, at Basing, on November 23rd, appeared in print shortly afterwards.

One of them thus addressed, "To the Tythingman of Lysturney (sic) haste, post haste, horse post, see these conveyed as aforesaid with speed," orders 300*l*. to be sent at sight from Odiham Hundred in part payment of contribution money, "Your part is 29*l*. 2s. 6d. William Gregorie, Constable." Two thousand horse and dragoons were to pay an unwelcome visit in case of refusal, but in the event of compliance, kind treatment was promised, and an allowance for any cattle previously taken. By a similar warrant the Constable of the Hundred of Odiham was ordered to send in by eleven o'clock on the following morning 100 qrs. of oats, 60 qrs. of barley or malt, 60 qrs. of wheat, 1000 lb. weight of cheese, 1000 lb. weight of bacon, and 20 loads of hay. "Your part is 10 qrs. of malt, 5 qrs. of wheat, cheese 100, and bacon 100 lb." The same terms were offered as in the former case.

It is said that the siege was raised by the unanimous decision of a Council of War, Lieut.-General Cromwell being specially in favour of this measure. Of Basing it was said "many brave sallies were made, and a multitude of men they slew, so that it was afterwards called Basting House. It was reported that during the 24 weeks' siege the besiegers lost not less than 1000 men." "Mercurius Britannicus" is satirical on Nov. 25th : " But by this time Basing House is relieved, and the Winchester Goose proud in conceit that his feathers shall not be pluckt this winter." Suspicions now arose in Parliament of the Earl of Essex "as careless or discontent," and on Friday, November 22nd, the Committee of Both Kingdoms were asked to give an account to the House of the operations at Donnington, Newbury, and Basing House. A letter was read from the Local Committee at Basing, with two warrants annexed concerning the remove of the forces, one under the hand of the Earl of Manchester only ; the other under the hand of the Earl of Manchester, Sir W. Balfour, and Sir W. Waller. " For Colonel Norton had writ a letter to them that he had received a warrant from a chief commander in the army, to withdraw from Basing, which was to him a thing unexpected, but yet he obeyed."

Colonels Norton and Jones " dispersed their forces into winter quarters at Farnham, Reading, Henley, and Abingdon, whilst the Cavaliers occupied Basing, Odiham, Blewbury, and Marlborough." Judging by the following paragraph, Lady Onslowe must have regretted the raising of the siege, quite as much, if not more, than her husband :—

" And Basing House now at liberty, when at London it was confidently reported it was lost. And the Lady Onslow reported that the Parliament had considered their good service in the cause, and therefore had given Basing House to her husband, and hoped the world should then see them in a better condition. But it proved otherwise, he being forced out of his Lines of Communication."

The King, having been rejoined by Colonel Gage, reached Oxford on November 23rd, and placed his troops in winter quarters.

No better words can conclude this chapter than those which end the "Diary of the Siege":—

" I shall end all with these observations, viz., that seldome hath been a Seige wherein the preservation of the place more imediatly might be imputed to the hand of God! That the souldiers in so long a Seige with all the sufferings incident thereto should never Mutiny. Nor that the customary Liberty at all our Parlyes for to meet and talke wrought any treachery, Wants of Provisions alwayes so supplyed as if by miracle, during the Leaguer ; wee not having lesse then scavenscore uselesse mouths, that had reliefe come at the time appointed, Waller then hovering with his force at Farnham, in probability a hazard whether they had releived us, or preserved themselves. Or had Norton (able to bring three times their numbers forth), when the next weeke they came, drawne out his strength, or had we not got Powder from them, that, by our Releife scarse serving till the Seige was raised ; or, when we were releived, had they not suffered us to possesse the Towne a weeke, thereout supplying ourselves for horse and man, before not having for above three weekes. Or had they when we first fetcht corn from Piats-Hill, or fired or removed it."

" But God that holdeth all things in His hand, appointing times and seasons ; ordereth all that tends unto those ends he wils ; in vain it therefore were to villify the enemy ; blaming his valor or discretion, or yet to say the care and diligence of the Lord Marquisse Governour, the skill and valour of the officers, the courage and obedience of the Souldiers (though all these did their parts) had thus preserved the place, in vain we watch and ward, except God keepe the House. Let no man therefore speake himself an instrument, onley in giving thanks that God had made him so, for here was evidently seen, *He chose the weak to confound the strong. Non Nobis Domine.* Not unto us, not unto us O Lord, but to thine owne name be all Glory for ever. Amen !"

NOTE.—Lysturney (page 194) is Liss or Liss Turney, near Petersfield.

CHAPTER XXVI.—DR. LEWIS—GORING IN HANTS—COURTESIES OF WARFARE—CAVALIER DEFEAT AT SALISBURY—LIEUT.-GENERAL MIDDLETON—REQUISITIONS—A CAVALIER PLOT—ISLE OF WIGHT AFFAIRS—GORING AT PORTBRIDGE AND CHRISTCHURCH—LUDLOW AT SALISBURY—DEATH OF COLONEL GAGE—CRONDALL IN FLAMES—CAVALIER RAIDS—WALLER PURSUES GORING.

On Friday, November the 1st, 1644, newspaper readers learned that a foraging party from Winchester Castle had appeared at Petersfield, and under cover of a fog plundered a Portsmouth road waggon, carrying off the eight horses which drew it. On November 14th an ordinance of Parliament was passed for displacing the Rev. Wm. Lewis, D.D., Master of St. Cross Hospital, at Winchester, because "he hath neglected the government of the said house, and adhered to those that have levied war against the Parliament, and are enemies to the King and kingdom." Dr. Lewis was a Welshman, born in Merionethshire, who was at an early age elected Provost of Oriel College. He was obliged to resign his post and to retire to the Continent on account of certain amours, but afterwards became Chaplain to the Duke of Buckingham, was created D.D., and was appointed to the Mastership of St. Cross. He accompanied the expedition for the relief of Rochelle, and on his return published "An Account of a Voyage to the Isle of Rhe." He was a staunch Cavalier, and a prebendary of Winchester Cathedral. Deprived of his office as Master of St. Cross, poverty and exile were his lot, until the Restoration sent him back again to St. Cross, where he died, and was buried in 1667. (Fasti Oxon.) Mr. John Lisle, M.P. for Winchester, remained Master of St. Cross until the year 1657, when he was called by Cromwell to a seat in the Upper House.

On Thursday, November 21st, 1644, both Houses of Parliament ordered 500 tons of timber and 6000 cords of wood to be cut on the estates of Papists and delinquents in Hants and Sussex, for the repairing of the defences of Portsmouth. The 500 tons of timber were to be employed in planking and fortifying the defensive works, and the 6000 cords of wood were to be sold by the Governor, Colonel Jephson, to provide money for the expenses of the garrison. The local Committees were ordered to see that the wood was cut equally in the two counties, and on the estates of the proper persons. No waste or spoil was to be permitted, and the work was to be done at seasonable times. No young trees or any fit for navy use were to be sold, and no timber was to be cut in the New Forest.

Sir William Waller had already sent some troops to Taunton in Somersetshire, where the Parliament had many friends, and where Colonel (afterwards Admiral) Blake was in command, and intended to go thither himself with the nucleus of an army to be raised for the purpose of reducing the loyal western counties to submission.

Clarendon says that the Parliament sent Waller out with such troops towards the west as they cared not for, and resolved to use their service no more. Lord Goring now persuaded the King to send him with 3000 horse and dragoons, 1500 foot, and a train of artillery through Hampshire to Salisbury, in order to keep Waller in check, saying also that he intended to advance into Sussex, where many friends to the Royal cause were, according to his account, ready to declare for the King, as were also the Cavaliers of Kent. He received a commission as Lieutenant-General of Hampshire, Sussex, Surrey, and Kent. He first attacked Christchurch, "a little unfortified fisher town," but was beaten off with loss and obliged to retreat to Salisbury, "where his horse committed the same horrid outrages and barbarities as they had done in Hampshire, without distinction of friends or foes, so that those parts, which before were well devoted to the King, worried by oppression, wished for the access of any forces to redeem them."

Goring permitted Vandruske, a German officer who had a command under Sir William Waller, to relieve Taunton, and then, pretending that his friends in Sussex and Kent were not yet ready to join him, requested and obtained orders from Oxford to proceed to Weymouth. This fortress too he lost "by most supine negligence at best." His forces, who were generally styled "Goring's Crew," committed unheard of rapine in Dorset, Somerset, and Devon, without attempting in any way to harass the enemy.

Warburton says:—" I am tempted to insert here, as apposite, a very characteristic anecdote of this time, told by Sir Richard Bulstrode. It shews the sprightly nature of the subordinate part of the war, and proves that even the Puritan general could enter into the spirit of his former associates.

'This winter (1644-5) General Goring was quartered at Bruton, in Somersetshire, at Sir Charles Berkeley's, an enclosed country, where the villages were thick, and great store of forage for horse. Sir William Waller was then quartered at Salisbury, in Wiltshire, where the villages are thin, standing only in the valleys, some distance from each other. General Goring, taking this advantage, sent out parties almost every night, to beat up the enemy's quarters in Wiltshire, which was done with such good success that in a short time we took many prisoners and colours, which occasioned Waller to write this ensuing letter to General Goring :

Noble Lord,—God's blessing be on your heart. You are the jolliest neighbour I have ever met with. I wish for nothing more but an opportunity to let you know I would not be behind in this kind of courtesy. In the meantime, if your Lordship please to release such prisoners as you have of mine, for the like number and quality which I have of yours, I shall esteem it as a great civility, being

Your Lordship's most humble and
obedient Servant,
WILLIAM WALLER.

A trumpeter (a humble sort of herald who transacted such messages between the hostile camps), arrived with this letter while Goring and Sir Richard were at dinner. "He had been often with us," says the worthy knight, "and was a pleasant droll, this trumpeter," so they told him to wait and he should have his answer after dinner. Meanwhile, a party of horse return from a foray on the enemy, bringing back "five colours and some prisoners of Colonel Popham's regiment." Whereupon Sir William Waller's trumpeter pressed that he might be sent back to his general, else probably he might find his general "a prisoner too." This transaction was followed by a general exchange of prisoners.'"

On Nov. 22nd, 1644, Colonel Jones, the Governor of Farnham Castle, asked for and obtained reinforcements from Sir William Waller, as 7000 Royal horse and dragoons, under Goring, had reached Odiham. Kent "now raised 3000 men to oppose the King's march into Sussex and Surrey, which was feared." Our old acquaintance, Col. Bennet, whose regiment of horse had been obliged "to bear off in some confusion" by Essex's cavalry at Newbury, on Oct. 27th, was now at Odiham, on Nov. 24th. The King's forces in that town were said to number 4000. Four days afterwards the armed Cavaliers in Hants were said to be 9000 strong, of whom 1800 were cavalry. The horse were quartered at Basing, Basingstoke. Odiham, and at various other places in the county. They made continual raids, and had threatened to proceed to extremities if a contribution of 40,000l. was not at once paid. Basingstoke is said to have suffered greatly. Sir William Waller sent out a detachment to the village of Crondall, near Farnham, which, finding the Cavaliers to be in considerable force. exchanged shots with them, and retired to Farnham. Many thousands were said to be taking up arms in Sussex for the Parliament. Mr. W. Cawley, at Chichester, was exerting himself to check the aspirations of the Royalists, and at the end of 1644 it was thought advisable to "demolish many strong houses in Sussex," where there was no garrison, allowing the delinquent owners to compound.

After the second Battle of Newbury (Oct. 27th, 1644), in which his regiment suffered severely, and his cousin, Cornet Gabriel Ludlow, was killed, Colonel Ludlow, at the express desire of Colonel Norton, took part in the siege of Basing House. After the raising of the siege he withdrew with the greater part of his regiment into Wiltshire, as the Committee of Both Kingdoms had ordered special care to be taken for that county. A party of Cavaliers, under Colonel Francis Cooke, had meanwhile reached Salisbury, and were busily fortifying the Cathedral Close. Early in December they sent out a detachment towards Southampton, which was repulsed near that town with a loss of 10 men and 12 horses. The victorious Roundheads, following up their success, marched on December 5th to Salisbury. Their leaders were Sergeant-Major (i.e., Major) Duet (Dewett), who belonged to Colonel Ludlow's regiment, and Major Wansey (Weinsford), who was in command of Colonel Norton's horse and some other cavalry. The whole force numbered 200 horse and dragoons. The Cavaliers, driven out of the town, retired into the Close, shutting the gates against their pursuers. The "Angel" Inn, at the Closegate, and the "George" Inn, at the Sand-gate (St. Anne's Gate), were both hastily garrisoned, the one by Captain Sturges' troop, and the other by Sir John Pollard's troop. The Puritan infantry forced open the Sand-gate, and their mounted comrades speedily entered the Closegate. The "George" and the "Angel" were then both set on fire, which, ere long, obliged those within to surrender, whereupon the assailants extinguished the flames. The prisoners taken here were Colonel Francis Cooke, Lieut.-Colonel Hooke, Lieut. Kelsall, Cornets Bame (Game), and Martin, Quarter-Masters Bower, Hollywell, and Berry (Derry), Master Alexander, a Gentleman Volunteer, and 40 common soldiers. Major Bower escaped, although wounded, as did many others, in the darkness. All the horses, 163 in number, some match and powder, 200 arms, and some other plunder were captured. A captain and about twenty others were killed on the King's side, but only two of the attacking party were slain. Capt. Feiler (Fielder?) and some others were wounded on the side of the Parliament. Some of the prisoners were set at liberty, and others, both officers and men, took the Covenant, and enlisted in the service of the Parliament. Elated with success, the victors retired with 80 prisoners to Southampton by way of Dean House, which was the home of Sir John Evelyn. Major Wansey had here found such good quarters that he neither cared to give up possession to the lawful owner, nor to take the

heʌpateld bidding of Colonel Ludlow. Ludlow therefore marched to aid in the relief of Taunton at the head of 200 horse, leaving the gallant major to take his ease at Dean House. Taunton being once more in safety, the forces raised in Wilts and Dorset returned at once to their own counties.

On December 5th a detachment of Ludlow's horse was quartered at Petersfield. Other Parliament forces were stationed at Arundel, Abingston, Reading, Henley, and Farnham, and active preparations were on foot for the relief of Taunton. On the next day complaints were made in Parliament that the counties of "Surrey, Sussex, and Hants, pay not the money due to Colonel Middleton," and on December 30th the Committee for the West and the Committee for Surrey, Sussex, and Hants were ordered to meet that afternoon "about preparing and furnishing the dragoons ordered from these counties, and to send money to Lieut.-Gen. Middleton." This officer afterwards represented Horsham in Parliament. He had been in May, 1641, the involuntary cause of alarming all London. "The report on a plot was reading in the House of Commons, when some members in the gallery stood up, the better to hear the report, and Middleton, and Mr. Moyle, of Cornwall, two persons of good bigness, weighed down a board in the gallery, which gave so great a crack that some members thought it was a plot indeed, and an alarm of fire, of the House falling, and of a malignant conspiracy, spread rapidly over the town, so that a regiment of trained bands was collected in the city upon beat of drum, and marched as far as Covent Garden to meet these imaginary evils." Middleton at first sided with the Parliament, and did good service against Donnington Castle and Basing House, but in June, 1648, he was concerned in a Royalist rising in Sussex, and was sent to London under arrest.

On December 6th, 1644, the Marquis of Winchester sent a warrant to the Tythingman of Chert (Charte, near Frensham), which is described as being a small hamlet of not more than 40 houses, ordering him to pay up eleven months' arrears of the assessment levied upon the neighbourhood by the Cavaliers. The required amount was 85l. 2s. 6d., and the township or precinct was required to pay an additional 60l. per month for eight months in aafit.ecn The whole sum of 565l. 2s. 6d. was to be paid within 30 days, "which if you fail to do, you must not expect any favour, but to be left to the mercy of the soldiers, which will take your goods and destroy your horses." On Thursday, Dec. 12th, Colonel Jones, Governor of Farnham Castle, came to London, and reported his garrison to be in a good state of defence, but he asked for a few horsemen to keep in check the Cavaliers from Basing House, who were constantly plundering, and carrying into the house much money and great store of provisions. There was no Royalist garrison nearer to Farnham than Basing, and he (Colonel Jones) had a few days previously sent out his scouts, who rode to Odiham, and went within two miles of Basing, without meeting with the enemy.

At 8 p.m. on December 17th, Harie Barclay wrote to the Earl of Essex from Reading, stating that a King's spy had been arrested on the previous day, and had confessed that he had formerly been a soldier in the Royal army, but was now living at Strattfeild Sea (Strathfieldsaye). On Friday, December 13th, he was "sent for by some of the Commanders of Basin House," and ordered to go to Reading to find out what guns, and how large a garrison there were in the town, "and what horse lay near." He was directed to ask for a brewer's house near St. Mary's Church, and was told that the owner thereof would send to four or five other friends of the King in the town to tell them that the messenger had arrived from Basing. A townsman promised "to be as good as their words." A large force of Cavalier horse and foot was to arrive about two o'clock in the morning of December 18th, in the hope of surprising the town. Several of the townsmen had been arrested, and all the guards had been strengthened. Barclay asks that cavalry may be sent, as scouts are urgently required. "One Mr. Bedford" had hitherto supplied intelligence, "who will be forced to put away his men for want of money."

On December 31st cavalry were also asked for at Farnham, in order to check foragers from the garrisons of Winchester and Basing. Thus ended the year 1644.

On New Year's Day, 1645, Speaker Lenthall was urging the Committee of Hants, Surrey, and Sussex to more energetic action, and on the next day it was ordered that Lieut.-General Middleton should have power "to raise the arrears due to the troop under his command raised by the county of Hants out of the quarters of the enemy in the said county, and that care be taken for the protecting of the people of that county, when the forces now there shall be drawn away from thence." The local Committees of Sussex, Surrey, and Hants were likewise ordered to raise 925*l*. 1s. 6d., in order to repay certain advances of money made by Waller to the troops of horse under his command which had been raised in those counties. From some of these loans we can ascertain the strength of various commands. In Sussex Major Ker, as captain, his commissioned officers, inferior officers, and 72 soldiers received 192*l*. 3s. as 14 days' full pay. Paid to Mr. John Crookshanks to send to him in prison at Bridgwater, 20*l*. Paid Nicholas Roberts, a wounded soldier of Captain Draper's, 17s. 6d.

In Hampshire Captain-Lieutenant Robert Parham, who was in command of the troop originally raised for Sir Richard Granville, received 117*l*. 10s. Lieutenant-General Middleton, as captain, his commissioned officers, one trumpet, three corporals, and 80 soldiers received 214*l*. 11s. Captain Jervoise's troop had in it 107 troopers on July 6th, 1644, but on December 12th of the same year he drew seven days' full pay for himself and other commissioned officers, and 14 days' full pay for two corporals, one trumpet, and 40 troopers, the total amount being 114*l*. 12s. 6d. In Surrey Captain Pavell received for his troop 37*l*. 10s.

On January 8th, 1645, Col. Norton was voted 14 days' pay for his regiment, and Sir Walter Erle and Mr. Lisle were to decide on the best means of raising the money. Colonel Norton and all commanders then in London were ordered to go to their respective commands at once. Two days afterwards 500*l*. worth of provisions were voted for the garrison of Portsmouth at the request of Colonel Jephson, the cost being charged against the garrison, which was also "to have all desired clothes." The provisions were to be sent from the Isle of Wight, concerning which we read that on January 25th the Lords sent down an ordinance to the Commons "for the making the borough of Newport, in the Isle of Wight, a parish of itself, and that Mr. Thompson may be minister."

On New Year's Day, 1645, Sir Arthur Haslerig's regiment of horse and the Kentish regiment of horse had their headquarters at Petersfield, whilst detachments were posted a

Midhurst, Petworth, and Tangmere, near Chichester. They were in great need of rest, their horses having marched hard and far, in order to check the atrocities of "Goring's crew."

On January 2nd orders were given by the House of Commons that the burden of billeting soldiers should be lessened in Hants, and that the forces raised in the county, then under the command of Sir W. Waller, should receive regular pay. On January 21st, complaints were made to the House "of many great outrages and insolencies committed by divers Walloons and strangers of Colonel Behr's regiment." The Committee of Both Kingdoms were directed "at once to secure the arms and horses of those Walloons and strangers and to discharge them of the service."

On January 2nd Major Philip Lower, who was in command for the Parliament at Christchurch, heard that a large force of Goring's Cavaliers from Winchester was only four miles from the town. A council of war at once resolved that as the garrison was but small and the town open and unfortified, and the soldiers but newly raised, a retreat must be made to Hurst Castle and the Isle of Wight. Having, therefore, sent away all their ammunition in boats belonging to Christchurch, the Puritans evacuated the town, pursued by the Cavalier horse, but with some loss at length made good their retreat. The Royalists soon afterwards left Christchurch, and fell back towards their main body.

On January 3rd Colonel Ludlow was defeated at Salisbury. On his return from the relief of Taunton to Salisbury he found that a Cavalier garrison had been established at Lord Coleraine's, "at Langford House, two miles from thence." It consisted of a troop of horse and 200 or 300 foot, who often entered Salisbury, pressing men for the King's service, taking beds, &c. Ludlow, therefore, determined to fortify the belfry tower, which then stood in the Cathedral Close, but hearing that some of the enemy were at Amesbury, he sent out Capt. Sadleir, who was the only captain of the regiment then at headquarters, to obtain information. Captain Sadler met the Cavaliers at Netheravon, and, contrary to his Colonel's expectation, was soon hotly engaged. Ludlow came in all haste to the rescue, and some men were killed and taken on both sides. The Puritans retired to Salisbury, and placed their prisoners in the belfry. Ludlow's force consisted of between 300 and 400 men, 100 of whom were quartered in the Close. They committed the fault of "thinking themselves too secure in their quarters." As Ludlow was reading a letter from Colonel Norton, asking for a cavalry reinforcement, a sentry gave the alarm, saying that some Cavaliers were entering the city. Mounting in haste, Colonel Ludlow rode up the street past the "Three Swans," but hearing a great noise of horses in Castle-street, he returned to the Market-place, which he at once perceived to be thronged with mounted Cavaliers. Whereupon, says Ludlow, " I went by the back side of the Town House (Council Chamber), through a street called the Ditch" to the guard in the Close. He there found that some of his men were in bed, whilst others had quitted their posts during the hours of darkness. Only about 30 horsemen could be collected, ten of whom were sent with a cornet to charge the enemy, Ludlow following with ten others, with a trumpet sounding in the rear, as if another body of cavalry was close at hand. Marching past the Butter Cross in single file, the colonel, with his men, entered the Market-place, where he found his cornet fighting desperately. Major Dewett was absent in London. The new comers charged the Cavaliers on the left flank and routed them. Ludlow, who escaped unhurt, checked his horse, which fell backwards, but he was speedily again in the saddle, and captured in Endless-street Lieut.-Colonel Middleton (a Roman Catholic), who said that he was in command of 300 men, that 300 others would soon arrive, and that a reserve of 300 additional troopers, under Sir Marmaduke Langdale, who was in supreme command, had halted in the outskirts of the city. There was now no alternative but to retreat, and Ludlow, at the head of 16 men, cut his way through the enemy, killing and wounding many of the Cavaliers. Captain Sadleir fired both his pistols, and then proved himself a skilful swordsman, as did also Major Dewett's lieutenant. Both these officers escaped, as did rather more than 100 men with their horses, and about the same number on foot. About 100 horses and 80 men remained in the hands of the enemy. Lieutenant-Colonel Read, Captain Jones, three or four "under officers," and a few troopers still resisted in the belfry tower, but the Cavaliers brought a cart laden with charcoal up to the door. Those within shot the luckless driver, who was by no means a willing agent in this transaction, but seeing that active preparations for roasting them alive by burning straw and charcoal were in progress, they discreetly surrendered.

Colonel Ludlow retreated over Harnham Hill through Odstock, losing the road upon the descent of the hill beyond Odstock, the snow lying deep upon the ground. He had a narrow escape from capture in a lane, but, passing through Fordingbridge, reached Southampton without further molestation, taking with him Colonel Fielding and certain other prisoners. His captured troopers were soon after exchanged for Colonel Cooke and the 60 other Cavalier prisoners who had been taken at Salisbury on December 5th, 1644, and who were still in durance at Southampton. Ludlow sent his best men to Portsmouth, and kept the rest with him near Lymington and Hurst Castle. He defeated an attempt made to surprise his force, and then went to the Isle of Wight, where he met with numerous friends.

On January 7th, 1645, Goring's head quarters were at or near Romsey, and on the following day the House of Commons heard that from 3000 to 5000 Cavalier horse were at Petersfield and Petworth, and were threatening to invade Surrey. The Kentish regiment of horse and Sir A. Haslerig's regiment had marched from Petersfield towards the west, and 6000 or 7000 Cavalier horse and foot were reported to be near Winchester, which was Goring's base of operations. The Earl of Manchester was officially asked "Why their forces lay quartered on their friends near London, and did not remove nearer to the enemy according to former directions."

"Mercurius Britannicus" said, on January 10th, "The enemy are very busy about Winchester, quartering within four miles of Portsmouth," intending to take Portbridge. Some foragers from Winchester Castle had been charged by Colonel Morley's troop, and routed with the loss of the cattle which they had seized, and of several prisoners. Goring's horse had now left Petersfield, and his army, consisting of 4000 horse, 2000 dragoons, and 1500 infantry, which had formerly been commanded by Prince Maurice, was marching towards Portsmouth, where Colonel Jephson and his garrison were thoroughly on the alert.

"Aulicus," on February 5th, said that Goring had taken numerous prisoners at Alton, Petersfield, and elsewhere, and amongst them Lieut. Langley, an engineer belonging to the garrison of Portsmouth. Having an iron substitute for a lost hand, his comrades styled him "Vulcan" and the "God of War," saying that he had made his own hand, but the Cavaliers called him "Bunny," because a namesake of his had been executed at Tyburn. He was released on parole, which he broke, whilst others observed it, and escaped, but was retaken in a house near Portsmouth. "A zealous woman," mistaking the Cavaliers for Roundheads, told them that the King's forces would certainly have surprised Portsmouth if honest Lieutenant Langley had not made his escape, and given information to the Governor. Extremely inclement weather and *other reasons* made Goring retire ere long.

The Parliamentary forces in Sussex were now reinforced by 1500 horse from Kent, and a strong force was also on the march from Reading to curb Goring's excesses. His headquarters were at Winchester, but some of his cavalry were quartered at Andover. About January 11th he retreated from Portbridge. The Governor of Portsmouth, with 140 horse, at once went in search of stragglers. They killed several, and returned to Portsmouth with ten wounded prisoners and about 20 horses.

The "Life of Sir William Penn" (Vol. I., p. 104) gives us a specimen of Goring's usual method of procedure. Penn was then in command of a Parliament's ship named the *Fellowship*, which had been, whilst laden with the plunder of Bristol, captured by the *Swallow* at Milford Haven in the preceding year. The *Fellowship* was of 400 tons burden, had 28 guns as armament, and a crew of 110 men. Captain (afterwards Admiral) Penn writes thus:—
"1644-5, January 6th, Colonel Goring, his forces came down and plundered the town of Gosport ; and about six o'clock at night fired some twenty-four (24) houses, and we, and the *Swiftsure* and the *Mary Rose*, shot divers pieces of ordnance to them." The *Swiftsure* was of 260 tons burden, mounting 48 guns, whilst the *Mary Rose*, Captain Phineas Pett, was of 320 tons burden, with 28 guns and 100 men.

Lord Winchester, on January 11th, lost a valued and trusty friend by the death of Sir

Henry Gage, who had been appointed by the King as Governor of Oxford, in the stead of Sir Arthur Aston.

The town of Abingdon, which was strongly garrisoned for the Parliament, is thus described:—" Abingdon, where a cruel custom had been practised of hanging all the Irish without any manner of trial, under which notion very many English also suffered, a barbarity so common that it grew into the proverb of 'Abingdon law'!"

The Governor of Abingdon appointed by the Earl of Essex was Major-General Browne, of whom frequent mention has already been made. Heath's Chronicle says that though he was at first a zealous partisan of the Parliament, he was "afterwards, when the war was ended and the King brought to Holmby, made one of the Commissioners to attend His Majesty, where he was so wholly gained upon by his princely goodness and virtues that from that time he was wholly changed and reduced from all false opinions concerning His Majesty, and afterwards proved a most cordial and loyal actor and sufferer for him and his cause."

Abingdon and its garrison had long been a thorn in the side of Oxford, and, with the approval of Prince Rupert, Sir Henry Gage proposed to construct a royal fort at Culham Bridge, to keep the Abingdon forces in check.

On January 11th, 1645, he marched out of Oxford at the head of a party of horse and foot. A traitor had, however, given warning to the enemy, and Major-General Browne was on the alert. A sharp skirmish ensued, in which Major Bradbury and at least thirty others were slain on the side of the Parliament. Of the King's forces not more than seven common soldiers fell, but Colonel Gage, marching at the head of his men, was wounded by a musket shot, and died a few hours afterwards. Clarendon says that he was shot through the heart by a musket bullet, and a third account states that he was wounded in the head, " of which he died as soon as he came to Oxford." "His body was afterwards interred at Oxford with funebrious exequies and solemnities answerable to his merits, who, having done His Majesty special service, was, whilst living, generally beloved, and dead, is still universally lamented. His daily refreshed memory makes me trespass on the reader's patience with this

E L E G Y
On the Never-Enough-Lamented Death of
Sir HENRY GAGE, the Most Desired
Governour of Oxford.

So Titus called was, " The world's delight,"
And straightway dyd ; The envious Sisters' spight.
Still the great favourite: The darling head
Unto the Fates is always forfeited.
Our Life's a Chase, where (tho' the whole Herd fly).
The goodlyest Deer is singled out to dye.
And as in Beasts, the fattest ever bleeds.
So amongst men, he that doth bravest deeds.
He might have lived, ha ! but a Coward fear
Kept him securely seulking in the rear,
Or like some sucking Colonel, whose edge
Durst not advance a foot from a thick hedge.
Or like the wary SKIPPON had so sure
A suit of Arms, he might (besiege !) endure.
Or like the politick Lords, of different skill.
Who thought a Saw-pit safer, or a Hill:
Whose valour in two organs too did lye,
Distinct: the one's in's ear, th' other's in his eye.
Puppets of War! Thy name shall be divine,
And happily augment the number nine.
But that the Heroes, and the Muses strive
To own thee dead, who wert them all, alive,
Such an exact composure was in thee,
Neither exceeding MARS nor MERCURY.
'Twas just tho' hard, though shouldst dye Governour
Of th' King's chief Fort of Learning, aud of War.
Thy death was truly for thy Garrison
Thou dy'dst projecting her Redemption.
What unto Basing twice (successful spirit)
Was done, thou hast effected here in merit.
The Bridge was broken down : The Fort alone
GAGE was himself, the first and the last stone.
Go, burn thy faggots, BROWN, and grieve thy Rage
Let's thee outlive the gentle grasp of GAGE.
And when thou rend'st in thy Britannicus
The boasted story of his death, say thus:
The Valour I have shewn in this was Crime,
And GAGE'S Death will brand me to all time.

Various changes seem to have taken place in the garrison at Basing. Cornet Bryan we shall see no more at Loyalty House, but methinks I catch a glimpse of him as Major Bryan, Governor of Wem in Shropshire, from which town Governor King, sometime a chandler in Chancery-lane, had been expelled. A gallant soldier ever! Many of our old friends will appear again.

To keep Goring in check, Waller in chief command, Cromwell, and Massey were sent westward with 6000 horse, with considerable success. On January 11th, the famous New Model Army was ordered to consist of 6000 horse, forming ten regiments, and of 1000 dragoons, arranged in ten companies. There was to be no Lieutenant-Colonel in a regiment of horse. The 12 regiments of foot, were each to have 10 companies, and to muster 1200 men. "Each trooper shall receive 2s. per diem for his entertainments." Horses were allowed to captains and other officers at the rate of 2s. each per diem. Colonel Rossiter's regiment of horse, 600 strong, was to be extra to the New Model. Sussex was to pay 3927*l.* and Surrey and Southwark 2000*l.* per month towards the maintenance of this force.

On January 15th, 1645, the Parliament had 6000 horse and dragoons quartered in and about Petersfield, in addition to a reserve of 1100 dragoons. A false report was prevalent on January 17th that Goring had surprised Christchurch, capturing 80 men and arms, together with two guns, but the truth was speedily known. After burning either 21 or 24 houses at Gosport, he marched westward, driving off all the cattle, horses, sheep, swine, and carrying away many men out of the hundreds of Titchfield, Alverstoke, and Fareham. Colonel Jephson arrested a miller, and certain others who had been heavily bribed by Goring to put him in possession of Portbridge, and of one of the defences of Portsmouth. Goring having plundered Romsey, "not leaving a sheep or a hog," marched into the New Forest, and on January 15th attacked Christchurch, which was again occupied by Major Philip Lower, and a garrison of 200 men, storming it on all sides," with about 1000 men. The town was "meanly fortified," and Clarendon calls it "a little unfortified fisher town." A townsman, who was the first man killed, guided the assailants to an open place, the town was quickly entered, and the garrison driven into the church, the castle, and Mr. Hastings' house. Such a bold stand was now made that a Major who led the stormers fell, together with many of his men. Bullets were flying thick and fast, when all at once a bright light as of a beacon fire was seen in the direction of Poole. This was hailed by the hard pressed garrison as a token of approaching relief, and a panic seized the Cavaliers, who were quickly driven out of the town with heavy loss. It was afterwards discovered that the fire which did such good service was not in any way intended to announce the coming of relief from Poole. Colonel Ludlow had already embarked his men in the Isle of Wight to relieve Christchurch, when he heard of the defeat of Goring, who retreated towards Lymington, taking as he went all the farmers' corn, and not leaving any for seed, so that the wretched peasants were obliged either to forsake their dwellings, or to starve. Lieutenant-General Middleton pursued the Cavaliers as far as Lymington, where he almost succeeded in hemming them in, but Goring at length eluded him, and on January 17th was at Whiteparish and the neighbouring villages, having lost at Christchurch a major, two captains, and many men. Clarendon says that he "was forced to retire to Salisbury, where his horse committed the same horrid outrages and barbarities as they had done in Hampshire, without distinction of friends or foes; so that those parts, which before were well devoted to the King's, worried with oppression wished for the access of any forces to deliver them."

On January 21st Goring was still at and near Salisbury. Essex's horse were at Alton, about to march to meet Sir William Waller, who was to advance against Goring with 6000 horse and dragoons, "and 1100 dragoons are to attend them as a reserve." Waller's infantry were about to march from Farnham, from which place a week afterwards Colonel Fortescue laments the "want of money and other provisions." It having been said by "Aulicus" that the Roundheads had stripped the lead from the roof of Basing Church and had then blamed the Cavaliers for it, "Britannicus," on January 27th, 1645, retorts that Lord Winchester, whom the journalist in very coarse terms charges with having taken shelter from bombardment for many months in a cellar, "gave order to have the church unloaded to make consecrated bullets to shoot away the Protestant religion." On the same day that this statement appeared in print 120 of Goring's horse sallied from Basing House and attacked two small troops at Crondall and Addershot (Aldershot), many of whom escaped, either by means of back doors, or by being quartered at scattered farmhouses. Either four or six men who asked quarter were killed, and 50 men and 40 horses were captured. Amongst the prisoners were a lieutenant, two cornets or colours, and a quartermaster. Some plunder was also obtained, but the alarm having been given at Farnham Castle the assailants retired, after setting the village of Crondall on fire in several places. The flames were extinguished after four houses and a barn full of corn had been destroyed. Another account says that but few escaped out of three companies of Roundheads, and that only 30 were taken prisoners out of 160, the rest being refused quarter. The leader in this bold enterprise was an Irish gentleman. A great panic prevailed in Farnham, of which several Cavalier prisoners took advantage to escape from captivity. Goring had been roused to action by hearing that Waller's infantry had marched from Farnham. Sir Marmaduke Langdale had therefore marched from Salisbury to Bishop's Waltham, whilst Goring, on the other side of Winchester, beat up the enemy's quarters. Goring and Langdale were said to be in command of 3000 horse. Passengers arriving at Portsmouth informed the Governor that recruits raised in Normandy for Goring were at Brest, intending to disembark near Portsmouth. The House of Commons ordered reinforcements to be immediately sent to Farnham Castle, and that Waller, who left London on January 30th, should "go west towards the enemy presently." About this time Captain Charles Price (not Capt. Rayden) was mortally stabbed at Basing (one account says Oxford) in a private quarrel. Colonel Ludlow was now posted at Odiham to check foragers from Basing House, and was frequently ordered to Godliman (Godalming) and other places. Colonel Devereux attacked near Marlborough a party of Cavaliers, who, on their march to join Lord Hopton from Donnington and Basing, were plundering road waggons. He captured Sir Anthony Sellenger, who commanded the party, Major Hyde, a captain, a lieutenant, and some other officers, 30 troopers, 50 horses, and about 40 stand of arms, retaking also the carriers' carts and waggons.

During the first week in February, 1645, Waller, at Farnham, asked for and obtained 6000*l.* from the excise duties, 3000 pairs of shoes, one week's biscuit and cheese, 200 backs, breasts, and pots, and 400 pairs of pistols. His men were to pay for their shoes, and "his surgeons were to be provided with medicaments that he may go into action." On February 2nd he was waiting for artillery before marching against Goring. On this day, which was Sunday, some troopers from Basing House rode up to Tilehurst Church during divine service, threatening to carry off the minister and the leading parishioners, unless 300*l.* was at once paid to them, which was accordingly done. Three more regiments of horse and foot were now being raised in Kent for the service of the Parliament. On February 4th Waller marched from Farnham to Alton, and was still demanding indispensable supplies. Some of his troops were skirmishing with and advancing against Goring's forces, who were retreating in a northwesterly direction beyond Salisbury. Goring himself, whose army, by the junction of Sir Thomas Aston's command, now consisted of 5000 horse and foot, was still at Salisbury. Sir Thomas Aston had been created a baronet on July 25th, 1628. A steadfast Cavalier, he died at Stafford on May 24th, 1645, from wounds received in the King's service.

Goring's army was thus described: "Such profane and blasphemous, villainous Irish, French, Walloons, and divers other nations as the world affords not the like." There followed the camp "a thousand women of bad character, many of them Irish, who carry much plunder upon horses!"

"Britannicus" says, on February 24th, 1645: "'Aulicus' tells of Goring scouring Hants, but Hants will never be scoured clean as long as that blaspheming wretch remains there, with collected filth of several countries, which the earth sure would vomit out, or take in, but that she is merciful to her native inhabitants."

The Cavaliers were, on February 4th, watching Southampton so closely that it was not safe to go a mile from the town. On February 12th Waller reported the loss of the outworks at Weymouth, and was ordered to march into the west with all his available horse and foot. If the infantry were as yet unprepared to march, a strong body of horse and dragoons was to go to the support of the garrisons in the west, leaving the infantry to follow with all speed. Some of Waller's officers refused to march with him from Petersfield, but the officers of Cromwell's regiments, and of some others, were willing to do so. To check such disorders in future, the Parliament on February 13th gave Waller full powers to enforce military obedience from all ranks, at the same time thanking him for so readily executing their orders and advancing against Goring, who was attacking Weymouth. Waller, who now had 3400 horse, 700 dragoons, and a large infantry force, found that 28 troops, numbering some 700 men, were in a mutinous frame of mind. They marched as far as Croydon, and the dwellers in Surrey and Kent fully expected to be plundered by them, but awed by the firmness displayed by the House of Commons, they implored pardon, and, promising better behaviour for the future, returned to their duty. Waller fully intended to obtain possession of Winchester Castle before marching against Goring, but the desertion of a trumpeter on the night before that fixed for the assault gave warning to the garrison, and the scheme was abandoned.

A letter from Waller was read in Parliament on February 12th, which stated that hearing that three regiments of Goring's horse were quartered at Andover, he sent a party thither to beat up their quarters, but, warning having been sent from Alresford, a retreat was made to Newton Toney, near Amesbury, and Waller's men were foiled in their purpose. Goring, evidently intending to march westwards, had requisitioned transport to assemble at Sarum upon pain of death. Waller himself was mustering his forces at Petersfield, intending to go westwards on February 17th or 18th: Goring pretended that his friends in Sussex and Kent were not yet ready to help him, and succeeded in obtaining orders from Oxford to march into the western counties, in which Lord Hopton commanded as Field-Marshal and General of the Ordnance. Goring was General of the Horse, and in order to prevent disputes, Hopton was, by special order, recalled to Bristol. Goring reached Weymouth with his full strength of horse, foot, dragoons and artillery, numbering more than 3000 horse and 1500 foot, in addition to local contingents, but most shamefully, "by most supine negligence at best," allowed the town, which was about to surrender, to be recovered for the Parliament. On February 20th Captain Batten, from Portsmouth, was lying there with either two or three ships from Portsmouth, which had proved a welcome succour to the beleaguered garrison. All the western counties were now practically lost to the King, "whilst the Lord Goring's forces equally infested the borders of Dorset, Somerset, and Devon, by unheard of rapine, without applying themselves to any enterprise upon the enemy."

It appears somewhat doubtful whether Tobias Baisley (see p. 117) was executed in February, 1644, or 1645. The following additional particulars are given concerning him. He had formerly been a pewterer by trade, then a porter to Nottingham carriers, at the "Ram" Inn, Smithfield, by which means he gained information about the traffic on various highroads, and lastly a corporal in Prince Rupert's own regiment. He was said to be skilful in poisoning, as well as in casting bullets. Whilst at Basing House he received a share of all the property captured through his information. He went to London as a spy, and "to buy military commodities, and by these gradations he is likely to go three steps higher. He was taken by man-catchers, as he called them." The Council of War which condemned him sat at Essex House. He died railing, full of imprecations, and refusing to join in prayer! On February 18th the Lieutenant of the Ordnance was ordered to send to the Isle of Wight 40 barrels of powder, a ton of match, 300 culverin shot, 1000 demi culverin shot, 2000 saker shot, and a ton of lead. The Portsmouth garrison was to receive 200 snaphaunce muskets (p. 70), and "arms and furniture" for fifty horsemen. Official demands were now made why Waller did not march. He replied from Petersfield on February 17th and 19th, and also from Portsmouth on February 22nd, reporting the condition of his own forces and of the enemy. On February 21st Parliament voted him 2000*l.*, but on the following day none of his men had advanced beyond Winchester, to which city it was reported that Goring paid a visit with a strong brigade on February 25th. Mr. Lisle was directed on February 24th to bring in an Ordinance "for the cutting down of woods belonging to delinquents for the service of Christchurch, in Hampshire," but no oak, ash, or elm timber was to be felled. Cromwell's Independents declined to march with Waller, remaining about Godleman (Godalming), but on February 27th both Cromwell and his men were ordered by the House of Commons to join Waller, who had given an alarm to the Winchester Cavaliers, taking some horsemen prisoners. On February 27th Waller writes from Wickham, saying that he is watching Goring's movements. On March 1st he writes from Owslebury, near Twyford, two days later from Farnham, and on March 4th he was, together with Cromwell, ordered to march at once into the west against the enemy, "all excuses set aside, with all available horse and dragoons." These two generals were said to have had four or five thousand horse and dragoons, and 2000 foot at or near Southampton on March 2nd, 1645. The "alarm" above referred to was as follows. About March 2nd a party of Cavaliers had "a great drinking day at Winchester, and being elevated in their minds" rode out 200 strong to engage a troop of 60 horse belonging to Waller at Marwell Hall, the seat of Sir Henry Mildmay, who bore the nickname of Sir Whimsey Mildmay, and was in 1649 one of the regicides. The Cavaliers marched so furiously, "divers being in their cups," that several of the party were left behind on the road. On reaching Marwell, there was a flourish of trumpets, and a trooper riding forth from the house was slain by one of the King's soldiers. Challenges and defiances were freely exchanged, and several single combats took place, in one of which Sir Thomas Phillips was shot through the head by one of Waller's troopers. The Cavaliers at length fled in confusion towards Winchester, losing a Lieutenant-Colonel and some men killed, and Colonel Gardiner captured, together with several others, as well as some horses and arms.

The weather was very wet, when on March 5th Waller was mustering about 30,000 horse and dragoons near Winchester, whilst Colonels Cromwell and Fiennes were not far off with their respective regiments. Waller was at Andover on March 9th, and his troops were said to be "a well disciplined and orderly army, that they behave themselves with all civility to the people, and gain much love." On the other hand, it was said that not long before, when some of Goring's men were drinking at the Catherine Wheel in Salisbury, one of them proposed the health of the devil. A comrade denied the existence of Satan, unless convinced by ocular demonstration, whereupon he was at once "mysteriously fetcht away!"

On March 9th Waller wrote from Andover that he had captured Lord Percy (Mr. Henry Percy) and 30 companions near that town. The prisoners stated that their destination was France. They had an old pass, which was, however, sanctioned by Parliament, and the captives were released. Christopher Love, M.A., was about this time appointed as "Preacher to the Garrison at Windsor Castle." He belonged to an old Hampshire family. Some of his relations dwelt at Basing, and he had made himself hated by the Royalists by having said, when preaching before the Commissioners at the Treaty of Uxbridge six weeks previously, "that there was as great distance between this treaty and peace, as between heaven and hell." On March 13th Waller reported to Parliament the defeat near the Lavingtons of Colonel Long, High Sheriff of Wilts, by, says Clarendon, "his great defect of courage and conduct." Colonel Long was captured, together with 300 men and 340 horses. Sir A. Haslerig was directed to write to Waller requesting him to exchange Colonel Long for Colonel Stephens, a prisoner to the King's forces. About 4000 men were ready to rise and join Waller and Cromwell in Dorsetshire, threatening to plunder those who did not join with them "to extirpate the Cavaliers." The Puritan Governor of Wareham was already aiding them with a cavalry force. Two of the King's ships bound from Dartmouth to France driven into the Solent by stress of weather were seized by Captain Baxter, Governor of Hurst Castle. The larger vessel, named the *Spirit of Dartmouth*, mounted six guns, and had on board 17 men, some letters, provisions, and a pack of hounds. In the other ship were 300 barrels of herrings, eleven pieces of cloth, four guns, and 23 men. This capture was known in London on March 15th.

Seven days afterwards the Earl of Manchester's treasury was to advance 14 days' pay to Colonel Wogan's regiment "for good service, being quartered about Farnham." It was now ordered that every pressed man should receive from the Committee of his county a coat, breeches, shirt, stockings, shoes, and snapsack. "The cost of these articles was not to exceed 24s. for each, besides the conduct money."

Captain Symonds writes thus: "Upon the King's coronation day, 27th March, 1645, Sir Robert Peake, sometime picture-seller at Holborn Bridge, and Lieft.-Colonel to the Marquis of Winchester, was then knighted in Christ Church, Oxon." An honour well deserved.

A letter written at Salisbury on March 28th complained that "the Winchester Horse do much mischief not only in Somborne and Thorngate Hundreds, in Hants," but even as far as Alderbury, near Salisbury, carrying off as prisoners to Winchester "divers honest, godly men." During the last week they came to Winterslow, near Salisbury, where they met a mounted carrier, "a godly, honest countryman," who had also "a baggage horse, and two men rid with him." They marched up to the amazed travellers and captured the carrier's horses and his two companions, but he himself, "for he hath formerly tasted of their cruelty," escaped into Buckholt Forest.

On March 29th, the "Granada shells remaining at present in the custody of Mr. Browne, gun founder," were ordered to be delivered to Sir Walter Erle, Lieutenant of the Ordnance. The gentlemen of Surrey and Hants received permission from Parliament to select and appoint a Governor of Farnham Castle. Colonel Jones, then in command complained that his pay and that of his garrison was in arrear, and thought himself unfairly treated. He asked that General Fairfax might appoint his successor, and that he might not be superseded by his own lieutenant-colonel.

Some of the dates given in this chapter are only approximations, but they are all correct within a day or two.

CHAPTER XXVII.—CROMWELL IN HANTS—DUCHESS OF CHEVEREUX—MILITARY CHANGES—
CAVALRY SKIRMISH—GORING RECALLED—RELIGIOUS STRIFE—COLONEL RAWDON LEAVES
BASING—FAIRFAX ON THE MARCH—STERN DISCIPLINE—BASING AGAIN BESIEGED—
LANGFORD HOUSE—DISTRESSED TAUNTON—MASSEY AT ROMSEY—CLUBMEN.

Though Sir William Waller was in chief command, Lieutenant-General Cromwell was the principal actor in the expedition into the west against Goring. He it was who captured Lord Percy and his friends at Andover, and now that he and Waller had about 10,000 men under their command, "Britannicus" hoped that they would "in time expel or bring up the Cornish ferret Grenvill with a halter about his neck." On March 18th Sir William Balfour was between Romsey and Winchester, and on April 1st Cromwell had reached Ringwood, where he was joined by Colonel Norton and Colonel Unton Crooke, with their regiments of horse. Further reinforcements had raised the number of his men to 4000 foot and 500 horse. Goring's army was not far distant, and Waller was marching to effect a junction with Cromwell, whose advance guard was said to be posted twelve miles beyond Dorchester. On this day also the estate of Sir Richard Norton, of Rotherfield, was released from sequestration, as he had for his loyalty paid a fine of 250l., and found security for 500l. more. Captain Blagrave was, on April 3rd, 1645, retained in garrison at Reading at the special request of the local Committee. Captain Daniel Blagrave was M.P. for Reading, Treasurer of Berkshire, and a vexatious persecutor of the clergy. He was one of the regicides, and at the Restoration fled to Aachen, in Germany, where he died in 1668, in an obscure condition.

On April 4th a man was arrested in Cheapside and remanded for further examination, on a charge of conveying strong waters to Farnham, and information to Basing House. A ship had been taken near the Isle of Wight by "Captain Hodges, that haughty and courageous man, in which was some of the worser sort of female stuff not worth the owning, many French ladies of eminent quality, said to be bound for Ireland." These were the Duchess of Chevereux and her attendants. It was from the hands of the Duc de Chevereux that Charles I. received his bride, Henrietta Maria, at Canterbury, on June 23rd, 1645. The Rev. Hugh Peters, being then in the Isle of Wight, spent divers hours with the Duchess, and persuaded her to make a statement. She stated that, belonging, as she did, to the Spanish faction, she had quarrelled with the Queen and Mazarin, both of whom she hated, and was imprisoned at Tours. Escaping, she tried to reach Dunkirk, but finally left France in a small vessel bound for Dartmouth. She had with her her daughter, who had been falsely reported to be Queen Henrietta Maria in disguise, and two servants, but only 80 pistoles in money. She had asked the Spanish Ambassador for a further supply. All things considered, Mr. Peters thought that the lady would be far better at Dunkirk than in the Isle of Wight, and arrangements were soon afterwards made to send the whole party to London. The Duchess was, however, still in the island on May 24th; sick, in want of money, "her 80 pistoles almost spent, as well as other monies received by her in England," and she wanted a pass for either Denmark or Spain. Colonel Jones, Governor of Farnham Castle, was on bad terms with the Committee for Surrey, who wished him to be superseded by Colonel Jeremy Baines. If this were done, the Committee would undertake to garrison the Castle with 200 or 300 men, to maintain 1000 men for the defence of the county, and also to have a troop of horse in readiness either to guard the borders of the county, or to garrison the Castle, as need might require. The House of Commons appointed a committee to induce Colonel Jones to resign honourably, and on April 5th the Committee of Both Kingdoms appointed Mr. John Fielder as his successor, and Lieut.-Colonel Whitehead, who had acted as lieutenant-colonel to Colonel Jones, was made Governor of Windsor Castle. Mr. Baynton and Sir Robert Harley were directed " to prepare a declaration in approbation of Colonel Jones his carriage, late Governor of Farnham Castle."

Some guns and infantry for Waller's army had reached Portsmouth by sea on April 4th. The House of Lords on the following day passed the ordinance for felling 1000*l.* worth of timber on sequestered estates in Hants. No oak, elm, or ash timber was to be felled except thirty tons of oak required for the defences of Christchurch, on the fortifications and garrison of which town the proceeds of this timber were to be expended.

The Self-Denying Ordinance was passed on April 3rd, 1645, by which Manchester, Essex, and Waller lost their commands, whilst Cromwell was still permitted to serve the Parliament. Essex and Waller were, however, in no hurry to send in their resignations, and some of Essex's foot at Farnham mutinied, and, demanding their arrears of pay, marched to Reading, in opposition to orders. Skippon, Major-General of the New Model Army, by his presence and rough but effective eloquence, induced these five regiments to submit once more to discipline on April 6th. Two days afterwards Lieutenant-Colonel Thorpe, in recounting his warlike exploits, stated that he had been wounded by a bullet in the stomach, and shot through the arm whilst leading on a regiment at Basing. He commanded the dragoons originally raised for Sir Richard Granvill at Cheriton Fight, where he captured Col. Beard's waggon laden with horse and foot arms, and his other carriages laden with powder and bullets. At Winchester, on the last march westward, he had the guard when a sortie took place from the Castle. He killed a lieutenant-colonel and six troopers, and captured another lieutenant-colonel and eight troopers, with the loss of one man killed and two wounded. Waller wrote on April 9th asking for money and supplies, which were granted, but he was informed that " the foot of Sussex come in so slowly that they are not considerable to be sent." He enclosed a letter from the Committee at Chalfield House near Bradford, stating that the Princes Maurice and Rupert had reached Marshfield. Prince Maurice seems not to have been present in person, but to have sent some troops to reinforce his brother Rupert. Cromwell also writes from Salisbury on April 9th, 1645 (ten o'clock at night), that Goring had retired to Wells and Glastonbury, " whereupon Sir William Waller, having a very poor infantry of about 1600 men —lest they, being so inconsiderable, should engage (entangle or encumber) our horse—we came from Shaftesbury to Salisbury to secure our foot, to prevent our being necessitated to a too unequal engagement, and to be nearer a communication with our friends. Since our coming hither we hear Prince Rupert is come to Marshfield, a market town not far from Trowbridge. . . . Sir, I beseech you send what horse and foot you can spare towards Salisbury, by way of Kingsclere, with what convenient expedition may be. Truly, we look to be attempted upon every day." Prince Rupert withdrew without fighting, and, on April 16th, letters reached London from Waller and Cromwell, at Salisbury, and from Colonel Norton, at Southampton, stating that they were anxious to divide their forces, so as to engage the enemy on all sides at once, but that their men's pay was sadly in arrears. Colonel FitzJames and Quartermaster-General Fincher presented a modestly-worded petition to Parliament from the officers of Waller's army, asking for 14 days' pay and a promise of arrears for all ranks. Waller and Norton added that " the garrisons of Winchester and Basing range and rage about the country."

From a very interesting letter written at Southampton, on April 15th, 1645, by John Eyres, " to his loving uncle in London," and from other sources we learn that Col. Norton having left Waller's army, and returned to Hampshire, marched to Romsey with six troops of horse on April 14th, intending to fortify the town " to stop the insolencies of the garrison of Winchester." Early in the morning Major Stewart was sent out wit three troops of horse to face Winchester, occupy the enemy's attention, and to bring them to action on equal terms at some distance from Romsey, where the other three troops of Norton's horse were hard at work. Meanwhile, Major Stewart having " otherwise dared them," the Governor, Sir

William Ogle, rode forth from the Castle, with all his horse, who were much more numerous than their opponents. Major Stewart " retired soberly" to a strong position, having but few men, but kept his fo. s at bay by a bold charge, retreating upon Romsey, with a view to reinforcements, and also to draw the Cavaliers from Winchester, so that their retreat might be cut off.

Norton's men did not arrive from Romsey as was expected, and Major Stewart charged thrice, disordering the enemy, until he was wounded, but not dangerously, in the thigh. Four or five of his men were taken prisoners, and seven or eight Cavaliers were killed. During the afternoon Norton's horse came up from Romsey, and the advance guard of ten or twelve men " between Hurstley and Winchester discovered the enemies' body, who sent out a forlorn hope to charge them, but were at first salute sent back faster than they came ; after this they drew out 40, and sent them against this small party of ours, led by my cousin Leon Green, a Reformado, who routed them, so that they fled, and disordered their main body." All Norton's men now followed in hot pursuit. Lieut. Coward, of whom Woodward says " few names recur more in the annals of Winchester than those of Coward and Simonds " was killed, with six or seven others, during the chase. Captain Heath, Lieut. Barnes, four or five other officers, and 30 soldiers with their horses (40 horses and 27 men), were captured before Winchester walls gave shelter to the fugitives. The Cavaliers were said to number 250, and their opponents only 130. The prisoners were brought on the evening of Tuesday, April 15th, 1645, " to the gaol at Southampton to sing another tune. Here's a gentleman (Norton) that will protect the country as well as the town in which he quarters, or of which he is Governor. Store of these would do well !"

On April 17th the 500*l*. per month first levied in August, 1644, on excise duties in Hants, was ordered to be continued for the pay of Portsmouth garrison as long as need requires. Colonel Norton was appointed Governor of Portsmouth, on May 10th, 1645, on which day Algernon Sidney became Governor of Chichester, and Colonel Morley of the town and castle of Arundel. Sir William Waller had been beating up Goring's quarters in Somersetshire, but towards the end of April he fell back to Andover. He had reached Windsor before April 25th, and resigning his command, as he was obliged to do by the self-denying ordinance, passed on April 3rd, went to London. On April 19th Cromwell was besieging Langford House, near Salisbury, and the garrison burned their barns, stables, and outhouses, in order to strengthen their position. On April 23rd all deserters from the armies of the Parliament were ordered to be executed without mercy. At the end of April Goring was recalled with his horse and dragoons towards Oxford by the King, who was anxious to join Prince Rupert near Worcester, but was hindered from so doing by Cromwell, who was at the head of a strong cavalry force, and had already thrice defeated the Royalists. On April 24th " merely by dragoons and fierce countenances he took Bletchington " from Colonel Windebank, who was, for thus surrendering, shot on May 3rd, at Merton College, Oxford. Islip-bridge on April 24th, Witney on the 26th, and Bampton Bush on the 27th, were scenes of Cromwell's victories, causing the King to exclaim " Who will bring me this Cromwell dead or alive ?"

Goring was unwilling to march to Oxford, but, says Clarendon, " However unwelcome soever these orders were to the Lord Goring, yet there was no remedy but he must obey them ; and it was now hoped that the west should be hereafter freed from him, where he was at that time very ungracious (unpopular)." He therefore commenced his march, plundering as he went, and making Beverston Castle, in Gloucestershire, a centre of devastation. Mr. Secretary Nicholas, writing from Oxford on April 30th, said, " Cromwell is now lying at Stamford and other places next to Farringdon, with six regiments of horse and four troops of dragoons, expecting the coming of Colonel Royden's (Rawdon's) regiment thither."

Religious dissensions had, alas ! arisen at Basing House, with the usual sad results ! Comrades, who had fought shoulder to shoulder against Waller and Norton, could not dwell together when all for the time seemed peaceful. " Mercurius Veridicus" says, on May 16th, " That Colonel Royden (Sir Marmaduke Rawdon) is cast out from being Governor of Basing House to some is already known, though the place of his new government, and the manner of his being put out of the old, will be true news to all that will be pleased to read it."

" Since the removing of the last siege against

Basing (the garrison being mix't Protestants and Papists), the Papists became jealous of the Protestants, especially of Colonel Royden, which by commission had the command of the house.

"This jealousie broke forth into a complaint against the Junto of Oxford that the Catholics of the Garrison were afraid to trust themselves any longer there amongst the Protestants, and for their better security presented a petition thus:—

'To the Right Honourable the Lords of His Majestie's Most Honourable Privy Council:

The Humble Petition of His Majesty's Catholic Subjects of the Garrison of Basing Hous·,

Sheweth that your petitioners, both during the time of the siege, which for some months was continued against this place, and since the raising thereof, hath (*sic*) had just cause to suspect divers persons of this Garrison, for by reason of their different opinions from us, we do generally hold it more safe that this Garrison, which hath been very serviceable to His Majestie, may consist of persons (both officers and soldiers) of one religion.

Therefore, to prevent such inconveniences as may arise, the Petitioners humbly pray that the premises may be taken into consideration, to the end it may be declared whether it be not requisite that your Petitioners, who are most deeply engaged in this present war, may not be thought the fittest defendants and maintainers of a place of that strength and concernment.

And your Petitioners shall pray, &c.,
WINCHESTER.'"

Upon which petition it was thought fit and so ordered, "That the garrison of Basing House should consist only of Roman Catholics, and that the Commander-in-Chief should be of that religion." This being declared a Popish garrison, Colonel Royden was ordered to depart thence with his troop of horse, since which he is made Governor of Farringdon." The Governor thus dismissed must have been a resolute soldier, for we learn from Lady Willoughby, "Sir Marmaduke Rawdon declared to the Marquis, who proposed to surrender, that he would not so long as a dog or cat or rat did remain." He successfully defended Farringdon, where his monument was formerly to be seen in the church.

The places of Colonel Rawdon and his veteran soldiers were but ill supplied. On May 15th, 1645, the "Moderate Intelligencer" is informed "that they have forced into Basing House, instead of those that are gone abroad with Col. Royden, almost as many out of the counties, and of them the most 18 years old, some not 12."

Truly these were "boys," but, in the hour of danger they proved themselves, like Napoleon's levies at Waterloo, "small, but biting." The most reliable estimates give 300 fighting men as the strength of the garrison during the final siege.

Colonel Rawdon was ordered to proceed from Basing to join Goring, and to march with him to Oxford in company with Colonel Bennet and Major Smith, as Cromwell was waiting near Farringdon to intercept the party from Basing. On May Day, 1645, some 500 horse and foot Cavaliers marched out of Loyalty House. As they were crossing the Kennet, between Thatcham and Newbury, they were attacked by Colonel Butler's Puritan regiment of horse, but succeeded in reaching Donnington Castle, where they were prudently refused admission by brave Sir John Boys, who was apprehensive of a siege. Fortunately for Sir Marmaduke Rawdon and his men, Fairfax's large army and about 32 guns did not reach Newbury until the following evening, so that they were able to pursue their march next morning, but were chased throughout the day by Colonel Butler, until, about five o'clock in the afternoon, they joined Goring's army near Lambourn. Col. Butler captured some prisoners, amongst whom was a Commissioner of Excise, who had about 25*l*. in his possession. Goring was on May Day at or near Marlborough "at dinner with his officers, roaring and drinking healths, and making themselves merry," and he mustered his army at Marlborough on May 2nd. Some of his men had penetrated as far as Farnham, but were obliged to beat a hasty retreat towards Oxford, abandoning three guns and some ammunition.

Goring, having been thus reinforced by the party from Basing, marched about eleven p.m. on Sunday to attack Cromwell at Farringdon, "but by the vigilancy and care of the Scout Master, they had such timely notice that they escaped him, Colonel Cromwell at that time being with Sir Thomas Fairfax, and sent for by him, but hasted to his quarters, and brought off his men without any loss, very little action, neither having at that time much mind to engage." ("Moderate Intelligencer.") Information of this intended attack was obtained from Lieut.-Col. Hacket, taken at Newbury. Cromwell was early in May near Blewbury, effecting a junction with the infantry, intending either to await the enemy or to advance. Prince Rupert was marching to join the King and Goring.

General Sir Thomas Lord Fairfax had been during the closing days of April, 1645, preparing at Windsor to take the field with the famous New Model Army, which was to consist of 21,000 effective men. 6000 horse, besides officers, made up ten regiments, 1000 dragoons besides officers, commanded by Col. Okey, who "were always counted the best men of the army." 14,000 foot were drawn up in regiments of 1000 each, besides officers, so says Colonel Edward Wogan, who held command in this army, but another account says that the infantry regiments were 1200 strong. 44,955*l.* per month, levied by assessment upon the whole kingdom, was the cost of maintaining this large army. Of this amount Surrey and Southwark contributed 2000*l.*, and Sussex 3,927*l.* 15s. 6¾d. The cavalry regiments were in all twelve in number, Col. Rossiter's horse and Col. Okey's dragoons being additions to the nominal strength. They were commanded by General Fairfax, the Commissary-General. Colonels Greaves, Sir Robert Pye, Whalley, Rich, Rossiter, Bourchier, Sheffield, Fleetwood, Hollis, and Okey. Col. Hollis's regiment was given to Lieut.-General Cromwell after Naseby Fight. The infantry regiments were commanded by General Fairfax, Major-General Skippon, Colonels Sir Hardress Waller, Pickering, Herbert, Ingoldsby, Fortescue, Montague, Welden, Hammond, Lambert, and Rainsborough. There was in addition a body of 400 pioneers.

The Rev. Joshua Sprigge, one of Fairfax's chaplains, seems to have been the author of "Anglia Rediviva," which has, however, by some been attributed to Colonel Nathaniel Fiennes. From this work, which gives copious details of the proceedings of Fairfax, we learn that in April, 1645, the King had in Wiltshire garrisons at Devizes, Lacock House, Langford House, and Highworth. The Parliament had only one garrison, at Malmesbury. In Dorset the King held Portland Castle and Island, Corfe and Sherborne Castles, whilst Poole, Lyme, and Weymouth had Parliament garrisons. In Hants the strong Royal garrisons of Basing and Winchester were opposed by troops at Portsmouth, Southampton, and Christchurch. In Berkshire the Cavaliers possessed Farringdon, Wallingford, Donnington, and Radcot, the Roundheads guarding Abingdon, Reading, and Windsor meanwhile. Oxford, Banbury, Woodstock, Gaunt House, Godstowe, and Boarstall House were confronted by the garrisons of Henley-on-Thames and Aylesbury. Bletchington House, another royal garrison, within four miles of Oxford, was captured by Cromwell on April 24th.

The King had between Oxford and St. Michael's Mount about 14,000 men under arms, and the clubmen (of whom more hereafter), favoured his cause. The Parliament had in the same district, under Waller's command, Waller's own regiment, the Plymouth regiment, and those of Cols. Popham, Fitzjames, and Cooke. There were also the weak cavalry regiments of Cols. Behr and Dalbier, which had formerly served under the Earl of Essex, but were now commanded by Lieut.-Col. Buller, and detailed for the army of Major-General Massey. These two regiments were brigaded just before Naseby Fight. But General Fairfax's New Model speedily turned the scale in favour of the Parliament.

Marching from Windsor to Reading on April 30th, 1645, Fairfax reached Theale on May 1st, Newbury on the 2nd, and Andover on the 3rd. He wrote from Newbury complaining that his march was impeded by the tardy arrival of provisions, and asking for the regiments of Colonels Cooke and Thompson, which had previously returned to Surrey. The Committee of Both Kingdoms were instructed "to dispose these regiments." Near Newbury he sent out good scouts and parties of horse, and without loss captured in a cavalry skirmish Lieut.-Colonel Hacket and six other prisoners, who gave seasonable information that Goring, to whose army they belonged, intended early next morning to beat up Lieut.-General Cromwell's quarters at Farringdon. Cromwell was speedily warned, and the night attack was repulsed. Fairfax marched from Newbury between noon and one o'clock on May 3rd. On the next day he had with him seven infantry regiments, numbering from 10,000 to 12,000 men, his cavalry having not yet joined him. At Andover the soldiers were quartered in the town and in the adjacent villages, and on the following day (May 4th) a muster of the whole force, which halted for two or three hours, took place a mile out of Andover on the Salisbury road. A Council of War was held, and five men were sentenced to death. One was a renegado or deserter, "and four more, authors of the mutiny in Kent, were cast, one of whom (whose lot it was) with the renegado was executed upon a tree at Wallop in the way of the army's march *in terrorem.* The deserter was "a parson's son," and was a native of Wallop. "Both of them died as they had lived, like sots. But how the Great Judge passed His sentence I have not to say." Summary punishment having been thus inflicted, the army marched forward to Salisbury. On the following day " was proclamation made throughout the army that it should be death for any man to plunder, at which our old Horse Dragoons, somewhat guilty, made answer " If the Parliament would pay truly let them hang duly." All ranks had received four months' pay, and nothing was permitted to be taken without payment. " No, not so much as grass for our horses." Not an ox, sheep, lamb, or even an egg was stolen, "save in our hard march hot days, vacancy of towns or houses over the Plain made them inordinately desire drink, or covet for water in the villages we past." The soldiers mostly slept in barns or under hedges for eight days. On May 6th the bivouac was at Sixpenny Handley, on the 7th at Blandford, and on the 8th at Witchampton, from whence a party under Colonel Welcher was sent to relieve Taunton, which was hard pressed by besieging Cavaliers. The army had now advanced 79 miles, "marching the whole seven days, and some of them very long marches, without any intermission, so willing were the soldiers to come to the relief of distressed Taunton, to Salisbury were they come before the enemy was aware, as was discovered by letters of Sir Ralph Hopton to the Governors of Winchester and Basing, wherein he desired them to send him word when he thought Fairfax would be able to take the field." General Fairfax had intended to relieve Taunton with his whole force, but two expresses from Westminster overtook him at Blandford with orders to retrace his steps towards Oxford. The King having marched northwards to join Rupert, the friends of the Parliament in Oxford promised to overpower the small garrison left in the city, if Fairfax appeared before the fortifications. Four regiments were at once sent towards Taunton under the command of Colonel Welden. How successfully this officer performed his task is admirably told in Mr. Hepworth Dixon's "Life of Admiral Blake." Fairfax being now weak in cavalry, avoided highways and marched through an enclosed country, as Goring's horse were now returning westward from Oxford to commit the same excesses as before. He reached Ringwood on March 9th, and a trooper was sentenced to death for burglary and murder. He was executed at Romsey on the following day. A fourteen mile march then brought the army past Winchester to Alresford, and we read, " I need not acquaint you with our hard march, hot weather and hard quarter, but in all our march we have not yet seen an enemy. We faced Winchester Castle as we came by, but no enemy appeared, nor any gun shot off against us." On May 14th the relief of Taunton was known in London, and Fairfax, who halted for one night at Whitchurch, had reached Newbury. At this place a foot soldier was sentenced " to have his tongue bored through with a red hot iron, for notorious swearing and blaspheming, all which was done as well for example and terror to others as for justice sake." But Fairfax, though severe, was a prudent general. Some regiment complained that constant rear-guard duty was exceedingly irksome. The General's own regiment refused to waive its privilege of being always in advance, but, " instead of severe discipline, the General alighted himself and marched on foot in the head of his own regiment about two miles, and so brought up the rear, and to this day his own regiment takes the turn upon all duties."

On March 16th, 1645, Prince Maurice wrote to Sir John Owen : " You are likewise to give strict order that every officer under the degree of a major march afoot with his company ; and that no officer or soldier presume to straggle or be found pistol-shot from his colours, upon pain of death. Hereof you may not fail."

On Saturday, May 17th, Fairfax marched to Blewbury, and from thence proceeded to the siege of Oxford and Naseby Fight.

The " Weekly Account" stated on May 16th, that Basing House being now declared a Popish garrison, the gentlemen of Hants and Sussex, grown wiser by experience, were about to besiege it again. Some persons were suggesting that instead of blockading the approach it would be more economical to spend from 500*l.* to 1000*l.*

in building redoubts, making shelter trenches, and employing a skilful engineer, who would speedily compel a surrender. The same newspaper stated on May 19th, three companies from Farnham Castle were quartered at Odiham to check foragers in that direction, and that on May 12th 100 men had marched from Odiham to Hackwood Park, within a mile of Basing, capturing two loads of hay and provisions which were going to the House. No large force of Cavaliers was met with, but four Parliament scouts met an equal number from the garrison, one of whom they secured, but the others fled. Colonel Ludlow, whose Major Dewett had some time previously deserted to the King, taking some troopers with him, was about this time stationed at Odiham. His standard bore the device of an open Bible with the motto " Verbum Dei" placed above a mitre, crozier, and rosary

On May 12th " the gentlemen of the Life-Guard to Sir William Waller, now quartered in Surrey," were ordered to receive 14 days' pay from " Sir Richard Onslowe, and the rest of the gentlemen of Surrey, and were then to be disbanded." The physicians, chaplains, surgeons, and scoutmaster-general of the army, late under the command of Sir William Waller, obtained by petition part of their arrears of pay. The Committee of the Army were " to consult and consider with the Assembly of Divines upon the speedy sending down and supplying the army under the command of Sir Thomas Fairfax with a convenient number and proportion of godly, learned, and able ministers." A humble petition was read from the officers and soldiers of the Portsmouth Garrison, and from the poor inhabitants of the town. Colonels Jephson and Norton were authorised to borrow money to be repaid before Midsummer by the Committee of the Revenue, in order to clear off the arrears of the old establishment. The gentlemen of Hants were to bring in an ordinance for selling the estates of Lord Worcester, and some other delinquents in Hants, to raise 2000l. of the garrison arrears of the new establishment. " It is but reason those incendiaries should have no wood left who strive to burn down the kingdom." The Committee of both Kingdoms soon afterwards decided that 600 men was a sufficient garrison for Portsmouth, and Colonel Jones, late of Farnham Castle, obtained command at the end of June of Sir W. Bereton's regiment of horse. On May 13th " 1000l. was provided as a fortnight's pay for Colonel Fienis his regiment." A week previously Col. Thompson, who had lost a leg at Cheriton Fight, asked for his arrears of pay, with either the command of a garrison or some civil employment, stating that he had, with the help of friends, raised a troop of horse for the service of Parliament, but that nearly 400l. was owing to his men. It was recommended by the Upper to the Lower House " that he may have relief and respect showed him."

Driven to desperation by Goring's excesses, the counties of Sussex, Surrey, Hants, and Berks were preparing to raise troops for the Parliament. On May 21st, 1645, Major Peter Baxter, Governor of Hurst Castle, was to receive 100l. in part payment of his arrears, and 100l. from the next sequestration of a delinquent's estate. Three days afterwards, in reply to a petition presented by 200 wounded and maimed soldiers in the Savoy Hospital, and by 1500 other soldiers and widows, 250l. per week was voted for the relief of maimed soldiers and widows, together with the collections at the three next monthly fasts, except one-half of the collection at St. Margaret's. Westminster, and at St. Martin's in the Fields. About May 23rd Colonel Norton, with a force of Southampton men, attacked Langford House, near Salisbury. His horse were commanded by Captains St. Barbe, Bettesworth, and Gertin, and his foot by the son of Captain Murford. Norton placed an ambush near the house. Then a small party of his men approached the garrison, as if levying contribution money. The Cavaliers sallied forth, led by the Governor, Colonel Griffith, who came out wearing linen stockings, without either horse or boots, and were all captured by the ambuscade. Captain Ludlow, who was probably a relative of the celebrated Colonel of that name, did the Parliament good service. The prisoners were Colonel Griffith, his captain, lieutenant, his own cornet, and eight other officers, besides soldiers, the total number being 74, together with their arms. Ten Cavaliers were killed, but Norton's loss was inconsiderable. The captives were sent to Southampton, and on May 29th were ordered to be sent up to London, exchange being prohibited without the consent of Parliament. Colonel Griffith was sent to Newgate, but his escape was announced on June 4th and all officers of forts and courts of guard were ordered to arrest him, and to send him up to the Parliament in very safe custody. On May 29th, 600 foot were ordered to form the garrison of Portsmouth, and the officers of Waller's artillery train were granted their arrears of pay, and were to be recommended to Fairfax for employment. On June 5th Mr. Edward Hooper, who had been appointed Governor of Southampton, obtained exemption on the ground of infirmity, and on July 5th Captain St. Barbe obtained the vacant post. The St. Barbes lived at Ashlington in Somersetshire, and at Broadlands, near Romsey. One of them was killed at Newbury Fight, on September 20th, 1643.

"Goring's crew" were now ravaging Somersetshire, and besieging Colonels Welden and Blake in Taunton. Great anxiety was felt in London for the fate of the town, and a deputation from the House of Commons went to the Committee of Militia to ask for 500 mounted musketeers. They were granted, and volunteers offered themselves on all sides. On June 7th the Committee for Surrey were ordered to send 100 dragoons, Sussex was to "send forthwith a troop of horse, consisting of four score, and one hundred mounted musketeers"; Wilts was to provide 150 horse, and Kent was "to send what force they can of horse mounted musqueteers for the relief of Colonel Welden and the brigade at Taunton." Thirty pair of pistols, with holsters, and a like number of saddles with their furniture, were to be at once delivered to Colonel Norton for his Hampshire horse by Lieut.-Colonel Owen Roe, who was in charge of the public stores. Colonel Whitehead acquainted the House of Commons that the Committee for Hants and Colonel Norton "had conferred together, and that they had resolved to furnish 100 commanded horse, under the command of Captain Thos. Bettesworth, to go upon this present expedition into the west for the relief of the brigade at Taunton." Fairfax wrote from Sherrington, and obtained permission for Cromwell to take command of all his horse. An ordinance now passed to collect the revenues of the sequestered estates of Hampshire Royalist delinquents. One-fifth and one-twentieth part of the proceeds were to be expended upon the county fortresses and defences and in the impressment of soldiers therein, the Isle of Wight being specially excepted. Another ordinance, passed through the influence of Col. Norton on June 12th, appointed "John Dove, gentleman, treasurer and keeper of the stores of ammunition for the town of Portsmouth." Two days later "600 soldiers and 40 gunners, comprehending the old establishment," were to be the garrison of Portsmouth, 50 soldiers being assigned to Southsea Castle. "£200 per week over and above the old establishment" was voted for the troops of Portsmouth and Southsea Castle. The Committee for Hants was to advance for this purpose 5000*l*., which was to be repaid from the Excise duties.

Colonel Massey, the well known Governor of Gloucester, was to come into Hampshire from the west, in order to unite with the forces from Kent, Surrey, and Sussex, which were intended for the relief of Taunton. Clarendon says that Massey was a soldier of fortune, who had formerly served the King in Scotland. When the troubles began he was at York, "with inclination to serve the King, but finding himself not enough known there, and that there would be little gotten but the comfort of a good conscience, he went to London, where there was more money and fewer officers, and was easily made Lieutenant-Colonel to the Earl of Stamford, and being quickly found to be a diligent and stout officer, and of no ill parts of conversation, to render himself acceptable among the common people, was, by his Lordship, when he went into the west, left Governor of the City of Gloucester, where he had behaved himself actively and successfully." Massey was, on June 13th, at Romsey; he had from 1000 to 1200 horse, and was expecting reinforcements.

On June 20th Colonel Webb was with the City Dragoons at Southampton, from which town the local contingent of horse was to march on May 23rd to Romsey; at which place a general muster was to take place on May 24th. Colonel Popham commanded the horse at Romsey during Massey's temporary absence. Clarendon calls him "Col. Edward Popham, a principal officer of the Parliament in their fleets at sea, and of a passionate and virulent temper, of the Independent party." Captain Pittman had on or about June 9th repulsed a sortie from Winchester Castle, and carried off 50 horses. The Pittman family owned land at Mapledenwell, and John Pittman, Esq., was one of the Commissioners appointed on November 6th, 1643, for making the weekly collection in Hampshire. Colonel Massey, on or about June 19th, marched to Winchester and carried off the sheep which Lord Ogle had collected in anticipation of a siege, but which he made no effort to defend. "Some 60 or more of the King's scattered horse" from Naseby Fight reached Winchester about this time. Colonel Massey was present on June 24th at the Romsey muster. He had been reinforced from Kent by 80 horse and 166 dragoons; from Hants by 100 horse, and Sussex, Surrey, Middlesex, and London had each sent him 100 dragoons. Captain Jervoise joined him with 340 horse, and 340 Reformadoes were a welcome accession of strength. These reinforcements together numbered 567 horse and 966 dragoons, and on July 2nd Massey joined with 3000 men at Blandford the army of Fairfax, which, after the decisive battle of Naseby, "turned westward to raise the siege of Taunton, crush Goring's crew, and recover the great strongholds of Somerset and Devon for Parliament."

The excesses of troops like those of Goring naturally brought about a reaction in the county, and on June 26th Mr. Secretary Nicholas, writing from Oxford, says, "The Clubmen in Hampshire and Wiltshire grow numerous, and, I hear, very stout. They have above 500 arms in Hampshire. The rebels have given orders for suppressing of them." It seems probable that the Royalist generals might have turned the movement to good account, but the opportunity was lost, as Goring issued a severe order against them from Exeter. These Clubmen wore white ribbons as a badge, and derived their name from being armed with clubs, flails, scythes, and sickles fastened to long poles. The county gentlemen and clergy headed the movement, which, according to Locke, was originated by Shaftesbury when a young man. The design was to form a third party, which should neither be Royalist nor Parliamentarian, an army without soldiers, for they were neither to wear swords nor to carry firearms. The Clubmen were about 14,000 strong, and were already ready when necessary to assemble in force in defence of their homes and granaries. Refusing to allow any armies to quarter within their districts, their banner, a white sheet, bore this motto :—

"If you offer to plunder or take our cattle,
You may be sure we'll give you battle."

The word "plunder," which had been introduced by soldiers of fortune from Germany, here first appears in our language. The Clubmen refused to submit to the Parliament, saying, "Our intentions are to go in a middle way; to preserve our persons and estates from violence and plunder; to join with neither; and not to oppose either side, until by the answer to our petition we see who are the enemies of that happy peace which we really desire." Fairfax negotiated with them, attended some of their meetings, and employed some of them as pioneers, but finally suppressed them.

On June 30th, 1645, Fairfax, returning from Naseby Fight to relieve beleaguered Taunton, marched from Marlborough to Amesbury. It was the day of Marlborough Fair, and some stragglers were in consequence left behind, who were speedily surprised and captured by Major Dewett or Duet, who, being Colonel Ludlow's major, had changed sides, and was now in garrison at Devizes. On July 1st there was a 12 miles' march to Broad Chalke, "and being drawn up that morning to a rendezvous to a place called Stonage (Stonehenge), marched in battalia upon Salisbury Plain." Chaplain Hugh Peters urged the destruction of Stonehenge, as being one of "the monuments of heathenism," but fortunately more pressing matters demanded attention. Some officers and others riding through Salisbury found the Clubmen there very confident, "wearing white ribands in their hats, as it were in affront of the army, not sparing to declare themselves absolute neuters, or rather friends to the enemy."

On Wednesday, July 2nd, Fairfax reached Blandford, where he was joined by Massey at the head of 3000 horse and foot. A soldier who had robbed a gentleman near Marlborough was here executed in a narrow lane. Mr. Penruddock and Mr. Fussell, two leaders of the Clubmen, were arrested, but, having acknowledged their error, were released. Five days afterwards Goring was beaten at Langport Fight, and the Royal cause soon became hopeless in the west.

CHAPTER XXVIII.—ROAD WAGGONS IN DANGER—CLUBMEN ROUTED.—WAYS AND MEANS—LORD OGLE'S REQUISITIONS—COLONEL DALBIER—BASING AGAIN BESIEGED—MINING OPERATIONS—HAMPSHIRE CLUBMEN—CHURCH PARADE—A SHATTERED TOWER—A GALLANT STRATAGEM.

On Saturday, July 12th, 1645, some scouts reported at Farnham Castle that a party of horse from Basing House were returning to that garrison with a Chichester road waggon, which they had captured near Hind-head. All the horse and dragoons in the Castle were at once sent out, and Cornet Stokam was despatched with a small party to bring up a detachment commanded by Captain Joyner from Alton to Tunworth Downs. Both parties arrived at the same time, and charged the Cavaliers both in front and rear, at a place two miles from Alton, routed them, retook the waggon, and pursued them to within half-a-mile of Basing, killing and wounding most of them, and taking nine prisoners and 15 horses. The retiring Parliamentarians had reached Bentley Green, when they were faced by 120 cavalry, belonging to the garrisons of Winchester, Basing, and Faringdon (Sir M. Rawdon's command). The new-comers prepared to charge, and took "Trooper Reeves, but received such a salute from our dragoons" that they fled. A Parliamentarian Major, whose name is unrecorded, was at the same time posted with 100 foot at Upton Gray, near Weston Patrick. He intercepted the Cavaliers as they retreated towards Basing, taking six men and four horses. Capt. Joyner (Joynet), who was shot in the arm, Cornet Stokam, whose head received a sword cut, James Mansurgh (Mansargh), who was shot in the leg, "were they who did most execution." One Puritan dragoon was killed.

On July 24th measures were taken to provide maintenance for 1500 horse and dragoons, to be employed in the blockade of Basing, Winchester, and other places. £5000 was, by an ordinance brought in by Mr. Lisle, voted upon Excise receipts "to be employed for the reducing of Winchester, Donnington, and Basing." The Committee of the Admiralty were "to take a speedy course for the reduction of the island of Jersey, and report the same to the House," as a petition had been presented from thence, to the effect that "many inhabitants, well affected, were remaining there in want and misery, ever since the revolt of the islanders, upon the forcible entrance which Captain Carteret made there against the Parliament."

On July 26th, 1645, it was ordered "Mr. Morris Jephson to be Lieut.-Colonel, and Mr. John Lobb to be Major of Colonel Norton's regiment of foot, now at Portsmouth." The Lobb family lived at Southampton, and one of them afterwards owned the Vine, near Basingstoke. On July 31st the Committee of the Navy were "to take care to bring about those prisoners that are on board the ships now at Portsmouth."

On August 1st our old acquaintance Major-General Browne was granted 2000 foot and 600 as the strength of his Abingdon garrison, and on the next day Colonel Fleetwood surrounded and dispersed 1000 clubmen at Shaftesbury. Cromwell attacked about 2000 others in an old Roman camp on Hambledon Hill. His men were at first repulsed, but were after an hour's fighting victorious, and brought 600 arms, 400 prisoners, 200 of whom were wounded, to Shrawton, where they were imprisoned in the church. Sixty clubmen were killed. They were said to have been stirred up by "malignant priests," and four vicars and curates were among the captives. Some were afterwards sent up to London, and others released, on taking the Covenant, and promising future quietness. Twelve colours were also taken. The Earl of Southampton was High Steward of

Winchester, but was on account of his loyalty disabled from holding office, and on November 27th, Robert Wallop, Esq., was elected in his stead. The Earl was now serving the King, and on August 4th a pass was granted by both Houses of Parliament to the Countess of Southampton with her two young children for 30 days to go from Oxford to Titchfield House. The reason assigned is a touching one, "It being the desire of the old Countess of Southampton to see them, which yet she never did." The Countess was permitted to take with her a coach, and a waggon, with ten ordinary servants and horses, but none of the party were to enter or remain in any of the Parliament's forts, castles, or garrisons. Six troops of light horse 670 in number, and three troops of dragoons, numbering 330, had been raised in several counties for General Fairfax. The sum of 9924*l*. 2s. was now voted for three months' maintenance of this regiment, "in all 1000, besides commissionary officers." The Kentish horse were on August 6th ordered "to be employed for the service of reducing the county of Southampton to the obedience of the Parliament," receiving pay meanwhile from the Committee for Hants. Colonel Jephson, M.P. for Stockbridge, was ordered to embark for Munster, with his regiment of horse. His men were to have quarters everywhere, paying for necessaries at reasonable rates. Not more than twelve pence per man and horse was to be paid for each 24 hours. Fairfax received some ammunition and battering pieces from Portsmouth, which aided in the capture of Sherborne Castle on August 15th, after a siege of 16 days.

About the middle of August much discussion took place as to the payment of some 60 poor waggoners who had been employed in several expeditions to Basing, Newport, Petworth, and the western counties. Their claim of nearly 3000*l*. was at last paid. Colonel Weare, who had been sent up from Portsmouth by the Earl of Essex under arrest in September, 1644, was still confined in the Comptor at Southwark. He was now removed to another prison, and was granted subsistence money from his arrears of pay. "Captain Bettesworth, having done very good service to the Parliament, to be enjoined not to go out of the Kingdom" on August 20th, and, nine days afterwards, mention is made of the "Masters and Governors of the Mystery and Commonalty of Barber Surgeons, London." A Common Assembly was held in the Guildhall, Winchester, on a certain Monday of this month to consider a warrant issued by the Governor, Lord Ogle. "It generally agreed by the whole assembly that Mr. Mayor (Longland) and whom of the rest of the Corporation he shall think fit, shall go, and to-morrow morning shall go to my Lord Ogle to inform him what things are here to be gotten, and what not concerning his warrant for necessaries for the Castle, and so to consider how they may be provided." Before this time only four constables had been annually elected at Winchester. But since the city had been garrisoned two others had been added, "to make up the number six during the tyme of these troubles."

Vigorous preparations for the final siege of Basing were now being made. The senior commanding officer was Colonel Dalbier.

Dol Beere, Dalbyer, &c. (his name is spelt in every possible way). He was a Dutchman by birth, and from him, according to Heath, Cromwell first of all learned the mechanical part of soldiering, and received help in the drilling of his Ironsides. At the outbreak of the war we find him in command of a troop of horse under Lord Bedford. He was also Quartermaster-General to the Earl of Essex, as well as an engineer. A most invaluable officer. He had been engaged some years previously, together with Sir William Balfour, in raising German horse. After the battle of Edgehill he urged the adoption of vigorous measures. In the same year the Lords desired the Commons that he being under accusation and restraint might be either tried or discharged. He took part in the burning of the village of Chinnor, in Oxfordshire, in June, 1643. The strength of his troop is given by Woodward as being 60 troopers, with two trumpeters, three corporals, a saddler, and a farrier. The officers were Lieut. William Frampton, Cornet H. Vanbraham, and Quartermaster John Downe.

In 1644 Colonel Dalbier was in command of a regiment of horse composed as follows:—

	Officers	Troopers
Colonel Dalbier	12	67
Captain Salkield	11	72
„ Pymm	11	80
„ Lukeman	9	18
Total	43	267 310

"Aulicus" and "Britannicus" are as usua

mutually satirical about the commencement of the siege. The former said that Dalbier complained of his design being " very much dampt by the alarms given to London, when His Majesty's horse was at Dunstable," whereupon the latter retorts that "the house is very much dampt, and the wise Marquis has taken up his damp lodging once more," adding that Lord Winchester spent his time in bed at the bottom of a cellar "out of reach of gunshot, for you know generals and governors should not be too venturous." "Aulicus" asserted that Dalbier had bargained not to receive any pay until Basing was taken, except 150l. to be paid at once to his wife, and that all Dalbier's projected mines were only plans to obtain money. "Britannicus" replies. "Upon such terms we will employ two or three colonels more, if they please to be in action, and to leave murmuring for arrears." "The engineer fell to his pretence, the work itself is money, August 20th" ("Aulicus"). On August 4th Dalbier brought in proposals to the House of Commons that the forces of Sussex and Surrey should block up Basing House, and that those of Hants, Middlesex, and the City of London should blockade Oxford, and on the 19th the Parliament ordered 400 bandoliers, 400 swords, 300 muskets, 200 pikes, and 10 drums to be issued from store to the forces from Portsmouth garrison employed for the reducing of Basing House. "Colonel Dalbier reached Basingstoke with 800 horse and foot on August 20th, but made no attack, and the provisioning of Basing House was not interfered with. "Which being completed, the Garrison resolved to visit the rebels, which it did on Thursday and Friday, and took a major and nine troopers, since which time Sir John Boys went from Dennington Castle (of which he was Governor) to alarm them, and brought away a colour, two officers, and seven other prisoners to Dennington. Basing daily beats up their quarters." Whereupon "Britannicus" retorts on September 22nd. "Are not these bare victories, think you ? But such they are glad to live upon."

On August 23rd it was ordered "Out of Reading, Captain Blagrave's company to be drawn for Basing." Dalbier was now in possession of Basing village, and "hath with him many good engineers and pioneers, such as use to dig in coal pits." Heavy rains favoured the besiegers, "the place thereabouts being hard and rocky." On August 28th more troops and materials for a siege were urgently required, and seven days afterwards 100 Southwark musketeers were ordered to Basing, those refusing to march being fined by the Committee of Militia and punished as usual.

On September 1st it was settled that the horse and arms of a dragoon were not to cost more than 6l., and on September 6th Waller received pay for 820 days as a Major-General, at the rate of 10l. per diem. By September 17th Dalbier had been reinforced, and hoped "to give a satisfactory account within a few days of that business," having commenced a bombardment and destroyed a great tower in the Old House. "That part of Basing House on the south called the New House is thought most seizable ; if we could gain that the other could not long hold out. There is a design to show the enemy there a gallant stratagem of war, but I had rather let them study to find it than let my pen tell tales out of school." The Clubmen were now rising for the King in Hants and Sussex, and vain hopes were formed of their coming to the relief of Basing House. Mr. W. Cawley and the Committee for Sussex on September 18th and 19th reported "divers outrageous proceedings" of 1000 Clubmen at Rowkeshill, near Chichester, enclosing the warrant issued by the Sussex Clubmen, and the declaration published by the men of Hants, Wilts, and Dorset. Colonel Norton was ordered to shift the quarters of the horse and foot under his command from Portsmouth to Bishop's Waltham, and to await orders from the Committee of both Kingdoms, to whom these documents were referred. The Committee for Hants, Sussex, and Surrey were directed to consult "how to prevent any inconvenience that may happen by reason of the Clubmen," and to sequester the estates of all recusants. Mr. Cawley again complained on October 13th of hindrances to the recruiting of Fairfax's army in Sussex. On September 25th we hear of Colonels Anthony Stapley, Morley, Norton, and others trying to disperse the Clubmen at Rowkeshill without bloodshed. Three days previously we read, "The Clubmen in Sussex and Hampshire are now numerous. A party is assigned to pacify them ; sure they have not so much to complain of as the more westerly parts, but if by this they draw troubles upon themselves, let them thank themselves."—*Mod. Intelligencer.*

The Hampshire Clubmen, although professedly neutral, were much more inclined to favour the King than the Parliament. "Idle Dick" Norton, otherwise Colonel Norton, took the field against them from Bishop's Waltham, with his cavalry and infantry, and on Wednesday, September 17th, Cromwell, who was now on his march from Devizes, sent him a strong reinforcement. On the 20th Cromwell and his brigade were at Andover. The reinforcement sent to the aid of Colonel Norton was the regiment commanded by Major Harrison, as will be seen by the following letter which appeared in the *City Scout*, of October 7th :—" The other news I hear of is, that of Wednesday last, the malignant (*i.e.*, Royalist) Clubmen rose and met at Loomer's Ash, within three miles of Winchester, countenanced by all the malignant gentry of Hampshire, to whom the Committee of Parliament for Hampshire, with noble Col. Norton, came, assisted by godly Major Harrison, with Colonel Fleetwood's regiment, where Colonel Norton used all means to send them home again; but the malignant towns of Bishop's Waltham and Petersfield would needs fight, who were soon surrounded by the horse. Then those Clubmen shot at them, which caused the horse to fall upon them, and killed four or five, wounded some others, and alarmed most of them. This day I hear worthy and religious Colonel Norton, with the Committee of Parliament, have given warrant to apprehend all the principall gentlemen of the Clubmen, to prevent further mischief. Winchester, the 29th of September, 1645."

The *Kingdom's Weekly Intelligencer* says that the horse "cut and hackt many of them, took all their chiefs, ringleaders, and about 1000 arms, which made their neighbours in Sussex to shrink in their heads, and we hear most of them are departed to their own homes."

The place where Colonel Norton dispersed the Clubmen is known as Waller's Ash, and is about 3½ or 4 miles distant from it. It is near the race course, and the first long tunnel on leaving Winchester by rail for London is called Waller's Ash Tunnel, from being near the place. The spot known as Waller's Ash is about three-quarters of a mile from it.

An Ordinance passed the Commons on September 30th to appoint Commissioners of Martial Law in Hants. Sir Henry Tichborne, who had been captured at sea after proving himself a loyal, skilful, and intrepid soldier in Ireland, was, together with Colonel Weare, on this day released from the Tower on exchange.

Sir Robert Peake, the Lieutenant-Governor at Basing, lost both his horse and groom at once.

"The Diary or Exact Journal" says, on September 20th, "Colonel Dalbeere is now intrenching himself before Basing House," and describes the Governor as "Robert Peek, who sold the pictures by Holborn Conduit," adding, "Sir Robert's groom is come in unto Dalbcir, and to make himself more welcome he hath brought with him his master's horse, on which he chargeth in the field, and another horse of good price."

The 21st of September, being Sunday, the besiegers assembled to listen to a sermon from their chaplain, who was then styled the Minister of the Army. The sermon was so much appreciated that it was sent next day to London, and was printed for John Wright, at the "King's Head," in the Old Bailey, on October 6th, 1645. A copy of it, with the imprimatur of James Crauford, September 26th, 1645, is now in the British Museum. Think not, oh most patient of readers, that I am about to inflict upon you 32 small qto. pages of small type. Far be it from me. The title is, "More Sulphur for Basing, or God will fearfully annoy and make quick riddance of His implacable enemies, surely, sorely, suddenly. Shewed in a Sermon at the Siege of Basing on the last Lord's Day, September 21, 1645. Together with a word of advice full of love and affection to the Clubmen of Hampshire. By William Beech, Minister of the Army there, Elect Minister of O., in the County of Suffolk." The motto of the sermon is Rev. xiv., 11. "And the smoke of their torment shall ascend evermore, and they shall have no rest day nor night which worship the beast and his image ;" the text being Psalm lxxxiii., 9, "Doe unto them as unto the Midianites, as to Sisera, as to Jabin at the Brooke of Kison." William Beech belonged to a Hampshire family, and had been a scholar under Dr. Love, at Winchester, to whose son, the Worshipful Mr. Nicholas Love, a Member of the Committee of Parliament for Hampshire, he dedicates his sermon in most fulsome language. Dr. Love is described as "the Learned and Most Orthodox Warden." Imploring the patronage of Mr. Nicholas Love, he says, "Malice hath dogged me these two years (the Lord knowes causelessly) by sea and land, and hath bespattered me exceedingly, and many are taken up and affected with Halifax Law."

These somewhat obscure concluding words seem to be synonymous with summary execution, as an old local law at Halifax in Yorkshire enacted that clothstealers to the amount of 13½d. were to be executed on the next market-day.

The preacher speaks of " the roaring of our cannon, or the terrible bursting asunder of the granado," no doubt alluding to the events of the week before, for on September 22nd, " By letters from Bazing, we were again advertised that Dalbier hath made divers shot against the Castle, and hath planted some batteries, and shot in some granadoes, some of which are believed to have done execution," as they in fact did, for " one granado burnt two hours before they could quench it."

The Rev. W. Beech " affirms that his county will be famous and sounding unto posterity for two things, viz., for sending burgesses and renowned champions that stood altogether, save one strange one that was lost, to defend it, and secondly, for two faithless garrisons and unworthy Catalines that laboured so much to destroy it.

" And ah ! poore Hampshire, deceived people, deluded countrymen ; for whom my spirit is in bitternesse, and my bowels yerne (for the first breathing of ayre I had among you), and once happy Hampshire, *Bona si sua norint Agricolæ* (*If farmers only knew when they were well off*), if they knew their happinesse, and how cans't thou endure a snake in thy bowels, a limbe of that cruell beast of Rome, and be silent and sleepe ? Nay, two garrisons of countrey destroyers, and not resolve against them, and not contribute your clubs towards the rooting of them out ?"

This pulpit eloquence somewhat failed of its desired effect, for on October 3, the " Scottish Dove" thus makes moan :—" The countrey people are base, and add nothing to Dalbier's assistance for their own freedome."

But a more famous soldier than Dalbier was at hand. Listen to the "Exact Journall"on Sept. 22nd :—" Colonel Dalbere hath raised a battery very near Basing House. He plays fiercely upon them, hath beat down one of the towers ; he wanted men and more great guns. It may be that Lieut.-General Cromwell may come or send him help."

Cromwell was even then ready to help surely and effectually. Prince Rupert had ridden forth from Bristol after its surrender on Sept. 11th, and soon afterwards Fairfax detached from Bath three columns, under Cromwell, Pickering, and Rainsborough, to take Devizes, Lacock House, and Berkeley Castle, all of which were successful. A fourth column reduced Farley Castle, near Trowbridge. Cromwell was despatched with a brigade of three regiments of foot and three of horse for the taking of certain Royalist garrisons, which, says Master Joshua Sprigge, " like vipers in the bowels, infested the midland parts. Of these Basing was the chief."

The tower above referred to as being destroyed formed part of the Old House, and was one of the largest belonging to the building. The "City Scout" of Sept. 30th says that " the great tower in the Old House was destroyed on Monday, Sept. 22nd, at which time he might have taken the House had he had a considerable party to fall on. Deserters and one of our troopers, which was then a prisoner in the House, and since released by his wife, for a month's pay, say that in the top of this tower was hid a bushel of Scots twopences, which flew about their ears. The Marquis of Winchester swears that Dolbier is a greater trouble to him than ever any was that ever came against the House."

The "Weekly Account" gives further details on Saturday, the 27th:—" From Basing it was certified that on Monday and Tuesday last, Colonel Dalbier played with the cannon very fierce upon the New House, and after many shots against the midst of the House, which loosened the bricks and made a long crack in the wall, he made another shot or two at the top of the House which brought down the high turret, the fall whereof so shook that part of the house, which before was weakened, that the outmost wall fell down all at once, insomuch that our men could see bedding and other goods fall out of the House into the court."

" The enemy in the house are extremely vext, yet at this time were they blockt up but on one side, and for want of horse they had often sallied out as far as Basingstoke and returned again, but by this they are confined to a less compass." According to the "CityScout," Dalbier had, on Friday, September 26th, not more than 1000 foot and some four troops of horse. He was unable to compass the house, the garrison of which was estimated to be half as numerous as were the besiegers, and could only besiege it on one side. On Tuesday, the 23rd, there was heavy firing, the result being "a very great breach," which was kept open by a vigorous cannonade. Colonel Dalbier now asked for further additions to his strength.

The "True Informer" hints at further destruction:—"Wednesday, September 24th. This day we understood by a messenger from Basing that Colonel D'Albere hath made several batteries against Basing House, or, as Aulicus calls it, Basing Castle. He hath beaten down one of the Towers of the Old House, and taken one of the works of the New House by storm. And we doubt not but that the House will, within 10 days, be in the Parliament's possession!"

"Mercuricus Veridicus" of Saturday, September 20th, adds:—"Those that come from the siege at Basing tell us that at the entering of one of the enemy's works in the New House, destroyed together with the Tower on September 22nd, they blew it up, but Colonell Dalbier made good the breach." The same newspaper somewhat prematurely reports the capture of the New House. "Mercurius Civicus" on the following day writes more cautiously:—"This evening we understand from Basing that Colonel Dalbier hath made several batteries upon Basing House, and hath beaten down one of the greatest Towers, and some say he hath taken the New House, but of that there is no certainty." The storming of the above-mentioned defence of the New House sufficiently accounts for these rumours. "The gallant stratagem of war," before referred to, was disclosed by the "True Informer" on September 24th:—"He hath a design to smoke them out, good store of straw being brought in from the country for that purpose."

The "Scottish Dove" two days later has the following:—"Colonel Dol Beer is in good action at Basing; he hath beaten down a Tower, and whilst he makes his works for the effecting his design he smokes them with the sulphur of brimstone, an emblem of their future vengeance!"

"Mercurius Veridicus" on Saturday, the 27th, is jubilant, yet cautious:—"But what? Will all the King's chiefest holds go to wrack together? Must they part with Basing House? All Papists? No treachery feared there? Yes, we are bidding fair for that, too, if the house will not burn the straw and other combustible matter will smoke, which, with advantage of wind, may seeme another element, and make the enemy scarce find their port-hole, but no more of this till we hear of the success. Dalbier sends into the house a compounded stifling smoake." Pass yet two days more, and "Mercurius Britannicus" adds insult to injury, "yet we must not call all yielding cowardice, because Winchester, the man of Basing, would needs be thought valiant, though he love not the smell of gunpowder, and therefore, in commiseration, Colonel D'Albier hath this last week tried to smoke him out with straw, just as they use to serve coles in old walls; and if this trick will not take, there is another nameless stratagem in acting, for the gallant Colonel is resolved to have his pay."

The "Parliament Scout" thus describes the siege on Sept 30th:

"They are all Papists in that garrison, and if there were purgatory upon earth, the Papists do find it and feel it there, for besides the thick and perpetual darkness which the wet and smoking straw doth make, the burning of brimstone and arsenic and other dismal ingredients doth infinitely annoy the besieged, which makes them to gnash their teeth for indignation; in the meantime the cannons do perpetually thunder one against another. On every side desolation dwells about them, and to subdue the place there are those things are put in execution which the nature of man doth tremble at."

The editor of "Perfect Passages" on Oct. 1st seems quite satisfied with the state of affairs:—

"800 are ordered by the Committee to be sent to strengthen D'Albere against Basing. Good reason he should have them, he goes on so hopefully."

On Friday, Oct. 3rd, the "Moderate Intelligencer" alludes to the siege:—"We hear the business before Bazing goes well! A battery upon one side, a breach made, if he had men to enter and storm, but they are wanting, that is a few more than they have!"

The "Exact Journal" says, on Oct. 4th:—"From Bazing we are informed that Dalbier expecteth more supplies, without which he cannot so easily go through the task he hath undertaken."

From "Mercurius Veridicus" (Mercury the Truthteller) of October 4th we learn that a heavy and effectual fire was maintained by the besiegers, and that the garrison were losing heart:—"I thought not at this time to have mentioned Bazing, for the defendants have been so used to the strong breath of old priests and Jesuits that straw and sulphur will not stifle them out of the house, therefore Dalbier daily sends pellets amongst them, and hath beat down part of the house, and so terrified some that they have stolen out of the house and got quite away. Others have come from Wallingford to us, and protest that they will never fight against the Parliament. No less than eight came in thus with their horse one morning, and say that more will come, and many are gone to other garrisons of ours."

The "Scottish Dove" of the same date says:— "Basing House is still besieged, not yet stormed, but continual battery, so that they have certainly made some breaches, and were it not that the besieged have good hopes to be relieved they would quickly yield it. Provisions are scarce with them, and want will make them do anything, but all is in God's hand, who guides all things by His own will." Things were looking badly for the Marquis.

CHAPTER XXIX.—CROMWELL AND HIS BRIGADE—COLONELS HAMMOND, FLEETWOOD AND HARRISON—HUGH PETERS—CROMWELL SUMMONS WINCHESTER—THE CASTLE BESIEGED—BISHOP CURLE—SIEGE OPERATIONS—BOMBARDMENT—PARLEY AND SURRENDER—BOOTY AND SPOIL.—HUGH PETERS AT WESTMINSTER—TROUBLES AT WINCHESTER.

We have before referred to the surrender of Bristol on September 11th, 1645, and noted the despatch of Cromwell at the head of his brigade of three regiments of foot and 2000 horse, with a view to the reduction of certain Royalist garrisons, of which Basing, if not the chief, was by no means the least important.

The character of Cromwell we need not discuss. Leave we Carlyle and others to that task. A portrait of "Old Noll" hangs at Hackwood House, not far from that of his gallant foe the Marquis, wherefrom all beholders may see what manner of man he was. Sir Philip Warwick thus describes his personal appearance in November, 1640, some five years before this time : "I came into the House one morning well clad, and perceived a gentleman speaking whom I knew not, very ordinarily apparelled, for it was a plain cloth suit that seemed to have been made by an ill country tailor. His linen was very plain, and not very clean, and I remember a speck or two of blood upon his little band (a linen tippet, properly the shirt-collar of those days), which was not much larger than his collar ; his hat was without a hat band, his stature was of a good size, his sword stuck close to his side, his countenance swoln and reddish, his voice sharp and untuneable, and his eloquence full of fervour." Mr. Hyde, afterwards Lord Clarendon, when Chairman of a Committee of the House saw another phase of his character : "His whole carriage was so tempestuous, and his behaviour so insolent, that the Chairman found himself obliged to reprehend him, and to tell him that if he (Mr. Cromwell) proceeded in the same manner he (Mr. Hyde) would presently adjourn the Committee and the next morning complain to the House of him."

A stern man, unyielding, and cast in iron mould, as the "merciless assault of Basing" and the storming of Drogheda give proof ; yet, as we would fain believe, a man of personal piety, and courteous to an enemy in defeat, as the following anecdote clearly shows : —" As the garrison of Hillesdon House, near Newport Pagnell, were evacuating it after the surrender, one of the soldiers snatched off Sir William Smyth's hat. He immediately complained to Cromwell of the man's insolence and breach of the capitulation. 'Sir,' said Cromwell, 'if you can point out the man or I can discover him, I promise you he shall not go unpunished. In the meantime,' taking off a new beaver which he had on his own head, ' be pleased to accept of this hat instead of your own.' "

" The tears of Cromwell appear to have been very constitutional, and must have produced a marvellous contrast on his rough-featured and heavy countenance ! "

"This brave commander, by reason of his resolution and gallantry in his charges, is called by the King's soldiers Ironsides. So Winstanley, in his "Worthies." says, ' One thing that made his brigade so invincible was his arming them so well, as whilst they assured themselves they could not be overcome, it assured them to overcome their enemies. He himself, as they called him Ironsides, needed not to be ashamed of a nickname that so often saved his life.' Heath also calls *him* by that name, and not his troop."

"In the beginning of November, 1642, the regiment had reached the number of 1000 picked men. Whitelocke thus describes them : —'He had a brave regiment of horse of his countrymen, most of them freeholders and freeholders' sons, and who upon matter of conscience engaged in this quarrel and under Cromwell, and thus, being well armed within by the satisfaction of their own consciences, and without by good iron arms, they would as one man charge firmly and fight desperately.' In May, 1643, a newspaper writer says, 'As for Colonel Cromwell, he hath 2000 more brave men, well disciplined. No man swears but he pays his 12d.; if he be drunk, he is set in the stocks or worse; if one calls the other "Roundhead," he is cashiered; insomuch that the countries where they come leap for joy of them, and come in and join with them. How happy would it be if all the forces were thus disciplined!'"

"A colonel of foot received 1l. 10s. the day; a lieutenant-colonel, 15s. the day; a sergeant-major (the present Major), 9s. the day; a captain, 15s. the day; a colonel of horse, 1l. 10s. the day, and for six horses 1l. 1s. the day; a captain of horse, 1l. 4s. the day, and for six horses, 1l. 1s. the day." Field officers drew the pay of a captain in addition to their own, besides other perquisites.

Cromwell's own regiment was steelclad, back and breast, with headpieces. Each man had a brace of pistols, the officers more, and each troop was 100 strong. Its officers were, Lieut.-General Cromwell, Major Huntingdon, Captains Jenkins, Middleton, John Reynolds, and Blackwell. The three regiments of foot under Cromwell's command were those of Colonels Pickering, Montagu, and Sir Hardress Waller. These regiments had been long together, and had seen much service in company. At Marston Moor "on the left was drawn up the Earl of Manchester's army from the Associated Counties under the general command of Lieut.-General Cromwell, consisting of three brigades of foot commanded severally by Colonels Montagu, Russell, and Pickering."

In a fiery charge by Rupert both on front and flank "the brigades of Colonels Montagu, Russell, and Pickering especially distinguished themselves, standing when charged like a wall of brass, and letting fly small shot like hail upon the Royalists, and yet, as an old account assures us, not a man of their brigades was slain."

This brigade sustained a severe check at the second battle of Newbury on the 27th of October, 1644, but on Naseby Field the Lord General's, Montagu's, and Pickering's regiments formed the right centre. Skippon's, Sir Hardress Waller's, and Pride's regiments formed the left centre. During the fight Sir H. Waller's regiment was broken by Prince Rupert. At the siege of Bridgewater, in July, 1645, the regiments of Cromwell, Pickering, Montagu, Waller, Hammond, and others attacked on the Somersetshire side, Lieut.-Colonel Hewson, of Pickering's, leading a forlorn hope. At Bristol, in the following September, the same regiments were to storm on both sides of Lawford Gate, and during the rest of the month they had simply marched from victory to victory. Colonel Montagu had raised his own regiment in 1643, took part in the storming of Lincoln, and distinguished himself at Marston Moor and Naseby. He is better known as the Earl of Sandwich, who brought over King Charles to England, and perished at the battle of Solebay in 1672. The officers of his regiment in 1647 were Lieut.-Colonel Grimes, Major Kelsey (since Major Rogers), Captains Blethen, Munney, Biscoe, Rogers, Wilks (slain at Basing, now Captain Cadwell), Thomas Disney, and Sanders. He was much influenced by Colonel Pickering in favour of the numerous lay preachers of his day, but changed his opinion on this point after Colonel Pickering's death. He disapproved of the King's execution, but held several important offices under the Commonwealth. In "A Narrative of the late Parliament (so-called)" we read as follows of Colonel Montagu and several others who played a prominent part at Basing:—

"Colonel Montagu, as one of the Council, 1000l. per annum; Commissioner of the Treasury, 1000l.; as General-at-Sea, 1095l.; in all, 3095l. per annum.

"Sir Gilbert Pickering, as one of the Council, 1000l. per annum: Chamberlain at Court, and Steward at Westminster.

"Lord Lisle, as one of the Commissioners of the Great Seal, 1000l. per annum.

"Sir Hardress Waller, as Major-General of the Army, 365l.; Colonel of Foot, 365l.; in all, 730l. per annum, besides other advantages."

In a list of "Persons not thought meet to be in command, though they much desire it, and are of such poor principles and so unfit to make rulers of that they would not have been set with the dogs of the flock, as Job speaks in another case (Job xxx., 1), if the Army and others who pretended to be honest had kept close to their former good and honest principles," mention is made of "Colonel Jephson, a man of better principles than the former, but for his good service in voting for a King (Cromwell), is lately sent Ambassador to Sweden."

Colonel John Pickering was a man of small stature. The celebrated Hewson was his Lieut.-Colonel. The other officers of this regiment were, in 1647, Major Jubbs, Captains Axtel, Husbands (now Captain Grimes), Toppington, Carter, Silverwood, and Price. Of Colonel Pickering, Sir Samuel Luke, so satirised in Hudibras, thus writes to the Earl of Essex after the storming of Hilsden House:—" We had no officer killed or hurt, save only Colonel Pickering, and that only a little struck under the chin with a musket ball. But, thanks be to God, he was dressed before I came away, and was very merry and cheerful."

Sprigge has an anagram—" In God I reckon happines—Johannes Pickering," together with some bad verses on the death of Colonel Pickering, which was caused by an epidemic which scourged Fairfax's army at the close of the year 1645. Colonel Pickering was reckoned one of the bravest and best officers in the army, and his death was very generally deplored. Sir Hardress Waller was concerned in the publication of the Army Manifesto in 1647, and two years later was one of the Regicides. At the Restoration he was brought to trial, and received sentence of death, but was not executed. The officers of his regiment were Lieut.-Col. Cottesworth, Major Smith, Captains Howard, Wade, Ashe, Gorges, Clark, Thomas, and Hodden. The three cavalry regiments were those of Colonels Hammond, Fleetwood, and Sheffield. Colonel Robert Hammond was the second son of Robert Hammond, Esq., of Chertsey, in Surrey, and was born in 1621. He spent three years at Oxford, but left without a degree. He has been well described as being " the nephew of two uncles," one of whom, Dr. Henry Hammond, was the favourite chaplain of the King, while the other, Thomas Hammond, had formerly commanded the 40th troop of horse, was now in 1645 Lieut.-General of the Ordnance in the service of the Parliament, and was afterwards one of the Regicides. Influenced by these two relatives, and by his wife, who was a daughter of John Hampden, Hammond's views were somewhat undecided. His uncle, Thomas Hammond, induced him to serve the Parliament in 1642, and obtained for him commissions, first as captain, and afterwards as major, under Col. Edward Massey at the siege of Gloucester. He here killed Major Gray for giving him the lie, but was acquitted by a Council of War in the Lord General's army. He was wounded at the first battle of Newbury, and was "shot with a brace of bullets in the arm" at Bristol, in September, 1645. He also took part in the second battle of Newbury, and greatly distinguished himself at Bristol. We shall hear more of him at Basing. Cromwell used to write to him as "Dear Robin." The officers of his regiment were, in 1647, Lieut.-Col. Thomas Eure, Major Sanders, Captains Disney, Charn, Smith, John Boyce, Puckle, Stratton, and Rolfe.

Colonel Charles Fleetwood was the son of Sir William Fleetwood, cupbearer to Charles I., and comptroller of Woodstock-park. He was appointed Governor of Bristol after its surrender to Fairfax, in 1645, did good service as Lieut.-General of horse at Worcester fight, on Sept. 3rd, 1651, commanded in Ireland, and married Ireton's widow. He aided the Restoration, and died in 1692. When he became Governor of Bristol, Major Harrison succeeded him in command of his regiment, every trooper in which was armed with pistols. The other officers were, in 1647, Captains Coleman, Laughton, Zanchy, and Howard.

Here is a picture of Harrison and his troop in 1648: "Another troop of horse was in good order drawn up between Alresford and Farnham, by which His Majesty passed. It was to bring up the rear. In the head of it was the captain gallantly mounted and armed; a velvet monteir was on his head, a new buff coat upon his back, and a crimson silk scarf about his waist, richly fringed, who, as the King passed him by an easy pace as delighted to see men well horsed and armed, the captain gave the King a bow with his head all à soldade, which His Majesty requited." Asking who the officer was, and being informed that he was Major Harrison, "the King immediately turned round, and looked at him so long, and so attentively, that the major, confused, retired behind the troops to avoid his scrutiny. 'That man,' said Charles, 'looks like a true soldier, I have some judgment on faces, and feel I have harboured wrong thoughts of him.'" Harrison escorted the King through Farnham and Bagshot, to Windsor. He was afterwards one of the Regicides, and on April 20th, 1653, said to Speaker Lenthall:

"Sir, I will lend you a hand" to leave the chair at the dissolution of the Rump Parliament, being as he was in command of "some twenty or thirty" grim musketeers. A member of the Council of State on November 1st, of the same year, he was the leader of the Anabaptists and Fifth Monarchy men. Imprisoned by Cromwell, he was put to death at the Restoration. "Several times he cried out as he was drawn along, that he suffered in the most glorious cause in the world;" and when a low wretch asked him "Where's your good old cause now?" he replied "Here it is!" clapping his hand on his heart, "and I am going to seal it with my blood!" He was cut down alive, his bowels torn out whilst he was alive, and then his quivering heart held up to the people! An heroic man in truth!

Col. Thomas Sheffield was a younger son of the Earl of Mulgrave. His regiment was in 1644 composed as follows: Colonel Sheffield's troop, 11 officers and 84 troopers; Captain Sheffield's, 10 officers and 70 troopers; Captain Hagles', 10 officers and 70 troopers; Captain Fynnes' troop, 11 officers and 71 troopers; Captain Robotham's, 9 officers and 63 troopers; Captain Wogone's troop, 10 officers and 53 troopers. In all, 61 officers and 414 troopers. The officers of this regiment in 1647 were Colonel Thomas Sheffield, Major Findler, Captains Robotham, Rainsborough, Martin, and Evelyn. Colonel Sheffield's standard bore the device of an armed horseman, with the motto "Deo Duce, Nil Desperandum."

Captain Richard Deane, who was afterwards killed in a naval engagement against the Dutch, was Comptroller of the Ordnance. (See his "Life," Longmans and Co., 1870.) "Master Hugh Peters, Chaplain to the Train of Artillery," must not be forgotten. He was "a man concerning whom," says Carlyle, "the reader has heard so many falsehoods." Born at Fowey, in Cornwall, he was publicly whipped and expelled from the University of Cambridge, and was obliged to leave England, having been prosecuted by a butcher in St. Sepulchre's parish for supplanting him in the affections of his wife. After some years spent in Holland and America, he returned to London in 1641, and became chaplain to Lord Brooke's regiment. He was the very pontiff of burlesque pulpiteers, and was indefatigable in stirring up the hatred of the soldiers against the King, whom he styled "Barabbas," comparing the army to Christ! In Ireland "he led a brigade against the rebels, and came off with honour and victory." He counselled the destruction of Stonehenge, said that the sword contained all the laws of England, and at Naseby rode from rank to rank "with a Bible in one hand and a pistol in the other," exhorting the men to do their duty. At the siege of Bridgewater he "improved the Sunday as much by Mars as Mercury." Clarendon calls him "the ungodly confessor," who contrived "the woeful tragedy" of the two Hothams. He was constantly employed to carry despatches announcing various victories. The Royalists called him "the ecclesiastical newsmonger." He had a few days before received 5*l*. for bringing "the good news" of the surrender of Winchester. Here is a specimen of one of his sermons: "He took for his text, 'Bind your Kings with chains, and your Nobles in fetters of iron.' Beloved, said he, this is the last Psalm but one, and the next Psalm hath six verses and 12 Hallelujahs—praise ye the Lord. And for what? Look into my text! There you have the reason for it. Because the Kings were bound in chains!" Such were the pulpit utterances of an Army Chaplain of the first class two centuries ago! Peters was one of the chief instigators of the execution of the King, which afterwards cost him his head on October 16th, 1660. Some have said that he was one of the masked executioners of Charles I. The following epigram shows what the Cavaliers thought of him. Dunn was the public executioner.

"Behold, the last and best edition
Of Hugh, the author of sedition,
No full of errors, 't was not fit
To read, till Dunn corrected it.
But now 'tis perfect—ay, and more,
'Tis better bound than 'twas before.
Now loyalty may gladly sing,
Exit rebellion in a string;
And if you say, you say amiss,
Hugh now an Independent is!"

After suppressing the Clubmen near Winchester, Colonels Norton and Harrison joined Cromwell's brigade, and now let "Perfect Passages," of October 1st, speak:—

"Lieut.-General Cromwell came before Winchester on the last Lord's Day at night, and with him a party of horse and foot, viz., of horse his own regiment, Colonel Sheffield's regiment, Colonel Fleetwood's and Colonel Norton's regiments, with some horse taken out of several other regiments to make them complete, 2000 horse; and of foot, Colonel Montague's regiment, Colonel Pickering's, and Colonel Waller's. Three regiments of foot."

Some of Colonel Okey's Dragoons were amongst the horse taken from other regiments. They had done the Parliament good service by lining Lantford hedges at Naseby Fight. Their officers were Colonel Okey. Major Moore, Captains Mercer, Abbotts, Farre, Bridge, Woggan, Shirmager, Captain Turpin (since Captain Neale). Col. Okey was afterwards surrendered to the English Government, and executed in a most barbarous manner, the principal witness against him being a former chaplain to his regiment, named Downing.

Cromwell writes as follows "To the Right Honourable Sir Thomas Fairfax, General of the Parliament's Army, these :—

"Winchester, 6th October, 1645.

"Sr,—I came to Winchester on the Lord's Day, the 28th of September, with Colonel Pickering, commanding his own, Colonel Montague's, and Sir Hardress Waller's regiments. After some dispute with the Governor, we entered the town."

As soon as he arrived, Cromwell wrote to Mr. William Longland, the Mayor, demanding admission into the city, and received a speedy answer :—

"Sir,—I come not to this City but with a full resolution to save it and the Inhabitants thereof from ruine. I have comaunded the Souldyers upon payne of death that noe wrong bee done, wch I shall strictly observe, only I expect you give me entrance into the City, wthout necessitateing mee to force my way, wich yf I doe, then it will not be in my power to save yon or it. I expect yor answeare wth in halfe an houre, and rest Your servant,

Sept. 28th, 1645. OLIVER CROMWELL.

Five o'clock at night. To the Mayor of the City of Winchester."

The answer to the said letter :—"Sr,—I have received yor Letter by yor Trumpett, and in the behalfe of the Citizens and Inhabitants return you hearty thanks for yor favourable expression therein. But wth all I am to signifie unto you that the delivry up of the City is not in my power, it being under the comand of the right hoble. the Lord Ogle, who hath the millitary Governt. thereof. In the mean tyme I shall use my best endeavour with the Lord Ogle to perform the contents of yor letter concerning the City, and rest

Your most humble servant,

WM. LONGLAND, Mayor.

Winton, Sept. 28, 1645."

The garrison was prepared for vigorous resistance. The "True Informer" stated on October 4th, 1645, "The enemy disputed, the city being fortified as well as the Castle, but the gate being fired our men entered." The "Exact Journal" wrote on October 7th, "The city made some opposition, contrary to his expectation, but having fired the bridge he quickly found a means to enter and subdue it." Another writer says, "Wee'l now come to Winchester. When Lieut.-General Cromwell came before it he found the town fortified, and the enemy upon their works. Here was found short dispute before entred, yet not long, but the enemy was driven off, and fled to the Castle, which our men close begirt, and have sunk two mines, and began their batteries." The besiegers entered the city on the morning of Monday, September 29th. "with the townsmen's consent we have cooped up in the Castle 120 horse and 400 foot, and all the malignant gentry and clergy of this Hampshire and Sussex, with many Papists and Jesuits. It is hoped the Parliament will give order these great delinquents shall trouble them no more!"

On Wednesday, October 1st, 1645, we read, " This day by letters from Winchester we understood that at General Cromwell's first coming against Winchester, having notice that Doctor Kirl, Bishop of that diocese, was in the city, sent to him, and proffered that in respect to his cloth (if he pleased) he should have liberty to come out of the town, and he would protect him from violence ; which the Bishop not accepting of, our men soon after forced their passage into the city, and the Bishop fled into the Castle, with the souldiers. The next day, when our battery was placed, the Bishop was so far awakened in his judgment by the thundering of the cannon that he sent a message to Lieut.-General Cromwell to this effect, ' That the Bishop was sorry that he had not accepted of Lieut.-General Cromwell's former proffer, and being better advised, did now desire the benefit thereof, &c.' Unto which answer was returned that he had refused the former proffer, and was gone with the soldiers into the Castle; he was not capable of that favour, and in case he were taken in the Castle he was to be esteemed a prisoner of war, and just now (the batteries being raised) be liable to such conditions as the rest of those that were in the Castle should be brought unto!"

The "Parliament's Post" thus moralises on Tuesday, December 7th: "The Bishop, who had before a guard to secure his person (with certain conditions), is now like to partake amongst them in the common distress. There is but little happiness to be expected from late repentance!"

Hugh Peters, Cromwell's chaplain, reports that amongst the prisoners taken at Winchester were "also Dr. Curle, the Bishop of Winchester . . . . and his chaplain, who were in their long gowns and cassocks." The Bishop and his clergy were referred to the mercy of the Parliament. Dr. Milner tells us that Bishop Curle retired unmolested, though he lost his whole income. He lived on the charity of friends, more especially that of his sister, at whose house at Soberton he died in 1650. "A reverend prelate, who resided amidst his flock, even in these days of danger and trouble, and quitted not his charge, until he was suffered no longer to continue in it."

Winchester Castle stood upon the site of the present Barracks, and the County Hall, the pride of the shire, was formerly a portion of it. In the County Hall hangs what is called "Arthur's Round Table," made of stout oak planks and perforated by many bullets, which are said to have been fired by Cromwell's soldiers. The picturesque West Gate is now the principal remnant of the ancient defences of the city but until 1824 the picturesque ruins of the city wall, intermingled with shrubs and ash trees, claimed the attention of every stranger. Running directly north from the West Gate, it retained in many places its original height, the ruins of several turrets, and its copings of freestone. Beneath this wall was the ditch or fosse, which extended as far as the North Gate, under the palace of Henry II., and was originally a stew for the King's fish. The entire site is now covered with houses.

The weather, as we shall presently see, favoured the besiegers, being unusually fine for the time of year. Cromwell writes: "I summoned the Castle; was denied, whereupon we fell to prepare batteries—which we could not perfect (some of our guns being out of order) until Friday following. Our battery was six guns, which being finished—after firing one round I sent in a second summons for a treaty, which was refused."

"On Saturday last, October 4th, Lieutnant-General Cromwell was in a posture of parlying with Col. Ogle, for surrender of Winchester Castle, Lieutenant-General Cromwell having planted his morter-piece and great cannon against the Castle, and one party at St. Thomas's going to the Minster and another at St. Lawrence, as also good strength on both the battle sides."

Hugh Peters says that "at the first Sir William Ogle, Governor of the Castle (lately made a Lord by his Majesty), refused upon summons to accept of any parly at all."

The following reply was returned to Cromwell's second summons to surrender: "Sir,— I have received a said summons, and desire that this inclosed may be conveyed from

Your servant,
Winton Castle, 4th October, 1645. OGLE."

"Sir,—Upon the opening of your sad message by your drum, there was a mistake between your men and mine, for there was a man making an escape from the Castle, at whom your men and mine did shoot, not knowing in the dark who he was, and the man is killed. OGLE."

The besiegers' batteries opened fire on the morning of Saturday, October 4th, and ere long Sir William Ogle hauled down the red flag which had been hoisted as a token of defiance, "and a treaty was going on for surrender, but just in the nick of time came the convoy into Lieutenant-General Cromwell, from Reading, which the enemy seeing (having had a promise of reliefs) hung out the red flag again and would not treat, whereupon Lieut.-General Cromwell prepared to storm. Sir Wm. Waller came to Winchester with the convoy, and was that night with the General."

Sunday, October 5th, must have been an exciting day in Winchester. Says Hugh Peters: "The Lord's Day we spent in preaching and prayer, whilst our guns were battering." Other accounts say: "Thereupon our forces began to play with the cannon, and played six continually, one after another, as fast they could charge and discharge, and made 200 cannon shot in one day against the Castle." The garrison were not idle, for, according to Hugh Peters, "The chiefest street of the town the enemy played upon, whereby divers passengers were wounded and some killed; in which street my quarters being, I have that cause to bless God for my preservation." Either upon the Saturday or the Sunday "a breach was made, the enemy sallied out, and beat us off from our guns, which were soon recovered again." Shell-practice was evidently very effective on this eventful Sunday.

"The flag was hanged out on Sunday, 5th October instant, the enemy being confident that a party was come to relieve them; we threw granadoes into the House, which broke down the mansion house in many places, cutt off a Commiss ry of theirs by the thighs, the most austere and wretched instrument in that country, and at last blew up their flag of defiance into the air, and tore the pinnacle in pieces upon which it stood."

Hugh Peters' account is, "They threw in granadoes which did very much good execution; one of them broke into the great hall and killed three men, and another beate the red flag of defiance which the enemy had hung out all to pieces, so that none could discerne what became of it."

"Summons was refused. . . . And another summons God sent them in the middle of our battery; his (Lord Ogle's) Lady (to whom our Lord General had given leave to come forth, and had gone some miles out of the town), died; by whom the Governor had during her life one thousand pounds a year with her, lost by her death."

The end of all this artillery practice was that Lieutenant-General Cromwell played hard against them with his great ordnance, and battered the house in many places, amongst the rest one breach (near the Black Tower) was so wide that 30 men might go in abreast, and then the enemy cried out "A parley, a parley, for the Lord's sake. O for God's sake grant a parley; articles, articles, O let us have articles, for God's sake; we will yield to any reasonable articles: will you not hear us for a parley?" "Indeed, the guns played so fast, and the business was so well followed, that we could not well hear them, and they, perceiving what a strait they were in, and how the house began to tumble upon their heads, thought that we should presently enter, and that they should be all killed."

One account says that this request for a parley was made on Monday night, but Cromwell himself says, "We went on with our work, and made a breach in the wall near the Black Tower; which, after about 200 shot, we thought stormable; and purposed on Monday morning to attempt it. On Sunday night, about ten of the clock, the Governor beat a parley, desiring to treat."

Mr. Francis Baigent, of Winchester, says, "The position of the tower designated the Black Tower is unknown. It could not have been the one at the back of the County Hall, as in an old lease I have seen it mentioned by another name. The Black Tower was probably one near the old drawbridge, or south of it."

Lord Ogle thus requested a parley:—

"Sir,—I have received formerly a letter from you, wherein you desire to avoid the effusion of Christian blood, to which you received my answer that I was as willing as yourself. But having received no reply (to advance) your desires, I have thought fit to desire a treaty whereby we might pitch up some means, both for the effecting of that, and the preservation of this place. And that I may receive your letter with all convenience, I desire that neither officer or soldiers of your party may come off their guards, and I shall take the like course with mine. Sir, I am.

Your humble servant,   OGLE.
Winton Castle, at eight at night,
October 5, 1645."

"Mercurius Britannicus," September 29 to October 6, 1645, speaks thus:—

"The two famous names of Fairfax and Massey united are a sure charm for victory. Put Cromwell in too, and then 'tis infallible. The people of Winchester know it well enough, and therefore they in the Castle cried a parley, and if that end not the difference, the next cry must be quarter."

Cromwell hereupon despatched Colonel Hammond and Major Harrison to draw up Articles of Surrender, with Sir Edward Ford, the Royalist High Sheriff of Sussex, and a Major of the garrison. The whole night was spent in negotiations, the victors wishing to secure Sir Edward Ford and Colonel Bennet as prisoners. The following terms were agreed upon: Lord Ogle was to deliver the Castle with all the ordnance, arms, and ammunition therein to the appointed officers, "without any embezzlement, waste, or spoil," at 3.0 p.m. on Monday,

October 6th. That the Governor and other officers should march forth with their arms only. That Lord Ogle should have his own colours, 100 fixed arms for his own guard, and 100 men to carry them as far as Woodstock. Hostages were to be given for the safe return of this convoy. That all the common soldiers should depart without their arms. Lord Ogle and all commissioned officers to have safe conveyance with horses, arms, and goods as far as Woodstock, six carriages being allowed to them. Dr. Curle, the Bishop of Winchester, and all the Cantory to be referred to the mercy of the Parliament. All officers, gentlemen, clergymen, and inhabitants of the city of Winchester, and all officers within the guards, desiring it, may be, at their own time, free from all violence and injury of the Parliament's forces. And the Castle being Sir William Waller's, the Lieut.-General delivered it into his possession by the Articles of Surrender, bearing date October 5th.

"What remained of the Castle," says a modern writer, "was conferred by the Parliament upon Sir William Waller, one of their partisans and generals. He was also brother-in-law to Sir Henry Tichborne, its real owner, who was in it during the siege, whose other property as well as this they had previously confiscated. Either this Sir William, or his son of the same name, sold the hall to certain feoffees for the purpose of a public hall for the county of Hants, and the rest of the Castle to the Corporation of Winchester."

On one point both Puritans and Cavaliers quite agreed, viz., that the defence was not as vigorous as it might have been. The Castle was "very well garrisoned," says Guthrie. "It surrendered on easy conditions," according to Clarendon. Wood thinks that it "was treacherously given up," and it was "likewise delivered on composition" says "Rusticus."

Cromwell writes thus to General Fairfax:—

"Sir,—This is the addition of another mercy. You see God is not weary in doing you good. I confess, Sir, His favour to you is as visible when He comes by His power upon the hearts of your enemies, making them quit places of strength to you, as when He gives courage to your soldiers to attempt hard things. His goodness in this is much to be acknowledged; for the Castle was well manned with 680 horse and foot, there being near 200 gentlemen, officers, and their servants, well victualled with 15cwt. of cheese, very great store of wheat and beer, near 20 barrels of powder, seven pieces of cannon; the works were exceeding good and strong. It's very likely it would have cost much blood to have gained it by storm. We have not lost 12 men. This is repeated to you that God may have all the praise, for it's all His due. Sir, I rest your most humble servant,
OLIVER CROMWELL.
Winchester, 6th October, 1645."

Hugh Peters took mental notes of all that passed. He says: "I was forthwith sent into the Castle to take a view of it. . . . Where I found a piece of ground improved to the best advantage, for when we had entered by our battery (or breach) we had six distinct works and a drawbridge to pass through, so that it was doubtless a very strong piece, very well victualled. The Castle was manned with near 700 men, divers of them Reformadoes (officers whose regiments had been disbanded); the chief men I saw there were Viscount Ogle . . . Sir John Pawlet, an old souldier; Sir William Courtney, and Colonel Bennett, also Dr. Curle, the Bishop of Winchester, . . . and his chaplain, who were in their long gowns and cassocks."

"There were in the Castle 700 men, officers and common soldiers. There was a great wall where the breach was made, which our forces must have entered, and three works, each higher than the other, before they could have taken the Castle; and by the judgment of knowing and experienced soldiers, they had made it the strongest architect (i.e., building) for that purpose, that the like is not in England; we lost not above two men in all the time of the playing so fiercely that day, nor about 12 or 14 in all the siege before it, which is to be lookt upon a great mercy."

The victors found in the Castle plenty of ammunition and provisions. They secured "four great pieces of ordnance, three less pieces, 17 barrels of powder, 2000lb. weight of musket bullets, 80 cwt. of match, 700 muskets (500 fire-arms), 200 pikes, halberds, and other weapons, 200 pairs of bandoliers, 100 horses, 15,000lb. weight of cheese, 80 lbs. of butter, either 40 or 118 quarters of wheat and meal, 700 lbs. of biskets, 30 loads of wood, 40 quarters of charcoal, 30 bushels of sea-coal for the smith, four quarters of beef, ready killed, and much powdered, 38 hogsheads of beef and pork, 14 sheep, great store of (20 bushels) oatmeal, 10 tun (qrs.) of salt, three or four hogsheads of French wines, 112 hogsheads of strong beer, 70 dozen candles, with divers crucifixes and Popish pictures." The surrender was delayed by the revelry of the vanquished Cavaliers. "Our men were to enter at eight of the clock the next morning, but they could not take possession till two in the afternoon, by reason the Governor and some of the officers, being unwilling to leave any wine behind them, had made themselves drunk." "700 men marched out of the Castle, and Viscount Ogle as drunk as a beggar." Hugh Peters said in the House of Commons: "Mr. Speaker. I cam from Winchester the last night late, but I had come sooner had not my Lord Ogle and his company been so unwilling to part with their sack and strong beer, of which they drank so liberally at their farewell that few of them, as it is their manner, could get up their horses without help, for the agreement was for their marching out at three o'clock, but it proved late through their debauchery."

Nearly 700 men, divers of them Reformadoes, marched out of the Castle, amongst whom were Viscount Ogle, the Governor, Sir John Pawlet, an old soldier, Sir William Courtney, Colonel Bennet, and Dr. Curle, Bishop of Winchester, "who came forth to our quarters in the morning," and with whom Hugh Peters "spent an hour or two, who with tears and much importunity desired the Lieut.-General's favour to excuse his not accepting the offer which he made unto him at his first entering the town; he desired of me a guard to his lodgings, lest the soldiers should use violence to him and his Chaplain, who were in their long gowns and cassocks, and he was accordingly safely conveyed home." Some of the departing Cavaliers both at Winchester and at Longford House complained of having been plundered by the soldiers, contrary to the articles of surrender. The stolen property was restored to its owners, and six troopers were convicted of the robbery at Blandford. One to whose lot it fell was executed next morning at the head of the army. He died very penitently, and his execution made a deep impression on his comrades. The five others were marched under escort to Oxford, and there handed over to the Governor, Sir Thomas Glemham, who sent them back, "with an acknowledgment of the Lieut.-General's nobleness."

As the prisoners taken at Alton took service under Waller, and fought desperately against their former comrades at Arundel, so Cromwell gained recruits at Winchester. "There went forth of the Castle, besides officers, 600 common soldiers, most of whom either went to their own homes or took up arms for the Parliament, so that it is thought the Governor will not have above one hundred (200) with him by the time he comes to his place of rendezvous (Woodstock). It did much affect us to see what an enemy we had to deal with, who, themselves being judges, could not choose but say that their God is not as our God."

Cromwell at once despatched Mr. Spavin, the Lieut.-General's Secretary, and Hugh Peters, Minister to the Army, with despatches to London. Mr. Spavin, "the messenger that brought the good news, had 5 l. given him by the Commons. A very good work to reward all men that do service." Intelligence of the surrender reached Fairfax at Lyme Regis in Dorsetshire. On his arrival at Westminster the Commons "forthwith called Mr. Peters into the House, who went in attended with the Serjeant-at-Arms with the mace before him, when the Speaker (Lenthall), giving him thanks for his unwearied labours in the preservation of this kingdom, and assuring him that the House took care for him who had so often brought them good tidings and hazarded himself so much, told him that he had liberty to speak freely what he had in command from the Lieut.-General. Mr. Peters spake in the House," and from his report many of the foregoing details have been gathered. He added, "The fruit of what is already done, amongst the rest what I saw upon the way: all sorts travelling freely upon their occasions to their own homes with carriages and wains, many inns filled with guests. The former face of things returning upon us in several kinds; yea, now we may ride with safety from Dover to the middle of Devonshire." Cromwell had ordered Peters to state certain facts, so "that you should be truly informed concerning the payment of the army, it being generally reported they are completely paid, and that army constantly enjoined to pay their quarters, in which there hath been much care taken, and by which much hath been gained upon the countries. It is most certain that of 21 weeks the horse are 12 weeks behind, and the foot have likewise their proportion of sorrow through want of pay. I know three score in one company lying sick by eating of raw roots and green apples through want of money to buy proper food." Peters wished a committee of each county to attend the army, in order to pay the soldiers from the assessment levied on the several shires.

Winchester being the 19th garrison taken that summer by the troops of Fairfax, "The Ecclesiastical Newsmonger" next asked for recruits, complaining that "when we have been promised and expected 4000, we have received but 900, and upon Friday last, when we were promised 3000, and did not expect less, we received but 1500." This latter reinforcement was before mentioned as the convoy brought from Reading to Winchester by Waller. "It may be easily conceived that such an active army needs be a great spender of men by sickness and otherwise, though blessed be God it appears at every siege the enemy's swords cut not off many. At this of Winchester, I know not of above two or three soldiers lost. Your recruits are so chargeable in the bringing to the army, that with half the money the officers would recruit themselves." Peters wished the strength of the army to be raised to 21,000, and spiritual provision to be made for the captured towns. "In this I am the bolder, because of the cries to me of the people in the places where I have been, and some of Winchester at my departure crying for help with them of Macedonia."

On October 14th Lieut.-Colonel Philip Lower, who had so bravely repulsed Goring at Christchurch, was appointed Governor of Winchester while it remained a garrison for the Parliament. Terrible was the havoc committed in Winchester after the surrender. Large portions of the Castle and of the fortifications were blown up, and, according to local tradition, horses were stabled in the Cathedral, whilst soldiers and others completed the destruction begun when Waller and Hopton held sway in ancient Winton (pp. 29 and 122). The Regicide, Nicholas Love, son of Warden Love, and one of the six clerks in Chancery, is said to have done good service to the College during these troublous times, as well as Colonel Nathaniel Fiennes', erewhile Captain of the 40th Troop of Horse for the Parliament. Walcott records the gift to the soldiers of Colonel Fiennes, in 1645, of 29l. 5s. 6d., and he is also said to have placed a guard at the College gate. Warden Harris, who built the Infirmary, and who died on August 11th, 1658, was described as being an orthodox divine and a fit person to be consulted by the Parliament about the reformation of Church government and the Liturgy. Having been ordered to preach before the House of Commons at St. Margaret's, Westminster, he excused himself on the ground of having a weak voice.

On October 18th, 1645, the House of Commons ordered Waller and the Committee for Hants to consider "of the garrison and Castle of Winchester, and also of Wolvesey House, and of Salisbury." The result of their deliberations is unrecorded, but Wolvesey Palace, which Leland describes as being "a castelle or Palace well tow'rd," speedily became the picturesque ruin which it has ever since remained.

Who that dwells by Itchen side knows not the great redoubt constructed by Lord Hopton (p. 126), but which bears for evermore the name of the great soldier who ran to himself master of Winton, "Oliver's Battery."

But the fate of hitherto impregnable Basing, alias Basting, House was now trembling in the balance!

CHAPTER XXX.—BASING AND LANGFORD IN DANGER—SEVERITY RECOMMENDED—CROMWELL'S ARRIVAL—TERRIBLE ODDS—A RECONNAISANCE — BASING SUMMONED — SUNDAY BOMBARDMENT—COLONEL HAMMOND TAKEN—THE FALL OF BASING—KILLED, WOUNDED AND PRISONERS—A GOOD ENCOURAGEMENT—PUBLIC THANKSGIVING.

Whilst Cromwell was constructing batteries at Winchester Colonel Dalbier was vigorously attacking the New House at Basing, but we learn on October 4th that "Colonel D'Albere hath made a great breach in Basing House, and when forces come up as was promised, that he may block them up round, he will storm, the want whereof makes him think the task too hard." The "Parliament's Post" stated on October 7th that the besiegers were "within half musket shot of the breach which he hath made in the New House. His cannon play with restless importunity upon it, and he hath beaten down a great part of the house." The writer believed that the garrison would have surrendered before if they had not dreaded hard usage, being Roman Catholics. "Many of them, fearing the sad effect of a sudden storm, are stolen away, and are got into Wallingford Castle," then held by Sir Marmaduke Rawdon, "but it is not the stubbornness of them that stay, nor the fear of those that fly that can long preserve them." The journalist adds that having no hope of relief, the King's garrisons hoped that severe weather would "prove their best friend for the raising of the sieges, but the fairness of the weather conducing to the designs of the Parliament, the besieged do begin to apprehend that the war they manage is unrighteous, and that Heaven doth, therefore, fight against them as well as men." On October 7th it was reported to Parliament that Surrey had only furnished 155 men out of a promised contingent of 250; and that of 400 men from Sussex only 269 had joined Fairfax's army. 200l. per week was now voted for the garrisons of Portsmouth and South Sea Castle.

The surrender of Winchester sealed the fate of Basing. From "Mercurius Civicus" we learn on October 8th that Cromwell had sent 800 men to reinforce Dalbier, and that with the rest of his brigade he intended to march against Langford House, near Salisbury, and from thence to rejoin the army under Fairfax. Langford House had been already reported in London as besieged on September 25th, and was falsely said on October 3rd to have been taken. The "Moderate Intelligencer" said on Oct. 7th, "They say there will be wagers laid that Basing is taken before Langford. When both are taken then the way is open, and passage for trade clear, which is worth a little more than thanks." On October 9th the "True Informer" writes: "This day we understand the valiant little Colonel Pickering is set down before Langford House, belonging to the Earl of Coleraine, within four miles of Salisbury," and the next day brought another false report of the capture of this steadfast ally of Basing. The "Weekly Account," on October 8th, confirms the expectation of reinforcements from Winchester at Basing. On October 9th it was ordered that there should be sent from Windsor Castle, to Chertsey Bridge, for service against Basing, 100 whole cannon shot of 63lbs., 300 demicannon shot (English) of 32lbs., 300 whole culverin shot of 18lbs., 200 granado shells of 13 inches, 200 demiculverin shot of 9lbs., 50 granado shells of 10 inches, and one great mortar piece," and on the same day "there went several carriages of ammunition and bullets, some of 63 pound weight, for the supply of the forces that besiege that house." The "Kingdom's Weekly Post" knew on October 15th that there are "some great bullets gone unto Cromwell that are six and thirty pounds in weight." The garrison had either nine or ten guns of various sizes, two of them being the culverin (18 pr.)

and the demiculverin (9 pr.). taken from Colonel Norton during the former siege. After the house was stormed "20 barrels of powder and match proportionable" remained unexpended.

The "City Scout" makes merry on October 9th : " Bazing is now close blocked up, and the country hope to come no more to petition Dalbier to keep their sheep for them. Whilst he makes his approaches, Lieutenant-General Cromwell makes his batteries, and hopes to put the Lord Marquesse into the same posture that Bishop Curle was in at Winchester, and within a few days you will hear that the House is as broken as the citizens that are in it."

The courage of the besieged supported them under all difficulties. for we are told by the "Weekly Intelligencer," on October 14th: " A day or two before Lieutenant-General Cromwell's setting down before Basing House, the enemy, being blockt only o" one side, sallied out a good distance from the House, and fetcht in 45 cows out of a gentleman's grounds adjacent to the garrison. It is believed that the Roysters (Cavaliers) therein are well supplied with provisions, but the Lieutenant-General's intentions being to storm, it is hoped they will imitate their neighbours at Winchester Castle, and accept of fair termes in due time before it be too late, for that otherwise, many of t at garrison being Papists, they are like to receive little favour from the besiegers."

The " Moderate Intelligencer," on Oct. 9th, recommends severity : " Several forces are going and gone to assist the siege of Basing, near 10). If we get that, there is good store of wealth in it. It were not amiss to hold that to hard meat ; it hath done so mu h mischief. One garrison dealt roundly with would fright the rest into a more sudden compliance. But to say truth, to begin and take a place, and all in a week, is not long work. They have one as skil 'ull at gr nadoes, who will make them fall at a near place according as desired." The " City Scout" wrote on October 11th : " Lieut.-General Cromwell goes on hopefully and truly against Basing, and they within as resolute to stand it out to the last man ; they are notable marksmen, and with their long pieces can take a man at half head, as one would kill a sparrow." The besieged stripped t e lead from the roofs and turrets, and the Marchioness and her ladies cast it into bullets.

The " Scottish Dove," on Oct. 10th, was of opinion that Cromwell had not sent more than 1000 men to reinforce Dalbier.

But now Cromwell himself came upon the scene. The manner of his arrival is thus described by "Mercurius Veridicus," on Oct. 11th: " The enemy being march away from Winchester, and Sir William Waller put into possession of his own Castle,it was agreed upon that we should march on Tuesday (October 7th) towards Basing, which we did accordingly, and came to Alfrod that night. (Alresford. ten miles from Winchester. Colonel Norton's home was at the Old Manor House, where he was frequently visited by Cromwell.) The next morning, about eight, our forlorne hope came into Basingstoke (11 miles distance), and drawing all our forces into a body in the field betwixt Hackwood Park and Basingstoke, three regiments of foot and two of horse were sent through the town, and drew up on the hill by the highway that leadeth to Andover. The rest of our forces kept on the other side of the river, and drew up towards the House by the Park, and Dalbier remained on the other side. where he had placed his battery next to Bazing Town." It is said that Cromwell made use of the old camp of Winklesbury Circle, between the South-Western Railway and Rook's Down, as a surveying station from whence to determine his best method of approach to the stubbornly defended fortress. Captain Richard Deane. Comptroller of the Ordnance, directed the artillery. " The great guns which Lieutenant-General Cromwell brought with him were drawn up on the south-east side of the house."

The "Moderate Intelligencer" thus estimates the opposing forces on Monday, October 13th. " They that write from Bazing say that Lieut.-General Cromwell makes the number now before it between six and seven thousand horse and foot ; he brought with him five great guns, two of them demi-cannons (30 pounders), one whole cannon (60 pounder). The enemy within is counted 800 f ot and 200 horse. Col. Dalbiere is much gladded at the Lieut.-General's coming, he wanting men and guns." The number of the garrison was in reality much near r 300 than 1000 ! Only 200 against nearly 7000 ! Terrible odds, indeed. As we shall presently see, the defences required a force of from 800 to 1000 men. Many of the gallant

300 were only 18, and some scarcely 12 years of age; priests, clergymen, women, sick, wounded, and helpless men were not wanting. It is marvellous that the place held out so long!

An attempt to relieve the garrison resulted in failure. Alas! gallant Colonel Gage was taking his rest in a soldier's grave, and Basing was left to her fate. Hear the "Weekly Intelligencer" on October 14th: "They having now no hope of relief, either from His Majesty nor from Oxford. The Oxford Roysters lately drew forth a party, intended to attempt their relief, but upon second thoughts they considered the difficulties of the service, and went back again."

Things now began to look uncommonly serious, and to make matters worse, shells from Dalbier's batteries were far too plentiful. Col. Ludlow says that Cromwell's batteries were placed on the eastern side of Basing House. One of his guns threw shot of 63lbs. weight, and "whole cannons make wide breaches." As soon as Capt. Deane had placed his mortars in position on the south-east side of the house he opened fire. One shell "brake in the Countesse of Winchester's lodgings, killed her waighting woman and her chamber maid and some others, the Countess herselfe very narrowly escaping." To save her life, the Marchioness tried to escape before the besiegers had finally closed round the house on that eventful Wednesday, October 8th. One account, given by some deserters, was to the effect that "she escaped quite out before the siege was close laid." Another version is that she was captured, duly exchanged, and then released. "The City Scout" says: "On Saturday, October 11th, they dealt ill with Cromwell to keep one of our men back, when the Marquisse's Lady was released, but the lady was stayed till all was properly performed." Another account expressly states that she escaped on Wednesday, October 8th.

"The name of Lieut.-General Cromwell was a terror to them; how much more will this unexpected presence be? This is a profest Popish garrison, wherein is good store of riches, and if the Marquis surrender not quickly, and we are put to storm, there is no doubt but our souldiers will venture well for it."

As soon as Cromwell had arrived he and Colonel Dalbier and the staff "rode round to view the house, to see how to plant the ordnance. A Cavalier of the garrison well mounted must needs peep out to see, and bid welcome our new supplies, which one of Cromwell's seeing, and not enduring to be star'd upon, rides up to him, pistols him in the neck, and brings off my gentleman and his horse. His body was buried, but not his clothes, for they were very good ones." ("Mod. Intelligr.," Oct. 13th.)

From the "City Scout" of October 14th and other sources we learn that Dalbier had made as good approaches, almost under their works, as the strength of his force permitted. For an account of the defences see pp. 6-9. The besiegers thought that the siege was protracted on religious grounds, as indeed it probably was. The "City Scout" on October 11th said: "I remember Winchester Castle was as strong a place as any in England, yet these being Papists, it may be will stand out longer," and the "Kingdom's Weekly Post," four days later, said; "We are certainly informed that there are many priests in Basing House, who knowing how ill it would go with them if that place were taken, do persuade the defendants to persevere in their obstinacy, telling them that it is meritorious, and that if they die in the defence of that place they shall be numbered in the catalogue of martyrs." It did indeed fare ill with Roman Catholic priests when Cromwell and Hugh Peters held sway in ruined Basing.

The reconnoitring party reported that the enterprise was feasible, and forthwith Lieut.-General Cromwell began his preparations to open fire from his siege guns, which were planted against the S.E. portion of the house, raising several new forts and redoubts. "Col. Dalbier continuing the battery which he had first begun on that side of the New House next the church. Our cannoneers shewed some excellent skill, and lost few shot, and in the interim our horse and foot stood entire, only some few, without command, rode down to the very walls and gave fire upon the enemy." (Messengers' report to Parliament, Oct. 14th.) The cannon baskets or gabions were filling and the guns planting on Thursday and Friday, and by Saturday night everything was ready. The lines of circumvallation were, according to Hugh Peters, above a mile in compass, but another account says that their length was a mile and a half in circumference. The area held by the besieged was 14½ acres. The garrison suffered daily losses by casualties and desertions, and on Oct. 11th some deserters falsely reported that "Sir Robert Peake, the Governor thereof, sometime a stationer near Holborn Conduit," had been killed by a shot from Dalbier's guns.

The "Moderate Intelligencer" stated, on Oct. 13th : " The house was summoned that (Saturday, Oct. 11th) night, the Lieut.-Gen. sending them a sharp summons, telling them they had been evil neighbours ; used the country people hardly ; they were a nest of Romanists, and so of all others could worst make good their arms against Parliament, and therefore they must look for no mercy if they stood out to the utmost period, but all the severity that in a just way of arms might be made good." Hard words these, and met by a firm refusal to surrender.

The church parade on Sunday, October 12th, must have been a remarkable sight. Hugh Peters was the preacher, but alas! we have lost his sermon ! But there was other work done on that October Sunday. "The guns placed Sunday ; we must have a breach or two before they will parley, and that's but reason, for other way they may stretch for it (i.e., be hanged for cowardice). We had from Bazing that Cromwell's cannon had beaten down the drawbridge, and killed in one afternoon 15 men with our granadoes ; they are resolved to storm this night (Oct. 13th) if the former resolution hold."

Was this drawbridge situated on the opposite side of the old house to the present entrance to the citadel ? Cromwell's guns were directed against the S.E. portion of the house, and traces of what may have been a drawbridge are still to be seen nearly opposite to the well on the outer edge of the moat. Let others decide this question.

The "Scottish Dove," on Friday, Oct. 17th, speaks strongly :—" The taking of the late habitation of devilish men, the sinke of English abomination, called Bazing House."

" Being got very near the enemy's works, they made many shot all day on the Lord's Day. The battle is not to the strong always, for then that House had been invincible. They that have seen and viewed it say that it was a piece made as strong and defensible as nature and art could imagine." Men could no longer be spared to guard prisoners, and on the morning of Monday, October 13th, a very dark and misty day, about 20 prisoners, all who were in the House, were duly exchanged. The besieged determined to make yet one more sortie. Without sound of trumpet, a party of horse rode quietly forth, possibly with a design to escape by cutting their way through the hostile ranks, and unexpectedly captured Colonel Hammond and Major King, who were riding from Basing village to inspect the cavalry posted on the opposite side of the House, and to visit Cromwell. Colonel Ludlow says :—" It was suspected that Colonel Hammond, being related to the Earl of Essex, whose half-sister was married to the Marquis of Winchester, had suffered himself to be taken prisoner on design to serve the said Marquis." Let the " City Scout" finish the story : " Coming to one of our sentries on the back side towards the highway, Col. Hammond asked if all was well He answered ' Yes,' so they rid on, but immediately there appeared a party of horse, who, it seems, had come out of Basing, but by reason of the fog they could not be discovered from whence they came, yet the careful contrey had them stand. Colonel Hammond and Major King being gone by, with only two boys to wait upon them, and the sentry having asked who they were for, they answered ' For the Parliament, but when they came near he knew them not to be friends, but of the House, and discharged upon them, and they made shot at him, and unhappily shot him in the back ; yet still he made good the pass, but the enemy sending out some to wheel about, surprised Colonel Hammond and Major King, who knew them not, nor scarce saw them till they were within pistol shot, and rode towards them, conceiving them to be some of their own soldiers. They carried them as prisoners into Basing House." Proposals for exchange were at once made, but were as promptly refused by the Governor, " as is conceived thereby to make better terms in case he be constrained to parley, of which there's a probability, for the Castle is judged feasible upon viewing."

Without loss of time Cromwell wrote to the Governor, saying that "if any wrong or violence were offered to these men, the best in the house should not obtain quarter."

The " Kingdom's Weekly Post," October 15th, says with truth :—" You see what desperate fellows they are that will adventure forth upon a sally, when our forces have besieged it round, and no less a soldier than Lieut.-General Cromwell before it."

Some say that Colonel Hammond and Major King had no cause to complain of their treatment at Basing. The newspaper just quoted says :—" They are both well, there are some it is like may fare the better for the good respect which they did find in their short captivity." The "City Scout" (Oct. 15th) somewhat ungenerously remarks:—" But, to speak truth, they used them well, for they have not neither stript nor plundered them, no not so much as took their rings from their fingers. But fear, not good will nor modesty, kept them from it, and within few days they will be exchanged."

On the other hand, Cromwell's official report to Speaker Lenthall says that Colonel Hammond "was taken by a mistake whilst we lay before this garrison, whom God safely delivered to us, to our great joy, but to the loss of almost all he had, which the enemy took from him." The House of Commons on October 15th awarded him 200*l*. as compensation for his loss at Basing.

All through that day of mist the cannonade continued, and " by Monday night our ordnance had done such execution, both on the part of the house, where Col. Dalbier placed his battery (his fire had been principally directed against the New House), and likewise where Lieut.-General Cromwell had placed his (on the S.E. side of the house), that our men might enter." One of Cromwell's largest guns broke, and became useless. And so the daylight faded, and the last day of the glories of Basing House came to an end.

Said Mr. Peters afterwards : " The Old House had stood (as it is reported) two or three hundred years. A nest of idolatry, the New House, surpassing that in beauty and stateliness, and either of them fit to make an Emperor's Court. In truth the House stood in its full pride ; and the enemy was persuaded that it would be the last piece of ground taken by the Parliament, because they had so often foiled our forces, which had formerly appeared before it."

Peace to the ashes of what Heath's Chronicle styles "'this fortress of loyalty,' the place being called by that name, 'Love Loyalty' being written in every window of that spacious house. It was commonly called 'Basting House,' and that truly enough."

The tragedy is at last nearly played out. During the hours of darkness, Hugh Peters, quoted by Carlyle, draws aside the curtain, and gives us a glimpse of Cromwell's quarters. "The Commander of this brigade had spent much time with God in prayer the night before the storm ; and seldom fights without some text of Scripture to support him. This time he rested upon that blessed word of God written in the 115th Psalm, 8th verse : ' They that make them are like unto them, so is every one that trusteth in them,' which, with some verses going before was now accomplished. 'Not unto us, O Lord, not unto us, but unto thy Name give glory ; for thy mercy and for thy truth's sake. Wherefore should the Heathen say, Where is now their God ? Our God is in the Heavens : He hath done whatsoever he hath pleased ! Their idols are silver and gold ; the work of men's hands. They have mouths, but they speak not ; eyes have they, but they see not ; they have ears, but they hear not ; noses have they, but they smell not ; they have hands, but they handle not ; feet have they, but they walk not ; neither speak they through their throat ! They that make them are like unto them ; so is every one that trusteth in them !' "

"These words, awful as the words of very God, were in Oliver Cromwell's heart that night !"

And yet, most strange to tell, above the west door of Basing Church may be seen by all passers by figures of the Virgin Mary and the Infant Jesus, together with an inscription to the effect that the church was built " to the praise of Christ and of Mary His Mother, by John Paulet, Knt., in the year of Our Lord 1519 !" Were these figures taken down during the troubles, and afterwards replaced ? We wonder whether the house afterwards the "Fleur de Lys," at Basingstoke, was the scene of Cromwell's stern midnight musings. Tradition has it that his head-quarters were there, but we know not of a certainty ! Not much sleep was there for Parliament soldiers that night. "Tuesday morning, about two o'clock, our forces, having agreed upon a storm before, prepared for the work. The great silence for some hours before and the great duty they within had been put upon caused them to fall to some repose, which was to us advantageous !" The last sleep in this world of many a brave Cavalier. Rumour tells us that whilst some of the guard were slumbering on " the swet hauckes," as guard beds were called, others were deep in the mysteries of cards. "Clubs are trumps, as when Basing House was taken," is a well-known Hampshire phrase. If such were the case, the push of pike and shot of pistol speedily ended both the game and the players !

The several posts of the various storming

parties had been previously settled. Colonel Dalbier, who was styled "the long besieger," was to be on the north side of the House next the Grange, little Colonel Pickering, with his regiment of blue coats, on his left hand. Woodward places Hartop's regiment next in order, but Cromwell's official letter makes no mention of this corps. Sir Hardress Waller's regiment of black coats came next, whilst Colonel Montagu's blue regiment was on the extreme left. The appointed signal for falling on was the firing of four cannon, which boomed suddenly out on the October air just at daybreak, as the church clock struck six. The stormers advanced "with great resolution and cheerfulness, and with undaunted courage got over the enemy's works, entered the breaches, and possessed part of the new house and the court betwixt that and the old house. It is affirmed we lost but one man e'er we got within their works."

The stormers are also said to have entered by two great breaches, one made by Dalbier being on the side towards Basing, the other on the side towards the Park."

"Mercurius Civicus" says "Tuesday morning, about five of the o'clock our forces began to storm the new house adjoining to Basing House, which they took after a hot dispute between them and the enemy, to whom upon the gaining of it no quarter was given." "Who first entered is uncertain, and to name were to disparage as worthy; all parts were entered, both by the Lord General's party and Col. Dalbier's. One letter saith that some of those who had been longest before the place (Dalbier's men) gave back upon a hot charge, yet the other parties getting farther ground, they came on again." —("Moderate Intelligencer," October 15.)

Cromwell says that Col. Pickering stormed the New House. The scene is thus graphically described :—"Immediately the dreadful battery began the great guns discharged their cholerick errand with great execution ; many wide breaches were made in an instant, and the besieged immediately marshalled themselves, and stood like a new wall to defend those breaches; our men in full bodies and with great resolution came on. The dispute was long and sharp, the enemy, for aught I can learn, desired no quarter, and I believe that they had but little offered them. You must remember what they were. They were most of them Papists, therefore our musquets and our swords did show but little compassion, and this House being at length subdued did now satisfy for her treason and rebellion by the blood of the offenders."— (The "Kingdome's Weekly Post." October 15.)

But as yet only a portion of the New House had been taken, together with "the court betwixt that and the Old House, where the enemy had lain a train of powder, which they blew up; the quantity was thought to be about three barrels, but, blessed be God, it did not much annoy us." Colonel Hammond, however, stated in the House of Commons that " the enemy blew up no mine, as was at first reported, only one of our men was killed by a barrel of powder which accidentally blew up.'

"This being done, our men slid in at the windows, and encompassed the New House round, for the enemy were fled thither ; then they in the House threw hand grenadoes at our men in the court, but we made our passage into the House among them, and by force of arms quenched their rage." Hand grenadoes have been discovered during the progress of the excavations. Cromwell says that it was Colonel Pickering who " passed through and got the gate of the Old House." Another account said "first we took the New House, the Old House being then all of a flame."

After gaining possession of the New House, Colonel Pickering attacked the Old House, or citadel. Here again he met with a desperate resistance. "They in the Old House hung out some black ensigns of defiance, and set fire on a bridge over which our men were to pass, disputing the passage at sword's point, and the rest in the house threw out grenadoes amongst our men, whereby many of them were killed." (" Mer. Civicus.")

Hugh Peters informs us that these ensigns of defiance were four in number. The bridge on which this fierce struggle took place seems to have been the archway brought to light some time since in front of the entrance to the citadel, for it was in gaining "the gate of the Old House" that this burning bridge had to be crossed.

"This great work (the storming of the New House) being done, the batteries were forthwith made against the Old House, and our men, flushed with taking of the New House, were more eager and resolute to subdue the Old. The great ordnance having torn down all before them, and made many breaches, our men did enter them. There the besieged showed incredible boldness, for although they knew that it was impossible for them to subsist, yet they fought it out to the last, and disputed every entry and pass with the edge of the sword, being all resolved to die, and as any of them fell their seconds, with infinite boldness, adventured to revenge their fellows' death. This made our men far more resolute, who, not minding their desperate fury, cried out 'Down with the Papists,' and by this means there were few of them left who were not put to the sword." ("Kingdome's Weekly Post," Oct. 15.)

Cromwell makes no mention of the success of Dalbier's attack, which makes it the more probable that, as already mentioned, he was unable to force an entrance until the other storming parties had gained at any rate a partial success, although one account says that his men and Cromwell's entered simultaneously.

The Gatehouse of the Old House being taken, Colonel Pickering "put those within to a parley, but the fight was hot, and the noise great; the souldiers could not hear!" Cromwell says plainly "whereupon they summoned a parley, which our men *could* not hear!"

In the meantime Colonel Montagu and Sir Hardress Waller, to whom Dugdale (Short View) gives the credit of the capture, with their respective parties were busily engaged. They attacked "the strongest work, where the enemy kept his Court of Guard" or main guard. Court of Guard is probably a corruption of the French "Corps de Garde," and about this time mention is made of a "Corps du Gard" near Heddington Hill, in Oxfordshire. Judging from the position assigned to the regiments of Sir H. Waller and Colonel Montagu this work must have been situated on the side near the park. The attack was made in force, and proved completely successful. The defenders were after a desperate resistance obliged to retire from that important post, leaving behind them a whole culverin, or 18-pounder, perhaps that formerly taken from Colonel Norton. Emboldened by success the assailants drew up their scaling ladders after them, and, having previously captured another portion of the defences, prepared to enter the Old House or citadel. This was no easy task, since the moat was at least 36 feet deep, and on the inner side there was a parapet four feet in height, in addition to other defences. In spite of all the efforts of the garrison the Old House was entered, as the New House had been shortly before. "At last our men came on with such courage that they entered the Old House too, crying 'Fall on, fall on ; all is our own,'" ("Mercurius Civicus.") "In this Sir Hardress Waller performing his duty with honour and diligence, was shot in the arm, but not dangerously." (Cromwell's letter.) A newspaper writer says that the Cavaliers intended the wound to be *mortal*, but that it would render him *immortal*, Cromwell and Dalbier's guns meanwhile kept up a heavy fire. Here is an honourable testimony from an enemy. Colonel Montagu and Sir H. Waller "take all, with the gallant Marquess, honourable, and an honest, faithful subject to the interest and cause he always undertook, and showed himself a noble enemy, and, therefore, Cromwell treats him kindly."

One account says that "the whole storm from beginning to end was not above three-quarters of an hour," and "Mercurius Civicus" states that "the old House was taken by 7.0 a.m., the attack having commenced about 5.0 a.m." Colonel Hammond informed the House of Commons that "the storm was violent for two hours."

Thus was Cromwell enabled to thank God that he could "give a good account of Basing," and the Cavaliers, surrounded and hemmed in on all sides, found that further resistance would be but vain. Many refused or could not obtain quarter, some succeeded in escaping, whilst other fugitives less fortunate were overtaken and cut down. Cromwell says, "We have had little loss ; many of the enemy our men put to the sword, and some officers of quality." Some accounts say that all in the garrison were either killed or taken, and one writer states, "The number of slain and taken are yet doubtful ; some say we have lost but 40 men, some say we have killed 300 of the enemy, some say more." On the side of the Parliament Captain Wilks was killed during the assault.

"The number slain on our side and theirs is variously reported ; those we most credit say some 10 of ours and 100 of theirs."—"Moderate Intelligencer," Oct. 15.

"October the 14th Basing House was taken by storm, the defendants not having a sufficient number within to man their works. The noble Marquess of Winchester, that had so long and gallantly defended that his own house, was here taken prisoner with about 200 others, and at least 100 of the defendants slain, many whereof in cold blood, not without some loss to the assailants." ("Mercurius Rusticus.")

Colonel Hammond reported that "We lost not above 40 in the first storm, and not many more afterwards, nor officers of note."

The number of the garrison was variously estimated at 600 common soldiers, besides many officers, at 800 and 300.

Hugh Peters spoke as follows : "We know not how to give a just account of the persons that were within. The works many, though not finished, and of too great a compass for so few men to keep, Sir Robert Peake swearing that they had but 300 fighting men in all."

Those slain on the side of the garrison were "Lieut.-Colonel Wiborn, Major Robinson, Major Cuffle, and in view about 74 others." Hugh Peters said " It may be, we have found 100 slain—whose bodies, some being covered with rubbish, came not at once to our view. Amongst those that we saw slain, one of their officers lying on the ground, seeming so exceeding tall, was measured ; and from his great toe to his crown was *nine feet* in length." *Est il possible !*

"Some soldiers were eager to plunder, otherwise there had hardly any in the place scapt with life. The soldiers or others that were in the house, seeing our men come, to save their lives would bring them to chambers where there was a good store of riches ; others minded not booty, but fell upon them and killed many."— ("Moderate Intelligencer," Oct. 15.)

Hugh Peters further remarked, "In the several rooms and about the house there were slain 74, and only one woman." Sprigge says that only 40 men were killed.

The "Moderate Intelligencer" adds, "The two prisoners of ours, Colonel Hammond and Major King, were courted in this sad condition of the enemy more than a great Court favourite: one crying ' Sir, save me,' another ' Me.' The Marquis kept close to the Colonel ; it's thought all had bin put to the sword but for these men's sakes of ours."

Colonel Hammond stated that divers Jesuits were amongst the slain, and six Roman Catholic priests were also put to the sword.

Major Robinson "was in Drury Lane a comedian, but here he acted his own tragedy." Colonel Hammond styles him, "one Robinson, son to the Clowne at Blackfriars Playhouse, and the Marquesse's Major." "The Marquesse's Major Robinson, the Player's Son, who a little before the storm was known to be mocking and scorning the Parliament and our army." He was shot by fanatical Major Harrison "as he was getting over the works," or, according to another account. " in cold blood, after he had laid down his arms, with the words. ' Cursed is he that doeth the Lord's work negligently.' " Yet another writer says, "Robinson the Fool slain as he was turning and acting like a player."

Player Robinson was probably a relation of " William Robinson, a Papist, Surgeon to the Lord Marquisse of Winchester," who was taken prisoner at Odiham in the preceding year.

Major Cuffand (called also Cuffle, Cuff, and Cuffles) had in the previous siege been in charge of the works facing the Park. " Divers that laboured to escape were slain, among others one Major Cuff," says the "Moderate Intelligencer," and " there lay dead upon the ground, Major Cuffle, a man of great account amongst them, and a notorious Papist ; slain by the hands of Major Harrison, that godly and gallant gentleman" according to Hugh Peters.

The prisoners were numerous. "Most of the rest we have prisoners, amongst whom the Marquis of Winchester himself, and Sir Robert Peake, with divers other officers, whom I have ordered to be sent up to you," are the words of Cromwell. " About 200 other prisoners, some of note," says a journalist. 400 says Heath, and " we have not quite 300 prisoners" reports Hugh Peters. The Marquis of Winchester. Sir Robert Peak, Inigo Jones, Wenceslaus Hollar, and Faithorne, Dr. Griffith, and four Roman Catholic priests were all taken. One statement makes the number of prisoners 180 men and 20 gentlewomen. The Marquis kept close to Colonel Hammond, who at length disarmed him, taking away his sword, " yet spared his life by reason he had before been used civilly. He (the Marquis) was afterwards stripped by our soldiers." " Yea, a soldier would needs change clokes with the Marquis of Winchester !"

A satirical pamphlet published 10 days after the house was taken speaks thus : " What served the religious and mighty Lord and Master for ? Could he invoke none of the saints ? It is wonder, for the man was very serious at his devotion, no Pharisee, I'le assure you, for he was found numbering his beads very privately in an oven!"

That "reverend Dragoon," Hugh Peters, was always equally ready either for sword exercise or religious controversy, and, according to his custom, he began " a large dispute" with the Marquis, but the brave old soldier "broke out and said 'That if the King had no more ground in England but Basing House, he would adventure as he did, and so maintain it to the uttermost, comforting himself in this disaster that Basing House was called Loyalty." Mr. Peters wished also to discuss the question as to whether the King or the Parliament had right on their side. He seems to have considered that he gained an easy victory in this argument, the Marquis probably having no particular inclination for debate at such a time. But neither threats nor persuasion could shake his loyalty to his King.

"He was soon silenced in the question concerning the King and Parliament, and could only hope 'That the King might have a day again.' What a glorious picture of

"A steadfast English Cavalier
All of the olden time."

"And thus" says Peters, "the Lord was pleased in a few hours to show us what mortal seed all earthly glory grows upon, and how just and righteous the ways of God are, who takes sinners in their own snares, and lifteth up the hands of His despised people. This is now the twentieth garrison that hath been taken in this summer by this army, and I believe most of them the answers of the prayers, and trophies of the faith, of some of God's servants."

Journalists and pamphleteers made merry at the expense of Sir Robert Peake, who had formerly lived as a neighbour to Hugh Peters in the parish of St. Sepulchre's. "The Governour, now a poor Knight, scarce so rich as when he sold picture babies for children, neer Holborn Conduit." ("Moderate Intelligencer.") "The wise Marquis of Winchester, Robert Peake, a new Knight, but an old ballad seller, of Snow Hill, London." Though he is styled "a poor Knight," he had plate to the value of 500l. at Basing. To save his life he gave to Colonel Hammond, or, according to another statement, threw to a soldier, the key of his chamber, saying that they would there find riches enough. But other plunderers had already broken open the door and taken all. One of them "first laid his hands on a bag of 300l. in gold, a good purchase for one" Sir R. Peake lost his "box of jewels, rings, and bracelets, and a box of graven brass plates," he being a skilful engraver (p. 66.) Wenceslaus Hollar was captured, but escaped, and Faithorne, his artist friend and comrade, was also in safe keeping.

"Inigo Jones, the famous surveyor and great enemy to St. Gregory, the great builder, the King's surveyor and contriver of scenes for the Queen's dancing barn," was amongst the prisoners. "He was gotten thither for help to the House. He was an excellent architector to build, but no engineer to pull down." The west door of Basing Church is said to have been designed by him. He "was carried away in a blanket, having lost his clothes," which had probably been "borrowed" by one of Cromwell's troopers. Poor Inigo was 72 years of age.

The Rev. Dr. Griffith, or Griffin, was also taken. On October 24th, 1642, mention is made of "Master Griffith, a minister, parson of St. Mary Magdalinn, Ould Fish-street, London, has been a long time very malignant against the Parliament, and preached of late divers seditious sermons full of invection and bitter language against the Parliament." Prince Rupert's Declaration in 1643 says, "Have they not by imprisonment or threats muzzled the mouths of the most grave and learned preachers of London, witness Dr. Featley, Dr. Hayward, Dr. Holdsworth, Master Shute, Master Squire, Master Griffith, for so I am informed these men are, because they preach that which their conscience tells them is the known truth."

Dr. Griffith had his share of troubles during these warlike days. He is thus spoken of in "A General Bill of Mortality of the Clergy of London, printed against St. Bartholomew's Day, 1661" ("Harleian Miscellany," vol. vii., p. 183):—"St. Maudlin's, Old Fish-street, Dr. Griffith, sequestered, plundered, and imprisoned in Newgate, whence being let out, he was forced to fly, and since imprisoned again in Peterhouse." Dr. Griffith was said to be the author of this list of persecuted clergy. The Journals of the House of Lords supply further details on March 3rd, 1643:—"Whereas Matthew Griffith, Rector of St. Mary Magdalin's, Old Fish-street, London, doth usually in his sermons endeavour to corrupt and pervert his parishioners and auditory by inveighing against the taking up arms in the present cause, in aid and defence of the Parliament, and against the bringing in of plate, horses, and money for that purpose, with great vehemency affirming them to be idolaters, rebels, and bewitched, and set on work by the Devil ; and that they who should be our law-givers (land-givers) and preservers have taken the King's crown from his head. That we have now no King in Israel, and that they have crowned him with thorns and rendered him contemptible to his people. And in his pulpit likewise usually scoffs at the public faith of the kingdom, and under the name of sectaries declaring against the Parliament for taking away episcopacy, which he affirms to be an ordinance of God, and the lands and revenues belonging to the prelates as a devouring of things consecrated to holy use. To the stirring and fomenting of seditious divisions and mutinies in the said City of London, hindering of the public defence of the kingdom, scandal of religion and of his profession, and dishonour of God." Sequestrators of the living were therefore appointed, and "Ithiell Smart, M.A., a godly, learned, and orthodox divine," was appointed "to preach every Lord's Day, and to officiate as parson, &c." Doctor Griffith was classed with "four other Popish priests," but was also spoken of as "a Godly divine, Protestant, for protection mixed with some Popish priests' profession." He was likewise "that Dr. Griffin or Griffith, that was for divers years the Diana of Dunstan's in the West," and " Dr. Griffin, some time of St. Dunstan's in the West, late of Old Fish-street."

His "three handsome daughters" accompanied him to Basing. The "Moderate Intelligencer" tells us that during the assault "divers women were wounded, who hung upon the soldiers to keep them from killing their friends. Of these women it's two of Dr. Griffin's daughters adventured very far without any hurt. Only their old father was dangerously wounded, if not mortal." Small wonder was it that one of "the handsome daughters, a gallant gentlewoman, fell a railing upon our soldiers at their entrance, calling them Roundheads and rebels to the King." This "provoked our soldiers, then in heat, into a further passion, whereupon one of our soldiers cut her on the head" and slew her, the only woman among so many men ! Heath calls her "a virgin, Dr. Griffith's daughter, whom the enemy shamefully left naked."

Hugh Peters says that there were in the house hiding places for priests, but "there were four Roman Catholic priests beside, who were plundered of their vestments, and themselves reserved for the gallows" ("Moderate Intelligencer"). Hugh Peters stated that there were taken "four Popish clergy priests," whom "Mercurius Veridicus" calls "four more old Reformation priests."

The ladies in the house received but scant courtesy. Hugh Peters admits that "eight or nine gentlewomen of rank, running forth together, were entertained by the common soldiers somewhat coarsely ; yet not uncivilly considering the action in hand," adding, "They left them with some clothes upon them," whilst "Mercurius Veridicus" makes mention of "the ladies' wardrobe, which furnished many of the soldiers' wives with gowns and petticoats." A hundred gentlewomen's rich gowns and petticoats were among the spoil. Sorry treatment this from English soldiers for ladies, some of whom had just seen their nearest and dearest slain before their eyes !

Some of the garrison escaped, as we learn from the "Scottish Dove," October 17th. "There were some soldiers that made escape out of Basing, and many that hid themselves in holes not found till afterward." There were also about 100 horse taken. The "Perfect Diurnall" on October 20th asserts that 200 steeds were here secured, whilst Sprigge says their number was but 80. Some of the garrison who were in hiding, finding that smoke and flames were invading their retreat, came forth and surrendered themselves ; but terrible indeed was the doom of their comrades. Hugh Peters says : " Riding to the house to Tuesday night we heard divers crying in vaults for quarter, but our men could neither come to them nor they to us. A truly hard fate for such valiant soldiers." The number of those slain and burnt is said to have been three hundred.

Having overpowered all resistance, Cromwell and his men began to estimate the value of the rich prize which they had secured, and speedily found that it was fully equal to their highest expectations. Oliver's letter to Speaker Lenthall says : " We have taken about ten pieces of ordnance, with much ammunition, and our soldiers a good encouragement."

This "encouragement" consisted of provisions, rich furniture, jewels, and plate, estimated to be worth at least 200,000*l.*, and which, considering the difference in the value of money, would be worth far more at the present time.

The number of the captured guns is variously given as seven, nine, 10, and 11. The much ammunition consisted of " 20 barrels of powder, with match proportionable, and good store of bullets." Colonel Hammond said that " 600 fire-arms. 100 pikes, and 100 halberds were taken." Spriggs says 500 arms, and the " Perfect Diurnall," on Oct. 20th, gave " 2000 arms as the number secured. Nine colours, and either 400 or 500 bandoliers were likewise taken." Hugh Peters found abundance, both in cellar and storehouse. He said " the rooms before the storm in both houses were all completely furnished; provisions for some years, rather than months, 400 quarters of wheat, bacon, divers rooms full containing hundred of flitches, cheese proportionable; with oatmeal, beef, pork, beer —divers cellars full—and that very good. There was a bed in one room furnished, which cost 1300*l*. There were Popish books many, with copes and such utensils." Much wine, and many hogsheads of beer filled the cellars. The aforesaid flitches of bacon were 300 in number, the cheese weighed 40,000lbs., and there were 200 barrels of beef. All this " afforded the soldiers gallant pillage." One hundred bags of malt, many firkins of butter, numerous crucifixes, Popish pictures and books, together with six copes and many friars' coats and girdles, formed part of the spoil. The beds, clothes, and goods, which filled 1000 chests, trunks, and boxes, were estimated to be worth 8000*l*., the Marquis's cabinet and jewels 50,000*l*., and that belonging to Sir Robert Peake, 500*l*. " One soldier found 300*l*. in a hole, and another had 120 pieces of gold for his share. The finder of the 300*l*. profited but little. Not able to keep his own counsel, it grew to be common pillage amongst the rest, and to make sport with this raw soldier, his comrades pillaged him by piecemeal to an half-crown coin." Some had plate, others jewels, for " the wealth of Basing House was of greater value than any single garrison could be imagined, in money, plate, jewels, household stuff, and riches. One bed valued at 1400*l*., and so orderly under rate of others." There was taken " 4000*l*. in money, as was judged," and four cabinets of jewels were burnt. All that sad Tuesday (Oct. 14th) the plunder of the soldiers continued.

The news of the capture soon spread, and a crowd speedily assembled from Basingstoke and the neighbouring villages. The Parliamentary troopers were anxious to turn their booty into money, and offered to sell the 400 quarters of wheat which they had found in the granaries. The farmers began to chaffer with them, hoping to obtain good bargains. But they soon found that they had to deal with men who knew how to take care of their own interests. No wheat could be purchased except at high prices, and it was not until the soldiers knew that they must march towards the west on the 16th that they consented to lower their demands. " The soldiers sold the wheat to country people, which they held up at good rates awhile, but afterwards the market fell, and there were some abatements for haste. After that, they sold the household stuff, whereof there was a good store, and the country loaded away many carts: and they continued a great while fetching out all manner of household stuff, till they had fetched out all the stools, chairs, and other lumber, all which they sold to the country people by piecemeal."

" Mercurius Veridicus" tells us " Plunder in abundance, both plate, hangings, and other goods, sold exceedingly cheap: the noise whereof caused one hundred hackney horse this morning to be hired in London for brokers to go purchase upon if the fair be not past. This frustrates the last hope of the Royalists, and will break their heart."

All this plunder and spoliation went on in Christian England under the name of Religion! But, as if the cup of misery and desolation was not already full to overflowing, a cry arose amongst those busy plunderers and bargainers of " Fire, fire, fire !"

During the assault some fireballs had been thrown by the besiegers, and one of them had been only partially extinguished by the garrison. It continued to smoulder, and towards evening clouds of smoke and red tongues of flame proclaimed that the hours of stately Basing House were numbered. The great beams were burnt through one by one, and dropped with a crash into the fiery gulf below, bringing down oaken floors and panelled ceilings with them in their fall. The beautiful windows, each bearing the motto " Aymez Loyaute," " Love Loyalty," were cracked and melted by the intense heat, whilst the roofs rained molten lead in showers. Oliver's men thought only of saving all they could for their own advantage, and the result was," In all these great buildings there was not one iron bar left in all the windows (save only what were on fire) before night. And the last work of all was the lead : and by Wednesday morning they had hardly left one gutter about the house, and what the soldiers left, the fire took hold on, which made more than ordinary haste, leaving nothing but bare walls and chimneys in less than twenty hours ;—being occasioned by the neglect of the enemy in quenching a fireball at first." (Hugh Peters' report.)

And, sickening to relate, many of the garrison were being slowly suffocated or burnt to death meanwhile in the vaults below, into which the flames penetrated, as the charred oaken curbs of the cellar steps give proof!

"Of the fate of the plunder, said to have exceeded 200,000*l.* in value, little is known. Mrs. Cromwell, the Protector's wife, is said to have had a voracious appetite for such 'pretty things,' as well as for Westphalia hams and similar articles with which 'the middle sort' presented her; and many of the Marquis's treasures are reported to have found their way to her hands." (Murray's Handbook for Hampshire.)

During the Civil War more than 2000 men are said to have fallen in and around Loyalty House. Whilst the spoilers were plundering the burning mansion "the Marquis of Winchester and Sir Robert Peake were carried to the Bell at Basingstoke." Until a few years ago this was the place of detention for prisoners awaiting trial. It contained a strong room, diagonally planked, with a massive door and ponderous lock. The fact that such important prisoners were in custody almost immediately opposite adds probability to the tradition that Cromwell lodged at the Fleur de Lys, on the site of which now stands the Falcon House.

On Tuesday, October 14th, Phineas Pain and W. Parker, both messengers to Lieut.-Col. Roe, scoutmaster of the City of London, reached Westminster in succession, with information for the House that Basing had been taken about six or seven o'clock that morning by storm. The messengers were both called into the House, and related certain particulars of the assault, saying "that at their coming away the storm was ended, and our men possessed of all."

The three messengers, two from Basing, and one from General Fairfax, were granted 20*l.* to divide between them.

On Wednesday, October 15th, arrived Hugh Peters and Colonel Hammond, the latter of whom was the bearer of Cromwell's letter to Speaker Lenthall. "Colonel Hammond, who was taken prisoner, came this day unto the House of Commons, and made a more full relation of the taking of Basing House." He was promised 200*l.* towards his losses. Hugh Peters was also called in, was requested "to make a relation to the House of Commons," and presented to the House the Marquis's own colours, which he brought from Basing, the motto of which was "*Donec pax redeat terris*," "Until peace return to the earth," the same as King Charles gave upon his Coronation money when he came to the Crown."

The bringing of these despatches from Basing was soon afterwards worth 200*l.* per annum to Mr. Peters.

A contemporary writer thus describes another mission of the "soldier's parson" of the same nature. "That Spiritual Newesmonger, Master Peters, the Lecturer, is come to Westminster from the Earl of Essex with such a stock of newes that on Thursday last it cost the Lower Members two full hours to hear it once over, though his fingers, eyes, and nosthrils helped his tongue to dispatch." A man of action, evidently! In "The Sale of Rebellious Household Stuff," he is thus referred to :—

Here's Dick Cromwell's protectorship,
And here are Lambert's commissions;
And here is Hugh Peters his scrip,
Crammed full of tumultuous petitions!

He was one of those preachers whom Bishop Corbet, in his ballad of "The Distracted Puritan" describes as saying :—

In the holy tongue of Canaan,
I placed my chiefest pleasure,
Till I pricked my foot,
With an Hebrew root,
That I bled beyond all measure.

The thanks of the House of Commons were voted to Lieut.-General Cromwell on Oct. 15th, the day after the final assault, and his letter to the Speaker was ordered to be read in all pulpits. It was further ordered "that on the next Lord's Day (Oct. 19th) public thanks be given to Almighty God for His great mercies and blessings upon the Parliament's forces under Lieut.-General Cromwell and Colonel Dalbeere in taking Winchester Castle and Basing House, in all churches and chapels of London and Westminster, and within the lines of communication." The capture of Chepstow was likewise remembered on this day of thanksgiving. But whilst London was jubilant, Oxford mourned the fate of Basing House, as we learn from "Mercurius Veridicus" "when he (the post) told them (in Oxford) that Basing was taken there was presently almost as bad a cry as when they heard of the loss of Bristol. And thus the poor ignorant people bemoaned the matter as if they had lost their gods, in which doleful condition we leave them." Such was the "sack of Basing House."

NOTE.—William Lilly, the celebrated astrologer, erroneously predicted that Basing House would be taken at 2.45 p.m. on September 11th, 1645.

In the register of Sherfield are the following interesting entries:—

"1644. John Worlye, a souldjer of ye Kentish Regimt. Buried, Octob. 26."

"1645. Mr. Amias Preston, slaine att Basinge Siege. Buried, Octob. 16."

CHAPTER XXXI.—BASING HOUSE DEMOLISHED—CROMWELL'S DEPARTURE—THE CAPTIVE MARQUIS — LANGFORD HOUSE SURRENDERS — SATIRICAL PAMPHLETS —CONFISCATED ESTATES—SUBSEQUENT EVENTS—THE KING AT CARISBROOK—ROYALIST RISINGS— THE CAPTIVE MONARCH—ARCHIVES OF WINCHESTER—SOUTHAMPTON AND PORTSMOUTH AFFAIRS—THE RESTORATION—DEATH OF THE "LOYAL MARQUIS."

Cromwell strongly urged the demolition of all that had escaped the fury of the spoilers and the flames, saying, "I humbly offer unto you (the Speaker) to have this place utterly slighted (i.e., pulled down) for these following reasons: It will ask about 800 men to manage it; it is no frontier; the country is poor about it; the place exceedingly ruined by our batteries of mortar pieces, and by a fire which fell upon the place since our taking it."

Another writer wonders that the defence was so long protracted, as not less than 1000 men were necessary to hold the position. The neighbourhood is "not worth the defence, nor able to support a garrison." All honour to the brave little garrison who fought so long and well.

Cromwell added: "If you please to take the garrison at Farnham, some out of Chichester, and a good part of the foot which were here under Dalbier, and to make a strong quarter at Newbury with three or four troops of horse, I dare be confident it would not only be a curb to Dennington (Donnington Castle, near Newbury), but a security and a frontier to all these parts; inasmuch as Newbury lies upon the river (Kennet), and will prevent any incursion from Dennington, Wallingford, and Farringdon into these parts, and by lying there will make the trade more secure between London and Bristol for all carriages. And I believe the gentlemen of Sussex and Hampshire will with more cheerfulness contribute to maintain a garrison on the frontier than in their bowels, which will have less safety in it." Chichester was, in fact, disgarrisoned on March 2, 1646.

Donnington Castle had long been the stout ally of Basing. Sir Marmaduke Rawdon, sometime Lieutenant-Governor of Basing House, was in command at Farringdon, and Wallingford was the last Royalist garrison that surrendered in Berkshire. Cromwell states that he is about to march westward with all speed on the morrow, and asks for recruits, and pay for his army. He concludes his tale of bloodshed and ruin with these words: "The Lord grant that these mercies may be acknowledged with all thankfulness. God exceedingly abounds in his goodness to us, and will not be weary until righteousness and peace meet; and until He hath brought forth a glorious work for the happiness of this poor kingdom. Wherein desires to serve God and you, with a faithful hand, your most humble servant, OLIVER CROMWELL." What he asked was done.

In the Journals of the House of Commons we find the following entries:—

"15th October, 1645.—Resolved, that the house, garrison, and walls at Basing be forthwith slighted and demolished."

"Resolved, that this House doth declare that whosoever will fetch away any stone, brick, or other materials of Basing House shall have the same for his or their pains."

Of course, when permission had been thus authoritatively given, the ruins were not long in being carted away.

It was also decided that orders should be at once sent to Cromwell to attack Donnington Castle. The despatch reached him late that evening at Basing, when all preparations had been made for the morrow's westward march, and he altered not his purpose. The Committee for Hants and Dalbier were directed to co-operate with Cromwell against Donnington, and to decide what portion of Cromwell and Dalbier's forces should be left to protect Hampshire. On

October 18th a letter was read in the House from the Committee for Hants, recommending the placing of a garrison at Newbury, as a check upon Donnington Castle, and on the same day it was ordered "That the Marquis of Winchester be forthwith sent a prisoner to the Tower." Action was forthwith taken, and the Marquis, in company with Sir Robert Peake and about 60 other prisoners, was sent up from Basingstoke to London under guard, in the custody of "Captain Terry, who is a person reported to have done many good services," and who on reporting his arrival in London was ordered to receive from the Sheriff of Hants 50l., wherewith to buy two good horses. Captain Terry probably belonged to a family long resident at Dummer. On the 25th of April, 1646, he is described as "Captain Terry, of Surrey." The prisoners reached London in the evening hours of October 19th, and on the following day the House of Lords gave order:

"That the Gentleman Usher attending this House shall bring the Marquis of Winchester to this House presently to acknowledge his offence committed against this House, he being taken in arms at Basing House, and then this House will take into consideration how to dispose of him further, and the Gentleman Usher to take him into custody wheresoever he shall find him."

The Gentleman Usher had not far to seek, and we read:—"This day (October 20th) the Marquis of Winchester was brought to the bar as a delinquent, and the Speaker, by the direction of the House, told him 'That for his high offence in deserting the Parliament, and for taking up arms against the Parliament and kingdom contrary to his duty, this House for the present doth commit his Lordship to the Tower of London, there to be kept in safe custody during the pleasure of the House.'"

"Ordered—That the Marquis of Winchester shall have one of his servants to attend him in the Tower of London."

Where, for the present, we will leave the noble master and his faithful servant to talk long and earnestly concerning the fate of stately "Loyalty!"

"The gallant little garrison was dispersed among gaols and hiding places at home, and the lands of refuge abroad."

Sir Robert Peake was sent as a prisoner to Winchester House, and his comrades in adversity were committed to various prisons. William Morgan and Edward Cole, two Roman Catholic priests, were "reserved for the gallows," and "amongst the common soldiers are two that are suspected Jesuits," with whom, doubtless, it fared but badly. Other prisoners were Capts. Cnfain (p. 66), Tettersall, and Tasborough (Peregrine Tasbury, p. 67), who were all Roman Catholics, and Capts. Tamworth, Raisby, Snow, (p. 166), and Payne. Also Lieutenants Hugh Glausie, an Irishman, Francis Massey, William Faithorne (p. 66), Rowlet (p. 66), and Beck. The Beck family held the manor of Woodcote in 1362, and in 1658 Gabriel Beck was M.P. for Andover. Cornet Francis Hide, a Papist, and Ensign Tunstall, of Foot. Some of the Hide family lived at this time at Yarmouth, Isle of Wight. Sergeant Henry Payne bore a well-known Hampshire name, and Sergeants Christopher Kenton, John Light, and Richard Foxall shared his captivity, as did also Quartermaster John Foy, and Corporals William Hare, a Papist, and James Ellis. One of the Ellis family rented Tylney Hall, in the last century. "Thomas Web, clerk," seems to have been Hampshire born, but assuredly Humphrey Vanderblin, whose servant, William Smithson, shared his master's fortunes, was a foreigner. Thomas Amtell, Roger Coreham (p. 67), John Weston, and Oliver Lloyd are all described as gentlemen. Lord Winchester's captive servants were "John Goldsmith, Richard Pickover, John Richards, Richard Read, William Eldridge, Robert Hodkins, the baker, a Papist, 15 Irish rebels and Papists, William Brown, a spy, Edward Pawlet, the hangman, and other common prisoners. (p. 138).

At dawn on October 15th, 1645, Cromwell's trumpets sounded "to horse," and the long columns of the Ironsides marched away from ruined Basing to join General Fairfax at Tiverton. A march of 20 miles brought them to Wallop, where the infantry halted for the night, but Cromwell, having sent off a despatch to Fairfax, made a forced march with the cavalry to Langford House, near Salisbury, where Lieut.-General Pell still held out for the King. On the 17th a summons to surrender was sent to the garrison, and "fair and equal conditions" were speedily agreed upon, Lieut.-Col. Hewson and Major Kelsey being deputed to act for Cromwell. The garrison marched forth at noon on October 18th, delivering up all arms and ammunition uninjured. 300 arms, four barrels of powder, bullet, match, and much provision were found in the house, of which Major Ludlow was now appointed Governor. The commanders-in-chief were to march out with horses and arms, other gentlemen, not more than 14 in number, might march out with swords, pistols, and horses, if they should lawfully possess them, but the soldiers were to march out without arms. The commanders-in-chief were to be allowed a cart or waggon to convey their property to Oxford, ten days being allowed for the march thither, under convoy for the first day's march of a troop of horse, and afterwards of a trumpet and pass. Any gentlemen might have passes for other Royal garrisons besides Oxford. Property left in the garrison was to be restored to its owners if demanded within two days. Lieut.-Colonel Bowles and Major Fry were to remain as hostages for the execution of this agreement. Lieut.-Colonel Hewson, who reported the surrender in London, got 50l. to buy two good horses. Basing and Langford had fallen, but Donnington Castle was not surrendered until April 1st, 1646. For details of the siege see Mr. Money's "Two Battles of Newbury."

On Oct. 18th, 1645, the House of Commons appointed Thos. Bettesworth, jun., as High Sheriff of Hants, and to command the horse raised in the county, and four days afterwards a letter was read from Mr. Wm. Cawley, of Chichester, complaining of the difficulty of raising local funds and recruits for the army of Fairfax. On Oct. 24th Sussex was ordered to provide men for the garrison with the country, and to send 200 foot to Donnington Castle as previously ordered. On Nov. 7th the same county was ordered to lend a troop of horse and 200 foot to Major-General Browne, at Abingdon, the Parliament undertaking to pay them. Hampshire was also ordered to at once pay the arrears due for service in Hants to the Kentish Dragoons, who were ordered to march to Abingdon. Sir Henry Wallop, M.P. for Hants, died in October, 1645, and most of the members of Royalist sympathies within the county were about this time disabled from sitting in Parliament. Richard Jervoise, Esq., M.P. for Whitchurch, died during this month. The Committees for Hants and Wilts were ordered, on Dec. 23rd, 1645, to arrest and return to their regiments all soldiers coming from the army without license. Fairfax's army, when marching to besiege Oxford, came from Salisbury to Andover on April 25th, 1646, and proceeded to Newbury after a halt of two days. On March 2nd, 1646, an order was given "that the ordnance at Chichester be brought to Arundel Castle, that Chichester be disgarrisoned, and the fortifications made since the troubles demolished."

A pamphlet was published in London on Oct. 24th, 1645, entitled " A Looking Glass for the Popish Garrisons, as held forth in the life and death of Basing House, &c." It speaks of " the tall walls, bulwarks, and ports that were cast up by the foreign engineer," says that the garrison could make the devil afraid, but could not make Cromwell bow, and that Lord Winchester was taken whilst " numbering his beads very privately in an oven." It taunts the garrison with the loss of all their contribution money and plunder, and says " the nest is now pulled down, the den is committed to the mercy of the fire ; there is scarce one stone left upon another." A satirical writer drew up pretended articles of impeachment for high treason against Sir Robert Peake, in the name of the Attorney-General.

The first charge was that he had wilfully betrayed Basing House, "having the fear of nobody but General Cromwell before his eyes." The second charge was that he " with an intention to weaken the King's most excellent irreligious army, did betray into the hands of the rebellious enemy the lives of many of His Catholic subjects, who very like hath neither been at prayer nor confession these seven years." The third charge was that he traitorously surrendered many of the King's "serviceable soldiers, and the best affected men in all his garrisons, who have faithfully served his Majesty this long time without pay, and carried themselves very honestly towards the country. They never plundered any man of more than he had, robbed nobody but friends and foes ; were never drunk but when they could get strong liquor ; scarce one word in three was an oath with them, though they were in extream passion, or upon any extraordinary occasion whatsoever ; they were ever ready to sally upon the least occasion, when the enemy was the farthest off ; and, to speak the truth, I think they would never have yielded had they been sure that the garrison would never have been stormed ; those men being so serviceable, loyal, and valiant, have been betrayed and delivered up into the hands of the enemy by the said Sir Robert Peake, as aforesaid." Lastly, that he had given up money, plate, arms, &c., "necessarily raised for the deluding of His Majesty, defence of his Catholic Council, maintenance of Popery, and subversion and ruin of the ancient laws and liberties of this kingdom." On these grounds the writer ironically prays that the accused may be sent to Oxford for trial. Sir Robert Peake was after a time released, and was succeeded in his business as an engraver and printseller by his younger brother. In the year 1662 William Faithorne dedicated to him "The Art of Graving and Etching, wherein is expressed the way of Graving on Copper," &c. Mr. Money says that his name "is attached to many prints and other engravings now rare. He died in July, 1667, and was buried with great military pomp in St. Sepulchre's Church, Holborn." He had long been a resident in the parish of St. Sepulchre.

The Marchioness of Winchester, who, by her presence and earnest solicitations at Oxford, had brought about the relief of Basing by Col. Gage, and who had herself helped to cast the lead from the turrets into bullets, could not expect to escape, sister to the Earl of Essex though she was, and accordingly we find the following entry:—"Friday, 9th Jan., 1646. To let them (the House of Commons) understand that the Lady Marquess of Winchester is restrained by the Committee of Examinations, and that this House (besides she being a Peeress of this Realm) gave her a pass to come to this town; and this House have now thought fit to commit her to the Gentleman Usher of the House, and desires that she may be delivered unto him accordingly." The pass referred to had been asked for by Lord Winchester on November 11th, 1645. He stated that he was in want of many comforts in the Tower, it being winter, and he being "for the present somewhat infirm," and asked that his wife may come to town, bringing with her some servants and certain necessaries. The pass was granted, as above mentioned.

The 15th of January discloses a sad state of things. The Marquis in the Tower, "having nothing to feed him but what his keeper voluntarily gives him," is by the Lords recommended to the House of Commons for an allowance out of his own estate, "that he may not starve." All his broad lands had lain under a sentence of confiscation ever since October 18th, 1643, since which date a charge of high treason had also been hanging over him. It was further ordered on the 31st of January, 1646, "that Mr. Lisle do bring in an ordinance for the full granting unto and settling upon Lieutenant-General Cromwell and his heirs the manors of Abberston and Itchell, with the rights, members, and appurtenances thereof, in the county of Southampton, being the lands of John, Marquis of Winchester, a delinquent that hath been in arms against the Parliament, and a Papist." In the lands round Basing House it was gradually found that the Marquis had only a life interest. Abberston and Itchell are respectively Abbotstone and Itchen Stoke. These only could be realised towards the 2500l. per annum promised to be settled on Lieutenant-General Cromwell. "On January 7th, 1646-7, the remainder of the 2500l. was ordered to be provided from the Marquis of Winchester's lands in general, which in a fortnight more was found to be impossible." Cromwell and Lieutenant-Colonel Joyce quarrelled about Fawley Park.

For Cromwell's management of these lands see Carlyle's "Letters and Speeches of Oliver Cromwell."

On September 25th, 1646, the estates of the Marquis of Winchester were ordered by the House of Commons to be sold for the purpose just mentioned.

On November 9th, 1646, it is a satisfaction to find that Edward Lord Pawlett, brother of the Marquis, "who designed to betray Basing House to Sir William Waller, is in such great want that he prays relief out of his brother's estate."

Released from the Tower, the "loyal" Marquis retired to the Continent to wait for better days.

William Faithorne, the father of the English school of engraving, and the pupil of Sir Robert Peake, with whom he worked for three or four years, and under whom he served at Basing, seems from his portrait, engraved by himself, to have worn long hair after the most approved Cavalier fashion. After the destruction of Basing House he was imprisoned in Aldersgate, where he was soon busy with his graver. Released by the interest of friends, he went to France until 1650, when he returned to England, married, and opened a shop without Temple Bar. He sold engravings, worked for the booksellers, especially for Mr. William Peake, a brother of his old master, became wealthy, and died in May, 1691. (*Chalmers' Biograph. Dict.*)

Hollar escaped to Antwerp, but on the death of his patron the Earl of Arundel returned to England. The Restoration benefited him not, and a mission to Tangier only earned for him 100*l.* and the barren title of the King's Iconographer. A conscientious, painstaking artist was he, for more than fifty years, engraving not less than 24,000 plates. He was a good man, but his life was one long struggle for bread, and he died beseeching the bailiffs not to remove him to any other prison than the grave. (*Book of Days*, vol. i., p. 432.)

Inigo Jones continued to design buildings and to theorise on the origin of Stonehenge until June 21st, 1653, when he died at the age of 80.

"Solid" Colonel Ludlow was afterwards Deputy of Ireland, and married Ireton's widow, but strongly opposed the Protectorate of Cromwell. At the Restoration he owed his escape to the Continent to his old friend Colonel Morley, and reached Lausanne, where he narrowly escaped assassination by Cavalier emissaries. Mr. William Cawley, of Chichester, died abroad, and the Duke of York seized his estates. Dr. Fuller, sometime Chaplain to the Forces at Basing House, remained at Exeter until the city surrendered in April, 1646. He had his share of the troubles of the time, and was silenced in 1647, but became Rector of Waltham Abbey in the following year. Dying on August 15th, 1661, he was followed to the grave by more than 200 clergymen. Colonel Richard Norton, "Idle Dick," lived to receive many a letter and visit from his old friend Oliver. He was Governor of Portsmouth, and on April 13th, 1647, it was "Resolved that there shall be no officer within any garrison above the rank of captain, but only the Governor." The Governor of Portsmouth was to receive 12*s.* per diem as Governor and 8*s.* as Captain, making in all 1*l.* From another entry it seems that the 8*s.* was drawn by the Governor of Portsmouth as "Captain of Southsea Castle." The Governors of Carisbrook and Calshot Castles received 12*s.* and 5*s.* per diem respectively. Colonel Norton sat in the Little or Barebones' Parliament, and was elected a member of the Council of State in the same year. He "dwindled ultimately into Royalism." Colonel Harvey, his comrade and ally in the first attacks upon Basing (if he be identical with "the poore silk man, now Colonel)," got the Bishop of London's house and manor at Fulham. For a time only!

Sir Marmaduke Rawdon defended Faringdon as successfully as he had done Basing House. Murray's handbook for Berkshire says that his tomb is in the nave of the church, but the Rev. H. Barne, Vicar of Faringdon, says "there is no extant monument of Sir Marmaduke Rawdon in Faringdon church as far as I can ascertain. There is a tradition that there was one; but I apprehend that when the church was restored in 1854 it was effaced!" Sir William Waller was one of the 41 Presbyterian members "purged out by Colonel Pride, and was imprisoned by the Independent party. He survived the Restoration, and died at Osterley Park, Middlesex, on Sept. 19th 1668." Sir Richard Onslowe, Kt., "of the old stamp, a gentleman of Surrey, of good parts and a considerable revenue," successfully weathered the tempests of the period. Purged out by Pride, he afterwards raised and led a Surrey regiment to Worcester fight in 1653. He spoke strongly in favour of Cromwell's becoming King, but was afterwards a member of the Convention Parliament which restored Charles II. to the throne. The history of Cromwell all men know. Col. Dalbier took Donnington Castle, friendly to Basing, on April 1st, 1646, and in the following year was ordered to bring in a list of persons willing to serve the Parliament, but in 1648 he joined the Royalist insurgents under Lord Holland, wishing to be revenged on the army, which some officers "despised for their ill-breeding and much preaching." The insurrection was speedily crushed, and at an inn at St. Neot's in Huntingdonshire, Dalbier was hacked in pieces, "so angry were the soldiers at him." There was a Berkshire tradition in 1759 that Dalbier was invulnerable, and that cannon balls were seen to rebound from his body! His head was struck off and exposed to public view. Sir Balthazar Gerbier, in 1663, congratulated Lord Winchester "that Dalbier is no more (nor a prince of the air, save the carcase of his head on a pole) drawing lines of circumvallation about your seats."

Lord Goring was brought to trial before the High Court of Justice in 1648-9, and was found guilty of treason. In the House of Commons the numbers for and against his execution were equal, but Speaker Lenthall's casting vote saved the prisoner's life.

The Cuffand (Cufford) family were long famous for their attachment to the House of Stuart, and one of the family refused in 1715 to take the oath of allegiance to George I.

Into the story of the residence in Hampshire of Richard Cromwell, who married Miss Dorothy Major, of Hursley, we have not space to enter, nor does it come within our province. For full details see Carlyle's "Letters and Speeches of Oliver Cromwell," "Duthy's Sketches of Hampshire," &c. One who knew him says, "He was a very good neighbourly man while he lived with us at Hursley." He rode hunting in a tie-wig, and in 1654 took part in the marriage of two of the parishioners of Eling.

The loyal High Sheriff of Sussex, Sir Edward Ford, had married the sister of the Parliamentary General Ireton. Dying in Ireland in 1670, his body was brought over to his native parish of Harting, in Sussex, for burial.

Sir Robert Wallop, of Hurstbourne, was one of the King's Judges. He was at the Restoration attainted of high treason, and sentenced to be deprived of his gentility and imprisoned for life. This sentence was put in force in January, 1662. His lands were forfeited by Act of Parliament, and placed in trust to the Earl of Southampton, for Sir Robert Wallop, his wife, and children. Old Sir Robert begged for freedom more than once, being old and diseased, but Hearst, the physician, certified that exposure to the air would hasten his death, he being weak with long illness. He was therefore not released until his death, in November, 1667. His sentence was reversed during the reign of William and Mary, and he was succeeded by his son Henry, who represented Whitchurch in Parliament.

Col. Herbert Morley was one of the King's judges, but did not sign the death-warrant. He met Charles II. when that monarch was a fugitive from Worcester fight, but did not recognise him. The King, on being told who it was, replied merrily, "I did not like his starched mouchates." He, with others, secured Portsmouth in 1659 for the Parliament, and made "incursions into Hampshire and Sussex, where he had many friends," and soon afterwards, marching to Hounslow with some horse, restored it to the Parliament on Dec. 26th, 1659.

At the Restoration he hesitated long, but at length purchased his pardon for 1000l., and died in peace at Glynde, in Sussex, on Sept. 29th, 1667, in the fifty-second year of his age.

Under the rule of the Parliament, as we learn from Dr. Milner, in Hampshire parishes the Directory was substituted for the Prayer Book in churches, chapels, and private families. Deans, chapters, and archdeacons were summarily abolished, together with bishops, archbishops, and even their dioceses. Certain presbyteries and classes were appointed in lieu of parishes. The Puritans styled themselves "abhorrers." They appointed a general fast on Christmas Day, and another to be held every month as an expiation for the crying sin of religious toleration. The use of the Book of Common Prayer either in public or in private entailed for the first offence a fine of 5l.; for the second a fine of 10l.; and for the third three years' imprisonment was the penalty. Quakers were whipped, whilst Roman Catholics were hanged and quartered. Between July, 1641, and June, 1654, no fewer than 21 priests were executed, besides others who also received sentence of death. Many of the city and cathedral clergy refused to take the Solemn League and Covenant, and to adopt the Directory, and were in consequence treated with severity as delinquents. Dr. Thomas Gawen, who was rector of Exton, and tutor to Bishop Curle's children, became a Roman Catholic (as did many other distinguished clergy), and wrote several controversial and devotional tracts. Church lands were sold for the benefit of the State between 1646 and 1651. John Lisle, Esq., M.P. for Winchester, was Master of St. Cross until 1657, when he was succeeded by John Cooke, Solicitor-General to the Parliament, who was executed at the Restoration. Mr. Lisle's widow was Dame Alicia Lisle, who was sentenced at Winchester, by order of Judge Jeffreys, on September 2nd, 1685.

On November 27th, 1647, a sum of money was at Winchester taken out of the coffers and delivered to Mr. Mayor to pay the soldiers, and 40s. was "expended about the city business in a journey to London concerning the removing of the said soldiers."

On June 2nd, 1648: "Taken out of the coffers five pounds, which was delivered to Mr. Mayor to go to London about the city business, for which he is to give an account." On

November 24th, "money was taken out of the coffers to pay Mr. Moggeridge in full of his bill for dressing of maimed soldiers and for ointment."

Mr. Hillier's able work on "Charles I. in the Isle of Wight," renders it quite unnecessary for us to enter upon that most interesting subject. Mr. Moody's "Sketches of Hampshire" should also be consulted. We need only note that Colonel Hammond, whom we have already met at Basing, was the King's gaoler at Carisbrook, having been appointed Governor of the Isle of Wight, of which his grandmother was a native, on September 6th, 1647. He was subordinate to Fairfax in military matters, and to the Parliament in civil affairs. When he dismissed the King's servants at Carisbrook, Capt. Burleigh, who had formerly commanded the King's ship *Antelope*, of 512 tons burden and 160 men, and had been dismissed when the fleet rebelled against the King, a man of good family in the Island, tried to rescue his royal master. He was "a man of more courage than of prudence or circumspection," and causing a drum to be beaten in the streets of Newport, cried, "For God, the King, and the people," and said "he would lead them to the Castle, and rescue the King from his captivity." This rash attempt was at once crushed, even the King's servants urging the people to return home, but poor Captain Burleigh was tried at Winchester on January 22nd, 1648, before Judge Wild on a charge of high treason, and sentenced to be hanged, drawn and quartered on February 2nd, 1648. He died nobly, and to the credit of the county Gregory, the executioner, was of necessity brought down from London, as no Hampshire man would carry out the sentence. The same Judge, and almost the same Jury, tried Rolph, Osborne, and Doucet, at Winchester, for attempting to withdraw the King from Carisbrook Castle. These men were actuated by very different motives. Osborne and Doucet wished to set the royal prisoner free, but Rolph avowed his intention to have pistolled the King. The Grand Jury "found an ignoramus upon the Bill," in consequence of the Judge's directions. (Clarendon, Book 11).

Several ships in the Parliament's service went over to the King, on May 27th, 1648, and not long afterwards Prince Charles arrived off Lymington (p. 119) with a fleet, but was repulsed at Yarmouth, and retired. The town supplied the Cavaliers freely with provisions, and the Mayor, Barnard Knapton, would have accepted a subordinate military command in the Prince's army if it had succeeded in gaining a footing in the Isle of Wight. The Duke of Monmouth was, in 1685, proclaimed King by the Mayor of Lymington, who also raised 100 men for his service. Not only was Charles I. a prisoner at Carisbrook, but his daughter Princess Elizabeth died there in captivity on September 8th, 1650. She was buried in St. Thomas's Church, Newport, where a beautiful monument by Baron Marochetti has been erected by Her Majesty to commemorate her hapless fate. On November 30th Colonel Cobbett conducted King Charles under escort to Hurst Castle (p. 52), which is thus described: "This castle stands a mile and a half in the sea, upon a beach full of mud and stinking ooze upon low tides, having no fresh water within two or three miles of it, so cold, foggy, and noisome that the guards cannot endure it without shifting quarters." Colonel Ewer, who had for nearly been left at ant-Colonel under Colonel Hammond, and of whom Firebrace gives a vivid description, here guarded the royal captive, who was, on December 17th, 1648, removed by Colonel Cobbett by way of Lyndhurst, Ringwood, Romsey, Winchester, Alresford, Farnham, and Bagshot to Windsor. Guizot says "Three miles from Hurst he found a body of horse charged to escort him to Winchester. Everywhere on his road a crowd of gentlemen, citizens, and peasants came round him. Some of them were sightseekers, who retired after they had seen him pass, without any particular observation. Others deeply interested, and praying aloud for his liberty. As he approached Winchester the Mayor and Aldermen came to meet him, and presenting him, according to custom, the keys and mace of the city, addressed to him a speech full of affection. But Cobbett, rudely pushing his way towards them, asked if they had forgotten that the House had declared all who should address the King traitors. Whereupon, seized with terror, the functionaries poured forth humble excuses, protesting they were ignorant of the will of the House, and conjuring Cobbett to obtain their pardon. The next day the King resumed his journey. Mr. Joseph Butler was the loyal Mayor of Winchester, and the then recent and barbarous execution of

Captain Burleigh in that city was amply sufficient to terrify even the bravest of Cavaliers. In the Corporation Records of Winchester we read, "7th day of March, 1650. Taken out of the coffers and payd to ye Clarke of Lawrance Church for toling ye bell for ye prisoners, 3s. 4d. More to Mr. Holloway for instructing the seven prisoners, 6s. 8d." The Corporation of Winchester had sent the city plate, valued at 58l. 6s. 3d., and other plate belonging to various citizens, of the value of 300l. more, to Oxford for the service of the King. They had also lent His Majesty 1000l., and had been several times plundered by the Parliament party, and the Castle and divers houses of great value by them demolished. After the city had surrendered to Cromwell a forced contribution of 1400l. was exacted by the victors, so that the city could not maintain the 200 poor families residing within the walls. On Nov. 5th, 1652, the sum of 5l. was paid to Mr. Richard Purdue in full of all monies lent by him to Sir William Waller for the service of the State. On December 19th, 1651, payment was made to Mr. Thomas Muspratt, the ex-Mayor, of 20s., "which was laid out by him in the business between the city and Sir Richard Tichbourne," and on December 3rd, 1652, a similar re-payment was made to Mr. Hussey. On February, 18th, 1653, "Taken out and sent to Mr. Humbridge, solicitor to the Committee of Plundered Ministers, the sum of 3.5l. for service done for the city at the Committee aforesaid, 1l. 15s." On December 23rd, 1653, re-payment was made to the Mayor of 12l. 14s. spent "for payment of the Dutch prisoners." On May 2nd, 1656, "Taken then out of the coffers to pay Sir William Waller for the purchase of the Castle, with the appurtenances and other material therein belonging, the sum of two hundred and three sovereigns, and on Sept. 9th, 1656, deeds and several copies of the value of 3l." Some of the purchase money was borrowed from Mr. John Complin, and repaid on October 30th, 1657.

On April 3rd, 1657, mention is made of 30l. paid to Captain Palmer, and of "an agreement with the Lord Richard Cromwell, in the behalf of the country." October 23rd, 1657. "To six several messengers for bringing proclamations, 15s." A lawsuit had been pending against Sir William Waller, the cost of which was 3l. 1s. 4d. Of this sum 1l. 11s. 3d. was paid to Mr. Champion, on July 9th, 1658, in part payment of his account, which was finally settled on December 23rd, 1658. On October 22nd, 1658, "For building the walls going to the Castle, 8l. 6s. 6d.," and on December 23rd of the same year 1l. 18s. was expended on the Dutch prisoners, and 14s. 6d. for "addresses to the Lord Protector," Richard Cromwell. But Colonel John Clobery, whose home was Clobery House, in Parchment-street, on the site of which the hospital was afterwards built, and who commanded a regiment in Scotland, was already planning the Restoration, with his friend General Monk. Charles II. was proclaimed King in Winchester, on May 12th, 1660, and the cost of the civic rejoicings was no less a sum than 34l. 2s. 6d.

Charles I. was not unknown in Southampton, for in 1625, the first year of his unhappy reign, he, says Mr. Moody, "fled from the plague then raging in London, and summoned his Parliament to meet at Oxford." Soon after he came with his Council to Southampton, to deliberate with Ambassadors from Holland. The house where he was entertained is No 17, High-street, and still contains specimens of carving that once profusely adorned it. In 1634 an order was "for Southampton to furnish a ship of 700 tons, armed and victualled, to aid in the suppression of the Turks and other sea rovers. 1957, was levied in Southampton as ship money, and in 1641 Charles I. granted to the town the last charter (now in force)." For several of these and other previously mentioned incidents in the history of Southampton I am indebted to the kindness of T. W. Shore, Esq., of the Hartley Institution. In 1647 the Platform took shape, and in 1649 Nathaniel Robinson, a friend of Oliver Cromwell, was settled in the Rectory of All Saints. For the correspondence between Robinson, Cromwell, and Richard Major, of Hursley, concerning the marriage of Richard Cromwell and Dorothy Major, see Carlyle's "Letters and Speeches of Oliver Cromwell." Robinson was ejected in 1662, and became the first minister of Above Bar Chapel.

It was proposed to send the King as a present on January 6th, 1647, he being then at Carisbrooke Castle, certain provisions for his household, but the cautious burgesses resolved that their Mayor should first write to their member (Mr. Exton) to ask his opinion of this. When Cromwell had schemed the government into his own hands, Southampton refused to give admission to his troops until Captain Jubbs from Portsmouth obtained an entrance into the town by means of a ruse. He surprised the Mayor and Council in their Council House, which he surrounded with troops, obliging them to surrender the keys of the town gates. William Higgins, the Mayor, and Edward Downer were hereupon deposed (in 1654) by order of Cromwell for disaffection to his Government. On March 11th. 1655, Robert Mason, of Southampton, of whom mention has already been made, was at Salisbury, taking a leading part in the rising in Wiltshire and Dorsetshire, under Ponruddock, against the Parliament. On May 5th, 1656, Major-General Goffe wrote to Thurloe, Cromwell's secretary, complaining of the wicked spirit of the Southampton Magistrates. Goffe was major-general of Hampshire and Sussex, for which he received 1141l. 3s. 3d. per annum, besides his major-generalship. At the Restoration he escaped to America, and in his old age, by his sudden appearance and military skill, saved a New England village from being destroyed by Indians. Thus closed a stirring and eventful career. In December, 1659, Portsmouth openly declared for the Parliament, and the leaders of the army at once despatched troops thither. The following extracts from a letter quoted in "Slight's History of Portsmouth" give some interesting details. Colonel Whetham was Governor of Portsmouth, and under his command were Sir A. Haslerig and Colonels Morley and Walton :—

"Chichester, December 9th, 1659.

Upon the arrive of this sudden change and alteration in so considerable a garrison as Portsmouth, it was ordered that a considerable body of horse and foot should be sent down forthwith into the western parts to reduce that garrison or to block it up, and accordingly the Lord Disbrow was made choice of, as Commander-in-Chief, for that expedition, who advanced with several troops of horse from Westminster, and on Tuesday night last Colonel Hewson's regiment of foot began their march from the City of London, and five companies of Colonel Gibbon's regiment from the borough of Southwark. . . . . Also all possible care is taken for the waylaying, stopping, and guarding the several avenues and passes fronting and leading to the town, that so the reducing of it may prove the more facile, and the work expedited. By these sudden and unexpected commotions, a translate of some forces are expected from the northern parts, and 'tis said that three regiments of horse and dragoons are already on their march. From whence it is affirmed that Lord Lambert's infantry consists of above 7000 foot, and that he hath a very considerable body of horse. And it is the expectations of many that there will be a mutual concurrence and happy accommodation. . . . . By the last express from Portsmouth, on Saturday last, it is certified that a party of horse came as far as Gosport and faced the town, but afterwards wheeled off at a further distance. Seven troops are also marched from Petersfield towards Chichester, and some commotions are feared about Exeter. The foot that marched from London was met on Saturday last between Lockhup (Liphook) and Petersfield, and intend to arrive before Portsmouth the 12th inst., which place is said to be supplied with great store of provision and ammunition, having above three-score pieces of ordnance."

Dissensions ran high in Portsmouth, but Colonel Whetham promptly arrested Captains Smith, Peacock, and Brown, with about six of the townsmen. He also secured the fifteen men-of-war then in harbour, which were the *Diamond, Ruby, Sapphire, Pelican, Dragon,* and ten others. 700 lansmen and 140 horse formed the garrison, for whose supply many of the neighbouring gentlemen furnished provisions, whilst others came to assist personally in the defence with horses and arms. "Major Colwell having notice thereof, immediately advanced with his own troop and two others towards Petersfield, to whose assistance some few withdrew from Farnham and those parts, with a resolution to block up the garrison if they can." Colonel Morley and his friends endeavoured to persuade the Governors of Portland, Isle and Castle, and of Cowes, Hurst, and Carisbrooke Castles to join them. Their head-quarters were at the "Red Lion" Inn, which stood on the site of No. 91, High-street. The siege was speedily raised, as nine troops of Colonel Ferry's (Terry's?) horse and five companies of Colonel Lago's foot joined the besieged garrison. On the Wednesday before December 23rd, 1659, Sir Arthur Hastings marched at 10 a.m with 5000 men to the assistance of the Parliament, leaving only 400 in garrison. He halted that night at Petersfield, and proceeded next day to Guildford. (Woodward.)

But the Restoration was ere long a great reality, and rejoicing Cavaliers could sing with impunity of "The Sale of Rebellion's Household Stuff:—

"And here are old Noll's brewing vessels,
And here are his dray and his slings;
Here are Hewson's awl and his bristles,
And diverse other odd things;
And what is the price doth belong
To all these matters before ye?
I'll sell them all for an old song.
And so do I end my story!"

On April 25th, 1660, the House of Lords thanked God for deliverance "from Thraldom, Confusion, and Slavery," and in 1661 a writ was issued amongst others to the Marquis of Winchester, summoning him to the House of Lords.

His brother, Lord Charles Pawlet, occupied the family residence at Abbotstone after the restoration, whilst he himself found a home at Englefield House, which had come to him through the Marchioness, from the family of Sir F. Walsingham, and which, according to Camden, he rebuilt and greatly improved. Captain Symonds, in 1643, calls Englefield "now the house of the Lord Marquis of Winchester," and Sir Balthazar Gerbier praises it highly in the dedication of his "Council and Advice to all Builders, qto. 1663." The Marchioness died here in her ancestral home on March 10th, 1661, aged 51 years, six months, and 19 days. John Milton wrote her epitaph:—

"This rich marble doth inter
The honoured wife of Winchester;
A viscount's daughter, and earl's heir,
Besides what her virtues fair,
Added to her noble birth
More than she could own from earth."

On March 5th, 1674, the Marquis died in his 77th year, and was buried in the little church in the park, as was also the second Marchioness, who shared with him the dangers of the siege at Basing. His tomb is described as being a neat monument of black and white marble, and in a compartment this inscription in gold Roman letters:—

"He who in impious times undaunted stood,
And midst rebellion durst be just and good,
Whose arms asserted, and whose sufferings more
Confirmed the cause for which he fought before,
Rests here, rewarded by an heavenly prince
For what his earthly could not recompense.
Pray, reader, that such times no more appear,
Or, if they happen, learn true honour here.
Ask of this age's faith and loyalty.

Which to preserve them Heaven confined in thee.
Few subjects could a King like thine deserve,
And fewer such a King so well could serve.
Blest King, blest subject, whose exalted state
By sufferings rose, and gave the law to fate!
Such souls are rare, but might patterns given
To earth, and meant for ornaments to heaven.
By JOHN DRYDEN, Poet Laureat."

"The Lady Marchioness Dowager (in testimony of her love and sorrow) gave this monument to the memory of a most affectionate, tender husband."

And on a marble stone on the ground at the foot of the said monument is this inscription, in Roman capitals:—

"Here lieth interred the body of the most Noble and Mighty Prince John Powlet, Marquis of Winchester, Earl of Wiltshire, Baron of St. John, of Basing, first Marquis of England: a man of exemplary piety towards God, and of inviolable fidelity towards his Sovereign; in whose cause he fortified his house of Basing, and defended it against the rebels to the last extremity. He married three wives," &c. (here follow various family particulars).

"He died in the 77th year of his age, on the 5th of March, in the year of our Lord 1674.

"By Edward Walker, Garter King at Arms."

Woodward and Wilkes say "Loyalty House was never rebuilt. The Dukes of Bolton preferred their fine new place at Hackwood, to say nothing of Abbotstone, to the ancient mansion of their stock. And then afterwards Basing passed away from the Paulets. But yet of the grand old mansion house and its former magnificence there are plenty of vestiges all around, and in local names some memory of the great siege still survives."

Now the grass grows green over the crumbling ramparts, but still may the lover of the past pace along the works which so often echoed to the tread of Cavalier sentinels. Still may he see the walks trodden by Good Queen Bess, Fuller, Inigo Jones, and the noblest and loveliest of the land. The Basingstoke Canal runs through the ruins, but much is still left of the moats, whose sloping sides were often reddened with English blood. The green ivy twines gracefully around the curtain and the ruined shells of the flanking towers. The Garrison Gate, through which rode many a Royalist troop of horse, still stands erect, bearing the family arms, warning all passers by to "Love Loyalty."

On two occasions, at least, treasure has been found within the memory of man.

Two excavators employed in digging the canal made a discovery and departed at once, not caring to claim the wages due to them, and a former inhabitant of Basingstoke was known to be in possession of a number of gold coins of the reign of Charles I.

FINIS.

Again thanking numerous friends and helpers for much valuable information most readily and kindly given, here ends this imperfect account of "The Civil War in Hampshire, and the Story of Basing House."

APPENDIX.

SIEGE OF PORTSMOUTH—DEFENCE AND DEFIANCE—FARNHAM CASTLE—ISLE OF WIGHT—MINSTEAD AND ANDOVER—LUDLOW'S SKIRMISH—CHICHESTER AND SUSSEX—THE "SANCTA CLARA."

A few facts gleaned from various sources, more especially from the Journals of the House of Commons and from "A True Relation of the Passages which happened at the Town of Portsmouth (August 12th to September 7th, 1642), written by one that was employed in that Service," may fitly be inserted here. They relate to the period between August, 1642, and March, 1643, and have been obtained whilst this volume was passing through the Press.

During the siege of Portsmouth, Goring's men are said to have carried off (p. 40) from Portsea Isle about 350 cattle, with many sheep and lambs, to Portsmouth. They killed the best, "and the rest they kept within the town upon some ground below the mounts that round the town, but the most of them were kept on a marsh near the town," guarded by musketeers. On August 12th the trooper who lost his horse (p. 18) had his hat cut, "and his head a little rased with a sword, but not much hurt." Two mounts were now raised at Portbridge to guard that important pass. The *Henrietta Maria*, pinnace (p. 40), was taken to Southampton, where six of her guns were landed and brought back to the neighbourhood of Portsmouth. Three of them were pointed towards the town, and the others towards "Porchdownue." The wheel of the abandoned gun (p. 40) had broken. Several skirmishes took place with foragers (p. 18), but "no great hurt done, though some cannon bullets came very near, and under their horses' bellies." The burnt mill (p. 18) was "a water mill, that only goeth at the ebbing of the sea." One Puritan trooper here lost his hat, which fell off, and another lost his sword, which the captor said was worth 5l., "a ribbon breaking at his wrist." Two days afterwards the Parliamentarians asked a parley for the exchange of prisoners. The garrison "knew not the sound of a parley from an alarum," and fired on the trumpeter, but missed him. The brave Scotchman (p. 18) was sent blindfolded "to a place called Newgate, exchanged, and mounted behind the trumpeter." Master Winter (p. 18) was Lieutenant of Southsea Castle. He was detained at the Court of Guard, which was a mile and a half distant from the town, close to a farmhouse, where Sir William Waller had established his headquarters. His son carried back intelligence to Portsmouth that the King was at Broadlands, if not nearer, and that a troop of Parliament horse had gone to bring His Majesty to Lady Norton's house, Southwick. Lord Wentworth's servant, disguised as a shepherd, reached Portsmouth together with his guide, and stated that the King would arrive from Oxford within four days with 12,000 foot, 6500 horse, and 3000 Dragooners. On August 18th the noise of pickaxes and carts at Gosport was plainly heard in Portsmouth. The man killed (p. 18), who is also said to have been shot by a sentry in mistake, was "Peter Baker, a very good ship carpenter." A blindfolded trumpeter was to no purpose sent by the besiegers to propose a parley on August 27th. On Monday, August 29th, the town fired heavily on Gosport and the Parliament Court of Guard, but the gunners only "made some holes into the tops of houses at Gosport, but killed not a man or a horse." A blindfolded trumpeter brought into Portsmouth, on Sept. 2nd, two bucks, which had been promised to Goring by the Parliamentary Committee on the previous Saturday (p. 42), and on the same day, about 4.0 p.m., the two gun battery at Gosport opened fire. The soldier who was killed (p. 19) was "carrying of earth on the great mount at the gate." Only a few shots were fired from Gosport during this night. On September 3rd, besides other damage, the besiegers "shot down the end of the church, and shot through a great many houses in the town, but killed not anybody." Vicars has written "Larvace" for "Jervoise" (p. 29), as appears from the original. Goring left Portsmouth for France and Holland at 6.0 p.m. on the day of the surrender. (P. 20.) His property was shipped on that and the following day. On Tuesday, September 6th, the decomposed body of a brave Dutch trooper, who had been missing for 11 days, and whose horse had returned with a blood-stained saddle, was discovered by his besieging comrades with 6*l.* still in his pocket. On September 8th two troops of horse reached Portsmouth at noon, and two companies of foot were posted in Portsea Isle. Hay and provender would not have lasted 14 days longer, there was not much butter or cheese in store, but salt and malt were abundant. Meal and biscuit were sufficient for at least three months, and large quantities of salt meat in powder were also found in the town. The Cavaliers boasted that they would retake the fortress before Christmas, but it was thought able to defy 10,000 men. The Earl of Warwick was also protecting it with "six goodly ships," which did not fire a single shot during the siege. (Grenville Library, 3830, Brit. Museum.)

Major Harbert and Captain Bushell (p. 42) promised quarter to the garrison of Southsea Castle (Grenville Library, 3803-40). On August 16th it was resolved that "Mr. Nicholas Weston did ill service to the Parliament in the business of Portsmouth and the Isle of Wight." He, Mr. Christopher Lewknor, and Goring now lost their seats. Sir William Lewis was on Sept. 8th, 1642, appointed Governor of Portsmouth, with 3*l.* per diem as pay, and within a few days the Committee for Hampshire and the officers and soldiers received the thanks of Parliament. Captains Martin, Swanley, and Browne Bushell were specially commended by name. The Sheriff of Hants had already, on August 13th, been called into the House and thanked for his good service and ready affections to the House, and on the same day the Mayor of Arundel received authority "for making stay of suspected persons, horses, or other warlike provisions going to Portsmouth." Mr. Lisle, M.P. for Winchester, carried this order of thanks with him, he and "Mr. Tulse, of that county" of Hants, having each obtained a pass "to have license to convey into Hampshire six horses, and to bring from thence household stuff without interruption or lett." Thanks were also voted to Colonel Sandys, of the Vine, "for his great service done in this last expedition into Kent." Mr. Button was ordered, with his regiment, to assist in the defence of Hurst Castle. On December 30th, 1642, Captain Swanley and others were ordered to be held harmless and rewarded for their services in the Isle of Wight and at Portsmouth. They were also to be commissioned "to land men and ordnance, and to use hostile acts on occasion for the service of the King and Parliament." Six days previously Captain John Lobb had been appointed Deputy-Governor of Portsmouth, and Sir W. Lewis was authorised to release, at his discretion, any of the private soldiers imprisoned at Portsmouth, on their promising not to serve against the Parliament. On February 6th, 1643, the Committees for Hants and Kent were ordered to be added to "the Prisoners' Committee, whereof Sir Robert Harley has the chair, to give not more than 6*d.* per diem to poor prisoners." Sir W. Lewis was on February 22nd, 1643, ordered to decide whether Captain Henry Chitty (p. 41) should command a Foot company at Portsmouth.

On October 19th, 1642, the Earl of Pembroke was placed in charge of Hants, Wilts, Somerset, Dorset, Devon, Cornwall, and the Isle of Wight. He was to have similar authority to the Earl of Essex "to raise and conduct forces for the suppressing of rebellion and preventing insurrections," and was ordered to pay his soldiers by seizing "the rents and revenues of Arch bishops, Bishops, Deans, and Chapters, and other notorious delinquents." On October 27th Sir Thomas Jervoise and Mr. Wallop were sent into Hants on Parliament service. A garrison was voted for Southampton on November 29th, and the members for the town were on the same day ordered "to attend the service of the House, all delays and excuses set apart." Three regiments of Volunteers, to be commanded by "Colonel Ruthen, Bainfield, and some other commander," were on December 5th, 1642, voted to be raised for Parliament service in Cornwall, Devon Somerset, Wilts, and Hants. The Deputy Lieutenants of these counties were ordered to disarm all Trained Band soldiers refusing to join this force, which had the power of martial law, and to give their arms to their respective regiments. The Colleges of Winchester, Westminster, Eton, and Christ Church, Oxford, were on October 29th, 1642, authorised to retain their revenues, but on February 22nd, 1643, an order was passed that the "young scholars" at Westminster Eton, and Winchester were not bound to wear surplices if they objected to so doing. Theodore Jennings, who first brought news to London of the capture of Winchester (p. 45), received 20*l.* A public thanksgiving was ordered for Sunday, December 18th, 1642, in London, Westminster, and Southwark, and Sir H. H. Vane was directed to prepare a narrative of this success." Sir Philip Stapylton, Colonel Hampden, and Sir H. Vane were ordered to thank Waller "for his care and vigilancy at Winchester," and 2000*l.* for his army was ordered to be advanced by some Southampton merchants. On January 5th, 1643, the Mayor and Sheriff of Southampton were forbidden to publish the King's proclamation prohibiting the receipt of tonnage and poundage, and another of grace, favour, and pardon to Hants and other counties which ordered notice of the approach of any rebel force to be given to the nearest Royal garrison. A third proclamation "for the better government of His Majesty's Army" was to be published forthwith. On February 10th, 1643, two troops of horse and a regiment of dragoons, to be commanded by Sir Thomas Jervoise, were voted for the defence of the county. On January 21st, 1643, the Associated Forces of Hants, Surrey, Sussex, and Kent "shall be drawn into a body." Waller was granted the power of martial law on February 23rd, but on the following day we hear that he had in some troops not more than ten men; in two other troops not more than 30; and that he had only received 100 dragoons of the 1500 promised to him. He had received the thanks of the House on January 14th for his services at Portsmouth, Farnham Castle, and Chichester.

Rushworth says (vol. ii., p. 82) that Waller reached Farnham Castle with only horse and dragoons, and summoned it (p. 23), "but, having no ordnance, they contemned the summons." After the gate was shattered by the petard yet they could not presently enter, by reason they within had placed at the gate great piles of wood." These being removed, the garrison asked for quarter. They took in the castle 300 sheep, 100 oxen, besides some warlike provisions of powder and shot." Sir Francis Williamson and twelve other gentlemen taken at Farnham were, on December 7th, 1642, ordered to be sent to Winchester House, the King's Bench, and the Lord Mayor's Prison in Southwark. Their names were to be given to the Speaker, who was to dispose of them. Mr. Hooke was to be disposed of by Mr. Pym, and the captive Irish Papists were to remain in the Gatehouse until further orders.

On August 13th, 1642, the Earl of Warwick was ordered to supply the town of Newport, in the Isle of Wight, with thirty barrels of powder, to be used for the defence of the island, as thought desirable by the Mayor (Mr. Moses Read), Mr. Bunckley, Mr. Thomas Boreman, and Mr. Robert Urry of Freshwater. Mr. Venn and Mr. Vassall were to thank the Mayor and others "for their care of the safety of that place and respects to the House." A Royalist declaration was extensively signed by the gentlemen of the island, and Sir Robert Dillington "for intending to send provisions into Portsmouth (p. 39), for putting his hand to

a declaration" was sent for as a delinquent, but was released on bail September 8th, 1642. Lieut.-Colonel Burk, Captain Burleigh, who afterwards tried to rescue the King at Carisbrooke, Colonel Brett, and Captain Humphrey Turney were also sent for. They surrendered to the Sergeant-at-Arms, were brought before the Committee of Examinations, and on September 26th " shall be forthwith discharged of their attendance." The name of the minister of Newport (p. 22) is variously given as Harvey and Harby. Col. Brett and the garrison of Carisbrooke Castle were allowed to go anywhere except to Portsmouth. The House of Lords was urged on September 2nd, 1642, to remove the Countess of Portland from the Isle of Wight. Friendly seamen at length gave her a passage to the mainland. On September 20th Sir J. Loe was ordered to the Isle of Wight, having been appointed Colonel of a regiment by the Earl of Pembroke, and on December 12th 20 men at 8d. per diem were to garrison Carisbrooke Castle. Mr. Peter Gard, collector in the Isle of Wight, is mentioned January 11th 1643, and on February 11th Captain Richard Swanley wrote a letter to the House of Commons on board "H.M.S. Charles, riding at Cowes." He stated that a Royal proclamation in 1639 had forbidden Englishmen "to sail with other nations." He had, therefore, sent his boatswain to " Captain Whittavell, Vice-Admiral to Van Tromp, now in Cowes Road, bound for East India," to demand the surrender of all English sailors. The Dutchman twice refused, whereupon Swanley ordered the Captain of Cowes Castle and the Mayor and Corporation of Newport to stop all supplies to the Dutch Fleet. Sir H. Vane, jun., and Mr. Lisle were ordered to write to Captain Swanley, bidding him countermand these orders without delay, and Mr. Pym was to write to Mr. Strickland "that he may satisfy the States herein." On February 15th, 1643, measures were taken for the relief of "such poor distressed Irish Protestants as are come out of Ireland into the Isle of Wight," and Mr. Samuel Cordell, maker of powder for the Parliament Navy, was on March 3rd, 1643, permitted to freely carry saltpetre to his works near Guildford.

" August 12th, 1642.—Whereas information was this day given to the House that Mr. Clarke, Vicar of Audover, doth obstinately refuse to obey the order of this House in admitting of Mr. Symonds to preach there as lecturer, and gives out that he, his wife, and children will be all put to death before they condescend to the said order." Mr. Clarke was cited for contempt, and on August 24th witnesses were called in " who testified that the said Vicar gave a command to lock the church doors. That he said "rather than Mr. Symonds should preach there, by order of Parliament, he would lose his life, and his wife and children should die in prison. That the church was as much his own as his own house, and he would hold his right, let the Parliament do what they would." Mr. Clarke being called in denied the truth of this information, whereupon he was ordered to withdraw. Being re-called, the Speaker told him that the House was not satisfied with his answer, the information having been proved by several witnesses. He was therefore committed to the King's Bench during the pleasure of the House, Mr. Symonds being duly installed at Andover. "Thursday, September 1st, 1642, ordered that Mr. Robert Clarke, upon his humble petition, expressing his sorrow that he had offended the House, be forthwith discharged from any further imprisonment." The parishioners of Minstead, near Lyndhurst, petitioned the House on February 15th, 1643, that Mr. Lake, a double beneficed minister, might be ordered to re-admit Mr. King as curate, to pay him arrears of stipend, and to allow him a competent maintenance in future. This information was referred to the Committee for Plundered Ministers, who were instructed to provide for the services at Minstead Church.

At an early period of the war Colonel Ludlow was Governor of Wardour Castle. He says (Memoirs, Vol. i., p. 66):—"Having notice that some of the King's forces were at Salisbury, I went out with six of my troop to procure intelligence, and to do what service I could upon the enemy's stragglers. When I came to Sutton (Mandeville), I was informed that six of them were gone up the town just before. Whereupon we made after them, and, by their horses, which we saw tied in a yard, supposed them to be in the house to which it belonged. Upon which I went in and was no sooner within the door but two of them shut it upon me; but my party rushing in, they ran out at another and escaped. A third mounted one of my men's horses and rid away; the other three, who were in a room of the house, upon promise of quarter for life surrendered themselves, with whom, and six horses, we returned to the Castle." The Mayor of Salisbury was directed "to keep Mr. Wroughton, now in prison, in safe custody until further order."

Mr. John Alford, Sir William Goring, Sir Thomas Bowyer, Sir William Morley, and others demanded the magazine at Chichester for the King's service on August 19th, 1642 (p. 11). In reply to a petition from the Mayor and Corporation of Chichester (p. 48), Mr. Henry Chittey was ordered to continue as Captain of Trained Bands at Chichester, and the Mayor was forbidden to publish a Royal proclamation of grace, favour, and pardon to the inhabitants of Sussex. Among the prisoners taken at Chichester (p. 51) not previously mentioned were Sir William Balnidine, Mr. Collins, a minister, Walter Monk, William and Richard Mayo, John Windsor, and Mr. Anderson. The inhabitants of the city offered a month's pay to the Army to escape being plundered, "which was accepted of." The money and plate taken at Chichester were sent up to London by sea. The Earl of Thanet was on November 29th, 1642, ordered to be called to account for sending forces to Chichester against the Parliament, and on the same day the security of the public faith was guaranteed to those in Sussex who aided the Parliament by their contributions. Sir Richard Lashley and his son were sent to London as prisoners on December 20th, and committed to Winchester House. "Mr. White to be keeper of my Lord Peter's house, and Mr. Dillingham keeper of the Dean of Paul's his house," where some of the prisoners from Chichester were confined. Twelve others were sent to Winchester House, but the Wood-street Compter and the Poultry received Majors Lindsay and Gordon, Captains Wolfe, Cooper, Ennies, Atkinson, Stephenson, and Moluin. Sir William Balnidine, Mr. William May (Mayo?), Lieuts. Withrington, Pridgeon, and Bird, Ensigns Goffe, and two Shelleys. Sir W. Balnidine, and Mr. Lowknor, who lost his Recordership were kept in close custody, being allowed to receive provisions and necessaries, but being forbidden to converse privately with anyone. Colonel Cockeram was likewise detained in Wood-street Compter. Sir Edward Ford was, in company with the Sheriffs of Kent and Devon, examined before the House of Commons in close custody on January 9th, 1643, and on the following day it was decided that "the 60 prisoners may go to Windsor in coaches if they will pay the cost" (p. 51). On September 7th, 1642, Sir John Caryll of Harting, obtained a pass for France, or beyond the seas, for himself, his lady, two men, and two maids, "provided he carry no prohibited goods with him, with his convenient necessaries." Deserters from the Cavaliers were to be welcomed, Papists and declared delinquents excepted. On October 10th, 1642, John Newman, clerk, of Rodmell, Francis Atkinson, Vicar of Firle, Henry Shephard, Vicar of Kingston and Pendinghoe, Walter Dumbleby, of East Aldrington, Antony Hugget, Vicar of Glynde and the Cliffe, and Thomas Russell, Parson of St. John's, in Lewes, were ordered 'to be sent for as delinquents, for denying to contribute or lend anything for this service in this time of imminent danger." They were discharged on petition on November 11th, 1642. Non-contributors to the Parliament in Sussex were to be deprived of their horses and arms. The local forces were to have the same discipline as the army of the Earl of Essex, and were to be paid by means of subscriptions and fines levied on the enemies of the Parliament. On February 15th, 1643, two troops of horse under Colonel Morley, and a regiment of foot under Colonel Anthony Stapley, all to be at the disposal of the Earl of Essex, were voted by Parliament for the defence of Sussex.

The cargo of the *Sancta Clara* (p. 41), Captain Benedict Stratford, was partly landed at Southampton, and carried to the house of Mr. Legay, who owned the ship. Two Committeemen, the Deputy-Lieutenants of Hants, and the members for the town, were ordered to ascertain the value of the cargo, so that it might be restored to the lawful owners when found. The captain, who was also part-owner, John Marston, and others, claimed the cargo, giving a curious account of the ship's voyage. Certain Spanish merchants, supported by the Spanish Ambassador, put in a claim, which was allowed, for the sale of the cochineal and the coining of the bullion in the Tower of London. They paid 50,000*l*. as security, and, after complicated proceedings in the Admiralty Court, the *Sancta Clara* was at length released in March, 1643, and proceeded on her voyage.

CHAPTERS.

	Page.
I.—The Ruined Fortress	5
II.—Basing in "Ye Olden Tyme"	10
III.—The Civil War Begins	13
IV.—The Capture of Farnham Castle, Marlborough, and Winchester	23
V.—The Generals and Their Forces	32
VI.—Events in Portsmouth—Colonel Goring Declares for the King—Skirmishes near Southampton, and in Isle of Wight—Capture of Southsea Castle—Surrender of Portsmouth	37
VII.—Outrages in Wiltshire—Surrender of Farnham and Winchester—Southampton Declares for the Parliament	44
VIII.—Rival Parties in Sussex - The Capture of Arundel and Chichester — Desecration of Churches—Hampshire Defences	47
IX.—Fighting at Alton—Sir William Waller Plunders Winchester and Defaces Romsey Abbey—Road Waggons Seized near Basingstoke	54
X.—Prince Maurice at Salisbury—Fast Day at Southampton and Portsmouth—Colonel Norton Repulsed—Basing House becomes a Garrison	57
XI.—Alarm at Southampton—Cavaliers Fined and Imprisoned—Colonel Powlet Slain near Winchester—Southampton and the Isle of Wight Fortified—Winchester Re-Occupied by the Cavaliers	61
XII.—The Governor of Basing House, and other Officers of the Garrison	64
XIII.—Sir William Waller's Preparations—Lord Crawford Defeated at Poole—Necessities of Portsmouth—The Associated Counties - London Trained Bands Ordered to Basing—Operations near Farnham—Desperate Assault upon Basing House—Repulse of Sir William Waller at Basing House—Capture of Lord Saltoun—Advance of Sir Ralph Hopton, Sir William Waller Beaten at Basing House—Retreat to Farnham	68
XIV.—Defence of the Isle of Wight—The Marquis of Winchester Accused of High Treason—Affairs at Portsmouth - Sir William Waller at Farnham Advance of Lord Hopton—Occupation of Winchester, Skirmish and Troubles at Odiham Expedition to Midhurst—Fighting at Farnham—Sir William Waller Reinforced	79
XV.—Defence of the Isle of Wight—Naval Estimates—Captain Swanley's Prisoners—The Sussex Cavaliers—Lord Hopton is Reinforced—Letter to Prince Rupert—Forays into Sussex—	

	Page.
Fight at South Harting	90
XVI.—Colonel Norton's Victory at Romsey—Lord Crawford Asks for Sack—Sir William Waller Attacks Alton—The Church Stormed—Disposal of Prisoners—Royalist March to Arundel—Siege of Arundel Castle - Skirmish at Havant—Warblington Castle - Arundel Castle Surrenders—Lord Crawford—Traces of the Conflict	98
(By a typographical error Chapter XVII. has been numbered XIX.)	
XIX.—Rival Parties at Winchester—H.M.S. Mayflower—Capt. Hall and Tobias Baisley—Colonel Ludlow Taken—Calenture—The Isle of Wight and Lymington—Governor Murford at Southampton—Royalist Plot—Skirmishes near Southampton—Outrages at Winchester—Preparations for Battle—Fighting at Basing House and Romsey—Sir John Oglander	116
XX.—A Battle Imminent—Sir William Waller's Advance—Lord Hopton's Reinforcements—Westmeon Occupied—Cavaliers at Alresford—Skirmish at Tisted—Cheriton Fight—Struggle in the Wood—The Tide Turns—Hopton Retreats—A Cavalry Charge—Keen Pursuit—Trophies of Victory—Losses on Both Sides—The Earl of Forth—Winchester Surrenders—Lady Hopton taken Prisoner—Rejoicings in London	126
XXI.—Dr. Fuller and Army Chaplains—Traitors at Basing House—The Associated Counties—Waller's Success at Christchurch—The Isle of Wight in Danger—Waltham House Taken—Recruiting in London—Opposition at Winchester—Affairs at Southampton, Odiham, Basing, and Salisbury—Opening of the Campaign of 1644	137
XXII.—Waller at Basing—Cavaliers Repulsed at Odiham—A Siege Imminent—Hostile Preparations Basing Village Occupied—Desultory Skirmishes—Watch and Ward—Sir Marmaduke Rawdon Night Attacks—The Siege Continues—Cropredy Bridge—Relief a Necessity—Buff Coats and Mortars—Rival Preachers	148
XXIII.—Forays in Hants—Winchester Castle. The "Golden Sun"—Affairs at Basing—The Siege Continues—Summons to Surrender—Bombardment—Messages to Oxford—Attack and Defence — Salisbury Cathedral — A Night Attack—Defence of Isle of Wight—Stubborn Basing — Expected Surrender — Successful Sorties Hopes of Relief—Cornet Bryan Captured—Hostilities Continue—Essex Surrenders	159

	Page.
XXIV.—Recruiting—Basing again Summoned—Renewed Bombardment—Proposed Relief—Sorties in Force—Lady Waller—A Puritan Army—Relief at Last—Colonel Gage—The Relieving Force—The March to Basing—Loyalty House Saved—Retreat to Oxford	171
XXV.—Fight in Basing Village—Lieutenant-Colonel Johnson—Renewed Blockade—Attack on the Church—Gathering Armies—The King's Advance—Andover Fight—Rendezvous at Basing—Welcome Supplies—Gage's Second Relief—The Siege Raised	182
XXVI.—Dr. Lewis—Goring in Hants—Courtesies of Warfare—Cavalier Defeat at Salisbury, Lieut.-General Middleton—Requisitions—A Cavalier Plot—Isle of Wight Affairs—Goring at Portbridge and Christchurch—Ludlow at Salisbury—Death of Colonel Gage—Crondall in Flames—Cavalier Raids—Waller Pursues Goring	196
XXVII.—Cromwell in Hants—Duchess of Chevereux—Military Changes—Cavalry Skirmish—Goring Recalled—Religious Strife—Colonel Rawdon leaves Basing—Fairfax on the March—Stern Discipline—Basing again Besieged—Langford House—Distressed Taunton—Massey at Romsey—Clubmen	208
XXVIII.—Road Waggons in Danger—Clubmen Routed—Ways and Means—Lord Ogle's Requisitions—Col. Dalbier—Basing again Besieged—Mining Operations—Hampshire Clubmen—Church Parade—A Shattered Tower—A Gallant Stratagem	217
XXIX.—Cromwell and his Brigade—Colonels Hammond, Fleetwood, and Harrison—Hugh Peters—Cromwell Summons Winchester—The Castle Besieged—Bishop Curle—Siege Operations—Bombardment—Parley and Surrender—Booty and Spoil—Hugh Peters at Westminster—Troubles at Winchester	221
XXX.—Basing and Langford in Danger—Cromwell's Arrival-Terrible Odds-A Reconnaissance—Basing Summoned—Sunday Bombardment—Colonel Hammond Taken—The Fall of Basing—Killed, Wounded, and Prisoners—A Good Encouragement—Public Thanksgiving	234
XXXI.—Basing House Demolished—Cromwell's Departure—The Captive Marquis—Langford House Surrenders—Satirical Pamphlets—Confiscated Estates—Subsequent Events—The King at Carisbrooke—Royalist Risings—The Captive Monarch-Archives of Winchester-Southampton and Portsmouth Affairs—The Restoration—Death of the "Loyal Marquis"	247
APPENDIX.—Siege of Portsmouth—Defence and Defiance—Farnham Castle—Isle of Wight—Minstead and Andover—Ludlow's Skirmish—Chichester and Sussex—The "Sancta Clara"	258

INDEX OF PERSONS.

Alexander, 198.
Alford, 261.
Amory, 167.
Amtell, 218.
Anderson, 112,261.
Appleyard, 129.
Archer, 70-8, 83, 85, 99-102.
Ask, 138.
Astley, 87, 92, 117.
Aston, 167, 173, 175, 204.
Atkinson, 261.
Audley, 131.

Bailey, 110.
Baines, 208.
Baisley, 117,205.
Baker, 96.
Balfour, 97, 123-8, 130, 131, 135, 139, 152, 187, 197, 208.
Ball, 117.
Balnidine, 261.
Bame (Game), 198.
Bamfield (Bamford), 105, 112, 259.
Barclay, 199.
Bard, 59.
Barnes, 210.
Barrow, 139.
Bartholomew, 48.
Batley, 86.
Baxter, 158, 206, 214.
Beard (Peard), 133.
Beck, 218.
Bedford, 199.
Beech, 220.
Behre (Hayne), 104, 108, 144, 200, 212.
Bellars, 158.
Bennet, 70, 28, 144, 197, 211, 230, 231.
Berry (Derry), 198.
Bettesworth, 94, 164, 214, 215, 218, 249.
Bird, 261.
Bishop, 112, 113.
Blagrave, 208, 219.
Boate, 111.
Bodley, 108.
Bodville (Bovill) 112, 132.
Bolle 99-101.
Boudman, 161.
Boreman, 260.
Bowen, 98.
Bower, 198.
Bowles, 219.

Bowyer, 261.
Boys, 151, 211, 219.
Bracebridge, 63.
Brandon, 117.
Brasier, 140, 141.
Braxton, 161.
Brentford (Earl of Forth), 123,126, 127, 133, 189.
Brett, 260.
Browne, 24, 49, 113, 117, 121, 126-130, 131, 141, 151, 155, 180, 202, 217, 218-9, 255.
Bryan, 67, 161, 163, 165, 167, 168, 181, 191-3, 202.
Buck, 260.
Buneklcy, 260.
Buncle, 175, 177, 178, 180, 181.
Burcher, 107.
Burleigh, 38, 253, 260.
Burton, 16.
Bushell, 39-42, 124, 259.
Butler, 105, 107, 131, 133, 172, 184, 211, 253.
Button, 79, 151, 259.

Campion (Champion), 175, 254.
Capcot, 96.
Capel, 14, 65, 159.
Carnarvon, 57.
Carne, 51, 79, 90, 118, 124, 125, 140, 154, 187.
Carr, 188.
Cary, 131.
Caryll, 91, 93, 95, 261.
Case, 136.
Cawley, 41, 47, 49-51, 197, 219, 219, 251.
Chase, 82.
Chevereux, 208.
Chidleigh, 131.
Chillingworth, 96, 105, 112, 113.
Chitty, 41, 47, 259, 261.
Clarke, 260.
Clerk, 61.
Clinson, 73, 74.
Clobery, 251.
Clubmen, 216-20.
Cobbett, 253.
Cochram (Cockeram), 111, 139, 261.
Cocken, 140.
Cole, 59, 218.
Coleraine, 260.
Collins, 261.

Complin, 140, 254.
Constable, 131.
Cooke, 111, 198, 201, 212, 252.
Cooper (Cowper), 91, 115, 131, 167, 168, 260.
Coram, 67, 149, 193, 248.
Cordell, 260.
Cornelius, 116, 120.
Cotton, 111.
Courtney, 98, 107, 231.
Coventry, 44, 139.
Coward, 210.
Crawford, 50, 68, 71, 84, 88, 93, 99, 100, 102, 110, 111, 185.
Crewe, 187, 189.
Crofts, 140.
Cromwell, 36, 172, 185, 186, 194, 205-12, 215, 217, 220-36, 237-40, 245, 217, 250, 252, 254.
Crooke, 208.
Crosfield, 158.
Cuffand, 66, 152, 163-7, 179, 184, 191, 192, 211, 218, 252.
Cully, 150.
Curle, 14, 96, 141, 228-32.

Dalbier, 57, 68, 132, 185, 188, 212, 218-223, 234-6, 239-40, 245, 247, 251.
Deane, 227, 235.
Denbigh, 61.
Denham, 23.
Devereux, 204.
Dillington, 260.
Dixie, 108, 141.
Doddington, 118.
Dolling, 116.
Dore, 119.
Doucet, 253.
Dove, 215.
Doven, 166.
Downer, 255.
Drake, 118.
Draper, 199.
Duckett, 131.
Duett (Dewett), 70, 198, 200, 214, 216.
Dunscombe, 150.

Eaton, 48.
Edwards, 158.
Egerley, 116.
Elizabeth, Queen, 11, 12, 119.
Elizabeth, Princess, 253.

INDEX OF PERSONS.

Eldridge, 248.
Elliott, 86.
Ellingworth, 85.
Ellis, 248.
Ennis, 110, 261.
Erle, 69, 79, 107, 199, 207.
Essex, Earl of, 16, 32, 41, 55-9, 69, 78, 96, 104, 110, 111, 118, 143-8, 152, 170-2, 181-91, 191, 203.
Eure, 226, 253.
Evans, 124.
Evelyn, 123, 198.
Exton, 13, 63, 117, 254.

Fairfax, 58, 211-18, 249.
Faithorne, 190, 209, 211-2, 248, 250.
Fane, 23, 172.
Fielder (Feiler), 61, 164, 198, 209.
Fielding, 201.
Fiennes, 29, 61, 206, 212, 214, 233.
Fincher, 190, 209.
Fitch, 140.
Fitzjames, 212.
Fleetwood, 185, 217, 226.
Fleming, 63, 132, 141.
Fletcher, 182.
Ford, 45, 48-50, 86, 91-6, 105, 109, 112, 113, 230, 252, 261.
Forth (Earl of), 123, 126-127, 133, 189.
Fortescue, 203.
Foxall, 248.
Foy, 248.
Fry, 249.
Fuller, 57, 137, 251.
Fussell, 216.

Gage, 173-181, 189, 191-4, 202.
Gallop, 13, 63, 117.
Gard, 260.
Gardiner, 206.
Gawen, 252.
Gerrard, 81, 92, 103, 186.
Gertin, 214.
Glansie, 248.
Goddard, 139.
Goffe, 255, 261.
Gogell, 139.
Goldsmith, 248.
Goodwin, 30, 49.
Gordon, 261.
Gorges, 187.
Goring, 13, 15-21, 37-43, 47, 112, 186, 188, 196, 200-206, 209-13, 216, 251, 258-9, 261.
Grandison, 21, 30, 45, 63, 64.
Graves, 154, 184.
Gray, 133, 143.
Green, 210.
Gregory, 191.
Grenville, 111, 122, 123, 138.
Griffith (Griffin), 214, 241-3.
Grose, 142, 150.

Hacket, 212.

Hammond, 226, 230, 237-41, 244-5, 253.
Harbert, 259.
Hare, 248.
Harrington, 186, 190.
Harris, 69, 233.
Harrison, 119, 185, 220, 226, 227, 230, 244.
Hartop, 239.
Harvey, 59, 123, 139, 143, 251.
Haslerig, 49, 51, 55, 58, 69, 80, 81, 85, 100, 103, 113, 114, 118, 128-31, 135, 141, 144, 155, 186, 188, 199, 201, 206, 255.
Hastings, 201, 255.
Hawkins, 175, 178, 179.
Head, 108, 141.
Heath, 210.
Hencocke, 140.
Hewson, 225, 226, 248-9, 255.
Heylin, 96.
Heyman, 108.
Higgins, 255.
Hill, 150.
Hitchcocke, 139.
Hodges, 208.
Hodkins, 249.
Hollar, 66, 241-2, 251.
Holloway, 254.
Holmes, 141.
Hooke, 260.
Hooper, 63, 215.
Hopton, 21, 32, 52, 58, 70, 75, 78, 80-97, 102, 106, 109-11, 116, 118, 121-37, 146, 159, 186, 188, 205, 213.
Horner, 57-8.
Howard, 131.
Humbridge, 254.
Hungerford, 57-8.
Hunt, 124.
Hussey, 254.
Hyde, 204, 248.

Imbor, 141.
Inchiquin, 80, 109, 118, 131.
Ivory, 66, 149, 184.

Jackson, 134.
Jeffrey, 162, 176.
Jenkins, 139, 140.
Jephson, 13, 144, 171, 179, 182, 196, 199, 201, 203, 211, 217, 218, 226.
Jervoise, 13, 20, 54, 79, 137, 154, 157, 179, 184, 199, 216, 249, 259, 260.
Johnson, 66, 74, 76, 140, 178, 182.
Johnston, 187, 189.
Jones, 62, 104, 149-51, 162, 168, 183, 194, 197, 198, 200, 207, 208, 214, 211-2, 251.
Jordan, 150, 154.
Joyner, 217.
Jubbs, 255.

Kaddens, 82.

Kelsall, 198.
Kelsey, 218.
Kenton, 218.
Ker, 199.
King, 50, 237-8, 244, 261.
Kingsmill, 69, 172.
Kingston, 134.
Kite, 134.
Knapton, 119, 253.

Lacy, 121, 156.
Lago, 255.
Lake, 261.
Lane, 110.
Langdale, 186, 200, 204.
Langley, 66, 149, 152, 204.
Lashley, 261.
Lockford, 49.
Lee, 80, 260.
Legate, 110.
Logaye, 61, 75, 121, 143, 262.
Lovesny (Livesay), 49, 85, 108, 126, 127, 111, 164.
Lovett, 85.
Lewin, 139.
Lewis, 13, 14, 20, 45, 49, 51, 57, 158, 196, 259.
Lewknor, 20, 23, 41, 47, 50, 51, 259.
Lilly, 246.
Lindsay, 261.
Lisle, 13, 51, 79, 80, 129, 140, 151, 158, 185, 196, 199, 205, 217, 225, 252, 259.
Lloyd, 218.
Lobb, 217, 259.
Long, 79, 206.
Longland, 218, 228.
Love, 69, 183, 206, 220, 233.
Lovell, 110.
Lower, 200, 203, 233.
Ludlow, 101, 110, 118, 159, 171, 177, 182, 191, 192, 197, 198, 200, 203, 204, 214, 237, 251, 261.

Maitland, 165.
Major, 63, 120, 254.
Manchester, 79, 143, 171, 172, 184-94, 194, 201.
Manning, 118, 133.
Mansurgh, 217.
Manwaring, 82.
Markham, 190.
Marsh, 134.
Marshall, 138.
Marston, 262.
Martin, 198, 259.
Mason, 63, 69, 120, 255.
Massey, 121, 215, 216, 248.
Matthews, 158.
Maurice, Prince, 55-8, 68, 94, 144, 145, 187, 213.
Mayo, 261.
Maynard, 158, 183.
Meldrum, 20, 42, 132, 159.

INDEX OF PERSONS.   267

Mellis (Millis), 124, 134.
Mercer, 61, 120, 143.
Michael, 110.
Middleton, 25, 64, 163, 186, 198, 200, 203.
Midley, 134.
Mildmay, 206.
Mill, 139.
Mills, 61, 139.
Milton, 130.
Moggeridge, 253.
Monk, 261.
Molum, 261.
Montague, 185, 225, 228, 239-40.
Morgan, 218.
Morley, 13, 11, 47, 53, 80, 83, 85, 92, 95, 96, 108, 113, 114, 119, 149, 151, 151-7, 161-3, 167, 178, 183, 201, 210, 219, 251-2, 255, 261-2.
Morsey, 134.
Mourton, 138.
Mullins, 112, 143.
Murford, 61-3, 98, 119, 120, 214.
Muspratt, 254.

Neale, 177.
Nevill, 131.
Northumberland, 91, 93.
Norton, 13, 14, 33, 34, 39-42, 58-60, 63, 79, 83, 85, 93, 95, 98, 104-11-116, 118-21, 131, 135-8, 141, 148, 164, 167, 172-9, 182, 183, 187, 194, 199, 208-210, 214, 215, 219, 220, 227, 251.

Oakley, 83.
Oglander, 125.
Ogle, 13, 63, 80, 81, 122, 134, 159, 160, 176-7, 210, 218, 229-232.
Okey, 188, 212, 228.
Onslowe, 150, 151, 155, 157, 161, 162, 173, 180, 183, 194, 214, 251.
Oram, 166.
Osborne, 253.
Outram, 173.

Palmer, 254.
Parham (Perham), 150, 198.
Paulet, 10-12, 52, 61, 62, 81, 91, 133, 137-9, 231, 236, 218, 250, 256.
Pavell, 199.
Payne, 248.
Peacock, 255.
Peake, 59, 66, 74, 78, 152, 180, 191, 206, 220, 236, 241-2, 244-5, 248-50.
Pell, 218.
Pembroke, 21, 38, 44, 52, 57, 124, 140, 164, 171, 187, 259-60.
Penn, 201.
Penruddock, 216, 265.
Percy, 91, 206.
Peters, 114, 158, 208, 216, 227-33, 237-45.

Phillips, 14, 133, 206.
Philpott, 139.
Pickering, 185, 225-8, 234, 239-40.
Pickover, 248.
Pittman, 215.
Pollard, 198.
Poore, 180.
Popham, 113, 144, 146, 159, 171, 197, 212, 215.
Porter, 95, 103.
Portland (Earl of) 14, 21, 38, 53, 189, 260.
Portland (Countess of) 22.
Portu, 9, 10, 39.
Puttley, 91, 113.
Poynet, 141.
Preston, 216.
Price, 134, 204.
Pridgeon, 261.
Prouse, 79.
Prynne, 46.
Purduc, 254.
Pyne, 144.

Rainsborough, 185.
Raisby, 243.
Ramsay, 108.

Rawdon, 59, 60, 64-6, 74, 148, 152-3, 210-11, 251.
Rawlence, 112.
Raymond, 61.
Read, 200, 248, 260.
Reeves, 51, 217.
Richards, 218.
Rigby, 184.
Robinson, 62, 67, 120, 149, 193, 241, 251.
Rodway, 105.
Roe, 171, 185, 215, 245.
Itolph, 253.
Roolfe, 79.
Rosewell, 66, 144, 184, 192.
Rossiter, 203, 242.
Rowlett, 66, 149, 184, 248.
Rupert (Prince), 44, 48, 50, 54-5, 171, 186, 191, 192, 209.
Russell, 185, 225.
Ruter, 160.
Ruthen, 259.

Sadleir, 200.
Saltoun, 75.
Sandys, 14, 133, 259.
Santbrook, 164.
Saye, 55, 165.
Scofield, 90, 124.
Scott, 133.
Scullard, 133.
Sedgwick, 135, 138.
Sellenger, 200.
Seymour, 134.
Sheffield, 226, 227.

Sheiling, 139.
Shelley, 50, 51, 261.
Simonds, 210.
Smith, 108, 111, 124, 132, 157, 211, 255.
Smithson, 248.
Snow, 166, 173, 248.
Southampton, 14, 63, 120, 218, 252.
Spavin, 232.
Springate, 108, 113, 118.
St. Barbe, 59, 62, 98, 214, 215.
Stanhope, 179.
Stanley, 119.
Stapleton, 111.
Stapley, 95, 114, 170, 219, 262.
Stawell, 124, 133, 139.
Stephens, 206.
Stephenson, 261.
Stewart, 209.
Stockam, 217.
Stonor, 179, 181.
Stourton, 41.
Strafford, 41, 262.
Strickland 58.
Strond (Strode), 111, 192.
Struce, 63.
Stuart, 124, 132.
Sturges, 179, 181, 198.
Swainely, 177.
Swanley, 39, 46, 91, 124, 157, 259-60.
Sydenham, 68.
Sydney, 51, 210.
Symonds, 260.

Tamworth, 248.
Tasbury, 14, 67, 218.
Temple, 187.
Terry (Ferry), 98, 218, 255.
Tettersall, 218.
Thanet, 48, 112, 261.
Thompson, 124, 128-30, 166, 199, 212, 211.
Thornburn, Thornbury, Thorneburgh, 110.
Thorpe, 209.
Tichborne, 13, 14, 63, 80, 124, 133, 220, 231, 254.
Todd, 110.
Tooker, 62.
Towse, 85, 116, 119.
Trayton, 15, 47.
Trenchard, 80, 85, 86, 91, 111.
Tulse, 259.
Tunstall, 218.
Turner, 118, 124.
Turney, 139, 260.

Urrey, 20, 25, 30, 39, 40, 49, 260.

Vanderblin, 76, 248.
Vandruske, Van Hust, Van Rowe, 87, 111, 110, 197.
Vavasour, 81, 91.

INDEX OF PERSONS.

Vicars, 17-20, 23-6, 49, 138, 169.
Vernon, 121.

Waller, Sir William, 13, 16, 20, 23, 24, 33, 39, 40, 45-59, 62-4, 68-89, 99, 102-118, 121-148, 155, 160, 166, 170-1, 184-191, 194-7, 203-10, 229-32, 251, 254, 259-60.
Waller, Lady, 107, 111, 114, 174.
Waller, Sir Hardress, 225-8, 239-40.
Wallop, 13, 57, 110, 157, 218, 249, 252, 259.
Walters, 176.
Walton, 255.
Wansey (Weinsford), 198.
Warn, 161.
Warren, 73, 105, 150.
Warwick, 17, 37, 79, 119, 121, 124, 157, 259-60.

Weare, 172, 218, 220.
Webb, 77, 85, 175-8, 189, 215, 218.
Welden, 213, 215.
Wems, 71, 96, 112.
Wentworth, 18-20.
Wesbrook, 150.
Weston, 13, 20, 37, 39, 218, 259.
Wetham, 255.
Whitby, 91.
Whitehead, 13, 61-2, 141, 154, 157, 162, 166, 168, 209, 215.
Wiborn, 241.
Wilkins, 138.
Wilks, 225, 240.
Williamson, 260.
Willis, 139.
Wilmot, 133, 146.
Winchester (Marchioness of), 31, 72, 167, 173, 235, 236, 250, 256.

Winchester (Marquis of), 13, 33, 59, 60, 72, 79, 117, 141, 149, 151, 160-2, 165-8, 172, 173, 177-81, 198, 203, 211, 219, 221, 240-5, 218-50, 256.
Windebank, 175, 210.
Windsor, 261.
Winter, 258.
Witherington, 261.
Wogan, 206, 212.
Wolfe, 261.
Worlye, 246.
Worsley, 54, 140.
Wroth, 63.
Wyatt, 104.

Yalden, 91.

INDEX OF PLACES.

Abbotstone, 250, 256.
Abbot's Worthy, 11, 158.
Aldershot (Aldershot), 203.
Aldermaston, 148, 176, 180, 191.
Alresford, 11, 87, 92, 99, 124, 128, 131, 134, 188, 213, 235.
Alton, 51, 69-71, 93, 99-103, 122, 124, 144, 187, 188, 201-4.
Alverstoke, 79, 203.
Amberley Castle, 113.
Andover, 13, 61, 70, 71, 91, 118, 124, 135, 143, 146, 151, 158, 160, 172, 186-7, 201, 205, 206, 210, 212, 213, 220, 249, 260.
Andwell, 151.
Arundel, 47-51, 92, 95, 105-111, 122, 123, 198, 210.
Avington, 132.

Basing House, 21, 56, 59, 61, 71-8, 82, 84, 91, 103, 117, 124, 132, 137, 138, 141-170, 172-181, 190-99, 201, 210-14, 217-23, 231-6, 237-50.
Basing Church, 152-4, 162, 163, 168, 179, 182, 183, 191, 203, 212.
Basingstoke, 21, 54, 55, 61, 72-5, 78, 111, 146, 148, 150, 161-7, 173, 171, 178-81, 187, 189-91, 197, 221, 235, 245, 247.
Bishop's Waltham, 123, 141-3, 201, 219, 220.
Blackdown, 91, 106.
Blandford, 171, 185, 213, 216.
Bramdean, 124, 129.
Bramley, 118.
Bramshill, 137.
Bristol, 59, 205.

Calshot, 46, 52, 57, 157, 251.
Carisbrooke, 21, 22, 39, 124, 251, 252, 255, 260.
Cheriton, 123-31.
Chert, 199.
Chichester, 40, 45, 49-52, 55, 109, 114, 122, 126, 127, 197, 199, 210, 213, 217, 249, 255, 260, 261.
Chinham, 176, 192.
Christchurch, 68, 139, 140, 171, 196, 200, 203, 209.
Cowdray House, 95, 106, 115, 122.
Crondall, 81-7, 197, 203.
Cropredy, 155, 157, 160, 162.

Delve, The, 166-8, 178, 189, 192.
Devizes, 58-9.
Ditcham, 91.
Donnington Castle, 64, 151-5, 160, 162, 181, 211, 217, 219, 217-9.
Dorchester, 58-9, 171, 208.

Englefield, 250.

Fareham, 123, 203.
Farnham, 23, 45, 53, 55, 59, 69, 70, 78, 80-7, 92, 94, 96, 99, 102-4, 129-4, 131, 143-6, 151, 160, 166, 148, 170-2, 181, 189, 197-9, 203-8, 211, 217, 217, 251.
Farringdon, 210-12, 251.

Godalming, 127, 150, 201-5.
Gosport, 18, 19, 42, 112, 201, 203, 255, 259.
Greywell, 111.
Guildford, 51, 70, 83-6, 126, 150-1, 255, 260.

Hackwood, 174, 191, 211, 235, 257.
Harting, 91-5, 110, 115, 252, 261.
Havant, 40-1, 48, 110, 127.
Hayling Island, 10, 171.
Hayward's Heath, 48.
Hinsley, 88, 252.
Hurst Castle, 52, 57, 79, 118, 119, 157, 172, 189, 200-1, 206, 211, 253, 255, 259.

Isle of Wight, 11, 21-2, 38, 55, 62, 79, 80, 90, 118, 124-5, 140, 157-8, 164, 171, 187 190-205, 208.
Itchen Stoke, 250.

Kingsclere, 180, 194, 209.

Langford House, 187, 200, 210, 211, 231, 248.
Lewes, 15, 17.
Liphook (Lippooke), 127, 255.
Liss, 194.
Lymington, 53, 68, 118-9, 171, 201, 203, 253.

Marlborough, 21, 144-5, 172, 185, 201, 211, 213.
Meon, East, 128.
Meon, West, 127-8.

Midhurst, 82-3, 125-7, 199.
Minstead, 251.

Netley, 46, 120.
Newbury, 75, 124, 135, 144-6, 180, 212-14, 247-9.
Newport, I.W., 22, 119, 199, 250.

Odiham, 69, 81-2, 84-7, 121-4, 144, 149-51, 188, 193-4, 197, 199, 204, 214.
Oxford, 45, 54-5, 83, 158-62, 167, 173, 181, 205, 210, 213, 232, 235, 246.

Petersfield, 13, 95, 99, 100, 111, 124, 127-8, 195, 199, 204-5, 224, 255.
Petworth, 83, 91, 93, 105, 121-2, 125, 199, 201.
Pool, 64, 85, 101, 109, 111, 118, 139, 203.
Portchester, 127.
Portsmouth, 13, 15-20, 37-43, 54-61, 68-9, 79, 107, 113, 125, 127, 111, 115, 157, 160, 171-2, 181-5, 196, 199, 201, 205, 209-10, 211-19, 234, 251, 253, 258-9.
Pyats Hill, 157, 191-2.

Reading, 45, 55, 57, 70, 117-18, 131, 137, 141, 145, 180, 181-3, 198-9, 208, 212, 219.
Ringwood, 119, 140, 143, 208, 213.
Romsey, 46, 54, 98, 121, 124, 126, 143, 201, 203, 208-9, 213-16.

Salisbury, 39, 56-9, 106, 118, 122, 135, 139, 144-5, 152, 163, 177, 182, 181, 186, 195, 198, 200, 203, 209, 213, 216, 249, 253, 261.
San lown, 52, 124.
Sherborne, 181, 191.
Sherfield, 154, 157, 181, 189.
Southampton, 14, 14, 38, 41, 46, 57, 61-4, 68-9, 75, 98, 101, 109, 117-21, 124, 130, 143-4, 161, 164, 170, 172, 181, 198, 201, 204, 209-10, 215, 251-5, 259-62.
South sea Castle, 19, 42, 57, 157, 215, 231, 254, 259.
Southwick, 39, 40, 58, 129.
Stanstead, 95, 113.
Stockbridge, 13.
Stoneham, 63, 120.

INDEX OF PLACES.

Stonehenge (Stonage) 216, 251.

Taunton, 197-8, 213, 215.
Tichborne Down, 126, 127, 130.
Tisted West, 13, 121, 128, 133.
Titchfield, 14, 187, 203, 218.
Troyford, 127.
Twyford, 107, 121, 205-6.

Upham, '52.
Up Park, 48, 91, 95.

Vyne, The, 11, 12, 75, 251, 917, 250.

Wallingford, 145-6, 176, 181, 231.
Wallop, 13, 248.
Warblington, 111.
Wardour Castle, 59, 110, 118, 261.
Weybill 118.
Weymouth, 59, 109, 118, 123, 139, 146, 171, 197, 204-5.
Whitchurch, 13, 139, 189, 213.
Wickham, 141, 205.

Wilton, 44, 57, 59, 135.
Winchester, 13, 24-30, 38, 45, 52, 54-5, 59-63, 87, 91, 105, 116, 118, 121-8, 135, 143, 158-60, 164, 176-7, 196, 201, 205-6, 217-8, 227-33, 145, 252-4, 259.
Winchester Cathedral, 26-30, 233.
Winchester Castle, 11, 26, 16, 80-1, 205, 213, 215-6, 223, 231-3, 216, 251.
Windsor, 19, 52, 68, 70, 245-6, 206, 212, 234.

www.ingramcontent.com/pod-product-compliance
Lightning Source LLC
Chambersburg PA
CBHW031946230426

43672CB00010B/2067